The United States and the State of Israel

The United States
and the
State of Israel

DAVID SCHOENBAUM

New York   Oxford
OXFORD UNIVERSITY PRESS
1993

Oxford University Press

Oxford   New York   Toronto
Delhi   Bombay   Calcutta   Madras   Karachi
Kuala Lumpur   Singapore   Hong Kong   Tokyo
Nairobi   Dar es Salaam   Cape Town
Melbourne   Auckland

and associated companies in
Berlin   Ibadan

Copyright © 1993 by David Schoenbaum

Published by Oxford University Press, Inc.,
200 Madison Avenue, New York, New York 10016

Oxford is a registered trademark of Oxford University Press

Library of Congress Cataloging-in-Publication Data
Schoenbaum, David.
The United States and the state of Israel / David Schoenbaum.
p.   cm.
Includes bibliographical references and index.
ISBN 0-19-504577-7
ISBN 0-19-5045769 (pbk)
1. United States—Foreign relations—Israel.   2. Israel—Foreign
relations—United States.   I. Title.
E183.8.I7S34 1993
327.7305694—dc20   92-9056

Printing (last digit): 9 8 7 6 5 4 3 2 1

Printed in the United States of America
on acid-free paper

To
Graham Hovey
James Joll
Lawrence S. Kaplan

If David, the King of Israel, who learned only two things
from Ahitophel, regarded him as his master, guide and
familiar friend, how much more ought one who learns from
his fellow a chapter, rule, verse, expression, or even a single
letter, to pay him honour.

Sayings of the Fathers, 6:3

Contents

Introduction, ix

1. In the Beginning, 3

2. Stopping the Buck, 34

3. Getting Acquainted, 63

4. To the Brink and Back, 92

5. To the Brink and Over, 125

6. From War to Watershed, 154

7. Yom Kippur, 183

8. Step by Step, 211

9. A Piece of Peace, 240

10. Perpetuum Stabile?, 269

11. Afterthoughts, 297

Epilogue, 320

Notes, 331

Bibliography, 381

Index, 395

Introduction

Certain books like certain people need no introduction. This is not one of them. Like many books, it began as a gleam in the eye of an editor, in this case a distinguished historian of U.S. foreign policy. He had just undertaken a series on significant bilateral relationships since World War II, for example, the United States and the Soviet Union, the United States and Germany, the United States and Japan. For practical purposes, it was assumed that each relationship was a tree, that is, an object for study in itself. But the idea was also to locate and study the tree within the forest. He was now looking for someone to write a book about the United States and Israel.

Had he turned to the professional Middle East hands, or what might be called Israeli-Americanologists, with their predominance of political scientists, this might well be a different book. Instead, consistent with the reflexes and conventions of a politicized subject and a balkanized profession, he had canvassed the academic borough he called home.

In practice, this meant a shortlist of the American-Jewish colleagues who, like himself, happened, to write about U.S. foreign policy. After one or more had turned him down, a common friend and colleague referred him to me. An outsider by most of the prevailing professional conventions, I had taken up the subject for my own reasons, prepared a course, and even published a few articles. But perhaps my outstanding qualification was a deep interest in reading a book like the one he was asking me to write. I was accordingly flattered, daunted, and tantalized. Hesitating briefly, I then accepted the invitation.

Independent of the original series, the project soon took on a life of its own, but its origins as a narrative, chronological history of the bilateral experience of the United States with Israel can still be recognized. Of course, as I soon discovered, documentation—be it published, microfilmed, routinely declassified, or pried loose by means of the ever-more-prohibitive Freedom of Information Act—had proliferated like the flowers in May since at least the early 1980s. Meanwhile, the literature on the relationship, both serious and otherwise, has grown like crabgrass. Earlier authors had also established benchmarks, among them Walter Laqueur's history of Zionism, Howard Sachar's history of Israel, Nadav Safran's *Israel: Uneasy Ally,* and Steven Spiegel's *The Other Arab-*

Israeli Conflict.[1] As regular readers in the field will surely recognize, I am heavily indebted to all four.

This is still a rather different book from theirs, both in purpose and conception. It is always hard to account for a negative, but if my experience is any guide, documentation is only part of the reason why I think no other book quite like this has appeared before. More basic, I suspect, has been a reluctance by both supporters and critics of the relationship to see it as historical at all, that is, as a product of frequently ambiguous, untidy, and fortuitous places, times, and circumstances rather than a timeless and self-evident feature in the landscape. In fact, the subject has turned out to be both protean and open-ended, and the project to be a voyage of discovery. But the book has remained what it was intended to be all along, an effort to explain to myself and others how that feature got there.

In addressing this, my premises have been both Rankean and utopian. In principle, I have tried to read everything, pursue things to their roots, account for all loose ends, lump (in John Gaddis's phrase) what needs lumping, and split (Gaddis again) what needs splitting. I have then tried to write the story *wie es eigentlich gewesen* (as it really was) in an era of hot and cold war, Auschwitz, television, postcolonial euphoria, existential hangover, microchips, petrodollars, international communism, missionary nationalism, renascent fundamentalism, global terrorism, PACs in general, AIPAC in particular, nuclear missiles, contentious bureaucracies, conservatism both neo and otherwise, and electorates with blood in their eye.

Since it is hard to know everything, and harder still to write it, the experience, predictably, has been an adventure in humility. Yet for all the inevitable surprises and disappointments, I think I can at least make a credible case that the relationship was not created in six days. On the contrary, it impresses me even more than it did when I began as a kind of Grand Canyon of international relations, whose vast and remarkable panorama is virtually inexplicable without some awareness of the vast and remarkable circumstances that put it there.

Inevitably, the conjunction of recent, and less recent, history with the urgency and immediacy of secular events has also left its marks on the product. In one of the twentieth century's great novels, Thomas Mann's *Doktor Faustus,* Dr. Zeitblom, the schoolteacherly narrator, recalls the eventfully calamitous history of a boyhood friend while World War II goes on outside his window. Writing with two Israeli elections and the fall of several governments, a couple of U.S. peace offensives, the hijacking of TWA 847 and the assault on the *Achille Lauro,* the end of the Cold War and the sunset of the Soviet Union, the Palestinian *intifada* and the PLO's reluctant embrace of Resolution 242, the Iraqi invasion of Kuwait and the Gulf war going on outside my window, I have often felt like Dr. Zeitblom. Reading proofs in the aftermath of the latest Israeli, and on the eve of another American, election has only enhanced the sensation.

Like Zeitblom's, my motives too have been personal, professional, civic, generational, even pedagogical in about equal parts. None of these requires a lot of explanation. Like innumerable other European Jews, my family discovered the United States in the early twentieth century when my grandfather, already forty and the father of eight, followed his ethnic German customers from the Black Sea to the upper Missouri Valley. Had he heard of Herzl? I have no way of knowing, but I doubt it would have affected his decision. Yet his decision virtually coincided with the birth of Zionism. Whether by sound instincts or good luck, the family arrived in Sioux City just ahead of the Kishinev pogrom, a landmark in the history of both Zionism and Jewish emigration. Far greater disasters, of course, were soon to follow.

The echoes and resonances of these secular calamities have inevitably shaped my choices and defined my horizons. A part of my psychic inventory in any case, they could hardly help make themselves felt when I was asked to write this book. It was no coincidence that I had earned my living, for the most part, as an American-Jewish practitioner of mostly German and mostly twentieth-century social and political history. On the other hand, I had pursued a short career in journalism after college, and still hung out with journalists at every chance. I had also spent some student years in Europe. The habit of writing about U.S. foreign policy, *ex tempore* if not *ex officio,* was a common legacy of all these experiences.

For me, like hundreds of grateful alumni before and after, St. Antony's College, Oxford, where Israelis, Arabs, Americans, and all possible Europeans talked about all possible politics at all possible hours in all possible permutations, was a quantum jump in my awareness of the world. So was Bonn, where it was impossible not to think about the world, the Cold War, the history of the Jews, the Middle East, and the twentieth century in ways that would not have occurred to me elsewhere.

Subsequent experiences only reinforced the habits thus acquired. One of the big ones was the U.S. Naval War College in Newport, Rhode Island. Thanks to another touch of serendipity, I had been invited there in the mid 1970s to teach "strategy," a discipline known elsewhere as history. I seriously doubt that I ever taught anybody there anything, but can hardly exaggerate what my students and colleagues taught me. Nor can I overstate for any interested reader how Thucydides and Clausewitz, then and perhaps still the specialties of the Newport menu, can illuminate the study of Israeli-U.S. relations as they illuminate so many other things.

Different as it is from Newport, the Woodrow Wilson Center in Washington, where I happened to be when asked to write this book, was another venue of self-discovery. Flanked by the busts of Wilson and Hubert Humphrey in the library, the Kennan Institute upstairs, and the national monuments all around me, I found it harder than usual to forget that history has something to do with public life, and that scholarship is also a civic activity.

That the Middle East was also so vividly real and present there was another stroke of luck. Among the resident cohort either on or soon after my arrival were a Palestinian-American historian recently arrived from Beirut; a Palestinian political scientist grateful for the respite from Bir Zeit; a distinguished Israeli Arabist, digesting his experience as civil administrator of the West Bank; an Israeli political scientist, who had served as secretary-general of the Foreign

Ministry; an Israeli aeronautical engineer whose self-defined mission was to make the best case possible for a homemade, state-of-the-art fighter bomber called the "Lavi"; a Jewish refugee from Tehran, who had been a lion of Iranian journalism before the revolution; the former director of the Iranian equivalent of the Council on Foreign Relations, and an Iranian historian, whose goal, already in view, was to rewrite the political history of the Iranian Shi'ite clergy.

I myself was there to reflect on how World War II had influenced U.S. foreign policy. But, not least with Ronald Reagan en route to Bitburg, I could hardly ignore the gravitational field, or the linkages, interdependencies, and concentricity of U.S., European, and Middle Eastern history being acted out around me. Each in his or her way, my Middle Eastern colleagues personified the impact of the United States, the region's historical fault lines, its claim to U.S. attention, and, incidentally, the startling provincialism of the U.S. academic job market. Of the group, only the Israelis had serious jobs to return to. The others, world-class square pegs, looked out on a landscape of round holes in a country that for forty years had been heavily engaged in, yet still remained invariably baffled by, the Middle East.

Their situation was cause in itself to think again about the United States and the Middle East. But, in fact, as I realized increasingly, I had been thinking about this for years. Now recycled as history, the current events of other times and places came back to me *seriatim:* student reminiscences of Suez; newsdesk colloquia on the 1958 revolution in Iraq, and the U.S. intervention in Lebanon that followed on its heels; Oxford table talk on the Lavon affair, and a sidewalk seminar with the late Yigal Allon, who was in Oxford, unlikely as this now seems, to learn something about India; ears to the radio during those wrenching and triumphant weeks between April and June 1967.

September 1970 had been a particular moment of truth. The airline hijackings and civil war in Jordan seemed to happen only a few weeks after the long hot spring of Cambodia and Kent State. Given the urgency of U.S. interests, the latest crisis looked like the overture to a long hot fall. A lot of difficult and very different histories were coming home to roost, it occurred to me, as I pored through the papers and newsmagazines, and stared at television. Historians needed to acknowledge and explain that. At the very least, I tried to persuade my colleagues, someone should be there to answer the questions from students, or the boys and girls at Channel 9. Realizing abruptly that there were no other volunteers, I then took up the subject myself. Crisis past, I clipped the papers, located the television transcripts, bumbled conveniently into a ticket to Washington, and interviewed the bureaucratic survivors.

The exercise had two salutary consequences. One of them was my first actual exposure to what academics coquettishly call the "real world" of policy-making Washington. The experience rather predictably became an article. The article, in turn, was later commemorated in an ego-warming footnote.[2] The second and substantially more important consequence was a colloquium I have since taught at the University of Iowa, the Naval War College, and the Johns Hopkins Bologna Center, but never the same way twice. Focused exclusively on the history of the Arab-Israeli conflict, the syllabus began with the

Book of Exodus, the birth of Islam, the Eastern Question, and the origins of Zionism and Arab nationalism, before even approaching the Balfour Declaration. It then extended open-ended to the present.

Rather more than most teaching commitments, the course, in turn, became an excuse to travel, read, and talk to groups that only rarely intersected: to Libyan, Iranian, Algerian, and Palestinian, not to mention American, students; to itinerant Israelis; to American Jews from across the hawk-dove spectrum; to visting experts and professionals, happy to visit what they coquettishly call the "real world" outside Washington; to high school and community college teachers, church groups, elected officials, and, in general, the constituents of a good state university, who vote, pay taxes, and read editorials.

Yet the operative questions have invariably been the same. Why is the region so difficult both for people who live there and people who don't? What is the Arab-Israeli conflict about, and what is the U.S. role and interest in it? How does the Israeli-U.S. relationship work, and how did it get that way? What were, and are, the options?

Various answers, theses, and speculations can be found in the succeeding chapters, but provisional impressions seem worth recording here, for example:

1. Of all the people in this story, Abba Eban has been the rightest longest.
2. The 1973 war need not have happened, and things might have come out quite differently had Henry Kissinger shuttled to Jordan, then Syria, in 1974; and had the PLO said yes to Camp David five years later.
3. The respective impacts of the 1967 war and Israel's 1977 election are hard to overestimate. So is the persisting inability of most Arabs to see why and how Sadat succeeded where Arab armies had consistently failed.[3]
4. As the 1992 Israeli election confirmed, the biggest question in the region for many years to come might well be who succeeds in addressing the hopes, fears, and imaginations, and thereby keeping the votes, of the latest wave of Soviet-Jewish immigrants.
5. The first-person memoirs of Camp David—including four by Americans, two by Israelis, and one by an Egyptian—should be mandatory reading a) for any serious student of history and historiography, b) for any administration that hopes to succeed and continue where its predecessors failed or stopped.
6. Aspiring students of international relations should be encouraged to study Israeli-U.S. relations for the same reason young violinists take on the Paganini caprices: because most other things seem easier afterward.
7. Joshua Sherman is not exaggerating when he notes how the subject has a tendency to generate to "an atmosphere where debate begins at a howl and escalates from there."[4] Neither is Tom Friedman, whose coverage of the region won him two richly deserved Pulitzers, when he observes that the Middle East makes most people a little crazy; that authors auda-

cious enough to write about it should therefore take care to know what they are talking about; and also not expect to be loved for their efforts.[5]

The author of this book is accordingly grateful for help and support, not only from Tom Friedman, who answered questions, and Joshua Sherman, who looked through chapters, but from

- the German Marshall Fund of the United States and the German Fulbright commission, which granted me money, and therefore time;
- the libraries of the University of Iowa; the German Society for Foreign Affairs in Bonn, and especially its librarian, Gisela Gottwald, a bibliographical force of nature; as well as Linda Weeks, the elemental force in Congressman Jim Leach's office, who connected me with the Congressional Research Service;
- Peter Bass, Asher Tishler, and Milton Viorst, who provided me with supplementary documentation and source material from their personal files; and John Henneman, who helped with material from the Dulles papers in Princeton;
- Rita E. Hauser, Robert Hunter, Gerhard Jahn, Samuel Lewis, Horst Osterfeld, and Stansfield Turner, who sat for interviews;
- Walter Eytan, Martin Hillenbrand, Marvin Kalb, Walter Laqueur, Sol Linowitz, George McGhee, Harry McPherson, William Quandt, Eugene Rostow, Cyrus Vance, and Paul Warnke, who answered questions;
- Bess Beatty, who shared cookies and listened to me talk (and talk and talk) when this began;
- Shirley McKim Gardner, Graham Hovey, Moshe Ma'oz, Leah Nathanson Marcus, Elizabeth Pond, Steve Rosenfeld, and Michael Wolffsohn, who made suggestions as it continued;
- Kevin Burnett, who was there to doctor fractured footnotes at the end;
- and my wife, who, as always, put up with a lot.

D. S.

Bologna
September 1992

The United States and the State of Israel

1

In the Beginning

In the cool, dry realm of juridical theory, all relations between sovereign states are special. But the realities of size, proximity, power, conflicting interests, economic resources, and cultural affinity inevitably make some relationships more special than others.[1] In the years since World War II, the Anglo-U.S., Canadian-U.S., Mexican-U.S., German-U.S., Japanese-U.S., and Soviet-U.S. relationships could all be reasonably described as special. Yet for most of that time, the relationship of the United States with Israel, a country neither large, close, powerful, hostile, richly endowed, nor culturally very near has been at least as special as any of them, and often more special than most. A unique but also fortuitous combination of acknowledged and unacknowledged values, interests, and memories, the whole of the relationship has regularly seemed to exceed the sum of its parts.

Even its patrons bear witness to its powerful resonances and historical exceptionality. But so do its critics. The former have included so odd a trio as Sen. Hubert Humphrey, a bellwether of postwar U.S. liberalism, James Jesus Angleton, the CIA's legendary counterspy, and the Reverend Jerry Falwell, the Protestant fundamentalist founder of the Moral Majority. The latter have included the equally odd trio of the Reverend Jesse Jackson, a sometime-aspirant to Humphrey's mantle; Secretary of State John Foster Dulles, a pillar of Cold War anticommunism; and Sen. J. William Fulbright, one of its most eloquent critics as chairman of the Foreign Relations Committee.

Actually, to judge by survey data since at least the 1970s, men, women, Republicans, Democrats, Protestants, Catholics, old people, young people, whites, and, although by narrower margins, blacks, have all been about equally supportive of U.S. support for Israel, and close Israeli-U.S. ties. Meanwhile, irrespective of their differences on other issues, hawks and doves, agnostics and believers, liberals and conservatives have learned to take the relationship almost for granted.

Widely and plausibly linked to decolonization and the Cold War, the relationship can as plausibly be traced to such obvious landmarks as the great wars of the twentieth century; the decline of the British, and the collapse of the Ottoman, empires; the French Revolution and the secular failures of German liberalism; the collapse of historic Poland and Lithuania; even the historic clashes of East and West, *ecclesia* and *sinagoga,* Christianity and Islam that are among the formative experiences of Western civilization.

Whatever its roots, neither U.S. experience nor the history of international relations has anything to show quite like it. The uniqueness and potency of its impact are measurable alike in symbols, polls, and aid figures. A kind of underground river in the deceptively tranquil 1920s, a close-run thing in the turbulent 1940s, a commitment of demonstrative tentativeness as late as the 1967 war, the relationship had evolved by the 1980s into a mutually ambivalent de facto alliance. Meanwhile, what both sides once believed to be discretionary and provisional had come to seem both normal and inevitable.

Yet for all its apparent timelessness, the relationship is scarcely older than network television, commercial air travel, and a genuinely metropolitan national capital. Measured in government-to-government aid, its current magnitude, in fact, goes back only to the 1970s. Between Israeli independence in 1948 and the civil war in Jordan in 1970, official U.S. aid barely peeped above the baseline of a graph. Since then, the annual foreign aid bill has both confirmed and documented the unique interdependence of a tiny Middle Eastern client and the world's last superpower, while incidentally turning Israelis into the world's biggest absolute *and* per capita consumers of U.S. aid. "We are no longer talking about a transformation in the relationship," Thomas A. Dine, executive director of the American Israel Public Affairs Committee (AIPAC), told a Washington audience in 1986, "we are talking about a revolution."[2]

Rising from under $100 million in 1970 to over $600 million a year later (about $500 million in 1967 dollars), U.S. aid reached its first peak in 1971. Rising from under $500 million in 1973 to over $2.6 billion (about $1.6 billion in 1967 dollars), it then reached a new peak three years later. At almost $5 billion (over $2 billion in 1967 dollars), it reached another peak in 1979. Since the middle 1980s, the annual level has never dipped below $3 billion.[3] So seemingly self-evident has the annual package become that few even remember its relative recency. Franklin Roosevelt and Chaim Weizmann, Harry Truman and David Ben Gurion, Dwight Eisenhower and Golda Meir would surely be amazed by the development of a relationship whose limits seemed so obvious in their lifetimes.

But money is hardly the only relevant measure. From 1947 to the present, U.S. support for Israel has outweighed sympathy for Arabs by margins as large as 10:1. Only in September 1982, with Israeli troops pounding Beirut and standing by as Maronite Christians slaughtered Palestinians, did public support for Israel fall close to 20%. Even then, support for Arabs only barely approached the same level.

Presented a menu of moral or other characteristic qualities in 1975, half the respondents identified Israelis with "like Americans"; 46% with "friendly"; 41% as with "peaceful"; 39% each with "honest" and "intelligent". Only 5–8% associated Arabs with the same qualities. At the same time, 47% identified Arabs with "backward" and "underdeveloped"; 41% with "greedy"; and 38% with "barbaric."[4]

Support for Israel has also shown consistent limits. Of 34% who favored close Israeli-U.S. cooperation in a 1953 survey, only 5% gave democracy as a motive, and nearly a third gave no motive at all. According to contemporary survey data, half to two-thirds of all Americans supported the partition of Palestine between October 1947 and March 1948, yet opposition to unilateral U.S. military involvement ranged from 61% to 83% over the same period. Between 1969 and 1975, substantial numbers of Americans were still willing to send troops to the defense of Canada,

Mexico, West Germany, and even the Philippines in the event of Communist invasion, but only 9–12% of respondents were willing to send U.S. troops to Israel, putting Israel in a class with Turkey and Taiwan. Between 1978 and 1983, significantly more Americans declared themselves willing to commit troops to resist an Arab oil embargo, or Soviet invasions of Western Europe or Japan, than to resist an Arab invasion of Israel. Only once between 1967 and 1985 did support for sending troops to Israel's aid reach 43%, while opposition never fell below 47%.[5]

Speculations on the sources of the relationship, both friendly and otherwise, go back to the beginnings of the relationship itself. Historical memories, Cold War politics, bureaucratic patronage, and Jewish money, votes, and organization have all been addressed and scrutinized as necessary, if not sufficient, conditions to account for it. "Practically every congressman and senator says his prayers to the AIPAC lobby," former Under Secretary of State George Ball told Mike Wallace of CBS in 1988. "Oh, they've done an enormous job of corrupting the American democratic process."[6] Shortly after, flanked by a former ambassador to Saudi Arabia, a former U.S. representative, and three other plaintiffs, he appealed to the Federal Election Commission, charging explicitly that AIPAC had skewed U.S. foreign policy. It was at least a year before the commission released its decision. It was then reported that the charges had been dismissed unanimously.[7]

Although none of the sources advanced and examined suffices in itself to explain the relationship, neither is any of them particularly mysterious. In reality, Jewish votes have mattered, not only because Jews vote in numbers disproportionate to their 2–3 percent representation in the census but because they benefit from an electoral college that favors the populous states where most Jews live.[8] Money has obviously mattered in a system heavily dependent on commercial television and direct mail, and averse to public finance and member-supported parties. Political know-how and organization, which American Jews first learned to master in the 1950s, matter too in a vast, centrifugal system, proverbially responsive to local interests and increasingly responsive to single-issue constituencies.

It is easy to exaggerate the magnitude and impact of Jewish money, votes, and organization. In 1988 it was estimated that Jewish political action committees invested $4.7 million in congressional campaigns. A seemingly impressive figure, it was still hardly enough to fund a single Senate race in a single middle-sized state. It is true that, at least in Democratic years, Jews have often voted with the winners. Yet from Truman to Bush, candidates of both parties have also succeeded without the Jewish vote or the electoral votes of states with major Jewish populations. Although few would deny that money is to politics what spinach was to Popeye, innumerable candidates can testify from experience that even large portions of it can be inadequate to win elections.[9]

Two midwestern Senate races in states with modest Jewish populations can be seen as a guide and a warning on the real, but elusive, facts of American-Jewish political life. In 1984, Congressman Tom Harkin of Iowa, a Catholic and liberal Democrat, successfully challenged incumbent Republican Senator Roger Jepsen, a volubly born-again Protestant and Reaganite Republican. In 1990, Senator Rudy Boschwitz of Minnesota, a Jew and incumbent Republican, was successfully challenged by Professor Paul Wellstone, also a Jew and a liberal Democrat. Both campaigns were marked by heavy spending, and "Jewish money," that is, contributions from the pro-Israel political action committees (PACs) that were conspicuous in both races.

Both Harkin and Jepsen boasted Jewish fund-raisers, and worked hard to establish themselves as declared and demonstrative friends of Israel, yet neither the Middle East nor Jewish money was even mentioned, let alone considered decisive, in the Iowa campaign.[10] In Minnesota, where the campaign coincided with the countdown to the 1991 Gulf war, Jewish and Middle Eastern issues did play a role, but the lessons for campaign consultants were, at best, equivocal. Unlike Wellstone, Boschwitz was a strong supporter of Israel with a long record of activism in Jewish community affairs. According to the Arab-American Institute, he was also the Senate's fourth-largest beneficiary among AIPAC-supported candidates for reelection. Heavily outspent, the liberal-populist Wellstone nonetheless pulled off a notable upset. On the eve of the election, Boschwitz informed Jewish voters that Wellstone had failed to raise his children as Jews. In the wake of his defeat, the mailing was regarded as a monstrous blunder.[11]

The impact of the "lobby," that is, the aggregate of Jewish organizations based on AIPAC and the Conference of Presidents of Major Jewish Organizations, is a similar challenge to theory and practice. By any Washington standard, it has been acknowledged as a prodigy of skill and motivation since its creation in the middle 1950s. Yet it would be hard to prove objectively that it left deeper marks on the electoral and legislative process than such other acknowledged forces of political nature as the farm lobby and China lobby, the civil rights movement and right-to-life movement, the American Medical Association and National Rifle Association. Well into the 1960s, its impact was actually quite modest, and popular presidents from Eisenhower to Bush have consistently inflicted memorable defeats.

Arguments from historical memory, national interest, and calculated advantage are equally ambiguous. It is hard to overestimate the impact of the Holocaust on both Jews and non-Jews. Yet survey data suggest not only consistent support for Israel over time but especially strong support among the youngest cohorts, that is, those furthest from personal experience of World War II, and least exposed to once-traditional images of Israel as "a bunch of kibbutzniks turning the desert into a land of milk and honey."[12] Significantly, Israeli-U.S. public relations have relied increasingly on realpolitik, emphasizing Israel's importance as a "strategic asset" since at least the 1980s.[13] In fact, both the intelligence and security establishments have had reason to take Israel seriously since at least the 1950s. Yet at ten-year intervals since 1951, the question "Is Israel a strategic asset to the United States?" would have produced quite different answers.

The differential impact of the Cold War is an object lesson. Notwithstanding the Truman Doctrine, the Prague coup, and the Berlin blockade, both superpowers endorsed the partition of Palestine and the creation of Israel in 1947–1948, as though Britain were a common adversary. In reality, Britain remained the major ally of the United States. Despite the concurrent Soviet invasion of Hungary, the superpowers again combined to censure the Anglo-French-Israeli invasion of Egypt in 1956. Yet France and Britain were still the major allies of the United States, and Israel was never regarded as an adversary.

The 1970s brought an even unlikelier metamorphosis. All four powers—Britain, France, the Soviet Union, and the United States—were now programmed for détente. Yet the Israeli-U.S. relationship had meanwhile become a quasi-alliance against the Soviet Union. More ironic still, the new relationship was both encouraged and welcomed by leaders of an Israeli Labor party, whose predecessors once dreamed of neutrality between the superpowers; by U.S. Republicans, who once feared and suspected Israeli socialism; and by U.S. diplomats, who traditionally regarded Israel as a Cold War handicap. In 1948, George Kennan, one of the intellectual fathers of postwar foreign policy, had opposed the very creation of Israel. Now, he argued, it was the responsibility of the United States not only to do everything possible short of direct military intervention to prevent Israel's destruction but to ensure that Israel continued to deter all challengers with bargaining power left to spare. It was also the responsibility of the United States, he added, "to assure that no other great power comes to dominate the Near and Middle East as a whole."[1]

In 1981, with both Israel and the United States now governed from well to the right of center, their defense ministers completed the transformation with a Memorandum of Understanding even secular Israelis might have prayed for thirty years before. It committed Israel to close support of the United States in the event of Soviet intervention in the region. Four years later, alone among non-NATO allies, Israel was offered, and accepted, a collaborative role in the Strategic Defensive Initiative, the touchstone and leading edge of the most advanced defense research of the United States.

Despite all affinities, the relationship remained as pragmatic, even paradoxical, as ever. In the aftermath of the Iranian revolution and the Soviet invasion of Afghanistan, U.S. aid for Israel was based on what Israel could do against Soviet clients, presumably including Iraq. Ten years later, when Iraq invaded Kuwait, U.S. aid seemed to be based on what Israel would *not* do, that is, respond to Iraqi rocket attacks. Fearful that untimely Israeli retaliation would compromise Arab allies crucial to the U.S. war effort, U.S. diplomats rushed to Jerusalem to urge restraint. At the same time, U.S. planners redeployed their forces to hit Iraqi launchers aimed at Israel,[15] and assigned both U.S. crews and Patriot antimissile systems to the defense of Israel, the first time that U.S. troops had been so deployed.

Yet in more than forty years, a formal alliance has never been formally proposed, let alone debated, and ratified by the constitutionally mandated two-thirds majority of the Senate. In this respect, like many others, the relationship recalls the Israeli constitution, also unwritten.[16] With specific agreements at stake, Israelis have demanded a precision and comprehensiveness legendary among diplomatic draftsmen,[17] but the precision has always existed within a larger and deliberate ambiguity. Both at home and abroad, the imprecision can be traced to common causes. Domestically, such basic questions as "Who is a Jew?" are a perennial threat to the very consensus a constitution is meant to confirm. Externally, the basic question "What—and where—is the Land of Israel?" has been a challenge and deterrent to both partners. Before Americans can be asked to defend Israeli borders, Israelis must define them to the Senate's satisfaction. Given the vast and passionate difference of views since the beginnings of the state, and especially since 1967, it is not surprising that both sides have chosen instead to leave ill enough alone.

Always difficult to characterize, the relationship has sometimes resembled a romantic fling, occasionally a formal wedding, complete with canopy, broken glass, and a *ketubah,* the traditional marriage contract. But perhaps its most persistent likeness is the common-law relationship of a very odd couple, hard-pressed to live together but unable to live apart. At least three times since 1948, U.S. presidents have gone to the brink to guarantee Israel's existence. Yet no president since 1948 has been willing to acknowledge Jerusalem as Israel's capital by moving the U.S. embassy from Tel Aviv; and none since 1967 has recognized Israeli annexation of East Jerusalem and the Golan, or the legality of West Bank settlements. If shared values, practical achievement, complementary interests, and great expectations by each of the other are among the common benchmarks of Israeli-U.S. relations, so is a trail of cross purposes and mutual suspicion reminiscent, for example, of Franco-U.S. relations, and perhaps unique in the history of democratic alliances.

Like the history of Zionism itself, the history of the relationship reflects both Jewish strength and weakness. Britain's Balfour Declaration, for example, the charter for a Jewish National Home in Palestine, is a tribute to the considerable power and influence of Jewish money and opinion, not least in the United States, at a crucial moment in World War I. Yet the Zionist movement and state can also be traced to historical weakness. In a world of tribal nationalisms, intolerant of Jews and all minorities, Zionists believed that a Jewish state was their last best hope. Even before World War I, they justified Zionism as the most modern and appropriate self-defense for what millions had come to see as a national, even a "racial," rather than a religious minority. The terrible decades after World War I seemed only to confirm that Zionist fears were understated. By 1939, British policy put even the promised National Homeland out of reach. By 1945, with Europe's Jews destroyed and survivors practically excluded from refuge elsewhere, millions of Jews and non-Jews alike saw a Jewish state as an axiom of self-preservation.[18]

In many ways, the development of Israeli-U.S. relations since World War II has only recapitulated the paradoxical history of Jewish strength and weakness. On the one hand, Israel's military power has not only made it an attractive ally but even made believers of U.S. officers and officials, who once regarded the relationship with deep ambivalence. At the same time, its exposed strategic geography, systemic economic frailty, and intrinsic political fragility have made it almost uniquely dependent on external support, from not only foreign taxpayers but the Jewish Diaspora the state was nominally created to defend.[19]

In practice, the peculiar history of the relationship makes even chronology a challenge. De jure recognition dates back to January 31, 1949; de facto relations to the first minutes of independence on May 15, 1948. But the U.S.-supported United Nations General Assembly resolution of November 29, 1947, authorizing partition of Palestine into a Jewish and an Arab state, is at least as credible a baseline. This only leads backward to the difficult summer of 1946, when U.S. officials first agreed to the principle of a Jewish state; or the spring of 1945, when Americans for the first time encountered directly the horrors of the Holocaust, and assumed responsibility for its survivors in their German and Austrian zones of occupation;[20] or the summer of 1944, when delegates to both the Republican and Democrat conventions wrote early Jewish statehood into their presidential platforms. This leads, in turn, to the watershed conference of world Zionist leaders at New York's Biltmore Hotel in May 1942. Thitherto, Jewish statehood had been an unspecific, distant aspiration.

Thenceforth, unlimited immigration and the statehood it implied would be the movement's immediate goal. The Biltmore conference thus helped define the course, and energize the process, of U.S. foreign policy in ways that eventually proved irreversible.

The backward trail extends still further, for example, to September 1922, when a concurrent resolution of Congress expressed overwhelming support for the establishment in Palestine of a Jewish National Home; or October 1917, when President Wilson assented almost surreptitiously to Britain's Balfour Declaration, the de facto charter of Jewish statehood. Yet these only reflect and confirm the heritage of still earlier experience, including the arrival and coming of age of an American-Jewish electorate in the nineteenth century, and a distinctly American style and process of foreign policy. And so, to a point, the Israeli-U.S. relationship can be inferred and extrapolated from the very sources—the pioneer tradition, constitutional institutions, liberal immigration policy, eighteenth-century political values, and seventeenth-century religious values—that most Americans still regard as indigenously American.

From almost any perspective, the one thing the relationship has never been is simple. Perhaps what Shakespeare said of men—that some are born great, some achieve greatness, and some have greatness thrust upon them—can also be said of the Israeli-U.S. relationship. Born great from the ashes of the Nazi Holocaust, it achieved greatness in the aftermath of Suez, when the United States inherited Europe's traditional predominance in the Middle East. The debacle in Vietnam then thrust greatness upon the relationship by causing the United States to subcontract its global burden to regional allies and clients. Since 1948, U.S. support has been essential to Israel's survival, but the interdependencies have grown since at least the 1970s. In 1975, Americans seemed almost unmoved by the fall of South Vietnam, where hundreds of thousands of Americans had served and tens of thousands died. Yet barely a year later, when Israeli commandos rescued airline hostages from terrorists in Uganda on the 200th anniversary of American independence, Americans greeted the raid on Entebbe as though it were almost a victory of their own.

Among the consequences has been a pattern of mutual respect and dependence perhaps unique in the history of patron and client. Despite Germany's incomparably greater political and economic weight, its relations with the United States had a somewhat similar quality between 1949, when the Federal Republic was created, and 1989, when the Cold War ended. Yet from Chancellor Konrad Adenauer to Chancellor Helmut Schmidt, Germans took for granted shocks and high-handedness that Americans only rarely thought to impose on Israel.

In Thucydides' classical paradigm of relations between the large and small, the representatives of mighty Athens tell the islanders of tiny Melos, that "the strong do what they have the power to do and the weak accept what they have to accept."[21] But not even in early 1957, when Washington seemed willing to threaten Israel with all means short of military intervention to make it leave the Sinai, or in early 1974, when Israel's dependence on huge infusions of U.S. aid seemed only to reinforce its unwillingness to trade land for peace, has there been anything like a Melian dialogue between the two countries.

If anything, it might be argued that the Israeli-U.S. relationship has been a

Melian dialogue in reverse. Now and again, the relationship has even recalled the legendary Serbian peasant who announced on the eve of World War I that "we and the Russians are a hundred million strong, and we will never desert them." Henry Kissinger, one of the most astute and authoritative students of the Israeli-U.S. relationship, has written that

> Israel sees in intransigence the sole hope for preserving its dignity in a one-sided relationship. It feels instinctively that one admission of weakness, one concession granted without a struggle, will lead to an endless catalogue of demands as every country seeks to escape its problems at Israel's expense. It takes a special brand of heroism to turn total dependence into defiance, to insist on support as a matter of right rather than as a favor; to turn every American deviation . . . into a betrayal to be punished rather than a disagreement to be negotiated.[22]

But as Thucydides himself might have added, and would certainly have understood, it also takes a special brand of national self-assurance to temper such overwhelmingly superior power with forbearance; to extend support as a matter both of democratic obligation and legitimate mutual interest; and to turn every Israeli lapse and provocation into a disagreement to be negotiated rather than a betrayal to be punished.

For all its uniqueness, it is hard to overlook how comfortably the relationship fits the U.S. historical landscape. What could be more American than the taste for biblical symbolism, entrepreneurial zip, pioneer settlement, national independence, democratic republics, and feisty underdogs that Israelis have shared and exploited since the beginnings of Jewish settlement in Palestine? Was there anything inherently mysterious to Americans in the aftermath of World War II about the Jewish concern for security and collective responsibility in a world of hostility, now German, now Arab, but consistently Russian, that generations of Jewish immigrants had brought with them and passed on to their children? Is there anything new about the inherent responsiveness of presidents and Congresses to voluble constituents, and the inherent tension between foreign policy and domestic politics? Seen in any of these perspectives, the roots of the relationship seem as much a part of U.S. experience as of modern Jewish history. It might even be argued that the relationship derives from the same facts of historical life that made Europe both dangerous and bad for Jews while making the United States both safe and good.

Although U.S. foreign policy, the U.S. political process, and the perennial questions of national interest and identity are all far older than the Israeli-U.S. relationship, all have defined and shaped it in ways that can still be recognized. As normative in its way as his Farewell Address, Washington's letter to the Jews of Newport in 1790 is a practical example. Far from a precocious exercise in ethnic politics, the letter first addresses its readers as citizens, and only then as Jews. "The citizens of the United States of America have a right to applaud themselves for having given to mankind an enlarged and liberal policy, a policy worthy of imitation," he declares as a kind of postulate. "All possess liberty of conscience and immunities of citizenship." Only after establishing this, does he move from the general to the particular. "May the Children of the Stock of Abraham . . . continue to merit and enjoy the good will of the other inhabitants, while everyone shall sit in safety under his own vine and fig tree and there shall be none to make him afraid."

By the mid-nineteenth century, many of the consequences of this "enlarged and liberal policy" were already visible in ways that retained their validity a century later. By that time, the United States had also become a global presence, and produced a largely, though not exclusively, Yankee and Protestant foreign policy establishment, whose members interacted easily and even interchangeably with their merchant and missionary fellow citizens. But official or unofficial, Americans abroad inclined to see themselves as an extension of national virtue, and their norms as an example to mankind.

The Monroe Doctrine of 1823 is another early and conspicuous example. At one level a symbolic benchmark of U.S. exclusiveness, it is also a declaration of support for the inviolability of independent nations. A generation later, the same impulse led to recognition, then asylum, for the European revolutionaries of 1848–1849. Sometimes practically, most often symbolically, Americans supported almost anyone who found, or was believed to find, or claimed to find the U.S. example worthy of imitation. Even the map, with its Bolivar, Lafayette, La Grange, Kossuth, Kosciusko, Ypsilanti, Parnell, and Elkader, reflected the national passion for colonial liberation and self-determination.[23]

Bathed in a glow of biblical nostalgia, and frequently linked to the secularized religious passion that so impressed Tocqueville, the same national reflex led to proto-Zionist initiatives before Theodor Herzl, the nominal founder of the movement, had even been heard of. Sometimes its sources were philo-Semitic, sometimes not. Among their sponsors were a Presbyterian minister in Albany, a mid-century Mormon sect, and a Methodist business promoter from suburban Chicago, who claimed John D. Rockefeller, Cyrus McCormick and J. P. Morgan among his supporters. As the stream of immigration from Eastern Europe grew, such initiatives were increasingly carried on an undercurrent of paternalistic nativism, whose basic message was "Better Palestine than here." In the case of blacks, the logic led to resettlement in Liberia. But in the Jewish case, at least, there seems to have been no practical effort to act on it.[24]

Especially outside Europe, the missionary impulse went well beyond symbolism, moral support, and practical example. Like West Europeans, and especially the British, from whom so many Americans took their cues, Americans maintained well-established commercial and religious beachheads in China, Iran, and various corners of the Ottoman Empire before the end of the nineteenth century. The American University of Beirut was both a prime and a representative example of American Protestant enterprise and dedication. Founded in 1866 as part of a missionary establishment that itself went back to 1831, it had become a seedbed of intellectual revival and national awareness for much of the Arab world by the 1890s.[25]

In themselves, American missionary colleges, archaeological institutes, consulates, and religious tourism fell substantially short of a deliberate and coherent foreign policy in the Middle East. Even as late as 1909, there was no division in the State Department with a specific mandate to take an interest in the region.[26] Despite two world wars, it was another forty years before the division became a bureau under an assistant secretary for Near Eastern affairs, and even then its mandate extended unspecifically from India to Greece. In 1943, at the height of World War II, the entire division employed fourteen officers, and the desk officer for Palestine was concurrently responsible for Egypt and Iraq.[27] Yet in one way or another, even before the twentieth century, the basically Anglophile U.S. establishment that was to dominate foreign policy well into the postwar era had already developed and acquired meaningful, if not especially coherent, cultural, religious, and economic views and interests in the Middle East. Their impact and legacy too were still reflected in U.S. policy generations later.

In many ways, the new immigration only reinforced existing American reflexes and dispositions, even among the Anglophile, which millions of Irish immigrants were not. Suspicion of British colonialism came as easily to an Adams as to a Kennedy. Both Wilson's diplomacy and Roosevelt's Atlantic Charter confirmed that the nation's anti-imperialist reflex was compatible even with Anglo-U.S. alliance. Reflexive suspicion of the continental European political and social order came at least as easily to most Americans. Practically by definition, the United States existed to be what Europe's *ancien régime* was not. Suspicion of princes, kaisers, and above all czars came as naturally to Mark Twain or the first George Kennan as it did to the Polish, Bohemian, or Ruthenian peasant just off the boat.

Immigration and the realities of technology, trade, and social change added their own weight to the process. If young Americans were less likely than their European peers to see the world beyond their shores, the world came increasingly to them. Not the least of the links between the United States and the world were the millions of new arrivals who remembered what they left behind in the old country, valued what they found in the United States and learned fairly early what representative government could do. It could hardly be a surprise that Irishmen, Poles, Serbs, or Greeks continued to take an interest in what went on at home, or that their feelings, like Yankee feelings before them, might be reflected in policy. The results were visible in World War I, the nation's threshold experience with global power and responsibility. So regarded, America's victory was a triumph of both idealism and ethnicity, and President Wilson, the minister's son turned professor and New Jersey Democratic pol, was the chosen representative of both.

Encouraged by Paderewski, the Polish statesman-pianist, to muster a Polish-American unit in the U.S. Army for service in the war, Wilson hesitated. This kind of ethnicity, he thought, was something the United States could do very well without.[28] But the postwar map was evidence enough of U.S. concern for ethnic politics, and U.S. feeling for the national concerns of Poles, Czechs, Serbs, Italians, and others could agree on what they wanted, and it could be accomplished without U.S. money, guarantees, or troops.

In the world of independent national states that appealed to most Americans, the case for Jewish nationalism was theoretically as strong as any other—naturally providing that the Jews, like all the others, were willing to define themselves as a nation, and could agree on what they wanted. Given the variety of Jewish experience, this was hard enough. And both the outcome of the war and the nature of the postwar conflicts assured more complications.

The prevailing style of U.S. diplomacy and public policy was only a further problem for American Jews in search of help abroad. Like the establishment from which it predominantly came, the U.S. foreign service was as talented, generous, and bright as any other. Like its foreign peers and models, it was also snobbish, anti-Semitic, and allergic to the radical politics that had rightly or wrongly been identified with Jews since the middle of the nineteenth century. In a variety of postwar confrontations, even the bona fide Wilsonians, who held the diplomatic high ground until the end of World War II, found it consistently easy to favor Germans, Poles, or Arabs over Jews.

Almost inevitably, a Jewish constituency in politics was the necessary condition for a Jewish issue in foreign policy. Yet the development of one was still fairly recent even in the 1920s. Until the mid-nineteenth century, there had been only about 50,000 Jews in the United States in a population of 27 million. It was only after Europe's abortive democratic revolutions that this began to change with some rapidity, first with the coming of German and Central European Jews in the 1850s, then of Jews from Eastern Europe in the 1880s. By 1860, the Jewish population was estimated at 150,000; by 1880, 250,000. Between 1881 and 1914, they were then joined by nearly 2 million more.[29]

Significantly, the Jewish newcomers were as different from their predecessors as any immigrant group before them. Children of an overwhelmingly rural culture, where they brokered livestock, traded horses, and peddled pins and needles from door to door, most central European Jews had arrived in the United States at least as poor and foreign as any group to date. Their success in the half century that followed became the stuff of legend. By the end of the nineteenth century, central European Jews had become pillars of the community, captains of commerce, patrons of the arts and sciences, and even a modest political constituency, respectably but not exclusively Republican. There was discreet embarrassment at a New York dinner when Jacob Schiff, the aged financier, acknowledged in the presence of President Theodore Roosevelt himself that Roosevelt had appointed Oscar Straus to a cabinet position as "the ablest Jew who would be most acceptable to my race," that is, Schiff's fellow Jews.[30] Jews were nonetheless proud of Straus's appointment.

Reflective of the nation's passion for a blend of foreign *and* domestic politics, the post of ambassador to Constantinople was also increasingly understood as patronage. The result, improbably, was to make the Ottoman Empire a kind of Liberia for politically deserving Jews with unanticipated consequences for all the interested parties. In 1912, after President Wilson's election, the process led to the appointment of Henry Morgenthau, Sr. An almost aggressive non-Zionist, like most of the German-Jewish establishment, Morgenthau has nonetheless already conferred with Rabbi Stephen S. Wise, himself a confidant of Wilson's, and it was not least on account of the small Jewish community already in Palestine that Morgenthau agreed to take the job.[31]

The newcomers who began arriving in the United States in the mid-1880s were at least as poor and foreign as their central European predecessors, but they differed from the German Jews, let alone the rather patrician Sephardic Jews of the original Jewish establishment, in language, custom, politics, religious practice, even physical appearance. Above all they differed in numbers. As early as 1894, there were enough of them to swing a New York election. Mostly Yiddish in speech and traditional in religion, the newcomers were often believed to be radical in politics. It was very soon clear, however, that most of them had come to the United States to make good, not revolution. Already uncommonly literate, skilled, and mutually supportive, and favored by a growing economy, they needed about fifteen years to overcome the economic gap between themselves and the native-born.[32] Within half a century, their grandchildren had become as middle-class suburban as they themselves had been blue-collar urban.

In most of eight consecutive presidential elections from 1900 to 1928, more Jews seem actually to have voted for Republicans than Democrats, with only 1900 and 1916 as possible exceptions. But at the local level, Jewish voters could behave quite differently when asked. By the 1890s, significant numbers of Jews had discovered Democratic machine politics and vice versa.[33] By the beginning of the new century, they had also discovered the possibilities of political self-help through such institutions as the American Jewish Committee, founded in 1906.

Different as the new and the established Jews might be, there was considerable, if implicit, agreement about the agenda of collective interests and self-defense. Religious or secular, German or east European, uptown or downtown, virtually all Jews shared common concerns, and a Washingtonian view of their place in American society. As the intensity of Russian and Roumanian *pogromchiki* increased, they also worried collectively and increasingly about the fate of Jews abroad. In theory, this could mean anywhere, including the Ottoman Empire, but unsurprisingly, it tended to mean the countries from which they had recently emigrated themselves.

As early as 1903, the conjunction of a credible American-Jewish establishment, a credible network of civic organizations, credible political weight, and a good cause led to a benchmark presidential intervention. In their way, both the U.S. initiative and Russian response anticipated dilemmas and exchanges almost seventy years later. First, in the wake of the infamous Kishinev pogrom, and on the eve of his 1904 election campaign, Roosevelt received a delegation of Jewish leaders, and promised to forward their petition to the Russian government. He then based his case on human rights, rather than argue from purely U.S. interest. The Russians were unmoved by the initiative.

Soon after, in the wake of the Russo-Japanese War and the 1905 revolution, there were even more violent pogroms. This time, concerned with a Russo-Japanese peace, Roosevelt declined even to repeat what he had done two years earlier. Nonetheless, at the request of Oscar Straus, he at least approached Count Witte, the Russian delegate, during the Portsmouth peace negotiations. On the other hand, under his successor in 1911, an initiative to abrogate the Russo-U.S. commercial treaty of 1832 was remarkably successful—at least as domestic politics. There was only one opposing vote in the House and, after the administration notified the Russians it would terminate the treaty within a year, support in the Senate was unanimous.[34]

Providing at least that no further activity was indicated, it was easy, of course, for Americans and Jews to agree on Russia. Zionism, which arrived with the new immigrants, was another story. Despite the movement's modest numbers, there was already evidence of the idea's potential resonance. When its prophet, Theodor

Herzl died in 1904, there was general mourning in Jewish immigrant neighborhoods, but as yet, the potential was mostly theoretical. As long as Ellis Island was open to immigrants, the United States remained a land of opportunity in ways that Ottoman Palestine was not. The immigrants' very choice of the one over the other could be seen as a way of voting with their feet.

Meanwhile, not only did Zionism divide Jews from Jews, the endless permutations of secular and religious, socialist and liberal Zionism divided Zionists from one another. Jewish constituencies only rarely saw eye to eye on public and community issues, but Zionism produced a rare consensus. Uptown grandees saw it as a threat to their American-Jewish identity. Downtown labor organizers saw it as a challenge to working-class solidarity and proletarian internationalism. In striking contrast to the robust political activism of their successors a few generations later, many of the pious Orthodox even inclined to see Zionism as a preemption of God's will, and therefore a kind of secular heresy. On the eve of World War I, there were only an estimated 20,000 Zionists in an American Jewish community of 2.5 million.

Yet who joined and why could be as important as absolute numbers. It was generally agreed that the accession of Louis D. Brandeis in 1910 was a benchmark in the hitherto undistinguished history of American Zionism. Already a prominent Boston lawyer, and remote from the Jewish grass roots as only a German-Jewish patrician could be, Brandeis inclined to see Palestine as a kind of second United States, with Zionism as a kind of alternative Progressivism. Then came the war in Europe. With the world Zionist movement in search of a neutral alternative to its current venue in Berlin, Brandeis was elected chairman of the Provisional Emergency Committee by 150 delegates to a special meeting in New York. The committee was to run the international Zionist movement for the duration of the war.

Heavily engaged in Progressive politics, Brandeis was appointed to the U.S. Supreme Court in 1916. His appointment led to a raucous debate in the establishmentarian American Jewish Committee on his role in Zionism, and the political role of American Jews. But what seemed really at issue was the implied threat to traditional German-Jewish hegemony. When the debate was over, Brandeis walked out. By the end of the war, a newly organized Zionist Organization of America claimed 175,000 members, and Brandeis had helped redirect the course of American policy.[35]

But it was the war as such, with the unintended help of Germany, that made the crucial difference. Before the war, Zionist efforts had inevitably focused on the Ottoman Empire, known in the diplomatic shorthand of the era as "the sick man of Europe." Now the sick man was about to die. In 1914 Turkey joined the Central Powers, Germany and Austria, in the war against Russia, France, and Britain. In May 1917, despite official interest from the State Department, and the engagement of Morgenthau, the former U.S. ambassador to Istanbul, as U.S. negotiator, a separate peace initiative with Turkey fizzled out. In December 1917, Allenby's British troops entered Jerusalem. At this point, the question of Palestine became a matter for British, not Turkish, decision.

By this time, Palestine had also become the object of competitive bidding. Extended to the limits of their manpower, resources, and domestic support, both

Britain and Germany were reaching frantically for any weapon in an effort to preempt the other. The result was an unprecedented speculation in Jewish sympathy by men not thitherto noted for their own sympathy toward Jews. Reflective alike of political calculus and a strong sense of urgency, their initiative also confirmed a deep and ambivalent conviction that Jews were powerful.

In fact, in 1904, German Jews in the United States really had affected world politics by their control of credits for Russia's war against Japan.[36] A decade later, Jews not only were a factor in their own right as publishers, editors, bankers, scientists, and revolutionaries but were even seen as an instrument for reaching and winning neutral opinion in a war that potentially polarized the globe.

At this point, Washington, London, and Berlin alike took German Jews seriously—including, ironically, the German Jews of New York. The same capitals were equally serious about the Jews of eastern Europe—again including those in New York. Francophile and Anglophile Americans saw the kaiser's troops as "Huns," and Germany as the scourge of civilization, but for millions of east European Jews, the German Empire was not just a land of relative liberalism, socialism, and economic opportunity, it was their last best hope against Russia.

In reality, the war on the eastern front exposed millions of Jews not only to unprecedented danger and privation but to the emancipated nationalisms of Poles, Ukrainians, and Lithuanians.[37] Yet inadvertent, contingent, or tactical as wartime policy often was, the relative liberalism and wartime philo-Semitism of both the western European and the Central Powers continued to keep Jews relatively safe. In a world where any serious threats came almost invariably from the East, the benefits of a seller's market now extended even to American Jews. Neither more hawkish than the Poles, Czechs, or Anglo-U.S. establishment, nor significantly more dovish than the Germans or the Irish, they could be seen by both Democrats and Republicans as a target of opportunity, and in each case, the addressees extended from eastern Europe to the Lower East Side.

What the Germans might, in fact, have offered is inevitably conjecture,[38] but the British had good reason to take the possibility seriously, and even take an interest in Palestine for reasons of their own. This inevitably led to Brandeis. An American Jew in touch with both Wilson and popular Jewish feeling, he seemed also promisingly remote from the old and by no means Anglophile German-Jewish establishment.

The results were a gradual tilt in U.S. policy, and U.S. support for a British initiative toward an Ottoman Empire still allied with Germany but with which the United States was never at war. After discussions with Balfour, Chaim Weizmann, the leader of British Zionism, briefed Brandeis by telegram. Balfour then saw Brandeis himself on a visit to Washington shortly after the entry into the war of the United States. Personally Anglophile, Brandeis had thitherto been scrupulously neutral, not least for fear of complications in Palestine, where Jews remained under Ottoman rule. Balfour, in turn, was at pains to reassure both Brandeis and Wilson about the innocence of Britain's long-term intentions in Palestine. Ironically, far from asserting imperial claims, the British were keen for a joint, or even a unilateral United States protectorate.[39] For reasons both contradictory and complementary, this idea had little appeal for either Weizmann or the Americans. Weizmann, who regarded British power as crucial to Zionist success, saw the United States as unreliable. The Americans, in turn, unconsciously confirmed his reservations. What they wanted, at most, was to be reassured of Britain's good intentions, while avoiding long-term commitments of their own. As late as September 1917, Wilson's preference for national self-determination seems to have led him one way, while his preference for open convenants openly arrived at led him in another. Balfour notwithstanding, suspicions that Britain might have designs on thitherto Ottoman territory was hardly unfounded. Yet British concern that the Germans might win the race for millions of Jewish hearts and minds mattered to Wilson too.

On October 13, the President finally agreed to the British proposal for a Jewish homeland in Palestine, but characteristically neglected to tell the State Department, which learned of the declaration only after its official publication three weeks later. Secretary of State Robert Lansing was predictably upset. It seemed to him a gratuitous provocation of the Ottomans, a no-win appeal to Jews, and, not least, the surrender of the Christian holy places to Jewish control.[40]

By this time, reports of the Balfour Declaration appeared in the London papers side by side with reports from Petrograd (formerly St. Petersburg but not yet Leningrad) on the Bolshevik Revolution. Reflecting months and even years of elaborate negotiation, the sixty-seven-word text of the declaration was as exquisitely balanced as any document in the history of diplomatic prose. Yet the Fleet Street headlines could hardly have been more forthright:"Palestine for the Jews," declared the *Times* and *Morning Post;* "A State for the Jews," declared the *Daily Express.* American, Russian, even German Jews welcomed the declaration as an epoch-making event.[41]

After first dispatching proxies to Paris, including his protégé, the later Supreme Court Justice Felix Frankfurter, Brandeis himself appeared at the peace conference to ensure that the homeland was formally legitimated. Decades later, Frankfurter's exchange of letters with the Emir Feisal, the later king of Iraq, not only retains its interest but continues to move the reader. Presumptive evidence for the complementarity of Zionism and Arab nationalism, the letters are at once an expression of postwar idealism, unstated cross-purposes, and at least a trace of wish-think. "Indeed I think that neither can be a real success without the other," Faisal declared. "We cannot but live side by side as friends," Frankfurter answered.[42]

In 1920, the San Remo agreement subsumed the Balfour Declaration in a British mandate for Palestine.[43] By this time, U.S. policy had approached and cleared a watershed after a triangular showdown between the president, the State Department, and Congress. Once Wilson declared himself on the subject, Zionism seems all but to have vanished from his thoughts.[44] But it remained on the mind of Howard Bliss, who, as president of the American University in Beirut, was one of the few Americans to take a long-term professional interest in the Middle East. In summer 1919, at Bliss's suggestion, Wilson dispatched a blue-ribbon commission to Palestine and Syria under the joint chairmanship of Henry C. King, the president of Oberlin College, and Charles Crane, an industrialist with Wilsonian views.

The commission's findings were outspokenly anti-Zionist. "It must be believed that the precise meaning . . . of the complete Jewish occupation of Palestine has not been fully sensed by those who urge the extreme Zionist program," the commission reported. "For it would intensify, with a certainty like fate, the anti-Jewish feeling both in Palestine and in all other portions of the world which look to Palestine as 'the Holy Land.' "[45] With little policy to influence, the report had little impact at the time, but at least in the State Department, it was quoted at length and with conviction as late as 1943.

By this time, postwar divisions had led insider-Democrats—Brandeis, Frankfurter, Rabbi Wise—to leave organized Zionism, but this mattered less in a post-Wilsonian, Republican era anyway. Leaving their marks on Wilson was one thing; getting to Harding was another. The same applied to the State Department, where Lansing's nephew, Allen Dulles, was now in charge of the Division of Near Eastern Affairs. Brother of John Foster Dulles, the later secretary of state, and himself Director of Central Intelligence during the Suez crisis some thirty years later, Allen Dulles was polite but cold to Zionist appeals.

Yet as long as the House of Representatives represented its constituents, and a third of the Senate came up for reelection every two years, domestic initiatives could be resoundingly, if misleadingly, effective. In 1919, some three hundred members of Congress declared their support for the Balfour Declaration. Despite a landslide election in the interim, and a sea change in U.S. politics, the support was still there three years later.

Ironically, it took a League of Nations initiative to prove it. In the wake of San Remo, a new colonial secretary, Winston Churchill, had convened a conference of senior British officials in Cairo, where they divided what had thitherto been understood as Palestine. Thenceforth, it was agreed, the area subsumed in the Balfour Declaration would stop at the Jordan. To the east there would now be a second mandatory territory, the Hashemite Kingdom of Transjordan under the Emir Abdullah, brother of Faisal. In September 1922, the new arrangement was finally ratified by the League of Nations council.

Concerned for U.S. support, the council had meanwhile turned to the United States and Congress for affirmation of the British mandate, and thus, indirectly, of the Jewish homeland. In April 1922, the Zionists won a first symbolic victory when the State Department agreed to negotiate a treaty with Britain, approving the Palestine mandate. This then led in 1924 to an Anglo-U.S. convention, superseding an earlier agreement with the Ottomans. A latter-day reaffirmation of the open door, its presumptive beneficiaries included traditional Protestant philanthropies; the Standard Oil Company of New York, whose claims in Palestine dated back to 1913; and the American Palestine Company, founded in 1921 to fund Zionist development projects. But in the terrible years that followed, it was also employed with indifferent success on behalf of American-Zionist constituents, and therefore of Jewish settlement in Palestine.[46]

At the same time, Congress acted too in explicit support of the Balfour Declaration. In this case, the campaign led to Henry Cabot Lodge, Sr., chairman of the Senate Foreign Relations Committee, who sponsored a resolution, declaring U.S. support for "the establishment in Palestine of the National Home." Not known till now for Zionist sympathies, Lodge had also led the fight against League membership. But in a year, as the *New York Times* unsubtly pointed out, when he was up for reelection, his feelings on the League were clearly not an obstacle. Congressman

Hamilton Fish, another impassioned isolationist, sponsored a corresponding resolution in the House. Of course, the texts were brushed and combed to avoid any hint of U.S. commitment to the League of Nations. As in the Balfour Declaration itself, there was also an obligatory reference to the rights of existing populations in Palestine, but neither the omission nor the qualification seemed to cause a problem for American Zionists.

In May, the resolution passed the Senate with no opposition. In contrast to the Senate, the House at least held hearings that produced not only pro-Arab testimony but anti-Zionist rabbis. In June, the resolution nonetheless passed the House. The congressional vote itself was inconclusive proof that American Jews were Zionists, though it at least confirmed that American politicians thought they were.[47] Yet, if numbers were a guide, the movement by now was clearly retrograde. From a benchmark membership of 175,000 at the end of World War I, the Zionist Organization of America had declined by the late 1920s to about 25,000.[48] It was September before the president signed the conference committee version, but the delay was rather a reflection of the Washington summer than the political heat.

Though few American Jews, and still fewer non-Jewish Americans, would have seen the connection, what mattered far more for American-Jewish politics and the future of Israeli-U.S. relations was immigration policy, both in the United States and Palestine. In theory, Americans still sympathized with the new nations and national movements, but it was increasingly clear that they preferred to sympathize from a distance.

Already under fire before the war from Ku Klux Klansmen, Progressive academics, and organized labor, mass immigration was a relatively easy and attractive political target in the Red scare and slump that followed. In 1921, Congress imposed proportional quotas on immigrants for the first time ever; the obvious purpose was exclusion of the less-Protestant, north or west European immigrants, that is, those immigrants a majority of Americans regarded as the more foreign of the foreign-born. Thenceforth, the United States would admit no more immigrants from a given country in any given year than 3 percent of those who already came from there according to the 1910 census. In 1924, Congress imposed an absolute limit as well. Five years later, the new law took effect on the eve of history's greatest economic crisis. Beginning in 1929, total annual immigration from overseas was set at only a little over 150,000. The practical results of the new system included Polish and Russian quotas of 6,524 and 2,784 respectively, compared to a British quota of some 65,000. But Poland and the Soviet Union, both increasingly difficult places for Jews, were still the countries where most Jews lived.[49]

The same year, for the first time, communal riots in Palestine approached the threshold of civil war. Their roots were a matter of controversy, but the apparent cause—a confrontation at, and about, the Western Wall of what once was Herod's temple—was both parochial and, in Christopher Sykes's phrase, "in full keeping with the time-honored squalor of religious dispute in Jerusalem."[50] As Arab riots and Jewish shootings were again to confirm in 1990, it was neither the first nor last such confrontation. But this time the struggle was something of a watershed, revealing familiar motifs and much larger issues that were to recur and reverberate far into the future.

As so often, the immediate issue looked trivial, even ridiculous, in retrospect. A year earlier, Jews had put up a screen at the Western Wall to separate men from women. Disingenuously asserting offense to the integrity of the site, Moslem clerics from the nearby Mosque of Omar exploited the opportunity to demand action from the British authorities. When singularly ill-advised police appeared to remove the screen in the midst of the Day of Atonement service, Jews protested premeditated British anti-Semitism. Haj-Amin al-Husseini, both the son of a prominent Arab family and the British-appointed grand mufti, countered with fabricated photos of the Star of David flying over the Mosque of Omar. Sanctuary officials then built an extension to the mufti's house on the Temple Mount above the wall, and the Supreme Moslem Council demanded that a blind alley leading to the wall be turned into a thoroughfare. To the indignation of the Jews, British legal officers ruled that the Muslims were within their rights.

In August 1929, the confrontation began in earnest. By coincidence, the Sixteenth Zionist Congress had decided just that month to include non-Zionists, though obviously not anti-Zionists, in its executive body, the Jewish Agency, after a typically strenuous debate. In practice, this meant the co-optation of rich and liberal Western, but especially American, Jews, whose political influence and money were believed crucial if the movement were to succeed. The vote was a major triumph for Weizmann, the movement's pragmatic president, and a defeat for Vladimir Jabotinsky, the leader of the movement's militant, Revisionist, wing. But it was not surprising either that Arab nationalist leaders, who saw Zionists as virtually interchangeable, should miss the point, and see it rather as a globalization than a moderation of Zionist aims.[51]

A few weeks later, Jabotinsky's supporters appeared to protest British policy at government offices in Jerusalem. The occasion was the ninth of Av, the anniversary of the destruction of the Second Temple by the Romans. Echoing their leader's opposition to any further concessions until there was a Jewish majority in Palestine, they then continued to the wall for an anti-Arab rally. The next day a Jew was stabbed to death during Arab riots at the wall; his funeral turned into a Zionist demonstration. The week after, crowds of Arab peasants arrived in town with clubs, knives, and even guns. From here, the disorder turned overtly murderous with the deliberate slaughter of some 60 Jews in Hebron and 20 in Safed. Before the fury subsided, Arabs had killed 133 Jews, including women and children, and wounded another 339; 116 Arabs were killed, and 232 wounded, mostly by police. Among the Jewish casualties, according to the U.S. consulgeneral, were 15 wounded and 8 dead Americans, all students at a *yeshiva,* a religious college, in Hebron.

The turbulence in Palestine seemed only to confirm both British and U.S. second thoughts. A product of increasingly distant wartime circumstances, the Balfour Declaration had been devised by Liberals and Conservatives, including Churchill, Lloyd George, and Balfour himself, who remained loyal to their creation. But Ramsay McDonald's fragile Labour cabinet was now in charge at 10 Downing Street, and a reflexive anti-Zionist—Lord Passfield, the former Sidney Webb—was now in charge at the colonial office.

American Jews were upset first by British negligence, then by the unhelpfulness of the U.S. consul general, then by the State Department's obvious unwillingness to challenge British policy, even to the point of representing American-Jewish views at the official British inquiry. They were equally upset by Vincent Sheean, whose eyewitness account is of interest for not only its sharp and vivid sense of time and place but its candid analysis of his impressions and sympathies.

Already among the stars of a golden age of foreign correspondents, Sheean had been moved to visit Palestine by a basic sympathy for Jews acquired in college and deepened by later experience in Europe and the Soviet Union. His experience of Palestine then disillusioned and embittered him for life. Acknowledging historical injustices to Jews, he concluded that Zionism was nonetheless an injustice to the Arabs, irrespective of the social and economic benefits that Zionists invariably asserted. "Even if it were *exactly* [italics in original] what the Zionists say," he reported telling American-Jewish audiences, "it would not affect the fundamental problem, which is one of nationalism against imperialism."[52] In editions of his memoirs published after World War II, he still described the mufti, who had spent the war years in Berlin, as levelheaded, deliberate, mild mannered, thoughtful, and humane.[53]

The successive appearances of the official report on the August riots, a follow-up study of the Palestine economy, and a White Paper on British policy in Palestine were only further provocations. The inquiry linked the riots to endemic Arab frustration, both political and economic. Jewish immigration exceeded the country's absorptive capacity, the commission concluded. Though a Jewish population of 17 percent contributed 44 percent of government revenue, this finding was reaffirmed a few months later, when the colonial office study concluded that arable land was virtually exhausted, and industrialization had little future. Asserting equality of obligation to Jews and Arabs, the White Paper then denied any political status to the Jewish Agency, in effect subordinating future settlement to Arab consent.[54]

As previous experience with the Balfour Declaration and subsequent congressional action suggested, U.S. intervention might imaginably have made some difference in London. Conservative or Labour, British governments had learned to heed U.S. opinion and American Jews were already taken seriously. But this presupposed a U.S., not to mention American-Jewish, consensus on Palestine and Zionism, and there was far too little of that for any effect. Like Sheean, non-Jewish liberals were increasingly skeptical about Zionism. Jews were also badly divided on both means and ends. Meanwhile, the deepening depression preoccupied all governments. Already averse to foreign initiatives and disposed to look to London as their major global ally, U.S. officials could hardly be expected to be more Zionist than American Jews.[55] In the end, parliamentary opposition led to a letter from McDonald to Weizmann, nominally interpreting, but effectively repudiating, the latest White Paper.[56]

The British reversal, and the coming of Hitler, led to a revival of Jewish investment and immigration, but also of violent Arab resistance. An almost unbroken series of commissions, investigations, and studies followed. The common direction was retreat from the Balfour Declaration, but the tempo of retreat only increased with the urgency of Jewish need and the pressure for immigration certificates. On the eve of World War II and the greatest disaster in Jewish history, a new White Paper in 1939 grudgingly agreed to admit 75,000 more Jews to Palestine over a five-year period. Further Jewish immigration would then stop altogether.[57]

De facto repudiation by traditional friends at the same time their enemies threatened literal annihilation was only one of the ghastly ironies that now confronted European Jews, and with them, the Jews of the United States and Palestine. Repudiation was not total, but new circumstances turned previous strengths into virtual helplessness. However reluctantly and laboriously, Britain finally accepted the challenge of Hitler's war. In the end, Americans too agreed to do their share, even to the point of demanding—and imposing—Germany's total surrender. In compensation for the stringencies of the White Paper, Britain showed a trace of traditional generosity: despite 12.6 percent national unemployment, almost 50,000 refugees from Germany and Austria, plus 6,000 more from Czechoslovakia, were allowed to enter Britain by October 1939.[58] In the years before the war, some 258,000 Jews were also allowed to enter Palestine, bringing the combined Arab and Jewish population there to about 1.5 million. For perspective, an estimated 169,000 additional central European Jews were allowed to enter the United States, with its population of 130 million, in the same period. European Jewry still constituted the majority of world Jewry, and the Jews of Poland, Lithuania, and the Soviet Union still constituted the majority of European Jewry. They were now in Hitler's path.

For all possible political, historical, and psychological reasons, U.S. unwillingness to resist the Nazi danger, and American-Jewish failures to respond to it more effectively, have baffled and haunted people ever since.[59] Even on the eve of U.S. entry in the war, a reluctant House of Representatives only barely renewed the draft that assured a modicum of military credibility. Responsibility can be traced from the particular to the general. Breckinridge Long, a strategically placed assistant secretary of state in charge of visa policy, might alone have saved thousands. Instead, his rigid interpretation excluded and so condemned them. Millions of his fellow citizens were equally unmoved by the Nuremberg laws, the annexation of Austria, and the Munich crisis. The same year as the so-called Kristallnacht pogrom of November 9, 1938, 83 percent of American respondents answered no when asked their willingness to raise immigration quotas to admit refugees. A year later, despite extensive lobbying, support from Eleanor Roosevelt, the president's wife, and bipartisan sponsorship, a bill to admit twenty thousand children above the quota limit sank in both the House and Senate.[60] Liberals frequently held their fire rather than risk a backlash that might only make the immigration laws still worse.[61]

Meanwhile, American Jews, both Zionist and non-Zionist, hauled and tugged on such intractable dilemmas as where and how to resettle refugees; whether or not to consider the British proposal for a Jewish ministate in a partitioned Palestine; and whether to boycott German exports or accede to the so-called transfer agreement between the Jewish Agency and the German government that authorized the Jewish Agency to buy German goods with German-Jewish assets in return for emigrant visas that would allow German Jews to leave for Palestine.[62] Evidence in itself of the new imperatives, the United Jewish Appeal cut funding for the Jewish community in Palestine from 35 percent to 20 percent of its annual spending.[63] The difference presumably went to meet the needs of recent immigrants.

The Jewish calamity extended well beyond the failings of individual leaders, or the blind spots, contentiousness, indifference, or natural inadequacies of groups, organizations, and even governments. The real problem was history itself. In its cumulative impact on Germany, Austria, eastern Europe, and the Middle East, World War I had engaged and threatened Jews as powerfully as any experience since the French Revolution. But the war was not itself about the Jews. On the contrary, belligerent governments on both sides saw Jews as significant allies, equivalent in their way to Italians, Irish, Indians, Roumanians, or Poles.

All this changed irreparably and irreversibly with the coming of Hitler. Acknowledged or not, war against the Jews was what the Nazi regime was about. Their social and economic, if not their overt physical, destruction was its basic and unnegotiable common denominator from *Mein Kampf,* the ideological prospectus of the 1920s, to the political testament of April 1945. A generation earlier, Jews had been an object of courtship by both sides. With Hitler in power, their anti-German position could be taken for granted. But it had also, perversely, become counterproductive. To a degree uncommon before the war, Jews had now become generally and explicitly unpopular in Western as well as Eastern countries.[64] For more or less representative governments, only barely recovered from World War I, and shoulder-deep in the world's worst depression, the first concern was avoiding war altogether, and only then persuading voters to resist and rearm. "Die for Danzig?" French graffiti asked on the eve of World War II. "Die for the Jews?" It was a question no democratically elected government could even consider.

In the new world of absolute choices, where the fate of the Jews was among the stakes, there could be only one Jewish position. But it inevitably turned the Jews into hostages of the allies. The nominal Zionist position—fight the latest White Paper as though there were no Hitler, and Hitler as though there were no White Paper—was at once bravado, absurdity, and a paradox of existential profundity. At the moment it was most needed, Britain had shown that it could take away in increments what it had given less than a generation earlier. By 1940, France had been defeated, the Russians were engaged in wishful collaboration with the Germans, and millions of Americans were still disposed to avert their eyes.

Like the Jews of Palestine, American Jews had already faced an impossible dilemma since 1933. For the United States and the other democracies to allow mass immigration from central Europe was arguably to legitimate and even disseminate Nazi anti-Semitism in a world where anti-Semitism was already endemic. In 1937, according to Gallup, 46 percent of Americans were unwilling (and 47 percent willing) to vote for a Jew for president. In 1939, according to Roper, 53 percent of Americans answered affirmatively, and only 39 percent negatively, to the proposition "Jews are different and should be restricted." According to another survey, 58 percent of Americans already regarded European Jews as at least partly responsible for their persecution.[65] On the other hand, to confront, resist, and even impose sanctions on the Nazis was only to confirm and thus assure the hostage status of central European Jews.[66]

At the same time, to allow more Jews to enter a Palestine already on the edge of civil war was arguably an invitation to the Germans to make Arab hay against the British, as the British themselves had made hay against the Turks a generation earlier. In 1936–1939, the British army and police, plus Jewish self-defense, finally mastered and put down the campaign of coordinated Arab attacks. It was a cautionary experience for planners. For the young officers and intellectuals in Baghdad, Damascus, and Cairo, the combination of imported fascism and indigenous nationalism really was heady stuff; military intervention really was needed to contain it, and the grand mufti, whom the British themselves had inadvertently installed as the titular spokesman for the Palestinians, was, in fact, to end up in Berlin as a Nazi client. From a British staff officer's point of view, commitments to defend the Jews of Palestine only exposed already overextended forces on yet another vulnerable front. On the other hand, there was no question but that Britain was determined to carry on the war, if necessary by itself.

By 1940, with Britain as the last remaining obstacle to the Nazis, it could also be credibly argued that only the United States could keep the British in the war, and that only Roosevelt could persuade Americans to support them. The result was a new dilemma. Alone among American voter blocs, Jews had increased their support for Roosevelt from term to term, not least because this seemed the surest alternative to isolationism, and now seemed the best way to keep Britain in the war. In 1940, according to contemporary surveys, Roosevelt carried over 90 percent of the Jewish vote.[67]

The limits of their choice inevitably disarmed the Jews against an administration that took their votes for granted and had no intention of challenging the immigration laws, let alone the White Paper. "It is so very easy to hold press conferences and to call meetings; but we must in advance consider what it will lead to—that it will utterly shut every door and leave us utterly without hope of relief as far as FDR is concerned," Rabbi Wise conceded a few years later in a resigned and candid letter to Nahum Goldmann, the Washington representative of the Jewish Agency. "He is still our friend, even though he does not move as expeditiously as we wish," he added. "But he moves as fast as he can, in view of the Congress on his hands, a bitterly hostile and in a very real sense a partially anti-Semitic Congress."[68]

Absurdly, Jewish support was a problem for Roosevelt, too. With the Jewish vote already committed by 1940, Jews had effectively lost what leverage they had, for example, on a State Department unwilling even to fill existing quotas on grounds that refugees might be German agents. Roosevelt also paid. Jewish support inevitably implied active opposition to Hitler. From here it was only another step to the active intervention a majority of Americans still opposed. Already resolved to take all steps short of war, Roosevelt met the challenge halfway. Support for Britain, he told Americans, was the best way to avoid the war. Under the circumstances, any suggestion of fighting for the Jews was a potential disaster.

In the end, ironically, it was neither the Americans nor even the Germans who resolved the Jewish dilemmas but the Japanese. Their decision to bomb Pearl Harbor on December 7, 1941, led four days later to Hitler's decision to declare war on the United States. In little more than a year, Hitler's eccentric but crucial expression of solidarity with Japan led directly and indirectly to Berlin's Wannsee, New York's Biltmore Hotel, and the Anglo-U.S. summit at Casablanca, where fundamental and radical decisions were taken by the Germans, the Zionists, and the allies, respectively.

Wannsee confirmed and made deadly clear what the Nazi regime had thitherto left vague and unresolved, despite nine years of racist anti-Semitism and a killing program under way in eastern Europe since at least the invasion of the Soviet Union in June 1941. Thenceforth, it was official, if undeclared, German policy that the Jews of occupied Europe were not, for example, to be resettled in eastern Poland or Madagascar, nor killed ad hoc as theretofore, but deported and murdered.[69] Casablanca, in turn, made public and explicit what had also thitherto been unresolved in the U.S. perception of the war and the world: that the destruction of Nazi Germany was an absolute goal, that the United States was in the war to stay, that the United States as a consequence of its new policy would assume coresponsibility as an occupying power for the postwar government of Germany, and that the United States would join the other victors as a power in the postwar world.

What happened in New York was a direct and explicit linkage of Europe and Zionism, but it was also a skirmish and quantum jump in the ancient struggle for definition and control of the Jewish community in Palestine. Like Brandeis's emergency committee a generation earlier, the Biltmore conference energized a movement that was again approaching entropy. Of some 650 delegates, about 600 were American, representing all Zionist factions but the Revisionist right. But it was the visitors, especially Chaim Weizmann from London and David Ben-Gurion from Palestine, who were decisive.

Since at least 1937, when Britain's Peel Commission first raised the possibility of a Jewish state in part of Palestine, both Weizmann and Ben-Gurion had favored statehood sooner, not later. They had differed significantly on when and how, and the future role of Britain. The latest conference was both a milestone and a watershed. Consistent with contemporary usage, the final resolution was discreetly coded: "The Conference urges that the gates of Palestine be opened; that the Jewish Agency be vested with control of immigration . . . and that Palestine be established as a Jewish Commonwealth integrated in the structure of the new democratic world." But it was clear from the outset that *commonwealth* meant state.

The resolution was important in at least three ways. With its vote for early statehood, the conference confirmed the transfer of responsibility and power from the Zionist diaspora to the Jews of Palestine, from the old, intrinsically European, establishment of Weizmann to the new, indigenously Palestinian establishment of Ben-Gurion, and finally from Europe to the United States. American Jews, who understood the politics of charity and philanthropy, had thitherto avoided the politics of politics. Thenceforth this would all be different as their leaders set out to reorganize their constituents, line up public opinion, and deploy the Jewish vote. Religious or secular, socialist or nationalist, uptown or downtown, the common goals would now be Jewish self-defense and unrestricted immigration to Palestine. It was less clear that rescue efforts, if only by default, would be left to other agencies.

Though its enormity was still unperceived, the crucial variable was, of course, the destruction of European Jewry. Until the war, there had been millions of Jews in Europe, and thousands in Palestine. The combination of the war and the Nazis now made Palestine the Zionist center of gravity. The homeland argument was as important as ever, Ben-Gurion told delegates, but it was no longer enough. Statehood was crucial to solution of the refugee problem that would presumably follow the war.

Yet the differences on statehood were also left unclear, and many were still reverberant fifty years later. There was little support for binationalism, but there was also little consensus on borders, partition, and federalism. There would be grave consequences if no solution were found to the Arab-Jewish problem, one Hadassah delegate declared. There could be "no deviation from the original plan for Palestine, even in the name of peace," replied a delegate from Mizrachi, the religious Zionist faction.[70]

There are times when headlines make history, and reporters are conscious of watching it, but it clear from the *New York Times* that this was not a simple game, and few outsiders even knew the players. For the first time, a *Times* headline reflected the magnitude of Ben-Gurion's role, yet a second-day story only confirmed how imperfectly the *Times* understood what it was watching. The outcome, the *Times* reported, could be "regarded as an indication of unity behind established leadership rather than as an expression of any new or surprising stand."[71]

The British, at least, got the message about statehood and immigration. From the perspective of their embassy in Washington they also concluded that the maximalists had won, and were now close to the revisionists.[72] This made sense only if statehood were seen as its own reward, irrespective of where, when, and how. In fact, what the conference confirmed was not that the center had failed to hold but that it had moved. The perennial cold war between the congress majority and the Revisionists was evidence not only that most Zionists saw statehood as a means, but that Zionism was, as it would remain until at least 1977, among the most centrist of national liberation movements.

By the end of the war, creation of the Jewish commonwealth was the consensus position of not only Zionists but most American Jews, who in turn found wide support among non-Jewish Americans. The shift reflected the dynamics of opinion making in a movement that was itself more united than ever before. In the wake of Biltmore, Ben-Gurion concluded an unprecedented alliance with both religious and labor Zionists that was later subsumed in the constitutive governments of Israel.

At the same time, American Zionists moved energetically to co-opt non-Zionist support. In August 1943, the thitherto centrifugal American movement reconstituted itself as the American Zionist Emergency Council (AZEC) under Abba Hillel Silver, a Cleveland rabbi of Republican sympathies, confrontationist disposition, and legendary forensic gifts. Despite a tentative agreement to pursue the course of moderation and emphasize non-Zionist rescue efforts, Silver persuaded the American Jewish Conference, an equally unprecedented assembly of thirty-three Zionist and non-Zionist groups convened at the Waldorf Astoria, to endorse the Biltmore program. Of the five hundred delegates, only the four-member delegation from the American Jewish Committee voted no.[73]

In the aftermath of the meeting, the dissidents walked out, and a further minority left even the American Jewish Committee to form their own bitterly anti-Zionist American Council for Judaism. Under Lessing Rosenwald, a former president of Sears Roebuck, and Arthur Hays Sulzberger, the publisher of the *New York Times,* the secessionists over the next eighteen months organized some 5,300 members in 3,400 communities. By comparison, by November 1943, AZEC could draw an audience of 15,000 to a single rally at Carnegie Hall.[74]

Meanwhile, the new consensus came under fire from the Revisionists under the leadership of Peter Bergson (Hillel Kook), who arrived from Palestine early in the war. Beginning with the American Committee for a Jewish Army, intended to bring pressure on the British by rallying U.S. support behind the old Jabotinskyite appeal for a British-armed corps of Palestinian Jews, Bergson eventually succeeded in lining up a remarkable collection of New York, Washington, and even Hollywood establishmentarians for an ad hoc army of his own. In the style of other mass organizations of the era, his first creation then led to a shrewdly targeted medley of affiliates. The American League for a Free Palestine demonstratively distinguished the "Hebrews" of Palestine from the "Jews" of the United States. The Emergency Committee to Save the Jewish People of Europe even avoided mention of Palestine.

Both a child of the Popular Front era and an anticipation of public relations campaigns to come, Bergson's League was an anti-White-Paper lobby with a typical roster of public figures on its letterhead. Among the more visible names were members of the House of Representatives, including Will Rogers, Jr., and the later Senate Minority Leader Hugh Scott; Senator Guy Gillette, a Democrat from Iowa, and the authors Louis Bromfield, Louis Untermeyer, and Lion Feuchtwanger. Decades later, one of the sponsors, Rabbi Baruch Korff, resurfaced as a quixotic Watergate-era defender of Richard Nixon.[75] Also launched in 1943 as a lobby for the creation of Allied and U.S. government agencies to rescue European Jews, Bergson's Emergency Committee too contended for attention in Washington. Declaring it unrepresentative of the Jewish community, a furious Stephen Wise testified against it before the House Foreign Affairs Committee, and the American Jewish Conference all but accused it of fraud.[76]

Perhaps the most widely admired of Bergson's achievements was a literal *coup de théâtre*. Recruited by Bergson as a man who knew his Hollywood and Broadway, Ben Hecht, the journalist and playwright, managed in turn to recruit Billy Rose, the columnist and producer; Kurt Weill, the composer; Moss Hart, the director; and an astonishing cast of collaborators, that included not only the actors Paul Muni, Edward G. Robinson, Sylvia Sidney, and Marlon Brando but even the jockey Eddie Arcaro. Their collaborative effort, a pageant called "We Shall Never Die," played beneath forty-two-foot tablets of the Ten Commandments. Like the prize fights and political rallies of the era, it even opened at Madison Square Garden, before touring the country in 1943.[77]

The same year, the Jewish Agency moved Nahum Goldmann to the United States to lobby political leaders. A diplomat in all but the formal *agrément,* Goldmann opened for business in Washington, where he saw Brandeis, Frankfurter, Under Secretary of State Sumner Welles, and the later Secretary of State Dean Acheson with some regularity.[78] In 1944, Bergson, who had acquired the former Iranian embassy on Massachusetts Avenue, opened his own "Hebrew embassy." Soon afterward, a page-one exposé in the *Washington Post* called attention to the million tax-deductible dollars Bergson acknowledged he had raised, the conspicuous elegance of the premises, the mysterious unaccountability of the money not invested in the property, the zoning problem occasioned by his ambiguous use of the building for residential and business purposes, and the thirty-four-year-old Bergson's own exemption from the draft, despite visible good health and physical vigor. It also reported that three U.S. senators, Scott Lucas, Harry Truman, and Albert Chandler, as well as Justice Brandeis's widow, protested unauthorized use of their names in a full-page *New York Times* ad denouncing U.S. government refugee and rescue policy. There were similar complaints from another New Deal senator, Robert F. Wagner, Sr., and several labor leaders.[79]

Challenged and provoked by non-Zionist inertia and Revisionist activism, mainstream Zionism rallied its own conspicuously liberal and impressively heavyweight support. Under its chairman, Emanuel Neumann, an American Palestine Committee lined up 67 U.S. senators, 143 U.S. representatives, and 22 governors in 75 local chapters with an aggregate membership of 15,000. Concurrently, the Christian Council on Palestine grew from circa 400 to 3,000 in the years that followed, and survived into the 1950s. Patrons and signatories included the theologians Paul Tillich, Reinhold Niebuhr, and Daniel Poling; Carl J. Friedrich, the Harvard academic; Senators Wagner and Charles McNary; the labor leaders William Green and Philip Murray; Eric Johnston, the spokesman for the movie industry, who would try a decade later to bring peace to the Middle East in the form of a comprehensive water plan; and even Sumner Welles, a personal friend of the president, and the State Department's second in command till his sudden resignation in 1943. In startling contrast to the department's official position, Welles even agreed to be Maryland state chairman. Helen Gahagan Douglas, the victim of a celebrated antiliberal backlash when she later ran against Richard Nixon for a Senate seat from California, was its national secretary.

Still another concurrent campaign aimed for minds as well as hearts. This one generated a petition from 150 college presidents and 1,800 professors from forty-five states, including Mortimer Adler, Hans Morgenthau, Arthur Schlesinger, Sr., and Albert Einstein; a widely distributed essay by Welles called "Palestine's Rightful Destiny," and a survey of Palestine's untapped potential by Walter Clay Lowdermilk, a senior official in the Department of Agriculture. Lowdermilk, who had toured the Middle East in 1938–1939, returned to the United States enchanted by Jewish agriculture, and convinced that a Jordan Valley authority, obviously based on the Tennessee Valley Authority (TVA), would support at least four million postwar settlers. Within a year of the Lowdermilk book's[80] publication, AZEC had done its part to assure that it had gone through seven editions, totaling 16,000 copies; appeared in Hebrew and Spanish translations; been distributed gratis to 1,500 members of Congress, government officials, journalists, diplomats, educators, and religious leaders; and been publicly approved by former Sen. George Norris, the father of the TVA and an almost iconic figure among U.S. liberals.[81]

Much as it had in World War I, organized Zionism had now grown from an extended family circle to the kind of numbers politicians notice. By war's end, the combined membership of the Zionist Organization of America plus the women's group, Hadassah, was an estimated 280,000, more than a fivefold increase since 1935. By 1948, the year of Israel's independence, membership had nearly doubled again, peaking at 500,000, or even 700,000, if the labor and religious Zionists, who continued to maintain autonomous organizations, were added to the total.[82]

Measured against the movement's basic agenda, the results were both impressive and inconclusive. Beyond anything to date, existential urgency, political skill, and even a subliminal sense of collective guilt combined to activate a population thitherto queasy about Jewish, let alone Zionist, political activity. They then enabled the Zionist mainstream to outflank Revisionists and anti-Zionists; co-opt non-Zionists; persuade Jews and non-Jews of a common sense of purpose; address; and make a visible impression on the political process.

By 1943–1944, seventeen state legislatures had passed resolutions supportive of a Jewish homeland. In 1944, as Peter Grose notes, over 3,000 civic organizations of all kinds, many in towns with no Jews to speak of, had passed pro-Zionist resolutions and notified their representatives in Congress. A year later, forty-one of forty-eight governors had signed an AZEC-sponsored petition that called for presidential action to "open the doors of Palestine." With amplification from AZEC, a single telegram from the Jewish Agency yielded coordinated mass demonstrations in thirty cities in a single month. These led, in turn, to constituent canvasses of some sixty U.S. senators on a given day, twenty-seven speeches on Palestine in forty-eight hours, and remarks from thirty-four more senators in the *Congressional Record*.[83]

Within two years of the May 1942 Biltmore conference, its resolutions had been written into the 1944 national platforms of both major parties. "We call for the opening of Palestine to . . . unrestricted immigration and land ownership, so that in accordance with the full intent and purpose of the Balfour Declaration of 1917 and the resolution of a Republican Congress in 1922, Palestine may be constituted as a free and democratic Commonwealth," the Republicans declared. "We favor the opening of Palestine to unrestricted Jewish immigration and colonization and such a policy to result in the establishment there of a free and democratic *Jewish* commonwealth," [author's emphasis] the Democrats replied, and the president added, "If re-elected, I shall help to bring about its realization."[84]

Though scarcely perceived as a decisive factor, the historical fortune that made Britain the mandatory in Palestine, and put Palestine on the margin of world affairs, was a kind of bonus. As the end of the war approached, Britain was still an acknowledged power in the world, a major partner in the diplomatic architecture of postwar Europe, and a uniquely popular ally with millions of Americans not thitherto given to Anglophilia. It was clear to insiders and newspaper readers alike that the Anglo-U.S. relationship was one of the foundations of postwar peace. At the same time, it was clear that the British could hardly help but carry on the war with Japan as well as Germany; that there was no question or danger that Britain would succumb to insupportable war weariness, or that it would yield to the temptations of an opportunistic separate peace. Yet the inexorable transition from U.S. partner to U.S. client was another fact of life. For better and for worse, Britain was in desperate need of U.S. support, and sensitive to U.S. influence on India and Ireland. It had been clear since 1917 that it was also sensitive on Palestine.

At each of these points, the British situation differed significantly from the Soviet Union's. The Soviet role in the war against Germany was both crucial and fundamental. Yet as late as 1943, Soviet willingness to carry on the war with Germany was arguable, while Soviet willingness to fight Japan remained a matter of vital interest as late as summer 1945. Had the fortunes of war made Russians the masters of the Ottoman Middle East in 1917, and thus imaginably the mandatory power in Palestine in the years thereafter, would Americans have had the same success persuading them to receive more Jewish immigrants, let alone concede a Jewish state in an area they traditionally regarded as crucial to their security? The question is obviously hypothetical. But it is not *ipso facto* silly in assessing the relative success of Jewish-American and Zionist politics between 1944 and 1948, and the failures of Poles and Polish-Americans to assert Polish national claims in the same period.

It was one thing to get congressional attention, another to get congressional action, another still to affect a foreign policy process that was itself inherently uncongressional. An obvious test case was the campaign in January 1944 to get Congress to oppose the White Paper, in part to preempt Bergson, in part to resume where Congress had stopped in 1922. Yet despite declared support "for a Jewish commonwealth" from 411 of 535 members of the 78th Congress; despite the demonstratively bipartisan cosponsorship of Senators Robert A. Taft and Robert Wagner, whose views on labor relations were benchmark alternatives; despite even an impending election, the Senate backed off. Senator Harry S. Truman was among the majority, reluctant to endorse a resolution "which affects the foreign relations program between Great Britain, the United States, and the Middle East." In the aftermath of the election, the Foreign Relations Committee tried and failed again. The vote was 10–8. In both cases, it was summit-level interventions by senior administration officials that made the difference. With the invasion of Europe a half year away, Chief of Staff George Marshall and Secretary of War Henry Stimson appealed against anything that might divert Allied troops. On the eve of Yalta, Secretary of State Edward R. Stettinius, Jr., intervened for the same reason. But so did the American Council on Judaism and even Rabbi Wise—the former out of concern for the status of American Jews; the latter out of concern for the patience of the president.[85]

The war among the Jews and the implicit deadlock among the political authorities almost inevitably created a dilemma for even such a highly professional Jewish practitioner as Congressman Sol Bloom of New York. A member of the House since 1922, Bloom was now chairman of the House Foreign Affairs Committee. What was he to do, he reportedly asked a friend, when Rabbi Silver told him to do one thing and Rabbi Wise told him to do the very opposite?[86] Though hardly a Zionist, Bloom took an interest in Jewish issues for every possible reason. But he was also a credible judge of what the political traffic would bear. Reflecting the postwar sea change and the urgencies of 1948, Bloom points in his memoirs to his services on behalf of a Jewish commonwealth, and pushing Britain to honor its obligations under the Balfour Declaration. But only 3 of his 327 pages address Palestine and Israel.[87] His circumspection during and immediately after the war is a revealing baseline for measuring the later activism of younger Jewish colleagues like Emanuel Celler and Jacob Javits.

A phone call to Stettinius in January 1945, with Bloom in the role of a Jewish Br'er Rabbit, affords a very different perspective into the realities of the day than the AZEC letterheads or Bergson's pageants. At issue was an ad hoc "Jewish" expert to advise senior State Department officials on the growing volume of Jewish démarches and initiatives. Unsurprisingly, Bloom had a candidate, an established businessman and former president of the Zionist Organization of America, with a long history of Jewish community activity and charitable engagement.

From the opening exchange of "Hello, Ed," and "How are you, boy?" to the closing wish for success at Yalta and goodbye, the prevailing tone is egalitarian American male bonhomie. The undertone is quite different. "I am getting sick and tired of these Rabbis . . .," says Stettinius. "Why don't you put one of those fellows in to deal with all of them?" Bloom replies with studied disingenuousness. Is the candidate—who was recommended, as it happened, by Wise, Roosevelt's confidant Judge Samuel Rosenman, and his Foreign Economic Administration counsel Oscar Cox—in fact the right man, Stettinius inquires? He lives in Washington, has no vote, contributes to Czech and Soviet war relief, is unbeholden to the New York and New Jersey political bosses, is rich enough to make it on his own, and is tough enough to say no, Bloom answers. This makes him independent, he emphasizes, and "the only Jew I know who is independent."[88] In the end, neither Bloom's nor anybody else's candidate was appointed.

The crucial priorities were naturally set in the White House, not the State Department. "If the proposal for the establishment of a Jewish State were carried through with determination and speed, the Arabs would in the end accept the accomplished fact of the existence of such a state," particularly if Britain and the United States provided "on broad and generous lines for the political and economic future of the Arab countries," Wagner wrote Roosevelt in January 1945. But "a long transition period," he added presciently, "would be disastrous."[89]

Although probably too sanguine by half, this was at least an arguable position. On the other hand, it was hardly one that Roosevelt was prepared to argue, despite the customary interview with Wise on the eve of his departure for Yalta. For the long run, the president fantasized characteristically about extending the New Deal to the Middle East. "When I get through being President and this damn war is over, I think Eleanor and I will go out to the Near East and see if we can put over an operation like the Tennessee Valley system that will really make something of that country," he reportedly told Frances Perkins, his Secretary of Labor.[90] Meanwhile he warned leaders of the American Jewish Committee that a Jewish state in Palestine was beyond accomplishment. The most that could be hoped for, they quoted him, was liberalized immigration secured through a world organization, and not only to Palestine but to other countries too.[91]

Roosevelt's hesitations were both general and specific. His health, the practical contingencies of present and future military operations, the unsettled fate of Central Europe, the ambiguous relationship with the Soviets, the presumed fragility of public support for any postwar commitment, personal memories of what Congress had done to Wilson—all were plausible grounds for caution. In Roosevelt's own lifetime, the futures of Poland and Germany had been at the heart of two world wars. He was hesitant to commit himself on either.[92] Was it surprising that he was also unwilling to go out on a limb over Palestine? A steady stream of foreign service reports from and about the Middle East could only reinforce his reluctance. "The one thing I want to avoid is a massacre or a situation which cannot be resolved by talking things over," the President wrote Wagner in cold acknowledgment of the senator's enthusiasm for forceful U.S. leadership.

On the eve of the February 1945 Yalta Conference, there was a prodigious campaign of letters, telegrams, and phone calls to put Palestine on the agenda. Not surprisingly, the State Department campaigned to keep it off. It was inadvisable for the

United States to take any definite stand on the future of Palestine, one memo concluded. It was therefore inadvisable to pursue any long-range settlement without Soviet approval. "We should not give the Soviet Government an opportunity to augment its influence in the Near East by championing the cause of the Arabs at the expense of both the United States and Great Britain," the author continued, anticipating arguments that would be heard more and more in years to come. In case a U.S. position was still required, he proposed enjoining the British to consult both Jews and Arabs, and make the results available to the Soviet and U.S. governments "so that a plan for a Palestine settlement can be worked out with the concurrence of all the great powers."[93] In the end, there was a single revealing, if inconclusive, exchange on Palestine at the last plenary session. "The President said he was a Zionist and asked if Marshal Stalin was one," the transcript reported. "Yes," Stalin answered cautiously, but he "recognized the difficulty of solving the Jewish problem," and incidentally regarded Jews as "middlemen, profiteers and parasites".[94]

En route home from the Crimea, Roosevelt conferred with King Ibn Saud of Saudi Arabia, whose country was already an object of official U.S. interest. It was also the only Arab state at the time with which the United States had a certain special relationship, and some considerable hopes for the future. The king confirmed Roosevelt's worst suspicions. Not only was he intransigently opposed to settling Jews in Palestine, he was even opposed to planting more trees there. Frustrated and chagrined, Roosevelt could only agree to "assure his Majesty that he would do nothing to assist the Jews against the Arabs and would make no move hostile to the Arab people." He then went home. "On the problem of Arabia, I learned more about that whole problem, the Moslem problem, the Jewish problem, by talking with Ibn Saud for five minutes than I could have learned in the exchange of two or three dozen letters," the president told Congress two weeks later in a deviation from his prepared text.[95]

The ad lib, with its implied concession of an Arab veto, caused both chagrin and bewilderment. On Roosevelt's death a few weeks later, it even caused a sense of betrayal as policymakers and frustrated Zionists alike behaved as though it were a kind of will. But there was both more and less to this than met the eye. Before the meeting, Roosevelt might really have believed that Arab opposition was exaggerated. But given his celebrated propensity for squaring circles, it is at least as likely that he left, resolved to muddle on till events forced his hand or something better turned up.

Meanwhile, it was a matter of normal prudence to avoid a no-win confrontation with any of a dozen foreign and domestic windmills, including Jews and Arabs, Congress and the State Department, the Soviets and the British. There was still, after all, a war with Japan to win and a need for allies to help win it. There were still twelve million Americans in uniform who wanted to resume their normal lives as quickly and safely as possible. Till proven otherwise, it was reasonable to assume that postwar isolationism remained a risk and hazard, and that the Arabs meant what they said about resisting Jews with force. Given the choices as Roosevelt might have seen them, there was no reason to yield to Congress. There was no reason to yield to the State Department either. And so the war ended far short of the Biltmore goals, for all their symbolic successes. There was still no Jewish state. There was barely a Jewish army. Repeal of the White Paper was nowhere in sight. The Zionists had failed not only to move Britain and the president but even Congress.

Yet skill, tenacity, and circumstances had also made the Zionist cause a fact of U.S. political life in a way it had never been before. With powerful allies across the national spectrum, and powerful adversaries in the administration itself, American Jews now had the full impact of history to exploit and contend with. After touring the United States in January 1945, Mordechai Ben-tov, editor of *haMishmar,* a leftish Jewish paper in Palestine, told the State Department's E. M. Wilson that Americans tended to a sentimentally humanitarian view of Palestine rather than an informed view of the Middle East.[96] This was surely true, but hardly surprising, and even crucial, if most Americans were to face the Jewish problem at all.

Sooner or later, decisions were inevitable, in part because the United States was democratic, in part because it was powerful. Like it or not, for better or worse, the United States was now in charge. Morally, politically, strategically, and administratively, there had to be an answer to the Jewish question. This inevitably led to Palestine. Alternatively, the president could try to resettle survivors in Europe, press Congress for immigration reform, and defy the Zionist agenda—not to mention his constituents, both liberal and Jewish. In fact, all three options were considered and even attempted, but they exceeded the stamina, resources, and imagination of even the United States in 1945.

That left an untested capacity to influence Britain with minimal cost at home. "Americans seemed to be searching for some solution to the refugee crisis that would not call on them to make any significant sacrifice," one American-Jewish historian noted decades later.[97] "The Zionists are counting heavily on Mr. Truman's sympathy for their cause, to which they add the conviction that, unlike the late President, he will not seek to play politics with them," the British embassy informed the Foreign Office. "This last represents pure wishful thinking rather than any basis of concrete evidence," it added.[98]

2

Stopping the Buck

Only three years later, on May 14, 1948, at 6 P.M. Washington time, Israel had become a state, and President Harry S. Truman, as Under Secretary of State Robert Lovett noted, had become its midwife, if not its father.[1] For reasons only incidentally related to Palestine, the United States had meanwhile become a major Middle Eastern power with formal commitments to Greece and Turkey, and a relatively clear and important stake in the stability and independence of Iran.

Ecstatically received in Israel itself, the proclamation of statehood appears to have been acknowledged in the White House with something like grim satisfaction. De facto recognition, announced almost immediately, was among the biggest and most obvious of the bucks that stopped at Truman's desk. Only two days earlier, a White House summit conference had ended in a draw. White House special counsel and Truman's principal campaign strategist, Clark Clifford argued energetically that the United States should recognize the new state before it had even requested recognition. General George C. Marshall, the legendary wartime chief of staff and secretary of state since 1947, was as adamantly opposed. "The counsel offered by Mr. Clifford was based on domestic political considerations, while the problem that confronted us was international," Marshall declared, according to the transcript. "I said bluntly that if the President were to follow Mr. Clifford's advice and if in the elections I were to vote, I would vote against the President."[2] Acknowledging the constitutional authority of the commander in chief like the good soldier he was, he nonetheless stayed on when the decision went against him. Clifford went on to a legendary career as a Washington lawyer's Washington lawyer and a short, but significant, tour as President Lyndon Johnson's secretary of defense.

Not surprisingly, Truman's victory a half year later was greeted with joy in Israel, if not necessarily the State Department. Writing to Chaim Weizmann, now Israel's president, shortly afterward, the victor over a supposedly invincible Republican challenger addressed the veteran Zionist, in effect, as one vindicated and triumphant underdog to another. Truman pleasurably recalled the wisdom of the "so-called realistic experts" and their assessment of "supposedly forlorn lost causes."[3] By the time he left office, his part in Israel's gestation and birth had become a matter of demonstrable and legitimate pride. "This is the man who helped create the State of Israel," his onetime comrade-in-arms and Kansas City business partner, Eddie Jacobson, announced in November 1953 as he introduced the former president at

34

the Jewish Theological Seminary in New York. "What do you mean 'helped create'?" Truman was remembered to have replied. "I am Cyrus," he declared emotionally, identifying himself with the Persian king who freed the Jews from their Babylonian captivity, "I am Cyrus."[4] By the time he wrote his memoirs, Truman's pride had subsumed and superseded most other recollections of the experience.[5]

Reality, if not exactly a different story, was at least less simple. With its two full chapters on Palestine and Israel in volume one, and three sentence-length references in volume two, Robert Donovan's history of the Truman presidency is itself a credible index of its priorities and preoccupations.[6] No one could deny that the new president was a man of strong views and firm principles, but faced with such perplexing and unfamiliar issues and circumstances as the struggle for Palestine, he had quite often entertained very disparate strong views and even contradictory firm principles.

Even Truman himself seemed in doubt about the implications. Long after their supersession by external events, he continued to refer to earlier agreements and compromises, for example, on resettlement of displaced persons (DPs) or continued British trusteeship in Palestine, as valid expressions of his policy, irresponsibly demolished by diplomatic cabals or Jewish zealots.[7] Yet, once recognized, the real, existing Israel really seemed to have vanished from his field of vision. "The Jews, Arabs, Egyptians and Syrians had been fighting a shooting war, and I was trying to get an agreement among those people to stop the shooting," he recalled in his memoirs. Even a subsequent index reference confirmed his selective memory. Ostensibly about Israel, its actual referent is a foreign aid package signed into law on June 5, 1950. The other beneficiaries included not only western Europe, Taiwan, and an aggregate of international children's projects but the estimated 750,000 Arab-Palestinian refugees from "the shooting war" with Israel in 1948.[8] Yet although funded by Congress like other aid bills, the Palestinian refugee appropriation was actually administered through a United Nations agency especially created for the purpose. Funding aside, the question of what to do with the huge—and growing—population of Palestinians that both the Israelis and their Arab neighbors refused to resettle testified in itself to the ambiguity of the achievement and its complicated legacy.

Actually, both Truman's convictions and his ambivalence went back to his years in Congress. Despite the urgings of Missouri Zionists and the resentment of some St. Louis Jews, the then-Senator Truman had already refused to endorse his party's Palestine resolution at the 1944 Democratic convention, regarding it as unjustified interference in foreign policy.[9] In fact, the convention then nominated him for vice president. For all his reservations about the "striped-pants boys," he also listened respectfully and even deferentially to the State Department, the Joint Chiefs, service secretaries, and the Office of Strategic Services when he assumed the presidency, and continued listening to them for the rest of his term of office.

During those nearly eight contentious years, his pursuit of the national interest and defense of the presidential authority caused even his adversaries to recall him as one of the nation's great presidents. But little suggests that he saw the creation and recognition of a Jewish state in Palestine as a logical consequence of either. "My soul [sic] objective in the Palestine procedure has been to prevent blood-shed," he ruefully declared on May 18, 1948, two days after the new state had been invaded by Arab armies. "The way things look today, we apparently have not been very successful."[10]

At a conference in Washington in summer 1948, Marshall referred to Palestine as "extremely complicated and perhaps insoluble."[11] Some months later, a new secretary of state, Dean Acheson, invited Ralph Bunche to leave the United Nations staff and join him in Washington as assistant secretary for Near Eastern affairs (NEA). Bunche, whose successful mediation of the conflict was to win him the Nobel Peace Prize, declined politely. He already had enough experience of the area to wish to avoid further involvement, he said. "How often I was to remember and echo his wish," Acheson recalled in his memoirs.[12]

Policy, of course, could only reflect the consensus of interests behind it. In the immediate postwar era, certain traditional principles stood out consistently, among them "freedom of the seas," the "open door," self-determination of nations, the inviolability of the Western Hemisphere, the defense of western Europe against hegemonial threats, and the rule of international law. The Middle East was hardly one of them. Already a headache in 1945, U.S. policy by 1948 had become both a mirage and a labyrinth. The paradoxical legacy of commitments and obligations to allies and constituents itself explains many of the seeming inconsistencies in a policy widely believed both then and since to have been irresponsibly erratic, if not deliberately duplicitous.

As president by chance, Truman struggled to find his way between the contingencies thrust upon him by Roosevelt's death, Europe's collapse, and impending global disorder. Among the very first of them were the Jewish survivors already in, or about to flood into, the U.S. zones of Germany and Austria. Literally within hours of his inauguration on May 12, NEA officials were pointing out to Stettinius "that the Zionists would attempt at once to extract some commitment from the new President and that he ought therefore to be briefed on our Palestine policy as soon as possible." Sure enough, only eight days later, with U.S. troops arriving at the gates of Dachau and Bergen-Belsen, Truman received Rabbi Wise, who left, according to Margaret Truman, declaring that "Dad supported Mr. Roosevelt's policy of unrestricted immigration to Palestine."[13] Yet by September, the president was already warding off solicitations forwarded via his family in Independence, demanding that he raise the issue of Palestine at the impending foreign ministers conference in London. " . . . There isn't a possibility of my intervening . . . " his mother and sister were firmly instructed to inform a neighbor. " . . . If the little country referred to is in any way involved it will have its day in court, but the call will come from the State Department and through regular channels."[14]

Perplexing in itself, the evolution of policy on Palestine was further complicated by the secular developments that increasingly crowded the presidential calendar. Between April and September 1945, other foreign policy briefings addressed the end of the war in Europe, future relations with the Soviet Union, the birth of the United Nations, the practical consequences of Germany's surrender, the impending summit conference in Potsdam, the dawn of the nuclear age, the last ghastly battles in the Pacific, and the surrender of Japan.

But the United States, of course, was never a place to separate foreign and domestic. By October 1945, Palestine had already become an issue in the race for mayor of New York.[15] At the same time, Zionist passion provoked its counterpassions. "It was not until the middle of World War II, that I began to realize the critical strategic importance of the Middle East to my country from a military and political point of view," recalled Virginia Gildersleeve, the president of Barnard College and a member of the board of the American University in Beirut. She now believed it essential to save the United States from a "movement which was to plunge much of the region into war, sow long-lasting hatred and make the Arabs consider America not the best-liked and trusted of the nations of the West . . . but the most disliked and distrusted," that is, Zionism. She therefore opposed resettlement of survivors in Palestine, she informed the *New York Times*. Such pillars of the American Protestant establishment as Harry Emerson Fosdick and Henry Sloane Coffin agreed, but so did "most of my Jewish friends," she added.[16]

Seemingly disingenuous, the appeal to "Jewish friends" was actually demonstrable and sincere. Milwaukee's Reform Congregation Emanu-el B'ne Jeshurun was an illuminating example. Not only did its senior rabbi refuse an invitation to Lowdermilk, he even dropped the traditional prayer "Etz Chayim" because the tune it was usually sung to recalled the Zionist anthem "HaTikvah."[17] In reality, the American Council for Judaism, with which he was affiliated, was relatively tiny, unrepresentative of not only American Jewish opinion but even his congregation. Its members were nonetheless wealthy, well connected, accomplished, acculturated, and earnest. They were therefore the kind of Jews establishmentarian Americans were likeliest to know.

Even Eleanor Roosevelt, who during her husband's presidency had been the conscience of the White House on questions of refugees and their resettlement, acknowledged her ambivalence. "I do not happen to be Zionist and I know what a difference there is among such Jews as consider themselves nationals of other countries and not a separate nationality," she advised Truman.[18] For Dorothy Thompson, too, the issue was a personal dilemma. One of the superstars of contemporary journalism, a liberal columnist with impeccable anti-Nazi credentials, Thompson was also among the first to attack Revisionist terrorism in Palestine. In reality, her concern was only an echo and amplification of Weizmann's, with whom she was acquainted. Responding to a well-targeted avalanche of reader protests, and himself reportedly close to Peter Bergson, the editor of the *New York Post,* her flagship paper, nonetheless dropped her column.[19] "I refuse to become an anti-Semite by designation," Thompson declared in her defense, but unfortunately, as Weizmann's confidant Murray Weisgal recalled, "this was more or less what happened."[20]

Still, although Palestine was the music of the times for a deeply concerned and committed minority, it was only a variation, counterpoint, or obbligato for most, including the president. Hardly more anti-Semitic than the vast majority of his peers and generation, Truman could affirm at least as credibly as Gildersleeve that some of his best friends were Jews. Among them was Jacobson, who enjoyed virtually unrestricted access to the White House. But what distinguished both from the president's Zionist constituents was their hesitation to see the survivors as a political issue. Instead, both inclined to see them as a fundamentally humanitarian problem, like the refugee problem before the war.

Meanwhile, as millions of Americans reacted to the early battles of the Cold War, postwar inflation, the price of steak, a wave of rail and coal strikes, housing shortages, and the reintegration of almost twelve million would-be civilians in schools, jobs, and families after fifteen years of global depression and world war,[21] Truman was harassed by party leaders and congressional spokesmen, warned of impending doom by military and diplomatic advisors, and suspected of duplicity or worse by the Jews and the British.

In the two and a half years needed to steer his way to a viable policy, neither Truman nor anybody else suggested that he acted elegantly, swiftly, or even well. Actually, despite an epic trail of gaffes, cross-purposes, and frustrations, administration policy reflected some logic and even consistency. As so often, both were apparent only after things had happened.

What made the problem ineluctable were, in a sense, the same circumstances that made it so intractable. In assuming global power, Americans had fallen heir to responsibilities for others that had thitherto been discharged by still others, and for whose consequences history had hardly educated or equipped them. Confronted by new challenges, Americans again reviewed traditional choices, from total war to splendid isolation. But nothing in their repertory, and least of all armed intervention, seemed very appropriate to Palestine.

On the other hand, both global and domestic politics made it practically impossible either to leave Palestine to others or to wait for it to go away. As a principal party to the Atlantic Charter of 1941, Americans acknowledged a commitment to self-determination. As a principal initiator and signatory of the United Nations Charter of 1945, they acknowledged a commitment to international peacekeeping. Yet self-determination cut both ways in a country with a Jewish history and Arab majority, and international peacekeeping was anyway chimerical so long as it was agreed that the British were responsible; no one else was prepared to take their place, and Jews, Arabs, and the British were already on the edge of triangular hostility.

In fact, given the alternatives, even the Zionists did their part to support the status quo at the constituent session of the United Nations in San Francisco in April 1945. In their quest for a formula that would yield nothing to the Arabs, they lobbied successfully for a trusteeship provision that actually reinforced the British mandate. Article 80 of the new charter thus stipulated that nothing "shall be construed in or of itself to alter in any manner the rights whatsoever of any states or any peoples or the terms of existing international instruments in which members of the United Nations may respectively be parties."

Ironically, in years to come, U.S. diplomats invoked Article 80 twice, but in contradictory ways. With all of Mandatory Palestine up for grabs in 1948, Ambassador Warren Austin was the first to use it, in this case as an argument against partition, and therefore Jewish statehood. In 1977, on the other hand, with all of Mandatory Palestine now under Israeli control and Jewish settlers crowding into territories occupied in 1967, Under Secretary of State Eugene Rostow invoked it in support of Jewish settlement, on grounds that the mandate's provisions still applied to the occupied territories.

Of course, both contingencies far exceeded anything foreseeable in 1945.[22] Yet deferral to foreign powers was already unhelpful and impractical even then. Britain, the logical candidate, did and said things that alarmed and offended growing numbers of Americans. Just as the Zionists intended, it was also losing its relish and capacity for the job. Scarcely two months after Jewish Agency delegates had stoutly defended the mandate at the United Nations, Ben-Gurion was again in the United States. Certain that the mandate would soon end with an Arab-Jewish war, he had come to raise funds and material to arm and equip a Jewish army from a covert ad hoc consortium of American-Jewish businessmen.[23]

For most Americans, arms sales were just another conundrum. There was still no legal Jewish army to receive them. There was great reluctance to take sides in any case. Both the public and policymakers also sincerely favored peaceful solutions, that is, those that reduced the likelihood not only of Jews and Arabs turning U.S. guns on one another but of both sides turning the guns on British troops.

Without British acquiescence and a formula that favored Arabs as well as Jews, money too was a dead end. In April 1945, Assistant Secretary of State Archibald MacLeish was reluctant to encourage the Interior Department's Bureau of Reclamation even to propose a survey of Mandatory Palestine's capacity for irrigation and hydroelectric development. A year later, then-Under Secretary of State Acheson solemnly reviewed proposals for a $25 million Jordan Valley hydroelectric project to be underwritten by the Export-Import Bank with an appropriation from Congress. He agreed with former Treasury Secretary Henry Morgenthau, Jr., and former Vice President and Commerce Secretary Henry Wallace that "trouble and unrest in the Near, Middle and Far East is a certainty . . . and Russia will continue to fish in troubled waters." He also agreed that "the way to offset it is not by counter-propaganda of our own, but by making use of our economic power." He warned that "our motives would be misconstrued and attributed to the pressure of Jewish groups." Perhaps it might work in conjunction with a Nile Valley and Tigris-Euphrates Valley authority, he speculated, but even then he favored turning the enterprise over to the not-yet-operational World Bank.[24]

For reasons already implied in Acheson's preference for the World Bank, mediation seemed hardly a hopeful course either. The Bavarian proverb "Lots of enemies, lots of honor" seemed the likeliest cautionary guideline for both policymakers and the public. The role of mediator was an honor with little appeal for either official or unofficial Americans at the end of World War II. When heavy weather showed up on their screens, postwar Americans preferred to look to international organizations for shelter. "My basic approach was that the long-range fate of Palestine was the kind of problem we had the U.N. for," Truman still insisted in his memoirs. Unilateral declarations of principle, like his somewhat ambiguous Truman Doctrine in February 1947, were more in keeping with the spirit of the era. Unfortunately, even after the murder of six million Jews, the principle in Palestine was as unclear as it had ever been, and the will and resources of the United States for defending it were at least as dubious. On the other hand, as Truman also acknowledged, someone had to do something if Jewish survivors were "to find a place to live in decency."[25]

What finding a place might mean in practice was open-ended. At the close of World War II, there were an estimated 30 million displaced persons (DPs) in Europe. Of these, Western military governments in Germany, Austria, and Italy were responsible de facto for between 7.5 to 9 million. Six million had been repatriated by the end of 1945, most willingly, some unwillingly. This still left military government responsible for dealing with 1.5 to 2 million under well-intended but frequently useless guidelines.

Of the remaining DPs, the Jews, unsurprisingly, were among the most wretched and unassimilable. Of 60,000 Jews still in camps at the time of liberation, it was estimated that 20,000 died within a week. The traumatized, demoralized survivors, in turn, were soon interned in camps and assembly centers with large east European populations that not only brought their own long histories of anti-Semitism but in many cases had actively collaborated with the Germans.[26]

For both the Jewish Agency and the British government, the Jewish DPs were a long-term issue, but their reasons were obviously antithetical. For the Zionists, practically by definition, the DPs were what the Jewish homeland was about. What stood in their way was the White Paper, still in force in 1945 as it had been since 1939. For the British, the Jewish Agency was not just a nuisance but an adversary, determined to take not only immigration but the law itself into its hands, at the risk of igniting the entire Middle East.[27]

For the United States, the problem was nominally short-term, but it was nonetheless urgent for all that. American Jewish relief agencies had already communicated something of the chaos and horror of the DP camps. The political process did the rest to assure some serious attention. Reluctant to appoint the cabinet-level committee on the problem proposed by Morgenthau, his secretary of the treasury, the president was at least amenable to a State Department initiative supported by the acting secretary, Joseph Grew. In June 1945, he appointed Earl Harrison, dean of the University of Pennsylvania law school, to inspect the camps as his personal representative.[28] Harrison's report, proposing 100,000 immigration certificates to Palestine, reached Truman in late August. A few weeks later, it reached London and the public, where it created a sensation, infuriated Britain's Prime Minister Clement Attlee and Foreign Secretary Ernest Bevin and, as it turned out, linked the DP problem irreversibly with the problem of Palestine's political future.

Round and large, but also arbitrary, the figure itself has been traced circumstantially to a conversation between Weizmann and Winston Churchill in November 1944. In August, Ben-Gurion proposed it to a flustered British Colonial Office, that then offered 20,000 in reply, naturally contingent upon Arab approval. Harrison's report, amplified by Truman's sympathetic reaction, now made 100,000 not only a symbolic target but a feature in the political landscape.

As it happened, at the moment Harrison's proposal surfaced, there were only some 50,000 identifiable Jewish DPs in western Europe, but in the months that followed, Polish pogroms, the Sovietization of eastern Europe, and Jewish Agency activity as such directed new streams of refugees toward the U.S. zones of Germany and Austria. By mid-1946, the Jewish DP population had grown to an estimated 250,000. A year later, Jews reportedly constituted a quarter of the remaining population of the camps. In early 1948, there were still an estimated 190,000 Jewish DPs in Germany, Austria, and Italy, plus 24,000 more in British camps in Cyprus. But by fall, the United States admitted only 13,000 as immigrants, half of these during the course of the year; Canada had admitted 10,000; and Latin America, 4,400.[29] After the fall of Saigon in 1975, by comparison, 130,000 South Vietnamese refugees were allowed to enter the country as immigrants.

Had the British acceded in 1945 before the east European exodus began, the whole story might imaginably have come out differently. The Truman administration would have scored points with Jewish voters. At least for the moment, the problem of the Jewish DPs would have vanished. The link between obstructed immigration and the need for Jewish statehood would have lost much of its force.[30] But the British resisted.

Not unreasonably, Bevin proposed instead to convene an Anglo-U.S. commission to look into the wishes of the Jewish survivors, survey the absorptive capacity of Palestine, and co-opt the United States in bilateral responsibility for the outcome. To the surprise of his colleagues, the Americans agreed, but only after imposing a deadline for action and rewriting the Commission's mandate to emphasize the centrality of Palestine.[31] Bevin seems to have hoped the experience would educate Americans to the realities of Palestine, Truman that it would establish the nexus between Palestine and the DPs beyond any further challenge.

Other expectations ranged from skepticism to overt hostility. Americans were incensed by Bevin's insensitivity at a press conference in November where he cautioned Jews against getting "too much at the head of the queue."[32] British officials were put off by Bevin's apparent determination to put a major British interest in U.S. hands. Meanwhile, the Jewish Agency was outraged by the delay and seeming co-optation of the Americans, and resolved to increase pressure on the British. Though this was the first official breach in Britain's monopoly since the Balfour Declaration, there seems to have been little appreciation of just how much the formal U.S. involvement really meant.

Appointed in December to avoid any conflict with the New York campaign, the commission started work punctually in January. But even its roster was a clue to how differently Britons and Americans saw their respective roles and mandate. Among the British were a Tory and a Labour member of parliament, an expert on Palestine's economy, a Labour peer admired for his tactical skill, and a friend of Bevin's from the International Labor Office. Respectively co-opted by the State Department and the White House, the Americans divided vaguely into Anglophiles and Semitophiles, with a slight common tilt toward pro-Zionist anti-imperialism. Among them were the secretary of the American Rhodes Trust; a Boston editor; a former ambassador to India; and the former League of Nations High Commissioner on Refugees, who would later become the first U.S. ambassador to Israel. Perhaps the most visible member was Bartley Crum, a Catholic, Republican corporation lawyer from San Francisco who had supported Roosevelt in 1944. Paradoxically, the British seemed to confirm their seriousness of purpose by including elected officials; the Americans, by omitting them. But as the former Senator James F. Byrnes, now secretary of state, reminded the former Senator Truman, now president, appointment of a member of Congress was not "a friendly service."[33]

Meanwhile, Congress itself pushed the president's hand. In mid-December 1945, with ecumenical sponsorship from Senators Wagner, the New Dealer's New Dealer from New York, and Robert A. Taft, the Republican's Republican from Ohio, a resolution in favor of Jewish immigration to Palestine again came before the Senate. This time, despite cautionary noises from Truman, Byrnes, Senate Foreign Relations Committee Chairman Tom Connally, and Senator Arthur Vandenberg of Michigan, who warned that it might lead to a British request for U.S. troops, it passed. A concurrent resolution then made it through the House. Revealingly, there was no roll call, and specific references to the Jewish people and a Jewish commonwealth were omitted from the text.[34]

A few weeks later, the Anglo-U.S. commission convened. In the course of hearings that took it to Washington, London, the European DP camps, Cairo, and Palestine itself, members listened to testimony from politicians, economists, civil servants, Zionist and non-Zionist Jews, Arabs, and survivors. Inevitably, much of the testimony was both predictable and contradictory. Professor Albert Einstein, at the peak of his public influence, warned equitably against British imperialism and Jewish nationalism. Walter Lowdermilk once again rolled out his plans for a Jordan Valley authority to demonstrate, and even underestimate, Palestine's capacity for economic development and absorbtion of immigrants. DPs, though not altogether spontaneously, registered their wish to emigrate to Palestine by majorities approaching unanimity.[35] Speaking for the Arab Office in Jerusalem, Albert Hourani uncategorically predicted Arab resistance to further Jewish immigration and a Jewish state.[36]

Within months, one member of each delegation had rushed into print with a personal account of his experience. Reportedly ghostwritten, Crum's was dedicated to the memory of Wendell Willkie, the globalist Republican who had challenged Roosevelt in 1940 and evoked the vision of "one world" in a best-seller published a few years later. A kind of anthology of contemporary liberal orthodoxy, Crum's book identified Jews with progress and democracy, Arabs with reaction and fascism, Britain with empire and anti-Soviet anxiety, and the State Department with Britain.

"There is one fact facing both the United States and Great Britain, Mr. Crum," he quoted Loy Henderson, the State Department's director of Near Eastern affairs, a wartime ambassador to Iraq, and a later ambassador to India and Iran. "That is the Soviet Union." Crum was unimpressed by Henderson's warning to "bear that in mind when you consider the Palestine problem."[37] What was needed in his view was "an American foreign policy," not what he regarded as a British Conservative one. "We cannot have peace with a Middle East divided, half Fascist, half democratic," Crum declared.[38]

R. H. S. Crossman, the maverick intellectual and Labour politician whose memoir appeared concurrently in London, was both more circumspect and more penetrating. Shrewd, opinionated, and fair-minded at once, he was exasperated by the posturings of his colleagues, ambivalent about the Arabs, and resentful of the formidable pressure from American Zionists. Why should Americans "from a safe position across the Atlantic lambast my country for its failure to go to war with the Arabs on behalf of the Jews?" he asked himself in Washington. "America was not prepared either to receive the Jews from Europe or to risk a single American soldier to protect them in Palestine."[39] Yet he was also willing to acknowledge the sincerity of the primordial sympathy of the United States for Zionism as a pioneer movement, the good faith behind Labor Zionism's promise to develop Palestine in the best interests of its Arab as well as its Jewish population, and the reality of the DPs' need, as well as passion, for the Jewish homeland.

Evan Wilson, who was in charge of the State Department's Palestine desk, noticed that members of the commission seemed about equally distrustful of their respective foreign ministries and of one another. The British saw the exercise "primarily as a means of getting the United States committed to a joint policy," he concluded. "They emphasized the Middle Eastern aspect, while the United States placed greater weight on the need for action concerning the homeless Jews of Europe."[40] Crum was, in fact, hell-bent on an interim report before the commission even reached Palestine, declaring the 100,000 immigration certificates an absolute priority. He then threatened to quit when the idea was turned down. Reportedly, it took a cable from David Niles of the White House staff, conveying the president's pointed hope "that you will do nothing rash," to turn him around.[41]

Both heartened and challenged by Bevin's assurance that he would act on a "unanimous" recommendation, and nudged along by a signal from Truman that "the world" expectantly awaited "an affirmative program to relieve untold suffering and misery,"[42] the commission brooded for three weeks in Switzerland over its intense and considerable disagreements before finally producing its report. In effect, its ten recommendations could be reduced to two. The first, immediate admission of 100,000 Jewish immigrants to Palestine, infuriated the Arabs. The second, continuation of the British mandate, pending a U.N. trusteeship and an eventual binational state, infuriated the Zionists.

The threatened Zionist rejection, in turn, infuriated Truman. He was nonetheless persuaded to endorse the first proposal publicly in return for American Zionist endorsement of his "humane and constructive approach."[43] Unsurprisingly, his unilateral statement and selective neglect of the other proposal enraged the British, who were struck as always by the U.S. tendency to "lay heavy burdens on us without lifting a little finger to help."[44] Bevin, who had staked his career on a solution of the problem based on Anglo-American cooperation, was especially infuriated. "I hope I will not be misunderstood in America if I say . . . they did not want too many Jews in New York," he declared in a famous speech at the Labour party conference in June.

Tactless and impolitic as this may have been, his taunt was hard to dismiss, if U.S. immigration policy was any measure. Each for their respective reasons, not only Catholics, WASPS, and organized labor, but Zionists too, were now arrayed against any modification of the exclusionary laws that had governed U.S. immigration since the 1920s. Jewish Americans divided fundamentally between Zionist supporters of the status quo, and anti-Zionist supporters of liberalized immigration, with the Zionists obviously seeing a threat to Jewish claims on Palestine in any liberalized admission of DPs. Most other Americans—by a majority of 72 percent, according to a poll in August 1946—opposed liberalized immigration altogether.

When Congress finally acted in early 1947 to consider an ambitious immigration reform, only two Jewish witnesses, New York's Senator Herbert H. Lehman, and the Jewish affairs advisor to the U.S. military governor in Germany, could be found to testify in its support.[45] At the same time, in the wake of Bevin's speech, Congress held up the British loan that was one of the pillars of administration foreign policy until Rabbi Stephen S. Wise, Morgenthau, David Dubinsky of the garment workers union, and other major Jewish figures intervened to save it.[46]

Thitherto unknown as an anti-Semite to even his closest friends and associates,[47] and anyway increasingly removed from policymaking by a combination of other official duties and bad health, Bevin was nonetheless compared with the great Jew-baiters of history. On a 1946 visit to New York, he was booed out of Yankee stadium. Dockers even refused to handle his baggage, a particularly bitter irony for a man who had devoted his life to the labor movement in general and dockers in particular.[48] In September 1946, a new Revisionist spectacular called "A Flag Is Born," featuring Paul Muni, opened at New York's Alvin Theater; its theme was the heroic struggle of Menahem Begin's Irgun against the British.[49] Yet even as Attlee took charge of negotiations with Truman, Bevin's colleagues were leaning increasingly toward partition, while waging their own small war against the army and British administration in Palestine.

Meanwhile, U.S. official opinion kept its distance from both 10 Downing Street and Yankee stadium. According to the Pentagon in May 1946, the British had all the troops they needed to keep order in Palestine. Staff planners asked only that the State Department keep the United States out of any trusteeship that would require commitment of U.S. forces. Though they assumed that the Soviet Union "would most likely . . . lend substantial aid to the Arabs," they also assumed nonetheless that the Jews were better armed, trained, and fortified, that is, that the Jews could handle the Arabs, and the British could handle both.

What was clear above all was that the Joint Chiefs of Staff (JCS) were unwilling to leave any scenario without a worst case. "We recommend that . . . the guiding principle be that no action should be taken [whose] repercussions . . . are beyond the capabilities of British troops," General—later President—Dwight Eisenhower informed the State Department's H. Freeman Matthews in mid-June. Use of military force in Palestine, he added, could lead to anarchy, general civil war, possible Sovietization of the region, including Turkey, and the loss of "probably the one large undeveloped reserve in a world which may come to the limits of its oil resources within this generation without having developed any substitute."

There were no funds or ships available either for moving 100,000 Jews to Palestine, the JCS noted—though an appendix conceded that they could, if necessary, deploy 52,000 men on four months' notice to help keep order on the ground. Order at sea was something else. A marine brigade, three cruisers, and six destroyers were available on five days' notice, the report continued. Intentionally or not, it was thus implied that there were forces available to help the Royal Navy stop the ad hoc flotilla ferrying DPs from European ports but none to help the British Army assure their safety in Palestine. Overall, it would take five to seven divisions plus air power for several years to protect British and U.S. interests, and principal centers of Jewish and Christian population, and "to crush Arab resistance," the report estimated.[50]

As the British were bound to see it, Washington also tolerated, and even encouraged, activities that could only make things harder for them. In the U.S. zones of Germany and Austria, U.S. policy effectively made the DP camps underground railroad stations en route to Palestine.[51] At the same time, private philanthropy was allowed to equip a Jewish army—in fact, two different and mutually antagonistic Jewish armies—to pressure, even terrorize, 100,000 British troops who, the British believed, were ultimately there to protect Jews as well as Arabs.

It was hardly irrelevant that it cost Britain nearly $500 million a year just to maintain the garrison in Palestine. By comparison, it cost only about $160 million to support all other British troops in the Middle East.[52] At the same time, private but tax-exempt Jewish philanthropy alone reflected the magnitude of the corresponding effort in the United States. From a relatively modest $14 million in 1941, United Jewish Appeal (UJA) contributions had risen to $35 million in 1945, $101 million in 1946, $117 million in 1947, and $148 million in 1948—all from an American Jewish population, including children, that was estimated at five million. For perspective, United Jewish Appeal contributions considerably exceeded the national receipts of the Red Cross. Of this, 75 percent funded overseas projects and relief, that is, went primarily to move and settle people still regarded officially as illegal immigrants.[53]

At the same time, more American millions—including as much as $100,000 a week in the last ten weeks of 1946 alone—flowed collaterally and independently to the Jewish militias the British army was trying hard, but unsuccessfully, to stamp out.[54] The combined private effort could be usefully compared not only with the $300 million in aid for Greece and $100 million for Turkey the president asked Congress for to implement the Truman Doctrine but the total federal budget of $36 billion proposed for FY 1947.

As British and U.S. government officials met in late June 1946 to discuss the Anglo-U.S. commission's proposals, the interests of all parties approached expectant impasse. For the moment, the British looked to the Americans, the Americans looked to the British, and, if only for lack of alternatives, both Arabs and Jews looked to the respective great powers. Meanwhile, most of the Zionist leadership— some 2,700 Jews, including three members of the Jewish Agency executive—was in jail after an all-points *razzia* against the Jewish militias. It was only because he happened to be in Paris that Ben-Gurion was not among them.

Given its mandate, the commission's short-term goal was a logistical arrangement to transfer the 100,000 to Palestine. From U.S. perspective, their resettlement was already the solution to a major problem. Quite apart from considerations of domestic politics, human charity, and taxpayer expense, according to Major General John H. Hilldring, the assistant secretary of state for occupied areas, "Our military and political interests in Germany and Austria require that we press for immediate implementation of the [anglo-American] Committee's recommendation."[55] The arrival of the U.S. delegation in the president's own plane was confirmation in itself of Truman's interest. As the president informed the U.S. representatives, he was also willing to commit the United States to a binational state, to $25–50 million in one-time-only U.S. matching funds to resettle the immigrants when they got to Palestine, and support for a World Bank initiative to develop the economies of the Middle East.[56]

Even this was problematic enough with a Jewish DP population as large as a quarter million in the U.S. and British zones. But with Arabs inalterably opposed to any further migration, no one could say what the immigrants would face when they got to Palestine either. The very idea of shared responsibility for their security there made the undermanned and overextended U.S. military turn pale.[57] Meanwhile, the intractable but unavoidable questions of not only Palestine's but Britain's future in the region inevitably plagued the Attlee government.

Sensitive to the constraints of their respective mandates, not to mention the anxieties in both Washington and London about Soviet intentions in Iran and Turkey, the professional civil servants in London took twelve days to reach agreement. The new proposals were associated with the names of Henry F. Grady, the career diplomat who led the U.S. delegation, and Herbert Morrison, the historically pro-Zionist Labour M.P. who brought the proposal before the House of Commons. For a time, the scheme made each notorious. Both sides now took it for given that the 100,000 would be resettled in Palestine. They also agreed that Britain would retain formal control of Palestine under a complicated federalization plan that allowed for autonomous Jewish and Arab provinces, while reserving defense, rails, customs and communications, immigration, and poublic security, to the central authority. After more than a year of frustration, embarrassment, harassment, misery, and injury to both life and property, this might nonetheless have been the basis for compromise had the Arabs shown willingness to settle on its terms, and Congress to liberalize U.S. immigration.

What also made the moment propitious was the growing weariness in both Washington and London for any solution that would make the problem go away. All the Americans asked, in principle, was that large numbers of Jews, currently on U.S. hands in Europe, be decently settled in Palestine, where they said they wanted to go. Even Whitehall was now so disposed to compromise that it resisted the urge to retaliate after the most dramatic Jewish challenge to date. On July 22, with the Morrison-Grady negotiations still in progress, Begin's Irgun bombed British administrative headquarters in Jerusalem's King David Hotel. The explosion collapsed a six-story building, killed ninety-one, and injured forty-five, men and women, British, Jewish, and Arab, as well as two Armenians, a Russian, a Greek, and an Egyptian. More than half the dead were hired staff, and Arabs constituted almost half the total dead.[58]

Like the Tet offensive in Vietnam, which represented a similar moment of truth for queasy Americans a generation later, the blast left its marks on British opinion, extinguishing much of the remaining light that mandatory authorities had hitherto believed to be or alleged to see at the end of the tunnel. Once, responsibility for Palestine had appeared a secular, imperial opportunity. It had then been declared a test of will and credibility, "A vital job—a MAN'S job," as one recruiting poster for the British Palestine police proclaimed.[59] Now, like India, and even the idea of empire itself, it was coming to resemble the heart of darkness.[60]

The credibility and moral self-assurance of much of the Zionist movement were among the further casualties of the Irgun bomb.[61] Ironically, this favored accommodation too. For all their shortcomings, the Morrison-Grady recommendations confirmed that the White Paper was a dead letter. For all their calculated ambiguity about federalism, binationalism, and provincial autonomy, they also implied at least the possibility of eventual Jewish statehood. Under the circumstances, even the current stalemate could be seen as a plausible incentive for a deal. With 2,700 Jews under indefinite detention, and 136 direct and immediate victims of Irgun terrorism, Ben-Gurion could now acknowledge the hazards of playing with paramilitary fire, put some distance between himself and the Revisionists, and above all, preempt British reprisals that might stall or even end a half century of Zionist enterprise.

There was ambivalent support for the new plan from the British, despite eloquent skepticism from Churchill, now leader of the opposition, and even Sir Alan Cunningham, the British high commissioner in Palestine. Churchill emphasized the crucial importance of U.S. support and the likely impossibility of sustaining the mandate without it. Cunningham warned against the impossibility of squaring Jewish immigration with Arab resistance under a British regime. If that meant partition, which the Jews supported, that ought to be recognized at the start, he argued.[62]

Like the Attlee government, Truman too was initially disposed to be supportive, despite challenges from his secretary of commerce, Henry Wallace; a front-page story in the *New York Times;* cautionary signals from the American members of the Anglo-American commission;[63] and earnest reservations from much of his cabinet. Morrison-Grady was nothing more than a conscientious implementation of the Anglo-American report, the president insisted. According to the skeptical Wallace, Truman saw the new report as a call for an autonomous Jewish province, sovereign as any U.S. state, in a Palestine under U.N. trusteeship,[64] "President Truman really thinks that the plan . . . is really fair," Wallace noted in his diary.[65] Truman was no less convinced, Wallace reported, that the plan assured the Jews the best and most historic part of Palestine. Consistent with the pieties of the era, Truman even assured Wallace that the report cleared away any remaining obstacles to a Jordan Valley Authority. Other visitors heard him repeat the same arguments with the same conviction, among them Senator Wagner and James Mead of New York, and James McDonald of the Anglo-American commission. McDonald warned of Jewish resistance to the Morrison-Grady scheme, both at home and in Palestine, if continued British rule were the price for the 100,000 immigration certificates. "The Jews aren't going to write the history of the U.S. or my history," the president replied truculently. He was not Roosevelt, and not from New York but from the Middle West, he added.[66]

A few days later, at a working lunch convened to discuss Morrison-Grady, a reluctant Truman agreed to shoot it down despite supportive arguments from Acheson and Navy Secretary James Forrestal. The latter, already worried about Saudi oil, was also increasingly worried about the Russians. But none of this could match the counterarguments, including "a sheaf of telegrams about four inches thick from various Jewish people," according to Wallace. "Jesus Christ couldn't please them when he was here on earth, so how could anyone expect that I would have any luck?" he quoted Truman. There was also a cautionary telegram from Byrnes in Paris.

Even Acheson, who favored Morrison-Grady, reportedly conceded that it would lead to Zionist protests. He was nonetheless prepared to believe that "the whole business would be forgotten by 1948 if the solution could be obtained right away."[67] Meanwhile, as Byrnes, Wallace, Treasury Secretary John Snyder, Secretary of Agriculture Clinton Anderson, and others pointed out, the problem was how to ignore the Republicans, who were already preparing a counteroffensive for the impending congressional elections. "The new British plan means not only complete frustration for the Jews of Palestine but deep despair for the million and a half surviving Jews of Europe," declared Senator Taft of Ohio, the home of Rabbi Abba Hillel Silver.[68] Once again, the British felt betrayed by the Americans, and Truman felt ill-used by the Jews.

The dilemma was that although acceptance exposed the president to charges of selling out principle for 100,000 immigration certificates, rejection exposed him to charges of failure to help even DPs. This time it was Niles, a protégé of Roosevelt's advisor Harry Hopkins and the residing expert on ethnic politics,[69] who came to his rescue. His solution was a joint meeting of the U.S. delegates to the Morrison-Grady talks and the U.S. members of the Anglo-U.S. commission. Duly convened, the latter informed the former that Morrison-Grady was not what they had in mind. Acheson then informed the British ambassador that the president considered it a political liability.[70]

In the meantime, the Zionist executive was reaching its own agonizing, but crucial, accommodation at a meeting in Paris. Inevitably haunted by the fate of European Jews both during and since the war, the delegates were now reminded of the spectre of Harry Truman. Alone in his proverbial kitchen, a message from Niles informed them, the president was facing the heat from Silver and the Republicans, with no help at all from traditional allies. Unless he got an acceptable proposal within the next few days, Niles reported, he would simply abdicate further responsibility to the British.

The implied ultimatum led to a cathartic debate. The third of its kind since the British offered Uganda in 1903, and a ministate in 1937, the debate ended in a cathartic resolution. While denouncing Morrison-Grady pro forma, it also backed off from Biltmore. Instead, it endorsed proposals for "establishment of a viable Jewish state in an adequate area of Palestine," and "immediate granting" of full autonomy—with full control of immigration—in "the area of Palestine designated to become a Jewish state." Certification and transfer of the 100,000 was declared a concurrent condition. Nahum Goldmann, still the Jewish Agency's quasi-ambassador to the United States and author of the compromise resolution, was then sent back to Washington from Paris to sell the plan as best he could to the administration.[71]

As it turned out, official sales resistance was nearly negligible. But significantly, Goldmann's crucial successes were with fellow Jews, including Niles. Primary targets included Silver, who by now had hopelessly alienated the White House but was still unchallenged as spokesman for the American hard-liners. Then came Judge

Joseph M. Proskauer in New York, the president of the non-Zionist American Jewish Committee and an old associate of Secretary of War Robert Patterson. Skeptical as ever about Jewish statehood, Proskauer was nonetheless concerned about civility, tranquillity, and the fate of the Jewish DPs.

In the course of their discussion, Goldmann persuaded Proskauer that the new proposal could both relieve the DPs and accommodate the Arabs. It was also superior, he argued, to an unworkable mandate, and no obstacle to eventual federation of a Jewish and an Arab state. A Jewish state, he assured Proskauer, would only be as Jewish as its majority; would assure minority rights; and would incidentally meet British military requirements in the area. Perhaps most important, "creation of a state would, once and for all, remove Zionism from American domestic politics."[72]

Convinced and reassured, Proskauer set off for Washington to line up Patterson with Acheson and Snyder in support of Goldmann's plan. What would happen, Goldmann asked, if things in Palestine got out of hand, the British began to shoot at Jewish immigrants, and there were a war between Britain and the Jews? Why not United States support for a United Nations solution? Acheson and Niles then went to work on Truman, who urged Attlee to support the proposal too. But meanwhile the president neither repudiated Morrison-Grady nor endorsed partition.[73]

This was still the case in early October when an obviously reluctant president was finally prevailed on to issue a public statement. The formal occasion was October 4, 1946, the eve of the Day of Atonement and the most solemn day in the Jewish calendar. The practical occasion was the threat of a preemptive strike by Thomas E. Dewey, the Republican governor of New York and the presumptive Republican candidate for president. Collectively instigated by Niles, Crum, Eliahu Epstein (later Elath), the new Jewish Agency representative in Washington, and Democratic National Chairman Robert E. Hannegan, the statement was successively drafted by Acheson, Niles, Epstein, and Judge Samuel I. Rosenman, who had stayed on at the White House after Roosevelt's death. The text was subsequently understood and even proclaimed as the first official declaration of U.S. support for partition. In fact, in its published version, the message emphasized continued concern for the 100,000 displaced Jews, expressed guarded support for the Jewish Agency proposal, and declared pro forma that "the gap between the proposals which have been put forward" was not "too great to be bridged by men of reason and goodwill." Two days later, Dewey conspicuously demanded immigration certificates to Palestine for not only one but several hundred thousand Jews.

As was widely anticipated, the 1946 congressional elections were nonetheless a Democratic rout, though there was little evidence that Palestine had much to do with them.[74] But if Truman's gesture failed even to impress the voters of New York, who defeated incumbents Mead and Herbert Lehman, and streamed to the Republicans like fellow citizens across the country, its impact in both Washington and London could hardly be overestimated. Within ten days, the president was cautioned twice by Walter George, chairman of the Senate Finance Committee, that Congress would not commit more money, let alone troops, "in the Palestine area." George's reminders elicited yet another affirmation from Truman that his only concern was the "pitiful plight" of the DPs, not to mention the burden they imposed on the U.S. taxpayer.[75] At the same time, London approached the flash point. Seen from Downing Street, Truman's statement was neither more nor less than naked opportunism, and a unilateral invitation to the Zionists to hold out against anything more the British might propose. Thenceforth, rather than continue the quest for Anglo-U.S. consensus, the British began looking for the exits.[76]

Dispatched to reply *ex officio,* the State Department's NEA responded with what the drafters themselves recalled as exemplary ingenuity. Resisting a powerful urge to roll their eyes upward and smirk, they duly informed Attlee that the president's gesture was intended only to acknowledge the frustration of his Jewish constituents, and emphasize the need for action before another winter. The statement's timing was governed by the fortuitous occasion of the "annual Day of Atonement," they added, "when [Jews] are accustomed to give contemplation to the lot of the Jewish people."[77]

Anodyne as it appears in retrospect, the Yom Kippur statement was a benchmark in the history of Anglo-U.S. cross-purposes and as clear an end as can probably be found to what till now had seemed the road to a common solution. In December, Bevin was invited to the White House for a serious and civil chat, but there was really little more to say. Strong and contrary as their own views may have been, both he and Truman were in harmony with the strong and contrary views of their constituents, and responsibly aware of the political constraints that operated on the other. Both men conceded that they had made incompatible promises to Jews and Arabs. While admitting that agreement between Jews and Arabs was unlikely, Bevin still felt obliged to try to reach one. Truman agreed, in turn, that immigration, and the unsolved problem of the Jewish DPs, remained the biggest problem that they faced. He promised to raise the issue of the U.S. quotas with the new and now overwhelmingly Republican Congress when it convened in January.[78]

As expected, 1947 brought only more deadlock. But it also brought crises and challenges to Britain, the United States, and Palestine alike, surpassing any since the end of the war. Each for its own rather different reasons, both Britain and the United States wanted a solution. But while Britain was unable to find one by diplomacy or force, the United States was both unable to address the problem or ignore it. With Britain already committed to evacuate its troops from Egypt, Palestine was arguably a strategic asset, but also a political liability, not least because of its impact on Americans. Paradoxically, the dilemmas facing both capitals not only made an untenable situation seem more insoluble but made solution all the more urgent before both everyone lost control.

Though there was increasing sympathy for partition on both sides of the Atlantic, this only led to more dilemmas. Eager to see the end of the British Empire, Americans were increasingly worried what might happen afterward, and profoundly reluctant to fill the empty space themselves. Although eager to be rid at last of their imperial burdens, Britons worried interchangeably about the costs of leaving and the costs of staying where they were. After India, Palestine seemed to pose the impossible test. If a binational solution (with its Arab majority) was understandably unacceptable to Jews, partition (with a Jewish state) was equally unacceptable to Arabs. War, with Britain in the middle, threatened Britain's credibility as a global power. All other costs aside, it was thus a potential blow to dominoes around the world. Yet withdrawal, the obvious alternative, could be regarded as an open invitation to outside forces of every kind to intervene in Palestine.

In the aftermath of history's greatest war, both powers meanwhile struggled with the unanticipated costs of victory and their differences with the Soviet Union. The destruction and unconditional surrender of Germany in itself made Americans unfamiliarly responsible, Britons unfamiliarly poor, and the European economy unexpectedly fragile. At the same time, Soviet policy in Europe and the Middle East required both Britain and the United States to reassess their global roles.

At least where Palestine was concerned, British policy preferences shifted increasingly to put up or shut up, dilemmas notwithstanding. On February 18, 1947, the same day the government set the date for withdrawal from India, Bevin announced his intention to refer the Palestine mandate to the United Nations. The message was presumably addressed to Jews and Americans alike, with their combined disposition to demand partition and let the British carry it out. Assuming that a U.N. majority, including the Soviet Union, would oppose partition, Zionists tended to regard Bevin's initiative with the deepest distrust. Instead, they saw it as a figleaf for a pro-Arab solution in Palestine, that would incidentally relieve Britain of any further obligation for a Jewish national home.

It was at least as reasonable to see it simply as a way for Britain to get itself off the hook and satisfy the yearning to get out that was quickly becoming irresistible.[79] By summer, public order in Palestine had virtually collapsed, and reverberations from the bloody counterpoint of terror and reprisal could be felt all the way back to Britain itself. In the steamy Zionist rhetoric of the time, it was fashionable and convenient to compare Bevin with Hitler, and the British with the Nazis.[80] But it was also disingenuous. In reality, the British could hardly have been more different in the two ways that most mattered. They were reluctant to kill people. They were equally reluctant to let their troops be killed. Each in their way, both Gandhi's Congress and Begin's Irgun were beneficiaries—of the British imperialism that allowed them to flourish, and the British scruples that allowed them to survive.

At the same time, no government involved with Palestine could deal with it in isolation, or make policy an exclusive function of domestic impact. Any government in London was bound to see the deterioration in Palestine as part of a larger deterioration in Britain's strategic position. This was linked, in turn, to an even more basic deterioration in Britain's ability to pay. On February 21, 1947, just three days after its decision to leave Palestine to the U.N., and leave India altogether, Britain also officially informed the United States that it was no longer able to aid Turkey and Greece.

For all their differences with the United States on local issues, British policymakers had no illusions about their dependence on U.S. money and goodwill. "It is far more important that there should be agreement [between Britain and the United States] than that there should be this or that variant of the ... various schemes of partition or cantonisation which have been put forward," Churchill declared almost self-evidently in the parliamentary debate on Morrison-Grady.[81] But the dependence was mutual. Americans too found themselves in an increasingly cold and unfamiliar world. In its historic prewar sense, isolationism too was among the casualties of World War II. Climatically weakened by two world wars, Britain was still a closer and more potent ally than any other. Its claim on U.S. support was as urgent and credible in 1947 as it had been in 1940.

The decision to refer Palestine to the U.N. was met with apprehension in official Washington, though Acheson acknowledged cautiously in January that "the American Government, for domestic and other reasons, would find it easier to support in the U.N. and elsewhere the solution of the Palestine problem calling for partition and the setting up of a viable Jewish state."[82] But the British decision to leave Greece and Turkey set off an extraordinary burst of U.S. activity. By March, in the form of a Truman Doctrine that ostensibly promised U.S. support wherever Soviet or Communist pressure threatened, the administration had persuaded Congress to come to the aid of Greece and Turkey. In April, the administration concluded from the foreign ministers conference in Moscow that agreement with the Soviets on the future of Germany was out of reach, and resolved to face the consequences. In May, Washington planners began the conception and gestation of the enormous program of bilateral and multilateral aid for European recovery and reconstruction that would be remembered as the Marshall Plan. By June, they were prepared to put it on the table, where the Soviets rejected it not only for themselves but for their clients and satellites in Eastern Europe. By summer, U.S. officials were thinking intensively about western Europe and anticipating a showdown with the Soviet Union.

The onset of the Cold War inevitably affected the U.S. view of Palestine as it affected everything else. Detailed reports from Jerusalem informed the State Department "that Communism is not at present an important movement in the political life of the country." This was presumably good news. Yet the question itself was an indicator of official fears and suspicions that only persisted as East European immigrants streamed into the country. Further reports that Jewish communists yielded to their Arab comrades on the question of immigration, that is, that communism supported the demands of Arab nationalism, might imaginably have been reassuring. Yet for those disposed to worst cases, they were proof that Arab nationalism was a Trojan horse.[83]

Years later, quoting Sumner Welles, the former under secretary of state, Elath [Epstein] saw the Truman Doctrine as a good thing for the Jews. By involving the United States in the big Middle Eastern picture, and making it a factor in Turkey and Iran, he argued, the doctrine also involved the United States in Palestine.[84] There was something to this, but the linkage was neither generally apparent at the time nor a conscious choice of direction. On the contrary, every self-preservative instinct in Congress and the administration alike warned against overextension. Americans were willing, even eager, to assume new responsibilities where the sides were clear and the global dangers seemed clear and present. For most Americans, however, neither condition applied to Palestine, and for most officials, the most obvious way to keep the Soviets out of Palestine was for Americans to avoid getting in.

Even a procedural memo from Dean Rusk, the assistant secretary of state for U.N. affairs and later secretary of state, reflected the resulting caution. The United States must ensure that only member governments participated in the General Assembly's special session on Palestine, he warned the president in April 1947. If

Jews and Arabs wanted to be heard, he advised, let them appear before a subcommittee as representatives from Palestine.[85]

U.S. reticence was again conspicuous in May when the U.N. General Assembly constituted a U.N. Special Committee on Palestine (UNSCOP), with a mandate to report its findings by September 1. Co-opted with the artful balance of a New York City election ticket, UNSCOP's members were drawn from western Europe (Sweden and Holland), eastern Europe (Czechoslovakia and Yugoslavia), the British Commonwealth (Australia and Canada), Asia (India and Iran), and Latin America (Guatemala, Peru, and Mexico). Among them, they represented democracy and communism, historical antiquity and fresh independence, colonial experience and anticolonial experience, Anglophobia and Anglophilia. It was generally understood, for example, that the Guatemalan member, Jorge Garcia-Granados, regarded it as his personal mission to expose British imperialism.[86]

It was clear, of course, that the UNSCOP report would constitute a moment of truth, but till then, Washington preferred to look the other way. The official position was that UNSCOP was a purely advisory body without executive authority, neither an agent of the superpowers nor an official arbitrator. The United States should address it only when asked, and take no position until the report appeared, Marshall advised the president on July 10, 1947. In fact, shortly afterward, UNSCOP was officially advised that the United States had rejected Morrison-Grady. But Marshall nonetheless informed an interested congressional group on July 31 that the United States position was no position.[87]

UNSCOP was meanwhile going over ground already covered by the Anglo-American commission a long fifteen months before, but its predecessors had at least heard both sides. This time, in contrast to the abortive talks in London where the Jews stayed away, the Arabs stayed home. Their absence only made the Jewish Agency's presentations more impressive. It was also hard to overlook the collapse of public order as UNSCOP went about its job.

An inadverent Goliath, the British were now almost purposefully involved in confirming the hopelessness of their situation. The arrival in Palestine in July of a superannuated Chesapeake Bay ferry, the *Exodus,* could only recall Talleyrand's aphorism about blunders that are worse than crimes. In July, the Jewish authorities decided to dispatch the *Exodus* from Marseille to Palestine with 4,500 refugees aboard. Conceived as a test of British resolve, it was really a no-lose situation for the Jews. If it penetrated the blockade, it would demonstrate Jewish determination and, incidentally, British helplessness. If it failed, it would document British brutality. In full view of the UNSCOP observers and the international press, the British provisionally disembarked the passengers at Haifa. But it was then resolved to send them back.

The question, of course, was where. In the end, since they refused to go ashore voluntarily anywhere else but Palestine, and the British were understandably reluctant to land them in a home port like Southampton, they were shipped back to Hamburg, the only alternative under British control. Apart from the political cost of forcibly disembarking Jewish survivors in Germany, the episode tied up four warships for nearly two months, disrupted training programs, and consumed a substantial part of the Mediterranean fleet's appropriation.[88]

On August 31, UNSCOP reported unanimously that Britain be relieved of the mandate. The minority of three proposed "an independent federal state." The majority of eight endorsed partition into Jewish and Arab states with an international trusteeship for Jerusalem. Czechoslovakia, not yet a Soviet satellite despite its coerced withdrawal from the Marshall Plan, voted with the Latins, West Europeans, and British dominions. Yugoslavia, still assumed to be a Soviet satellite, voted with Iran and India. On September 20, the British cabinet resolved to get out of Palestine come what may and, as in India, let the locals work things out among themselves.

Though hardly a surprise in Washington, the British decision was hardly welcomed either. The administration knew perfectly well that overt opposition to the majority report was out of the question. Yet it also understood, as Eisenhower put it, that "the United States would be under strong pressure to assume joint responsibility or at least provide assistance in putting the plan into effect because of the past efforts of the United States to achieve solution of the Palestine problem, and because the plan to partition is strongly supported by a numerous and influential racial group of United States citizens."[89]

The question, as Clifford spelled out in successive memos to Truman, was how to do well by doing good. The only place where one could realistically speak of a Jewish vote was New York, he reminded the president. On the other hand, nobody had run successfully for the presidency since 1876 without the electoral vote from New York. In any case, as he argued at length the following March, support for partition, that is, for Jewish statehood, had been U.S. policy for decades; it was still the policy likeliest to enhance the credibility of the United Nations; and it was therefore the policy likeliest to contain the Soviet Union, restore public confidence, and minimize the risk of war. Because support for partition was the correct position anyway, Clifford concluded, good policy was likely to be the best politics.[90]

At the same time, the military and the State Department made sure that the White House was as forcefully reminded of the potential costs of support for the UNSCOP plan. Pentagon studies took it for granted that the General Assembly would approve partition, that Britain would propose a joint Anglo-American trusteeship plus military and economic aid for a two-year transitional period, and that the United States would have six months to decide whether to put troops in Palestine. The premises led to the inexorable conclusion that a positive decision would limit U.S. influence "to that which could be maintained by military force," and potentially lead to Soviet "influence and power throughout the area." In an area where the Soviet advantages included geography, land mass, and numbers, the analysts informed the Joint Chiefs, this would also risk a buffer area, and loss of Saudi, Iraqi, and Iranian oil, thus threatening United States loss of an "oil-starved war."

Members of the Joint Strategic Survey Committee were appalled at the idea that Britain would say no to partition while the United States said yes. They were equally appalled that the Soviets might agree to joint trusteeship and so sneak into the Middle East as part of a multilateral agreement. Suitably edited and homogenized, the official report from the joint chiefs accordingly favored U.S. silence on the matter of troop commitments, British responsibility for administering partition, and U.S.

financial and material aid as the most acceptable alternative to full British responsibility.[91]

Reports from the intelligence community reached similar conclusions. Palestine, the infant CIA reported *ex officio,* was a "small weak country whose war potential is almost nonexistent, but whose geographic position gives it a strategic significance out of all proportion to its size and wealth." It could potentially turn the Arab world from "evolution in cooperation with the West to revolution with the support of the USSR," the report added predictably. What was clear was that the Arabs would resist partition and that any effort to enforce it would therefore lead to armed conflict. CIA analysts were reluctant to project the outcome. Both sides were dependent on external support, they acknowledged. The Arabs also were likely to get more of it, while the Jewish forces were superior in numbers and training. But the authors' real concern was that the United States could be forced to intervene in support of the Jews.[92]

Presumably, this was also one of Truman's concerns, but it was hardly the only one. His ambivalence was reflected in the undignified series of fits and starts that were to mark U.S. policy for the next half year. Where did the United States stand on partition? In favor, the White House seemed to say as it demonstratively added Eleanor Roosevelt and General Hilldring to the U.S. delegation in order to balance off the pro-Arab expertise of its State Department advisors.[93] Marshall, sent personally to urge support for the UNSCOP plan, nonetheless cautioned delegates not "to show their hand." In fact, Mrs. Roosevelt was only reluctantly persuaded of the case for a Jewish state, though concerned for the credibility of the United Nations. Marshall, on the other hand, was primarily concerned with the vulnerability of the United States. What would happen, he wondered, if the Soviets should join the Arabs, the British should throw in their hand, and the United States, after voting for partition, should then be left by alone to enforce it?[94]

In the end, ironically, what seems to have carried the partition resolution was an unplanned, uncoordinated, but nonetheless effective conjunction of Soviet opportunism and U.S. ambivalence. On October 13, to nearly universal surprise, the Soviets declared for partition. Though openly suspicious of Soviet motives, Americans thereafter could hardly oppose what the Soviets supported. The only issue now was the extent and sincerity of U.S. support.

Even as the vote approached, only three of the seven U.S. delegates, including Hilldring and Mrs. Roosevelt, seem to have been clearly for partition. Two more, Marshall and Ambassador Warren Austin, were apprehensive. As his later career confirmed, John Foster Dulles was undecided. Later to serve as secretary of state under Eisenhower and already a shadow candidate for the job, he was skeptical how Jewish statehood might affect the region. Yet as advisor to Republicans, including Dewey, the presumptive candidate in 1948, he was inevitably aware what it could cost to surrender the issue to the Democrats. As a former ambassador to Iraq, consumed with anxiety about Soviet ambitions in the region, Loy Henderson was naturally opposed to partition. Herschel Johnson, the chief U.S. delegate, reportedly burst into tears under the pressure of contrary instructions.

Truman's intervention in November 1947 was a model of what drove Johnson to tears. Concerned about British plans to reassign the Negev to the Arabs, thus linking Egypt and Jordan, and incidentally cutting off Israel from the Red Sea, Chaim Weizmann had taken the matter directly to the president. Impressed with Weizmann's presentation, Truman then called Hilldring, who called Charles E. Bohlen, who informed Robert A. Lovett of the president's decision that afternoon. But since presidential and departmental instructions were now in diametrical conflict, even Hilldring advised a brief delay in announcing the new U.S. position.[95]

Fearing the worst, American Zionists pressed Hilldring to delay the final vote on partition till Saturday, November 29. Meanwhile Democratic congressmen, partly officials, and the president's old friends from Kansas City turned the heat on Truman. But it seems to have been November 26 before there was any systematic action. Then, with at least the tacit permission of the president, Niles, Clifford, Clifford's assistant Max Lowenthal, and other White House staffers began calling in the IOUs with a resourcefulness clearly mixed with desperation.

In the next few days, Emanuel Neumann of the American Zionist Emergency Committee turned his acquaintance with a former U.S. governor general of the Philippines into pressure on Manila, and two justices of the U.S. Supreme Court and twenty six U.S. senators informed the Philippine president that a vote against partition would risk offending American friends. Goldmann got Adolph Berle, the onetime New Deal economist and former State Department official, to pass on a similar message to Haiti. Reportedly threatened with a Jewish boycott, Harvey Firestone of Firestone Rubber acceded to pressure from former Secretary of State Edward Stettinius, and leaned heavily on Liberia's President William V.S. Tubman. Meanwhile Niles himself activated old Boston connections to put some heat on Nicaragua and Greece, and appealed to Bernard Baruch, the legendary financier, to try to influence the French.[96] With the outcome still uncertain, several Latin American delegations also reported offers of money. On November 29, the General Assembly finally voted to accept the UNSCOP plan by 33–13, with ten abstentions. But unanimous Arab opposition made it clear before delegates had even left the room that there would be no partition without a fight. An undeclared civil war in Palestine began almost immediately thereafter.

On the other hand, comparing the effort with the arms Americans had twisted in pursuit of other goals, Thomas J. Hamilton, the *New York Times* correspondent at the United Nations, was impressed with how little pressure was exerted in behalf of partition. In fact, at least two heavily dependent U.S. clients, Greece and Cuba, had voted against partition, while equally dependent Mexico, China, Honduras, and El Salvador were among the abstentions. Arabs took it for granted that U.S. extortion and bribes had been decisive. Yet Garcia-Granados, the Guatemalan UNSCOP member and a particularly fervent supporter of partition, could only report in his memoirs how grateful he would have been for more of the support the others so self-evidently alleged. The United States "did not use very much pressure, if any at all," reported the delegate of another Latin country that had chosen not to support partition.[97]

If the vote for the UNSCOP plan ended one phase of U.S. policy that "the foreign observer might be excused for regarding as ambivalent," as Acheson later wrote,[98] it only introduced another in which ambivalence reached open crisis.

Reconsideration seems to have begun before the partition resolution had even passed. By now, the impact of partition on U.S. defense planning was an obvious question. Though majorities of Americans favored partition when Gallup asked them, virtually none, save Jews, were also prepared to fight and die, or send members of their families to fight and die, for it. Yet this, increasingly, seemed what was involved. So, each in its way, the combination of Jewish military setbacks, the U.S. political calendar, and the imposition of a U.S. arms embargo—actually effected in mid-November, 1947, but not acknowledged in public till December 5—only made the question more urgent.

The deepening Cold War also made the question more urgent. By coincidence, the debate on partition practically coincided with the creation of the Cominform. A club in both senses, the new collective was meant less for western than for eastern Europe, where the merest hints of national independence were now regarded with the deepest suspicion. The Cominform could hardly help but recall the prewar Comintern, and it was hardly surprising that Westerners should see it as a challenge. Sure enough, its creation was followed in December by continued deadlock at the Big Four foreign ministers meeting in Moscow.

By February 1948, the U.S. military establishment was already sounding alarms, while the State Department anticipated disaster. U.S. prestige was in retreat, the JCS reported. Under the circumstances, new commitments in Palestine were naturally out of the question. Because Americans believed both in partition and the United Nations, and the Arabs were in armed opposition to both, this was obviously a problem. On the one hand, the JCS took it for granted that the Soviets would oppose U.S. troops in Palestine, from where they could attack the Soviet Union. On the other, the JCS saw little chance for an international force without contingents from the superpowers. It would therefore be impossible to enforce partition, they concluded, without damaging such basic principles as noncommitment of U.S. troops, exclusion of Soviet forces from the region, continued access to oil, and friendly relations with Arab governments, "which will facilitate our use of strategic base areas and lines of communication . . . in the event of war with the USSR."

By the end of March, considered military opinion had determined that, even irrespective of organized intervention from neighboring Arab countries, peacekeeping in Palestine would require more than 100,000 troops plus sizeable naval, air, and support contingents. For perspective, the Haganah, the main Jewish force that was to carry the day against four Arab armies, had decided in January 1948 to establish an infantry of 15,000 and a home guard of 3,000. Meanwhile, the U.S. Army, which numbered 3.5 million in May 1945, had been cut to about 400,000 by March 1946.[99]

In the view of the State Department's policy planning staff, the United States had three courses: to support partition, oppose it, or adopt neutrality. The first course, its director, George Kennan, argued, would end in disaster. Either the United States would be "militarily responsible for the protection of the Jewish population of Palestine against the declared hostility of the Arab world," he explained, "or of sharing that responsibility with the Russians and thus assisting at their installation as one of the major powers of the area."[100]

Seen from the State Department, the third course looked little better. Not only did it foreclose any U.S. influence, it left the initiative to the Soviets. This left option two, and a new U.S. policy based either on a cantonized federal Palestine as envisaged by Morrison-Grady or a new trusteeship vested in the Western powers or the United Nations. Although opposition from "Zionist elements" was taken as given, it was assumed that these would be outweighed by support from the Arabs and "world opinion in general".[101]

Robert McClintock, Rusk's assistant in the State Department's U.N. office, challenged Kennan's view. As he saw it, the proposed reversal of stated policy, not to mention implied toleration of Arab resistance to a U.N. resolution, would be bad for U.S. credibility. Predictably, his view was shared by Clifford, who argued forcefully and persuasively that the Arabs needed the United States at least as much as it needed the Arabs. In both the diplomatic and defense establishments, this still remained a minority position. "[U]nless we had access to Middle East oil, American motorcar companies would have to design a four-cylinder motorcar sometime within the next five years," Defense Secretary Forrestal speculated grimly in January 1948, after breakfast with a major oil executive.[102] Certain both chaos and the Soviets were waiting over the horizon, U.S. diplomats accordingly pursued trusteeship with frantic ingenuity from February to mid-May.[103] The Security Council was responsible for international peace, Austin informed the United Nations in late February, with Truman's approval. It was not responsible for enforcing partition.

At the same time, an eccentric but conspicuous special election in the Bronx inevitably seized the administration's attention. Running to fill a congressional vacancy in a heavily Jewish district, the Wallaceite candidate of the American Labor party trounced the regular Democrat, and former Vice President Wallace himself, who was soon to run against Truman as the candidate of American Labor party voters, declared that "Truman talks like a Jew and acts like an Arab."[104] Truman declared himself to be unmoved by reminders of his need for Jewish votes and money and even the seeming defection of large sections of his constituency. "The Palestine issue will be handled here, and there'll be no politics involved," he stiffly informed one party official. Meanwhile, opinion polls showed that support for partition had declined from 65 percent to 38 percent, while 83 percent—including 61 percent of the Jewish respondents—were opposed to unilateral U.S. intervention.[105]

Whatever the president's personal credibility, the meanderings that followed did little for the credibility of his administration. At a famous White House meeting on March 18, 1948 resourcefully brokered by the ubiquitous Jacobson and almost aggressively kept from public view, Truman reassured the aging Weizmann that U.S. policy was unchanged. The next day Austin announced to the Security Council that the United States no longer considered partition a viable option; he therefore proposed international trusteeship.

In the public uproar that followed, it was easy to blame confusion, and suspect still worse. On March 20, Truman even called an extraordinary Saturday morning staff meeting to try to control the damage. "This morning I find that the State Department has reversed my Palestine policy," he wailed to his diary. "There are people on the 3rd and 4th levels of the State Dept. who have always wanted to cut my throat," he continued darkly. "They've succeeded in doing it."[106]

It was as at least as reasonable to blame the real-world pressures of overwork and bureaucratic politics for the general embarrassment. In February, Czech Communists had carried off a coup in Prague. In March, General Lucius D. Clay had warned of the risk of sudden war in Berlin. On March 17, Truman himself had gone to Congress to appeal for universal military training, support for the Marshall Plan, and enactment of a draft. The same day, the nation's major West European allies signed a mutual defense treaty in Brussels. On March 18 came the interview with Weizmann; March 19, Austin's speech in New York; March 20 the final stormy meeting of the Allied Control Council, which had once been hopefully conceived to coordinate four-power military government of Germany.

During the same period, the foreign policy establishment hauled and tugged not only on its policy in Palestine but its obligations under the U.N. charter. One basic issue was already clearly drawn: whether the United States should challenge the legality of the General Assembly resolution of the previous November 29. Rusk said yes. The Office of the Legal Advisor, which usually felt itself ill-used and unconsulted anyway, said no. In February, the issue had been thrashed out in a series of meetings with Under Secretary Lovett. In the lawyers' opinion, the Security Council was obliged to intervene to keep the peace. Sincerely or disingenuously, the United States then asked the Security Council for a clear declaration of its intentions. On March 17, while Marshall, Lovett, and Rusk were all away from Washington, their deputies prepared instructions that were dispatched to New York the next day. It was these that led to Austin's bombshell on March 19. Truman seems to have been right that he was uninformed of the new instructions, and also that the decision that was to cause him such memorable chagrin was reached well short of the State Department, let alone the White House, summit. But it hardly helped. Ironically, at least two of the responsible inhabitants of the "3rd or 4th level," including Loy Henderson and Charles E. Bohlen, were later to take their places in the pantheon of postwar U.S. diplomacy, and the State Department even named a lecture hall in Henderson's honor.

In the aftershock of Austin's speech, it was agreed to back off from any request for a special session. Senior officials assured the president "that it would be possible to secure both Arab and Jewish agreement to a Palestine truce and trusteeship." Truman seems to have given them a week to try it. They were then to return to the original U.S. position in support of partition. Meanwhile, Lovett denied that U.S. policy had changed.[107]

As late as early May, the State Department was still hell-bent on preempting Israeli independence and the war that was expected to be its inevitable obbligato. A quarter century was to pass before a secretary of state engaged himself in actual Arab-Israeli negotiations. Marshall was nonetheless prepared to put the presidential plane at the disposal of Jewish, Arab, and U.N. representatives if that would advance negotiation of an unconditional cease-fire. Yet even as the State Department was asking the British to extend their mandate by ten days, Truman was informing Weizmann—though not the British or the State Department—that he would recognize a Jewish state. The Jewish Agency passed over the truce proposal, but the Arabs rejected it too, as though determined once again to snatch defeat from the jaws of acceptable compromise. Meanwhile, the British proved unwilling to extend their stay another quarter hour. Transjordan's King Abdullah, the one Arab head of state who stood to gain from Palestine's partition, declined to stand against the truce, but he left the matter of accepting it to those members of the Arab League who were already members of the U.N. Taking their cues, as always, from the grand mufti's Arab Higher Committee, the Arab states then forfeited a chance to put Abdullah and the British on the spot by saying yes. By this time, it was May 12.[108]

What saved the day for all but the Arabs was neither official consensus nor public opinion but an improbable combination of the Communist coup in Prague and a victorious Jewish army in Palestine. The former, which led to an eleventh-hour arms sale to the desperate Haganah, allowed the Jews to outflank the U.S. arms embargo that remained in place despite the pressures of an election year. The latter, as Arnold Rogow noted, "broke the deadlock in United States foreign policy."[109]

Certainly among the more romantic dimensions of Israel's war of independence was the private initiative of a cast of characters who sometimes recalled Jack Armstrong, the All-American Boy, and sometimes an odd combination of Damon Runyon's Nathan Detroit and Isaac Babel's Benya Krick, the Gangster. Sometimes successful, sometimes not, they were at least hard to fault for commitment and resourcefulness. Between 1945 and 1948, they located, acquired, and processed small arms, machine tools, explosives, spare parts, whole bombers, and even a surplus aircraft carrier. They then shipped them via unreported air and sea routes as far afield as Panama, the Azores, and Prague.

During the same period, an estimated 1,000–1,500 Americans also volunteered to serve with, though not in, the Israeli army. Of these, 37 combatants and a Hadassah medical team were killed. Among the casualties was Colonel David (Mickey) Marcus, a former aide to both Governor Dewey and General Eisenhower, now buried at the U.S. Military Academy at West Point. One volunteer actually went to jail in Florida for violating the embargo. Another, Hank Greenspun, the subsequent editor and publisher of the *Las Vegas Sun,* was fined $10,000 for the same offense but later pardoned by President Kennedy.[110] Still another volunteer, Al Schwimmer, later a founding father of Israel Aircraft Industries, resurfaced in the mid 1980s as an accessory to Irangate, an arms deal more fantastic than anything either his earlier comrades in arms or Israel's founding fathers could have imagined.[111]

Although there could be some question about the practical impact of American arms, there could be little doubt about the impact of American money. On a single afternoon at the Council of Jewish Federations and Welfare Funds in Chicago, Golda Meir raised $25 million, still an impressive figure decades later, and an astonishing figure for the period. It was the improbable constellation of available dollars, Soviet political support, German military surplus, Czech exclusion from the Marshall Plan, and the chance for the new Communist regime in Prague to earn some hard currency that now yielded a double bonus for the Israelis. The Soviet-approved, Czech sale of German-surplus planes and artillery led to a stream of military-age immigrants from eastern Europe who supported the socialist—and consistently anticommunist—legitimacy of Mapai, Ben-Gurion's mainstream Labor party. In early April, the arms too began to help to turn the tide, supporting a series of offensives that linked the thitherto isolated islands of Jewish settlement. On May 14, as the last British troops embarked in Haifa, Ben-Gurion resolved to declare a state in the area held by Jewish forces, and the United States and Soviet Union extended recognition almost immediately.

There was a bizarre scene at the United Nations, where the U.S. delegation, under instructions from the State Department, was still in dogged pursuit of a formula for trusteeship. Informed of the president's decision by Clifford a quarter hour before the official announcement, Rusk passed the message on to Austin, who then, as Rusk recalled years later, "simply went home." Meanwhile there was pandemonium in the hall, where a U.S. delegate reportedly sat on the Cuban delegate to keep him from leaving. The other U.S. delegates may or may not have sympathized with the Cuban. Marshall nonetheless thought it prudent to send Rusk to New York in case they did.[112]

With more or less plausibility, containment of Soviet communism, preemption of early Soviet recognition, speculation in Jewish votes, and personal triumph over the diplomats who tried to outflank him, have all been advanced as motives for Truman's decision. But common sense should not be left out. It was clear that trusteeship required a trustee, that the United States was not a candidate, and that volunteers were not readily available. It was also clear that the Jews of Palestine wanted a state, were in control of the territory on which it would be established, and that others, including the Soviet Union, were about to extend recognition.[113] Hard as it may have seemed to make the case for recognition under such circumstances, it was harder still to make a case against it.

De facto recognition opened a third phase of U.S. policy. Yet even a week after recognition, Kennan was still convinced that administration policy was heading the United States toward unilateral responsibility for Israel's survival, conflict with the British, and collision with the Arabs. "It thereby threatens not only to place in jeopardy some of our most vital national interests . . . but to disrupt the unity of the western world and to undermine our entire policy toward the Soviet Union," he informed Lovett. "This is not to mention the possibility that it may initiate a process of disintegration within the United Nations itself."

By now, events, including the 1948 presidential election, were in the saddle. "As I understand it, we have no long-term Palestine policy," wailed one member of the State Department planning staff in July. "We do have a short-term, open-ended policy which is set from time to time by White House directives."[114] This was true, but only part of the truth. U.S. policymakers, including Truman, favored anything that would stop the war in Palestine, but they also opposed anything that would force unilateral responsibility, let alone direct intervention, on the United States. This left responsibility with such U.N. mediators as the Swedish Count Folke Bernadotte. But this was no solution either, since good intentions led only to such bitterly divisive initiatives as Bernadotte's proposal that Israel surrender the Negev in return for the western Galilee. On September 17, Bernadotte was assassinated by Jewish terrorists, among them Yitzhak Shamir, Israel's later prime minister. Political justice Israeli-style, the aftermath was also a grim anticipation of things to come. Though arrested within twenty four hours, the murderers were then allowed to escape, and their leader, sentenced to five years imprisonment, was simultaneously amnestied and elected to Israel's first parliament a few months later.

Till well into 1948, practical opposition to the U.N. plan came not only from Jews and Arabs in Palestine but even from such powerful U.N. supporters as Mrs. Roosevelt at home.[115] Meanwhile, Truman resisted the urgings of political allies and advisors to lift the arms embargo, extend de jure recognition, or announce the loan the new Israeli state had requested almost concurrently with its declaration of independence. Revealingly, it took a tactical lapse by his opponent to coax the president from a tacit moratorium with the Republicans. Almost on the eve of the election, Dewey hinted broadly that Truman had undercut the assurance in the Democratic platform that Israel would get the Negev. On October 24, Israel's extended borders were then reaffirmed by a presidential statement. Two days later, at a rally in Madison Square Garden, Truman added zestfully, but unspecifically, that Israel "must be large enough, free enough and strong enough to make its people self-supporting and secure."[116] He was reelected shortly afterward, the most remarkable comeback in the history of U.S. presidential politics. But ironically, the crucial votes came, for example, from Iowa, where it was the farm, and hardly the Jewish vote, that was decisive; while he lost New York, where the Wallace vote effectively threw the state to Dewey.

By the end of the year, with Israel both victorious and irreversibly recognized, it appeared that U.S. policy had at least been jolted into a new and more hopeful ambiguity. The problem of Palestine, it now appeared, was no longer a matter of discerning reality but legitimizing and learning to live with it. This meant an official end to the Arab-Israeli war and conclusion of a peace that would not only be acceptable but presumably preferable to all parties. Soon to be secretary of state himself, Dulles tried to explain the U.S. position to the Lebanese delegation at the U.N. "The American people and the government were . . . convinced that the establishment of the State of Israel under livable conditions was a historical necessity," he argued patiently. This involved "certain injustices to the Arab world," he conceded, and he acknowledged that there was no single solution that would make everybody happy. "Nevertheless," he concluded, "there had to be a solution and, we believed, a peaceful solution."[117]

3

Getting Acquainted

Like a lot of new beginnings, the turbulent transition to state-to-state relations was an anthology of loose ends. Though Israel's juridical status might still be open-ended, its borders indeterminate, and its survival itself a matter of touch and go, there was now, at least, a Jewish state in Palestine with its own currency, flag, and postage stamps, and recognized missions in all the world capitals that mattered.

It was hardly a coincidence that Jews were particularly sensitive to the gravitational pull of the new state. Born of circumstance and sustained by desperation, relations between American Jews and the Jewish community in Palestine had thitherto reflected the improvisation, contentiousness, and urgency of the Zionist movement. With Israel's creation, the Zionist organizations and even the movement itself were suddenly redundant and even potentially disruptive. Concerned alike to demonstrate Israel's sovereignty with respect to foreign Zionist funding, and to insulate its political system from targeted cascades of foreign Zionist votes, Ben-Gurion himself took care to put the American organization virtually out of business within a year or two of independence. Henceforth, the United Jewish Appeal (UJA) was to be the vehicle of Jewish community support, assisted by a wide variety of autonomous civic and philanthropic groups. Distribution of American Jewish funds, in turn, was to be determined by a formula that was eventually to reserve to Israel two-thirds and more of the money it collected.

Meanwhile, as official Washington learned to deal both with official Israel and a radically reorganized and energized American Jewish community, the American Council for Judaism, the institutional voice of American Jewish anti-Zionism since 1943, too sank into anachronism. Zionism had been a dream and then a movement. Israel was now a fact. The birth of Israel thus transformed the whole matrix of Jewish-Israeli-U.S. relationships in ways that were both dramatic and paradoxical.

Among the obvious consequences of independence was the challenge to both Israeli and American Jews to debate, negotiate, and assert their respective identities and inevitable differences. The result was a new demarcation on both sides: Israelis here, Diaspora Jews, of whom organized Zionists were no longer more equal than the others, there. Years later, Walter Eytan, the first director general of the Foreign Ministry, recalled proposing from the start that Israeli diplomats acknowledge a triple demarcation—between Israeli Jews, Diaspora Jews, and American Jews as a separate category. Unlike British, French, and Italian Jews, who remained Jews no matter how long they lived in Britain, France, or Italy, he argued, it was in the nature of the United States that American Jews became American practically on arrival.[1]

This continued to be a minority position. The special status of American Jews was nonetheless acknowledged de facto in a 1950 document, negotiated at the summit between Ben-Gurion and Jacob Blaustein, the president of the American Jewish Committee. Reflecting eight hours of strenuous discussion, their "exchange of views" read rather like a diplomatic communiqué, in which Blaustein no less than Ben-Gurion represented a sovereign party.

If the binary distinction between Israeli and Diaspora Jews had been among the first principles of Israeli identity and constitutionality, the statement was a tacit concession that the United States too was a promised land. "The Jews of the United States, as a community and as individuals, have only one political attachment and that is to the United States," the document declared. "They owe no political allegiance to Israel." To this, Blaustein added, "If democracy should fail in America, there would be no future for democracy anywhere in the world, and the very existence of an independent State of Israel would be problematic."[2] The particularity of both countries was reaffirmed in U.S. law, which rejected dual-citizenship altogether till 1967, and then approved it only in circumscribed cases.[3]

Ironically, the circumstances that made organized Zionism redundant also made the Zionist enterprise legitimate and uncontroversial as it had never been before. The vast majority of American Jews now not only accepted and supported the idea of a Jewish state in Palestine but also came increasingly to regard it as "the cherished inheritance of nearly all Diaspora Jews," "the least common denominator of their collective identity," and "the one sure sign that an American Jew still retained allegiance to the Jewish people."[4] In practice, only a tiny minority of American Jews—1,711 of the 686,739 immigrants to the new state between 1948 and 1951—were prepared to go and live there.[5] Few more were willing to learn its language with any fluency, or even make a serious effort to understand the new state's formidable complexities and stresses.[6] Yet for every possible reason of solidarity, admiration, concern, historical memory, subliminal fear, or vicarious pride, almost all American Jews were now prepared to regard, accept, defend, support, and, above all, pay for Israel as an acknowledged extension of themselves.

Beginning in May 1951, private support for the state now took the form of Israeli bonds. The bond program was unveiled in September 1950 at a three-day "Ben-Gurion Conference" in Jerusalem for some sixty American-Jewish business and community leaders. The official Israeli presence only emphasized the significance of the occasion. Not only did the prime minister, foreign minister, and finance minister of Israel appear at the King David Hotel to address the conference in person but the whole United States division of the Foreign Ministry and a substantial cadre of the ministry's senior officials closed up shop in Tel Aviv for most of a week in order to be present. Ben-Gurion himself appeared at the opening session to propose a three-year plan, which Finance Minister Eliezar Kaplan anticipated would cost $1.5 billion, for bringing 600,000 more immigrants into the country. The prime minister was confident that Israel could raise a third of this from its own resources, but there was little doubt where the rest would come from. Though

Moshe Sharett too counted on "the ever-present good will of the Government and people of the United States," he explicitly acknowledged "the two collective partners in the great joint enterprise, American Jewry and Israel," in expressing his hope for "an overwhelming measure of active support from all constructive elements in American Jewish life."

After the former U.S. Treasury Secretary Henry Morgenthau, Jr., assured him that the administration in Washington was amenable, Ben-Gurion toured the United States to kick off the campaign. In his report on the Jerusalem conference, the U.S. chargé pointed demonstratively to a headline in the local press. "America Has Enough for Israel and Local Needs," it declared. The "local" seemed to refer not simply to the American-Jewish community but the whole United States, he added with official jocularity.[7]

The mode of payment turned out to be an initial irritant for both fund-raisers and presumptive contributors. Symbolic of Israeli sovereignty, Israeli bonds, like any other public issue, were theoretically available over the counter to both private and institutional investors. But banks and other large financial institutions were unwilling to underwrite them. As a result, Israel Bond and UJA volunteers competed for public attention. Contrary to expectation, their success was impressive, although the exchange rate on of the Israeli pound declined from $2.80 to $0.60 in 1951 alone. In part as a consequence, bond sales fell far short of their $500 million target in 1951. Still, the combined receipts from bonds and UJA contributions amounted to nearly $100 million, and in 1963, the Bank of Israel began redeeming bonds on schedule. By 1967, Americans had bought $850 million worth of Israeli bonds, and Canadians, West Europeans, and others, another $150 million. Between 1946 and 1962, it was estimated that American Jews contributed at least $1 billion more through UJA.[8]

At the same time, public support for Israel extended across the American political spectrum. Mrs. Franklin Roosevelt, the patron mother of U.S. liberalism, found Israel "like a breath of fresh air after the Arab countries." George Sokolsky, a raucously right-wing columnist for the Hearst syndicate, already saw it as "another potential island of defense against aggressive Communist penetration."[9] The resonance even extended to popular culture. "Tzena, Tzena," a slightly synthetic Israeli hora in a thundering arrangement by Mitch Miller was high on the "Hit Parade" in 1951. *Exodus,* Leon Uris's large, sentimental novel about the war of independence, sold some four million copies on its appearance seven years later. Otto Preminger, the Hollywood producer-director, and his writer, Dalton Trumbo, then turned it into a screenplay and four-hour film epic featuring Paul Newman, Sal Mineo, Peter Lawford, Lee J. Cobb, John Dereck, and Eva-Marie Saint. In time, even the score, by Ernest Gold, had become ubiquitous, while the film, first released in 1960, could still be seen occasionally on late-night television well into the 1980s.

The very different experience of those relatively few Americans with pro-Arab sympathies was a revealing index of public attitudes and expectations. In 1948, Virginia Gildersleeve, the old Middle East hand from Barnard College, helped organize the Committee for Justice and Peace in the Holy Land with herself in the chair, and Teddy Roosevelt's grandson Kermit as executive secretary, but even she conceded that it left few traces. Only a new administration "with Mr. Dulles as Secretary of

State" was likely to effect a change of course, she reflected in her memoirs four years later. Compared to their Democratic predecessors, she added, the Republican new-comers seemed at least aware "that the situation in the Middle East is very danger-ous to our country, and that the plight of hundreds of thousands of Arab refugees is a running sore."[10]

Roosevelt's career was in fact de facto evidence that someone was listening in Washington. As an official of the newly created CIA, he had already been co-opted in 1951 for a top-secret interagency committee on U.S. policy in the Middle East. A year or so later, the job led him to Egypt, where he made it his mission to make friends with the young officers who had just overthrown the monarchy. A year later, with a new administration firmly established in Washington, he took charge in Teh-ran as executor of the coup that restored the shah of Iran to power after a self-imposed and short-lived Roman exile.[11] For years afterward, the coup was regarded in Washington as wonderfully successful.

Rejected by her old liberal readership for incorrect views on the Irgun, the partition of Palestine, and the plight of Arab refugees, Dorothy Thompson too was quietly adopted by the State Department to produce a series of articles, intended to tell American readers what they should know but had not yet learned about "the seething Middle East." But not even her offer to omit her views on Israel was enough to attract a buyer. The only readers with any interest in the region were Jews, the *Saturday Evening Post* informed her in a politely regretful rejection letter, "and their prime interest was the future of Israel rather than the plight of her foes." Ironically, the only alternative immediately available was *Commentary,* an intel-lectual monthly published by the American Jewish Committee, where Thompson appeared in March 1950 in a symposium with the historian Oscar Handlin. A few months later, this time supported by Rabbi Elmer Berger, executive secretary of the American Council for Judaism as well as a subsidy from Aramco, the Saudi-Amer-ican oil giant, she surfaced again as cofounder of American Friends of the Middle East.

It was 1967 before it became publicly known that the new organization, like the National Student Association and the Congress for Cultural Freedom, was also a ward of the CIA. In a letter to the president of the United States, Rabbi Philip S. Bernstein, chairman of the American-Israel Public Affairs Committee (AIPAC), contended that he had actually known of the funding since at least 1962 but had been assured—misleadingly—that it had long since stopped. Lyndon Johnson guardedly conceded that a review committee, already at work, was "likely to be responsive to some of the points you make."

In fact, it was unclear if the founding members of American Friends of the Mid-dle East really knew where their money came from,[12] but given the temper of the times, it is also not certain that they would have cared. What mattered, as Thomp-son insisted at an inaugural press conference, was that it be generally understood that the new group was not directed against Israel, that it received no Arab subsidy, and that it was not a propaganda organization. It existed, she emphasized, because the United States, the most popular foreign country in the Middle East after World War I, had become the least popular country in the region after World War II, "largely because of its lead in sponsoring the state of Israel." But the *New York*

Times, whose publisher himself had been an aggressive anti-Zionist, failed even to send a reporter to her news conference.[13]

Since the confused and demoralized days of 1947, U.S. policy had changed almost beyond recognition. In September 1949, apparently on his own initiative, Dean Rusk drew up a comparative résumé of declared goals and ostensible achievements, and sent it to Clifford at the White House. "Dear Clark," it began, "As a fellow veteran of an ancient war, I think you will be interested . . ."

The memo matched the language of the 1948 Democratic platform to the current state of U.S. policy. Sure enough, as Rusk now saw it, each successive pledge—recognition of Israel, borders consistent with the UNSCOP plan, the arms embargo, Israeli U.N. membership, the international status of Jerusalem—had been "liberally and fully carried out." Yet, in its way, each point also reflected just as clearly how much and how many things had changed in barely a year, and how many loose ends were left to tie.[14]

The issue of borders showed how far events had raced ahead of political purpose. Since May 1948, Israelis' military skill had extended the new state's frontiers beyond anything foreseen in the original partition plan. It was already clear that there could be no possible reversion to the UNSCOP map short of another war with a radically different outcome from the first one. With the collapse of Arab resistance, the U.S. arms embargo had meanwhile become something of an anachronism. Internationalization of Jerusalem under U.N. supervision had lost its relevance too because Israel and Jordan had agreed de facto to occupy and divide the city between them. What kept the issue alive was its continuing significance for other parties, not only Arabs but also Latin Americans, Catholics in general, and U.S. Catholics in particular, who tended, like Jews, to be traditional Democratic voters. Israel's U.N. membership was subsumed in the logic of the UNSCOP plan and the consensus of the superpowers rather than any particular policy of the United States.

Even the extended process of recognition—from May 1948 to January 1949—testified to conflicting pulls of political gravitation. De jure recognition was nominally withheld for reasons of democratic principle, pending the general election required to confer legitimacy on a provisional government. But it was also delayed for reasons of diplomatic practice, while the administration tried to extract Israeli accommodations on borders, U.N. mediation, and all the other unresolved puzzles in the continuing struggle for Palestine.

There were persisting differences between the White House and the State Department on the very status of the mission. Clifford wanted Class I, like London, Paris, or Moscow; the State Department, Class IV. Between them, they settled on Class II. In practice, this meant a dozen U.S. officials in Tel Aviv, provisionally housed in the same hotel as their Soviet colleagues. Even two years later, the working climate could best be described as difficult. "[U]ntil overcrowded, underfed, pioneering, intensively exigent Israel shall have solved some of its pressing economic problems," one senior officer informed the department, "American objectivity here will best be realized by specifying clearly each staff member's period of assignment." What this meant, he explained, was a maximal eighteen-month tour, guaranteed in writing.[15]

Both the rank and choice of the chief-of-mission were further indicators of official ambivalence. James G. McDonald, who advanced from minister to first ambassador with the conferral of de jure recognition, had served on the Anglo-U.S. commission. A former League of Nations commissioner for refugees from Germany from 1933 to 1935, and editorial writer for the *New York Times,* his person and career were a signal to both Israelis and Americans of how the White House understood the job. Even the omissions in his résumé were clues to what was expected—and not expected—of him. Not a career diplomat, a fat-cat campaign contributor, or a token ethnic like the once-traditional Jewish ambassador to Ottoman Turkey or the still-traditional black ambassador to Liberia, he was nonetheless regarded with habitual suspicion by the professional foreign service, who dismissed him as "a professional Zionist." Now and then, he was even cut off from cable traffic by his colleagues in the Arab capitals.[16]

Notwithstanding shabby treatment by old Middle East hands both in and outside the State Department, McDonald established a benchmark of independent judgment and good sense that could still be a standard for his successors. Openly skeptical that Israeli concessions would have any effect on Arab neighbors, he was also at a loss to see why Israel should be any more vulnerable to communism than France or Italy, with their vastly larger Communist parties, and openly contemptuous of what he described as "Alice in Wonderland" schemes to get Israel to concede territory for matching grants of $50 million. Official speculation to the contrary, he doubted too that American Jews would stop supporting Israel, and warned specifically against trying to use them against Israel as a source of pressure.

Yet he was far from the one-man Israel lobby his colleagues claimed to see. On the contrary, his views and priorities put him at odds not only with the State Department but with conventional Jewish wisdom both in Israel and the United States. His mission, as he saw it, was to move the State Department to a more flexible position on the status of Jerusalem, and to urge "realistic moderation" on the Israelis. For a start, this meant some accommodation of what were now estimated as 900,000 refugees from the first Arab-Israeli war. It then meant getting Israeli officials, with their commitment to mass immigration from both the Arab world and Europe, to listen to U.S. experts before they vastly exceeded Israel's economic capacity. Not least, McDonald wanted Israelis to know that U.S. benevolence had limits.

Save for Iraq and Saudi Arabia, McDonald envisaged formal peace between Israel and its neighbors within ten years. He even foresaw a degree of Israeli-Arab rapprochement, though he assumed it would be born of economic, not cultural, complementarity. But what he saw as Israel's long-term destiny was neither martial nor messianic. It was, rather, the genial provincialism and modest significance of a Middle Eastern Switzerland. Perhaps most remarkable in retrospect is the omission of any hint of a special, let alone strategic, relationship with the United States.[17]

Within two years, McDonald had returned to private life. His successor, Monett Davis, was a career officer like most of the ambassadors who were to follow. Yet for at least another two decades, McDonald's circumspection established and defined both the possibilities and limits of U.S. policy. Even for so publicly uncritical and supportive a friend as Minnesota's Senator Hubert Humphrey, it was clear that the "1949 armistice boundaries constitute inviolable political boundaries subject to change only by joint agreement," and that Israel "should be told unequivocally that we would be unalterably opposed to . . . expansion."[18] However ponderously, Americans had established a principle in Palestine by the early 1950s. Before 1948, a Jewish state in a partitioned Palestine had been a speculative option. With the achievement of Israeli independence and the armistice agreements that followed, it had now become the status quo.

The interdepartmental paper flow was further evidence of how views had changed. Scarcely a year and a half after CIA analysts had advised the president that partition was unattainable, an agency assessment acknowledged that "the present state of Israel represents a remarkable accomplishment."[19] Only a year before the Pentagon had feared for Israel's survival without U.S. intervention. Now the U.S. Air Force chief of staff himself declared that "Israel has demonstrated by force of arms its right to be considered the military power next after Turkey."[20]

By 1952 both the State Department and the JCS had even acknowledged that "Israel's ability to defend itself and to participate in the defense of the area of which it is a part is important to the security of the United States." But the formula was code. It meant that Israel qualified, like Syria and Saudi Arabia, for reimbursable military aid under the terms of the Mutual Defense Assistance Act. The State Department referred explicitly to "the need for impartiality"; the JCS to the eighteen-to-twenty-four-month lead time involved in any new request for aid, given NATO, Korean, and—already—"Indo-Asian" priorities, a code in this case for aid to embattled French forces in Indochina.[21]

As both the principle and the qualifications confirmed, the new consensus left room for a policy that acknowledged and accommodated Israel with a minimum of tilt. Its common denominators were (a) limited liability for (b) a secure and peaceful Israel in a (c) stable, friendly Arab Middle East on (d) terms that were compatible as far as possible with the UNSCOP resolution. As an immediate result, the problems that had only recently led to war—immigration, borders, statehood itself—were now subsumed in the problems of negotiating peace, and the United States, the only foreign power credible to both sides, was inevitably engaged both as catalyst and broker.

Ironically, the new role only anticipated what would again preoccupy U.S. policymakers a generation later. Just as they would again in late 1973, priorities included an Israeli-Egyptian armistice; disengagement of a major Egyptian garrison from Israeli siege; and restraint of a foreign power, though in this case Britain, from resupplying an embattled and humiliated Arab client. According to U.S. officials, the idea was to save Egyptian face.[22] According to Israelis, the question was whether "the UN can restrain Egypt in the future any more effectively than in the past."[23] A few weeks later, the priority issue was getting Syria to withdraw from Lebanese territory so Israeli troops, still posted there, could conclude an armistice with Lebanon.[24] But there was little common sense of obligation to any status quo. On the contrary, both Zionists and Maronite Christians had speculated since the 1920s on a mutually advantageous partition of the French-created Greater Lebanon, at the presumable expense of both Sunni and Shi'ite Lebanese Moslems. The same sense of opportunity applied to the British-created Hashemite kingdom of Trans-Jordan. So Jordanians and Israelis too fought and parleyed interchangeably.

Contingent on the outcome of a peace settlement that never came, Israeli solutions ranged from the maximalist goal of a border on the Jordan to the minimalist goal of an ad hoc border dividing both Jerusalem and Palestine. In their hearts, most Israelis continued to favor the former. But *faute de mieux,* they were also prepared to accept the latter, if this were the price of peace and international legitimacy.

The *Atalena* incident of June 1948 was as different from the *Exodus* affair the year before as the former's name—the Italian word for "seesaw"—was from the flight from Egypt. The episode proved that Ben-Gurion was determined to live with partition, even at the risk of civil war. A onetime U.S. LST, made over to the Irgun by the French, the *Altalena* had set sail from Port-de-Bouc near Marseilles with a cargo of arms, not people. The $5 million shipment, in Begin's phrase, was intended "to put the nation in command of the whole country."[25] In full view of reporters, U.N. observers, and hotel guests on Tel Aviv balconies, Ben-Gurion ordered Palmach and commando units to fire on it to keep it from landing.

The episode was hardly proof that he considered the borders optimal. Just a few years later, after the assassination of Jordan's King Abdullah, he reportedly proposed taking advantage of the killing to seize not only the West Bank but even the Sinai. In 1954, according to his foreign minister's diary, he was ready to exploit the latest coup in Syria by dividing Lebanon with the Maronites. By 1956 he was even prepared to liquidate Jordan altogether. Meanwhile, he still fantasized about a Lebanese-Christian state that would allow Israel to advance its border to the Litani River.[26]

Yet the *Altalena* episode confirmed the essential pragmatism of a democratic Bismarck. To keep options open, and the Arab Legion at a distance, Israelis even dallied rhetorically with Palestinian independence. The "principle of self-determination should be observed for Arab Palestine," declared Walter Eytan, the first director general of the Israeli Foreign Ministry and Israel's representative to the U.N. Conciliation Commission in Lausanne. "Its future must be left to its inhabitants."[27] Regularly informed of secret negotiations by the Jordanians, who wanted support for themselves and pressure on the Israelis, U.S. officials grimly stayed in touch with both sides, though persuaded, as one reported, that one side was remarkable for its "utter perfidy," the other for its "utter stupidity."

By the spring of 1949, the situation had seemingly crystalized for years to come. First was the question of Jerusalem. Its division looked solid enough. On the other hand, internationalization seemed ever more remote. Historical associations aside, wartime experience had settled the question for both sides. "No government in Israel which agreed to [internationalization] would last five minutes," John H. Hilldring informed Dean Acheson.[28] It remained for both Israel and Jordan to struggle for their respective shares. Otherwise, they only ganged up on outsiders who sought to get between them.

Count Folke Bernadotte, the late Swedish U.N. mediator, who had called for

6,000 "well-armed and fully-trained troops," had been accordingly disappointed by U.S. unwillingness to provide them. Given the opposition of "a large segment" of the [Jerusalem] population to other arrangements, internationalization would require 4,000 policemen at an annual cost of $30 million, Truman informed Francis Cardinal Spellman of New York. "Unfortunately," he added pointedly, "the countries most directly concerned" were unable or unwilling to pay the price. It was clear from the context that the price referred to was primarily political. But a dollar price could also be advanced with appropriate effect. Commitment of 124 men to a U.N. force alone would cost the taxpayer nearly $300,000 a month, Secretary of Defense James V. Forrestal replied *ex officio* to a State Department query on the subject. Over half of this would be required just to operate the three destroyers needed to support them, he added.[29]

The reluctance of Americans and others to get involved was inevitably an invitation to the belligerents to settle de facto on their own terms. At the same time, the inconclusive outcome of the war was an invitation to reopen questions deferred, if not forgotten, since the end of the Ottoman Empire and the creation of Syria, Jordan, Iraq, and Lebanon. Irrespective of defeat, Syria and Lebanon still lusted for the western Galilee, Egypt for the Negev, Jordan for Lydda, Ramle, and a corridor to the sea at Haifa or Jaffa. In the U.S., British, and also U.N. perspective, peace for land was at least a possibility at the respective negotiating tables assembled under U.N. supervision in Rhodes and Lausanne. But Israel remained intransigent. "[I]t was immoral that anyone should think of rewarding the Arabs for . . . aggression," declared Abba Eban, the chief Israeli U.N. delegate. At once uncertain of themselves and profoundly suspicious of one another, the Arabs dug in. Unable to deal with Israel collectively and unwilling to confront it directly, they waited instead for the United Nations or the United States to solve their problem for them. Private conversations tended to be conciliatory as Arab leaders tried at least to avoid sawing down their bridges. Jordan "had more to worry about from other Arab states than from the Jews," King Abdullah told U.S. diplomat. Meanwhile, Egypt's King Farouk sounded out American visitors on whether existing demarcation lines between Egyptian and Israeli forces might be negotiable. "Of course, we could not admit to the other Arab states that we are talking of this," he quickly added.[30] In public, as might be expected, the Arab answer was simply no.

The most intractable problem was the Palestinian refugees. By the end of 1949, U.S. and U.N. officials estimated that there were 700,000 of them, though Arab estimates predictably ran higher and Israeli estimates lower. In Washington, the issue was seen as an opportunity for confidence-building on the basis of an implied division of labor. Israelis would compensate most refugees and repatriate a few. Arabs would resettle the majority. Americans, as unobtrusively as possible, would pay the bills.

But neither Arabs nor Israelis were prepared to buy it. Israelis considered the refugees a security threat. So did neighboring Arabs, though they were understandably reluctant to say so in public. Nor, despite the obligatory declarations of Arab solidarity with the Palestinian cause, was there any likelihood of Arab or Palestinian consensus on a Palestinian state. The Egyptians and the Arab League convened a

Palestinian congress in Gaza to establish an "all-Palestinian government." Abdullah convened a Palestinian congress in Jericho to declare Palestine and Jordan united, and incidentally declare Abdullah king of Palestine.

In the resulting vacuum, this seemed to leave but one solution: Jordanian annexation of the territories, known to right-wing Israelis as Judaea and Samaria since 1967, and to the rest of the world as the West Bank. De facto or de jure, annexation was what Abdullah presumably intended all along. But Israelis were clearly prepared to live with it, and Palestinians, Syrians, Iraqis, and Egyptians were unable or unwilling to challenge it.

Gaza meanwhile came under Egyptian administration. Otherwise disposed to a strict interpretation of the 1947 partition resolution, U.S. officials were disposed to acquiesce in the Jordanian intervention by summer 1948 and to ratify it de jure afterward, if only because, compared with all other options, it seemed the least bad. "Arab Palestine standing alone could not constitute a viable independent state," George Marshall noted in an internal policy statement.[31] Though the U.S. consul in Jerusalem reported reservations among the Palestinians themselves, there was little disagreement.

Seen from the Middle East, on the other hand, the question of Arab Palestine and the Palestinian refugees was not an opportunity but a circle. In Israeli perspective, there was no solution without peace. In the Arab perspective, there was no peace without a solution—which nominally meant complete repatriation of all refugees in what was now Israel. Under pressure, the Israelis agreed in principle to compensate the refugees and provide for their resettlement—with money, to be sure, that would inevitably come from the United States. The Arabs, in turn, hinted repeatedly that they were willing to accept U.S. and British aid for domestic development projects, whose purpose presumably included resettlement of refugees. But nothing happened.

By summer 1949 Washington had effectively concluded that it was dealing with eggs and chickens. The refugee chicken appeared to precede the peace settlement egg. In Lausanne, a variety of implied U.S. sticks persuaded the Israelis to agree, in reluctant principle, to the repatriation of 100,000 Arab refugees in the context of a general settlement. A variety of implied U.S. carrots in the form of promised aid also persuaded Arabs, for example, Syria, to agree in equally reluctant principle to settlement of Palestinian refugees on its territory. But U.S. negotiators were unwilling either to put the screws to the Arabs or go public in blaming Israel for the deadlock.

In August 1949, in tacit recognition that U.N. mediation was a loser, Washington proceeded to an alternative course, when the president announced the appointment of Gordon Clapp, chairman of the board of the Tennessee Valley Authority, to lead an economic survey mission. Like the bulk of the regional diplomacy of the United States, the new initiative was linked circumspectly to the United Nations. In its way, Clapp's appointment brought U.S. policy back where it began scarcely four years earlier, when President Roosevelt first discovered the region's quandaries, and government planners were at least half-persuaded by Walter Clay Lowdermilk's vision of regional development. Perhaps, it was now hoped, a Jordan Valley Authority, if not a whole Middle Eastern New Deal, might be the solution.

Consistent with its vision, the administration sent Interior Secretary Oscar Chapman to address the American Zionist Council in New York on the second anniversary of Israeli independence, while Ben-Gurion himself insisted on visiting the Tennessee Valley Authority when he toured the United States in 1951.

"On my return from the Middle East, the question most often asked me by Christians was: What's behind the policy of Israel toward the world?" Kenneth Bilby of the *New York Herald-Tribune* reported in one of the earliest American books on Israel. "My answer was always: self-interest." Defiance, as Bilby saw it, already constituted the essence of Israeli history to date: "defiance of the Arab armies, defiance of Truce Commission edicts, defiance of Security Council orders, defiance of General Assembly decisions." There was no question, he conceded, that the Arabs would behave the same way if they could. It was also clear why the Arabs, who had so intransigently opposed the UNSCOP plan, now looked to the United Nations as their last best hope, while the Israelis, who derived their original legitimation from a U.N. vote, now took U.N. resolutions or left them alone with sovereign disregard. But somewhere the process had to stop, he said.

With the rightful claim to Palestine effectively resolved by force of arms, Bilby argued, Israel could now choose between the military temptation to occupy all of Palestine, and the political prudence it needed to secure the support and sympathy of the United States. "As long as it remains patently obvious that the Arabs are the aggressors . . . Israel can confidently rely . . . on American support," he predicted. He nonetheless hoped not only that the Israelis might show some self-restraint but that circumstances would permit them to. "Nothing, in fact, would be more helpful to Israel than to disappear for a few years from the front pages of the world press," he concluded.[32]

In principle, both Ben-Gurion and the vast majority of Americans saw it this way too. Since the beginnings of Zionism, normalization of Jewish life had been the movement's very purpose. Reaching it was another story, given the inexorable realities of global politics and Arab hate, and the elemental needs of a nation-state literally engaged in self-creation. In many ways a new nation like dozens of others in the postimperial world of the late 1940s and early 1950s, Israel was in other ways a phenomenon that defied or qualified almost any category of previous historical experience. Even the population was sui generis. Normal postcolonial circumstances suggested that people came first and statehood afterward. But for Israel, in the aftermath of independence, immigration was both a necessary condition for the new state's survival, and its very *raison d'être*. Within its first two years, the new state had absorbed 400,000 new immigrants from Europe and the Middle East. Their arrival, resettlement, and acculturation brought the population to 1.2 million, about a million of them Jews, who set about straightaway to transform and redefine the nation's identity and self-image, as Irish, Italian, Polish, and Jewish immigrants had once transformed and redefined the United States.

The historical affinities that made Israel attractive and meaningful to Americans were also ambiguous. Whatever might have been the case in 1776 or 1787, Americans in 1948–1949 took security, stability, continuity, legitimacy, domestic consensus, international recognition, not to mention the world's most desirable currency, a global economy, and history's highest living standard, for granted.

These were things Israelis could only dream of. At the same time, Israeli normality was beyond American imaginings. For most Israelis, British austerity seemed almost sybaritic, yet their optimism was among the wonders of the world. A kind of Ellis Island in a tiny southern California, their country was already a medley of bazaar, shtetl, Main Street, and Viennese café, where the American visitor might be reminded of the Bible and Frederick Jackson Turner's frontier theory over the same glass of tea. The psychic landscape alone—a blend of Auschwitz and renascence; victory over five invading armies and the persisting hate of a hundred million neighbors; the Minuteman consensus of citizen soldiers and threshold civil war; entrepreneurial zip and socialist fundamentalism; the European urbanity of Eban and Eytan, and the Oriental remoteness of any new immigrant from the Yemen or Morocco—defied traditional historical cartography. It was reflected, in turn, in the national image: a blend of idealism and pragmatism, ruthlessness and *chutzpah,* Walter Mitty and self-irony. "Tough on the outside and tender on the inside, his hair . . . blowing in the wind as he rode his jeep, part cowboy in a western movie, part epic hero in a great Soviet novel," one Israeli historian recalled it forty years later. It was clear that his readers were meant to smile.[33]

Even without the psychodrama, reality was challenge enough. "Let's cut out all the crap and have a good talk," a shirt-sleeved Truman told a morning-coated Eban as he accepted his accreditation. The president of the United States and leader of the free world then sat Israel's first ambassador down to an aggressively informal forty-minute conversation.[34] Like the conversation itself, Truman's suspenders and Eban's striped pants were a kind of *tableau vivant* of working relations between established states with common interests. Even the ambassador's new rank testified to the particularity of the relationship. With the extension of de jure relations in January 1949, McDonald had been promoted from minister to ambassador. "It was realized at once that this was not an offer that could or should be refused," Eytan recalled, "especially as at that time the U.S. was represented in several Arab states by ministers only."[35] Although the Israeli Foreign Ministry had originally not even planned for ambassadors, the Washington job was upgraded.

The problem was making the pieces fit, where substance and style were so oddly matched, and the respective burdens of domestic expectation, global circumstance, and historical memories were so hard to reconcile with any remembered normality. In the abstract, Israeli and U.S. definitions of *normal* approached identity. In practice, they tended to ambivalence, cross-purpose, even collision. Israel, like the United States, favored representative democracy, national self-determination, and genuine independence. The United States, like Israel, aspired to Middle Eastern peace. But the more things seemed the same, the clearer it became to both how many were different.

The basic asymmetries of power alone made normality not only elusive but nearly a contradiction in terms. In the aftermath of World War II, the United States had become a superpower almost against its will, whose capabilities and burdens alike exceeded any in previous experience. Almost by an act of will, a tiny, poor, and unstructured Israel had meanwhile become an independent state and even a regional minipower. Scarcely born, its impact on the Middle East already inspired ambivalent awe. By 1949 the CIA was convinced that Israelis could move their borders eastward to the Jordan, as they actually did in 1967, and northward to the Litani, as they sought to do in 1982.[36]

But Israelis could neither believe, nor afford to let others believe, that they had actually become a power, despite the panicky terror they inspired in their neighbors. In fact, for all their numbers, their nominal wealth, and their presumed access to British officers and weaponry, the Arabs were even more dependent and disorganized than Israel itself. Yet it was hardly surprising that Israeli scenarios should lean toward worst cases.

It was therefore no surprise that Israel should also be interested in the United States—though the interest was mutual, for a variety of reasons. Postwar Americans now acknowledged responsibility for Greece and Turkey, Britain and Europe, even Germany and Japan, both as objects in the Cold War and good causes in themselves. To most Americans who thought about foreign policy officially, the Middle East was a means rather than an end in itself. But the habits of history and the premises of U.S. policy increasingly disposed Americans to think of it increasingly as the source of Europe's oil, a locus of its colonial entanglements, and a focus of that Soviet *Drang nach Osten* that once again threatened a peaceful postwar order.

By a kind of Bernoulli's Law of politics, even the European legacy thus led to a certain sense of grudging responsibility for Israel per se. Ben-Gurion's calendar—which included appointments with Marshall, Acheson, W. Averell Harriman, a visit to both houses of Congress, meetings with labor and business leaders and several governors—confirmed that Israel, the victor over five Arab neighbors in a strategically situated part of the world with a long history, was something more than a newly independent Third World state.

It was also both obvious and self-evident that the relationship was spectacularly asymmetrical. For most Americans, the new relationship was still largely discretionary. For a variety of reasons, many passionately wanted Israel to exist, and the vast majority accepted it without any problem. Yet few Americans would argue that the United States needed Israel in any of the hundred ways nations have declared they need one another. Whatever the assertions of credibility, history, sentiment, or bad conscience, whatever the assertions of democratic ideology, postwar geopolitics, or Cold War opportunity, Israel was neither a natural ally nor conventional client, a buffer, satellite, colony, beachhead, market, or supplier.

Yet for all its local superiority and bristly independence, Israel needed the United States not only for its further survival but for its very existence. United States aid and above all American-Jewish aid were crucial if Israel was to avert starvation for want of oil, markets, and hard currency. "The United States is going to have to grant sufficient financial support to the present Israeli regime to avoid seeing the country go bust and perhaps swing into Communist hands," the *New York Times's* Cyrus L. Sulzberger reported even before the Korean War and European recovery had begun to erode world raw material supplies and inflate commodity prices.[37]

By this time, in ways most Americans were scarcely even aware of, U.S. officials were already putting in a good word for Israel with oil companies, cautioning Arab boycott planners, helping out with civil aviation and with access to planes and commercial air routes, and approving and processing a considerable—though by Marshall Plan standards quite modest - $100 million loan from the Export-Import Bank.[38] There was even a de facto military liaison in the person of Fred Grunich. An American-Jew, then thirty-two, and a former colonel who had served on Eisenhower's wartime staff, Grunich had been recruited in New York by Micky Marcus and Teddy Kollek.

Practiced in regular warfare as Israelis were not, he now stayed on as "Fred Harris" after Marcus's death, putting his experience at the service of the Israelis like a kind of latter-day La Fayette. His situation reflected both chance and design. In fact he had no acknowledged status in either country. Under U.S. law, Americans in the service of foreign governments at war with states at peace with the United States were subject to fine. Despite some squeamishness about the likely impact on Arabs and legal constraints that precluded active service in the Israeli army, the State Department was nonetheless willing to allow a retired officer like Hilldring to make his expertise available to the Israelis. On the other hand, the Pentagon preferred not to be seen there at all, on both political and legal grounds. The JCS, somewhere between the two, acknowledged that an American advisor without official status would be hard for Washington to control. On the other hand, when it was considered both dangerous and unnecessary to send an official advisor, they were hesitant to put even an unofficial advisor in harm's way.[39]

Ben-Gurion had reservations too. Eager as usual for U.S., and American-Jewish, expertise and support, he was equally ambivalent about both. "We cannot reveal all our secrets to an American soldier," he told Kollek. "They will reach the British and perhaps the Arabs." Grunich, the Jewish-American soldier, was thus both a private advisor and a kind of second military attaché, whose activity was probably unknown to the State Department. Yet it was known at least to individual officials in the Pentagon, where Elath, now Israel's ambassador, and Grunich himself lobbied unsuccessfully for a regular military mission to Israel.[40]

Officially-unofficially posted at the Israeli-U.S. fault line, Grunich registered the stresses like a walking seismograph. A private one-man military mission by grace of Ben-Gurion and Washington alike, he was hauled by the prime minister himself to meetings of the Knesset, the General Staff, and Palmach, the elite strike force that constituted or dominated the formative cadres of the Israeli army. Yet it was soon obvious that both Left and Right regarded him as a target of opportunity rather than a strategic asset. Given Palmach's inherent leftward tilt, that mesalliance was practically inevitable. It was estimated that 80–90 percent of Palmach members had some sort of leftist affiliation; large numbers came from Mapam, the leftmost of the labor Zionist parties with a well-developed fellow-traveler wing. It was bad enough, Grunich recalled with a slightly inapposite sense of metaphor, that "I stood out like a red cow," but "as an American," he added, "I stood for everything they loathed."

Before long, it was rumored that Grunich was really in Israel as an agent of the Pentagon, if not the CIA. Resolved at most to keep their distance from both superpowers, the Palmach chiefs inevitably saw him as a Pied Piper who would lead Israel down the Cold War path to de facto integration in the United States alliance system. In a way, there was even something to this. Like a lot of American Jews, Grunich sincerely believed it in Israel's interest to seek maximum compatibility with U.S.

practice and equipment, especially considering that it stood alone with no other allies in view. But it was only one more of the ironies of his situation that, for rather different reasons, the liaison that was feared and resisted in Israel also met intransigent resistance in Washington.

In July 1949, with the Israeli struggle to transform existing political militias into a reliable national army at its height, Grunich became a political liability for Ben-Gurion, and a symbolic target for those Israelis determined to see him as a personified violation of Cold War neutrality. "Every Jew has a share in this state, and it seems to me that spiritual slavery to an anti-American attitude goes too far, if it ends by disqualifying the Jews of America," Ben-Gurion replied to a parliamentary questioner. Testifying in itself to the robust political partisanship for which Israel was to become famous, a Communist paper nonetheless charged the prime minister with treason for engaging "a foreign espionage officer at GHQ." The issue of Grunich's status then led to a slander suit. As might be expected, the court eventually found in Ben-Gurion's favor, though hardly with flying colors. The judges conceded that "Harris's" presence did not itself confirm Ben-Gurion's guilt, but by this time it was clear to Grunich himself that his presence had outlived its value, and when Ben-Gurion, against his advice, appointed Yigal Yadin the new army's first chief of staff, he left for home.[41]

Meanwhile, with fine impartiality, increasing success and growing self-assurance, Israelis said no to Arabs, U.N. resolutions, and the great powers, as though self-assertion were itself a way to make their fragile sovereignty grow and flourish. Demonstrative nonalignment crested in early 1950 when Israel became the seventh state to recognize the People's Republic of China. U.S. aid nonetheless continued, though there was also no improvement in relations with the Soviet Union.

Only a few months later, in response to a word from Truman, personally conveyed via David Niles, the Israeli delegation endorsed the U.N. intervention in Korea. This time, revealingly, with Israelis divided as usual on Left-Right lines, the principal opposition came from Begin's Herut, on grounds that Israel should avoid identification with the United Nations.

Even after the Israeli change of heart had led to advances and initiatives unthinkable before Korea, Israel was the only noncommunist state to join the Soviet Union, the Ukraine, Byelorussia, Czechoslovakia, and Poland in December 1951 in a six-vote minority opposing a General Assembly resolution calling for appointment of an international commission to investigate the possibility of free German elections. A year later Ben-Gurion dispatched concurrent telegrams to Washington and Moscow. The first congratulated Eisenhower on his election as president. The second, recalling both the Soviet role in World War II and "support given to the State of Israel since its inception," congratulated Stalin on the thirty-fifth anniversary of the Bolshevik revolution.[42]

Given the peculiar conjunction of superpower support that had led to Israel's independence, Israel's legitimate concern for the security and mobility of east European Jews, and many Israelis' traditional affinities for both the Russian and the Marxist classics, Third World neutrality seemed, in fact, the better part of prudence. But even before Korea, and especially in the aftermath of the Prague coup and Berlin blockade, it set American teeth on edge. "Most annoying of all," one senior embassy official noted at the end of a lengthy report on leftist activity in Israel, was that Israel's aggressive neutrality made it practically impossible even to get reliable information on what Communist activity there was. It was bad enough, he noted, watching Israeli officials chatting easily in Russian with representatives from the Soviet embassy, but "when such requests are made officially, one is generally looked at coldly"—"down a long curving nose," he added for good measure.[43]

From the moment of independence, it seemed to official Washington that Ben-Gurion took particular pleasure in defying U.S. appeals on incursions into Egyptian territory, resettlement of Arab refugees, the volume and tempo of new immigration, and, perhaps above all, Jerusalem. On December 11, 1949, Ben-Gurion resolved unilaterally to move Israel's capital to Jerusalem, despite U.S. and U.N. pressure and warnings from Sharett and Eban. To Israelis, history and the city's Jewish majority were already reasons to show the flag in Jerusalem. Then came precedents established since the state became independent, the assignment of a military governor, a Knesset session, and the swearing-in of Weizmann among them. None had run into serious opposition. Then came the unlikely coalition of Arabs, Latins, Soviet bloc delegations, and Cardinal Spellman that was seen in itself as a reason to act.

Designed to preempt any U.N. initiative for internationalization, the decision was already typical of Israeli style and motives. Interpreting the inactivity that followed their initiative as acquiescence, the Israelis then moved the Foreign, though not the Defense, Ministry from Tel Aviv to Jerusalem a few years later. Frustrated and exasperated, the State Department imposed a boycott of official Foreign Ministry functions in Jerusalem, but it collapsed after a couple of years.[44]

The U.S. embassy in Tel Aviv nonetheless stayed in Tel Aviv, where it still remained more than forty years later, despite recurring efforts, often by Democratic presidential contenders, to reconsider its status. Ben-Gurion, unsurprisingly, drew his own lines on how far he was prepared to go to accommodate U.S. reservations. Israel was neither the result of a U.N. resolution nor of U.S. help, he noted firmly in his diary for June 1949. He observed bitterly that neither the United States nor anybody else had intervened to enforce the partition resolution or stop the Arabs who violated it. Had Israel gone under, the United States would not have come to save it. On the contrary, he recalled, the United States had imposed an arms embargo while the United Nations let the Arabs trample the UNSCOP borders under foot.

The Arabs had had their chance and passed it up, Ben-Gurion noted grimly. At this point there were no refugees. There were only Arabs who had tried to destroy Israel.[45] The same arguments applied by extension to Jerusalem. In November 1947, he had been willing to regard the trade-off between a Jewish state and an internationalized city as an acceptable tactical concession. After the 1948 siege and the devastation of the Old Jewish Quarter, he considered it a nuisance and an insult.

If Americans, for all their postwar idealism and Cold war passion, had little taste for new responsibilities toward a demonstratively independent Israel, Israelis had few illusions about the almost desperate dependency that underlay their independence. Yet if anything, Israeli initiatives only increased U.S. ambivalence. It was not only an article of Israeli faith but a premise of Israeli existence that immigration was crucial to Israel's identity, let alone to its defense. At the same time, the prevailing scale of immigration assured a perennial payments deficit that was to become a kind of national institution and lead a growing stream of Israeli visitors to official Washington. By 1949 the deficit already constituted more than 30 percent of the Israeli budget; by 1950, more than 40 percent.[46]

Still, neither the most fervent Mapamnik, convinced of the hopeless corruption of Wall Street capitalism, nor the most dedicated Revisionist, convinced that U.S.-imposed partition and U.S.-extorted retreat had cost Israel half of Mandatory Palestine, could imagine life without the United States. Even the most impassioned Canaanite, from a tiny intellectual sect that was convinced that their Middle Eastern identity was totally distinct from the world of Diaspora Jews, had to acknowledge that the importance of the United States was a fact of life very much like the law of gravity.

"Continued dependence on philanthropy violated the most elementary concepts of Zionism, of self-reliance, and self-labor, to say nothing of national independence," Golda Meir announced emphatically and sincerely. From the war of independence to the end of her public career, she nonetheless campaigned with brilliant success for American Jewish funds and ultimately U.S. weapons.[47] Israel's security rested on two pillars, the army and the American-Jewish community, an Israeli diplomat told a visiting congressman. "The Almighty placed massive oil deposits under Arab soil," another Israeli spokesman explained to a State Department official. "It is our good fortune that God placed five million Jews in America."[48] Two years after independence, McDonald reported, tears still came to Weizmann's eyes when he described Truman's help as "providential" and even after a decade, one of Israel's senior diplomats still described U.S. recognition in 1948 as "a near miracle."[09]

For all the declarations of affinity and awareness of dependency, the foreign policy environment and the security threshold only increased the distance between Israeli and U.S. normality. Unsurprisingly, both sides tended to see what they wanted to see. Contingent on their ideological preference, Israelis looking toward America saw democracy, power, wealth, but also Gentile disinterest, at least potential perfidy, and capitalist seduction. Americans, looking in turn toward Israel, saw founding fathers and pushy Jews. "These aggressively urgent people," Richard Ford, the chargé in Tel Aviv, called them in a typical cable.[50]

Yet for many Americans, Israel was also a tiny extension of their nation's own hopes and history. "We too once proclaimed our own independence in a ringing declaration which is still an inspiration to freedom-loving peoples throughout the world," Truman told the National Jewish Welfare Board on the fourth anniversary of Israeli statehood in 1952—though the message was conveyed through a middle-rank proxy, who appeared at the meeting to read the speech.[51] For Senator Hubert Humphrey, returning in 1957 from a tour of the Middle East, Israel was "reminiscent in many ways of the old American West." The association was obviously intended as a compliment. "An American can feel very much at home in Israel—that is, an American who loves adventure, and who realizes that our own great country was once a little nation wedged between the sea and the wilderness," he added.[52] Adaptive from the start, Israelis learned early on to turn such expectations to their own advantage. However tempting, the images frequently obscured reality as much as they illuminated it.

Probably nowhere were the differences of perspective more dramatic than in the respective definitions of national interest and priorities. For Israelis, the United States was uniquely, almost absolutely important if Israel were to survive and flourish in the Middle East. But for both countries, the Middle East was itself a challenge on its own, very un-Western, terms.

Haunted by the global threat, Americans wanted primarily that the Arab-Israeli conflict should go away; and that Israel, so far as possible, should be seen, not heard. Haunted by recent history and the open-ended conflict with its neighbors, Israel's worldview was another variation of Steinberg's famous view of New York, with Ramle, Lydda, and Eilat in the foreground, and even the superpowers only dim on the horizon. In any Israeli security equation, the Middle East was the inevitable constant. Global circumstances of even Cold War magnitude were the variables. Given the balance of domestic opinion and the fundamentally adversarial relationship between them and their Arab neighbors, Israelis tended to an unsentimentally pragmatic, contentious, and consistently tough view of their security needs with a preference for worst cases.

This was a view official Washington found hard to share. It was also one that drove it to increasing frustration and impatience as Israel mortgaged its economy, turned immigrants into social facts, exploited the armistice agreements and borderless status quo to local advantage, and stonewalled on repatriation of Arab refugees. For Americans, Israel and the Middle East were the variables, the global picture was the constant. Apart from the tiny cohort of Zionists, missionaries, oil prospectors, and academics with an intrinsic stake or interest in the region, the idea of looking at the Middle East on its own terms and for its own sake not only was unfamiliar to Americans but seemed vaguely frivolous or even dangerous.

Be it as a touchstone of postwar liberalism, a peaceable kingdom for land-grant economists and hydraulic engineers, be it as a provocation to the Arabs and a threat to the European oil supply, Israel was of interest for extrinsic rather than intrinsic reasons. Theoretically, this still allowed a full spectrum of choice from benign neglect to formal alliance. For most, though not all, American liberals in the first flush of postwar liberalism, support for Israel was almost second nature. Recent history, the Israeli style of social democracy, even the collective hostility it inspired among sheikhs, pashas, commissars, and oil companies, made it a natural liberal cause. Given Israel's style and origins, its historical coordinates included both the New Deal and the war with Hitler. Though Soviet Communism and the east European Jewish labor movement alike had been consistently anti-Zionist for nearly half a century, it seemed perfectly natural to Americans like Bartley Crum and Henry Wallace that Israel, the United States, and the Soviet Union should now be on one side, that foreign imperialists, domestic reactionaries, and international oil companies should be on the other. Like the Israeli Left, American liberals could even believe that peace would come only when the Arabs too felt the benefits of the global New Deal. From the great Wilsonian middle of the United States to its fellow-traveling fringe, Israel was itself a definition of what most Americans meant when they said *national independence, democracy, socialism,* and *progress.*

Yet almost from the moment of Israel's independence, Soviet second thoughts and the Cold War itself increasingly framed and limited U.S. options. As usual, Soviet motives were a riddle wrapped in an enigma. In fact, this may well have been because both riddle and enigma were enveloped in dilemmas complementary to those so perplexing to the West. Andrei Zhdanov, the presiding custodian of the Soviet party-line, was conspicuously silent on the future of the Middle East in a programmatic speech delivered "somewhere in Poland" in 1947 at the founding conference of the Cominform. If anything, his remarks could be understood as resignation to the inevitable, that is, that an invincible United States, "with the help of intimidation, bribes and chicanery," had already crowded Britain out of its traditional positions in "Greece, Turkey, Egypt, Iran, Afghanistan, [and other countries]."[53] At least till something else showed up, Israel, the "objective" victor over British imperialism and Arab reaction, and a place where people still talked Marx and drank their tea from glasses, was a special case.

If sympathy for the Arabs was something less than a natural reflex of Russian history, sympathy for Jews had not been among its outstanding characteristics either. In a culture that found both Jews and spontaneity suspect by their nature, the sight of enormous crowds welcoming Golda Meir as Israel's first ambassador to Moscow can only have added an element of xenophobic urgency to what was already a policy of calculated opportunism. Change was not long in coming. "Whole Israel shocked and pro-Russian sections stunned by success of Russian-Vatican-Muslim combination," McDonald cabled the State Department with evident satisfaction as he reported the local impact of the U.N. General Assembly vote on Jerusalem.[54] In the Orwellian logic of Stalinist style, it was only another step or two to overt anti-Semitism of a kind most recently practiced under Hitler, and from there to self-fulfilling alienation of even the most resolutely neutralist-socialist Israeli fellow travelers.

By the time Stalin died in March 1953, Jewish doctors were atop the Moscow hit list, and thoroughly assimilated Jewish Communists, who had devoted their lives to the revolution, had become the featured defendants in show trials all over eastern Europe. Meanwhile, the adjectives *Zionist* and *cosmopolitan* had become interchangeable expletives in party-line vocabularies, though their synonymy was not only artificial but positively ridiculous in any other context.[55]

Despite the changing climate, U.S. liberals generally continued to see Israel as a liberal cause, but especially with the coming of the Korean War, their arguments were increasingly clothed in Cold War expectations. Liberal and conservatives alike inclined to make their case in global terms, but the focus now was not on British but on Soviet imperialism. It thus seemed both a corollary of the Truman Doctrine and a logical extension of the North Atlantic (NATO) Treaty that Illinois's redoubtable liberal Democrat, Senator Paul Douglas, could propose—at a China Institute dinner, at that—that the United States should form an alliance with Turkey, Greece, Israel, and "as many Arabs as would come in."[56]

In the same way, Ohio's no less redoubtable Mr. Republican, Senator Robert A. Taft, argued unabashedly for viewing Israel as a first line of defense in the event that the Soviets, say, should grab for the uranium reserves of what was still the Belgian Congo. It was "important that if we ever have a war we somehow defend the

Suez Canal," he told his largely acquiescent colleagues on the Foreign Relations and Armed Services committees. "In that defense, a state that is able to fight in a very strategic position, even though small, presents, I think, a very useful assistance for us from the military standpoint."

Only Iowa's equally redoubtable Republican Bourke Hickenlooper expressed a hint of skepticism with respect to "the probabilities of Israel being able to support itself at a future time." Taft was quick to reassure him. "They should have tremendous possibilities of becoming a leading manufacturing center for that area of the world," he replied. This was not least because "they are much more familiar with and are likely to follow American methods." If seven million New Yorkers could support themselves without natural resources, Taft argued, it was likely that two million Israelis could do the same.[57]

As might be imagined, things looked quite different down the hill from the Capitol, let alone across the Potomac at the Pentagon. Fully preoccupied with the war in Korea and the defense of Europe, policymakers found reason enough to regard the Middle East as an extension of both, and add it to their list of worries. But Korea and Europe, at least, were fairly clear choices. Whatever the immensity of the challenges they presented, there was little question of what was presumably at stake or which side was "ours" and which was "theirs." Where the Middle East was concerned, let alone the new Jewish state in Palestine, things could hardly be more different. The inevitable dissonances between Washington's global picture and the specific complexities of the Middle East led policymakers to gallop off ambivalently in a half dozen different directions.

Among their most far-reaching initiatives was the Tripartite Declaration of May 1950.[58] Laboriously negotiated to co-opt both Britain and France as established and interested Middle Eastern powers, the document was an early effort at coordinated crisis management. Western consensus was both a premise and intention. Despite well-developed U.S. misgivings about the British, and still more the French, presence in the region, so was continued Western hegemony, at least pro forma. Without it, in fact, there could hardly have been a Tripartite Declaration.

What Washington wanted from its allies was a semblance of regional order. The idea was to contain, if not resolve, the Israeli-Arab conflict while the Western powers went about the larger business of containing the Soviets. Despite substantial differences between the British and French presence in the area, as opposed to the still quite modest U.S. presence, the idea was to preclude an Arab-Israeli arms race by a common policy between the only three powers believed capable of tilting the fragile status quo. Whether London and Paris were as concerned as Washington is arguable, but in Washington, at least, where a Democratic administration had stuck to a bona fide arms embargo despite a uniquely difficult election campaign, the concern was genuine.

Given the dilemmas of the recent Arab-Israeli war and the unresolved frustrations that followed it, the question of how a new war might affect Western interests, and what to do if it broke out, was reason enough for official concern. It was only complicated by the variety and potential incompatibility of Western interests and commitments in the region. Britain, by treaty, was patron-defender of Arab clients from the Fertile Crescent to the Persian Gulf. France was at least an interested party from Morocco to the Levant. However indirectly, recent experience seemed only to reinforce a U.S. tilt toward Israel. It followed that a regional arms race would turn the Western allies into political adversaries and economic competitors.

The apprehensions of the United States were reflected in each of the declaration's three principles. The first was that sales of arms to regional clients and customers would thenceforth be governed only by considerations of internal order and self-defense. The second, no less solemnly whistled in the wind, was that assurances of peaceful intent must precede any arms sale. The third, and in many ways most interesting, was that the signatories themselves, both as independent sovereignties and U.N. members, would intervene immediately against an aggressor in the event "that any of these states was preparing to violate frontiers and armistice lines."

At the same time, the question of containing Jews and Arabs was inexorably linked with the larger problem not only of containing communism but of containing the Cold War itself. Theoretically, the United States might pursue any of three courses, a tilt toward Israel, a tilt toward the Arabs, or a demonstrative, if well-intentioned, distance from both. From both the Western and the Middle Eastern perspectives, each, in its way, was compatible with Cold War logic.

Beginning with Ben-Gurion, who never questioned Israel's need for at least one major ally, Israel's partisans left no argument unturned in their quest to establish Israel's credentials as a Western, and above all U.S., asset. Israel, it was argued, was the very opposite of the Arab world in every way that mattered: democratic, tough, efficient, anti-Soviet, and pro-Western by nature. Unsurprisingly, these arguments went down well in the Jewish community, and had their resonance in Congress, if not beyond it.

Arab partisans made the same case in reverse. But they could also embellish theirs with arguments Israelis could hardly match: the Suez Canal, the absolute and relative size of the Arab compared with the Israeli population, the crucial link between Middle East oil and European recovery, the fragile domestic order that could momentarily drive desperate Arabs into Soviet arms, and the attendant threat of that proverbial power vacuum that Western officials always assumed was irresistibly attractive to the Soviets. These arguments had little resonance in Congress or public opinion, but they invariably found some listeners in the administration.

A third option, whose intrinsic interest is largely historical, was a kind of global tripartite declaration that would preclude a Middle Eastern Cold War by encouraging external powers to stay out. Ironically, a practical variation, almost reflexively invoked in Washington during the collapse of the British Mandate and the Arab-Israeli war that followed, was itself a Cold War strategy. Any U.S. presence in any form—troops, advisors, arms sales, even under a U.N. flag—would only bring in the Soviets it was argued whenever the subject arose. It was therefore counterproductive.

There was also a countercase with rather different implications. In this variation, the superpowers were adversaries only in circumscribed areas, for example, central Europe. In the Middle East, on the other hand, they were accomplices, if not potential partners. For a recent example, the serendipitous pursuit of common interests not only helped put Israel on the map in 1947 but spared both superpowers a lot of trouble. Although it was also clear until at least 1953 that both the United States and the Soviet Union were willing, even pleased, to see Britain leave the Middle East, each for its respective reasons, there was little evidence that either was eager to be the replacement.

In the abstract, the case for any one position was as strong as any other. But European, Asian, and, increasingly, domestic realities had already made some arguments more equal than others. Even before Korea, the Truman Doctrine and the creation of NATO were clearly seen as precedents for an extensive U.S. presence. Paradoxically, U.S. choices were defined both by British strength and decline, but it was especially the latter that increasingly turned Anglo-American thoughts toward a coordinated "Command Structure in the Middle East" on the model of SHAEF, if not of NATO. Variously known as Middle East Command, Supreme Allied Command–Middle East (SACME), and even Middle East Defense Organization, it was destined from conception for a long and troubled gestation, as well as an unlikely reprise, this time under a Republican administration, in the 1980s.

In principle, any number could join. Pakistan, even South Africa, Australia, and New Zealand, were mentioned speculatively among its prospective members. So, self-evidently, were the United States, Britain, France, Turkey, Egypt, Lebanon, Syria, Jordan, Iraq, and Saudi Arabia. Israel, to be sure, was not included—nor did it wish to be, if common membership required it to share defense information with its Arab neighbors—but it was at least officially informed of what was going on.[59]

In practice, membership proved more exclusive than originally planned. But self-selection too was unusually rigorous. Anglo-U.S. planners expected that presumptive members would share their sense of real and present danger from the Soviet Union and world communism. But it was also hoped, and even expected, that they should see eye to eye with one another. The predictable result was a very short list of candidates. By the time the project, now known as the Baghdad Pact, finally saw daylight in early 1955, there were only three signatories: Britain, Iraq, and Turkey. By this time, revealingly, even the United States was unwilling to join.

The trick, according to Paul Nitze, then director of policy planning in the State Department, was to attract the voluntary support of the Arab states, Israel, Iran, Pakistan, and contiguous land areas.[60] The policy rationale could hardly be more obvious, that is, that the administration was unwilling or politically unable to make any formal commitment to Iran, Pakistan, the Arab states, or Israel. It was equally obvious that Israeli interest was itself a deterrent to interested Arabs.

The de facto exclusion of regional clients, be they Israelis or Arabs, from U.S. planning could only lead to more dilemmas vis-à-vis Britain on the one hand, and what would soon be known as the Third World on the other. As Pentagon planners were perennially aware, Britain was the area's traditional strategic bird in the hand. At the same time, the British—and European—recessional from Asia and Africa was not only acknowledged as an inevitable fact of postwar life but even welcomed by large numbers of Americans.

Under the circumstances, one dilemma led unavoidably to another. Even before the 1952 revolution replaced the sodden administration of King Farouk with a new and seemingly more congenial regime of young officers, there was a *prima facie* case for U.S. aid to Egypt. It was an "important, strategically located nation of 20 million," as Acheson reminded the then-Congressman and later Senator Jacob Javits of New York.[61] Acheson was equally aware that it would "require considerable forbearance on the part of Israel" to stand by while the United States and even Britain groomed Egypt for "a major role." It might even prove necessary for the United States, the United Kingdom, France, "and possibly Turkey" to remind the Israelis that the Tripartite Declaration was a security guarantee, and ask them to back off from "a prominent role" of their own.

But forbearance was increasingly remote from Israel's thoughts. On the contrary, by the early 1950s, senior officials like Teddy Kollek, later mayor of Jerusalem, Chaim Herzog, later chief of state, Foreign Minister Moshe Sharett, and even Ben-Gurion himself, were turning up with awesome regularity at the Capitol, the State Department, and the Pentagon. Eager to buy any arms they could get, they were no less eager to sell any security relationship Americans might take. The prospectus extended from coordinated production of small arms and industrial cooperation to depot rights in Israel in return for an assured supply of oil and wheat, and NATO membership per se.

The more importunate the Israelis became, the more their American interlocutors typically took shelter behind the Tripartite Declaration. Only recently, U.S. officials had brooded about Israel's Cold War neutrality, or worse. Now, ironically, they inclined to pedal backward and in circles whenever Israelis expressed their own Cold War concerns and declared their Western loyalty. "The best means whereby the US could facilitate peace in the Near East was by extending economic aid to the Israelis," and so show the Arabs that Israel was there to stay, Ben-Gurion insisted. Israel's outstanding contribution to the stability and defense of the region, would be "to control and prevent the border incidents which continue to occur with its neighbors," George Marshall, now secretary of defense, replied.[62] The Israeli counselor mentioned that "Israel is in a particularly vulnerable position with regards to food, oil, etc." a typical State Department memo noted at the conclusion of a briefing on Korea. Israeli vulnerability "is very much on our minds," Assistant Secretary George C. McGhee countered *ex officio,* and "Israel should consider carefully what concessions it might make . . . in order to have the Arab economic blockade lifted."[63]

Despite the apparent impasse, it could not be overlooked that some things moved, not only in Congress. Starting with the loan from the Export-Import Bank in early 1949, aggregate U.S. government aid to Israel through the end of 1950 was already estimated at over $158 million.[64] By comparison, the government's entire program of foreign loans and grants in 1950 was about $1.1 billion, and the entire federal budget for fiscal year 1951 totaled a little less than $43 billion. At the same time, Israelis acknowledged discreet disappointment with their relegation to Point Four, the State Department's Third World development program. Between 1951 and 1962, Point Four brought some 340 U.S. technicians to Israel and 640 Israelis to the United States. But what Israelis really needed was money.

The course of the 1952 foreign aid bill was an illuminating guide to ways and means. Jointly sponsored by Robert Taft and Paul Douglas, the Senate version proposed $150 million in aid to Israel, a quantum jump on anything to date. It was hardly a coincidence that the congressional figure matched the figure Israeli officials presented Acheson in March. It was understood that the aid request would coincide with a half-million-dollar bond issue and the annual UJA campaign. The bill's success reflected a congressional-relations campaign that, for the first time, enlisted the leadership of both parties in both houses for more than symbolic purposes. "I took pride in the way our campaign was carried out—without the press, through personal contacts, and without strong pressure," Kollek recalled in his memoirs. It was, he said, "just friends speaking to friends." Their request, the Israelis emphasized, was based not only on anticipated population growth and heavy defense obligations but on the "declared willingness to contribute generously in payment of compensation to the Arabs."[65]

Unsurprisingly, the State Department looked on with a mixture of discreet distaste and unfeigned horror. It was bad enough, one member of the planning staff informed Nitze, that the proposed grant "would increase by 15,380 per cent Israel's portion of economic aid as contemplated in the foreign assistance program put forth by the Executive," and that a proportional increase of contemplated aid for neighboring countries would "entail a grant of more than $40,000,000,000 to the Near East." What was worse, he continued, was that such a grant would presumably finish off any support for the United States in the Moslem world as far away as Pakistan, and so "militate against . . . the security and other interests of the United States not in a slight but in a drastic degree." He implored intervention at the highest levels before Congress itself got rolling, and urged "every legitimate effort to ensure defeat" of the bill.[66]

What State instead proposed was a Mutual Security Act appropriation of about $50 million: half for Israel, half for the Arabs. As the summer heat settled on the Capitol, the predictable accommodation was reached. In the end, the compromise appropriations for aid to Israel, including technical assistance under Point Four, came to $72.2 million. Sharett expressed his gratude in a short speech that incidentally left "strong impression final relatively favorable sum reached thanks to efforts Israel's friends in US and Washington Emb.," as Ambassador Monett Davis cabled.[67] By this time, Congress was already well into the next budget cycle, the new Israeli request was for $125 million, and the State Department was talking about an $80 million appropriation for 1953.

Meanwhile, a more interesting and even dramatic political process was under way elsewhere. It too reflected Israel's economic desperation. It began in early 1951 when Ben-Gurion decided not only to approach the United States for $150 million in government aid but to approach the four occupying powers collectively for $1.5 billion in German reparations, including $1 billion from the Federal Republic. As expected, the proposal met unqualified rejection from the Soviet Union and its East German satellite. Its initial reception in Washington was unpromising too. And yet, as the State Department could hardly overlook and one official even spelled out in a memo, "there would be a definite political advantage to making a contribution to the Israeli economy indirectly through Germany . . . " since "direct contributions gave rise to requests from neighboring Arab states."[67]

On the other hand, there were innumerable obstacles to overcome, from domestic politics to international law. Henry Byroade, a former army colonel now serving as director of the Bureau of German Affairs, was typically and officially discouraging. Later to be assistant secretary for Near Eastern affairs and ambassador to Egypt, Byroade was hard put to see how the German economy could pay in kind, let alone cash. On the contrary, he expected that the German trade deficit, not to mention heavy demands for German support of Allied forces, would stretch resources to the limit. In any case, given its traumatic reminiscences of the reparations quagmire after World War I, official Washington had reacted neuralgically to even the hint of reparations from current production since at least 1944.

Acheson's own reservations were both legal and economic. As per the Potsdam agreements, he solemnly informed Eban, there was already a binding international agreement on Germany—to which Israel, incidentally, was not even a party. It effectively precluded U.S. action with respect to any claims until conclusion of a peace treaty. "It was impossible to predict when such a settlement would be possible," he added. He also reminded Ben-Gurion that "any German deficit would have to be made good by the US."[69]

On the other hand, as the U.S. side duly noted, none of this precluded a direct approach to the Germans. Or vice versa. Sure enough, in April 1951, a meeting mysteriously materialized in Paris between Chancellor Konrad Adenauer of West Germany and David Horowitz of the Israeli Finance Ministry. By late June, John J. McCloy, the U.S. high commissioner was reminding the chancellor that "there were still serious doubts in the USA about a real change of heart in Germany."[70] In July the Allies officially ended the state of belligerency, despite Israeli appeals for a public expression of German *bone fides.*

Unsurprisingly, Adenauer was unwilling to concede collective guilt. On the other hand, he was not one to underestimate American, including American-Jewish, opinion either. On September 27, he went before the Bundestag to declare German responsibility for formal reparations, and propose a settlement with the state of Israel and world Jewry. At a meeting in London in December with Nahum Goldmann, now president of both the World Jewish Congress and the Conference on Jewish Material Claims against Germany, he then agreed unilaterally that the Federal Republic would negotiate on the basis of $1 billion. In the twelve months between proposal and final signature, the symbolic importance of the issue was clear to American correspondents in Germany, and even outside New York and Washington news coverage was both thorough and comprehensive.

Actual negotiations with Israel began in Luxembourg in early March, practically concurrent with parallel negotiations in London and the Hague that were convened to settle the totality of reparations claims against Germany, and Germany's prewar debts respectively. "Believe it desirable you shld inform Adenauer of serious polit difficulties confronting Israel Govt and that US considers it important that conference not be allowed to fail," Acheson instructed McCloy as the German-Israeli talks began.

Given the enormousness of the expectations confronting them on every side, the Germans had their problems too. Not the least of these was the DM 13 billion, that is, the circa $3 billion, claim under negotiation in London. Another DM 13 billion was projected in fiscal 1952–1953 for rearmament and support of Allied troops. Marshall Plan aid itself had totaled about $2.7 billion between 1948 and 1952. It was true that the medicine was working. It was also true that the "economic miracle" was just over the horizon, and that the German economy had produced a modest trade surplus in 1951, but it was far too early to take any of this for granted. By comparison, the 1950 deficit had totaled DM 601 million.

Meanwhile, the presence and potentially explosive demands of twelve million refugees from East Germany and German territories since annexed to Czechoslovakia, Poland, and the Soviet Union imposed their own consequences on the federal budget, and the Arab states threatened both political and economic sanctions with sufficient credibility that Adenauer too felt moved to ask for U.S. help.

It was still no surprise that the Israelis showed little sympathy when the German negotiators opened with an offer of DM 100 million in kind, to be delivered over a period of years. Nor was it surprising that they suspected the Germans might even be trying to get other creditors to shield them from Israeli claims. As might be imagined, the Israelis dismissed the German offer out of hand. The result was a deadlock that threatened to end the negotiations only weeks after they began.

While American-Jewish agencies appealed to government officials and Congress, Jacob Blaustein pleaded directly with Truman for public intervention, and even proposed the State Department as mediator and the U.S. government as arbitrator between Israel and the Federal Republic. But Acheson and Goldmann opposed the idea. Acheson was afraid both Germans and Israelis might get the idea that the United States would cover the checks. But he was at least as worried about what would happen if the chancellor's adversaries should get, or exploit, the idea that Adenauer—"the Chancellor of the Allies," as the Social Democratic leader Kurt Schumacher had once called him from the Bundestag floor—was capitulating to U.S. pressure.

At the same time, Acheson endorsed a discreet expression of the U.S. hope "that the negotiations will reach a successful conclusion." Goldmann, in turn, believed that Israel would do far better by letting the Western Allies confine themselves to moral reminders, and leaving the outcome to the negotiators. On May 19, he addressed his own letter to Adenauer with a copy, as usual, for McCloy. Two days later, as Goldmann recalled in his memoirs, McCloy hinted on the phone that an important message was expected momentarily.

As promised, it announced the long-awaited breakthrough. In fact, the formula had been devised by Goldmann and Franz Boehm, the principal German negotiator. On May 23, Adenauer got his cabinet to accede. Apart from compensation to individuals, the Federal Republic of Germany undertook to pay the State of Israel over DM 3 billion in kind over a twelve-year period, over $800 million at the current rate of exchange. On May 25, Acheson, who was in Bonn to negotiate both the European Defense Community and the restoration of German sovereignty, warned Adenauer of "unfortunate consequences" if the Luxembourg talks should fall through. But while his intervention was welcome, and surely effective, it was not decisive.

According to Goldmann, Byroade expressed open astonishment at the news. Had he been called in to arbitrate himself, he reportedly told Goldmann, he would have asked the Germans to pay at most DM 300 million. En route to ratification, the agreement set off turbulent debates, but barely a year after its emergence as a public issue, the reparations settlement had passed both the Bundestag and the

Knesset. Support from the opposition Social Democrats inflated Adenauer's majority to 239, though 86 government deputies abstained, and his finance minister, Fritz Schaeffer, even voted with the minority. In Jerusalem, the furious opposition of both Right and Left limited Ben-Gurion's rather smaller majority to the government parties,[71] but by this time, American attention had wandered. Save for the Yiddish papers, the American press handled the story with a combination of indifference and objectivity, notwithstanding the intrinsic significance of the German payments, the unique importance and multiple ambiguities of the U.S. role, and the furious drama of the Israeli debate. Yet ironically, as Lily Gardner Feldman has noted, the settlement with the Federal Republic was to make the Germans a "more reliable and more generous donor and supporter than even the USA" until 1967.[72]

A memorably abrasive foreign policy debate, a memorably confrontational primary and general election campaign, and the coming of the first Republican president in a generation did little to focus the Israeli-U.S. picture. But what the 1952 election did assure was a Republican administration, resolved like none before it to abjure traditional isolation. Taken at its campaign word, the new administration undertook to master the untidy realities of the postwar world from the Straits of Taiwan to the heart of Europe. It even undertook to win back what its predecessors had allegedly lost or conceded, The mandate, as the new administration defined and sincerely understood it, was not only to maintain U.S. virtue, wealth, and power but to use them to maximum advantage in a bipolar world. The idea was to punish freedom's enemies and reward its friends. Before Korea, when U.S. officials were still capable of distinguishing between the Soviet Union in particular and communism in general, these categories still allowed bit of subtlety with respect to Yugoslavia and even China, but there was little subtlety left by 1952. By this time, the categories were presumably settled, and *friendly* was understood as basically synonymous with Western allies and clients.

The new administration's short-run priority was self-evidently to end the inconclusive war in Korea. To accomplish this, it hinted broadly, it was even prepared to risk nuclear war. In the long term, in effect, it proposed to do the same on a global scale. This first meant surrounding and confronting the communist world with prosperous and well-armed allies from the Black Sea to Southeast Asia. Presumably, it then meant Soviet retreat after negotiations from positions of unassailable Western strength.

But in this respect too, although the world had changed dramatically since the previous election, the United States vision of the Middle East remained occluded. Even in Europe and East Asia, where the Cold War landscape was now relatively established and familiar, the distinction between "our side" and "their side" was often arbitrary. In the larger, postcolonial world already visible in 1952, where anti-communism, anti-Western nationalism, and traditional fear of the Soviet Union swirled and merged, the certainties were more obscure than ever.

Iran on the Soviet border, where an anticommunist premier nationalized the British-owned Anglo-Iranian oil company in 1952, was a practical example. For the moment, at least, the United States preferred to mediate and negotiate rather than to confront him. Egypt was another case. In the course of seizing power from the ineffable King Farouk in 1953, young nationalist-revolutionary officers in Egypt had incidentally seized the American imagination. For partisan constituencies, the choices might be as easy as ever, but in the real world of U.S. electoral politics, where presidential candidates were neither Jews nor oil executives, and their advisors and presumptive cabinet members, for the most part, were neither "old Arab hands" nor "professional Zionists," the choices only got harder. In 1948 exceptional circumstances, Democratic realities, and Republican initiatives alike had all made the Middle East an inevitable campaign issue. By 1952 both regional circumstances and domestic circumspection confined it to the margins.

This hardly meant that official Washington was unaware of the Middle East, or that the new administration, like its predecessors, was from Missouri. On the threshold of the new administration, a revealingly ambivalent National Security Council study confronted the challenges of the Middle East. However reluctantly, it pointed to continuities rather than liberating new departures. Reasonably certain that the Soviets would shy away from war, its authors were also certain that local instability, anti-Western nationalism and the Arab-Israeli conflict per se were fertile ground for Soviet intervention; that local forces would have to do the fighting in the event of attack; and that there was no saying who these local forces would be. It was certainly not the Israelis, swamped by a flood of immigrants. Nor was it the Arabs, whose societies and states they believed were already coming apart. They were skeptical as well that it would be the European powers.

Anglo-American differences, they continued, only made the choices harder. "Gunboat diplomacy" was obsolescent and new relationships were indicated. But continued Western power and prestige were needed too, they speculated, hence the necessity for U.S. participation to stiffen Middle Eastern backs. The United States could offer staff, training missions, and equipment, they mused, but if military support were actually requested, they feared that "token forces" would be required.

"The task is not so much to prevent the changes that now impend as to guide them into channels that will offer the least threat to Western interests," they submitted bravely. But this was understood to mean that "we should work with and through the present ruling groups, and while bolstering their hold on power, use our influence to induce them to accommodate themselves as necessary to the new forces that are emerging." Yet, they conceded, this, in turn, could not be allowed to preclude association with new groups, though who these might be was yet another conundrum. They recognized that agricultural development must clearly be top priority but also acknowledged that local elites gave top priority to industrial development. Meanwhile, they feared that Middle Eastern peasants might take their cues from the Chinese.

What was certain, at least, was that "our principal aim should be to encourage the emergence of competent leaders." This meant continued aid. The consequence seemed certain too, that is, that "care should be taken to avoid the appearance of partiality to Israel," and to avoid a local arms race. This, in turn, could require U.S. influence "to secure some modification of Israeli policies, particularly the immigration policy."[73]

Meanwhile the Israeli request for $121 million in fiscal 1954 was already on the table, and the Middle East was prominent as never before on policymakers' plates.

"[T]here was a general feeling . . . that the United States could always be counted upon to come to Israel's rescue when the latter got into trouble," Ambassador Davis informed the State Department in January.[74]

A few weeks later, John Foster Dulles was already preparing to visit the region *ex officio,* the first secretary of state ever to visit the Middle East.[75] Originally planned for thirteen days. the expedition had grown to twenty by the time he actually took off on May 9. Over the next three weeks, the secretary's party descended *seriatim* on Cairo, Tel Aviv, Amman, Damascus, Beirut, Baghdad, Riyadh, New Delhi, Karachi, Ankara, Athens, and Tripoli. On June 1, Dulles returned to Washington, where he immediately reported his findings to the National Security Council in the presence of the president, vice president, and secretary of defense.

Western prestige was "in general very low," Dulles announced, but he hoped that "we could regain our lost influence if we made a real effort." He also favored a reaffirmation of the Tripartite Declaration, though he acknowledged that it had not thitherto been a "notable success" with the Arabs. Eisenhower immediately seized the cue. "There should be a quick follow-up to remove the causes of Arab hostility," the president said. As he had only recently reminded Egyptian visitors, "There were five million Jewish votes in the United States and very few Arabs," but he had no intention of taking sides between Israelis and Arabs, he added.

Before the day was over, Dulles had gone on national radio and television to report on his trip. "The people usually greeted us with friendly smiles and applause," he noted reassuringly. But he continued, pointing to the area's largest population, its mineral and oil resources, its strategic geography, and religious history, he still considered it "high time that the United States Government pay more attention to the Near East and South Asia." Americans had been surprised when China fell to the communists, he recalled. "There could be equally dangerous developments in the Near East and South Asia."

With respect to the area per se, the secretary was pleased to report that Egypt faced a "great new future," though contingent, for example, on a peaceful solution of the Anglo-Egyptian differences on the future of the British base at Suez. Israel too was doing fine, he added—providing that something were done about Jerusalem, refugee resettlement, and water supplies.[76]

Israelis acknowledged the speech with open ambivalence. An embassy spokesman in Washington pointed unsurprisingly to the familiar injunctions on Jerusalem and refugees, but he especially regretted the secretary's implication that previous U.S. policy itself had been mistaken. He feared Dulles's signals would only make the Arabs hang tougher. His American counterpart was unmoved. Israel might like to call the Arab bluff with a well-timed peace initiative of its own that would then confirm the Arab unwillingness to settle, he countered archly. The Israeli "immediately exploded," the American noted, insisting that Israeli domestic opinion would never take it. As for the implication of previous U.S. error, the American continued, "I replied that purely aside from the fact that it might actually be a fact, we, like the Government of Israel, had the problem of public reaction to consider, and this could be viewed as the statement of the Secretary of State of the new Administration."[77]

4

To the Brink and Back

Within weeks of Eisenhower's inauguration, Stalin died. The confused circumspection of his successors and the near-collapse of the Soviet client regime in East Berlin could only enhance the self-assurance of an administration already committed to "negotiation from strength."[1] Unlike its predecessors, it was also almost proudly unbeholden to Jews. An estimated 75 percent of Jews had voted in 1952 for Adlai Stevenson, the Democratic loser, and even more were to vote for him again in 1956. It was true that Cleveland's Rabbi Silver, still one of the nation's most aggressive Zionists, remained a Taft Republican, but given the hard feelings left over from a bitter campaign for the nomination, that was unlikely to win any points with the new administration either.

Considering the underrepresentation of Jews in its electorate and the eccentric profile of the relatively few Jews among its supporters, it was no surprise that the new administration saw the American Council for Judaism *faute de mieux* as representative of American Jews. There were no Jews in the Eisenhower cabinet, nor any Jewish appointees particularly involved in foreign policy. Had they raised the issue, at least two relatively senior officials, Lewis L. Strauss, the chairman of the Atomic Energy Commission, and Max Rabb, the secretary of the cabinet and the administration's liaison to the Jewish community, might still have influenced the president's views on Israel, but at least till Suez, there is no evidence that they did.[2]

The impact of the new administration could soon be sensed in the growing touchiness of the Israeli-U.S. dialogue. In his inaugural visit to the new men at the State Department, Israel's Ambassador Abba Eban expressed a now-familiar interest in their views of Israel's place in U.S. defense planning, regional security, and economic aid. He also wanted to know more about recent talk of U.S. military aid to Egypt. But what was really wanted, as an *aide mémoire* made clear, was "an early statement that abandonment" of previous policy was not contemplated. It was not forthcoming. A few weeks later, Eban was back to inquire about a proliferation of newspaper articles on "a new approach to the Middle East." Their tenor, as he read them, was "to discredit United States-Israel relations, thereby winning Arab friendship." Eyes turned heavenward, U.S. officials were at a loss to explain how the press might have got such an idea. They nonetheless wondered if Israel itself might not share some responsibility for it, considering how recent Israeli statements had themselves emphasized U.S.-Israeli differences.[3]

Secure in its popular mandate, congressional majorities, and serene good conscience, the new administration meanwhile leaped in with self-confidence and apparent success where its predecessors had trod with little luck and indifferent results. During more than two years of strategic stalemate and inconclusive armistice negotiations, U.S. troops had continued to die in Korea. For about the same period, oil-rich and strategically located Iran seemed to teeter on the brink of anarchy or communist takeover, while U.S. mediators sought vainly to reconcile the expropriated owners of the Anglo-Iranian Oil Company with the government that nationalized it. By summer 1953, a bit of nuclear sabre rattling had helped end the Korean War, at least de facto, and a locally improvised but wonderfully effective, covert action had restored the shah to power after several months of Roman exile.[4] The administration saw both the end of hostilities in Korea and the successful coup in Iran as examples of what worked, and was quick to internalize and generalize their apparent lessons. For years to come, both nukes and spooks were to be among the favored instruments of U.S. policy.

In many ways, the continuities with previous policy were as striking as the new departures. In the full rhetorical flight of the election campaign, it was at least implied that the new administration, if elected, would unleash the Nationalist Chinese from their Promethean rock, liberate eastern Europe from the shackles of Yalta, and generally roll back the communist empire. In fact, as it was to confirm by its demonstrative nonintervention in East Germany just months after taking office, it was hardly less committed than its predecessors to both the European and the East Asian status quo *post* bellum. As before, the rearmament of (West) Germany and the reconstruction of (western) Europe and Japan remained top U.S. priorities. By comparison, neither the Third World in general nor the Middle East in particular were matters of much intrinsic concern. But the new administration was also prepared to live with, and even occasionally encourage, the decolonization of Asia and Africa, providing it took an appropriately anticommunist course; and to pursue an Israeli-Arab compromise in the Middle East, despite deep skepticism that it was actually possible to reach one.

What distinguished the new administration from its predecessors were not so much the ends as the means. Korea itself was a watershed experience, a lesson in both the foreign and domestic costs of a conventional war in what the Joint Chiefs of Staff themselves referred to as the wrong place at the wrong time. If "no more Munichs" remained a conspicuous watchword of the new policy, "no more Koreas" inevitably became another after three years of bloody inconclusiveness in a place most Americans had a hard time even finding on the map. Within the next half decade, the Munich logic led to what Dulles personally called "the brink" in places as far apart as West Berlin, the Straits of Formosa, and the beaches of Beirut. Korea's logic too became ever more apparent. It included a system of global alliances, both de facto and de jure, that were intended to redistribute the strategic load; a quest for local proxies to share and shoulder local burdens; creation and deployment of "battlefield" nuclear weapons that would assure "more bang for the buck," while minimizing draft calls and, above all, casualties; further demonstrative noninterventions in Indochina, Hungary, and Egypt, as well as East Germany, that might lead to risky complications, and a profusion of dirty tricks, from Vietnam and Guatemala to the Persian Gulf and the eastern Mediterranean, whose legacy was to haunt U.S. policy for generations afterward.[5]

Remembered alike for its confrontational zeal and exemplary restraint, the new administration was actually remarkable for a combination of both. On his inaugural tour of the Middle East, Dulles personally explained the connections to Ben-Gurion in the prime minister's office in Jerusalem. The main priority, he said, was long-term vigilance toward an adversary, whose goals had presumably not changed with Stalin's death. What this required was military strength without economic damage, "concentrating on buildup of quality rather than quantity." If only for reasons of strategic geography plus access to oil and bases, this was clearly where the Arabs came in.

As the Jerusalem venue confirmed, the secretary was tactically prepared to meet Israel halfway, despite cautionary noises about the potential hazards from U.S. diplomats around the region. From Amman, Dulles was officially warned of Jordanian anxiety that U.S. acceptance of Ben-Gurion's lunch invitation could be seen as recognition of Jerusalem as Israel's capital. Beirut was meanwhile convinced that the "Arab world . . . would be so hurt and emotionally upset by such a move" that it could prejudice the entire trip.[6] His finger raised circumspectly to the desert wind, Dulles readjusted his schedule to allow for an hour's visit to Arab Jerusalem before proceeding to Amman, but his first priority was obviously to get his own message to its reluctant Israeli addressee.

Though aware as ever of the need for good relations with Washington, Ben-Gurion nonetheless remained committed to a course the new administration was even likelier than its predecessors to find willful, provocative, and self-destructive, not to mention inopportune. By the time Dulles arrived for lunch, Jerusalem was already the seat of Israel's parliament, prime minister, and president. Previously disposed to assert their presence in the city in order to preempt external pressure, Israelis felt only the more justified in extending it as external pressure appeared to decline.[7] The transfer of the foreign ministry in July 1953 inspired an earnest but unavoidably awkward U.S. boycott of Israeli diplomatic proceedings, plus diplomatic soul-searchings, and injunctions to American journalists on what to do on a social or personal visit to the city if an Israeli host or colleague should start talking business. "Your present policy is blasphemy," an antic Prime Minister Sharett informed a startled American at what the official report called "a casual meeting" in Tel Aviv soon afterward. "Christ himself came to Jerusalem," he continued cheerfully. "So did Dulles, a religious man. . . ."[8]

Americans were again infuriated by a seeming disregard for international opinion as Israeli engineers and settlers went about the unilateral business of making facts in the demilitarized zones of the Jordan Valley, and the government continued full tilt with an ambitious program of domestic development. Ambassador Manett Davis himself, a respected career diplomat and the nominal opposite of the "professional Zionist" his colleagues deplored, reminded Washington that Israel's problems were not all of its own making. "It seems quite clear that we are confronted by something more serious than mere 'Arab prejudice' . . . that presumably could be overcome by a few minor territorial adjustments, resettlement of refugees, payment of compensation, etc.," he cautioned. Davis feared that the new administration's intended display of "impartiality" could send entirely the wrong signal, if it implied any diminution of the aid that Israel genuinely and urgently needed to avoid "immediate financial collapse with far-reaching political consequences."[9]

For all that Dulles told Ben-Gurion he was there "to learn and listen," his visit to Tel Aviv and Jerusalem left no doubt that he was also there to teach and talk. "Secretary expressed appreciation Sharett's presentation, remarking that as judge might not agree with all his arguments but as lawyer admired presentation of case," the transcript noted after the two foreign ministers had met for an opening exchange of views.[10] But whether implied or explicit, Dulles's message was invariably the same. The transcripts recall a dutiful but inevitably preoccupied family lawyer explaining the facts of life to a bright but querulous adolescent ward. "Trust us," was the common message, be the subject borders, refugees, the status of Jerusalem, Israeli security, or U.S. aid. "With respect to the U.S. Military Agreement with Iraq, the Secretary could only say that it was his belief that when the final chapter to this topic was written, it would be found to be in the best interests of Israel," the official U.S. transcript noted after a particularly candid exchange with Eban in May 1954. "He would not undertake to explain why this was so," it continued, "but requested the Government of Israel to accept it on faith."[11]

In his talk with Ben-Gurion, Dulles prophylactically assured the prime minister of his admiration for "Israel's history and present creative activity," which "created [a] feeling of common debt which was more binding than [a] formal treaty of alliance." But there could be no useful U.S. role in the region, the secretary continued briskly, unless the United States enjoyed the goodwill and confidence of the Arabs. Because the Arabs believed that Democratic Jewish voters under Roosevelt and Truman had tilted the United States in favor of Israel, the conclusion was obvious. "New administration was elected by overwhelming vote of American people as whole," Dulles declared in the terse language of the official transcript, "and neither owes that type of political debt to any segment nor believes in building power by cultivating particular segments of populations."

Ben-Gurion would surely agree, the secretary continued, that "best interests of Israel would be served by healthier, friendlier United States-Arab relations." In fact, Dulles believed they were in reach, but "ability accomplish this purpose may depend on understanding of United States Jews," he signaled broadly, "and suggested that Prime Minister might be able to help United States to help Israel in this regard."[12]

In the months that followed, the putative differences between Israeli and American Jews became a recurring theme of U.S. public diplomacy. It thus became a major source of American-Jewish anxiety and Israeli-U.S. contention. "If we are to be accused of 'pro' anything, let us make it amply clear that that prefix can only apply to one thing, and that is that our policy is first and foremost 'pro-Americam,'" Henry Byroade, now assistant secretary of state for NEA, announced in a widely noted speech to the Dayton, Ohio, World Affairs Council in April 1954. In the spirit of enlightened candor, he then informed the Israelis that they should "look upon yourselves as a Middle Eastern state . . . rather than as headquarters . . . of a worldwide grouping . . . who must have special rights within and obligations to the Jewish state." The injunction to the Israelis led, in turn, to an injunction to the

Arabs. They should "accept the State of Israel as an accomplished fact," Byroade told them, and make peace with Israel. A few weeks later, Byroade appeared at the annual meeting of the American Council for Judaism in Philadelphia. This time he warned the peoples of the Middle East, both Jews and Arabs, of the common threat from the Soviet Union, and again admonished the Arabs to drop their "negativism." But the Israelis seemed still to be the principal addressee; they could advance their cause by reassuring their neighbors and curtailing immigration, Byroade told them.[13]

Though noted only casually in the United States, Byroade's speeches reverberated in both Israel and the Arab world. But what was heard there varied with the audience. Save for one pro-Western Christian paper in Beirut that reportedly found the Dayton speech "nearly perfect," Arab commentators from Damascus to Jordan were outraged at the idea of making peace, although the Philadelphia speech seems to have made a more positive impression.

Israeli commentators, including Ben-Gurion himself, took offense at Byroade's views on the whole range of Israeli policy, but especially his views on immigration and Israeli-Diaspora relations. With official circumspection, Eban protested "a certain lack of scholarship and of sensitivity." It was bad enough that the Dayton speech neglected to advise the Arabs against raiding Israel. Considering the failures of British immigration policy when it most mattered, and the cataclysmic circumstances that had brought the vast majority of immigrants to Palestine and Israel in the first place, Eban thought it particularly insensitive of Byroade to make an issue of immigration. Given prevailing restraints in eastern Europe, new immigration was not a current issue anyway, he noted. But if it were, he added with a well-tuned sense of his audience, the "Middle East would be better off as a result, for these people would be true anti-Communists."[14]

With Independence Day approaching, and at least a subliminal civil-military crisis in progress at home, Israeli sensitivity was arguably heightened by the need for political distraction. Yet the issue was real enough. "It is not within the realm of possibility to snap the link between the Jewish people in its Dispersion and Israel," the usually affable Teddy Kollek, now chief of staff in the prime minister's office, cautioned Parker T. Hart, the State Department's director of NEA. "[T]his is a matter about which even a chap like me feels pretty deeply."[15]

The relative indifference of the editorial writers notwithstanding, there were evidently Americans who felt pretty deeply about it too. In late May, Thomas E. Dewey, the former presidential candidate and still governor of New York, passed on a memo to Sherman Adams, the White House chief of staff. According to Dewey, its source was a "man of real substance, loyalty and intelligence." There was no further identification. The anonymous author called for a statement from President Eisenhower before it was too late. What was needed, in his view, was a statement supportive not only of Israel but also of American Jews, constructive criticism, and free speech. "At this moment there is widespread belief (I assume unfounded) that America has abandoned its traditional friendship for Israel," the memo warned. It noted incidentally that, with an election coming up, it might be wise to issue such a statement quickly in order to preempt any impression that it was politically motivated. With Dulles gone, Adams passed the memo on to Walter

Bedell Smith, the under secretary of state, "for the benefit of your sagacity." Three weeks later, Smith noted, both men had decided "that the storm had subsided and that it would be best to do nothing further about it." But it would be opportune for Smith to see the still redoubtable Silver when he was next in Washington.[16]

In July 1954, as the French effort in Indochina collapsed, the foreign ministers of the major powers gathered in Geneva to divide Vietnam, and the French Assembly rejected the European Defense Community that was to integrate new German contingents in a European army, a top-secret policy statement by the National Security Council confirmed that the administration line remained unchanged. "Settlement of outstanding political disputes" required that "the United States convince the Arab states that it is capable of acting independently of other Western states and of Israel,"[17] the paper declared.

"And of Congress too," it might have added, considering the administration's experience as it tried to fit the round peg of economic pressure into the square hole of Israeli external debt. As early as summer 1953, Washington had genuinely feared Israeli default with all its ramifications. But it was also resolved that U.S. aid not be used to pay outstanding debts, that Israel not be rewarded for seemingly willful disregard of U.S. concerns and interests, and that aid go where the administration wanted it to go. The problem, according to the U.S. embassy in Tel Aviv, was that, as long as Israelis believed that the United States would not allow default, they would simply go on borrowing.[18]

Dulles held firm. The United States could maintain pressure on Israel by keeping track of its foreign exchange expenditures and exercising careful control of aid, he informed the embassy. In August, Eisenhower even made pressure statutory by signing an executive order, prohibiting use of U.S. grant-in-aid funds for payment of debt. Pending solution of the debt crisis, another U.S. government loan was out of the question. The secretary advised Israelis to "seek relief through arrangements with present holders [of] debt or other private sources." The purpose of U.S. aid, Dulles insisted, was to make Israel "self-supporting in shortest possible time."

Though Israel was not the only addressee of the new policy, the Israeli reaction was conspicuously irritable. Israeli policy would continue to be determined "by statesmen motivated by faith in Israel and not by experts, bookkeepers and statisticians," Finance Minister, and later Prime Minister, Levi Eshkol announced at a meeting with U.S. officials. In a testy conversation with Kollek, Francis Russell, the embassy counselor, replied in kind. The United States had not already invested over $300 million in Israel in order to see it go under, he declared emphatically. At the same time, the United States was fed up with Israeli secrecy, disregard of U.N. armistice commissions, an "'over our dead bodies' attitude toward negotiating outstanding issues with Arabs," transfer of the foreign ministry to Jerusalem, Israel's apparent "impatience with US desire to devote economic aid to goals of sound economy," not to mention "Eban's high-handed disregard ... of half million American boys in Korea," he continued with evident relish.

By now, the embassy acknowledged, there were signs that the Israelis were coming around to U.S. views on reduced consumption—though not of food, Eshkol qualified emphatically—as well as increased exports, agricultural development, and short-term payoffs. The administration continued to hang tough, despite cautionary noises from Harold Stassen, its aid director.[19] The new bill proposed a $100 million package of military aid for the Middle East, exclusive of Greece, Turkey, and Iran, which were funded separately. Because no funds for Israel were planned, the beneficiaries were all Arabs by default. The bill soon ran into trouble in the House, but was eventually saved, though cut by half and heavily amended, in the Senate. Meanwhile, Stassen omitted any mention, not only of Israel and the Jewish people, but even of UJA itself at the annual UJA dinner. Soon afterward, the same omissions recurred in Eisenhower's message to the annual convention of the Zionist Organization of America. In apparent reprisal for the relocation of the Israeli Foreign Ministry, the State Department even dropped the American Zionist Council from its briefing list.

The other shoe dropped a few weeks later, when the administration submitted an economic aid package, heavily reworked to reflect what it considered the priority needs of Iran after the CIA coup in August. On October 20, it then suspended technical assistance to Israel altogether. Attributed to Ambassador Loy Henderson in Teheran, the idea was ostensibly to divert the bulk of U.S. aid from both Jews and Arabs to the new regime in Iran. The story was first leaked to the Jewish Telegraph Agency, a news service for the Jewish press. It then surfaced in the *New York Times* by way of Tel Aviv. I. L. Kenen, the Zionist lobbyist in Washington, had meanwhile activated friendly members of Congress. Pointed inquiries from Minnesota's Democratic Senator Hubert Humphrey and Michigan's Republican Senator Homer Ferguson soon reached Dulles. Both were up for reelection the following year.

By that time, Ferguson was clearly scared. Attaching the predictable pro-Israel statement from his Democratic opponent, Patrick V. McNamara, he requested the secretary's "comments" at the "earliest opportunity." Dulles's provisional cabled answer left Paris eight days later. His office then needed another two days to dispatch a disingenuous eight-page handout from a downtown Washington consultant to the Republican National Committee. The text called attention to Democratic shortcomings during and immediately after World War II, and emphasized Senator Robert A. Taft's yeoman services to Jews and Israel. "I must ask that the attached not be attributed to the Secretary personally or to the Department," the cover letter added. In November, Ferguson lost his seat.[20]

Meanwhile, bipartisan congressional consensus had at least spared a collision on foreign aid. In October 1953, there was a further avalanche of mail from both sides of the aisle, both sides of the Capitol, and even an occasional state legislator. Among the dozens of signatories were the later presidential candidate Barry Goldwater and the later Presidents John F. Kennedy and Lyndon B. Johnson. He was "amazed to read in the New York Times" of the Administration's plans, Congressman Melvin Price of East St. Louis, Illinois, informed the State Department in a typical letter. As a member of the Armed Services Committee, he wanted it known that he applauded "all attempts by U.S. to bolster the economies of both the Arab states and Israel."

For the moment, the administration held its ground. On the one hand, it called attention to the special need "to prevent Iran from falling into the Soviet orbit." On the other, it enumerated what it regarded as the special derelictions of Israel. These included a head-to-head confrontation with General Bennicke, the U.N.

chief of staff in Jerusalem, over a disputed Israeli water project on the Syrian border in the northern Galilee, and a particularly bloody reprisal raid on the Jordanian border village of Kibya under the command of Ariel Sharon, a twenty-five-year-old reserve major, whose unusual combativeness had already drawn ambivalent but admiring high-level notice from Israeli officials. In a pro forma telegram of congratulations to a regional Hadassah conference in his native New Hampshire, Adams indicated that Eisenhower would "proceed with allocation of funds as soon as he was informed that Israel had assured the United Nations of its policy to cooperate with the efforts of the Security Council."

For all the huffing and puffing, the suspension was brief. Within a few weeks, the Israelis had retreated tactically in the Galilee; Stassen had informed Dulles that U.S. intervention was needed to stave off imminent default; and Dulles, himself a former Republican senator from New York, had emerged from a reportedly tense meeting with New York's incumbent Republican Senator Irving Ives and its future Republican senator, incumbent Congressman Jacob Javits. It was likely that aid for Israel figured prominently in the discussion.

On October 28, Eisenhower announced his decision to resume scheduled payments, but in contrast to the $73 million appropriation the year before, the 1953 appropriation was $54 million, $52.5 of it in grants, the rest in technical assistance. Ironically, both Jewish leaders and State Department officials regarded the settlement as a tactical defeat for Israel. Clearly concerned that Israel's partisans might overplay their hand, Eban cautioned Congressman Emanuel Celler of New York that Israeli-U.S. relations had recently improved. His letter was "not for attribution or quotation in any form," he added. Yet the file copy at the State Department suggests that someone, and presumably not Celler, made sure that it came to the department's attention.[21]

By the end of 1956, U.S. evenhandedness, in the sense of action independent of "other Western states and of Israel," as envisaged by the National Security Council staff and recommended to the administration just two years before, had nonetheless transcended anything to date. In early 1957, the administration had even confronted Israel directly, as no U.S. government had done before, and none was to repeat with quite the same self-assurance. Yet the Arabs were as unpersuaded as ever of U.S. intentions,[22] and U.S. policy was no closer than ever to its stated goals.

To a far greater degree than most Americans realized, the administration also made a serious effort during the same period to diversity and hedge its bets, and even to address some of the region's basic problems. Yet its initiatives constituted not only a practical anthology of the contemporary diplomatic repertory but a short course on the limits constraining even a superpower in the postwar Middle East.

Given the presumed success of the covert operation in Teheran, it was unsurprising that more of the same enjoyed high priority in Washington. Between 1953 and 1958, Americans undertook a variety of schemes to co-opt, as well as suborn, allies in Lebanon, Syria, and Egypt with money, arms, aid, and diplomatic favor. Arguably among the most colorful U.S. initiatives of the era, they may also have been among its most counterproductive, directly and indirectly enhancing the very Soviet influence they were presumably intended to contain.

Among the era's most constructive and imaginative U.S. initiatives, on the other hand, was a comprehensive regional development program, all the more deserving of attention for its near success. Now virtually forgotten, it was a direct successor to the previous grand designs of Walter Clay Lowdermilk and Gordon Clapp. In October 1953, just a week before the disastrous raid on Kibya, the plan was entrusted to Eric Johnston, a former spokesman for the motion picture industry. Johnston thus became the first in what was to be a long line of personal presidential representatives to the Middle East with ambassadorial rank.

Despite suspension of U.S. aid to Israel a few days later, Johnston set immediately to work within extensive guidelines prepared for him by Dulles himself. His mission was to "secure agreement of the states of Lebanon, Syria, Jordan and Israel to the division and use of the waters of the Jordan River Basin" and to secure "agreement from Jordan and Israel on plans that may be prepared for the internationalization of Jerusalem, if"—a significant qualification—"it is subsequently decided by the Department that this subject should be discussed." Lebanon's Litani River was explicitly ruled out as a chip to put on the table.

The idea, Dulles explained, was to divide the water equitably, eliminate the previous demilitarized zones, and maintain the armistice lines. "States concerned" were to understand that future U.S. aid would vary according to the warmth of Johnston's reception, and that administration action, in turn, was constrained by Congress. There was also the implication that Syria would get an extra carrot in the form of military assistance—though contingent on "assurances that the arms would be used to meet the prime objectives of the U.S. Government" and not, that is, for attacking Israel, Dulles specified. Incentives for Israel included the direct and indirect payoffs it could expect from resettling refugees, the advantages of a practical scheme for making resettlement possible, and the assurance of both water and U.S. support for "immediate, important development assistance in the form of irrigation works." Arab incentives presumably included the benefits of water and hydroelectric development for Jordan and Syria, plus border security, access to Lake Tiberias, and an assured claim to water that Israel might otherwise preempt.[23]

In the two years and four rounds of negotiations that followed, Johnston actually got Israel to agree. In summer 1954, the United States and Israel concluded a draft memorandum of understanding on the basic conditions of water allocation, storage, supervision, and sovereignty that the Israeli cabinet then ratified without a vote. But the quest for a solution by enlightened technocracy turned out again to be a mirage. Only a few weeks after Israeli ratification, the plan fell victim in part to inter-Arab skirmishes, in part to Arab reluctance to reach any agreement with Israel at all. On October 11, 1955, almost two years after the mission began, the Council of the Arab League expressed its gratitude for Johnston's patience and its "hope that continued discussions and efforts will lead to satisfactory results." At least one Israeli analyst tried manfully to read a "maybe" into the communiqué, but it was perfectly clear to Johnston that the message meant no.[24]

By this time, the administration was already deeply engaged in mediation between Israelis and Egyptians. The list of intermediaries included at least three British Labour MPs, a couple of Commonwealth foreign ministers, one Nobel Peace Prize winner, and one future prime minister, as well as a leading Quaker,

Jacob Blaustein, the relevant embassies, and the CIA, with its own interest in heading off alternative Israeli initiatives before they reached the U.S. government.[25]

In the aftermath of the Anglo-Egyptian treaty of 1954 and the attendant withdrawal of British forces from Egypt, there was also an Anglo-U.S. initiative known as "Project Alpha." Unlike the mediation efforts, "Alpha" was actually unveiled in public, and its sponsors included both Dulles and Britain's foreign secretary, the later Prime Minister Anthony Eden. Intended as a comprehensive political solution to the whole Arab-Israeli conflict, it proved to suffer from terminal deficiencies of realism and judgment, but there was no denying it a certain wrongheaded dash and boldness.

As its creators always emphasized, its goal was a "settlement," not "peace." At the heart of the scheme was a package of guarantees and incentives, including almost exclusively Israeli territorial concessions. Though U.S. officials could be coy in admitting it,[26] "Alpha" was to link Egypt and Jordan in the Negev, without threatening Israeli control of Eilat at the head of the Gulf of Aqaba; to get Israel to cede about four hundred square miles of territory, including Jerusalem's Mount Scopus, to Jordan, with further concessions in the event that Israel should end up in control of Gaza; to impose demilitarized zones along both sides of the new borders; to repatriate an unspecified number of refugees, and to end the Arab boycott and Egyptian exclusion of Israeli shipping from the Suez Canal. At the end of the rainbow came a pot of economic aid for all signatories plus Anglo-American guarantees of the new borders.

The premises were as flawed as they were compelling, yet they were uncritically accepted by policymakers in both London and Washington, who obviously wanted to believe in them. Among the common denominators was the conviction that Arab nationalism was an aberration born of communist agitation and the Arab-Israeli conflict. It followed from this that solution of the Arab-Israeli conflict was itself the high road to exclusion of Soviet or communist influence from the area, and restoration of the presumably pro-Western status quo. A second premise was that Israel was the primary, if not the exclusive, cause of the conflict with its neighbors; and that Israelis could be induced to trade territory and more for external guarantees. Assuming that the United States could deliver these, a third premise was that Nasser would then buy the package. Meanwhile, it appeared that Ben-Gurion, who assumed that U.S. and British policy were fundamentally divergent, had no idea what was going on.[27]

The immediate initiator of this unlikely scheme was Evelyn Shuckburgh, a senior career officer in the British Foreign Office. But at least initially, Americans were willing to cooperate all the way to the top. The two governments had about a year to accomplish something before the next presidential campaign, Dulles reportedly told a small and distinguished Anglo-American dinner party in late 1954. Within weeks, Shuckburgh was on his way to Washington for the first round of negotiations.

Shuckburgh nonetheless assumed from the beginning that Americans would be soft on Israel, be it from conviction or prudence. Even Russell, his immediate negotiating partner, came directly from assignment in Tel Aviv, Shuckburgh told himself, where he saw "their, i.e., Israel's, point of view very clearly." Dulles, for his part, wanted to press the Arabs too. They should understand that all U.S. efforts to "deflate the Jews" would end with the coming of the election campaign, the secretary reminded Shuckburgh.

The other problem, as Shuckburgh also acknowledged, was that the Arabs were unlikely to make peace. This, in turn, meant that the United States was unlikely to offer the guarantees on which the plan depended. As Russell understood only too well, Egyptian demands for a corridor through the Negev would also cause trouble, not least because Israelis were sure to oppose it. That, for once, was not a problem— at least for Shuckburgh, whose casual indifference to Israeli views, and even sovereignty, derived from a conviction that Israeli independence had itself been a product of British war-weariness and bad conscience. Because he believed that Israel was founded on "a false premise and in unnatural, impermanent condition," he accordingly concluded that "the Jews are doomed if they don't change their ways"— though Israelis showed no sign of appreciating this.[28] He nonetheless lost no opportunity to tell Shimon Peres, director general of the Defense Ministry and a later Israeli prime minister, that the Western powers could not "sacrifice their major interests for Israel."[29]

Preoccupied as he was with U.S. squeamishness, Shuckburgh thought first of U.S. politics when Dulles announced his intention of unveiling "Alpha" in a speech to the Council on Foreign Relations on August 28, 1955. The speech may actually have been meant to preempt the famous Soviet-Egyptian arms deal that became public a few weeks later, but Shuckburgh took Dulles at his word that his target was domestic. The point of the speech, he explained to himself and presumably London, was to get Americans, including Democrats, committed to "Alpha" while the going was good, for example, while Adlai Stevenson might still be supportive of it, and before Stevenson's presumptive challenger, New York's then-Governor W. Averell Harriman, lined up with the Israeli hawks. What worried him was what would happen if Israel, unlike the Arabs, should actually agree to "Alpha," and then ask Western guarantees without the settlement it was supposed to bring about.

What killed "Alpha" in the end was neither Republican cold feet nor Democratic unilateralism, but its basic unattractiveness to its presumed beneficiaries. Given its stake in U.S. goodwill and its speculative interest in both U.S. arms and settlement with Egypt, Moshe Sharett's government hesitated to say no. But Israeli skepticism about external guarantees, anxiety about transfer of Western arms to Arab neighbors, and genuine passion for the Negev, nonetheless assured that the idea would go nowhere without a major Arab breakthrough.

An Arab breakthrough was at least as unlikely. Arguably, Nasser had something to gain by negotiating with the Western powers, but agreement on their terms seemed likely to bring him little but trouble and opprobrium. Palestinian refugees were hardly among his top priorities. Acquisition of a few more miles of desert territory was no incentive either. Domestic and foreign opinion were already on his side. There was no pressing reason at this point to sacrifice a promising role as champion of the Arabs for a flawed and unrewarding settlement with Israel.

In September 1955, the Egyptians delivered the coup de grace to "Alpha" with their concurrent threat to blockade the Gulf of Aqaba, and the spectacular public announcement that the Soviets had agreed to barter hundreds of trucks and armored vehicles, 200 late-model jet aircraft, 500 guns, 230 tanks, plus submarines and other naval vessels for Egyptian cotton. In its way, the sale was a watershed for both parties. Like collateral Soviet initiatives from India to Guatemala, it seemed to confirm for the first time since Stalin that the Soviet Union meant to be something more than a European power. By outflanking the Tripartite Declaration, it also seemed to confirm the end of Western hegemony in the Middle East.

Despite the public uproar, the CIA had actually been aware of the impending deal at least since May. There were plausible reasons that the Egyptians should want the CIA to know about it, despite the potential risk of alarming both the United States and Israel. The CIA also knew that the Soviets had offered to deal via Warsaw or Prague, in case direct contact embarrassed Cairo. It was meanwhile reported that the Soviets had made similar offers to Syria and even Saudi Arabia.

Then and after, Soviet expectations and motives have been a source of impassioned debate.[30] Yet an analysis of the larger implications by State Department Intelligence and Research (I&R) was almost demonstratively unperturbed. The Soviets were worried about the Baghdad Pact, I&R explained. Egypt was an unexpected opportunity to challenge, even bust it. At the same time, the Soviets were not giving anything away, nor could they have any illusions about Nasser's basic anticommunism. Considering their vulnerability to Western reaction and local embarrassment alike, I&R continued, the Soviets also had every reason to be discreet. It even considered that the Soviets might want the deal to fail, thus assuring it full value as public relations, while avoiding the attendant risks of a practical commitment.

Nasser too had reason to worry about the Western reaction, but there was nothing mysterious, at least, about his expectations and motives.[31] As I&R noted, he was already in bad economic and military trouble. His effort to coax substantial military aid from the United States was also going nowhere.[32] Beyond this, as an Arab nationalist, a veteran of the war with Israel, and an Egyptian, he obviously resented the Baghdad Pact. Not only was he bound to regard it as a symbol of continued Western hegemony, he was also likely to see it as a tilt to the "Northern tier," and particularly the Fertile Crescent, which had challenged Egyptian hegemony since Babylon. Of course, he resented Israel too, which, like virtually all Arabs, he associated with Western hegemony.

Genuinely persuaded that Britain's last best hope to remain a global power was ingratiation of the Arabs, a frantic Shuckburgh could only register the growing stress. He resented that Britain too had to acquiesce while Egypt threatened Aqaba, and, at the same time, to restrain the Israelis from unilateral action. "The process of betraying Israel is going to be both dangerous and painful," he conceded balefully.[33] The Soviet-Egyptian arms deal only made things worse. Dulles, he noted, now brooded openly about a spontaneous alliance of those thitherto unimaginable bedfellows, the Jewish lobby in the United States and the McCarthyite right wing. "Would it not be a good long time before our public opinions regarded the Arabs as Communists?" Shuckburgh asked him consolingly. "Not in the United States," Dulles snarled back.[34]

As always, U.S.-Israeli differences were reflected in money, arms, and symbols.

Circumstances allowed, even compelled, Americans to separate what for Israelis was practically inseparable. For all their incidental passion, most members of Congress and most policymakers in any given administration could still regard the annual hauling and tugging over Israeli aid as basically discretionary, a question of means, not ends. Given the nature of U.S. constitutionality, law, and political culture, the annual mix and numbers could then be negotiated within increasingly familiar parameters of bureaucratic and electoral politics.

In Israeli perspective, the margins were far narrower, and the political imperatives quite different. It was the irony, if not the tragedy, of Sharett's incumbency that even the most dovish of Israeli premiers had no occasion to exercise his dovishness. Gloomier, in fact, than Ben-Gurion about the long-term recalcitrance of the conflict, Sharett was nonetheless prepared to respect, and even accommodate Arab nationalism, if only to maintain the international, and especially U.S., goodwill on which he believed that Israel's security ultimately rested.

Yet personality aside, Sharett's failure as prime minister testified to domestic, regional, and international restraints guaranteed to discourage and frustrate the hardiest of doves. The defense establishment was practically beyond his control. Irrespective of its intention, U.S. "evenhandedness" had meanwhile become a virtual invitation to Israeli activism. But the insuperable obstacle was a world of Arab adversaries, unwilling to recognize, and possibly incapable of recognizing, an Israeli dove when they saw one.

Seen in its own terms, Israeli politics allowed for considerable and meaningful choices. Hawkish as it might seem to Arabs, Ben-Gurion's pragmatism had allowed for partition of Palestine. Ben-Gurion was also disposed to regard the United States as an incomparably more equal ally than any other, favor a pro-Western orientation in the Cold War, and pursue a pluralist economy and society. To his right were the former Jabotinskyites, now followers of Begin, who still believed in an undivided Palestine extending far across the Jordan. To his left were the unreconstructed socialists, if not fellow travelers, who had dominated the Palmach, and continued to believe in a largely neutralist Israel of collectivized yeoman farmers in all of Palestine west of the Jordan.[35] Within their shared domestic habitat, relations between the respective groups ranged from chilly coexistence to cold civil war.

It was the tragedy and irony of both Arab and U.S. policy that both Arab and U.S. leaders ignored such differences rather than exploit them. For anyone who read the papers or the election returns, it should have been clear that the Israeli majority was pragmatic, not fundamentalist in either a religious or nationalist sense. Yet Americans like Byroade tended to pose questions that threatened all Israelis, while the Arabs made both their own and Israeli fears self-fulfilling. In his inaugural conversation with Dulles, Sharett called attention to the Arab paradoxes. On the one hand, Arabs posited an insatiable and unviable Israel, unable to live within existing borders. On the other, they demanded territorial concessions. Terrified of Israeli expansion, they nonetheless refused a peace that would itself impose constraints.[36]

Unrestricted by treaty, and fearful that the Arabs might read self-restraints as weakness, Israelis tended to increasing self-assertiveness. Revealingly, even the bureaucratic status of the cease-fire agreements was a matter of contention. Sharett thought the matter belonged in the Foreign Ministry; Ben-Gurion in Defense. Ben-Gurion emphasized that he was in favor of peace, opposed to war, and committed to faithful compliance with the armistice agreements, but if the other side broke them, and the United Nations failed to enforce them, he was for force, "regardless of the consequences."[37] Israelis candidly acknowledged their intent of sending a message to the Arabs, but after generations and millenia of powerlessness, they were as plausibly sending a message to themselves. Progressively indifferent to U.N. resolutions and alert to the open ends in the armistice agreements with their neighbors, they therefore created still more new facts on the borders with Egypt, Jordan, and Syria. Their neighbors then responded with economic boycott, denial of access to the Suez Canal, and ad hoc warfare.

Between the War of Independence and the Sinai campaign of 1956, the undeclared war on Israel's borders cost a total of 1,237 Israeli casualties, including 162 in 1953, and 230 in 1954. Given the relative populations of Israel and the United States, the rate could be credibly compared with U.S. casualties in Korea. But unlike Korea, the border war went on in full Israeli view, and civilians, women, and children not only were among its casualities, but seemed to be its favored targets. Unsurprisingly, there were calls for action. In the 1920s, as even the dovish Sharett warned his colleagues, it was Weizmann's self-restraint that helped lead to the growth of Revisionism. He himself was clearly worried where more border incidents might lead. "The disease of dissent might be revived in the state if we attempt to pull the string too taut," Weizmann had noted in his diary.[38]

At the same time, as Sharett knew better than most, Israel lived on its diplomatic and moral credit with the Western powers, particularly the United States. It also lived on its credibility at the United Nations, which was still clearly recognizable as a U.S. creation. Yet the unending war with its neighbors successively put it in conflict with allies and supporters, then with the other new nations that were soon to dominate the U.N. General Assembly. Britain's commitment to Jordan was a practical example. Israel wanted good relations with Britain. In time, it would even be prepared to defend Jordan itself. Yet British guarantees to Jordan effectively meant war with Israel in the event that Israeli-Jordanian tensions should require Britain to come to Jordan's defense.

Britain's waning presence in Egypt posed a different dilemma. In July 1950, Britain had hinted that Israelis might exploit the war in Korea to attack Egypt themselves.[39] This in itself was reason for Israel to wish the British gone. On the other hand, there was the question of who and what would succeed them. Now the coming of Nasser and his colleagues, and the demonstrative interest of the United States in coming to terms with them, seemed reasons to do whatever possible to assure that Britain stay.[40]

Threatened and challenged alike, Israelis responded to their security dilemmas in three ways. Eban, who was to use the United Nations like no Israeli before or since to capture the public imagination, was a valid reflection of Israeli priorities. One was to adapt to foreign norms and expectations, at least tactically. Itself a creation of U.N. consensus, Israel was already deeply ambivalent about the role and objectivity of the United Nations. But it nonetheless—and therefore—continued to make sure it was visibly and effectively represented there.[41]

At the same time, Israelis pursued external, particularly U.S., military assistance as a self-evident priority, if not an end in itself. Unsurprisingly, it was uphill work. No-strings grants were out of the question. Sales were constrained by Israeli liquidity and the Tripartite Declaration, but even pro forma reciprocity at the interservice level met serious resistance. Israelis bristled, for example, at U.S. itineraries that took U.S. generals and admirals to British and other Middle Eastern, but not Israeli, installations. U.S. generals, in turn, grew huffy at their exclusion from the Israeli loop. Pleading security and reciprocity alike, Israel's chief of staff, the still relatively unknown Brigadier General Moshe Dayan, vetoed a series of U.S. requests, apparently including a request for Israel's order of battle. The U.S. Army countered by rejecting some twenty-five of thirty requests from Israel's military attaché, Colonel Vivian (later Chaim) Herzog, who subsequently became Israel's president. A test of vanity, sovereignty, national interest, and bureaucratic politics on both sides, the squabbles soon demanded the attention of officials as senior as Eban and Walter Bedell Smith. "Isn't there something I can do to loosen up the Army?" Smith scrawled demonstratively at the bottom of a memo to NEA's John Jernegan. "Do we *want* to loosen up the Army?" Jernegan replied.[42]

Security guarantees, offshore contracts, and, above all, arms sales remained the definitive test of commitment for both sides. The last, of course, was also an issue that "would have to be taken up at the highest Governmental level," as a relatively junior State Department official reflexively pointed out after a Sunday stag lunch in Moshe Dayan's honor in late 1953. Reflective alike of dilemmas and disingenuousness, Dayan based his case on Israeli strength, not weakness, vis-à-vis the Arabs. Off the record, he was "confident that the Israeli forces, if they so desired, could occupy 4 out of 5 of the major Arab capitals within two weeks of the commencement of hostilities." The point of U.S. arms, he emphasized, was helping Israel resist "possible future Soviet aggression in the Near East, whereas the Arab States would not and could not resist such a move."[43]

Byroade hammered back. "Even with help on a very small scale" for Turkey, Pakistan, and Iraq, he told both Israeli visitors and American Jews, U.S. aid could work wonders in an area that constituted "a great vacuum in our security set-up." He meanwhile warned Eban and others that Israeli interest in U.S. jets could only complicate relations with Iraq, since Iraq could expect nothing comparable.

In June 1954, after weeks of ambivalence, Byroade finally came to a decision. Sale of planes not only would give Arabs the wrong idea, he concluded, but would also give Israel air superiority over "all the Arab states put together." Anyway, he added, it was the collective view of U.S. ambassadors in the region that the real threat to regional security lay "in some foolish move on the part of Israel." Meanwhile, he argued, Israel could buy what it needed elsewhere, "probably from the Swedes or the British." Dulles concurred. A few weeks later, the Defense Department politely brushed off Israeli bids for U.S. contracts.

Confident both of his cause and his calculations, Dulles was baffled by the persistence of Israeli anxiety. It was true, he conceded to Eban, that pending U.S. proposals might "not all [be] to Israel's liking, but [they were] in essence to Israel's benefit."[44] At the same time, Defense Department analysts pointed, like Dayan himself, to Israel's capacity for "effecting tactical victories over any one or combi-

nation of Arab forces deployed on or near Israel's borders," and to the likely impact
of French jet fighters that would make Israel capable of challenging not only the
Arabs in toto but even "existing RAF aircraft in the Middle East."[45]

Like official sensitivity to foreign opinion, reaction to the Egyptian dilemma too
remained ambivalent. The Foreign Ministry favored diplomatic contacts, the military favored unconventional confrontation.[46] To a point, there was even a disposition to try both courses at once, permitting, but also ultimately frustrating, U.S.
mediation.

Between 1954 and 1956, U.S. representatives actually tried at least twice to get
Nasser and Ben-Gurion to meet face to face. Elmore Jackson, a Quaker official, was
the first intermediary; Robert Anderson, an Eisenhower confidant and secretary of
the treasury, the second.[47] Not only a former secretary of the navy and of defense,
and later secretary of the treasury but a man the president "would be pleased to see
succeed him,"[48] Anderson was as close to the top as the administration could manage. Preceded by an offer of U.S. funding for Egypt's premier development project,
a high dam on the Upper Nile, he set off with a mandate from the president and a
briefing from the CIA. His mission, in effect, was to negotiate bilaterally the terms
that Dulles had proposed in his "Alpha" speech.[49]

But diplomacy was among the casualties as Israelis struck back at border raiders
with increasing fury and efficiency, and Egypt raised the stakes.[50] In principle, each
Israeli counterraid was supposed to "exact twice the price—or more—for every
attack." Uncertain if their targets were Palestinian irregulars, Syrian, Egyptian, or
Jordanian army units, or Arab civilians, the Israelis tended to hit all three.[51] Still,
the security dilemma remained insoluble. Only a tiny minority of Israelis found
retaliation politically counterproductive, yet it undeniably had its costs, both in
casualties and political attrition. Even the soldiers progressively recognized it as an
imperfect answer to the problem of Israel's porous borders. Their frustration led to
a gradual escalation, both in scale and conception, by a security establishment that
was itself increasingly disposed to define its own agenda.

By summer 1954, it was clear that Sharett had lost control of the Defense Ministry, that Defense Minister Pinhas Lavon had apparently lost control of the army,
and that the army itself, under the command of Dayan, seemed increasingly uncon-
trollable. Concurrent with the withdrawal of British forces from Egypt and what
Israelis tended to see as the U.S. courtship of Nasser, the volatile compound of fan-
tasy, brutality, stupidity, and political irresponsibility finally exploded in July. Like
France's Dreyfus affair or Watergate in the United States, the so-called Lavon affair
was to preoccupy first Israel's politicians, then its public, then its historical profession for years to come. The search for the smoking gun led instead to a jungle of
forgery, intrigue, and personal animus that was eventually to subvert Ben-Gurion's
authority, destroy a few political careers, and shake the nation's confidence in its
own good conscience.

Like Watergate, the idea behind the operation was almost embarrassingly simple. It was also in transparent violation of what was, purportedly, a basic rule of
Israeli covert operations. In theory, Israelis resolved to avoid involvement of local
Jews, both because they were already obvious targets of suspicion and to avoid putting other Jews at risk.[52] With the help of Egyptian Jews, Israeli agents nonetheless

arranged now for covert provocations of Britons and Americans, including fires at United States Information Agency (USIA) libraries in Cairo and Alexandria. Suspicion was supposed to fall on anti-Western Egyptians. The resulting damage was then supposed to leave its marks in London and Washington. Instead, the whole nasty business backfired almost literally. Shortly after a bomb exploded prematurely on the person of its bearer outside a Cairo movie theater, Egyptian authorities rolled up the operation altogether. Over the turn of the year 1954–1955, the defendants were tried and convicted. Eventually, two were executed, and others sentenced to long prison terms.

In January 1955, Israel countered with a particularly violent raid on the Egyptian garrison in Gaza. Egyptians later argued unpersuasively that it was the raid itself that led to the celebrated "Czech" arms deal. What seems a good deal more certain is that the raid led to Egyptian control of commando raids, which meant, for the first time, that an Arab state assumed direct responsibility for Palestinian guerillas.[53] Egypt also seized an Israeli ship and crew.

The CIA, which probably understood the Israeli situation as well as any agency in Washington, acknowledged Israel's paradoxical situation. It was a strategic asset to the United States in time of war; it was a political handicap in time of peace. The agency was also quick to recognize the inextricable linkages between Israel's security, economy, and psyche. There was just not enough money around to settle immigrants, provide for the common defense, and support the standard of living, a report prepared for the National Security Council in summer 1953 noted clinically. Reduced aid inevitably meant cuts in military expenditure, economic development, or the country's already austere standard of living. "Israel, however, regards national survival as its major problem" with predictable economic consequences, the report qualified. The authors were modestly optimistic about the prevailing strategic balance. At the same time, they acknowledged that outside aid would be a major determinant in any outcome, and even speculated that Israel might provoke an incident to increase the flow of aid.[54]

In the event, it was reasonable to assume that outside arms would leave their mark. The impact of demand was clear already as Israel and Egypt, each for its own reasons, looked abroad with increasing urgency. Ironically, as successive missions and intermediaries came and went with neither apparent progress, nor definitive rejection, Cairo and Jerusalem even seemed prepared to consider diplomatic contact, if it would make a favorable impression in Washington, and thereby advance the chance of getting U.S. arms. But unlike Israel, Egypt was also prepared and able to test the Tripartite Declaration. Fully engaged in the heady experience of Third World self-discovery, the new regime in Cairo discovered that it could negotiate pragmatically with East and West, naturally making sure that its potential suppliers were at least partially visible to one another.

In the short run, at least, the Soviet-Egyptian deal promised the dawn of a new buyer's market. For the Israelis, on the other hand, and certainly for Ben-Gurion, it was a moment of truth.[55] In October 1955, Sharett pursued Dulles to Paris to press his case against sale of arms to Egypt, and incidentally to confer with the French on possible purchase of their newest jet. For the Israelis, the talks in Paris were both good news and bad news. The French, it appeared, were happy to sell. On the other hand, their hands were tied by U.S. conditions. Till July 1956, new planes were reserved for NATO members. There was also no way to divert them surreptitiously without raising the questions of landing rights and supplementary fuel tanks. These only led back to the issue of U.S. approval.

From Paris, Sharett proceeded to the Big Four foreign ministers conference in Geneva to appeal for redress against encroaching isolation. The results were again both anticlimactic and alarming. Molotov denied that Soviet arms were any of Israel's business. Dulles reportedly refused even to discuss the matter, lest he thereby legitimize the Soviet initiative.[56] In December, Dulles rejected an Israeli request to send the arms, particularly planes, which at least one Israeli commentator believed might have prevented the Sinai campaign ten months later.[57]

Instead, Eisenhower resolved to send Anderson, his treasury secretary, as a personal emissary in January 1956. By this time, Ben-Gurion was hinting broadly at preventive war, as he had been since his return to power as defense and prime minister in November 1955. "If we should get a negative answer from the President on our request for arms, or none at all," he told Anderson in March, "we will have only one task: to look for our security." How literally this was meant is questionable. But it was clear that Israel at least reserved its options.

Yet supply was quite different from demand. By their own choice, the Western powers had locked themselves into a cartel. Stalin's successors, on the other hand, now seemed as mobile and sovereign as the czars. Mutual interest was reason enough to see a postcolonial world as a target of opportunity. But West German rearmament, the Baghdad Pact, and a Western military presence from Gibraltar to Pakistan were still more reasons to rediscover the Middle East for the first time since the Bolshevik revolution.

In time, after the Egyptians showed themselves unexpectedly independent, expensive, feckless, and ungrateful, the relationship proved both a tar baby and a Pandora's box. But in the short run, at least, Western consternation seemed only to confirm the brilliance of the Soviet move. Trying to match it could only deter presumptive clients in the "Northern tier," while alarming Israel and its U.S. supporters. A corresponding increase in Western aid to Syria and Iraq was also hard to reconcile with Israeli sensitivities. Given the inevitable impact on the Arabs, aid to Israel was no solution either. Allan Dulles, Director of Central Intelligence even conceded as much. "There is no good solution immediately available to us, but if the Egyptian-Israeli situation can be kept from erupting into open conflict," there might at least be a chance to "explore alternatives" with Egypt and Israel, he informed his brother.

A few months later, State Department I & R generated one of the era's most interesting introspections on the choices and possibilities then facing U.S. policy in the Middle East. Ironically, the document owed much of its originality to I & R's peculiar status as a loyal, but only lightly regarded, official opposition. Yet for all its marginality, the document is a benchmark of not only policy debate but freedom of discussion in Dulles's State Department. A road not taken in an age of Cold War conformity and anticommunist fundamentalism, it is striking in retrospect for appearing on contemporary maps at all. Within a year, anything like it would be virtually unimaginable. Meanwhile, all three authors had resigned in frustration from the department.[58]

At a time when U.S. debate revolved almost exclusively around containment of the Soviet Union, the paper instead proposed containment of the Cold War. The United States had three choices, the authors argued. It could increase its efforts to win clients in the Northern tier. It could seek to neutralize the Middle East on the basis of the status quo by making the Soviets, in effect, accessories to the Tripartite Declaration. Or it could go about its business in the Northern tier, irrespective of the deal between Cairo and Moscow.

Refreshingly unconventional even here, the authors saw their nominal middle course as the likeliest to make things worse without corresponding gain. To the extent that Northern tier beneficiaries believed the Egyptians got a better deal, the authors argued, they would only lean toward neutralism. At the same time, non-participants like Israel, Egypt, Syria, and Saudi Arabia would either become more dependent on the Soviet Union or take action that would exacerbate existing frictions, increasing the danger of local war.

The first course, the authors conceded, would presumably reassure states and regimes disposed to the West already. But they saw little military gain as a result. More U.S. aid might be good for Turkey, they acknowledged, which was anyway the only serious local source of resistance to the Soviets. But it could only be bad for Iraq, whose main reason for adhering to the Northern tier system, as they saw it, was "early annexation of Syria." This, in turn, only meant trouble with Egypt, Saudi Arabia, and eventually the Soviets. "Thus," they continued, "there would result a division of the Middle East, an arms race between Soviet-supplied states, and possibly local war."

Accordingly disposed to the second course, the authors conceded that neutralization would probably discourage Western clients, and incidentally confirm their most cynical view of Western reliability and motives. They were nonetheless willing to face the political costs. Local forces already sufficed to contain domestic communists, they argued. There was also at least a chance that reduced arms spending might pay off in badly needed domestic investment and nation-building, even if the affected states were less than friendly to the United States.

At the same time, the authors anticipated considerable, even dramatic, benefits to the region and the West. "Deprived of the means of altering the status quo, the Arabs and Israelis would in time come to accept it as fixed and unalterable, the only basis upon which they are likely to become reconciled to it," the authors contended. "And if the USSR became by implication a coguarantor of Israel's continued existence and territorial integrity, it would have taken on some of the obloquy attaching to a situation that has hitherto turned Arab opinion against the West. . . ."[59]

Later administrations were to show themselves more receptive to such flights of fancy, but in the aftermath of the Soviet-Egyptian arms deal, the audience for such arguments in Washington was close to zero. By September 1955, it was taken virtually for granted that the Middle East was a theater of the Cold War. More, not less, engagement was accordingly the order of the day, contingent only on the shifting local scene.

Meanwhile, even Israel had become a modest presence in the international arms market. In 1954, the Israeli air force acquired twelve new Meteor aircraft from Britain. The same year, it acquired a shipment of Ouragans from France on the condition that they not be used against Syria or Lebanon. By the end of 1955, Eban believed, Sharett was close to a deal with all three Western powers, save for an ill-timed reprisal against Syria.[60] On his return to power, Ben-Gurion was nonetheless able to exploit the prevailing U.S. distinction between "offensive" and "defensive" weapons to get even Eisenhower to supply Israel with antitank artillery.

To everyone's surprise, the real Israeli breakthrough came in Paris. Given prevailing constraints, the new connection was as considerable a coup as the Soviet-Egyptian liaison. Actually, its genesis owed a good deal to both the United States and Egypt, though in ways neither Eisenhower nor Nasser had imagined. Like Israelis, the French had long concluded that they lived in the shadow of U.S. favor. Though with radically different implications, they had also concluded—like State Department I & R—that U.S. pursuit of a Northern-tier defense would split the Middle East, and open it to the Russians. In a region where both superpowers seemed hell-bent on acquiring Arab clients, the French were fairly quick to see Egypt as a menace and Israel as a likely, and untapped ally.

Israel, in turn, was quick to reciprocate. The mutual discovery was favored by the disjunctions of government and civil service, civil arm and military arm, that were among the specialties of both countries. In both cases, the prime movers—Abel Thomas on the French side, Shimon Peres on the Israeli—were neither diplomats, parliamentarians, nor generals but thoroughly political young civil servants. Within a few years, the peculiarities this reflected were to help destroy the Fourth Republic. But till then, at least, they let the French Defense Ministry, much like its Israeli counterpart, conduct its own foreign policy, virtually independent both of parliaments and the nominal foreign policy establishment.

If French diplomats, like their Anglo-American peers, tended to debate the relative benefits of Arab and Israeli connections, French defense planners worried independently about the security of Suez. They then looked at the map of the region between Djibouti and the Mediterranean, took note of Israel's potential and France's strategic situation, and drew their conclusions. Contrary to popular assumption, the Israeli link preceded serious concern for the rebellion in Algeria. But indirectly, at least, it could be traced to memories of the traumatic defeat of 1940, long-term fear of French decline, the impact of Asian guerrillas on French strategic thought, and a reflexive disposition to link Arab nationalism with communism.[61] As so often in the arms trade, commercial interests also played a role: Israel was a market, Britain had already tapped it, independent French production required foreign sales.[62]

What clinched the relationship was as much the natural affinity of Social Democrats as the competitive advantage of Dassault, or the damaged identity and bone-deep anticommunism of conservative French soldiers, many of whose grandfathers had presumably taken it for granted that Captain Dreyfus was guilty. Committed alike to the legacy of the Resistance, a special relationship to Israel going back to the war and immediate postwar period, and their own Jacobin version of the *mission civilisatrice*,[63] French Socialists returned to government in January 1956, suspicious alike of appeasement, communism, and Nasser.[64] The title of Thomas's memoirs "How Israel Was Saved,"[65] may be somewhat disingenuous as a statement of what really moved French cabinet ministers en route to Suez. His career, on the other hand, was authentic Fourth Republic. Outside of Laborite Israel, or the Kennedy-era Pentagon, it is hard to imagine an equivalently young and dashing left-of-center technocrat in any other contemporary defense establishment.

By February, Christian Pineau, the new Socialist foreign minister, was asking Washington to approve diversion of twenty-four new Mystères IV for sale to Israel. In fact, without U.S. consent, Peres had already signed a contract for twelve in late December. Although U.S. approval came in May, Israel had already received the first twelve planes by April. By that time, Israel had signed a second contract for twelve with Bourgès-Manoury, again without U.S. consent. At a meeting in June, French and Israeli negotiators then agreed on another seventy-two planes, plus tanks, guns, rockets, radar, and other equipment.[65]

If French policy fell short at times of its proverbial clarity, U.S. policy also tended to the opaque. Eisenhower himself recalled the fuss in February 1956 when a consignment of eighteen tanks inadvertently left Brooklyn for Saudi Arabia. A cash sale, the shipment had apparently been approved years earlier by both the State and Defense departments. Under Israeli protest, the shipment was momentarily stalled, pending review of the Tripartite Declaration. It was then approved again a few days later.

"Soon after," the president added, Under Secretary of State Herbert Hoover, Jr., approached him about the sale of what Eisenhower recalled as "twelve" Mystères. Eisenhower had no objections, but was pleased that the French had asked. Only later, he noticed, did the original shipment "display a rabbit-like capacity for multiplication." Thomas nonetheless insisted that the French had scrupulously informed the Americans of their actions till September, and that the Americans had even assured spare parts, including extra fuel tanks, "should force be needed."

Eisenhower referred to the policy of the United States as "arms in escrow," that is, a program for laying away "appreciable quantities of military equipment" on U.S. ships in the Mediterranean for "instant dispatch" to any victim of regional aggression. Pentagon reservations notwithstanding, he regarded the scheme as visible demonstration of the "complete impartiality" of the United States between the Arabs, especially Egypt, and Israel. By July, when the rest of the Mystères reached Israel, a U.S. ship was already on station.[67] But it was not there long, the president added, since "aggressive acts by Nasser" had forfeited any claim to U.S. arms. On the other hand, it was clear that Eisenhower had no intention of supplying Israel either.

By summer 1956, an extended escalation was already well under way that tended only to confirm and exacerbate the respective suspicions of all sides. Though the choice of first step is inevitably arbitrary, it could be dated back at least to March, when Jordan's King Hussein infuriated the British by dismissing the British commander of his army at the behest, it was assumed, of Nasser. In April, Nikita Khrushchev, the new Soviet party secretary, had then worried Egypt by discussing regional arms control with Anthony Eden.

Dulles was delighted, but Nasser, understandably, was not. He was especially upset by the sale of French planes to Israel. In May 1956, he therefore recognized the People's Republic of China, the bugbear of U.S. conservatives, and itself still years away from U.N. membership. This time, it was the U.S. Congress that was infuriated. With White House acquiescence, Congress countered by blocking funds for the Aswan Dam on the Upper Nile. Only recently proposed as an incentive to peace with Israel and better relations with the United States,[68] the offer was now, in effect, left to die by attrition.

Among those opposed to it was a whole coalition of primarily domestic interests, including the Cold War lobby, which saw the People's Republic as the devil's work; the antiforeign lobby, which was opposed to spending U.S. money on foreigners per se; the cotton lobby, which saw no reason to help Egyptians raise more for export; the Israeli lobby, whose opposition was self-explanatory; a public works and power lobby that wanted its dams built close to home; and a foreign aid lobby, prepared to let the State Department have its way on aid to neutralist Egypt or neutralist Yugoslavia but not both.[69]

Given the constitutional weight of the executive branch, Dulles might still have tried to change some votes, had he seen a likely payoff, for example, exclusion of the Soviets from the Middle East or an Egyptian settlement with Israel. But Nasser was plainly unready for either. Contrary to post-facto legend, Dulles's denial of aid on July 19 was neither particularly abrasive nor an absolute rejection. Nasser's response, on the other hand, was in the grandest style. On July 27, the anniversary of the 1952 revolution, he took dead aim at a still more ancient sacred cow before an estimated audience of a quarter million in Alexandria, plus a radio audience of millions more. This time, he announced his country's intention to nationalize the Suez Canal, and use its revenues to finance the new dam.

The impact on Britain and France, as well as Israel, was immediate and dramatic. With an election already in view at the end of a very short tunnel, Dulles set to work to defuse the crisis, or at least win time. His chosen instrument was an international conference, where the global community of user-states, Britain and France self-evidently among them, could discuss alternatives. Among these was an elaborate escrow fund for collecting and holding canal fees, pending what would presumably be extended adjudication. But time, for once, was no concern. A war in the Middle East was about the last thing the U.S. administration needed. It could be reasonably assumed that the secretary was willing to see the conference continue indefinitely, or till election day, whichever came first.

For the British and French, not to mention Israelis, the priorities were quite the opposite. Anglo-French military talks began almost immediately. For the Europeans, Suez was both a fact and symbol. To Socialists in Paris no less than Conservatives in London, Nasser's provocation not only invited action but positively required it, if the world were to see how cause led to effect.[70] For the Israelis, barred in any case from Suez, the canal mattered only relatively, but a cocky Egypt mattered plenty. So did the risk of allowing Nasser's armed forces to receive and absorb their new Soviet equipment without challenge.

At the same time, Israelis had to face the risk of offending the United States. For Israeli Socialists, whose ambivalence contrasted oddly with the self-assurance of their French comrades, the imperialist overtones of the impending action were yet another problem. So was Britain. Ben-Gurion took Britain's hostility almost for granted. He also saw its commitments to the defense of Jordan, Iraq, and even Egypt as an insoluble obstacle to any agreement with Israel. In the best of all worlds, one advisor surmised, Ben-Gurion would far rather have awaited a danger more real and present than nationalization of the canal. He would also have liked more time to absorb the new French arms and to persuade the United States to support Israel in the event of war with Egypt.[71]

But Ben-Gurion could only work with what he had. What settled the case was the chance to act in concert with not only one big power but two, while the United States was busy electioneering. Time was passing; both France and Britain were already committed to action; France was even looking sympathetically at Israel. Who knew when there would again be such a chance? By September, Franco-Israeli military talks had led to an alliance.

The United States already preoccupied with the president's health, the impending election, and momentous events in eastern Europe, where both Poland and Hungary were close to open revolt against Soviet hegemony, remained in the dark. This was exactly where France and Britain wanted it. Unhappy with the role of aggressor assigned it by the Anglo-French scenario, ambivalent about embarrassing Eisenhower in midcampaign, and confident of U.S. aid thereafter, Israel was still for telling Washington. But in the end, Ben-Gurion too acceded to the majority. It took the United States till 1917 to enter one war, till 1941 to enter another, Mollet reminded him.[72]

Meanwhile, Israelis made a persuasive show of an impending war with Jordan. The signals were intended for both foreign and domestic audiences.[73] Even after all the beans were spilled, and "the Suez affair," "the Suez expedition," and even plain "Suez" were history, "Sinai Campaign" remained official Israeli usage. It was only months after it was over that Israelis finally learned of the triangular collusion negotiated at Sèvres October 22–24, 1956. Till then, even the immediate purpose of the exercise remained a closely guarded secret. Though individual ministers took part in planning it, the Israeli cabinet learned of the war only a day before action began on October 29. Soon afterward, at the United Nations, Eban unleashed his prodigious eloquence on behalf of an enterprise of which he himself had scarcely heard, and whose conduct was to fill him with growing ambivalence.

In fact, the inherent dissonances had only been resolved at Sèvres, where the hosts split the differences between the guests. It was clear that the Europeans wanted Israel as a fuse; its unilateral invasion of Egypt would then presumably both justify and ignite the Anglo-French charge.[74] It was no less clear that the Israelis were deeply uncomfortable about assuming the role of designated aggressor, whose allies would then ride to the rescue of world peace without acknowledging their relationship with Israel. As least as obsessed with historical memories as any of the other participants, Ben-Gurion was also anxious about the physical risk. There was no chance in the world of Egypt's bombing Paris or London. There was at least a possibility that it would bomb Tel Aviv.[75]

In the end, the Israelis agreed to proceed even without the British assurance they demanded. French pressure for action was one major factor. An ingenious operational compromise by Dayan was another. The idea was to avoid Gaza altogether.

Instead, Israeli paratroops would invade the Sinai behind Egyptian forces. Their attack would thus threaten but not physically jeopardize the canal, supply the "act of war" required by the British, and minimize Israeli casualties. The third decisive factor was a British concession. Visibly embarrassed even to be seen in the odd company with which historical circumstance, Nasser, and imperial decline had now presented them, the British agreed on paper to advance their strike on the Canal Zone by a day, and assure that there was no threat to Israel from Jordan. The gesture, reinforced by French planes and pilots assigned to defend Israeli air space, relieved Israeli anxieties. According to his chief of staff, Ben-Gurion carried away his copy of the British commitment like a trophy. Only a day after the meeting, Egypt, Iraq, and Syria announced a military treaty and a joint command. They thus inadvertently confirmed Ben-Gurion's disposition to proceed.[76]

On October 29, 1956, Israeli forces struck. Two days later, Egyptian forces were in panicky retreat and Israeli units were within striking distance of the canal. On November 5, they lifted the siege of the gulf at Sharm el-Sheikh. By then, the French and British had become both redundant and ridiculous, a victim at once of Israeli success, their own extravagant planning, and a last-minute crisis of British purpose.

On the other hand, the diplomatic war had just begun. By October 26, U.S. intelligence was already aware of Israeli mobilization. Directly challenged by Eisenhower himself, Ben-Gurion insisted that the buildup was strictly defensive, while British sources hinted that Jordan might be the intended target. In fact, this had been Eisenhower's suspicion all along. By the morning of October 29, Dulles had also become suspicious of the French. By early evening, the indignation was general. Since 1950, the president declared, the United States had assured its support to any victim of Middle East aggression. The question now was how to deliver it. Given the Israeli initiative, it seemed to him both a matter of logic and honor to invoke the Tripartite Declaration.[77] Had Israel moved alone, Eisenhower later speculated, the United States would have acted anyway, "possibly initiating a blockade."[78] But as the picture gradually cleared, he only became more furious at what he clearly viewed as a marriage of stupidity and betrayal. It was bad enough that the French and British were so reckless as to jeopardize Europe's oil supply. He was horrified that they should also risk Soviet intervention in support of Nasser.

"What was the point of offending the entire Muslim world?" he asked Eden rhetorically in an unsent cable he nonetheless cited in his memoirs. To his horror, he discovered not only that the British were unwilling to act against the Israelis but that they regarded the Tripartite Declaration "as ancient history."[79] He was equally appalled to be so deceived by his closest allies, and especially outraged that the Israelis might think they could get away with such a thing on the eve of a U.S. election. "I gave strict orders to the State Department that they should inform Israel that we would handle our affairs exactly as though we didn't have a Jew in America," he informed an old friend a few days later.[80]

While Dulles raised the issue of financial sanctions against Israel, the State Department prepared a draft resolution, identifying Israel as the sole aggressor, and calling on U.N. members to suspend all military, economic, and financial assistance till Israeli forces had withdrawn. By the time the Security Council convened, U.S. Ambassador Henry Cabot Lodge, Jr., included Egypt in the call for withdrawal, and the U.S. resolution condemned not only Israel but, by implication, Britain and France. The Soviet Union, on the threshold of a memorably brutal intervention in Hungary, meanwhile dispatched notes to Eden, Guy Mollet, and Ben-Gurion, threatening the use of "every kind of modern destructive weapon."[81] The Soviet text converged with the U.S. resolution. After the predictable French and British vetoes, the matter then went to the General Assembly.[82]

By the evening of October 31, Eisenhower was on the air, proclaiming to the world the nation's opposition. "Allright, Foster," he reportedly announced to his closest associate, "you tell 'em, goddamit, we're going to apply sanctions, we're going to the United Nations, we're going to do everything that there is so we can stop this thing."[83] It was a policy that would "lose some Israeli votes," Vice President Richard Nixon conceded in a call to Dulles from the campaign trail. But "there weren't many" of those, and anyway "at such a time you don't want a pipsqueak for Pres.," he added. "How wonderful the Pres. has been," Dulles chimed in. "He will not sacrifice foreign policy for political expediency."[84]

But this still left room for prudence. "We should not do anything that makes us look as if we are trying to get an excuse to pick on Israel," Eisenhower warned Dulles after reading Walter Lippmann, Washington's most influential columnist and reviewing the latest speech by Adlai Stevenson, the Democratic candidate. "If we do anything against them, then we have to do something against Fr and Br." At an NSC meeting within the hour, he was still adamant about "any kind of aid to Israel, which was an aggressor." On the other hand, the indignation was already qualified. "Israel had not yet been branded as an aggressor, had it?" he asked disarmingly. In fact, as the president concluded before the meeting ended, he was genuinely anxious about "the prospect of imposing a blockade against Israel." Nor did he "want the British and the French to be branded aggressors." Treasury Secretary George Humphrey favored leaving the question to the United Nations. Stassen, now a special presidential assistant, preferred to go easy on the British, steering instead toward a cease-fire and negotiated peace. "He was compelled to point out to Governor Stassen," that it was the British and French who had just vetoed a cease-fire proposal, Dulles answered "with great warmth." Yet it appeared that Dulles had his own reservations. "The Sec. is afraid it will prove a disaster but they may prove they are right—the Sec. does not know," Senator Walter F. George, the chairman of the Foreign Relations Committee, was told.[85]

As the debate moved to the General Assembly, the United States was trying to regain the initiative, not least to buffer its embattled allies, and Eban was trying hard to control the damage. It was true that Mrs. Franklin Roosevelt defended the Israeli invasion; and even George Kennan, no friend of Israel *or* the Soviet Union, condemned U.S. policy for the odd company it now kept at the United Nations. But by this time, the damage extended to Israel's most loyal supporters. Editorial opinion was mixed. Measurable public opinion was confused and ambivalent. Although surveys revealed that nearly half of all Americans had no determinable opinion, a third disapproved of Israel's action and fewer than 20 percent were clearly supportive.[86]

Even American Jews were upset and confused. Unilateral Israeli action with respect to guerrilla raids, Egyptian arms, and Arab politics made sense. The Anglo-

French intervention was something else. It was the first time Israeli representatives had encountered American-Jewish resistance to an Israeli initiative.[87] As spokesman for the organized minority of American Zionists, Emanuel Neumann took to national radio on November 4 to identify Israel with the United States that had sent an expeditionary force to Mexico to counter Pancho Villa's bandits under President Woodrow Wilson. Recalling the Czechoslovakia so fatefully sacrificed to Hitler in 1938, he appealed in the interests of the whole free world for U.S. support against "The Hitler of the Nile." The non-Zionist Jewish majority meanwhile began to search for a face-saving exit from the conflict.[88]

Picking his way from Joseph M. Proskauer and Jacob Blaustein to Thomas E. Dewey, Eban discovered and reported the president's concern for a permanent occupation of the Sinai plus the Pentagon's concern that the Soviets too might intervene in the Middle East.[89] Ben-Gurion was accommodating, but only to a point. Before he withdrew, he announced, he wanted a peace treaty, including clear assurances that Egypt would abstain thenceforth from raids, boycotts, blockades, and any further acts of war against Israel.

Meanwhile, Eban appealed to Dulles to think of how Nasser's collapse would advance both peace and containment. But rather than let him collapse, the United States was actually resolved to save him. As always, Eban's speech to the General Assembly was an artistic success. The vote was nonetheless 64–5 with six abstentions. France, Britain, Australia, and New Zealand joined Israel in the minority. As in 1947, the majority included both the United States and the Soviet Union.

Given France's political and military dependence on Britain, and Britain's political and economic dependence on the United States, disengaging France and Britain proved relatively easy.[90] Disengaging Israel was another story. To Eban's dismay, Ben-Gurion hung tough in a Knesset speech on November 7, declaring unilateral abrogation of the 1948–1949 armistice lines and opposition to U.N. intervention.[91] Eisenhower and the State Department hung even tougher. Outraged and exasperated, the president convened his senior officials, and threatened suspension of all private as well as government aid. "The Secretary, having in mind the election results, stressed that this was the right moment to take this step with the Israelis," it was noted at Dulles's Walter Reed Hospital bedside.[92]

Meanwhile, the administration set out to navigate its new course through the ruins of the Trilateral Declaration, the wreckage of the regional balance it had pursued since taking office, and the ever-more-baffling landscape of a postimperial Middle East. "The Bear is still the central enemy," Eisenhower emphasized.[93] The strategic priorities followed from there: keep the tankers moving, keep the Soviets out, keep the "moderate" Arabs moderately happy. In theory, even practice, there were discernible links between the status of the canal and Israel's right to use it. Logically, these led to the collateral issues of Israeli-Egyptian relations, Israeli security, and the Straits of Tiran.

Law and fact were a practical nuisance. For the moment, Washington saw the reopening of the Canal as its own reward. After foreign troops were out, a buffer force in place, and the Canal appropriately cleared and dredged, it was argued solemnly, the other issues could be taken as they came. There were obbligato declarations of loyalty to traditional allies, and even pro forma invitations to Mollet and Eden. November was nonetheless devoted to squeezing the French and British so hard that Parisian cabbies refused American fares, and London's Conservative government disintegrated.[94]

From December on, it was Israel's turn to take the heat, as Arthur H. Dean, a senior presidential assistant, made clear to Eban and Israel's new foreign minister, Golda Meir. Did they really want to be "arrayed against Northwest Europe, who would say if it weren't for Israel, they could get the Canal cleared?" Dean asked.[95] He added preemptively that the administration felt no friendliness toward Nasser; that there was no way back to the status quo; that it was time for another crack at the Arab-Israeli conflict; and also time for substantial investment in development aid to the region to advance the likelihood that such an effort would succeed. But the United States still seemed tilted toward the Arabs—providing a suitable addressee could be found to tilt back.

"One of the measures that we must take is to build up an Arab rival of Nasser," Eisenhower announced in a personal note to Dulles. "If we could build him up as the individual to capture the imagination of the Arab world, Nasser would not last long." It was obviously not the first time the subject had come up. The president added that the administration even had a "natural," if unspecified, candidate. This was presumably Saudi Arabia's King Saud, who was invited to visit the United States a few weeks later.[96] The idea that the United States could help make, and that the region would accept, Saud as surrogate king of the Arabs is not only a clue to U.S. problems in the Middle East. With the more or less concurrent choice of Iran's Shah Reza Pahlavi and Vietnam's Ngo Dinh Diem for more or less similar roles in other places, it also suggested a general cause of U.S. problems in the world.

Meanwhile, Ben-Gurion was all but invited *not* to come to Washington; Eden only rarely found someone to talk to above the assistant secretary level; and it was nearly the end of the year before Meir managed even to see Dulles. Their exchange, in its way, was prototypical. Meir concentrated on the future of Gaza, where she wanted the Egyptians out; and access and security in the Straits of Aqaba, where she wanted international guarantees in. While conceding on Aqaba, Dulles focused on high principle. "The Secretary," the transcript records, "could not see where Israel's present course could bring about any solution to Israel's problems."[97]

Eban got the message. After huddling with congressional leaders and Americans as diverse and ecumenical as Dulles's legal advisor, Herman Phleger, Eisenhower's old associates Walter Bedell Smith, Robert Murphy, and Anderson, and even the generic establishmentarian wisemen John J. McCloy and General Lucius D. Clay, he began preparing his strategy. Israel's long-term goal, as he saw it, was orderly withdrawal from the Sinai and assurance of access to the Straits of Tiran. Its priorities were oil, the Gulf of Aqaba, and access to East Africa and Asia. The last of these, he added, was "one of the central visions that had inspired us in accepting the UN partition idea."[98]

At a four-hour meeting on January 1, 1957, Eisenhower and Dulles unveiled the administration's new plan before gun-shy congressional leaders. The president made every effort to be reassuring. His only concern was communist intervention, he told his ambivalent listeners. Four days later, he presented an "Eisenhower doctrine" in a special message to Congress. It called for $200 million in special economic aid to the region plus a pledge to meet "overt armed aggression from any nation controlled by International Communism."[99]

The trick was to reconcile the administration's vision of regional dynamics with the Israeli view of regional stability. What Israel demanded—from a U.N. force in the Straits of Tiran to de facto annexation of Gaza—was, in fact, incompatible with assurances Israel really wanted, U.N. Secretary General Dag Hammarskjöld informed Lodge. What was also clear, the frustrated Hammarskjöld added, was that the Israelis were "apparently counting on American support."[100]

Of this, at least, Dulles needed no reminding, particularly after February 2, when the General Assembly by 74–2 demanded immediate Israeli withdrawal from Egypt. Only France and Israel opposed the resolution. The United States voted with the majority. With Arab and Soviet-bloc abstention, a second resolution then called for reinstatement of the 1949 Israeli-Egyptian armistice agreement and deployment of a U.N. peacekeeping force.[101]

On the contrary, Israeli expectations were the unstated premise of three contradictory, yet complementary, lines of U.S. argument in the weeks that followed. Israel should stop demanding assurances of the United States, Dulles repeatedly told Eban, because the United States had no mandate to supersede the United Nations. The United States was the key to effective U.N. action, he told Lodge, since the Arabs would otherwise turn to the Soviets. Meanwhile, he told himself, unless the administration could make the Israelis back down, it was all up with the U.S. position in the region.[102]

William F. Knowland, the Senate Republican leader and a member of the U.S. delegation to the U.N. General Assembly, and even Henry Luce, the redoubtable publisher of *Time,* warned Dulles against sanctions. He was "well aware how almost impossible it is in this country to carry out [a] foreign policy not approved by the Jews," the secretary of state moaned into the phone on February 11. "That does not mean I am anti-Jewish," he told Luce prophylactically, "but I believe in what George Washington said in his Farewell Address that an emotional attachment to another country should not interfere."[103] "It was impossible to hold the line because we got no support from the Protestant elements of the country," he informed a friend a few weeks later. "All we get is a battering from the Jews."[104]

Cagey, equivocal, high-minded, and pessimistic in turn, Dulles tended accordingly to look out on a landscape of erosion, descending spirals, and slippery slopes. Israeli adamancy meant the end of the United Nations as a credible peacekeeping body, the threat of European economic collapse, Soviet hegemony in the Middle East as the Arabs turned to the Russians, and renewed hostilities leading to general war, the administration argued to increasing effect. But its position also risked war with a Congress so opposed to sanctions that a continued stall, as Dulles spelled out to Lodge, seemed the only way to avoid exposing the administration's weakness.[105]

Ben-Gurion, on the other hand, seemed genuinely baffled by U.S. obtuseness. It was obvious, he assumed, that Egypt, the aggressor, had effectively voided the 1949 armistice; that there was therefore no way back to the status quo; that the only way to stop renewed incursions was an Israeli presence in Gaza; and that the Straits of Tiran must be internationally policed from the western side of the Gulf of Aqaba. In the prime minister's eyes, pressure on Israel not only constituted a double standard but subverted the U.N. credibility it was intended to confirm.

In return for a civil role in Gaza, an *aide mémoire* declared both touchingly and a bit disingenuously on February 15, Israel was even prepared to "make a supreme effort" on behalf of the population of Gaza, that is, to integrate as much as a third in the Israeli economy, repatriate an unspecified number, and somehow resettle the rest.[106] Searching as usual for a neutral way to route economic aid to the region, the Americans were unimpressed. "I couldn't get through to the Americans—least of all to the U.S. secretary of state, that cold, gray man, John Foster Dulles—that our very life depended on adequate guarantees," Golda Meir recalled.[107] For its own part, executive-branch Washington demanded that Israel pull out unilaterally and, neither for the first nor last time, deplored Israeli unreasonableness.

Neither for the first nor last time, congressional Washington meanwhile saw things differently. In early February 1957, seventy-five House Democrats and forty-one Republicans asked the administration to refrain from sanctions. On February 11, the Senate Democratic policy committee and Senate Republican leadership took the same position unanimously. In Eban's view, the breakthrough came the same day when the State Department handed him an *aide memoire* assuring right of passage in the Straits of Tiran, declaring the Gulf of Aqaba an international waterway, and endorsing a U.N. peacekeeping force between Israel and Gaza.[108] Murphy encouraged the ambassador to regard it as "sensational." Even the *New York Times's* James Reston "called me three times . . . to emphasize, with some emotion, that Israel would make a grave error if she neglected a historic opportunity to transform her status in the Red Sea and Gulf of Eilat and—no less important— to achieve a new atmosphere of understanding with the U.S.," Eban reported.[109]

To Eban's horror, Ben-Gurion remained unwilling to take yes for an answer. The prime minister continued not only to oppose any Egyptian return to Gaza but to demand an Israeli civil administration. Convinced that further concessions would only confirm a Jewish mortgage on U.S. policy, Dulles too refused to budge and the United States again threatened global economic sanctions.[110] But if the administration held the Israeli economy hostage, Congress held a pistol to the Eisenhower doctrine.

On February 20, the impasse led to a two-and-a-half hour White House summit with Vice President Nixon and twenty-six congressional leaders in attendance. The meeting opened with a statement from the president, but Dulles and Lodge did most of the talking. As president himself a half generation later, Nixon concluded that Eisenhower and Dulles had made a bad mistake.[111] But squeezed symmetrically between Eisenhower, who was determined to put Israel on the spot, and Knowland, his patron and fellow California Republican, who was resolved to do the contrary, the vice president was remembered only for his silence.[112]

Once again, the administration expressed fear of general war if the Israelis remained in Egypt, and the Arabs appealed for Soviet help, while Dulles held out for consistency, order, and symbol in U.S. foreign policy. The double standard argument—that Israel took the heat for invading Egypt while the United States voted with the Soviets, who invaded Hungary—was left bruised but standing. It was a fact of diplomatic life, Lodge explained, that the United Nations would never vote sanctions against either superpower. It was also true, as Dulles pointed out, that the prerogative to use the veto, without which the United States would never have joined the United Nations, constituted a double standard in itself. The United States had still found innumerable ways to impose sanctions on the Soviet Union far beyond any considered for Israel. Fumbling for alternatives, the legislators successively considered postponement of the U.N. debate, a negative vote on the pending General Assembly resolution, and a new and less specific text. Dulles waved them off. In case of failure, the United States "will inherit the disaster," he argued. One way or another, the United Nations would act. "The United States effort should be to get the best resolution that would satisfy the U.N. majority even though it fell short of what the United States would like."[113]

In the end, the legislators found themselves reluctant either to support administration policy or call for Israeli withdrawal. An agnostic on Middle East affairs as in others, Arkansas's Senator William Fulbright inquired about getting the message across to Israel by congressional resolution, and so avoiding a U.N. shoot-out. But both the pressures of time and the explosiveness of the issues spoke clearly against that idea, as did the obvious hesitation of all present to suggest the United States would go to war to enforce Israeli withdrawal. As Fulbright himself pointed out, it was not even certain there was a consensus for withdrawal unless "it could be certain that Israel would get justice in the future."[114]

The consensus instead was to let Eisenhower bell the cat. The president was not averse. In fact, he had been thinking about the speech for the past ten days, he admitted, "and ran briefly over the possible highlights of such a statement." Georgia's Senator Richard B. Russell, the formidable chairman of the Armed Services Committee, and Sam Rayburn, the legendary Speaker of the House, fell in line. The president could "crystallize the thinking" of the American people, Russell said. "America has either one voice or none," Rayburn added, "and the one voice was the voice of the President even though not everyone agreed with him."[115]

At 9:00 P.M. the same evening the president accordingly appeared again on national television. High-minded by default, as its principal author, Emmet John Hughes, later recalled, the president's speech was, in fact, an improvisation. Its genesis, he added, was only complicated by the secretary of state, "a lawyer," who "largely ignored the word 'law.' " Himself disposed to "relate the U.S. position to the concept of 'law' in an international community," Hughes opted instead to dump Dulles's draft in favor of his own. Warming to the task in the ambiance of a White House on deadline, Hughes made equality before the law his operative principle. "No other reasonable approach occurred to me . . . *without* vilifying our allies," he later explained. To its author's surprise, the speech came out "surprisingly coherent," and Eisenhower himself remembered it as tough.[116]

In the end, there were no sanctions, in part because the administration blinked, in part because the Israelis did. At a meeting of the National Security Council on February 22, Dulles again held forth on the need to limit immigration to Israel, if only to make a positive impression on the Arabs. In the same spirit, George Allen, a former assistant secretary for Near Eastern affairs and now director the U.S. Information Agency, even proposed lifting tax deductibility on private American contributions to Israel, then estimated at $100 million.

At this point, Lewis L. Strauss, the chairman of the Atomic Energy Commission and the administration's most senior Jewish member, spoke up. It was the first time he had been known to address the subject of Jews and Israel on record. Considering that only Israel had made room for survivors of the Holocaust, he declared, and that only Israel was likely to make room for Jewish refugees from Arab countries, he believed that constraints on U.S. philanthropy would be "resented by people of both political parties, of all religions and all nationalities." Dulles conceded the point. Allen later apologized for his proposal.[117]

Meanwhile, as Eban made clear on his return from Jerusalem, his government's position too had changed. The Israelis were now prepared to waive their claim to guarantees, subject only to U.S. recognition of Israel's right to defend its ships, and assurances by the United States and other maritime powers of their intent to defend their own ships in the Gulf of Aqaba. The Israelis also demanded only that Gaza not revert to the status quo ante. While warning that Egypt would not let itself be pushed out of Gaza, Dulles commended the ambassador for "a constructive and masterly" presentation.[118]

From here, the action moved to the United Nations, where Dulles and Eisenhower made French Foreign Minister Christian Pineau their authorized agent.[119] In collaboration with U.N. Secretary General Hammarskjöld, Pineau was to work out a withdrawal formula acceptable to all parties. At the same time, mindful of Walter Bedell Smith's admonition to soften up Ben-Gurion, Eban negotiated with Dulles on the settlement in the gulf, while testing U.S. resolve on an Egyptian return to Gaza.

By the end of February, the deal was in place, its clincher discreetly attributed to Canada's Foreign Minister Lester Pearson. The package included Israeli withdrawal from Gaza and Sharm el-Sheikh, a U.N. buffer force (UNEF) on the Egyptian side of the Israeli-Egyptian frontier, and U.S. assurance of unrestricted navigation in the Straits.[120] Looking back on the arrangement from his memoirs, Eban found it good: "an American-Israeli contract in every real sense."[121] Meir, on the other hand, recalled "a compromise of sorts" that assured passage in the gulf, but failed to keep the Egyptians out of Gaza.

But save in the furious world of Israeli domestic politics where Ben-Gurion asserted it jeopardized his government,[122] it was hard to believe that keeping Egypt out of Gaza was ever a real alternative. As Dulles spelled out to Eban with icy consistency, exclusion of Egypt would not only threaten Egyptian compliance with the rest of the deal but risk the whole status quo so laboriously negotiated eight years earlier. If the armistice agreement went, the status quo ante went, and so on back to the partition resolution of 1947, he argued. In whose interest was that? If the United States could live with the Korean armistice, he declared, Israel could surely live with the Egyptian armistice.[123]

On March 1, after intense consultation between Eban and Dulles, Meir finally declared Israel's intention to withdraw as per an agreement that deferred to Israeli sensibilities by neatly substituting "international obligations" for "armistice agreement" wherever the issue came up. Lodge's acknowledgment, a few degrees cooler than Israelis anticipated, then set off a final crisis, but Eban, who pointed to what Israeli reconsideration was likely to cost in Washington, won set and game. "I believe that Israeli will have no cause to regret having thus conformed to the strong sentiment of the world community," Eisenhower cabled Ben-Gurion March 2. Two days later, the Israelis finally confirmed their withdrawal.[124]

In the event, the Israelis left Gaza and the Sinai on schedule. They were replaced by Egyptian administrators, but not soldiers. Navigation rights then passed the test when Israeli-chartered U.S. tankers called without incident at Eilat. Thenceforward ten years of relative peace obtained on the Israeli-Egyptian border. Meir, who, as prime minister seventeen years later, would again be concerned with withdrawal from Egypt, had nonetheless reached her own ambivalent conclusions on the solidity of U.S. assurances.[125]

Undeterred both by Israeli ambivalence and Senator Richard B. Russell, who wanted to cut aid, the Eisenhower doctrine now passed the Senate by 72–19, after having passed the House by 355–61. Because support for Israel was ordinarily subsumed in the foreign aid package, this was the only law specific to the Middle East to pass the 90th Congress. Yet for all its subtlety, it was the first U.S. policy statement of any kind to declare Israel a strategic beneficiary and presumptive partner.

The key was Israel's candidacy for aid in the event of communist aggression. Ironically, it was just this that caused Israelis to regard the breakthrough with ambivalence. Familiarly, the left-wing parties, Mapam and Achdut haAvodah, were reluctant to provoke the Soviets with a claim on U.S. support, while the right-wing opposition, for all its sturdy anticommunism, was unwilling in principle to support the government. On the other hand, rejection of the U.S. offer was no solution either, for both domestic and diplomatic reasons. On May 21, 1957, the ambivalence found expression in a communiqué of almost aggressive blandness. It then being agreed that it was neither in Israel's interest to embarrass the government nor to offend the United States, there was a stage-managed ratification in the Knesset: fifty-nine deputies voted for the government's tepid resolution, five Communists predictably voted against it, and the opposition abstained.[126]

It was perhaps at least as ironic that the Eisenhower Doctrine remained a square peg in a world of round holes. Within months of its ratification, official Washington saw threats to the stability and even independence of both Syria and Jordan, and growing evidence of Soviet influence in Syria and Egypt. Yet Lebanon, in March 1957, was the only Arab state to accept the U.S. offer officially, and both Moslems and domestic leftists saw President Camille Chamoun's acceptance as a provocation.[127]

In summer 1958, the administration actually sent troops to Lebanon after the Iraqi monarchy collapsed. Jordan too looked shaky. If Washington looked on with concern, its Middle Eastern clients, particularly the royal ones, reacted to events in Baghdad and Amman with threshold panic. At a White House briefing for congressional leaders, CIA Director Allen Dulles reported that Chamoun wanted U.S. troops within two days; that Jordan's Hussein had only barely preempted a plot against his life, and that Saudi Arabia's King Saud demanded immediate U.S., U.K. and Baghdad Pact intervention in Jordan and Iraq. His country would otherwise simply go along with Egypt.

Dulles was particularly concerned about Israeli reaction. "There is no doubt that Israel will be alarmed at the prospect of being surrounded by Arab states under Nasir influence, and if Jordan falls to Nasir, might move to take over West Jordan to the Jordan River," Dulles speculated. "Israeli mobilization is probable."[128] Within a few days, U.S. marines were en route to Beirut, despite serious reservations from U.S. Ambassador Robert McClintock,[129] and although even Eisenhower recalled that the decision was unpopular in Israel, Ben-Gurion expressed his concern by letting Britain overfly Israeli airspace to come to Jordan's aid.

The purpose of the Lebanese expedition, in Eisenhower's words, was "to stop the trend toward chaos,"[130] but there was little support, though also little overt opposition, for U.S. intervention. Speaker Rayburn feared intervention in a civil war. Fulbright, now chairman of the Foreign Relations Committee, was doubtful even that the crisis was communist-inspired. His skepticism was confirmed by Robert Murphy, Eisenhower's representative on the spot.[131] The troops went nonetheless, and unlike their successors a generation later, came home intact.

In the end, Lebanon was the single case of U.S. intervention on behalf of the single government that officially accepted the Eisenhower Doctrine. But rather than justify its action by the doctrine's stricture against "international communism," Washington instead found it prudent to fall back on the Mansfield amendment, its fail-safe or umbrella clause: "The United States regards as vital to the national interest and world peace, the preservation of the independence and integrity of the nations of the Middle East."[132] After all the Cold War fear and trembling that produced it, the Eisenhower Doctrine was never officially invoked.

5

To the Brink and Over

Europeans, Mideasterners, and Americans alike learned something from the Suez campaign, but it was practically inevitable that the lessons would be different. For at least three of the protagonists, what the United States was believed to have done and not done was still among the basic lessons of the affair.

No less ambivalent about Nasser, no less apprehensive of Krushchev's adventurism than their European allies, Americans had nonetheless ended up saving the former and voting with the latter, and in the face of nuclear blackmail at that. Given the number of weapons in its arsenal, not to mention the technology available for delivering them, the Soviet threat was dubiously credible. Like all nuclear threats, it nonetheless got people's attention, and not only in Jerusalem and Tel Aviv, with its reference to a "question mark against the very existence of Israel as a state." At least symbolically, the threat was seen as a first potential test of the will of the United States to risk New York for Paris. Had the Soviet Union, in fact, hit Britain or France, it would have been destroyed "as night follows day," General Alfred Gruenther, the Allied supreme commander in Europe, made clear.[1] But as Guy Mollet, the French prime minister, warned Ben-Gurion before the action even began, the Americans had taken years to get to Europe, despite the impending threat of two world wars. All subsequent experience only confirmed that U.S. support, like fire insurance, commanded a stiff premium—assuming, as the Israelis themselves might have added, that the Americans were even prepared to sell.

But life without U.S. insurance was no choice either. Though Suez was sui generis, and the Franco-Israeli relationship would survive another decade, it was already clear that, sooner or later, the partners of 1956 would again go separate ways. Meanwhile, as Americans noted with growing discomfiture, Britain, France, and Israel alike had arrived independently at at least two, and even three, common conclusions. The first, and most obvious, was that U.S. reservations must not again be allowed to frustrate or deflect them from independent action in what they believed to be their own best interests. The second, implied rather than explicitly posted, was the need to acquire some countervailing options, incentives, and instruments to relieve, or even reverse, American pressure.

The third was the logical and the practical consequence of the other two: acquisition of the independent deterrent in its most contemporary form. Britain, already in possession of a bomb, set out to build a missile of its own to carry it. France, already equipped with considerable nuclear infrastructure, but as yet with neither bomb nor missile, set out to devise and manufacture both. The project was already under way before the men of Suez had even left office. It only gained in single-mind-edness and official favor with the collapse of the Fourth Republic in 1958, and the coming of a new regime under Charles de Gaulle.

Meanwhile, with French assistance that presumably included illegal reexports of U.S. heavy water, Israel had undertaken its own nuclear program, not least on the basis of Franco-Israeli exchanges reaching back to the late 1940s. Franco-Israeli conversations on the first step, a nuclear reactor at Dimona, seem actually to have begun in mid-September 1956, and to have resumed immediately after Suez.[2] The decision was so controversial that six of the seven members of Israel's nuclear regulatory agency had resigned by 1957. Contested on political, strategic, and economic grounds alike, the nuclear option reportedly divided both the government and the Labor establishment. Yet despite challenges from the current and future finance ministers, Levi Eshkol and Pinhas Sapir, and the current and future foreign ministers, Golda Meir and Yigal Alyon, Shimon Peres, Moshe Dayan, and, above all, Ben-Gurion, not only got their way, but even, reportedly, got private contributors in New York and elsewhere to put up the money.[3]

By the time Dimona came on-line in 1963, it was capable of producing weapons-grade plutonium in substantial quantities. Because the reactor was fueled by natural uranium that Israel itself could provide, Dimona was also insulated against U.S. interference.[4] By 1965, Arieh Dissentchik, the editor of *Ma'ariv,* acknowledged in a conversation with William C. Foster, the director of the newly created U.S. Arms Control and Disarmament Agency, that Israel was "four or five years ahead in know-how in the nuclear field and could quickly take the last steps take make the weapons." He considered it a "vitally important deterrent."[5]

Dimona itself was the logical consequence of a program under way at the Weizmann Institute since 1948. In 1952, the government had created the Israel Atomic Energy Commission under the Ministry of Defense. A year later, reportedly, the new agency, in turn, signed a cooperation agreement with its French counterpart. In 1954, an Israeli heavy-water plant went into operation. Under President Eisenhower's Atoms for Peace plan, the United States even supplied Israel a small research reactor at Nahal-Soreq in 1955, which started operation in 1960. Though technology and treaty constraints alike made Soreq virtually unusable as a weapons plant, it nonetheless remained a place where Israeli nuclear scientists learned their trade.[6]

By all indications, Ben-Gurion had already decided for a bomb by the middle 1950s, although the decision for Dimona *per se* was only taken after Suez. In 1957, the French and Israelis agreed on a common project that would make French expertise in the production of plutonium available to the Israelis, and Israeli expertise in the production of heavy water to the French. Though under continual surveillance from American U-2s, the project remained secret till December 19, 1960, when it appeared for the first time among the news the *New York Times* saw fit to print. Two days later, Ben-Gurion acknowledged Dimona before the Knesset.

The news of Dimona made a considerable impression in Washington. Only days before leaving office, the Eisenhower administration reportedly wanted the reactor dismantled, and backed down only after Ben-Gurion agreed to de facto inspection by U.S. scientists. Desalinization of sea water and general export competitiveness were plausibly numbered at least among the collateral motives for the Franco-Israeli program. But Israel's strategic isolation and Ben-Gurion's own Gaullist turn of mind in security matters assured continued concern, especially in Washington, with its growing anxieties about worldwide nuclear proliferation.[7]

For all the drama of 1956–1957, and the potentially momentous consequences of a nuclear program, the Israeli security equation and the Israeli consensus remained virtually unchanged. The memorable success of Israeli preemption and the U.N. buffer force on the Egyptian border assured, at least, that there were no more raids from Gaza. But there was no resumption of the Israeli-Egyptian flirtations of the pre-Suez period, and certainly no peace with Egypt or any other Arab state. By early 1957, official Washington took it for given that hopes for a comprehensive peace had died between Rhodes and Lausanne years earlier in the aftermath of the first Arab-Israeli war. Instead of peace, what Americans offered was the piecemeal pragmatics of crisis management—buffer forces, security guarantees, arms sales both direct and indirect—with the American profile itself kept low to the ground. Considering what went before, Abba Eban had reason to regard these as a watershed success. "The understandings we reached became an American-Israeli contract in every real sense," he recalled.[8] But for the moment, at least, the days of front-burner attention and red-carpet U.S. emissaries with a presidential mandate were over. The coming of Secretary of State William Rogers, the plausible successor to Mark Ethridge, Eric Johnston, or Robert Anderson, was to await another two wars, and at least ten years.

If Israelis felt relatively secure, it was in part because Egyptian energy, aspirations, and policy had turned to what seemed more fertile fields both in the Arab world and far beyond it. The ostensible goal was Arab unity, as much for its own reward as for any specific purpose. Yet it was perfectly understandable that Israelis should see themselves as the ultimate target of Arab unity, if only because hostility to Israel was the one common denominator all Arabs officially agreed on.

Meanwhile, Israel continued to claim water from Lake Tiberias and the headwaters of the Jordan as per the Johnston plan of 1954. Syria remained determined to challenge and resist the Israeli claim. The Soviet Union remained willing to help Syria, where Egypt was first invited to be senior partner in a United Arab Republic in 1958 and then asked out again in 1961. Egypt intervened in the civil war in Yemen. Communists and various Arab nationalists slugged it out for control of Iraq. Jordan and Saudi Arabia, the region's surviving monarchies, feared for their own security in the interactive and hyperactive new world of Arab nationalism and Egyptian ambitions, and looked anxiously to the United States. Israelis worried as a ring of Egyptian clients, Soviet weapons, and pan-Arab rhetoric seemed to close around them. Americans feared, as always, that Israelis would again strike first and perhaps hit the Soviets. Threat and counterthreat, global and regional politics assured that, at least long term, the region was as potentially explosive as before.

Irrespective of how the Soviet weapons that continued streaming toward the Middle East were used, it was only logical that the Israelis should also see themselves as their ultimate targets. By the early 1960s, the Egyptians had undertaken their own domestic arms program. It was arguable that the appearance of recycled German scientists and engineers, and the production and demonstrative test of a surface-to-surface rocket were a plausible reaction both to Israeli reactors and Egypt's own dependence on the Soviets.[9] Even Shimon Peres conceded post facto that the Americans were right to have been unconcerned about the German scientists, and that Israelis had wildly overestimated them,[10] but it was again not surprising that they awoke the Israelis' primal fears.

The first generally acknowledged Arab hero in living memory, Nasser was as determined as ever to lead the Arab world to independence from its old colonial masters. As his global visibility itself made clear, he was equally determined to play an appropriate role in the new, postcolonial, Third World that was apparently emerging between the postwar superpowers. But to Washington's inevitable apprehension, the Soviets stayed with him, despite repeated tensions, rebuffs, and frustrations. Between 1954 and 1972, they invested nearly $1.2 billion in economic aid and $2.7 billion in military aid to Egypt; plus $549 million in economic aid and $1 billion in military aid to Iraq; and $317 million in economic aid and $15 million in military aid to Syria. The United States, by comparison, invested $1.2 million in economic aid and sold $2 billion in weapons to Israel alone in the same period.[11]

Soviet support and weapons for Egypt notwithstanding, the ride had nonetheless become memorably bumpy long before the Arab-Israeli collision of 1967. The United Arab Republic of Syria and Egypt, contrived to preempt a possible communist coup in Damascus, ended in mutual disillusion. Syria, with nine coups between 1949 and 1966, was a fragile reed before and after. The revolutionary carousel in Baghdad brought Arab unity no closer. By the mid-1960s, Egyptian involvement in Yemen had become messily inconclusive, and the real fault line in the Arab world was the one dividing the new secular "progressive" regimes from the conservatives. Yet divided as they might be among themselves, Arabs remained as bitterly anti-Israel as ever.

Former Prime Minister Moshe Sharett expressed his own doubts about Suez and its aftermath in an eloquently tentative speech at a school for party officials in 1957. It was surely no coincidence that a party journal should republish it nine years later as Ben-Gurion's heirs dithered once again over whether and how to approach the Arabs. It was surely no coincidence either that the U.S. embassy called the speech and its republication to the attention of the State Department and U.S. stations around the Middle East, or that Harold Saunders of the National Security Council staff should bring it to the attention of Walt Rostow, President Johnson's national security advisor, with the suggestion that Rostow might "even" like to pass it on to leaders of the American-Jewish community.[12]

It was true that security was Israel's first priority, and uncategorical repatriation of Palestinian refugees was out of the question, Sharett had acknowledged. Yet even the Revisionists and their successors now agreed that Israel's ultimate goal was peace with its neighbors. The problem, he argued, was that Arabs too had their national consciousness. Not only had Israelis typically disregarded it, they had also overlooked the damage that they themselves had inflicted on it by creation of their state on what had once been Arab land.

Instead, Sharett continued, Israelis had drawn their own conclusions, among them that the Arabs understood only force, and would make peace only when they were conclusively defeated. He conceded that this had paid off en route to Suez. If one took Arab hostility for granted, Israel would, in fact, have been in trouble but for armed and active retaliation and preemption. But it was at least imaginable, he suggested, that Israeli policies themselves had something to do with "the Egyptian buildup and the attitude that produced it," and that conclusive defeat had only made Arabs the less willing to make peace.

The alternative, according to Sharett, was political restraint in place of reflexive military preemption. Ben-Gurion was "quite right," he added loyally, "in saying that only the Powers are capable of relieving the tension." But with all respect for the role of big powers, Sharett believed, Israelis would be wrong to underestimate the importance of what they did and said or to oversimplify what was intrinsically complex.

Given the intrinsic complexity of their own situation, Israelis, in fact, did a little of both. Long since disabused of their hopes and dreams of Third World equidistance between the superpowers, they had discovered a couple of basic truths about themselves and the world that seemed at least to define the parameters of their security. Allies were one. Weapons were the other. Paradoxical as always, the logic of Israel security made these both complementary and antithetical.

Repeated disappointments notwithstanding, the transcendent importance of good relations with the United States was nonetheless an obvious consequence, if only because Soviet policy made it unavoidable. Unwilling to concede the Middle East to the United States, as a Foreign Ministry paper argued, the Soviets had entered the postcolonial vacuum left behind by the departing British and French. They concentrated their resources on political and military aid, knowing they were unable to compete economically with the United States. "This was a sphere in which Washington was unable to outdo Moscow," the paper argued, "because American public opinion would not allow its government to take steps endangering Israel's security."[13]

Sharett's signature and legacy could be seen in Israeli diplomacy at all levels. Natural inclination and practical calculation alike disposed his diplomatic heirs to counsel self-imposed restraint, if only out of consideration for U.S. sensibilities. At the same time, they applied themselves beyond the wildest dreams of any Dale Carnegie to the existentially serious business of making friends and influencing people. The anthology of names and places attached to successive Independence Day celebrations was in many ways a sequel to the Revisionist spectaculars of the 1940s. Be it at the ambassador's Washington residence, be it at Yankee Stadium, Harry Truman, Herbert Hoover, Adlai Stevenson, Lyndon Johnson, John Foster Dulles, Stuart Symington, Jacob Javits, William Knowland, Felix Frankfurter, George Meany, John F. Kennedy, even Marilyn Monroe successively appeared to see and be seen. Their presences were savored post facto like the centerpiece at a catered dinner or the inevitable gallery of photos on a Washington lawyer's wall.[14]

Ben-Gurion's signature was unmistakable too, not least on the perennial quest for weapons and an acceptable strategy for using them. The prevailing U.S. distinction between "defensive" and "offensive" weapons hardly made things easier. It was true, as a by-product of the alarums and excursions of summer 1958, that Peres was able to turn an exception to good advantage. "For the first time, I received weapons which shoot!" he later told his biographer, Matti Golan. In response to Ben-Gurion's appeal, Eisenhower agreed to sell a hundred 75 mm. antitank guns with ammunition—though not the 350 originally asked for—on grounds that the weapon was both defensive and unavailable from any other source.[15]

Given all that had gone before, any U.S. weapons were welcome, almost by definition. Their practical utility was another question, given what the generals, particularly Moshe Dayan, believed they had learned from the Sinai campaign. In any case, it was Israeli doctrine that Israel's best defense was a good offense. Time was too short, numbers too disparate, strategic space too limited, and the population and economy too vulnerable to allow Israel the luxuries of leisurely mobilization or even of forward defense. By the middle 1950s, it was clear to planners that Israel must be ready to strike first. The logic of this pointed, in turn, to the need for strategic superiority against neighbors on three sides, unchallengeable air superiority, and an armored, mechanized army.[16] The continued introduction of Soviet arms only raised the stakes. So, in principle, the Israelis were where they were before: in urgent need of reliable suppliers of modern planes and tanks.

After Suez as before, Ben-Gurion's first choice was some kind of treaty with the United States. Next best, in his view, was membership in NATO. At least de jure, of course, neither was remotely attainable.[17] But de facto association with NATO members was another story. For the time being, the French connection held firm, though the coming of the Fifth Republic accelerated the decline and disarray of that odd coalition of Socialists and defense establishment that had been its firmest supporters.[18] But by this time, Peres's urgent wanderings had led him to a new and even odder source of what he wanted than the grandsons of the anti-Dreyfusards.

The new source was the Federal Republic of Germany. Each state for its own reason continued to avoid exchange of ambassadors, Israel for reasons of domestic sensitivity, West Germany for fear that the Arabs would recognize East Germany. But it was already clear that a meaningful relationship did not require ambassadors. In late 1957, Peres had his first, understandably secret, meeting with Franz Josef Strauss, the Federal Republic's new minister of defense. His country's first-ever minister for nuclear affairs, Strauss had also only recently conducted his own nuclear conversations with the French. By spring 1958, Strauss had formed a Franco-German-Italian consortium for joint production of conventionally armed antitank and antiaircraft missiles, ground vehicles, and tanks;[19] and Strauss and Peres had agreed concurrently on a program of joint development, German deliveries and Israeli sales to the Bundeswehr. Their insignia painted over, German planes and helicopters were flown to France, Strauss recalled in his memoirs. They were then shipped to Israel from Marseille. Other equipment simply vanished from Bundeswehr depots by dark of night. The United States was opposed to the idea, Strauss told his party's convention a few weeks after the Six-Day War. It would only cause trouble, he said the United States had asserted. The Israelis already had a U.S. guarantee, and that was enough.[20]

Two years later, when Strauss and Peres met again to agree on a military aid program, the Americans took a different view. In mid-March 1960, the arrangement was ratified by Konrad Adenauer and Ben-Gurion at a meeting in New York, which served at the time as the political midpoint between Jerusalem and Bonn. Buyer and seller agreed on a bill of sale. The Germans then charged payment to the Israeli reparations account.[21] Deliveries began in 1961, though only the leadership of the three parliamentary parties and a few senior officials were officially aware of them. By the mid-1960s, Washington not only tolerated and welcomed German military aid to Israel but positively demanded it.

"If America gives us funds, but not arms, and if France gives us arms for cash, the Germans give us arms without remuneration," Peres told the Israeli general staff. There were nonetheless political strings attached on several sides. If the deal became publicly known, Peres added presciently, it was as good as dead. In 1962, it faced but also passed a meaningful test. According to Peres, Fritz Erler, the parliamentary security spokesman for the opposition Social Democrats in the Federal Republic, made his own, and thus his party's, support for the deal conditional on U.S. approval. Possessed of unchallengeable anti-Nazi credentials, Erler had nothing against aid to Israel per se, let alone solidarity with fellow Social Democrats. But it was no surprise that an opposition party should think twice about sharing responsibility for a high-risk policy undertaken entirely on government initiative. Historical experience alone made Germans squeamish about arms exports, particularly outside the NATO area. Given German fears that the Arabs would retaliate by recognizing East Germany, the conjunction of Middle East and Israel only made Germans more apprehensive. But there was no resistance from Washington. On the contrary: . . . "Since German-Israel relations are in any case out of the ordinary, I see no reason to oppose this arms policy," President Kennedy reportedly declared.[22]

By this time, the United States was no longer a mere observer either. By conscious choice, it had weighed the trade-offs and become a player, though it was years before this too was publicly acknowledged and its implications were generally realized and appreciated. Submerged among the high-visibility themes of East-West relations, the nuclear arms race and the early dawn of a test ban and nonproliferation, the Berlin and Cuban missile crises, the perplexities of the newly decolonized Belgian Congo, buoyant hopes for an Alliance for Progress in Latin America, and the deepening quagmire in Vietnam, the Middle East is scarcely even visible in the standard biographies that followed Kennedy's assassination. Even by liberal estimates, Ben-Gurion and Nasser, Israel and Egypt appear on only seven each of Theodore C. Sorensen's 758, and Arthur M. Schlesinger's 1,031 pages of text.[23]

Yet, U.S. diplomacy was approaching, then crossing, a watershed in its choice of means, if not of ends. "The decisions taken by Kennedy regarding Israel . . . amounted to a reversal of U.S. policy," Mordechai Gazit has argued.[24] Given what American opinion and administrations had both wanted and expected of Israel and the Middle East since the 1940s, this is open to question. By 1962, the new administration had nonetheless agreed to sell major arms systems and guarantee Israel security as had no administration before it. Yet the reversal was only marginally noticed and acknowledged, even by its apparent beneficiaries. For reasons of diplomatic prudence, it was also scarcely publicized.

The U.S. reappraisal was at least an indirect by-product of Suez. But it was also an indirect acknowledgment, even by Dulles, that there might be more things between the Bosporus and the Khyber Pass than were hitherto dreamt of in his philosophy. As so often in the United States, the reconsideration included domestic politics as well.

Among the grounds for reconsideration was the discovery that the Israelis could be useful, just as they had always claimed, and in ways that Washington had hardly anticipated. Israel's performance in the Sinai also left an impression, particularly compared with the heavy-footed meanderings of the Anglo-French. Hitherto unknown to most Americans in, let alone outside, the Pentagon, Moshe Dayan was now to become an almost legendary figure. Israel's willingness in 1958 to allow British overflight to Jordan was noticed too, both in Cairo, where it was read as a kind of second coming of Suez, and in Washington, where Israeli influence helped persuade Congress to swallow the concurrent U.S. intervention in Lebanon. "The United States was obviously coming to regard Israel not as a burden . . . but as an asset in the global and ideological balance," Eban later remarked, again looking down from his memoirs and finding it good.[25]

In 1956 Israeli intelligence pulled off a coup that scooped the world, profoundly impressed Washington, and may even have astonished the Israelis themselves. It was, as one knowledgeable contemporary historian notes, "the beginning of a long period of close collaboration, the history of which will perhaps one day be written . . . or maybe not."[26] In a legendary secret speech to the 20th Congress of the Soviet party in late February 1956, Krushchev had shaken the Communist world with a massive indictment of Stalin's crimes. Reported by word of mouth, and distributed to foreign parties under top-security classification, it had already attained relatively wide, if unofficial, circulation by June when it appeared in the *New York Times* and other major Western papers.[27] By autumn, the speech had shaken both Poland and Hungary to their political foundations.

Reverberations from the speech reached the West within days of the conference, yet weeks passed before the CIA managed to get a full text. One request was reportedly rejected by the Yugoslavs, and a reputed Polish source apparently passed on an abridged version. In the end, according to many sources, it was none of the Western intelligence agencies but Israel's Mossad that was first to get the unabridged text.[28] Recalling early postwar days in Italy when he kept professional company with James Jesus Angleton, later the CIA's director of counterintelligence, Mossad's Isser Harrel reportedly hand-carried the precious text to Washington in April or May. Already known both as an authority on the Soviet KGB and as a friend of Israel, Angleton had the document authenticated. He then took on "the Israeli account," as it was known in the office, and handled it himself until his forced resignation in 1974. By this time, it had grown to legendary dimensions, and Israeli colleagues dedicated a little monument to his memory after his death.[29] Only after his departure were Israeli affairs again reintegrated with the rest of the Middle East.

The apparent result of Harrel's gesture was a double payoff: a formalized exchange agreement on all Middle East information short of the very highest security classification; and an archipelago of bureaucratic sympathy in an agency where Jews were regarded with some suspicion,[30] and other Old Boys, from Kim Roosevelt and Miles Copeland to Allen Dulles himself, leaned temperamentally toward the Arabs. By the mid-1960s, Israeli-U.S. intelligence cooperation reportedly sufficed to support an elaborate, and successful, plot to acquire an example of the Soviet Union's latest-model MIG-21 via Iraq.[31]

With the coming of a new, and comparatively Third World–minded Democratic administration, there was also a growing rediscovery that the United States might have a prophylactic role in the region. It was in any case for Americans to help maintain the regional balance before things again approached the slippery slope as they so recently, and so memorably, had. Hence aid to Israel increasingly became a function of aid to Arab clients. Both for reasons of size and circumstance, Egypt was the first coordinate. But by the middle 1960s, with Jordan too coming under Egyptian pressure, Israelis learned to link their own supplies to King Hussein's, though the idea required some fancy selling before the Israelis acceded.

Prudence alone suggested a new approach to Israel and Egypt alike. It was not for nothing that U.S. policymakers had worried consistently about the likelihood and potential hazards of Israeli unilateralism since at least the declaration of statehood. What was relatively fresh and original was the idea that the United States could, and should, do something about it.

"Kennedy reasoned that it was much wiser to respond to Israel's security problems before they became so serious that it would be too late for the United States to control or even to influence what Israel did about them," according to Mordechai Gazit, then chief of staff in the Israeli prime minister's office.[32] Ironically, the disposition to think again was favored by the outcome of the revolution in Iraq. Profoundly suspicious of Nasserite urgings among his younger associates, Colonel Qassem, the leader of the revolution, found himself more and more dependent on Communist support. Nasser's intervention on behalf of Arab nationalists led, in turn, to a demonstrative public squabble between Nasser and Khrushchev over the respective roles of communism and nationalism.[33]

But, in principle, this was Kennedy's position all along. Among the first of his political generation to think new thoughts about the postwar world, he had endorsed Jewish statehood relatively early, visited Israel as early as 1951, and pressed Dulles to lift the U.S. embargo on arms to Israel five years later as a response to the Soviet-Egyptian deal. In 1957, he supported Israel's insistence on guarantees as a condition for leaving the Sinai.

At the same time, he was among the first Americans to express some understanding of the Algerian war against France. By the late 1950s he had also concluded that Nasser and his United Arab Republic were a fact of life. With a courage far from common among members of Congress with ambitions for higher office, he had carried the message even to Zionist audiences that U.S. Mideast policy must acknowledge the realities of strategic geography, oil, economic underdevelopment, and Arab nationalism. He had also tried to explain the Third World's seemingly inexplicable weakness for Soviet-style or Communist Chinese–style modernization, and even put in a sympathetic word for the plight of the Palestinian refugees.[34]

There is no evidence that it hurt his candidacy. Just as he had confronted Protestants head-on in Texas, Kennedy let his advisors Myer Feldman, Senator Abraham Ribicoff, and Abraham Feinberg organize a meeting at Manhattan's Hotel Pierre with thirty "top Jewish leaders." For up to ninety minutes, he then patiently held his ground under heavy grilling that included even his father, the appeasement-minded ambassador to Britain before World War II. In November, Kennedy carried New York by 384,000 votes, including an 800,000-vote plurality in Jewish precincts. His 9,000-vote majority in Illinois, a key to the election, subsumed an estimated Jewish advantage of 55,000. According to a Michigan survey, Kennedy had actually run stronger among Jewish voters than had Adlai Stevenson at the height of the Suez crisis. "I owe my victory to the support of the American Jews," he reportedly told Ben-Gurion at their first meeting. "How can I repay them?"[35]

Then came reality, including Khrushchev's assurance of global support for "wars of national liberation," the humiliating failure of a U.S.-proxy invasion of Cuba, the confrontation with the Soviet party chief at their introductory meeting in Vienna, and the escalating crisis in East Germany and Berlin. The Middle East remained, of course, as real as ever, but its priority, under such circumstances, was something else. "Should [Egypt's] Ambassador Kamel suggest that the U.S. avoid actions or statements which might stir up the Arab-Israel issue," a briefing paper advised the president only months after he took office, "you emphasize that we are not interested in complicating an already difficult problem. . . . "[36]

Two days before construction of the Berlin Wall in August 1961, the president received Amos Elon, the U.S. correspondent for *Ha'aretz,* Israel's most prestigious daily, for a private talk. Published only after Kennedy's death, the transcript might be regarded as a baseline of U.S. policy, not only on the Middle East per se but on its place in the administration's view of the world. The interview revealed an informed and thoughtful president in a mood of cautious, and even overt, resignation. He acknowledged that Jordan, Lebanon, Iraq, and Saudi Arabia were unanimously negative, if not overtly hostile, to a discreet expression of U.S. interest in a new Palestine conciliation commission. Kennedy expected nothing of Egypt either. While he liked the idea of ending the Cold War in the Middle East, he also saw no reason that the Soviets should accommodate him. " 'What would it give them?' " he asked Elon, "raising his hands in a gesture of despair."

What the United States could do was resist aggression, and maintain a strategic balance between Israelis and Arabs, the president said. He conceded Elon's point that Israeli nervousness, for example in 1954–1956, was itself a factor to contend with. "Israel should be certain that the United States will not abandon it," he emphasized. *Ha'aretz* printed this sentence in boldface type.

At the same time, the question of Israeli neutralism led him to contradictory answers. Kennedy was hard put to see what Israel had to gain from it. "Israel's close ties with the United States help it more than they do us," he noted. "We are often in trouble because of our close ties with Israel." *Ha'aretz* again reached for the boldface type. On the other hand, the president added, he welcomed anything that could contribute to an Israeli-Arab settlement. "That's all we want," he said.[37]

The new men set out to meet the Third World at least halfway—while at the same time tightening the screws on Cuba and seemingly equivocating on the independence of the formerly Belgian Congo in ways that did little to advance their credibility with their target audiences. In motive and form, their approach to Egypt resembled their approach to Yugoslavia, but in each case, motifs and instrumentation—student exchange, technical assistance, economic development, central planning, national independence—recalled the complicated legacy of earlier administrations as far back as the New Deal.

"If Nasser can gradually be led to forsake the microphone for the bulldozer," Under Secretary of State Chester Bowles reported after a conspicuously high-level visit to Cairo in early 1962, "he may assume a key role in bringing the Middle East peacefully into our modern world." For an old liberal Democrat like Bowles, this was practically its own reward. Not only were the new leaders "extremely competent," "sincerely dedicated to the improvement of conditions," "pragmatists," in Bowles's view, "we have underestimated the basically revolutionary character of the regime," he added approvingly.[38] This was the language of Franklin Roosevelt. It was even the language of Ben-Gurion. It was hardly the language of Anthony Eden, Guy Mollet, or John Foster Dulles.

In Cairo as in Belgrade, even the choice of experienced, professional, and regionally expert ambassadors—George Kennan in Yugoslavia; John Badeau, the Arabic-speaking former president of the American University in Cairo, in Egypt— was a signal and a new departure. In the world of Dulles, and Congress too, as it turned out, neutralism tended to be seen as a moral failing. In the new administration, friendly intentions were to be presumed till proven otherwise.

Of course, Egypt was aware of "our initial and continuing support for Israel," Bowles acknowledged. Of course, "the UAR takes the same view of Israel that the U.S. takes of the USSR," he added. But this was no reason to write off so important a place as Egypt as a hopeless case. On the contrary, it was an argument for more aid, more understanding, even an invitation to Washington, and certainly an effort to persuade "key Jewish leaders in the U.S." to see "the advantages for Israel should a visit result in genuine relaxation of tensions."[39]

In reality, Nasser may well have been less impressed than skeptical of an Arabist ambassador whose American-accented classical Arabic was itself an obstacle to understanding. By the ambassador's own account, Nasser had nonetheless received him at least twenty-five times in twenty-two months. He obviously had nothing against U.S. aid either, delivered in a form the Soviets, for all their latest-model fighters and light bombers, could scarcely match. Between 1946 and 1960, Egypt had received an estimated $254 million in economic aid. Now between 1961 and 1963, it received an estimated $500 billion, despite congressional grumbles, Jordanian and Saudi anxiety that they too were on Nasser's hit list, and the French conviction that the new U.S. policy was a positive incentive to regional war. In fact, more than two-thirds of U.S. aid took the form of surplus grain, exported at government cost under Public Law 480.[40]

If only out of gratitude for what Eisenhower had done in 1956, Nasser himself would have voted for Nixon in 1960, his confidant Mohammed Heikal reported. On the other hand, he added, Nasser had also been impressed by Kennedy's performance in the campaign's first television debate. He was curious, impressed, even flattered by Kennedy's idealism, youth, and intellectual style. An irony in itself, considering Walt Rostow's later role as national security advisor to President Johnson, Heikal recalled that Nasser even had Rostow's *The Stages of Economic Growth: A Non-Communist Manifesto* translated into Arabic, and distributed to his cabinet.[41]

As interdependent as a watch mechanism, U.S. policy sought to harmonize Israeli and Arab concerns with more general American hopes and fears. As always, it was uphill work. Within days of Kennedy's inauguration, as the president prepared to meet Ogden Reid, his predecessor's ambassador to Tel Aviv, a briefing paper already noted Israeli nuclear activity as "an item of special interest." The theme recurred as Kennedy was briefed for his first conversation with the Egyptian ambassador a few months later. "Express the view," it instructed the president, "that as presently projected, Israel's atomic program represents no cause for special concern."

This was clearly disingenuous. An Israeli bomb, the CIA's Office of National Estimates was to argue in early 1963, would only advance the strategic polarization of the Middle East by making Israelis tougher; and Arabs more resentful, not least of the United States, and therefore more receptive to the Soviet Union as a patron-protector of last resort.[42] In the shadow of the Cuban missile crisis and the early dawn of nuclear détente, the potential hazards of an Israeli bomb were bound to be both an incentive and constraint in U.S. relations with Israel.

Atoms aside, the January 1961 briefing paper, with its collateral references to arms, aid, and regional security, already resonated with the familiar counterpoint of Israeli-U.S. relations. Secretary of State Dean Rusk, himself a veteran of the Truman era, confirmed the now-established formula: European weapons and U.S. aid in return for Israeli restraint. Reid, he advised the president, was to be "commended for his efforts during various incipient crises in persuading Ben-Gurion and his government to follow courses of moderation."

The question, as always, was the price and even the practical meaning of moderation, where space, lead times, and political culture alone assured vast differences between Israeli and U.S. thresholds of risk, temptation, and threat perception. Kennedy's first meeting with Ben-Gurion—at the prime minister's instigation, not Kennedy's, and in New York, not Washington—only confirmed the traditional U.S. view of quids and quos. Ben-Gurion wanted the Hawk, the latest-model U.S. surface-to-air missile. Reassured for the moment on Dimona, the president also wanted accommodation on refugees as symbolic down payment on his proposed Palestine conciliation commission. Ben-Gurion, who had been through this all before, agreed reluctantly, but to nothing in particular.

Over a year later, the refugee stalemate was still the subject of a six-hour meeting in Israel between Myer Feldman, the first presidential aide specifically appointed to be responsible for Jewish affairs, and Foreign Minister Golda Meir. The duration of the meeting alone, plus an "eyes only " report for Kennedy and Rusk, at least implied sincere U.S. interest. But, as usual, the text itself did little more than reaffirm the traditional Israeli view that the relationship of peace and refugees was the relationship of eggs and chickens. Two years into the Kennedy administration, its special representative to the Palestine Conciliation Commission had resigned with inconspicuous dignity, while Ambassador Walworth Barbour, still mandated to pursue the matter *ex officio,* continued whistling gently in the dark.[43]

On the other hand, the security relationship did move. At least indirectly and in part, this was itself a consequence of the refugee problem. "Status of Jerusalem," "Lake Tiberias Sovereignty," "Israel-Arab Military Balance," "UNRWA [the United Nations agency responsible for Palestinian refugees] questions," and "Jordan's Anti-UAR Propaganda" constituted the literal agenda of a normal government-to-government conversation between Israel's Ambassador Avraham Harman and the State Department in July 1962. The sequence only confirmed again how the question of Israeli security and the corollary question of arms supply were linked to all the others.[44]

This led, in turn, to a political and a military calculation on both sides. From an Israeli point of view, "the real key was our willingness to supply something that would be a demonstrable indication of our concern for supporting Israel and maintaining a military balance," William P. Bundy, the deputy assistant secretary of defense for international security affairs, quoted Peres after Peres's visit to the Pentagon in May 1962. But while there were "all sorts of collateral political motives (such as a desire for a gesture of support from us a time when they are bulling through their Jordan Valley development project)," he added in a memo to the State Department, even the Pentagon agreed that there was "a valid military basis" for Israeli concern and acquisition of the Hawk air defense missile they requested.[45]

From a U.S. point of view, spelled out with remarkable candor in a seventy-minute conversation between Kennedy and Meir in Florida in late 1962, arms were clearly the means to a political end, and the key was reciprocity. "We have to concern ourselves with the whole Middle East," the president explained. "On these questions—of water, of the UN role and reprisals, of refugees and of missiles . . . —we are asking the cooperation of Israel in the same way that we are cooperating with Israel. . . . " The idea, he added, was "to see if we can make some progress on refugees and maintain our friendship with Israel without constantly cutting across our other interests in the Middle East."[46]

In the effective division of labor, the United States undertook beyond any commitment to date to be Israel's guarantor of last resort. As Feldman later acknowledged, provision of the Hawk was made contingent on an Israeli undertaking not to develop nuclear weapons. But in practice, this proved to be increasingly remote and disingenuous. More generally, in return for U.S. support, Israel was expected to practice self-restraint, not only toward its neighbors but toward U.S. policy elsewhere in the region. As the Johnson years, particularly, made clear, help in other forms was welcome too, from support in Vietnam to collateral help with American Jewish voters. But it was never a condition for aid.

The practical result was a deliberately unobstrusive but nonetheless unprecedented flow of presidential assurances and guarantees, first of the Jordan water project in June 1962, then of Israel itself in the event of invasion a half year later. Meir's memoirs, while silent on the quo, are nonetheless explicit on the quid: "He took my hand, looked into my eyes and said very solemnly, 'I understand, Mrs. Meir, don't worry, nothing will happen to Israel.' ' ' " On October 30, 1963, he reaffirmed the commitment in a letter to Prime Minister Levi Eshkol.[48]

Also beginning in 1962, the guarantees found practical expression in an unprecedented flow of hardware. In living memory, private Americans had practically conspired to bootleg small arms and war surplus, while official America had not only declared but enforced an embargo. Only a few years before, White House, Pentagon, and State Department had imposed a regional cartel by trilateral action, and had been reluctant, when not adamantly opposed, to sell Israel anything at all. Over a five-year period, Israelis now advanced from surface-to-air-missiles to modern tanks to the promised land of latest-model aircraft.

At least by comparison with what followed, sale of the Hawk was relatively simple. As consecutive State Department and embassy cables recorded laconically, Feldman left on August 16 for Israel, where the embassy was to "offer services," and avoid social arrangements, unless otherwise instructed. The British were officially informed of the sale August 17. The Tel Aviv embassy was instructed that the British should get a chance to make a competitive offer August 18. Feldman reported "eyes only" to Kennedy and Rusk August 19 on his three-and-a-half hour meeting with Ben-Gurion, Meir, and Teddy Kollek. "[T]he President had determined" that the missile should be made available, he told them. It would nonetheless take time before it arrived. Nasser would meanwhile be informed of the decision, Feldman added, "in the hope that we could prevent escalation of weapons in the Near East." Ben-Gurion had nothing against the idea. On the contrary," he declared, he would gladly agree to no missiles at all if Nasser could agree to "arms limitations and controls."[49]

If only with respect to the reaction in Washington, it is fascinating to think what might have happened if Nasser had now declared a peace offensive. In fact, the vast expectations and Hobbesian contentiousness of intra-Arab politics alone were driving Egyptian policy in directions that made other Arabs, let alone Israelis, anxious.[50] In time, both Washington and the Israeli military concluded independently that Nasser's German missiles were militarily ineffectual. They nonetheless left their political marks on Israel, setting in motion a train of events that first forced Mossad's Isser Harrel, then Ben-Gurion from office.[51] The proximal result was a new, improved package of U.S. aid, and a revised schedule of quids and quos.

"Hawk is appreciated but Government of Israel regrets that in light of new offensive weapons being prepared by Israel's neighbors, Hawk alone is not a deterrent," Ben-Gurion informed Kennedy in spring 1963. In the months that followed, the Israelis made clear that they were also interested in up to five hundred current U.S. tanks. Ben-Gurion was particularly concerned with the announced formation of a military union of Egypt, Syria, and Iraq, whose nominal purpose was to "liberate Palestine." His proposed solution was a joint Soviet-U.S. declaration, guaranteeing the integrity and security of all states in the region, and the suspension of aid to any state that threatened or refused to recognize its neighbors.[52] Kennedy, unsurprisingly, was skeptical.

In time, the request for guarantees vanished again from the agenda, but the tanks remained. Peres, in Washington to discuss delivery and deployment of the Hawk, raised the issue of weapons and guarantees in conversations with Feldman, national security advisor McGeorge Bundy, Attorney General Robert Kennedy, Vice President Johnson, and the president himself. According to Peres, Kennedy replied with more than forty questions of his own on the range of new Soviet missiles, the reasons for Israel's fear of the German scientists in Egypt, and the grounds for Moscow's apparent success in Egypt.

What, the president asked, did Israel really want? A general security guarantee, Peres answered. If the United States guaranteed Israel, would this not have to apply to Egypt too, the president countered? What if the Soviets guaranteed Egypt? What about Lebanon, Jordan, and Saudi Arabia?[53] Yet events confirmed his willingness to undertake commitments in Vietnam as though the stakes there were clearer, and the danger real and present, in ways Washington was unprepared to see in the Middle East.

When the official dialogue resumed in 1964, the situation in Southeast Asia had, in fact, deteriorated dramatically; both Ben-Gurion and Kennedy were gone, and the aid agenda included not only arms and development loans but "practical processes" of desalinating seawater. Though the CIA's Office of National Estimates winced at the conjunction of "nuclear energy, water and Israel" in a single speech, the new president himself confirmed in public that "discussions" on "cooperative research in using nuclear energy to turn salt water into fresh water" were already underway. "Water can banish hunger and can reclaim the desert and change the course of history," Johnson told the American Friends of the Weizmann Institute at a New York dinner in February 1964.[54] The idea was clearly meant as another incentive for Israelis to move back from the brink, but his entire career proved that he believed it too. It was absolutely true, as Under Secretary of State W. Averell Harriman told the Israelis a year later, that "President Johnson [has] a keen understanding of water."[55] All at once, nuclear desalinization was the confluence of Walter Clay Lowdermilk, the Johnston plan, and the president's New Deal past, the latest route to that Middle Eastern TVA Johnson's predecessors had once dreamed of.

Nuclear desalinization had its strategic logic too. If it worked—in itself no trivial qualification, as things turned out—the project was the answer to everybody's fears, Israeli, Arab, and American alike. In the Middle East, of all places, water really did matter. Israelis were ready to fight for it. So were Arabs, if only to deny it to Israelis. On the other hand, if Israel could get its water from the sea, there was no further need to risk a preemptive strike over diversion of the Jordan and the Yarmuk. If Israelis could use atoms for peace, it was imaginable they could even be diverted from using them for war.

In the end, the project generated some heat but little desalinated water, and both parties learned a little more about the world and each other than they knew before. It began with a joint communiqué remarkable for its restraint, and a cautionary tale from a U.S. firm already engaged since 1959 in a joint desalination venture in Eilat. The communiqué noted emphatically that the International Atomic Energy Agency was invited to participate "from the beginning," and that "all countries with water deficiencies" were to have access to "the knowledge and experience obtained from this program." The businessmen thought the State Department might like to know that dealing with Israelis was no picnic. Not only had the Israelis persuaded them that they were "dealing with partners almost as tough and shrewd as the Japanese" but the resulting differences seemed to be "making a mockery out of the ordinary meaning of joint venture."[56]

By the time the experts reported officially in October 1964, it was nonetheless clear that they meant to think big. Engineering consultants were instructed "to study alternative dual purpose plants which would provide between 175 and 200 megawatts of electricity and between 125 and 250 million cubic meters of fresh water a year." Significantly, a year and a half later, the focus had switched to "dependable numbers relating to costs, demand and future trends of water and power consumption." The cost of a plant could run as high as "$200 million and up," a joint study concluded.

In fact, according to H. S. Rowen, the president of RAND, the California think tank, Israelis themselves had concluded that the estimates were too low, and "that the project makes sense for Israel only if it is given to it by the US." On the other hand, they were also prepared to consider an oil-powered alternative. There turned out to be no real consensus on national water needs anyway, and the Ministry of Agriculture was seriously interested both in shifting to tropical fruits, vegetables, and flowers for export, and new techniques for targeted irrigation. Under the circumstances, it seemed to Rowen, the United States should commit itself only "to helping Israel with its *water* problem" and "avoiding commitment to any specific technique." By August, Ellsworth Bunker, a negotiator almost as venerable and establishmentarian as W. Averell Harriman, was en route to Israel with a mandate from Rostow to look at financing "or continuing subsidy," and "look especially closely at the problem" of getting the Israelis to accept the International Atomic Energy Agency safeguards not only on the desalinization project but on Dimona and "all future reactors."[57]

Meanwhile, irrespective of the strategic logic of water, the political logic of weapons was virtually unchanged. As spelled out for the White House by Under Secretary of State George Ball in anticipation of a 1964 visit by Israel's new Prime Minister Eshkol, it was to satisfy Israel "of our continued interest and ability to safeguard Israel against attack"; to "maintain U.S. influence among the Arabs . . . and promote trends toward accommodations;" and to "prevent stimulation of the Near East arms race by Israeli acquisition of missiles or nuclear weapons."[58] The respective points were enumerated discreetly, but implicitly, at least, they were clearly linked.

The tanks Israelis wanted were a test case of the political and military trade-offs between Israeli wishes and U.S. hopes and fears. As always, the interagency surveys breathed caution. For all its putative special relationship with the Israelis, the CIA was as circumspect as ever on meeting Israeli needs. Any accommodation of Israel in an election year was likely to be bad for U.S. interests, the Office of National Estimates warned. Tanks would only make the Arabs demand more revenues from U.S. oil companies, and cooperate less on U.N. aid to Arab refugees and continued isolation of mainland China. Carl Rowan, director of the U.S. Information Agency, saw delivery of U.S. tanks as a disaster waiting to happen. The Joint Chiefs acknowledged the case for modernization of Israel's obsolescent armor but not for increasing numbers.[59]

Meanwhile, Eshkol's visit, like the U.S. presidential election, approached, and the Israelis turned up the heat. "I have rarely been exposed to as much pressure as I have had recently on the question of tanks for Israel," Feldman informed the president. "It has been only after considerable effort that members of Congress have been restrained against making speeches . . . , the Anglo-Jewish press has killed several articles, and responsible leaders of the Jewish community have demonstrated their confidence in the Administration by keeping silent."[60] In the end, both the

Israelis and the administration got what they wanted. But clichés to the contrary, the acknowledged price on all sides was the sacrifice of domestic political advantage. Notwithstanding conventional wisdom about Israel, Democrats, and election years, official U.S. aid actually bottomed out in 1964.[61]

As the prime minister's visit neared, with its first formal White House reception of an Israeli prime minister, Americans and Israelis tended increasingly to circle each other like porcupines negotiating a *mariage du convenance.* If Israel backed off from Ben-Gurion's request for a security guarantee, the U.S. embassy reported, it was in part because there was no chance of getting it anyway; in part, and "probably more importantly," because Israelis preferred "having in own hands the means . . . adequate to deter and if necessary defeat war." Official Washington countered with whole inventories of potentially "reassuring moves," including intensive—but not too intensive—briefings, guided tours of some of the nation's most inaccessible military installations, and a tour of an emphatically nonnuclear desalination plant. The idea, a background paper explained, was "to reassure the Israeli Government of the intent and capability of the United States to come to Israel's aid in the event of an unprovoked attack (Short of combined planning or commitments restricting U.S. freedom of action)."

Meanwhile, Israelis viewed developments in Syria, Jordan, and the Yemen with official concern. In conversation with Assistant Secretary of State Phillips Talbot, Harman even "expressed his increasing concern" about the "dangerous potentialities in [Ahmad] Shuqairi's movement to launch a Palestine entity." The "entity" was the Palestine Liberation Organization (PLO), whose recent creation by Arab leaders was as plausibly motivated by the wish to avoid confrontation with Israel as to provoke it. Jordan's King Hussein alone, with his large Palestinian population and long border with Israel, had reason enough to keep it under firm control. Shuqairi himself, an upper-class Palestinian lawyer variously described as "demagogic, venal," "an opportunist," and "a charlatan," was a former Syrian delegate and Saudi ambassador to the United Nations.[62] In one of the earliest Israeli-U.S. exchanges on the PLO on record, Talbot was unimpressed. How much Palestinian autonomy, he asked Harman, was Arab traffic likely to bear?[63]

By the time Eshkol reached Washington on June 1, the White House kitchen was ready at least with a demonstratively kosher dinner. The menu was authentic, as Peres noted, but for the camembert at the end that inadvertently violated the separation of meat and milk.[64] In reality, few Jews in the United States or Israel in 1964 consistently practiced *kashrut,* and lifelong socialist Zionists like Eshkol and his party neither expected nor particularly valued it. Like the open collar, that was itself a kind of uniform, its nonpractice had actually been a kind of self-definition. The appropriation and public display of an imperfect *Kashrut* under the circumstances, was a clue to the actual state of things: a signal to the president's Jewish constituents that Jews *qua* Jews were welcome at the White House table; a symbolic accommodation of Eshkol's coalition partners from the religious parties; a civic expression of that reflexive public piety that Americans have always favored, and that has impressed and baffled foreign observers since Tocqueville; even a bridge to the increasingly romanticized past both Israeli and American Jews had consciously left behind. Yet, lapse and all, it was also a little metaphor of the larger relationship, a reflection at once of sentiment, cynicism, good intentions, cross-purposes, and mistaken identity.

The tank arrangement was surer-footed but only by comparison. Johnson assured his guest that Israel would get its tanks. In fact, the decision had long been reached, not least in Bonn, though there was reluctance to talk about it even a generation later.[65] Not for the first time, Washington looked to the Germans and especially to Chancellor Ludwig Erhard, Adenauer's successor. Not for the last time, Erhard hesitated to say no to Johnson. As always, the decision was a headache, and even Johnson knew it hurt.[66] Sliding irresistibly into a major commitment of both credit and credibility in Vietnam, the Americans wanted German help. But the Vietnam war was already unpopular with Germans, and the German budget was tight. Apart from national squeamishness about the sale of arms in general, Germans also knew only too well that arms to Israel meant potential embarrassment in the Arab world. On the other hand, West Germany's booming export trade was inexorably linked to the dollar, and the continued presence of U.S. troops was practically a condition of West Germany's mental health.

The Pentagon continued to tell Peres, in Washington with Eshkol, to find his tanks in Europe. Peres continued to tell the Pentagon that he wanted U.S. tanks from U.S. sources "with all its political implications." For the moment, at least, he got half of what he wanted. The solution may well have been his own: an indirect deal with the United States with the Germans and Italians as intermediaries. The Americans undertook to supply the tanks—directly, if necessary. The decision was probably reached in July, when Erhard visited Washington, and saw Rusk, Secretary of Defense Robert S. McNamara, and the president. Under pressure to relieve U.S. burdens, he was anyway disposed to do something nice for Johnson, but he probably responded with special sensitivity to three U.S. arguments, a senior aide surmised: U.S. forces in Vietnam needed all the tanks they had; the Federal Republic was keen to replace its own aging inventory; and the United States should not have to take all the heat in the Middle East. Besides, it was understood, no one was supposed to know about it anyway—though, even a generation later, it was a mystery to the aide how anyone could have believed such a matter would stay secret.[67] Shortly afterward, the West German cabinet ratified the decision, despite resistance from Foreign Minister Gerhard Schroeder, and agreed to sell the Israelis 150 used U.S. tanks.

Before things went wrong, as they soon did, about forty U.S. tanks from West German inventories were delivered to Italy where, in the language of a U.S. briefing paper, they were "up-gunned" for transshipment to Israel.[68] Then the leaks began, though their source, and even motive, remained a matter of speculation. A first story appeared in the left-liberal *Frankfurter Rundschau* on October 26. It was followed by a succession of stories in the *New York Times.* Meanwhile, the State Department pursued its own fragile campaign to make hay with Nasser, including a visit to Cairo by the elder statesmen's elder statesman, John J. McCloy. It was terribly important that Eshkol understand what this was about, Rusk cautioned the embassy in Tel Aviv. "If Nasser convinced Israel going down dangerous road of sophisticated weapons or feels he being put under intolerable Western pressure [he is] likely [to] decide [to] give priority to military weaponry."[69]

As they invariably did when embarrassed in Third World capitals, the Germans countered with money, conveyed in this case by Eugen Gerstenmaier, the Speaker of the Bundestag. But he was followed to Cairo in early December by the Soviet deputy prime minister, and the Egyptians then brought Bonn to its knees altogether. In late January 1965, they invited Bonn's nemesis, the East German leader, Walter Ulbricht, to Cairo to sign a $78 million credit package.

By the time, Ulbricht arrived a month later, the German arms deliveries to Israel had stopped and both Washington and Bonn were engaged in heavy activity. The German reappraisal began, predictably, with Erhard's suspension of arms transfers on February 12, combined with an offer of monetary compensation. On February 23, the day before Ulbricht's arrival, the chancellor then dispatched his special representative, Kurt Birrenbach, to Jerusalem to find a mutual solution. Though his hosts made sure he visited the Holocaust memorial at Yad v'Shem, and Dayan himself took him on a helicopter tour of Israeli airspace, Birrenbach hung tough.[70] A few days later, a blue-ribbon U.S. delegation turned up in Israel to negotiate about not only the promised tanks but even planes.

By that time, Birrenbach had been to the United States, where he laid out German policy to senior officials, elder statesmen including McCloy, and Jewish leaders. Bonn wanted to suspend arms transfers and recognize Israel, he explained. It was only afraid that recognition of Israel would lead to Arab counterrecognition of East Germany, and thus the risk that Germany's irreversible division would be blamed on the Jews. The only solution, Birrenbach told his American interlocutors, was that they arm Israel themselves. On his return to Bonn, he reported that the Americans had told him that the Federal Republic should hold its ground as the last Western state with much political capital in the Arab world.[71] A few weeks later, after a strenuous debate in the cabinet, West Germany had increased aid and recognized Israel. Meanwhile, Washington was en route to becoming Israel's—and Jordan's—major arms supplier.

In late February 1965, Robert Komer, a senior White House aide, and W. Averell Harriman, who had once negotiated with Churchill and Stalin on behalf of Roosevelt, arrived in Israel on behalf of Johnson. They carried a mandate from a president who had just won a landslide victory, and who now, as Harriman pointed out, "was contemplating a fundamental change of U.S. policy." They faced an Israeli government that was looking ahead itself to elections the following November. What followed were nearly three weeks of the kind of talks diplomatic communiqués conventionally call "open and frank," and whose intensity so impressed Komer that he called it to the attention of McGeorge Bundy as a phenomenon unto itself.[72]

The conversations confirmed a relationship where politics led to weapons and back again, almost despite the intention of the vendor. In previous administrations, Harriman's opening statement might actually have been understood as a way of saying no. In a world where the Sino-Soviet split led to increasing pressures in Vietnam, Latin America, and Africa, it was important that the Middle East not "become polarized along East-West lines," he declared. "It would be most unfortunate if Israel became a point of East-West conflict as Berlin had."

In practice, the larger argument turned out to have three corollaries. The first was that the United States would deliver weapons to Jordan, to be paid for by Kuwait. There was no question of arming Jordan anyway, Harriman explained; it was only a matter of where Jordan chose to get its weapons. The second consequence was that Israel would shut up about it. "No public discussion," Harriman announced. " . . . It was most important to the President that the Prime Minister put these matters into proper perspective for the key leaders of the [Jewish] community," he added. The third consequence was, nonetheless, that "for the first time the President was willing to consider the direct sales of military equipment Israel needed at an appropriate time and with appropriate coordination of the publicity problem."

His presentation was met with a barrage of questions about payments and schedules, but what really mattered was water, and its threatened diversion. The Israelis wanted weapons, they wanted aid, but above all they wanted public support. Harriman was adamant. Israel had made its point in the Gulf of Aqaba. It had also made its point on use of the Jordan. But there was no need for publicity on arms, he repeated. Eshkol was quick to note the inconsistency: deliveries to Jordan would not be secret. "Governor Harriman asked if the Prime Minister would prefer that Jordan received Soviet tanks."

Golda Meir, who had once watched Americans climb down from their position on Gaza, now thought she saw them climbing down again. First, Americans had pledged to resist Arab diversions, she argued. Now they were telling Israel to avoid preemption and take its case to the United Nations. As far as she was concerned, Hussein got water and now was getting U.S. weapons too. Komer and Harriman reformulated their brief: Israel would announce that the United States supported Israel's claim and opposed the use of force. The arms would remain a private matter. What happened, Meir asked sensibly, when Israelis realized that Jordan was getting tanks while the Israeli government was bound to silence? "We would consider this to be a mutual problem," Harriman answered.

When the conferees regathered the next morning, it was hardly by chance that the talks began with a heavily detailed briefing by General Yitzhak Rabin, the military chief of staff. "What was important was not to contain an enemy attack but to destroy the enemy on its own ground," Rabin emphasized, totting up the numbers, ranges, and specifications of weapons already in Jordanian, Syrian, and Egyptian hands. Israel, he made clear, needed tanks and planes at least of comparable quality. Peres began from a similar position. Better weapons with secrets than secrets without arms, he declared. "Rather than complicated words about a change in U.S. policy," he argued, "let's have the hardware, bombers and tanks." Harriman countered firmly. "He came for a discussion of basic political issues, not military details," the transcript recorded.

But weapons were a political issue, Eshkol answered, as he had the day before. This seemed to him to apply especially to weapons delivered to Jordan, when Jordan was also preparing to divert water assigned to Israel by the Johnston plan. "We must have an answer," Harriman answered implacably. "Should we abandon Jordan to a Moscow-U.A.R. [Egypt] axis?" At this point, the conversation threatened to stall. By nightfall, an agreement had nonetheless materialized. The United States undertook to supply the rest of the promised tanks and maintain the military balance, planes included; to support the "integrity and independence of Israel"; and defend Israel's claim to water under the Johnston plan.

To this, both sides appended their wish lists. Israel asked that the United States conclude a "detailed agreement" before selling arms to Jordan; receive assurance from Jordan that it would not deploy tanks on the West bank; announce the deal with Israel concurrent with public announcement of the deal with Jordan; publicly reaffirm Israel's integrity, independence, and water rights; and exercise all possible influence on Jordan. The United States wanted Israel to honor its reasons for coming to Jordan's aid; to try as best it could to continue meeting its arms needs in Europe; to keep quiet about any Jordanian agreement to desist from deploying tanks on the West Bank; to shut up on the terms of its agreement with the United States; and to acknowledge U.S. opposition to "any military action against the Arab diversion works."

A few weeks later, the Pentagon had agreed to the sale of tanks, serious consideration of the aircraft order was already under way, and the Israelis had come around on Jordan. What Israel needed, according to the Pentagon, was a fighter or fighter-bomber capable of reaching targets around Cairo and as far south as Luxor. Given Egypt's growing air defense, it also had to be capable of low-level attack. Though the Pentagon was willing to sell up to twenty planes, Komer was nonetheless to offer only "a few," if only because of the potential "open-endedness" of any commitment to be Israel's supplier of last resort.[73]

The deal progressed like a fugue with three subjects: the sale itself; apprehension of what the Israelis might do if the sale were not forthcoming; and anxiety about what might happen if news of the sale got out. It was taken for granted that, sooner or later, the sale would become public. In the event that it did, the Pentagon should also be prepared to entertain a similar request from Jordan, a memo recommended. Sure enough, the alarm bells rang in mid-April, though in retrograde motion. The Israelis discovered that John W. Finney of the *New York Times* was about to report the sale of arms to Jordan, and believed that public announcement of the sale to Israel might "provide useful balance." The State Department urged discretion, and the matter again retreated to the inside pages.[74]

Given apparent Arab brinksmanship, the risk of Israeli preemption was another story. Arab diversion projects were no cause for military action, Rusk again warned demonstratively in March. In mid-May, ostensibly in connection with the official opening of the Israel Museum, former Ambassador Ogden Reid, now a member of Congress from New York's 26th District, felt the need to return to Jerusalem to make sure the Israelis were not about to move. He went straight to Rusk on his return. "In the absence of substantial reassurances from the United States, including provisions of military equipment, chances for an Israeli strike against the Arab diversion projects were enhanced," he reported. "If Israel will eschew provocative attacks across frontiers, we'll talk," Rusk answered.

Meanwhile, as the Israeli shopping list grew, and the State Department solemnly underlined the incompatibility of "military talks" and "military initiatives,"[75] each side wrestled with its own dilemmas. The administration was as apprehensive as ever that the alternative to U.S. supply of conventional weapons was Israeli development of nuclear weapons.[76] Unequivocally embarked on its own relentless warpath in Southeast Asia, it was also even more anxious than usual for stability, at least, in the Middle East, not to mention Jewish sympathy at home. Squeezed between contentious neighbors and demanding constituents, Eshkol's government dithered, in turn, about the political price of U.S. weapons versus the marginal utility of preemptive action. The plane negotiations shambled on through the year, leaving a trail of cross-purposes and mutual irritation.

The agreement reached on June 2, 1966, was "a graphic example of the painstaking and agonizing arms decisions we are forced to make by the realities of Near Eastern politics" a presidential background paper declared on the eve of an unofficial visit by Israel's President Zalman Shazar. The sale was "a deliberate exception," it repeated, adding almost reflexively, "We have no intention of becoming Israel's principal supplier of arms." By this time, the Pentagon's twenty-plane ceiling had risen to forty-eight, and military-credit assistance, till 1962 an unknown component of the annual aid package, now constituted about two-thirds of the total.

In fact, 1963 and 1966, the years of the Hawk and Skyhawk, were also the first since 1949, in which U.S. government aid to Israel had exceeded $100 million. Of the more than $1.2 billion in U.S. government aid to Israel since independence, more than 40 percent had been appropriated since 1961, already making Israelis the world's leading per capita beneficiaries of U.S. aid.

In the process, Congress itself had become *a* bank of Israel. Under a whole bouquet of programs, U.S. loans were now invested in a power plant and the Technion in Haifa, the Industrial Development Bank of Israel, the Weizmann Institute, the University of Tel Aviv, the American-Israeli Cultural Foundation, and local-currency loans to private American investors in Israel, the Agency for International Development (AID) reported. In a number of cases, the capital was itself a by-product of previous loans; including proceeds of aid under Public Law 480, the farm-export program. These local-currency repayments, in turn, were reinvested in new projects, but they would eventually be repaid in dollars, which would "ultimately" benefit the U.S. balance of payments, AID's director, David Bell, pointed out.[77]

It was no coincidence under the circumstances that aid itself figured increasingly in presidential briefing papers. A growing traffic in high-level visitors drew particular attention to Israel's substantial external debt and a defense burden that then constituted a quarter of the budget and 11 percent of GNP.[78] The rolling thunder of American-Jewish concern for Israel's security that followed each visit also played a role in focusing official attention.

Though only indirectly acknowledged, Vietnam too had its effect on Israel, the White House, and the Jews. The budgetary impact was self-evident. As war spending rose, once-cherished hopes for the Great Society sank with it. In the process, aid funds became "increasingly tight," as Walt Rostow acknowledged with becoming understatement.[79]

The political nexus was more subtle but at least as telling. He had recently learned that Israelis were passing the word that the government of South Vietnam was anti-Israel, Vice President Hubert Humphrey informed Rusk in March 1966. Actually, Israel had offered a bit of aid, he said, but was willing to supply much more. He proposed that Washington encourage the South Vietnamese to recognize Israel, not least for the "constructive effect amongst the leadership of the Jewish community in our key cities." The problem seemed, on the contrary, to lie with Israel, Rusk replied, where the left-wing coalition parties opposed involvement in Vietnam. Obviously on cue from Washington, Ambassador Barbour actually raised the subject in April in conversations with Eshkol and Eban, now Israel's foreign minister. Eshkol only replied that Israel was itself a small country at the gateway to Asia, and that "Israeli relations with Asian and African developing nations would suffer" by support for Vietnam. Vietnam had done nothing for Israel either when it mattered, Eban added, and Israeli opinion had generally been impressed by American, particularly intellectual, opposition to the war.[80]

Convinced that the matter "had a bearing on some of the reactions of the leaders of the American Jewish community," Humphrey nonetheless persisted. "We should urge upon South Vietnam that she exchange Ambassadors with Israel and vice versa," he proposed to Rostow in May. Rostow reported to Johnson, in turn, that Humphrey was "ready to mount a systematic campaign" to make sure American Jews understood what Johnson had done for Israel, and that "the whole fate of Israel depends on the credibility of U.S. commitments." A few weeks later, when Shazar arrived in Washington, aid was in third, Vietnam in sixth place of six recommended "talking points."[81]

The Israeli economy was itself among the reasons that aid was again an issue. Nourished by Jewish philanthropy, U.S. loans and grants, and German reparations payments, it had become one of the world's success stories with annual growth rates of 10 percent and more. Israel's per capita GNP now exceeded Japan's and Italy's. Since the early 1950s, the export-to-import ratio had also grown from scarcely 20 percent to more than 50 percent, though Israelis understandably hoped to increase that. In fact, by normal statutory criteria, Israel no longer qualified for U.S. aid at all. But "we have still found ways FY 62 through FY 66 to put in a *total of $304 million*," Rostow reported with satisfaction—with an additional $350 million in support for Arab refugees, plus $520 million in collateral aid to Jordan, that he considered support for Israel too.[82] He believed that there were still a lot of useful things for the United States to do, but it was not by chance that many of those he now proposed—endowed chairs, medical research projects, permission from AID to let Israel bid on potash sales—came relatively cheap.[83]

Seen from Washington, the problem was part a matter of getting this across to Israelis, part of getting it across to American Jews, part of getting both to accommodate to changing circumstances. Like Eshkol's appearance two years before, Shazar's visit accordingly became another barometer reading of global as well as bilateral expectations. Given Arab reaction to the sale of planes, original plans for the visit called for Shazar to be received by Humphrey. The decision to involve the president directly, after weeks of staff debate, could therefore be seen as a signal of U.S. favor, not least by the Israelis, who had loyally resisted the temptation to show off their new weapons in the annual Independence Day parade. Johnson rose familiarly to the occasion with a 440-word toast on the biblical injunction to morality, peace, and social justice, whose text included not only references to the book of Leviticus and the prophet Micah, but three displays of laboriously transliterated and phoneticized Hebrew.[84]

In the weeks that followed, Jewish Democrats devoted increased attention to the administration's neglect of Jewish hearts and minds, or at least systematic consultation with the organized Jewish community. In principle, said Philip M. Klutznick, a Chicago lawyer and later secretary of commerce, the White House appeared pro forma on public occasions, delivered "a few speeches" and accepted some medals. It otherwise confined any discussion of Jewish affairs to Jewish members of the administration. This might have been enough where there was little to talk about anyway, as under Eisenhower. It was a mistake where it had a record to defend. But, in fact, Israelis had a better idea what the administration had done for Israel than American Jews, Klutznick noted. The approach assured the worst result: the administration got inadequate credit for its accomplishments plus inadequate support when it was needed. Within days of their appearance Colonel Jacob M. Arvey, a very big man in Chicago Democratic circles, saw that Klutznick's views reached Marvin Watson, one of the president's special assistants.[85]

In April 1967, at Johnson's behest, Rostow presented both Rusk and Secretary of Defense McNamara a voluminous inventory of U.S. policy toward Israel for comment. In its choice of issues and solutions, and its filigree of foreign and domestic policy both in the United States and Israel, the memo was an almost uncanny prefiguration of the next decade's, and next administration's, agenda.

With another presidential election on the horizon, the survey began with an overview of American-Jewish politics and some thoughts on former Vice President Nixon as the probable Republican candidate. It seemed likely that Nixon would appeal to Jews as he had not in 1960. The White House also expected to pay for Vietnam. If the war went on, the memo noted, "a special effort to hold the Jewish vote will be necessary." American Jews worried *inter alia* about Israeli security, Soviet arms for Syria and Egypt, Israel's deteriorating economy and defense burden, it continued, but also about "the condition of Soviet Jewry." Their expectations, in turn, were likely to meet resistance from "enclaves of resistance and suspicion" still installed in both the State and Defense departments. Yet Israelis continued to look to the United States for military and economic aid.

For example, the Israelis wanted two hundred latest-model armored personnel carriers (APC), needed to phase out old British tanks, and wanted to upgrade their aging French aircraft. Israeli requests, of course, had always required strenuous negotiations and White House intervention. Now the Defense Department was reluctant even to sell APCs. One solution, the memo proposed, would be to let the Israelis buy parts and assemble APCs on a royalty basis, and to buy new U.S. motors for both the British tanks and French planes. Not only would Israeli industry, employment figures, and the balance of payments be the better for it, there would be "a collateral opportunity to offer repair and rehabilitation services, and other support, to the U.S. military in Europe and in the Eastern Mediterranean, and perhaps in the Far East."

The Israelis also wanted U.S. farm surpluses, the option to bid on South Vietnamese and South Korean requests for fertilizers, and the chance to pay off outstanding debts in goods and services that the United States would otherwise buy abroad: equipment and services for the Air Force, potash and phosphates for AID, small arms and ammunition as well as farm products, port facilities, and repair and overhaul of communications equipment. Perhaps, the memo continued, Americans could let the Soviets know they would advance the cause of détente by a more liberal policy of family reunification. Perhaps there was a case for an "American university" in Israel that not only would match the existing institutions in Beirut and Cairo but would train Africans as well as Israelis.

Israel could otherwise help the United States in two ways, the memo went on. It could transfer foreign exchange reserves to U.S. banks, and so help the U.S. balance of payments. It could also "(with difficulty however)" take a more positive view of Vietnam, and maybe send a medical team. "This action would be of importance to the Jewish community in the United States," the memo repeated. At the same time, the memo concluded, the White House could presumably help both Israel and itself by inviting Jewish guests to White House occasions, dispatching Americans other than "candidates and operating-level officials" on official visits to Israel, and arranging another Eshkol visit for the coming fall.[86]

By the time Eshkol actually arrived in early 1968, events in the Middle East had themselves made clear that there were more urgent priorities than the White House guest list. On June 5, 1967, the war that some had yearned for, but most had not, had finally broken out. When it ended slightly less than six days later, many things were different, though some were not, and such recent preoccupations as water-diversion plans and a United Arab Command seemed suddenly irrelevant.

As many observers noted soon afterward, the war was only in part a product of Arab-Israeli differences. Odd Bull, the Norwegian general in charge of U.N. forces on the Syrian-Israeli armistice line, saw it as a struggle for control of water resources. According to Theodore Draper, the real *casus belli* "was a struggle against history" that variously subsumed the rivalries and mutual grievances of Israelis and Arabs, Arabs and Arabs, Arab and non-Arab Moslems, Soviet and Chinese Communists, and the postwar superpowers.[87]

At the moment, Arab-Israeli differences seemed almost subordinate to the Hobbesian differences between Arab "revolutionaries" and Arab "conservatives" that had agitated the region since the coming of independence. It was widely assumed, according to Malcolm Kerr, that Palestine was the Arabs' last common denominator. On the contrary, he argued, it was only when Arabs inclined to cooperation, that they also inclined to consensus on Palestine, that is, a general abstention from any action that would itself upset the consensus. Conversely, Kerr contended, when Arabs were quarrelsome, they also tended to squabble about Palestine, secure in the knowledge that belligerency between any Arab state and Israel would also threaten their Arab competitors and enemies.[88]

Once the war was over, it was generally agreed that just such an inter-Arab squabble, in this case a coup in Syria in February 1966, had been at least its proximal cause. In themselves, Syrian coups were nothing new or particularly alarming. What proved fateful about this one was both that Syria was the only Arab state seriously determined to divert the Jordan headwaters, and that the new men in Damascus, for their own reasons, were keen to confront Arab "reactionaries." In a decade that had already seen the success of revolutionary guerrilla warfare in Cuba and Algeria, and its impressive promise in Vietnam, they therefore hit on the scheme of using Shuqairi's newly founded PLO for a "war of national liberation" against both Jordan and Israel. The result was a series of incursions across the Israeli border from both Jordan and Syria.

Predictably, the Israelis demanded action. From a Syrian point of view, the raids and the inevitable Israeli reaction had the double virtue of putting both "reactionary" Jordan and "progressive" Egypt on the spot. In November 1966, Egypt concluded a mutual defense treaty with Syria, if only to make sure it would be consulted.[89] But the Soviets too came ostentatiously to Syria's defense, and the attacks on Israel continued. On April 7, 1967, a border skirmish escalated to the point that planes went into action, and the Israelis shot down six Syrian MiGs over Syrian and Jordanian territory. Under the circumstances, even a concerted display of restraint, like the Israeli Independence Day parade of 1967, could be interpreted as a signal of belligerency. Where, Arabs asked, were those troops deployed?[90] As the escalation continued, the Soviets informed the Egyptians that Israelis were massing large forces on the Syrian border, and encouraged Nasser to make his own show of force in Syria's support.[91] By May 16, the Egyptians had deployed considerable numbers of troops and tanks in the Sinai, and the Israelis were becoming clearly anxiou'. That night, the Egyptians requested that Secretary General U Thant remove the U.N. buffer force installed in the aftermath of Suez. "Our first effort must be to keep him out in front and stiffen his spine," Walt Rostow declared in a memo to Johnson on May 19.[92] When the secretary general nonetheless complied with the Egyptian request, the Israelis grew tenser still, and foreign proposals to transfer the U.N. troops to the Israeli own side of the border did not reassure them. Meanwhile as Egyptian troops and tanks continued moving into the Sinai, the Israelis were advised to consult the U.N. The U.S. position, as Eban understood it, was that Israel not use force "*until* or *unless* Egyptian forces attempt to close the Straits to Israel-bound shipping." Both for what it said and what it implied, the Israelis liked this so well that they then adopted it as their own.[93]

On May 22, Nasser decided to close the Straits of Tiran, and things turned climactically for the worst. For the Israelis, the conjunction of straits, Sinai, and buffer forces constituted an instant and automatic test of the 1957 guarantees. At the Israeli cabinet meeting of May 23, Eban, who understood the U.S. assurances better than anyone else, at least persuaded his colleagues to give diplomacy a chance. The issue, he explained, was whether Israel should go it alone or with the support of others. It was also important to test Soviet intentions, the reliability of the 1957 guarantees, and U.S. willingness to supply both arms and diplomatic reinforcement. Given "the rising tide of Soviet penetration, and the trends in Arab politics that such penetration encouraged and fortified," as then-Under Secretary of State Eugene Rostow later described it, it was generally acknowledged in Washington that a new Arab-Israeli war had global implications. At the same time, Rostow "advised the President that he had to choose between . . . war or an international force to convoy ships through the Straits."[94] Johnson's preference, at least, was clear already: that the United States would not be responsible for unilateral Israeli action.

As Eban set off to canvass the Western capitals, Johnson, whose circumspect first draft had provoked a small tantrum from Minister, and later Ambassador, Ephraim Evron,[95] issued a statement proclaiming the straits an international waterway, and declaring the blockade not only illegal but "potentially disastrous to the cause of peace." Meanwhile, official Washington was silent as Johnson tested both the political and the international waters, and even dispatched General Andrew Goodpaster to test Eisenhower's memory of the commitments made ten years before.

Bruised by a cold shoulder in Paris, then warmed again by London's willingness to cooperate with Washington, Eban was to reach the United States on May 25, 1967. As his arrival approached, there was general consensus that the straits were an international waterway, whose security required international action. But the Americans also preferred that the Israelis stay out. At this point, reportedly, Ambassador Avraham Harman began to mobilize American-Jewish leaders, who began, in turn, to call the White House.[96] Senate leaders were basically sympathetic to Israel, but especially with a war on in Vietnam, they were also opposed to U.S. unilateralism.

Armed with the minutes of the 1957 agreements Eban found warnings from home of impending Egyptian attack already awaiting him in Washington.[97] A test of U.S. willingness to regard an attack on Israel as an attack on the United States, the signals from Israel sent Rusk directly to Johnson and General Earle G. Wheeler, the chairman of the Joint Chiefs of Staff. Both acknowledged Israel's sense of urgency, but neither shared it. The Pentagon was unconvinced that Egyptian attack was imminent. After running aground in pursuit of a multilateral NATO fleet many had never believed in anyway, the military was also congenitally suspicious of multilateral anything.

Paradoxically, their own hesitations only made the military the more tolerant of unilateral Israeli action.[98] But more tolerant hardly described the president. Mindful of the potential stakes and liabilities, Johnson had actually written out the essential part of his message for Eban.[99] The United States would meet its commitments, the president emphasized, but congressional participation was required, and the United States would have to consult the United Nations at least pro forma. Till then, Israel was either to avoid preemption or be on its own. By now the Israelis too were on the spot. As Arab rhetoric soared and escalated, NATO headquarters in Naples announced that six U.S. ships with two thousand marines aboard had sailed for the Mediterranean.

On his return to Jerusalem, Eban reported the U.S. intent to act on the straits, as well as suspicions that Israel might be trying to involve the United States in an unwanted conflict. At a six-hour cabinet meeting beginning at 10:30 P.M. on May 27, he proposed a forty-eight-hour delay to see what the Americans might accomplish. The vote was 9–9. By the time the cabinet reconvened the next day, Johnson had notified Eshkol both of expressed the Soviet Union's intentions to aid its Arab clients in the event of Israeli attack, and of the intent of the United States "to make every possible effort" to organize an international naval task force to open the straits. Johnson's message sufficed to tip the cabinet in favor of delay. As the Israeli embassy in Washington fended off anxious queries about when Israel meant to react, and both Walt Rostow, the national security advisor, and his brother Eugene, the under secretary of state for political affairs, whistled hopefully about impending naval plans, Jordan's King Hussein arrived in Cairo to sign a defense agreement with Nasser. "As I have said, Israel's existence in itself is an aggression," Nasser declared at his press conference on May 28. By this time, anti-American rhetoric too had reached a pitch and volume like none since 1958, and Washington looked on in bafflement. Nasser was "shrewd but not mad," Walt Rostow reflected. The CIA even speculated that he might simply be trying to extort more grain and credits.[100]

By the beginning of June, it was clear that the international naval force was going nowhere. Washington and London had consulted more than eighty governments. Israel apart, only two, the Netherlands and Australia, were firm. New Zealand, Belgium, and Iceland were willing to support a declaration of innocent passage. West Germany, Portugal, Argentina, and Panama were still considering. Canada, Italy, and Mexico had withdrawn.[101]

As U.S. hopes receded, and Israeli confidence in U.S. intentions with them, Eshkol dispatched a second emissary to Washington incognito. This time it was Meir Amit, the head of the Mossad. Amit was confident he could figure out what the United States really intended, he later told an interviewer.[102] He also thought he could persuade the Americans how serious things had got. By now, this was something of an understatement. The Americans were clearly concerned that the Israelis were about to force their hands.[103] The Israelis were clearly concerned that their deterrent advantage was a wasting asset. On June 1, for the first time, they formed a National Unity government of all parties, even Menahem Begin's hitherto proscribed Gahal. Dayan, the hero of 1956, agreed to succeed Eshkol as defense minister.

Robert Anderson, once vainly sent to see Nasser on behalf of Eisenhower, now vainly met him again on behalf of Johnson, though it was at least announced that Egypt's vice president would visit Washington the following week. Meanwhile, Eugene Rostow emphasized to Harman how much the president wanted to avoid not only an Arab-Israeli war but another diplomatic victory for Nasser, which would threaten the Arab clients of the United States. But this was clearly uphill work. As Harold Saunders of the NSC staff soberly explained to Walt Rostow on June 3, it was first necessary to persuade Nasser that the United States was immovable on the straits, while still leaving room for a broader settlement. It was then necessary to begin and end the U.N. debate on rights of passage, a job further complicated by the French, whose own opposition to a Straits resolution frustrated the State Department's test of a Soviet veto. Finally, it was necessary to determine whether a naval probe was necessary, and if so, get Congress to support it.[104]

Returning from Washington the same day, Amit had accordingly concluded that the United States would not resist if Israel acted alone. Since May 28, there had been no more U.S. warnings against Israeli action.[105] The cabinet was also in general agreement with Eshkol and Eban that the United States would be diplomatically supportive when the war was over, and that the Soviets would not intervene militarily. By this time, Wheeler had told Johnson that war was inevitable, that Israel would win within two weeks, but that destruction might be very heavy. On Sunday, the Senate Foreign Relations Committee released a report on testimony by Vice

President Humphrey and Secretaries Rusk and McNamara. With regard to an international declaration and the use of force, it clearly distinguished between passage of U.S. and of Israeli ships through the straits. At its meeting that day in Jerusalem, the cabinet voted unanimously for war.

"None of the great, not-so-great and no-longer-so-great" powers, as Theodore Draper observed, had meanwhile covered itself with glory. The Soviets, who had committed themselves since the 1950s to a kind of Baghdad Pact in reverse, now faced the risks and hazards of regional confrontation or worse. The Americans, who had consistently avoided commitment to Israel in the interest of credibility with the Arabs, now proved unable to deter either side. Speculations on conservative Jordan and revolutionary Egypt had both failed,[106] though paradoxically, Hussein's decision to enter the war on Nasser's side, while costing him the West Bank and East Jerusalem, may also have saved him his kingdom. By June 1, only a concerted action by both superpowers could have stopped the war. Yet this, under the circumstances, was among the unlikeliest of eventualities, for all that Johnson enjoined the Soviets to caution on May 22 and followed with hot-line messages to the same effect after the war had started.[107] In fact, since at least the early 1950s, both sides had done almost everything in their power to make concerted action impossible. The result, on the face of it, was a proxy Cold War in the Middle East. If anything, as Draper noted, the nearer their clients came to war, the less the superpowers could do about it.[108] For the second time in barely ten years, they nonetheless shared the liabilities for their clients' actions. Now, once again, they had to face the consequences.

6

From War to Watershed

It was one of the little ironies of U.S. politics that Harry McPherson, a presidential aide of Candidean temperament and impeccably Anglo-Saxon, Texas Democratic origins, had meanwhile succeeded Mike Feldman as the White House "resident specialist on Jewish affairs."[1] It was one of the little ironies of the 1967 war that he now arrived in Jerusalem the day the war began, en route home from Vietnam. Assigned to inform Prime Minister Levi Eshkol *ex officio* of White House concern about the growing strain on U.S.-Israeli relations, he was met and briefed on Monday morning by Israel's chief of military intelligence, Aharon Yariv. "Did the Egyptians attack?" McPherson asked. Yariv replied with an order of battle. "But did they attack?" McPherson persisted. Johnson obviously needed an answer before releasing any statement of his own. The answer came to McPherson as he noticed that his briefer, rather than hustling him to a bunker, was simply studying his watch. Realizing that this could only mean the Egyptian air force had ceased to be a threat, McPherson cabled the president accordingly.

Like it or not, the White House had already been aware of the war since 4:35 A.M. Washington time. By then, the Israelis had effectively destroyed the Egyptian air force on the ground. Secretary of Defense Robert McNamara confirmed receipt of the first serious signals on the newly installed Washington-Moscow hot line by 8:00 A.M.[2] At this point, the Israelis had established unchallengeable air superiority over the whole Middle East.

Although military planning was both thorough and brilliant, strategic and political planning was minimalist. Israel had no intention of expanding its borders as a result of the war, Ambassador Ephraim Evron informed Walt Rostow on June 5. Given both the urgency and oppressiveness of the political and military situation as Israelis understood it, and the war plans General Staff officers actually presented the political leadership, there was no reason to doubt Israeli sincerity. In anticipation of bombing, mass graves had already been prepared in Tel Aviv parks, and schoolchildren were drilled on what to do in case of air or gas attack. The agenda, according to Gideon Rafael, was neither more nor less than to beat the Egyptians, avoid withdrawal before conclusion of real peace, resist reinstatement of the previous armistice, and stay close enough to the United States to avoid "reactivation of that fatal American-Russian vice" that had made things so difficult for Israelis ten years earlier.[3]

The same night, McPherson and Ambassador Walworth Barbour conferred with an unnamed senior official in an unnamed Jerusalem hotel amidst a general blackout. Aware that external pressure would only increase with Israeli success, General Moshe Dayan himself had seen to it that information was at a premium. For the moment, Israeli victories were unannounced, while the Arabs reported victories that never happened.[4] Unsurprisingly, McPherson and Barbour complained about the scarcity of information. "The official" expressed his regrets, McPherson recalled, "but suggested that Israel had spared the United States considerable embarrassment by taking matters into its own hands." There was something to that, McPherson conceded.[5]

Revealingly, Washington's war began with a briefing error. "Our position is neutral in thought, word and deed," a State Department spokesman announced on June 5. Given the entire history of U.S. commitments to Israeli security, not to mention the obligations to assure freedom of passage on the Straits of Tiran undertaken in 1957, this was "an oversimplified approach to a complicated situation," as the president himself later noted in his memoirs. "We were certainly not belligerents," Johnson qualified. But "neutral" was obviously "the wrong word." Before the day was over, Secretary of State Dean Rusk himself had intervened to correct any misapprehension.[6]

It was unclear to what extent Johnson was really surprised by the Israeli preemption. But it was still harder to prove he welcomed it. Months later, receiving Abba Eban in the privacy of the Oval Office for the first time since their dramatic meeting in May, the president was still upset. The Israeli initiative had occasioned "the most awesome decisions he had taken since he came into office," the sanitized transcript disclosed. He found the Israeli decision unwise in June, the president declared. Looking back in October, he still found it unwise, victory notwithstanding.[7]

"I have never concealed my regret that Israel decided to move when it did," Johnson recalled. "I always made it equally clear . . . that I did not accept the oversimplified charge of Israel aggression," he added.[8] Years later, his national security advisor still insisted that the administration really believed it had from Monday to Friday to deter the Egyptians, move the United Nations and carry a reluctant Congress.[9] Yet there were equally credible reports that Johnson had conceded defeat after meeting Eban on May 26. "I've failed, they'll go," he told one senior advisor. Another recalled his saying, in effect, that "Israel is going to hit them."[10]

A working politician of legendary sensitivity, Johnson could hardly help but be aware that his Israeli peers were under superhuman pressures to act unilaterally. A consensus builder and political manager of mythic virtuosity, he must also have realized the almost other-worldly unlikelihood of finding meaningful and timely support for his own multilateral alternative. At the same time, he would surely have seen, as a number of U.S. ambassadors in the Middle East and Evron of the Israeli embassy alike told Walt Rostow, that it was better for both U.S.-Arab and U.S.-Soviet relations if the Israelis solved the straits problem themselves, rather than let the United States act unilaterally for them.[11]

Virtually irrespective of the outcome, it was clear, at least, that Washington was likelier to see the Israeli initiative as trouble than as opportunity, and that no one in any position of authority was likely to see it as a windfall for the United States.

The last thing Johnson could possibly want under such circumstances was a new international crisis. U.S. military resources were already hopelessly enmired in Southeast Asia. Rightly or wrongly, senior officials like Eugene Rostow inevitably saw the Middle East as a target of opportunity for the Soviets. "The administration was reasonably certain it could keep Vietnam from spreading," as the president himself recalled. "Conflict in the Middle East was something else."[12]

Meanwhile, a significant part of the electorate was suddenly alert, active, even existentially involved, as it had not been since World War II. At the same time, Congress, already a couple of years into the proverbial Southeast Asian tunnel, was nearly panicky at the thought of being asked to sign another blank check. Notwithstanding the intelligence community's conviction that Israel would win, any president faced the intimidating question of what to do if it should nonetheless run into trouble. On the other hand, as ten years before, there were the vexing questions of what to do if Israel won, and how to deal with a Soviet adversary, whose own chestnuts were now so clearly in the fire.

McNamara, no mean student of international tension, ranked the 1967 war with the Berlin crisis of August 1961 and the Cuban missile crisis of October 1962 as the high point of his seven years at the Pentagon.[13] Given the relative magnitude of Soviet and U.S. interest in the outcome; the likely calculus of risk and hazard; the actual Soviet record, both before and after; and the daunting strategic and political problems confronting any Soviet leader who might actually intervene militarily on behalf of his Arab clients,[14] the equation is at least arguable. On the other hand, given both the strategic situation of the United States and the administration's institutional memory, it is hardly surprising that Washington moved quickly to inform Moscow of its surprise, demonstratively avoided military movements in the Mediterranean, and reacted smartly to the Soviet reply on the hot line. Between them, both sides were to use the hot line almost two dozen times during the war's six days.[15]

By Tuesday, June 6, when the president was informed that Soviet Premier Alexei Kosygin was trying to reach him, Vice President Hubert Humphrey, Rusk, McNamara, Attorney General Nicholas Katzenbach, and Walt Rostow were all assembled in the White House situation room. Reflective itself of how seriously things were viewed, so were Rostow's predecessor, McGeorge Bundy, recalled from the Ford Foundation; Ambassador Llewellyn Thompson, recalled from Moscow; and the perennial wise man Clark Clifford, this time as representative of the President's Foreign Intelligence Advisory Board (PFIAB). Kosygin reported that he was working for a cease-fire. The Americans replied that they were doing the same.

On Monday, it was at least imaginable that the United States would have supported the Arab demand for Israeli troop withdrawals, had Egypt agreed to withdraw its troops from the Sinai and lift the blockade of the straits.[16] But neither was a real possibility. By Tuesday, as the Israelis continued their triumphant advance across the Sinai, the U.S. position had shifted to favor a cease-fire in place. But the Egyptians refused to consider it, and American thoughts began turning to a postwar order beyond the improvisations and hair-trigger status quo of the past twenty years. As Eban took up contact with Arthur Goldberg, the ambassador of the United States to the United Nations, on Wednesday, the text of the draft resolution quickly metamorphosed from "revitalized armistice" to "stable and durable peace," and Columbia Records rushed out an LP version of Eban's speech to the Security Council.[17]

Instead of coming closer, the United States and Israel stumbled into a confrontation whose consequences were as bloody as its causes, motivation, and even eventual settlement were obscure. On June 8, Israeli planes and torpedo boats attacked and devasted U.S. signals ship, the USS *Liberty,* off the Sinai coast. The Pentagon was informed of the attack by the *Liberty*'s commanding officer, with subsequent confirmation from an on-site U.S. submarine. But the submarine hesitated to break radio silence by calling for help. Concerned that the *Liberty* might actually be under Soviet attack, McNamara reportedly dispatched carrier-based F-4s. The Soviets were then notified via the hot line that the planes' movements were not hostile.[18]

Despite heavy damage, the ship survived to be towed away, though thirty-four crew members and specialist personnel died in the episode, and another seventy-five were injured, many severely. Not the least of the crisis was a minifailure of public information, occasioned by the smoke of battle and official disingenuousness alike. Immediately on learning of the attack, ten officials from the Navy, Joint Chiefs, and secretary's office gathered in McNamara's office, only to discover that they knew too little to respond, let alone retaliate. Meanwhile, another debate reportedly proceeded in the Oval Office.

Though McNamara and Phil Goulding, the assistant secretary for public affairs, favored admission that the *Liberty* was in the war zone to monitor electronic communications, even this was obscured in the initial briefings. Only when reporters demanded to know whether the respective coastal states had been officially informed that the ship was on station, was the point eventually conceded. No, Goulding acknowledged in a background briefing, they had not been informed, but the ship was both unarmed and in international waters. It was another day or more before the Pentagon, with a jog from the White House, finally reached a consensus position: that the attack on the ship was not "plausible," as had been asserted in an unattributed wire service story, but an outrage; and that failure to identify the ship as an intelligence collector had been "a major public affairs error."[19]

Each party for its own reasons, neither the Israeli nor the U.S. was exactly forthcoming on what had actually happened. Despite reports from the Pentagon and Clark Clifford, speculation and debate smouldered on for years.[20] In 1976, the Navy finally released 707 pages of top-secret material from hearings before a court of inquiry. But only 28 unclassified pages emerged from the sanitized transcript. On the other hand, there were grounds enough for disingenuousness. It may have been true that the *Liberty* was clearly identifiable as a U.S. ship and in international waters when attacked. A message to position itself one hundred miles off Gaza had nonetheless been misdirected to the Philippines, and then to Washington; a follow-up message never arrived because the ship was unequipped for messages from the "top-secret" communication system that dispatched it, and the U.S. flagship in the area had then passed on the message by ordinary teletype.[21]

As so often in such cases, it was easy enough to spike the excuses after the fact. If the Israelis really believed, as they said they did, that El Arish was under naval bombardment; that the *Liberty* was moving at suspicious speed; that the *Liberty* was a significantly smaller Egyptian supply ship; that the smoke of battle obscured the target, and so on, there were good reasons to question their judgment and responsibility. But deliberate malice, while easy to assume, was also hard to prove. Given Israeli concern for the security of their signals and their war plans; external pressure to accede to a U.N. cease-fire; and both the leadership's eagerness and domestic pressure[22] to take on the Syrians while the going was good, there was a circumstantial case that the Israelis knew very well what they were hitting.[23] There were also reasons as various as protection of Israel, the Navy, and the CIA, to infer U.S. cover-up.

It was no less plausible that the Israelis, from their own point of view, were acting in strategic good faith. Understandably reluctant to let an ambivalent Washington read their hand, they took the *Liberty* under observation, made sure that Washington knew it, then ordered the ship from the area. But the message from Washington failed to arrive, the ship remained in the war zone, and Israel attacked it, possibly calling the bluff in full awareness that it was a U.S. ship.

It could as plausibly have been a case of honest error with yet another U.S. source. According to an interview almost a quarter century later with a former Israeli major, who had served in the operations room in Tel Aviv, Israelis had been unable to identify the ship. They therefore sent photos by courier to the nearby U.S. embassy with a request for confirmation. The embassy—which may not, in fact, have known—denied the ship was American. The Israelis, with no reason to doubt the embassy's word, then attacked it.[24]

Consistent with either argument, Israel claimed error pro forma, and expressed official regret for the "tragic accident" in an apology submitted June 10. It then indemnified the injured and the families of the dead at about $3.5 million each. Yet it consistently refused to pay damages for a ship it had tried to warn away. Eban spoke of inadvertent attack and damage. "But it seemed inevitable that those who took risks might sometimes incur tragic sacrifice," he added.[25]

Nothing conclusive was ever proven, and credible evidence of that battle-specific and universally reported confusion that Clausewitz refers to as "friction" proliferated too. "Friction" at least suggested why the *Liberty* had failed to get out of harm's way. Arguments on U.S. concern for Syria are fragile too. According to Eban, who understandably called the White House in the aftermath of the attack, an unnamed presidential advisor actually found it strange "that Syria, the originator of the war, might be the only one which seemed to be getting off without injury." Assuming that Washington would "not be too grieved" if Syria took some punishment, Eban reported the conversation to Jerusalem the same day.[26] Yet Ze'ev Schiff, an Israeli reporter of notable authority and courage, argues plausibly that Dayan deferred the attack on Syria till June 9 for reasons as diverse as cloud cover, respect for Soviet sensitivity, and the course of the war against Egypt and Jordan. It was only then, according to Schiff, that Dayan "suddenly" changed his mind.[27]

As with many post facto arguments from effect, it is also hard to overlook a basic inconsistency in admittedly partisan premises. Arguably, the United States was a passive accessory to the Israeli campaign against Egypt and Jordan on June 5–7. Arguably, the Israelis saw the *Liberty*—and the CIA *a fortiori*—as a potential obstacle to their campaign against Syria on June 8. But conclusive evidence is thin for either proposition, and it takes a leap of faith as well as logic to believe in both at the same time.

Once under way, Israeli forces nonetheless managed to breach the Syrian lines by noon on Saturday, establish themselves on the Golan Heights, and take the town of Kuneitra after twenty-seven hours of heavy fighting. By this time, Damascus itself was only thirty miles and, according to the estimates of Israel's Major General David Elazar, no more than thirty-six hours away. Expectedly, Soviet concern grew apace with Israeli progress, while U.S. anxiety grew apace with Soviet concern. "If you want war, you will get war," Kosygin's hot-line message of June 10 declared in effect. Immediately alert to the overtones and resonances of words like "catastrophe," and "independent decision," Johnson took the precaution of ordering the Sixth Fleet from its current position three hundred miles off the Syrian coast to a new position just fifty miles away, while making clear to Kosygin that the United States supported a Syrian-Israeli cease-fire.[28] Meanwhile, Rusk was reportedly "in near panic." Unpersuaded that the Golan operation was either wise or necessary, he contacted Eban to urge Israeli compliance. The president of the United States "does not want the war to end as the result of a Soviet ultimatum," Goldberg reportedly warned. But Rusk himself assured a subsequent interviewer that he could "find no substance to this idea."[29]

At 6:00 P.M. on Saturday the shooting officially ended, with Israel victorious beyond anything imaginable when the week began. Its Arab neighbors, including an estimated 100,000 to 200,000 new refugees, were variously humiliated, stunned, and terrified. The region's strategic geography had been virtually turned upside down. Where most of Israel had hitherto been under Arab guns, Damascus was now in range of Israeli artillery and Cairo of Israeli tanks. In 1956, Israelis had abstained from taking the Suez Canal, and incidentally avoided the need to secure it. Now they stood at the canal as well, impervious to Dayan's prescient arguments that it could yet prove a strategic liability.[30] From the sea to the Jordan, all of what once was Mandatory Palestine was under Israeli control too. In 1966, Congress had appropriated $126.8 million for economic and military aid to Israel. Between May 27 and June 10, 1967, American Jews collected over $100 million in emergency funding, and a total of $317.5 million by the end of the year. The year's total dollar transfers came to $430 million, a burden on the balance of payments of such a magnitude that Johnson was advised to ask Eshkol's help in seeing that a good part was reinvested in long-term dollar holdings.[31]

The question of how to turn military victory to political advantage was the same as it had been for nearly twenty years. In principle, all options seemed open, save return to the status quo ante bellum. Yet as McPherson realized after a victory party at the Weizmann Institute, it was already clear that they were not. "Of course, you'll have to give it back if you want peace," he told his host as Jerusalem was toasted. "Never," his host replied.[32] On June 27, with only three Communist deputies opposing, the Knesset declared East Jerusalem part of Israel. Both Johnson and Rusk were forthrightly critical of Israeli failure at least to consult religious leaders or friendly states before unilaterally taking the city into their own hands.[33] Further pursuit of that "mutual trust and intimate consultation with the United States" that

Israelis saw as "the indispensable prerequisite" for achieving the "state of good-neighborly peaceful cooperation" that was "Israel's central goal,"[34] only made both Israeli-Israeli and Israeli-U.S. differences more apparent. It was even true that nearly all Israelis, from Menahem Begin's Gahal on the right to Mapam and former Brigadier General Yigal Allon's Achdut ha'Avodah on the left, agreed to the formula "territories for peace." The issue was which territories. Gahal was willing to concede parts of the Sinai, and no more. Mapam was determined to keep Gaza and Jerusalem, and no less. Achdut ha'Avodah's "Allon Plan" proposed continued strategic control of the West Bank combined with Palestinian self-government in the territory's populated areas.[35]

Subject to demilitarization of such areas as Israel might evacuate, and a special status for Sharm el Sheikh, the government was nonetheless prepared to return to the status quo ante with Syria and Egypt in return for a peace treaty, Eban informed senior U.S. policymakers in July. But he delicately conceded that Jerusalem and the West Bank "raised problems that transcended strategic interest." Where these were concerned, it was obvious that the Israelis were at odds with one another as they had been all along—or at any rate since their reluctant agreement to the partition of Palestine some twenty years before. In fact, the astonishing outcome of the war only reopened a debate as old as Zionism.[36] The Israelis could settle with Hussein, Eban informed Rusk. Contingent on unspecified "constitutional precedents," they could also pursue a settlement with the Palestinians on the basis of autonomy and an economic union, he added. "Rusk's response was brief and to the point," a witness noted in his memoirs. " 'There is a constitutional precedent for letting people themselves decide,' " he told the Israelis.

On the other hand, without obvious incentives and alternatives, the same principle applied to democratic Israel. "Without regard to political factors," General Earle G. Wheeler, chairman of the U.S. Joint Chiefs of Staff, reviewed the options in late June in reply to a query from McNamara. "Solely on military considerations from the Israeli point of view," he concluded, there was a strong case for Israeli retention of the high ground, hitherto Jordanian, directly east of Jerusalem; the high ground, hitherto Syrian, as far east as the border with Lebanon on the Golan Heights; the entire Gaza strip; and even an enclave in the Sinai, adjacent to Eilat.[37]

If professional opinion was firm, public opinion ranged increasingly from stiff to intransigent. By February 1968, over 90 percent of Israelis favored holding onto some or all of the West Bank, Sharm al-Sheikh, and the Golan, and 85 percent to holding onto some or all of Gaza.[38] "Attitudes towards Israel's present border shift as one goes up the social ladder," Congressman Joshua Eilberg of Pennsylvania noticed on a visit to Israel a few months after the war. At the bottom, people were opposed to giving up an inch. "At the top," he noticed, "there is realization that Israeli concessions in return for a real peace settlement would be worth making."[39]

As they had long since learned to do when at odds with one another, Israelis looked expectantly to the White House. The White House, in turn, looked circumspectly toward Congress, the Middle East, and the Soviet Union. "Let me emphasize that the U.S. continues to be guided by the same basic policies which have been followed by this Administration and previous Administrations," Johnson informed Senator Mike Mansfield preemptively in a letter on June 8, after Mansfield solicited the president's views on the Middle East.[40] Yes, the president told a press conference on June 13, the United States remained committed "to the territorial and political integrity of every nation in the Middle East." But what happened would "depend a good deal on the nations themselves," and he had no "rule of thumb or arbitrary formula" to offer.[41] "I am for peace, territorial integrity, political independence, and unrestricted navigation in the Houston Ship Channel," he jocularly informed a Texas Democratic party dinner in Austin on June 16.[42]

Only on June 19, after a foreign policy *tour d'horizon* embracing the Americas, Africa, and Asia, did Johnson turn specifically to the Middle East. In a speech to an invited academic audience at the State Department, the president now proposed "five great principles of peace." The first, consistent with previous policy, was "the recognized right of national life." No nation would be true either to the U.N. Charter or its own best interests, Johnson declared, "if it should permit military success to blind it to the fact that its neighbors have rights." The second was "justice for the refugees." Without it, he announced as had three presidents before him, "there will be no peace for any party in the Middle East." The third principle, expectedly, was maritime rights, not least, Johnson emphasized, because he considered the closure of the Straits of Tiran "a single act of folly . . . more responsible for this explosion than any other." The fourth, clearly intended as a successor to the Tripartite Declaration, was a collective regime of arms control in the Middle East to be administered through the United Nations. Finally, the president concluded, there had to be "peace between the parties" with "recognized borders" and security arrangements, as well as a special status for the holy places in Jerusalem.[43]

A few days later, the grand design had already run into heavy weather. At an ad hoc summit in Glassboro, New Jersey, in late June 1967, Johnson and Kosygin confirmed and acted out the now-traditional superpower stalemate. Johnson talked about limiting arms transfers. Kosygin talked about the Middle East. Johnson unrolled his plan for a settlement. Kosygin concentrated on Israeli withdrawal. "I must report that no agreement is readily in sight on the Middle Eastern crisis," Johnson reported on his return to the White House. He was nonetheless determined to keep on trying. Only two weeks before, there had been agreement on a cease-fire. There was agreement now on "such simple propositions" as the right of every state to live, the need for an end to the war in the Middle East and withdrawal of troops "in the right circumstances," the president declared.[44]

By mid-July, Johnson's continued pursuit of what Israelis saw as "dubious diplomatic compromise,"[45] and the administration saw as a basic expression of global responsibility, had led to a near breakthrough, to what Eban recalled as "one of the most embarrassing discussions which the United States and Israel had ever held," and to a document that persuaded Eban "that we were in serious trouble."[46] After intensive talks with the Soviet Union's perennial Foreign Minister Andrei Gromyko and its almost equally perennial ambassador in Washington, Anatoly Dobrynin, Goldberg produced a draft text, adapted from a previous Latin American resolution that failed to find a majority. Perhaps revealingly, Rusk had quite forgotten it when reminded by an interviewer years later.[47] An ironic principle for the superpowers themselves to have acceded to, as Goldberg admitted,[48] it declared that territory acquired through conquest was inadmissible. It then demanded immediate withdrawal from occupied territories and asserted the right to independent existence of national states, though without specific reference to Israel. Emphatically informed by Eban that the United States was "on a course incompatible with Israel's security and with the interest and dignity of the free world," Goldberg replied diplomatically that the United States was interested in any Soviet initiative plus a formula that would split the Arabs. Besides, he anticipated correctly, nothing would come of the statement anyway.[49]

In late August, the Arabs proved him right. At a summit meeting in Khartoum, the assembled heads of state, including Jordan's King Hussein and Egypt's President Nasser, agreed that Kuwait, Saudi Arabia, and Libya would resume suspended oil deliveries to Western customers, and divert the proceeds to Jordan and Egypt. They then resolved that there would be no recognition, no negotiations, and no peace with Israel on any terms. Arguably, the three negatives were a bargaining position. But the furthest Arabs would go was to allow Hussein a free hand to negotiate through the United States on terms for an Israeli withdrawal.[50]

Since putative "extremists" like Algeria's head of state, Colonel Houari Boumedienne, demonstratively stayed away, and the Syrians left the meeting altogether, the outcome could even be seen as a victory for Arab "moderates."[51] But it was no surprise that Israelis failed to see it this way. In June, as the Israeli chief of staff and later ambassador to Washington, Yitzhak Rabin, claimed to have learned post facto from U.S. sources, the Israeli government had been amenable to substantial withdrawals from Syrian and Egyptian territory, contingent on demilitarization of the affected areas. In August, after Khartoum, it changed its collective mind.[52]

By the time the General Assembly convened for its annual session in September 1967, correspondingly little of the U.S. plan was still in view, and there was little evidence of consensus even in Washington. Israel had emerged from the war in fine economic shape, the administration concluded. Given historical anxieties about the Israeli balance of payments, this seemed good in itself. Yet it could also be one more reason for Israel to persist in positions that already worried Washington. "[T]he concern of Israel's friends is reinforced by increasing [Israeli] emphasis on form of settlement (direct negotiations and formal peace treaties) rather than substance (peaceful borders and Arab renunciation of belligerent rights and actions)," an unsent instruction to Ambassador Walworth Barbour noted.[53]

At the same time, for reasons as various as Arab intransigence, superpower stalemate, fears that the Soviets would make hay of the Middle Eastern impasse, the hovering memory of 1957, an impending presidential election year, and growing congressional and public frustration with Vietnam, it was hard to make a case for putting the screws to Israel either. There was desultory consideration for extending the regional arms embargo. Imposed on the outbreak of the June war, its impact fell hardest on Israel. But there was an equally plausible case for resuming credit sales, including the Skyhawks agreed to some fifteen months before. As always, the administration preferred to make delivery to Israel contingent on sales to "moderate Arab states" as well, including Jordan. But Congress, clearly taking its cues from Israel, was not about to have any of that either, particularly as evidence grew that the Soviets were resupplying Arab forces, and three Soviet missiles from an Egyptian vessel based in Port Said sank an Israeli destroyer on October 21.

The dilemmas practically shone from the briefing paper prepared for Eban's White House visit a few days later. Almost in consecutive sentences, the paper declared a decision on aircraft "imperative," acknowledged "a sense of urgency about moving toward negotiations," and expressed concern that Israel's "post-war policies may have the cumulative effect of undermining this opportunity." In effect to build Israeli confidence, it endorsed continued firmness at the United Nations and relaxation of the arms embargo. At the same time, it reflected real anxiety about Jordan, and acknowledged not only a strong but possibly "unique and non-recurring," case for indirect negotiations with the Arabs, particularly given the impossibility of direct settlement.

"Failure to achieve a reasonable settlement . . . could lead to further fragmentation of that state and a consequent land grab and conflict among its neighbors," the president was told. "Similarly we see no advantage in the creation of yet another tiny, unstable and only semi-independent state on the West Bank," the paper added. Conceding grounds for Israeli disenchantment with King Hussein, it was equally emphatic that "any imaginable alternative would be worse, not only for us but Israel." Israel would have "to understand Jordan's importance to the U.S. position in the area and to do nothing to undermine the Hussein regime," it declared.

In his meeting with Eban, Johnson was characteristically forthright about his situation. Congress was serious about aid cuts, he emphasized. Domestic opinion was increasingly keen to "'come home,' whether it be from Saigon, Berlin or elsewhere." Meanwhile, increasing numbers of Americans looked on arms sales as the equivalent of "joining the Mafia." For all that the Soviets assumed that the United States had a lot of influence with the Israelis, and the Israelis assumed it had a lot of influence with the Russians, both were wrong, the president added.

Johnson acknowledged, under prodding from Eban, that the Sixth Fleet "had not harmed the situation" in June. The Israelis would nonetheless have to understand that Americans' tolerance for foreign commitments was in decline, and that the United States had to maintain its position in the Middle East "to keep the USSR from putting its tentacles on other nations," the president emphasized. They would also have to understand that "the further they get from June 5, the further they are from peace."[54]

The same day, October 24, 1967, Robert McCloskey, the State Department press officer, circumspectly announced release of "end items," that is the embargoed Skyhawks, to a roomful of aggressive reporters at the daily briefing. Their reactions were as revealing as they were predictable. "Bob, what exactly do you mean by end items?" asked one. "In that connection, Bob, what's the rationale for omitting Jordan . . .?" asked another. "You're totally at the mercy of the Soviet Union in this thing, aren't you, Bob, if your policy is subject to reaction to whatever they do?" asked a third. "Does this . . . mean the Administration has now clarified all the outstanding elements of arms sales or credits which are involved in pending legislation?" asked a fourth.[55]

Actually, nothing was very clear save general stalemate. For both domestic and diplomatic reasons, the Israelis refused to budge from their original demands, contingent on recognition by their devastated neighbors, and a phone call from Amman that never came. For their own domestic and diplomatic reasons, the Arabs, in turn, found it as irresistible as ever to make immobility their common position. The Soviet Union, with its own credibility at stake, could hardly back away from its humiliated Arab clients. The United States, which had implicitly linked Berlin and Israel, could hardly agree to a position unacceptable to Israel. Since the United States insisted on a resolution acceptable to both Israel and at least a token representation of Arabs, this meant, in effect, that Israel now exercised a veto over U.S. policy.[56]

As so often, the bottlenecks were on full view at the United Nations where, between June and November 1967 both the Security Council and General Assembly failed to muster the majorities required for any action. Yet even here, as parliamentary Galileos grudgingly acknowledged, things moved. From mid-September on, the one idea that did find general favor was the idea of a U.N. envoy. The breakthrough was nonetheless two months away. Seemingly born about equally of idealism and desperation, the compromise text was immeasurably assisted by two assets that had hitherto gone unnoticed and unappreciated. One was the circumstantial credibility of a British delegation, suddenly rehabilitated beyond anything imaginable eleven years before. The other was the professional resourcefulness of an ambassador, Lord Caradon, who nearly forty years before had first experienced the Middle East as a very junior colonial officer in the Palestine administration, and who in 1957–1960 had tested his stamina as British governor of Cyprus.

In contrast to previous would-be mediators, including the superpowers, with their prior commitments to their clients; the French, who had abruptly switched sides on Israel in June; the Indians, whose prime minister, Indira Ghandi, was associated with Nasser; the Danes and Canadians, whose Aqaba initiative had inspired Arab suspicion in May; and the Nationalist Chinese, who inspired distrust from much of the United Nations practically by definition, the British now proved acceptable to contending parties, who themselves had only recently regarded the British as the enemy. But it was Caradon's ability to doctor, coax, and tailor the chosen instrument from a variety of Third World, Latin American, and superpower oddments going back to the previous summer that clearly turned the tide.

The secret, as Caradon acknowledged, was language of such calculated, even inspired, ambiguity as to satisfy the increasingly modest expectations of the contending parties. Henry Kissinger could later describe it with some reason as a "symbol of deadlock, more an expression of stalemate than a means of its resolution."[57] Yet, at the moment, it looked not only clever but hopeful. Tidily divided into "preambular" and "operative" language, Caradon's draft both declared that conquest was inadmissible *and* recognized "the need for a just and lasting peace in which every state in the area can live in security." It called for Israel to withdraw "from territories occupied in the recent conflict" *and* for "termination of all claims or states of belligerency" with corresponding "respect for and acknowledgement of the sovereignty, territorial integrity and political independence of every State in the area and their right to live in peace within secure and recognized boundaries. . . . ." It affirmed "the necessity" for freedom of navigation, "a just settlement of the refugee problem," and guaranteed "territorial inviolability *and* political independence of every State in the area" by means of measures including establishment of demilitarized zones.

Finally, the new text authorized the secretary general to "designate a Special Representative" to "establish and maintain contacts . . . in order to promote agreement and assist efforts to achieve a peaceful and accepted settlement. . . . ." Given the prevailing code, this was still another exquisitely balanced package. Neither a mandate to oversee Israeli withdrawal, as the Arabs wished, nor to confine the envoy's role to "matchmaking," as the Israelis wished, the job description was a compromise between the undesirable activism of autonomous diplomacy and the equally undesirable passivity of pure stenography. With its hint of negotiation, the mandate to "promote agreement" could even be understood as an incentive for the Israelis. As it happened, Gunnar Jarring, an experienced Swedish mediator, was already in place. Appointed a full month before the Security Council officially requested him, he was currently Swedish ambassador to Moscow, had already held several posts in the Middle East, and had previously served as U.N. intermediary between India and Pakistan. Paradoxically, although little was expected of the resolution per se, much was expected of the mediation. Yet long after Jarring had returned to Moscow, and his mission had vanished in oblivion, the text continued to serve as baseline for what was itself now referred to with consistent ambiguity as "the peace process."[58]

After the fact, it was easy enough to fault Caradon's text for three conspicuous omissions. There was no reference to specific postwar borders. There was no reference to the Palestinians per se. There was also no reference to Jerusalem. Yet, in the real world of 1967, these were among the very virtues of the draft. A passionate exegetical debate over the relative priority of "territories" in the English text versus *"des territoires"* in the French text[59] itself confirmed that there was no consensus on how things should come out. On the contrary, the eventual outcome, with or without the services of the secretary general's special representative, was to be the object of the negotiations. Omission of any reference to the Palestinians *expressis verbis* was no coincidence either. "We all took it for granted that the occupied territory would be restored to Jordan," Caradon credibly insisted years later. In fact, an independent Palestinian presence was hardly visible at the time from Amman, Jerusalem, or Cairo, let alone from the East River. As for Jerusalem, "we all assumed that East Jerusalem would revert to Jordan," Caradon added.

The Americans' own incremental drift—from support in June for the Latin American formula, "all forces from all territories," to its own formula, "withdrawal of armed forces from occupied territories," in early November—only underlined the arbitrariness of the "we."[60] But by this time there was little disposition to pedantry. On November 22, with a vote of 15–0 and the cheers of a crowded gallery, the Security Council accepted Caradon's draft as Resolution 242. Nasser accepted it, while demonstratively keeping his armed forces at the ready, and making any solution contingent on a formula acceptable to the "Palestinians themselves." Presumably, this meant the PLO, which itself rejected Resolution 242 shortly afterward.[61] With Eshkol's approval, Eban also accepted for Israel, but the acceptance was so discreet and indirect that Johnson felt a need to request its reaffirmation in

April 1968, and Eshkol himself seemed virtually unaware that he had authorized Eban to go ahead.[62] Unable to agree either to endorse or reject Eban's action, Eshkol's cabinet instead rewrote the resolution unilaterally to meet desiderata that included direct negotiations, a peace treaty, "secure," that is, new borders, right of passage through the Suez Canal, and resettlement of refugees outside of Israel's final borders.[63] Since no actual borders were specified, consensus was no problem, even for Begin and Dayan, who had powerful, if differing, views about withdrawal from the West Bank and elsewhere.

As might be expected, the unmediated ambiguities on both sides tended to turn the diplomatic dialogue into a kind of dialogue of the deaf about eggs and chickens. The Arabs demanded withdrawal as a condition for negotiations. The Israelis demanded negotiations as a condition for withdrawal. Jarring's best weapon in such circumstances was the threat to quit.

By the time Eshkol appeared for his last talks with Johnson in early January 1968, both sides were whistling in the dark. With peace nowhere in sight, Israel was even more dependent on U.S. arms than ever. Yet as half a million U.S. troops sank ever deeper in the jungles of Southeast Asia, and the president sank ever deeper in the opinion of his fellow citizens, the United States in general and its president in particular discovered unanticipated dependencies of their own. Democrats should take advantage of Israeli polls, reflecting Johnson's popularity, Congressman Eilberg informed the White House on his return from Israel. At the same time, calling attention to Dayan's views on the salutary role of the United States in Jordan, Harold Saunders urged Barefoot Sanders, a fellow White House staffer, to make full use of them when making the administration's case to Congress on why Jordan should get U.S. arms.[64] As always, Walt Rostow's briefing paper on the eve of Eshkol's visit was a little barometer of "who" and "whom," not to mention quid and quo. "What we want," was neatly itemized under the first rubric: Israeli concessions, Israeli accession to a nuclear nonproliferation treaty, Israeli toleration of U.S. support for Jordan, "some quiet words to American Jewish leaders" on Vietnam. "What we'll give," the second rubric continued: twenty-seven more Skyhawks and a promise to deliver the follow-on Phantom; revision of the old desalinization plan to accommodate the entire Jordan Valley; a bit of Food for Peace aid. Peace itself was explicitly identified as the administration's top priority, but "We can't support an Israel that sits tight," the paper warned.

As always, public rhetoric was a barometer too. Received around the family table at Johnson's Texas ranch, the Israeli guests were the addressees of an afterdinner speech as heavily rewritten as Beethoven's overture to *Leonore,* and with similarly inspirational intent. "We are both of pioneer stock," the president noted. "We both admire the courage and resourcefulness of the citizen-soldier," he added. He even compared the Alamo with Masada and the Israelis with Texans. But the real Israeli-U.S. link, the president continued hopefully, was a common vision of peace.[65]

Unfortunately for hosts and guests alike, the vision was at least premature. Before the month was over, the enemy's biggest offensive of the war had irreversibly crushed U.S. confidence in Vietnam. A few weeks later, the president drew his personal consequences. On March 31, 1968, he announced his decision to surrender the White House almost concurrently with Rabin's arrival in Washington as Israel's new ambassador.

As chief of staff in June, Rabin had been, almost by definition, among the public heroes of the recent war. Still untested in the political combats that were to follow, he was nonetheless a man of formidable self-assurance in a job that both favored and required it. As such, he was both a model and a trial to the Americans he met, even including Henry Kissinger, himself no slouch at self-assurance.[66] Either way, Rabin could hardly have differed more starkly from the Americans around him, who seemed to him to populate "a country in the throes of disintegration." Some, like Joseph Alsop, the syndicated columnist, looked to Rabin for wisdom. Others, like Senator Robert F. Kennedy, the former president's brother and one of the year's Democratic presidential candidates, looked to him for vicarious support. On the eve of the California primary, Kennedy's campaign staff called for a photo opportunity. No believer in the political celibacy of ambassadors, Rabin would, in fact, have accepted. But a day later, on the evening of Kennedy's climactic victory and the first anniversary of the Six-Day War, the candidate was assassinated in Los Angeles by a radicalized Palestinian. "The American people were so dazed by what they perceived as the senseless act of a madman that they could not begin to fathom its political significance," Rabin recalled with some justice.[67] As it was, he attended both national nominating conventions as an observer, where he noted with distaste that Democrats reflexively believed that a candidate's views on Israel were the principal determinant of Jewish votes, and that Republicans, for all purposes, had practically written off Jewish voters.[68]

With respect to peace, Rabin defined his mandate according to priorities rather different from anything envisaged in either Resolution 242 or Johnson's speech of June 19. As he saw it, his first responsibility was to see that Israel got what was needed for its defense. Only then came coordination of policy in preparation for peace talks—"or at the very least, preventing the emergency of too wide a disparity in policies" between Israel and the United States. The rest of his self-defined charge included U.S. financial support "to cover our arms purchases and buttress our economy," U.S. strategic support to deter direct Soviet intervention, and devising "a plan for maintaining Israel's leverage with the American Administration and Congress."[69]

The last, of course, was a necessary condition for all the others, if not a sufficient condition in itself. Yet unlike 1948 or 1957, the established political landscape and the prevailing political climate were on Israel's side. Domestic and Asian turmoil notwithstanding, the June war and its open-ended aftermath brought unusual visibility to the Middle East.[70] They also led a new U.S. Left to regard Israel with growing skepticism, and the White House to identify the friends of Israel as "Doves for War."[71] Yet even this now worked to Israel's advantage, endowing it with a rare and priceless image as underdog, as hero, and as test. "There are those who believe that if the United States allowed Israel to be eliminated, nobody would have any trust in American security commitments anywhere else," the social democratic Eban declared in an interview with William F. Buckley, one of the pillars of U.S. conservatism. "Like Vietnam?" Buckley followed up predictably. "Yes, and Asia, Europe, Latin America," Eban replied. Given his actual views both on Vietnam and Israel's role there, Eban's answer was at least a little disingenuous. But this was clearly no concern of the interviewer, or the interviewer's researcher. "Amen!" Buckley answered.[72]

Under such circumstances, U.S. opinion was a virtual open door for a can-do Israeli like Rabin, who only recently could and had so spectacularly done. "I always thought Jews were yaller," declared an admiring South Georgia gas station attendant in the aftermath of the war. For the moment, at least, Israel enjoyed the sympathies of conservatives *and* liberals, hawks *and* doves, provided, that is, that the United States remained out of the line of fire and, above all, refrained from sending troops. "You Hebes really taught those guys a lesson," an associate told a Jewish businessman." It was abruptly clear to countless thousands of American Jews that this was a collective compliment.[73]

Meanwhile, amidst the centrifugal pulls of presidential politics, urban riots, Vietnam itself, and the Soviet invasion of Czechoslovakia in late summer, a discredited administration sought to win the Israelis for indirect talks on substance as opposed to direct talks on procedure. The incentives included both arms and diplomatic support, but especially in an election year, Congress found it irresistibly easy to reward friends and punish even indirect enemies. In October 1967 and again in July 1968, the House voted to reduce the year's import quotas for cotton from Egypt and the Sudan, and transfer them instead to U.S. producers. Ironically, it took Johnson, the long-time senator from cotton-producing Texas, to veto the initiative "on grounds that it would unecessarily politicize a purely economic matter." Conversely, Israel was one of a select group of U.S. clients exempted in 1968 from a requirement that U.S. economic aid be withheld in amounts equivalent to the respective beneficiary's expenditure on sophisticated arms acquisitions.

Established aid programs continued, and even flourished. In December 1967, the Senate endorsed a proposal going back to the Eisenhower administration for provision of desalination and power plants to both Israel and the Arab states, contingent on their mutual cooperation. In 1968–1969, this was specifically rewritten to favor a dual-purpose desalination and power plant for Israel, and incorporated as a $40 million request in the foreign aid bill. In the end, $20 million, was even appropriated for the purpose, although the administration had not requested it, and the State Department opposed the idea on both budgetary and technical grounds. For the first time, Israeli institutions were also subsumed in the traditional package of aid for Middle Eastern schools and hospitals. Thus, Congress appropriated about $10 million for Arab, but $12.5 million for Israeli, schools and hospitals in 1970. Specific items included about $9.5 million for the American University in Beirut, but nearly $5 million for expansion of the Hadassah Hospital in Jerusalem and, after internal debate on the wisdom of indirect aid through forgiveness of outstanding loans, a further $2.5 million for the Weizmann Institute, Israel's premier research center.[74]

As always, arms were a bellwether issue. At his meeting with Eshkol in early 1968, Johnson had agreed to supply Israel with America's latest high-performance jet, the F-4 Phantom. But terms, timing, and political conditions were unspecified, contingent on a possible arms-limitation accord with the Soviet Union. There was some support for trading the planes for territorial concessions, and alternatively for accession to the nuclear nonproliferation treaty. As usual, the ideas met especially stiff resistance. In fact, as was credibly acknowledged some ten years later, agents of Israel's Mossad were already resourcefully, if unconventionally, procuring the stocks needed to make a bomb.[75] Meanwhile, it was reported that the Israeli government volunteered to abstain from "introduction" of nuclear weapons in the region. But, on closer examination, this turned out to mean neither more nor less than that Israel would not be the first to "test" or publicly acknowledge possession of a nuclear device. In his memoirs, Rabin was to assert that the Pentagon, represented by then-Assistant Secretary Paul C. Warnke, demanded a written explanation of Israel's request for planes, and Israel's accession to an inspection regime that would have put U.S. observers in virtually every Israeli research facility. Years later, Warnke denied Rabin's slightly disingenuous version pro forma. But their encounter seems to have been the last American effort to link arms aid to nuclear abstinence.

In any case, the search for a quid pro quo had been abandoned by October 1968. By this time, Senate endorsement of the plane sale had already been on record since July, Soviet resupply of Arab forces was well advanced, Israeli positions on the Suez Canal were under fire from Egyptian guns, and the November election was approaching. On October 8, the Senate voted "that the President should take such steps as may be necessary" to "provide Israel with an adequate deterrent force," offset new Arab weapons, and replace losses incurred in 1967. The same day, in a speech at the United Nations, Eban agreed to substantive talks with Jarring. As he anticipated, there was no response from the Arabs and a barrage of flak from the Israeli Right. A day later, Johnson announced approval of the Phantoms, and for a year thereafter, Eban noted, "Israel was immune from charges about her obduracy and intransigence."[77] The official deal, concluded in late December only weeks before Johnson's departure, provided for delivery of sixteen planes in 1969 and thirty-four more in 1970.

A few weeks later, a new administration took over the White House, and with it a global agenda as perplexing as any in memory. Meanwhile, according to declassified documents released a few years later, the CIA had informed Johnson of an Israeli nuclear arsenal, but the president had explicitly asked that the information be withheld, even from Rusk and McNamara. Within a year, U.S. inspections of Dimona had reportedly stopped too, and Johnson's Republican successors neglected even to mention the nuclear issue until 1970, when Richard Helms, then Director of Central Intelligence, reported the existence of an Israeli bomb to the Senate Foreign Relations Committee. From the mid-1970s on, there was a series of similar official revelations and confirmations. In no case was there any threat of sanctions from an Administration prepared in the French as well the Israeli case to accept and even encourage what it could no longer stop.[78]

It was credibly estimated in 1968 that 90 percent of Jewish voters supported the Democratic loser, Hubert Humphrey.[79] Yet four years later, only 60 percent—and as few as 25 percent among the politically and religiously conservative *hasidim*—supported his successor, Senator George McGovern, like Humphrey an upper-middle-western populist with unexceptionable liberal credentials.[80] Meanwhile, to the Democrats' dismay, Nixon, the 1968 winner, had co-opted such traditional liberal initiatives as guaranteed income and the opening to mainland China. Yet apparently it was not for these that he won the votes of Jews who previously had spurned him but because of the basically conservative, lower-middle-class values thousands of them had arguably shared with him all along.[81]

Revealingly, Nixon, the Republican winner of both elections, regarded his 1968 failure to reach Jewish voters as a positive advantage. "I was in the unique position of being politically unbeholden," he recalled in his memoirs. "I had more flexibility to do solely what I thought was the right thing."[82] Both then and after, this was a matter of debate. Yet it was just another irony of his presidency that, less than two years after his landslide reelection, Jerusalem and Cairo, as well as Moscow and Beijing, were among the last places on earth where he was still welcomed by cheering crowds.

In fact, as his Jewish secretary of state was to notice, a president who "stood by Israel more firmly than any other President since Harry Truman," not only did not especially like Jews but seemed at times positively obsessed by them.[83] Golda Meir's announcement within a year of Nixon's election that the new president was "an old friend of the Jewish people" came "as startling news to those of us more familiar with Nixon's ambivalences," Kissinger recalled.[84] For a man who suspected Jewish liberalism, Jewish loyalty, and, perhaps above all, the hostility of the putatively Jewish media for all his public life,[85] it was just another irony that he had not only hired Kissinger but acquired him from the eastern Republican establishment he had always abhorred as well.

Yet it was also true that Nixon included Israelis in his well-documented regard for toughness. "He had a real machismo thing for the Israelis," recalled Roger Morris, a member of Kissinger's NSC staff. "He liked to see them shed blood."[86] As noted by William Safire, a White House staffer and later columnist for the *New York Times,* Jews were also prominent among Nixon's heroes, from Benjamin Disraeli and the Supreme Court Justices Benjamin Cardozo and Felix Frankfurter to the novelist Herman Wouk. Jewish staff and senior officials were prominent too— even conspicuous by the standards of just eight years earlier. Apart from Kissinger as national security advisor and secretary of state, they included Arthur Burns as chairman of the Federal Reserve; Herbert Stein as chairman of the Council of Economic Advisors; Leonard Garment as White House counselor.

Yet irony again, while reluctant simply to let Jarring and the strategic balance take their course, Nixon was equally disinclined on taking office to run personal risks in the Middle Eastern minefields.[87] For the moment, U.S. policy was based on "genuine peace," Israeli withdrawals, U.S. brokerage, and an indeterminate role for the Soviets. "It is high time that the United States stop acting as Israel's attorney in the Middle East," one White House staffer was heard to say. Kissinger himself was reportedly both withdrawn and skeptical. "Look, anyone who has been through what I've been through has some very special feeling for the survival of the state of Israel," he told a friend.[88] At the same time, he was concerned that Israel's strength was ultimately counterproductive. He was also convinced that U.S. diplomacy was a potential winner, and that there were practical limits to Soviet influence in the Arab world. Each in its way, the United States could influence Israelis and Arabs, both moderate and radical, Kissinger argued.

For the moment, at least, this too left Nixon unpersuaded. He saw the Middle East, like Africa, as a part of the world where the stakes were elusive, and the price, not least the domestic one, was high.[89] He chose to be active, but indirectly. On the one hand, with reassurances to the Israelis[90] and at least nominal support for Jarring and Resolution 242, the administration set out to see what could be done in concert, particularly with de Gaulle and the Soviets. At the same time, it conferred responsibility on a State Department for which Nixon himself had no more than qualified regard, and whose own view of the Arab-Israeli conflict struck Kissinger as dangerously skewed.

In part, as the president explained and Kissinger confirmed, he subcontracted the Middle East because "Kissinger's Jewish background would put him at a disadvantage during the delicate initial negotiations for the reopening of relations with the Arab states." In part, as Kissinger added though Nixon did not, it was because he believed that Jews would be unappreciative of anything he did anyway, and he wanted to be seen resisting domestic Jewish pressure. "We've got to help the king," he reportedly declared in April 1969 on the occasion of Hussein's latest visit to Washington. "We cannot let these American Jews dictate policy."[91] Less than a year later, after France sold Libya a consignment of over one hundred jets, some once intended for Israel, he not only demonstratively attended a dinner for French President Georges Pompidou but reportedly suspended relations to American-Jewish groups that protested Pompidou's appearance in New York.[92] But his main reason for reluctance to intervene directly and personally in the Arab-Israeli conflict, Nixon argued at least as credibly, was because he believed Vietnam, strategic arms control, and superpower relations in general had priority over the Middle East.[93]

Yet such was the logic of the new administration's view of the world that its priorities both demanded, and effectively precluded, a Middle East initiative per se. Instead, they subsumed such seemingly diverse issues as U.S. disengagement in Vietnam, stable deterrence, Soviet-Jewish emigration, and Arab-Israeli peace in a concurrent system of superpower negotiations. Their "linkage," to use the new administration's favorite code word, presumably allowed the contending parties to pursue their mutual give and take on a global level.[94] Intellectually compelling and operationally elusive, the premises were at once direct and subtle. For the moment, at least, the president took it for granted that the Soviet Union, not the United States, was the political winner of the Six-Day War. With rather more reason, he also took it for granted "that further wars would be fought . . . for repossession of those conquered and occupied territories." Since, as he told his new secretary of state, it was equally clear that *"we* want peace," but *"they* want the Middle East,"[95] the Middle East could impress him only as a spontaneous combustion waiting to happen. "I consider it a powder keg," the new president declared within a week of taking office. "I am open to any suggestions that may reduce the possibility of another explosion, because the next explosion could involve . . . a confrontation between the nuclear powers," he added emphatically.[96] Yet it followed from the logic of his own position that the way to Jerusalem, Damascus, and Cairo first led to Moscow, and that the road to peace was paved with superpower negotiations.

Meanwhile, the Middle East showed no sign of coming to rest. At once secure and insecure, Israeli forces, for the first time in their history, confronted the challenges of a more or less static defense along impermanent and permeable borders, and especially the Suez Canal. As the Egyptians appreciated quite correctly, not only Israeli forces but Israeli morale and the Israeli economy were highly vulnerable to a war of attrition, whose purpose, by definition, was to tie down manpower and inflict casualties. They also speculated, Kissinger assumed, that they could bring pressure on the Soviet Union, and hence the United States, by continued military activity along the canal, thus leading to external pressure on Israel.[97] Armed for the moment both with patience and superior artillery, the Egyptians managed at least to generate casualties, though many, including the Egyptian chief of staff, were inevitably their own.

For the first time, Palestinian irregulars also attained and asserted a certain degree of practical autonomy. A political cipher since 1957, they now resumed the little war across the cease-fire lines that had been virtually suspended after Israel's withdrawal from Gaza. Their new self-assurance was clearly linked to the debacle and humiliation inflicted on the Arab states, "progressive" and conservative alike. The new strategy and self-image, in turn, were inspired by such disparate examples as China, Vietnam, and Algeria, themselves reflections of prevailing political fashion. In the brave new world of Palestinian politics, Amman was accordingly seen as the Palestinian "Hanoi," and Jerusalem as the Palestinian "Saigon," awaiting its liberation.[98] The new campaign was militarily negligible. Yet politically, the PLO waged an increasingly effective war of attrition on Israel's traditional left-of-center support and image at the very moment when the traditional Israeli Left had arguably attained its most comprehensive political ascendancy.

Among the results of the war were an extended draft term as compulsory service was extended from two and a half to three years, and a bigger, not smaller, military budget. In 1966–1967, military spending had stood a little below 11 percent. In 1968–1969, it grew to nearly 19 percent, in 1971–1972 to nearly 25 percent. The war of attrition meanwhile exacted its own bloody and specific toll on both sides. Between the end of the 1967 war and the cease-fire of August 1970, Israeli forces sustained about as many casualties as they had during the legendary six days, but this time, many of the casualties were civilians.

Domestic opinion alone required retaliation in force. But by now, an election in October 1969 had not only tilted power to the left but to the hawks. Their views on strategic borders and new Jewish settlements, though deliberately and admittedly ambiguous, were subsumed, in turn, in the Labor platform, codified in an "oral doctrine," and sketched out on a map. Apprehensions of U.S. "even-handedness" were themselves a catalyst in turning a near-even left-right split into a new National Unity government after weeks of postelectoral dithering. Yet Labor animals—Meir, Dayan, Yigal Allon, Eban, and Minister without Portfolio Israel Galili—were more equal in the new government than others.[99] Not for the first time, few Americans, Jewish or otherwise, had much comprehension for what might be called Jacobin Zionism. But if only via Rabin himself, an ambassador who reported directly to the new prime minister, Golda Meir, rather than to Foreign Minister Eban, the tendency left its marks on American opinion, and had a powerful impact on the Israeli view of Israeli-U.S. relations. It was, in fact, among the generic characteristics of the new relationship that official dovishness was left to Eban and William P. Rogers, the respective foreign ministers, while each became increasingly marginal to his own government.

As Israel reacted to Egyptian artillery, first with its own guns, then with U.S.-provided airpower, the conflict escalated accordingly. By January 1970, Israeli planes were embarked on deep penetration raids against targets in the Nile Delta and in and around the Egyptian capital, and the frantic Egyptians were both calling for, and getting, substantial Soviet help. Rabin himself claimed credit for the idea, proposed not least in order to "shore up America's status in the region and thus block its retreat in talks with the Soviet Union."[100] In the meanwhile, the Libyan monarchy, one of the most conservative and pro-Western of Arab regimes, fell abruptly to a camarilla of passionately anti-Western young officers, including Muammar Qaddafi.

The U.S. reaction was both direct and indirect. In September 1969, the first Phantoms reached Israel, and Meir was officially and demonstratively received at the White House, though without the usual communiqué on her departure. At the same time, Secretary of State Rogers and Assistant Secretary of State Joseph Sisco conferred with their Soviet counterparts at the United Nations on a joint venture in delivery of their respective clients. With little apparent encouragement, the Americans nonetheless went about their business, and drafted a document that was eventually presented to both the Egyptians and the Israelis. Identified as the Rogers Plan, it consisted of a preamble and ten points, both procedural and substantive, on withdrawal, peace, borders, navigation in the Straits of Tiran and use of the Suez Canal, indirect negotiations between the parties, "fair settlement of the refugee problem," and mutual recognition and validation in international law. Final ratification was reserved to the Security Council, that is, the Four Powers.

Publicly revealed in a speech by Rogers on December 9, 1969, the proposal almost immediately sank like a stone, as both Kissinger and Nixon had evidently anticipated it would from the beginning. Rabin plausibly assumed that the Rogers Plan had the president's approval. In fact, the White House saw it as a trial balloon. Kissinger himself was unhesitant in encouraging Rabin to shoot, should he feel an urge to do so; he should just make sure to aim at Rogers, not at Nixon.[101]

As far as Nixon was concerned, the Rogers Plan at least served the purpose of telling the Arab world "that the United States did not automatically dismiss its case regarding the occupied territories or rule out a compromise settlement of the conflicting claims."[102] But apart from Jordan, the Arabs were unprepared to see it that way. The Egyptians, whose first priority was restoration of their military credibility, seem not to have replied to it at all. The Israelis, who could scarcely help acknowledging it, did so almost within hours of Rogers's speech. Rabin, who read the speech as a post facto signal for Israeli action, immediately called for "an extensive information campaign." Israel's failure to heed his advice and land a heavy blow on Syria had left the United States with no option but a political initiative, he argued.[103] This seems to have been a little much, even for a hawkish majority. The Israeli government nonetheless rejected the Rogers Plan explicitly, feeling itself distinctly and unfairly under pressure from an administration that "seemed resolved to play the role of mediator, negotiator and map-maker in one."

Back again at the drawing board, the administration sought to learn from its experience. As so often, it found itself confronted with long-, middle-, and short-term dilemmas, whose horns were deeply embedded in the fabric of U.S. foreign policy. On the one hand, so long as Vietnam remained at the top of the national agenda, there was the clear and present problem of limits. To a greater degree, perhaps, than any predecessor since World War II, the new administration regarded the world as a seamless web. To a greater degree, for certain, than any administration since Eisenhower's, it also appreciated the nation's declining willingness and ability to take literal arms against a sea of troubles. "We should assist, but we should not dictate," the president declared in July 1969 at a press conference on Guam. "We must avoid that kind of policy that will make countries in Asia so dependent upon us that we are dragged into conflicts such as the one that we have in Vietnam," he added. The solution, soon acknowledged and recalled as the Nixon Doctrine, was that the United States would continue to assert its global interests, but it would act in concert and, at least implicitly, by proxy. In contrast to such illustrious predecessors as the Monroe, Truman, and even Eisenhower doctrines, the Nixon Doctrine was unassuming in both the form and venue of its appearance. It was nonetheless a watershed in postwar U.S. policy.[104]

The second dilemna, as always, was the role of Israel. Since the coming of the Cold War, there had been two schools on that. In one traditional view, widely represented in the State Department, Israel was not an asset but a nuisance, an embarrassment, and even a menace that continually threatened to involve the United States in the wrong war at the wrong place at the wrong time. Be it as an obstacle to Arab-American relations or a standing excuse for Soviet intervention in the Middle East, it seemed hardly the answer to any of the problems of the United States but rather a problem in itself.[105]

The alternative position was that Israeli values, geography, and military competence virtually predestined it to be a U.S. ally. For obvious reasons, Israelis themselves had always argued this way, but given the circumstances of early 1970, more Americans than ever before were prepared to listen.[106] The argument became Rabin's stock in trade. To the obvious anguish of the Foreign Ministry, with which he had little contact, Rabin both believed, and let it be known at home, that Americans in and around the White House wanted Israel to bash Nasser till he went under or came around.[107] Not only was there something to this, it was red meat for the Israeli Right. But it was also a red flag for U.S. policymakers.

Their problem was how to stop the fighting and somehow move toward a settlement, while streams of Soviet arms and support personnel showed up in Egypt, and Israel feared for the military balance. Any step toward peace required a gesture of accommodation toward Egypt. This in itself was no easy trick at a moment when newly supplied U.S. planes were dumping four and a half to six tons of bombs per sortie on Egyptian targets. Yet, at the same time, American credibility required that Israel be resupplied, especially because Israeli pilots now encountered latest-model Soviet SAM 3's, whose mobile launchers made them that much more difficult to locate and destroy. At the beginning of 1970, there had been no Soviet pilots or missile crews in Egypt. By year's end, Egypt was host to more than 200 Soviet pilots flying the latest-model MiG-21J, and an estimated 12–15,000 Soviet officers and soldiers, assigned to man some eighty missile sites.[108]

It was clear, at least in retrospect, that official Washington had badly underestimated the potential risks of Israeli escalation. At least in part as a result, it thus failed both to deter Soviet intervention or to persuade Israel to cease and desist. Either might have spared a major international crisis.[109] In fact, U.S. policymakers seem to have tried a bit of almost everything in addressing their Middle East and global dilemmas. But as so often, the "intelligent neglect" proposed in a letter from former Secretary of State Dean Acheson was not on the shortlist of options. Instead, both concurrently and consecutively, the administration warned the Soviet Union, renewed its call for restoration of the 1967 Israeli-Egyptian cease-fire, deferred resupply of arms to Israel, but nonetheless rejected unilateral constraint. Kissinger himself, who proposed demonstrative opposition to the introduction of Soviet military personnel in any form, and support for the Israeli air force if it were threatened, heard only one hand clapping. "Most of the government blamed the impasse on Israeli intransigence," he recalled, while the president himself was ambivalent.[110]

Clearly exasperated by the Soviets' resupply of their Egyptian client, Nixon was nonetheless prepared to use Jewish protests against France's president Georges Pompidou, a hint of affirmative signals from Egypt, and Jordanian instability alike as grounds for inaction. In vain, Rabin went to the proverbially hawkish Senators Barry Goldwater and Henry Jackson, House Republican leader Gerald Ford, AFL-CIO Chairman George Meany, "and even the Reverend Billy Graham, whose unreserved support for Israel never failed to move me."[111]

Cast in its ever-more-familiar role as Cassandra, the Israeli Foreign Ministry looked on with apprehension. Rabin might argue as he wished that Nixon was disillusioned with Jewish voters and primarily acting on domestic motives, Gideon Rafael speculated, and Meir could dismiss U.S. concerns with a suitable aphorism from her ever-ready repertory of Yiddish folk wisdom. "However, the United States had its own idiom," he noted. It included demonstrative silences, delayed deliveries, and unanticipated policy reviews. Silent or not, Rafael believed, these meant exactly what they said, which was that "the Administration wanted to persuade Israel to de-escalate its air strikes."[112]

By his own account, Nixon reassured Israelis just like Kennedy and Johnson before him. Yes, the United States would be there if and when it mattered. But this was obviously something for Washington to decide. At the same time, the president battened down the White House hatches for the storm of protest he assumed his hesitation would provoke. "One of the main problems I faced . . . was the unyielding and short-sighted pro-Israeli attitude prevalent in large and influential segments of the American Jewish community, Congress, the media, and intellectual and cultural circles," Nixon recalled in his memoirs. What he was after, he added revealingly, was nothing less than "a new set of power relations in the Middle East—not only between Israel and the Arabs, but also among the United States, Western Europe, and the Soviet Union." Meir and Rabin, not to mention congressional critics and domestic friends of Israel too blind to see who their real friends were, would just have to trust him, Nixon announced in a huffy memo to Kissinger. He intended to see that Israel retained "'an edge,'" he emphasized, because "Israel is the only state in the Middle East which is pro-freedom and an effective opponent to Soviet expansion." But, as Nixon could not help but add, this required not only the support of a Jewish constituency that opposed him by 95 percent, "but the 60 percent who are in what's called the silent majority."[113]

In late April 1970, the growing Soviet role in Egypt led to a revealing minidifference between Jerusalem and Washington over the suitable form of a warning to Moscow. Concerned that Soviet embarrassment might actually make the problem worse, the Israelis favored discretion. Conceivably speculating that public awareness of the Soviet escalation might strengthen its position, the White House instead favored publicity, and the story appeared in the *New York Times* on April 29. Attention then turned to the president's decision to invade Cambodia on April 30, and the spasm of domestic protest that followed. It was the third week of May before the White House was in any condition to concentrate again on the Middle East. But by this time, there had been a general review of the Soviet role in Egypt, and Meir herself had done her part to meet U.S. expectations in a speech to the Knesset. If only to propitiate the White House, she now accepted Resolution 242 for the first time in parliament, agreed to indirect negotiations, and asked for resumption of U.N. mediation. "We needed Mr. Nixon and Mr. Rogers much more than they needed us," she explained to the recalcitrant Begin, "and Israel's policies couldn't be based entirely on the assumption that American Jewry either could or would force Mr. Nixon to adopt a position against his will or better judgment."[114]

On April 21, Eban was received at the White House with a test question straight out of the Nixon Doctrine. Was it still Israel's policy, the president asked the foreign minister, that U.S. troops not be involved? Eban passed with flying colors. "Well, in that case, you'll get the stuff so long as you don't insist on too much publicity," Nixon answered. Clearly apprehensive of direct confrontation with the Soviets, Dayan nonetheless took exception when Eban reported his success to his colleagues in Jerusalem.[115]

And yet things moved again. Indirectly heartened by indications of Egyptian interest, Nixon authorized Rogers to have another try. On June 19, the secretary proposed at least a ninety-day cease-fire and resumption of talks under Jarring's auspices. On June 25, the initiative was publicly announced. Yet only a day later, "the Administration's top officials" let it be known at a background briefing that the continued presence of Soviet troops was a threat to U.S. interests per se. The idea, according to Kissinger, was to "expel the Soviet military presence" in Egypt. Though the "expel" was recanted at a follow-up briefing the next day, its inadvertent publication in the *Washington Post* a few days later predictably caused a sensation. The premise, as Kissinger explained, was that the United States could put the heat on the Soviets *and* influence the Israelis, contingent on serious Egyptian concessions. The Egyptians would then come around when they realized that the Soviets preferred détente with the United States to a new war in the Middle East.[116]

The Israeli reaction, at least initially, was predictable, prompt, and negative. In part, this was because the new U.S. initiative came once again as a surprise—not least because of Rabin, who had neglected "at least three requests from the Foreign Minister to clarify Washington's intent." There was also understandable anxiety that the new initiative might be linked both to arms supply and the previous Rogers initiative of December or, in Rabin's terms, between capitulation to a new U.S. initiative and capitulation to SAM 3's.[117] Yet in part, as Kissinger noted, rejection was an acquired Israeli reflex, virtually irrespective of issue. The huge asymmetries in the relationship assured that any Israeli government felt practically obliged to stand its ground, preempt further demands, and generally "limit the freedom of action of a rather volatile ally five thousand miles away that supplies its arms, sustains its economy, shelters its diplomacy and has a seemingly limitless compulsion to offer peace plans." Historical experience, fragile coalitions, and the understandable desire to dump responsibility for difficult decisions on its superpartner also played their part.[118] This time Rabin himself intervened demonstratively to avoid gratuitous offense to an embattled president, and it was agreed for the moment that Israel would take no position at all.[119]

The initial Egyptian response was negative too, but not absolutely, and it softened progressively after Nasser visited Moscow for medical treatment and serious consultation in late June. On July 19, Egypt agreed unconditionally to the Rogers initiative, and Jordan followed a week later. Motivated by an elaborate package of carrots and sticks, the Israelis too saw no alternative but to come around in early August. The Egyptian decision was itself a powerful motivator, exposing Meir's government not only to foreign but even domestic censure if it once again dismissed a peace initiative out of hand. The military situation, as Soviet pilots appeared over the canal and the SAM 3's began to do their work, was another stick. Now, the Israelis could cross the canal to attack the missile sites, but incidentally risk direct confrontation with the Soviets, which in turn, required U.S. support and resupply. Or they could back off from the canal.

A final important consideration was a direct appeal from Nixon. On July 23, Nixon assured Meir that the United States would not impose a peace, a refugee settlement that altered the fundamental Jewishness of the state, or a return to the borders of June 4, 1967; that it would support secure and recognized borders as the outcome of negotiations between the parties; that it would meanwhile assure supply of arms and a strategic balance, continue economic aid, and also provide troops to observe the cease-fire line. Meir replied, characteristically, with a request for "clarifications" and "assurances," for example, on delivery both of planes and air defense missiles, withdrawal of the previous December's Rogers Plan, and U.S. willingness to veto any Security Council resolution unfavorable to Israel. The administration complied only on arms. Its accommodation nonetheless sufficed to produce conditional Israeli consent, including the Knesset's acceptance of Resolution 242 "in all its parts" on August 4; Gahal's withdrawal from the government coalition; and an ambiguous cease-fire. The cease-fire, actually a U.S. commitment to Israel rather than a bilateral Israeli-Egyptian agreement, provided for complete military standstill to a depth of 50 km on both sides of the canal, effective August 7.[120] Israel's acceptance was a cause of satisfaction for Eban, who saw it as a basic choice between more war, Soviet-Israeli confrontation, and erosion of U.S. support, on the one hand, and the principle of land for peace on the other.[121] "A major accomplishment for Rogers and Sisco," as Nixon instructively referred to it,[122] the cease-fire was a source of short-lived jubilation in the State Department.

The complaints began almost immediately when Israelis noted missiles in the canal zone, where none had been before. But remarkably and embarrassingly, Washington had no obvious means to confirm them. Neither the State Department nor CIA had thought to order satellite photos on August 7, 1970. Existing photos, taken a week earlier, were of little use, given the buildup on each side before the cease-fire took effect. Sisco himself conceded in an interview years later that the United States and Israel had agreed to the standstill principle on the basis of different maps. The Egyptians transmitted their agreement directly to the United States. The Soviets agreed neither to the cease-fire nor the standstill principle.[123] The United States refused to see or acknowledge violations[124] but also lost no opportunity to blame the Soviets for violations that occurred.

"The American reaction was bizarre," the journalist Tad Szulc later declared with reason.[125] Not least of the problems, as Kissinger himself noted, was the odd division of labor, going back to the very beginnings of the administration, when a president distrustful of the State Department and unwilling to rely on his National Security Council staff, put the State Department in charge of the Middle East.[126] By mid-August, Washington had already assured Israel of an appropriate arms package in case the cease-fire broke down. "I have no illusion about Soviet motives," Nixon told Rabin. Considering the importance of public opinion, he nonetheless wanted scrupulous Israeli compliance.[127] By the end of the month, both the State Department and CIA had turned over "incontrovertible evidence" of violations, and Washington had officially protested to both the Soviets and the Egyptians. Hitherto circumspect about Israeli arms requests, Nixon now reconsidered with a vengeance, and informed Nasser accordingly.

At this point, odd things began to happen in a different corner of the region, and Washington found itself face to face with its second major international crisis in four months. The basic elements had been at least subliminally familiar since the very beginnings of the Arab-Israeli conflict. One was Jordan. The other was the Palestinians. In many ways a by-product, a victim, and a beneficiary of the same circumstances that created Israel, Jordan was also uniquely exposed to the currents swirling around the region. But as heir in itself to the Palestine Mandate, it was particularly vulnerable, both to Israel, with which it coexisted de facto, and to the Palestinians displaced by Israel's creation. Between 1948 and 1951, Jordan had even tried to coexist with Israel de jure. The effort ended with the assassination of King Abdullah on the steps of Jerusalem's Al-Aqsa mosque. He was succeeded in 1953 by his grandson, Hussein, a witness to the murder. Hussein, himself the target of assassination attempts as recently as September 1 and June 9 of that very year, had been living dangerously ever since.

Economically frail and militarily exposed, Hussein's kingdom was heavily and increasingly dependent, both on fellow Arab monarchs and his British, then U.S., patrons. Since at least the war of 1948, the Palestinians had been at once the kingdom's hope and its conundrum. An estimated half of Jordan's total population, they were Jordanians by reason of flight and annexation rather than any positive choice. Their circumstances made them a kind of colonial population *malgré eux,* neither loyal nor disloyal as such but, in fact, a bit of both. The rise of Nasser, and the fall of the Iraqi monarchy, confronted Jordan with another existential challenge. Since June 1967, the kingdom had confronted two more insoluble dilemmas in turn. The first was a war with Israel it could neither avoid nor win. The second was a peace with Israel it could neither accept nor reject out of hand, if it were to recover the territories now occupied by the Israelis.

In part, Jordan's equivocation reflected acquiescence in a consensus imposed from outside by variously bigger, richer, and tougher Arab neighbors. It also reflected internal pressure from a coalition of contentious and differentially radical Palestinian guerrillas. Little more than an Egyptian lapdog before 1967, the Palestinian Liberation Organization (PLO) had found its political voice thereafter, and its message was loud, clear, and unequivocal. Unlike both Egypt and Jordan, it rejected Resolution 242 both in toto and out of hand, and declared both the 1947 partition of Palestine and the establishment of Israel "fundamentally null and void."[128] Only precariously united under the umbrella of the PLO, the guerrillas were nonetheless resolved to see Jordan as a staging area, and even to take over altogether. By 1969, they were already far enough on their way to becoming a state within a state as to scandalize a basically sympathetic visitor from Damascus, Syria's air force chief of staff and later head of state, Hafiz al-Asad.[129]

The Palestinian problem, as such, was hardly unfamiliar in Washington. Nixon himself, according to Kissinger, regarded the collective inability to deal with "the problem of the Arab refugees" as one of the major failures of the postwar period.[130] Yet Under Secretary of State Eliot Richardson, who left Rogers a secret memo on the subject before taking over as secretary of health, education, and welfare, seems to have been the only senior member of the administration to take the Palestinians seriously as a political factor in their own right.[131] Preoccupied as they were, first with the cease-fire, then with what appeared to be its imminent disintegration, U.S. officials were otherwise unaware that the Popular Front for the Liberation of Palestine (PFLP) took the cease-fire and its potential for a comprehensive diplomatic settlement at least as seriously as they did.

A radical *groupuscule,* as grimly concerned that Rogers's cease-fire and all it represented should fail as the State Department was concerned that it should succeed, the PFLP now seized two American and one Swiss airliner on a single day, September 1970, and a British airliner three days later. Though a collateral attempt to seize an Israeli plane failed, there was no doubt, at least, that it had the world's attention. After blowing up one of the American planes in Cairo, the hijackers landed the rest on an abandoned Jordanian airstrip, secured their British, German, Swiss, American, and Israeli hostages and demanded release of Palestinians held prisoners in several countries.

Between September 6 and September 23, when things again had simmered down, the crisis passed through three stages, each more dramatic than its already-dramatic predecessor. The first was a hostage crisis, which confronted the administration with its own dilemma. Nixon reportedly ordered a demonstrative raid on PLO bases from carriers in the Mediterranean, but Defense Secretary Melvin Laird pleaded bad weather.[132] As all responsible officials were aware by now, there really was no acceptable military solution to the hostage problem, not least for lack of reliable information. On the other hand, there was also no way for the United States, and particularly an administration as dedicated to law and order and the survival of small allies as the incumbents in Washington,[133] to give way without major political damage. At the same time, given the bilateral negotiations under way between the hijackers and the respective governments, there was real anxiety in Washington that the British and Germans would back down at the cost of the United States and Israel. On September 9, Kissinger convened a Washington Special Actions group (WSAG) of senior officials. It continued to meet at least once almost daily for the next seventeen days.

Despite reservations from both the State and Defense departments, it was agreed to move ships in the Mediterranean and supply planes in Turkey, if only so the Soviets would notice them. There was also a serious discussion of Israel's role, both for and against. Given the situation of the United States in Vietnam, Kissinger favored Israeli action, in case action was required. "Since I considered an Israeli response to an Iraqi or Syrian move almost certain, I thought the best use of our power . . . was to deter Soviet intervention against Israel," he explained. Given the likely political costs, Nixon initially favored U.S. action. On September 12, however, he also lifted the freeze on arms deliveries to Israel, while Kissinger prudently prepared a choice of plans, in case the president might reconsider.[134]

The next stage of the drama, a potential declaration of civil war in Jordan, began three days later, September 15, when Hussein, under pressure from the army, announced his intention of establishing a military government and proclaiming martial law. On September 17, he then ordered the army into Amman and civil war broke out. In itself, this should have been no problem. On the contrary, from its origins as a British-led Arab Legion, the Royal Jordanian army of 50,000 had been regarded as one of the most efficient in the area, and it was widely agreed, even in Jordan, that the king's reaction was long overdue. A few thousand undisciplined, ill-coordinated, and underarmed guerrillas were no match—unless the Palestinian population itself made things impossible for the army, which was considered unlikely. What mattered was what happened if Syrian, Iraqi, let alone Soviet outsiders came to the aid of the PLO, and whether Jordan's underdeveloped air force could stand up against substantially superior Syrian resources. To Washington's relief, Iraqi troops in Jordan not only held their fire but demonstratively withdrew across the border. There were also reassurances from both a Soviet note and the Soviet *chargé* that there would be no Syrian intervention.

By coincidence, Meir was in Washington. Disquieted by the situation above and along the Suez Canal, she was preoccupied as always with arms, and concerned to "find out just what the American people thought and felt about us and what they were willing to do to help us."[135] Nixon assured her that the United States was already in contact with the Soviets on the matter and that he intended to maintain the military balance in the region. "We were prepared to work with her in developing a military aid program . . . appropriate for the strategy the Israelis adapted," he added significantly. Israel would not move "precipitately" in Jordan, the prime minister reportedly replied.[136]

On September 19, Syrian tanks nonetheless crossed into Jordan and took their first town. The Syrian intervention introduced a third stage of crisis. Kissinger concluded that the Soviets had double-crossed him. Hussein's frantic calls at least for air support only added to the common sense of urgency. His predicament once more thrust U.S. policymakers before a dilemma that revealed how startlingly things had changed since 1958. Especially in the wake of the spring's Cambodian incursion, neither the foreign nor domestic climate was exactly propitious for U.S. intervention in yet another Third World civil war. The defense establishment was also close to physical pain as it tried to match the attenuated resources at its disposal to the mission it now seemed called upon to face.[137] Yet the United States, and Israel too, could hardly afford to let Hussein go under.

The alternative, though never specifically acknowledged as such, was clearly the Nixon Doctrine. The Israelis were the obvious candidate, particularly if they could carry out the mission by air, and so minimize the risks of both explicit U.S. commitment and their own intervention on the ground. With Nixon's authorization, Kissinger called Rabin in New York in the night of September 20, and proposed Israeli reconnaissance flights. The ambassador, "who was nobody's fool," as Kissinger noted, anticipated Nixon's actual mandate. Contingent on circumstances, Rabin asked Kissinger, would Washington look favorably on an Israeli air strike? The provisional answer from Kissinger, Rogers, and Sisco alike, was yes.[138] Beyond anything known to date, the United States now needed Israel. The dependence was already apparent in the intelligence deficiencies that made policy-making so hard. In the days after September 20, Rabin briefed Kissinger twice daily on latest Israeli intelligence.[139]

But the new liaison only introduced more problems. Middle East specialists worried especially whether Israeli ground forces, if they crossed the Jordan, would ever leave again, and what Israel might expect of the United States in return for its strategic services.[140] At the same time, Israelis were understandably anxious to know who would replace their losses; what the United States proposed in the event that air strikes proved inadequate; what the United States proposed especially in the event that Israel intervened on the ground; and whether the United States was prepared to hold off the Egyptians, and even the Soviets.

Whether implied or explicit,[141] the answer was evidently satisfactory to both sides. By the early morning of September 22, 1970 Nixon was ready to support Israeli ground action unilaterally. On consultation with senior officials, urged on him by Kissinger, it appeared that Rogers had serious reservations and Laird was ambivalent. Yet Kissinger himself regarded the situation as basically auspicious. If things turned really bad for Hussein, he assumed, Israel would act almost irrespective of U.S. views. For Israel to act, it also had to mobilize in full view of the Syrians. So, as troops massed on the Golan, and tanks moved toward the Jordan, Israeli mobilization alone might deter the Syrians without further action. Meanwhile, mobilization itself was worth two days, during which Egypt and the Soviet Union would face their own hard choices.[142] The same morning, Hussein unleashed his air force against unsupported Syrian tanks. By afternoon, the Syrians were withdrawing from Jordanian territory. Shortly afterward the air hostages, who had almost been forgotten,[143] were released; the PLO demanded a cease-fire; and an Arab summit ratified Hussein's victory.

For the United States and Israel, at least, the crisis was now not only over but widely regarded as a triumph of Israeli credibility and U.S. crisis management.[144] Years later, observers could still find traces of its impact. One was a modified U.S. nuclear doctrine that aspired to extend flexible response beyond its traditional

European venue.[145] Another, in 1982, was the overt mutual hostility between Syria's Asad and the PLO's Arafat[146] that contributed to Arafat's expulsion from the Lebanese sanctuary that was itself a consequence of the disaster in Jordan. Yet there was surprisingly little consensus on what had actually worked in September 1970.

In retrospect, the Syrian intervention turned out to be a model of ambivalent cross-purpose.[147] The Jordanians had also put up a surprisingly good fight. It was even arguable that there had been less crisis than met the eye; that the Jordanian and Israeli intelligence the United States depended on *faute de mieux* was not unchallengeably objective; that the Syrian-PLO relationship was at least ambivalent; that the Soviet influence on the Syrians, let alone the PLO, was overrated; and that the Soviets understood as well as anyone that they shared the risks if Hussein went under.[148] It could be argued too that there were Israelis, including Rabin, who had wanted to hit the Syrians for months. There were certainly Americans who were keen to bash the Soviets.

What did seem clear from the events of September 1970 was that Jordan, Israel, and the United States, each in its way, were winners, and that Syria, the Soviet Union, and certainly the PLO were losers. More secure than he had been in years, Hussein drove the last of the guerrillas out of Jordan in 1971. Though the special Israeli-U.S. relationship of September 21 was canceled four days later,[149] Israel had meanwhile attained the coveted status of "strategic asset."[150] With it, virtually for the first time, came an assured supply of U.S. arms and relief from pressure for political initiatives. As official America turned once again to *Ostpolitik,* Asia, arms control, and reelection, its self-esteem gained proportionally with the success of its clients. For the moment, peace plans were out of style and military balance was Washington's major preoccupation.[151] Meanwhile, the indigenous problems of the region continued on their own course out of view, and largely beyond control, of the superpowers.

7

Yom Kippur

It took another war, in October 1973, to make people aware that what was remarkable in the aftermath of Jordan was not so much what had happened as what had not. In some ways, the new war was the most frightening to date, a kind of geopolitical Big Bang, that not only shook the earth from Gibraltar to the Persian Gulf but rattled windows as far away as Moscow and Washington. The aftershock was felt around the world. But this time the impact was compounded and amplified by political, economic, even social fallout as diverse and spectacular as suspension of diplomatic relations between Israel and twenty-three black African states, an awkward face-off between the United States and its NATO allies, a worldwide nuclear alert, a 7 percent decline in oil supply, a 300 percent jump in oil prices,[1] carless Sundays in most of Western Europe, and block-long lines at U.S. gas stations.

Ironically, up to the eve of the war itself, Israelis, American Jews, and official Washington had rather believed themselves witnesses to a golden age of Israeli-U.S. rapport and the preliminaries of a hopeful new U.S. peace offensive. In living memory, the Pentagon had been reluctant even to let Israeli officers see the inside of a staff college. Now Israeli Ambassador Yitzak Rabin was invited to lecture at military academies, brief the Pentagon on Israel's experience with reserves, fly in a Phantom jet, visit an Air Force nuclear command post, and "become acquainted" with the communications systems of nuclear submarines.[2]

When the dust finally settled after three weeks of the most violent fighting since World War II, the worst had been avoided, Israel—and the United States—had again prevailed, and Egypt had at least avoided humiliation. Although Israel had come out weaker, it was hard to say its adversaries had come out stronger, let alone that there had been any breakthrough or catharsis. While Syria had ended up as Egypt had in 1967, fending off more and worse defeat by a postwar battle of attrition, Egypt had come out rather like itself in 1956, when only timely foreign intervention had saved it from disaster. Actually, in many ways, Israeli forces had performed as impressively as they had in 1967. Yet while the Egyptians regarded themselves practically as winners, the Israelis practically behaved as if they had lost.

Despite anticipations, threats, and apprehensions since 1956, it was the first time that oil really had proved to be a weapon. The collateral damage it inflicted on currencies, capital markets, and trade and consumption patterns in both developing and industrial countries left Israel more isolated than before. The spasm of mutual blame and self-castigation that followed all but recalled the France of 1870 or 1940. The questions Israelis avoided were as revealing as those to which they directed their attention. Reflecting both the state of Israeli nerves and the constraints on Israel's field of vision, a blue-ribbon commission of inquiry addressed only the vexatious issues of military preparation and operations, avoiding the hard but crucial questions of whether and how political priorities and foreign policy might themselves have contributed to the recent trauma.[3]

Irrespective of their political sympathies or regional venue, all members of the Organization of Petroleum Exporting Countries (OPEC), Arab and otherwise, were direct beneficiaries of the sellers' market that followed the war. As oil exporters struggled with a payments surplus in the hitherto unimaginable amount of $60 billion, and oil-thirsty importers struggled to cope with the consequences of their dependency, floods of petrodollars now made their way to Zurich, Franfurt, London, and New York, where they were processed and filtered through the world's great banking centers. They then rolled over both the Second and Third World. The mountains of debt and grand canyons of social and economic erosion they left behind could still be seen from Warsaw to Buenos Aires years later.

The explosive trade in two of the world's most desirable commodities, oil and arms, contributed at least indirectly to an unanticipated Islamic revolution that first swept away a shah of Iran, and then a president of the United States. From Afghanistan and Lebanon to Gaza, Egypt, and Algeria, it now rattled the rest of the region too. The politics of oil crisis led, at best, to mixed results.[4] By virtually any standard, the politics of Islamic revolution were a general nightmare.

One political message, at least, was heard and understood in Washington more clearly, perhaps, than ever before. Once again, U.S. policymakers had come face to face with a destructive potential now literally measurable in megatons, and experienced firsthand the risks of leaving ill enough alone. Once again, they returned from the diplomatic drawing boards with hopes and plans for comprehensive action, but this time the result included some of the most creative U.S. diplomacy since the golden age of the Marshall Plan and NATO. Though neither adversaries nor allies showed much appreciation or understanding, U.S. negotiators managed between 1974 and 1979 to impose, cajole, and broker at least a piece of that Arab-Israeli peace that had evaded their predecessors since the end of World War II.

As always, there was a wrangle about who, if anyone, was to blame for what had preceded the war, and whether and how it might have been avoided. As always, the answers were in the eyes of the beholder. Yet even by the maddeningly elusive and ambiguous standards of Arab-Israeli conflict, the new war seemed rather more evitable than some of its predecessors. Granted that political plates were full, and regional walls were covered with graffiti, it nonetheless seemed clear, at least in retrospect, that things might have come out quite differently if a couple of the more prominent and self-occupied diners had read the handwriting visible there for months. For a variety of reasons, Israelis, Americans and even the Soviets had nonetheless persuaded themselves that the Arabs had nothing to gain from another war, and that war was therefore unlikely. When at last they saw the message, their inability and even refusal to take it at its word only added to the effectiveness of the Arab surprise.

Meanwhile, U.S. negotiators scrambled summitward in pursuit of détente with

the Soviet Union, and even rediscovery of China after a generation of mutual alienation. The common destination—or itinerary, since neither the United States nor
the Soviet Union was very clear about whether they understood détente as a process
or an end in itself[5]—included Berlin and eastern Europe, disengagement from Vietnam, and contractual limits on antiballistic missiles deployment. Cautious, conciliatory, and confrontational at once, the peculiar course of superpower politics was
naturally reflected in the Middle East. Of course, with the coming of another presidential year, the peculiar contingencies of the U.S. electoral cycle too could be felt
again around the region.

For all its seeming inconclusiveness, there was no shortage of regional activity
in the three years between the Jordan crisis and the new Israeli-Arab war. In the
conventional sense of summit-level coming and going, the region, in fact, was as
busy as ever. Between April 3 and September 12, 1973, alone, local media reported
at least eighteen high-level Egyptian and Syrian visits to one or another Arab capital.[6] Airport honor guards, public statements, and the occasional trial balloon all
belied the apparent standstill. There was also a stretch of unusually heavy political
weather in Cairo, Damascus, and Jerusalem. For the moment, domestic politics in
all three countries seemed both a distraction from the persisting conundrums of
peace and war, and a kind of extension of the status quo by other means. Yet in
each case, the longer-term outcome could be seen post facto as a watershed in the
politics of the region.

After three and a half wars with Israel since 1948, and nearly twenty years of
heroic exertion, rhetorical self-intoxication, and furious activism since the coming
of Nasser, it appeared that the Egyptian revolution had finally run out of steam.
And after a couple of decades of violence, sectarianism, carousel politics, and pursuit of phantoms remarkable even by regional standards, Syria was meanwhile
about to settle into its longest period of domestic stability since independence.

After twenty years of comprehensive domestic consensus and exemplary
nation-building, Israel too was ready for new departures. But these took a rather
different direction. While the secular victory of 1967 may have brought Israel a new
Jerusalem, it had not ushered in one. On the contrary, the occupied territories and
all they represented confronted the parties, society, and the nation itself with
choices and challenges unlike any before in Zionist history.[7] From Labor left to
Revisionist right, it was still the Zionist goal to create a country like other countries,
and incidentally live in peace with Israel's neighbors, but Israelis had never agreed
on what this meant in practice.

The new situation both allowed and required choice, yet there was little in Jewish history to guide it. The heroic exertions of the past had prepared Israelis only
imperfectly for the unheroic realities that most of the world considered normal, and
the muddle-through pragmatism that most of the world considers peace. Still less,
had their exertions prepared them for the dilemmas of victory and occupation.
"Governing proves more difficult than conquering," as Yehoshafat Harkabi, a onetime chief of military intelligence turned professor of international relations,
observed years later. His personal transformation from unblinking hard-liner to
bleak, unsentimental dove was itself a measure of the difficulty.[8] "Israel chased the
illusion that it could both acquire territory and achieve peace," Henry Kissinger

noted. "Its Arab adversaries pursued the opposite illusion, that they could regain territory without offering peace," he added.[9] Each proposition naturally tended to make the other self-fulfilling.

As always, domestic politics was both an effect and cause of foreign policy. Issues, stakes, and national style were as different as the respective countries. Yet common to all three nations was the same problem that haunted Hamlet. Since 1967, each for its own reasons had found it equally impossible to suffer the slings and arrows of historical fortune or to take arms—naturally supplied by their respective superpower patrons—against a sea of troubles, and by opposing end them.[10] Arms supply was, in fact, a problem common to both sides. The United States was still disposed to link arms transfers to political concessions. The Soviet Union was reluctant to risk both new arsenals and political capital on Arab clients without adequate security. Yet domestic change in both Egypt and Syria led inexorably toward a new war, intended by its initiators to correct the previous one.[11]

The new era began once more in Egypt. On September 28, 1970, Nasser suddenly died only hours after brokering a disengagement agreement between Hussein and Arafat. His death threw Egypt into spasms of public grief so passionately genuine that it actually alarmed an old *apparatchik* like Alexei Kosygin.[12] The constitutional succession was orderly, at least in form, but it was still some months before Anwar al-Sadat asserted his authority over adversaries generally regarded as Soviet protégés, and persuaded foreign states that he was in power to stay.[13] Meanwhile, Egypt's crisis again spilled over into Syria, where Hafiz al-Asad, the air force chief of staff, ended a cold civil war of some years' duration with a cold coup d'état in November.[14]

In Israel, the regional cold war collided increasingly with reawakened domestic passions. The resulting fog of ideology and party politics tested elected officials, professional diplomats, political generals, and ordinary citizens alike. The Arab adversaries, who themselves rejected partition out of hand in 1947, had inadvertently allowed Israelis to reopen questions believed answered, for better or worse, at the time of independence. In the 1940s, the secular compromise on partition was rewarded with statehood. Now the secular victory of 1967 was a challenge not only to the nation's self-image but to the principle of partition itself. Just as the UNSCOP lines of 1947 were among the casualties of the war of 1948, the armistice lines of 1948–1949 were among the casualties of the war of 1967. Within ten days of the war, Moshe Dayan himself referred to the new borders as "ideal."[15] Israel's determination to maintain its grip on the bird in hand was only reaffirmed by the War of Attrition, the civil war in Jordan, and Palestinian terror in general. In November 1971, PLO terrorists assassinated Jordan's premier in a Cairo hotel lobby. In summer 1972, at the Olympic Games in Munich, they first kidnapped, then murdered eleven Israeli athletes on worldwide television.

In Israeli perspective, the demonstrative absence of any Arab to talk to, the windfall of U.S. arms and favor since 1970, and the apparent impregnability of Israel's strategic position each did its part to legitimize the status quo post bellum. For hawks, who never believed in Resolution 242 in the first place, the territories were their own reward. For doves, committed to the principle of land for peace, there was no point in conceding one without some reasonable prospect of the other. In a world where the representatives of 210 million Americans were about to negotiate as equals with the representatives of 22 million North Vietnamese, Kissinger himself saw the basic absurdity of a situation where perfectly reasonable demands like direct negotiations and policy coordination practically assured an impasse with the Arabs and an Israeli veto of the United States.[16]

If the remembered past was one argument for hanging tough, the intractable present was another. Any Israeli old enough to ride a bicycle could recall the impending abyss of June 5, 1967 and the suspension of French arms deliveries when they were most needed. Any Israeli old enough to vote could remember the U.S. pressure to leave the Sinai in 1956–1957. The birds in the bush of the Rogers Plan, the successive lessons of the War of Attrition, the duplicitous Soviet-Egyptian missile fiasco, and the civil war in Jordan were seen and used as so many more reasons both for assertive self-reliance and for doing nothing.

Beyond any state in memory, Israelis had shown themselves adequate to existential military challenge. In theory, the secular victory of 1967 might even have been grounds for self-confidence. Yet the persisting intensity of Arab and Soviet hostility only made many more sensitive to their own vulnerability. With the Eichmann trial of 1961 still fresh in the national consciousness, captured Egyptian nerve-gas arsenals inevitably had their impact. It was no problem either to imagine Soviet preemption scenarios that would wipe out Israel's Dimona reactor as Israel itself was to wipe out Iraq's Osiraq reactor in 1981. The enormous decision to move from potential to actual construction of nuclear weapons is believed to have been taken in the aftermath of the Six-Days War, though only after a strenuous debate in the cabinet.[17]

At the same time, a windfall of imported money from the United States, West Germany, and foreign Jews in general minimized the need for any urgent choice between guns and butter. Though the intended beneficiary was the embattled Israel of June 5, the de facto beneficiary was the victorious but nonetheless anxious Israel of June 11. In the six years that followed, American-Jewish aid alone was estimated to average circa $300 million, before soaring to a new record $1.8 billion in 1973, the year of the October war.[18]

Almost coincidentally with Nasser's death, Congress also assured that Israel could buy missiles, tanks, and aircraft on credit without limits on cost or number. The perpendicular increase in military credits after the crisis in Jordan constituted another quantum jump in U.S. support. In fiscal years 1968, 1969, and 1970, Israel had received $25 million, $85 million, and $30 million in U.S. military aid respectively. In the three years thereafter, the figures rose respectively to $545 million, $300 million, and $307.5 million.[19] By 1973, Israelis could and did spend nearly 30 percent of their GNP on defense[20] while still enjoying guns *and* butter to an extent unknown before.

Even as Labor's traditional establishment of agricultural settlements, union movement, public sector, and military seemed to enjoy their secular vindication, the heady brew of social change and imported money was dissolving traditional loyalties and constituencies. By 1970, multinational corporations predominantly

U.S., were annually investing about $150 million in Israel, a figure exceeding 10 percent of Israel's net imports. Between 1968 and 1973, the surge of foreign capital, in turn, fueled growth rates averaging nearly 12 percent.[21]

It was symptomatic of the postwar scene that Ben Gurion himself grew increasingly isolated after declaring in public that Israel should surrender all conquered territories save Jerusalem in return for peace. His position was shared by perhaps 6 percent of the Israeli public.[22] Inflation, social envy, legitimate grievance, and the new assertiveness of the huge non-European immigration Ben-Gurion had himself promoted and encouraged between 1947 and 1955 only contributed to a domestic stalemate that all but precluded diplomatic initiative.[23] By 1967, more than half a million Jewish refugees from Morocco, Iraq, the Yemen, and the rest of the Arab world had settled in Israel, effectively transforming the country. In 1948, the ratio of foreign to native-born Jews had been about 2:1, and 80 percent of the Jewish population was of Western origin. By 1972, the ratio of foreign to native-born was about 1:1, and Western Jews constituted about 44 percent.[24]

Measured against the hawkishness of early 1968, opinion on the Occupied Territories actually grew more moderate. By early 1969 only 75% of respondents still declared their determination to keep most or all of the West Bank and Gaza, compared to the earlier 91% and 85% respectively; by early 1971, the figures for the West Bank and Gaza had fallen to 56% and 70% respectively, and only 31% still indicated a desire to keep most or all of the Sinai.[25] Yet the new immigrants' endemic fear of, distrust of, and contempt for Arabs only added to the natural caution of Ben-Gurion's heirs and the national security establishment, and so reinforced the new status quo.

Paradoxically, the sense of liberation and malaise that was alike the product of the victories of 1967–1970 now confronted Ben-Gurion's heirs with a virtually insoluble dilemma. As their ideology grew quaint, and their competence was challenged by some of the world's most ferocious domestic bargainers, their legitimacy increasingly became a hostage to their defense and foreign policy. Yet there was little consensus on what to do about this either, save a common determination not to return to the status quo of June 5 under any imaginable circumstances, and a fundamental refusal to consider international guarantees as a substitute for real peace with secure borders.

Both propositions sufficed to sustain a government, but neither sufficed either to create new facts or to launch an initiative likely to overcome the stasis. Immobility was nearly self-fulfilling. So, as a result, were pressures from both Arab neighbors and the superpowers, with their own respective stakes in making something move. The bleak and anticlimactic history of Egyptian, Israeli, U.S., and Soviet, not to mention Palestinian, initiatives between the civil war in Jordan and the new war in the Sinai and the Golan Heights is a textbook case of how powerless an idea can be whose time has not yet come.

Of all the possibilities of 1970–1973, the most promising was an Israeli-Egyptian initiative for an interim settlement along the Suez Canal. The idea both anticipated the breakthroughs of 1974–1979, and recalled the Israeli-Egyptian liaisons of the early 1950s. Kissinger himself acknowledged post facto that it could have prevented another war.[26] An indirect product of the War of Attrition with its obvious costs to both Israel and Egypt, the principle behind it amounted to a bit of bilateral peace. But in ironic contrast to the 1950s, it was now Dayan who undertook the discreet and highly contingent role of dove, and Americans, for no less contingent reasons, who looked on with deep skepticism.[27]

At successive levels, Dayan's initiative reflected the outcome of the near-confrontation in Jordan, the death of Nasser, and Israeli anxieties about the continued interest of the United States in both the Jarring talks and the Rogers Plan. But it also reflected his own longtime reservations, only confirmed by the War of Attrition, about the strategic and political cost-benefit ratio of Israel's position on the canal. A package of modest quids and quos, the scheme was intended to make choices a little easier both for Nasser's successor and President Nixon. The heart of the plan was restoration of the canal to Egyptian sovereignty after a huge and counterproductive escalation that had abruptly swollen Israeli defense spending from under 30 percent to over 45 percent of the public budget without appreciably enhancing Israeli security. It was thus an appeal both to Egyptian prestige and self-interest.[28]

What was envisaged within its calculated limits was that game theorist's delight, a positive sum game. Israel, Dayan proposed, would withdraw toward the strategic passes in the Sinai. In return, Egypt would pull back westward, clear and reopen the canal to traffic including Israeli ships, and rebuild the cities on its eastern bank. At least in theory, there would be something in it for all interested parties—save Jordan, Syria, and Palestinians of the Occupied Territories. In the process, of course, Israel would open some daylight between the Egyptian position and the general Arab party line without damage to its own military security.

On the other hand, the Egyptians stood to recover revenues, territory, and self-regard. Though Washington was unlikely to welcome this so long as the Soviets continued to supply Hanoi, the Soviet Union would regain access to the canal. On the other hand, the Americans, who had felt good about Israel since September 1970, had also been restive and ambivalent about Israeli immobility since June 1967. So the new initiative would reassure them too by proving things could move, which, in turn, might make Washington a little less anxious about another superpower confrontation. This would then help assure Israel a steady supply of latest-model weapons, while relieving pressure for another of those U.S. peace initiatives that always made Israelis anxious.[29] Though Dayan's plan got nowhere with his Israeli colleagues, and he even felt obliged to deny that any plan existed, Assistant Secretary of State Joseph Sisco and U.N. Ambassador Gunnar Jarring alike made sure that his proposals got at least as far as Cairo.

On January 5, 1971, the Jarring talks resumed. This was mostly, it appeared, because the United States wanted them to. At U.S. instigation, Jarring even turned up the heat before the current cease-fire elapsed.[30] To the surprise of both the Israelis and the Americans, Sadat replied with an initiative of his own. Though its larger implications became clear only as time, and perhaps opportunity, passed, it was apparent that he had been thinking seriously about his predecessor's difficult legacy. Mohamed Heikal, the editor of what Western reporters inevitably called the "semi-official" *Al-Ahram,* had already urged "neutralization" of, that is, de facto reconciliation with, the United States as a preferable alternative to superpower polarization in the region.[31] But Sadat seems hardly to have needed much persuading before deciding to take a chance on Washington.

In the years that followed, Sadat was to show repeatedly that he not only understood what U.S. opinion was worth but how to reach it to a degree unmatched by any previous Arab, let alone his predecessor, Nasser. Anyway, as he later explained, a diplomatic offensive was his only alternative, given the impossibility of a military one. The question was whether he should start with Jarring, the Soviets, or the Americans. Characteristically, he tried all three.

On February 4, 1971, the day before the expiration of the Israeli-Egyptian cease-fire, Egypt's new president accordingly went before the National Assembly to announce his willingness to extend the cease-fire by thirty days, reopen the canal, and allow U.N. troops to police the Straits of Tiran. In a follow-up interview with Arnaud de Borchgrave of *Newsweek,* he even indicated readiness to guarantee the passage of Israeli ships. But it was all conditional, he emphasized, on Israeli withdrawal beyond the Sinai passes, deployment of Egyptian troops on the east bank of the canal, and above all, Israel's fulfillment of "its obligations" under Resolution 242. In any case, as he explained to James Reston of the *New York Times,* it was one thing to negotiate peace through a mediator; diplomatic relations were something else. "Our people here will crush anyone contemplating such a decision" as diplomatic recognition, Sadat declared.[32]

Rather typically, Israelis were both impressed and skeptical. Experience and habit disposed them to see Sadat's new strategy at once as a new departure and a war of attrition by other means: "The answer is 'no'—now, let's hear the suggestion," as Golda Meir tells Sadat in a cartoon by the *Denver Post*'s Patrick Oliphant.[33] As most analysts were quick to appreciate, it was the first time since the death of Jordan's King Abdullah that any Arab had even come close to de facto recognition of Israel within the borders of 1948. At the same time, Israelis could hardly help notice that what appeared in *Newsweek* did not appear in the Egyptian papers.[34]

Meanwhile, the Jarring talks self-destructed after a last effort to breathe life into Resolution 242. Apparently activated by U.S. expectations, Jarring undertook his own initiative just days after Sadat's speech to the National Assembly. He proposed an appropriately hedged but unmistakably direct Israel withdrawal from Egyptian territory in exchange for Israeli-Egyptian peace. Egypt accepted in principle. Pleading both procedural and substantive objections, Israel predictably balked on the issue of withdrawal as a precondition for negotiations. On March 25, Jarring returned to his job as Swedish ambassador to Moscow and a place in the diplomatic footnotes. Since he took with him any surviving hopes for the comprehensive settlement once envisaged with his appointment, Americans were left holding the bag, virtually by default.[35]

Hopes now turned to an interim Israeli-Egyptian agreement, almost as its own reward. It was clearer than at any time since 1955 that the Egyptians were also looking to Washington. But as always, the Israelis were as concerned to insure themselves against U.S. activity as they were to make peace on any terms short of face-to-face talks and full recognition.[36] It was clear again that the further the parties got from the canal itself, the further apart they were on such basic issues as linkage of an interim settlement with a peace agreement, the depth of Israeli withdrawal from the canal, the presence of Egyptians east of the canal, and access of Israeli shipping to the canal. On a last grand tour of the region, U.S. Secretary of State William P. Rogers and Sisco managed only to elicit an anthology of just how basic the differences were.

It hardly helped that the White House, as Kissinger observed, had thitherto "acted as if the State Department were a foreign sovereign power."[37] Now, unbeknownst to the State Department, the White House was pushing it aside. By early 1973, looking for the Egyptian-U.S. dialogue was a little like trying to find the source of the Nile. As only Kissinger himself was aware, there were no fewer than three channels linking Washington and Cairo, including the State Department, the CIA, and a special link between Kissinger and Soviet Ambassador Anatoly Dobrynin.[38] Meanwhile en route respectively to China, a Moscow summit, and what was expected to be a hard-fought campaign for reelection, the administration was reluctant to get involved in any enterprise unlikely to pay off.[39] Instead, after taking office in 1969 less beholden to Jews than any president since Eisenhower, and determined to keep the Middle East at arm's length, Nixon now tilted so heavily toward Israel that Ambassador Rabin, the Labor Zionist, came alarmingly close to endorsing him for reelection.[40]

Successively hopeful, resourceful, energetic, and desperate, the State Department soldiered on under heavy fire from Egyptians, Israelis, and the White House alike. This time it proposed "proximity" talks, that is, a kind of three-headed dialogue through U.S. mediators, that would allow reluctant Arabs to save their face and use it too. Once practiced with some success by Ralph Bunche to produce the armistice agreements of 1948–1949, the technique was later to be used to spectacular effect by President Jimmy Carter to produce an Israeli-Egyptian peace treaty. But it was clearly going nowhere in 1971–1972, not least on the eve of a U.S. election.

Reportedly, Rabin and Sisco actually came to terms. But from Egypt's perspective, their agreement got Israel off the hook by providing only for interim settlement without total withdrawal, while assuring Israel a $300 million credit to finance forty-two Phantoms and ninety Skyhawks.[41] As Egyptians lost confidence in U.S. credibility and ability to deliver, Sadat lost interest and his initiative withered. The dialogue with Washington continued, but talks with the Soviets continued too, as Egyptian thoughts turned steadily toward military options and the Soviets grudgingly yielded.[42]

In later years, there was a serious question of whether another chance was lost. As the evidence gathered before that proverbial court where history judges, Tad Szulc and Seymour Hersh arrived independently at the same grim and critical conclusion: the war of 1973 need not have happened.[43] Industrious reporters and experienced diplomatic correspondents, both were credible witnesses, though their premises and arguments were too different to support a common brief. On the other hand, it was no coincidence that both cases rested heavily on Kissinger's role, first as Rogers's adversary and then as his successor. Long before he left office, his priorities, motives, judgment, and character were matters of lively debate, but there was never any doubt of his importance.

"What finally got me involved in the execution of Middle East diplomacy was that Nixon did not believe he could risk recurrent crises in the Middle East in an election year," Kissinger himself explained disarmingly. "He therefore asked me to step in, if only to keep things quiet."[44] Once in, he was to remain for five full years, leaving a deeper mark on the region than any foreign statesman, perhaps, since Balfour. His mandate itself was a partial explanation for the processes and policies that were now to lead once more to war.

In the complicated, if nonetheless finite spectrum of U.S. options, the generic choices had nonetheless changed remarkably little in twenty years. What was at issue in each case was a strategy of containment, whose implied choice of ends subsumed a choice of means. But the ends tended to be mirror opposites. In the first case, the priority was containing the Cold War. In the second, it was containing the Soviet Union.

The first case implied approaching the Middle East as something other than a Cold War battlefield, and even extricating it from the Cold War altogether. Neither superpower had exactly covered itself with glory there. Whatever Americans had set out to do in the region, it had presumably been—or like the Baghdad Pact would never be—accomplished. Reflexive fears of Soviet penetration had anyway proved wildly overstated. Syria, Iraq, and Egypt were no more communist than Hungary or Poland, and were significantly harder to control.[45] Yet the conjunction of outside arms and local politics had produced more and lower flashpoints than anywhere else in the world. On the face of it, the case for détente in the Middle East was least as compelling as it was in central Europe.

Under the circumstances, there was every reason for the United States, and the Soviet Union too, to seek to limit liability. With or without the Soviet Union as its preferred and acknowledged partner, the United States could look to the United Nations as the venue of Middle East diplomacy, internationalize responsibility, broker regional security guarantees, and pick up the check for buffer forces as necessary. *With* the Soviet Union as its acknowledged partner, it could even try to restore that lost innocence of 1950–1955, when a tripartite cartel of external arms suppliers had imposed some limits on their clients. In itself, this was no guarantee that the Arab-Israeli conflict might not continue anyway, but it could at least be disengaged from the superpower arsenals with reduced risk of collateral damage.

Alternatively, the United States could approach the region's Cold War first, accepting the polarization of the Middle East as a given. As in Eisenhower's time, this too led to alternative choices. One, as Israelis never ceased to argue, was a tilt toward Israel as the only natural ally and strategic asset of the United States in the region. The other, as much of the Washington establishment never ceased to argue, was "evenhandedness," that is, a de facto tilt to the Arabs that effectively meant containing the Soviet Union by containing Israel.

Itself a casualty of the Cold War, and the receding regard for the United Nations that went with it, the former position had last enjoyed a certain popularity during the partition debate of 1947 after the Soviet Union had backed away from Turkey and Iran. In those days, it seemed both reasonable and desirable to look to the United Nations for solution of the Arab-Israeli conflict. It also seemed both reasonable and possible to isolate the Middle East from the Cold War, just as it seemed desirable and possible to Israelis to stand between the superpowers. The consensus extended ecumenically across the U.S. political spectrum. For intrinsically conservative reasons, official Washington, like Moscow, chose to keep its distance from the conflict and the region. At the same time, in the afterglow of wartime idealism, American liberals not only favored the United Nations, superpower unanimity, and a Jewish state but took for granted that they were mutually compatible, if not interchangeable. The Israeli establishment did the same, and saw itself as the beneficiary.

A generation later, nearly everything had changed, including the venue of support for a policy that had once seemed almost self-evidently left of center. By now, even Jews recalled their previous allegiances with a combination of nostalgia and embarrassment. After a quarter century of global and Middle Eastern Cold War, Vietnam and the politics of race had finally and irreparably cracked the old New Deal coalition. Its New Left splinters now looked askance at both Israel and détente. Israel, many now decided, was just another imperial power, a kind of Middle Eastern South Africa. Détente, as many decided, was a latter-day Holy Alliance, in which both superpowers together constituted the ancien régime. Right or left, the United Nations was meanwhile among the last places Americans looked to revive their flagging idealism.

Yet for at least some Americans, the underlying premises of Soviet-U.S. consensus, partition of Palestine between Jews and Arabs, common liability and shared responsibility for the Middle East were as compelling as they had been in 1947. Vermont's Republican Senator George Aiken had already declared it time to call Vietnam a victory and come home. Americans of similar temperament now reached the same conclusion about the Middle East, and for much the same reasons. Many had actually inclined to such thoughts all along: natural conservatives of a kind Americans have always found hard to recognize and classify—their European counterparts might have been socialists or Christian democrats. In the United States, they tended to be seen—and frequently see themselves—as liberal Democrats, but their common denominator was a vision of U.S. foreign policy not easily classified as left or right.

Adlai Stevenson was an example. Spokesman and symbol of a thoughtful American liberalism from 1952 to his death in 1965, Stevenson had been a Middle Eastern skeptic since the early 1950s.[46] Each in his way, so were his friend and one-time campaign aide George Ball, who served as under secretary of state in the Johnson administration; George McGovern, the South Dakota senator who ran so calamitously against Nixon in 1972; and J. William Fulbright, chairman of the Senate Foreign Relations Committee.

Though hardly a liberal by standard American definition, Fulbright was a lifetime maverick, Cold War agnostic, and bellwether critic of U.S. efforts in Vietnam. A natural adversary of both Democratic and Republican administrations since his election to the Senate in World War II, his skepticism about U.S. efforts in the Middle East reflected still larger doubts about the unilateralism, Sovietocentrism, and calculated unclarity of the nation's foreign policy since the very beginnings of the postwar era.

In Fulbright's view, the Middle Eastern Cold War was a case of mistaken identity. Each for their respective reasons, both superpowers had deceived themselves about the reality of their interests, and allowed themselves to be taken captive by their clients. The Soviets needed Israel as "their admission ticket to the Middle East." Americans had been any easy mark for a combination of "cultural and sentimental attachment," "the impact of the most powerful and efficient foreign policy lobby in American politics," and "some of the same old communist-baiting humbuggery that certain other small countries have used to manipulate the United States for their own purposes."[47] But both superpowers had a real interest "in a settlement which gives security to Israel, restores lost territories to the Arabs, removes the Middle East as an issue of contention between themselves and breathes life into the United Nations."[48]

The first step, as Fulbright predictably saw it, was a negotiated settlement on the basis of Resolution 242 in all its ramifications. The second was a bilateral U.S. commitment to guarantee "the territory and independence of Israel within the adjusted borders of 1967," that is, a treaty with all that implied, including ratification by a two-thirds majority of the Senate. But, Fulbright qualified, the treaty was to take effect "after—and only after—" the U.N. guarantee had "been agreed on and ratified by all parties."[49]

In the real world of both Israeli and U.S. politics, his prescription was plausible, audacious, hardheaded and otherworldly all at once. After years of experience in the region, neither Washington nor Moscow needed Fulbright to tell them that the Mideast policeman's life is not a happy one. But the design was aimed at the clients, as well as their frustrated and disillusioned patrons. For the Arabs, it promised at least a chance of regaining territories and self-regard they had lost not only to Israel but to their own bravado and fecklessness. For Israelis, it promised a degree of security beyond any to date, plus assurances that would have looked like the gates of heaven not only in March 1948 but as recently as June 5, 1967.

Repeated experience since 1947 had already shown that superpower consensus was attainable. As experience already suggested, and the future was to confirm, impending disaster could also do wonders to concentrate the mind. Since the early 1950s, both superpowers had learned to see the Middle East as another of the game theorist's constructs, the zero-sum game where one side's gain is the other's loss. Successive confrontations from 1956 to the present now pointed to an alarming new possibility, the negative-sum game, that is, the game both players lose. Yet, in the cold dawn of nuclear détente, its opposite, the positive-sum game, was imaginable too—if only in the bleak and qualified sense that both superpowers stood to win by keeping the lid on the Middle East and containing their regional clients.

Even assuming the superpowers were able and willing to come to terms with one another, square the circles of Resolution 242, "adjust" the borders of 1967, enlist support from third countries, and deploy troops, money, and good offices where appropriate, it was hard to see how either half of Fulbright's scheme could work without making history itself run backward. Americans might regard Israeli behavior as irresolute, ungrateful, exploitative, contentious, and bloody-minded. There were Israelis too who found it shortsighted, even self-destructive. It was nonetheless a matter of objective fact that their current situation reflected the precipitous decline of U.N. credibility and prestige since 1947 and the demonstrable inadequacy of U.S. guarantees in 1967 and 1970. Even assuming a minimum of sixty-seven U.S. senators could be found to pronounce a new international guarantee in the long shadow of the Bay of Tonkin Resolution and tens of thousands of dead Americans in Indochina, it was stretching both credibility and comparative strategic advantage to believe that it would work. The very terms that Fulbright proposed implied choices that both sides preferred to avoid. In their present state of mind, guarantees were rather the problem than a solution.

Donald Bergus who, as minister in the ambassadorless Cairo embassy of the United States, had done his best to represent the State Department in the negotiations with Sadat, nonetheless believed an agreement was possible in summer 1971. The insuperable obstacle, he contended, was not the Egyptians, the Soviets, or even the Israelis; it was Kissinger, who had overestimated the Soviets and hijacked responsibility from Rogers.[50]

Hersh, who took Bergus's word for it, and also took a dark and comprehensive view of Kissinger, predictably reached the same conclusion. It was true, he conceded, that Sadat's initiative posed a prodigious dilemma for Nixon. On the one hand, pushing Israel was risky for anyone, let alone a president now counting on Jewish votes and money he had never before enjoyed. On the other hand, it was Nasser's successor, of all people, who was offering him "the chance for a wondrous triumph—Middle East peace would isolate the Soviet Union and further disarm the Administration's antiwar critics." And still, Hersh argued, the White House let the chance go by because it feared that Rogers would get the credit; feared to take on Israelis and American Jews, who were up in arms about Rogers's and Sisco's alleged pro-Arab tilt; and feared the fire of Henry "Scoop" Jackson, a contender for the Democratic nomination in 1972. The Washington senator not only was a traditional New Deal liberal with a credible claim on Jewish voters and money by virtue of his irreproachable hard line on defense, Vietnam, and support for Israel, but also was a crucial vote if the Senate were to ratify the impending arms control treaty with the Soviets.[51]

There was some validity to Hersh's critique and alternative scenario too. For the first time, a major Arab leader was signaling interest with both hands. With the progressive collapse of the liberal consensus, Democrats, American Jews, even Israelis were visibly disoriented. Arms control and central European détente were clearly good politics. After a generation of inconclusive and dangerous hot wars and Cold War, Middle Eastern peace on plausibly honorable terms was arguably good politics too. Within three years, Nixon himself was to confirm its potential with many of the rewards that Hersh described.

Arguably, Sadat's initiative might even have had a special appeal for a man of Nixon's temperament, history, and competitiveness. It was not for nothing that the larger-than-life figures of Disraeli, Bismarck, and de Gaulle[52] occupied a special place in the White House pantheon. For Nixon, the self-made Tory, who had already discovered welfare reform, the environment, and the volunteer armed forces, and was now about to rediscover China, Sadat was yet another chance to dish domestic Whigs. For an Administration with dreams of a new Republican majority, the Egyptian opening was a chance to make peace, embarrass the Soviets, steal the Jews, and beat the Democrats all at once. Potentially, it therefore meant a place for Nixon too in the great conservative pantheon, among those other "white revolutionaries" who had not only won the game but rewritten the rules for their successors.

Yet it followed from the administration's own agenda and the expectations it confronted that 1972 was not the year for it. Nixon's reelection was still far from inevitable. The White House was still shaky from the aftershocks of the disastrous Cambodian invasion of 1970 and the calamitous domestic reaction that followed it. By 1971, Nixon, a Republican president, had imposed wage and price controls, suspended what was left of the gold standard, and effectively devalued the dollar. Foreign policy, domestic politics, and bureaucratic logic all spoke against further experiments and adventures. If Middle East peace was good politics, arms control, the opening to China, and, above all, extrication from Vietnam were still better, and significantly more attainable. But they were also linked, both functionally and conceptually, to the administration's view of a world whose geopolitical gravitation was determined by the superpowers. For all its acknowledged importance, the Middle East could wait.

As so often, Kissinger was almost disarmingly candid about both his action and inaction. There was no point, he explained, in trying to impose a solution on the Israelis, even had Nixon felt adequate to the task, which he did not. So long as Egypt was a Soviet client, the United States had nothing to gain by pressuring an ally. Neither side was likely to comply, and only the Soviets would gain, whether by demonstrable U.S. impotence or what seemed to be an effective show of Soviet pressure.[53]

The alternative, he argued, was deliberate stalemate, pending Soviet interest in compromise or Arab interest in Washington. "By the end of 1971, the divisions within our government, the State Department's single-minded pursuit of unattainable goals—and the Soviet Union's lack of imagination—had produced the stalemate for which I had striven by design," he noted in his memoirs.[54] From there on, détente worked as Kissinger thought it should. Through their respective "front" and "back" channels, negotiations proceeded with Israelis, the Soviets, and Egyptians.

Meanwhile, the Soviets kept their distance. They were keen for cheap U.S. grain and U.S. support for West German *Ostpolitik* with its de facto recognition of central Europe's postwar borders. They were also anxious about Israel's capacity to humiliate the Arabs once again, and reluctant to risk another confrontation with the United States in a part of the world where it had the tougher client.

It was both sad and funny under such circumstances that Sadat's very interest in making a deal could be taken as grounds for procrastination. On July 18, 1972, Sadat reversed seventeen years of Egyptian policy, and threw out some 21,000 Soviet military advisors without asking for U.S. reciprocity. The gesture, one of the most spectacular in living memory, accomplished everything he could have wished. A huge success at home, it also did wonders to get attention in Moscow, while thoroughly misleading both Israelis and Americans.[55] Barely a month after the Watergate break-in, the White House was already fully occupied with the campaign. For the moment, it acknowledged Sadat's coup as a free good. Gratified, on the one hand, that an Arab leader had finally seen things its way, it was puzzled, on the other, that he had done it unilaterally without even asking a price. Sadat was given to understand that something would happen when the election was over. Yet even assuming that his gesture meant the very opposite of what it seemed to mean, which it plausibly did, and that it was really meant to tell the Soviets that he wanted more, not less, from them in the future, the decision to assure Israeli military superiority seemed adequate in itself to keep the Middle East on hold till the United States was ready to take the next initiative.[56]

With Nixon's landslide reelection in November 1972, and the nominal outbreak of peace in Vietnam in January 1973, Kissinger now began to take the Middle East seriously in a way he never had before. His negotiating formula would be "sovereignty" for "security," and his strategy both incremental and comprehensive. Nixon had spelled out his own position in a memo to Kissinger the previous February. "The time has come to quit pandering to Israel's intransigent position," the president had informed his national security advisor. "Our actions over the past have led them to think we will stand with them *regardless* of how unreasonable they are."[57] Yet his decision to let Israel have another forty-eight Phantom jets had been leaked by mid-March. By election day 1972, the administration was taking credit not only for having sold Israel everything Meir requested but for having provided more aid in four years than all predecessors put together had provided in nineteen.[58]

"Some issues and disputes could be resolved on a priority basis," the president told Congress in May 1973. But he emphasized that "all important aspects of the Arab-Israeli conflict must be addressed at some stage, including the legitimate interests of the Palestinians." The issues were "formidable, interlinked and laden with emotion," he acknowledged. He nonetheless believed there was "room for accommodation and an overwhelming necessity to seek it."[59]

Even as he spoke, evidence of "overwhelming necessity," if not necessarily "room for accommodation," was piling up around the region. On March 2, Palestinian terrorists murdered two senior U.S. diplomats, including the ambassador to the Sudan, at the Saudi embassy in Khartoum. In early April there was a government crisis in Lebanon after Israeli commandos raided Beirut, in effect the new PLO capital, blew up Palestinian offices, and killed three leaders of Arafat's Fatah. Within weeks, both Syria and Egypt had provoked Israel to partial mobilization.

Meanwhile, Defense Department analysts warned that the United States faced a serious squeeze on domestic oil reserves, and Saudi Arabia's King Faisal, usually among the most unobtrusive of clients, threatened for the first time to use oil as a weapon unless the United States started twisting Israeli arms. But the former were reluctant to link energy policy to Mideast policy, and the latter was not taken very seriously in Washington. In May 1973, State Department I&R correctly predicted that, without early diplomatic progress, Sadat would go to war by fall. In June, participants at a prestigious international conference in London agreed that oil prices were likely to rise, that Saudi production was crucial, and that consumer countries could be made to scramble for scarce supplies at considerable cost to alliance solidarity. Yet by September, paradoxically, Faisal's threat was actually read as evidence that things were again under control. If oil, with Faisal's help, were to be a big gun in Sadat's strategy, and the United States remained substantially independent of Arab oil, it would be several years at least before the strategy worked. Therefore, it was reasoned, resort to the "oil weapon" made war less imminent, not more.[60]

In June, when Leonid Brezhnev, the Soviet party chairman arrived for his first visit to the United States, the Middle East nonetheless not only was on the agenda but was the object of three hours of emotional debate. Brezhnev was clearly impaled on a dilemma. Soviet credibility demanded large-scale support for Syria and Egypt. Yet large-scale support for Syria and Egypt was likely to lead his clients into another disaster, and the Soviet Union into another unwanted confrontation with the United States. He accordingly informed his hosts that Syria and Egypt were determined to fight, and that only U.S. pressure on Israel could prevent a war. Though the latter was surely arguable, the former, at least, was true. Nixon nonetheless understood the argument in toto as a bluff or threat.

What Brezhnev seems actually to have had in mind was a joint settlement, imposed by the superpowers. Nixon and Kissinger too wanted movement, though Brezhnev's brief was not one they were ready to buy.[61] Yet by this time, summit or near-summit level talks with Jordan, Egypt, and Israel had only confirmed how hard it was likely to be for the United States to produce real movement. External constraints aside, the impending Israeli election could hardly make the Meir government more accommodating. At the same time, Egypt's sense of national interest and the requirements of Arab consensus imposed constraints on Sadat. By October, it was clear that U.S. military and political calculations, based on the deterrent effects of Israeli superiority and Soviet restraint on Arab initiative, had been little more than self-deception.

Though the official decision to go to war was taken only in late August 1973, Sadat and Asad had effectively decided to go to war together in February. Shortly after, Egypt and the Soviet Union reached a compromise: the Soviet Union would supply what was necessary for a cross-canal operation, and Egypt would confine its war aims to a defensible strip of the east bank, adequate to reopen the canal. In part for reasons of Soviet squeamishness, in part for fear of an Israeli bomb, there were significant differences between the Syrian and Egyptian goals. Egypt looked ultimately to the United States to get Israel out of the Sinai. Syria looked to itself to get Israel out of the Golan. Though kept in the dark about the actual start of operations till almost the very eve of the attack, the Soviet Union had nonetheless agreed months earlier to support the enterprise.[62]

The flood of weaponry already rolling down on the region confirmed not only that Sadat's grand gesture had worked but that Syria too was a beneficiary. Between December 1972 and June 1973, the Soviet Union delivered more arms to Egypt than it had in the preceding two years; the shipments included latest-model battle tanks, SAMs, and MiGs, as well as the hand-carried precision-guided missiles that were to play such a spectacular role in the war itself. "They are drowning me in new arms," a gratified Sadat told Heikal, *Al-Ahram's* editor. Asad's return from Moscow in May, accompanied by the Soviet air force commander, was a further benchmark of Soviet commitment.[63]

When the guns finally went off at 2:05 P.M. (8:05 A.M., Washington time) on October 6, 1973, the effect was spectacular beyond the planners' dearest hopes. Within an hour, Egyptian units had already overrun Israeli positions in what was generally acknowledged to be one of the great water crossings in the history of warfare. By evening, two Egyptian armies were established along a 170 km front on the east bank of the canal, and 80,000 men had penetrated the Sinai to a depth of several kilometers. Meanwhile, a formidable Syrian attack on the Golan had overrun Israeli headquarters and almost reached the Jordan.[64]

As with all great military surprises,[65] not only deliberate deception but the evidence of impending attack itself—even the possibility that the adversary had seen the war plan[66]—worked to the attackers' advantage. The Americans had scarcely less reason than Israelis to hold Israeli intelligence in high regard. They also had every reason to assume that Israelis would let them know if they felt threatened. Since they took their cues from Israel, they were naturally as surprised as the Israelis. "October 6 was the culmination of a failure of *political* analysis on the part of its victims," Kissinger observed later.[67] Where political logic made it impossible to see how the Arabs could win, and cultural reflexes made it hard to believe they could fight, it was not surprising that military intelligence should fail too, even as Soviet dependents were seen to leave Egypt and Syria, while technical and military advisors stayed behind.[68]

Alone among senior U.S. intelligence officials, Ray Cline of State Department I&R foresaw the imminence of war the night before it began, but he was unable to reach Kissinger, who was in New York for the General Assembly session, or Nixon, who was in Florida, trying to manage the very different crisis that was to end with the resignation of Vice President Spiro T. Agnew. "I was disappointed by our own intelligence shortcomings, and I was stunned by the failure of Israeli intelligence," Nixon recalled disarmingly in his memoirs. Israelis were stunned too, not least as they came to realize how they had let themselves be deceived by their own earlier successes.[69]

Roused by Sisco with a cable from Ambassador Kenneth Keating on the imminence of war, Kissinger first called Nixon. At 6:30 A.M. he then talked to Abba Eban, who, like him, had just arrived for the annual General Assembly session. Suspected of dovishness since at least 1967, the foreign minister had already been crowded toward marginality by Rabin. Now Israeli-U.S. relations effectively ran from Kissinger to Ambassador Simcha Dinitz to Meir. But Dinitz, for the moment, was in Israel and Eban in New York. Through the foreign minister, Kissinger cautioned against preemption. Save that Israel had nothing of the sort in mind, and that Eban was practically removed from the conduct of Israeli-U.S. relations,[70] it was a kind of reprise of 1967.

Before 7 A.M. Kissinger was on the phone to Dobrynin to confirm that the Israelis planned neither to attack nor preempt attack.[71] The answer, according to Kissinger, was disingenuous; that embassy communications were inadequate for quick contact with Moscow. Kissinger thereupon offered the White House switchboard. At Israel's request, Egypt's U.N. ambassador was notified too of Israel's intention not to preempt, and there were further appeals to Jordan's King Hussein and Saudi Arabia's King Faisal for moderation. Severely tested as in 1967, Jordan chose and managed this time to stay out of war.[72]

By 9:00 A.M., the U.S. crisis managers were already in session. Kissinger, now both secretary of state and national security advisor, was the conveyor belt to the absent and heavily preoccupied Nixon. Others present included Sisco; his deputy, Alfred Atherton; Defense Secretary James Schlesinger; Director of Central Intelligence William Colby; Admiral Thomas Moorer, the chairman of the Joint Chiefs of Staff; and Deputy Secretary of State Kenneth Rush. It seemed probable or certain to nearly everyone present that Israel must have struck first, and even the Israelis assumed that the Syrian and Egyptian moves were unconnected.[73] Only Atherton, who was later to be both assistant secretary for Near Eastern affairs and ambassador to Egypt, deviated from the consensus. An old Middle East hand, whose personal experience went back to the Damascus embassy in the early 1950s, Atherton also happened to be the closest thing to an area expert in a roomful of globalists.[74]

The group reconvened toward dinnertime. Even after reality was unscrambled, there was little sense of the urgency a Saturday-night meeting in Washington might and did imply, when the president fired Archibald Cox, the Watergate special prosecutor just two weeks later. "All the Israeli government was asking . . . was to have confidence in our early triumph and to avoid complications in the Security Council," Eban was later to recall self-critically. As long as the Israelis reported, and sincerely believed, it would all be over in a few days, it was easy for Americans to fudge the question of resupply, be it on grounds that there were no shortages, that resupply would compromise effective mediation, or that supplies would arrive too late. Kissinger, by his own account, was the only advocate of immediate action, but his reasons were political, not military. If the Arabs won, there would be no rewards for U.S. restraint. If the Israelis won, they would be obliged to the United States. "The time to show understanding for the Arab position was *after* the war," Kissinger contended. For the moment, at least, the Sixth Fleet was nonetheless instructed to keep its distance from the conflict, just as the Soviets too avoided any demonstrative movement of warships from the Black Sea to the Mediterranean.[75]

Taking the Israelis at their word, policymakers tended rather to worry what would happen if the Arabs suffered another disaster. It was clearly a moment of truth for U.S. credibility in the Middle East, requiring the United States to support Israel "in such a way that we would not force an irreparable break with the Egyptians, the Syrians and the other Arab nations," Nixon noted in his memoirs. It was also, as Kissinger warned Dobrynin, a moment of truth for détente. Yet, for the same reasons, it was no time to bash the Soviets, even if they were accessories to the attack, and still less to bash Arabs, even if Nixon declared post facto that the Israelis were "victims of aggression."[76]

In the best possible world of Middle East belligerency, it was accordingly assumed and hoped that the Soviets would exercise restraint; that the superpowers would avoid confrontation; that the Israelis would roll back the Arab tide, and that the Arabs by then would positively welcome the status quo ante. By the end of the week, when it was time to propose a cease-fire, the United States would then be in a no-lose, the Soviets in a no-win situation. If the Soviets said no, they risked détente and the Israelis won more time to wallop their clients. If the Soviets said yes, they shared the blame and responsibility for the outcome.

Or so it seemed when Dinitz, Rabin's successor as Israeli ambassador, returned from home leave Sunday with a request for two hundred tons of small arms, ammunition, and spare parts to be sent by air in the event of emergency. By this time,

Kissinger had already consulted Schlesinger on ways and means that would be both credible and unobtrusive. These included Sidewinder air-to-air missiles and landing rights for unmarked El Al airliners at an unobtrusive Virginia naval base. But there was no particular sense of urgency. On the contrary, as reported by Bernard and Marvin Kalb and Kissinger, Dinitz's argument seems to have been almost platonic, warmed only gently by a discreet threat to turn up the congressional heat if nothing happened. Israel had complied with the U.S. request to resist preemption, Dinitz argued; the United States thereby incurred "a special responsibility . . . not to leave us alone, as far as equipment is concerned."

In the meanwhile, only 100 of the 265 Israeli tanks in the Sinai when the battle began were still operative, and Dayan had offered to resign. There are even suggestions that Israel had readied nuclear missiles, if only as a signal to the Soviet Union to stay away and to the United States to show up quickly to resupply Israel with conventional weapons.[77] By Monday it was clear that the traditional instruments of Israeli superiority—the tank and fighter-bomber—had failed to overcome a new generation of antitank and antiair missiles. As the counterattack stalled short of the canal, the Syrian front—and the potential threat to Israeli population centers, and the possibility that Jordan might enter the war—was the obvious alternative. Preceded by an air offensive, Israeli forces reconquered the Golan the next day, and even extended their position, but this was hardly enough to end the war. Political discretion alone deterred Israel from marching on Damascus, and losses on both sides were staggeringly high. By Tuesday morning, it was estimated that Israel had lost five hundred tanks, by Thursday that the Syrians had lost a thousand. Aggregate loss of tanks over the war's three weeks was estimated at three thousand, three-quarters of it Arab. Israel alone lost more tanks than the United States produced in a year. By the end of the first week, Israelis had also lost sixty to eighty planes, as many as a third of them Phantoms.

Paradoxically, as Washington reacted to Israeli failure, Soviet activity seemed to reflect Israeali success. As the Syrian front threatened to collapse and Israeli planes bombed Damascus, Soviet transports from as far away as Hungary and Yugoslavia began to arrive in Syria, then Egypt; freighters began to load at Black Sea ports; and the entire Soviet airborne force of fifty thousand troops was alerted. The prospect for Israel at this point appeared to be a new and unwinnable war of attrition.

It was only in the night from Monday to Tuesday, October 8–9, that Israel, then Washington, began to appreciate and react to a situation radically different from what they had assumed just a day or two before. Between 1:45 and 3:00 A.M. Dinitz roused Kissinger twice. A few hours later, a meeting with Dinitz and Mordechai Gur, the Israeli military attaché, gave some idea of the immensity of losses. To this point, the United States had assured Israel of two new Phantoms and electronic equipment—no tanks, artillery, or other weapons. Meir was now threatening to fly to Washington incognito, Congress was audibly restive, and the question of resupply was threatening to supersede all others.

Confident as anyone of Israeli victory just the day before, Nixon had already informed Kissinger that something would have to happen when the war was over. "We must not get away with it just having the thing hang over for another four years and have us at odds with the Arab world," the president declared inelegantly but emphatically in a memo. By Tuesday evening, he had agreed to replace Israeli losses and assure access to everything in the U.S. conventional arsenal, save laser bombs. "Is Israel going to lose?" a congressional leader reportedly asked the president the next day. "No," Nixon says he replied, "we will not let Israel go down the tubes." But save as the Israelis themselves provided the planes, there was still no decision on an airlift.

It was October 14 before the advance end of an air bridge with a thousand-ton daily capacity reached Israel. Prepared only two days before its arrival to accept an immediate cease-fire, Meir acknowledged the first C-5 with tears. "Thank God I was right to reject the idea of a pre-emptive strike!" she told herself. "It might have saved lives in the beginning, but I am sure that we would not have had that airlift, which is now saving as many lives."[78] By October 25, the U.S. effort had yielded about eleven thousand tons of equipment. The Israelis acquired another forty Phantoms, thirty-six Skyhawks, and twelve C-130 transports, though fewer than two dozen tanks, during the same period. By November 15, when the arrival of seaborne supplies made the airlift unnecessary, an additional eleven thousand tons had reached their destination. Meanwhile, the collateral Israeli airlift delivered another eleven thousand tons of military supplies.[79]

Like the abortive interim agreement and the outbreak of the war per se, the air-lift too was balefully scrutinized in the years that followed, not least by a security establishment unpleasantly aware that it would need till 1981 to replenish stock-piles and inventories redirected to Israel in 1973.[80] Presidential distraction only added to the confusion. While the Israeli security establishment debated war plans till after midnight, and the U.S. security establishment began in earnest to debate the airlift needed to support them, the commander in chief of the United States was fully engaged on the home front. On October 10, after extended negotiations, amounting in effect to plea bargaining, Agnew finally agreed to resign. His resig-nation was the first of its kind in U.S. history. But the whole double fugue of con-stitutional and international crises was also without precedent. Itself little more than an echo of Watergate, Agnew's resignation confronted the White House with two existential challenges. The first was proving that Washington could act. The other was proving that U.S. actions were something more than a distraction from domestic politics.

In the event, Agnew's exit had its impact even on the airlift, if only to the extent that Nixon's attention was intermittent or somewhere else. In the president's de facto absence, decision making devolved on Kissinger, Schlesinger, and Schlesin-ger's deputy, William Clements, a former Texas oil executive. Beyond this, there was little agreement, least of all about who was at fault for the delay. The debate about who might be deceiving whom left a trail of suspicion, blame, and even demonology peculiar to, and characteristic of, the Nixon administration.

Four contemporary journalists, all of them insiders, effectively anthologized the judgment of instant history. In Bernard and Marvin Kalb's version, the nominal obstacle was an apprehensive Schlesinger. Equally fearful of provoking the Arabs to an oil boycott and needlessly drawing down U.S. inventories, according to the authors, the defense secretary both heeded his deputy and dragged his feet.[81] In Tad

Szulc's version, the principal obstacle was an overconfident and disingenuously manipulative Kissinger. Still persuaded on Monday that the Israelis would win by Thursday, according to Szulc he first blamed Schlesinger for his own omissions, then deliberately procrastinated to maximize leverage on the Israelis.[82] In Matti Golan's version, too, Kissinger is a master of duplicity, but his victims include himself. Wishfully determined to misread Soviet intentions, according to Golan, he persisted in his misreading until October 11. He then deceived Dinitz, until an exasperated Nixon intervened on October 13.[83]

Admiral Elmo Zumwalt, then chief of naval operations, was at least a witness in Schlesinger's defense. Already persuaded by October 10 that Israel faced trouble without immediate U.S. resupply, Zumwalt learned from Moorer that "we are to be overtly niggardly and covertly forthcoming," that is, the opposite of what was generally believed. Yet Schlesinger told Zumwalt only that "his hands were tied." Uncertain at this point whether "Richard Nixon and not unelected, unaccountable Henry Kissinger was making national policy," Zumwalt then turned on his own authority to Jackson of the Senate Armed Services Committee. He never doubted Kissinger would come to Israel's aid, Zumwalt added in his memoirs. But he believed he had at least hastened the U.S. decision.[84]

The principals' versions are differentially enlightening. In Kissinger's, as might be imagined, Kissinger himself was the hero, but his story includes both a shrewd and generous appreciation of Dinitz and a redeeming dollop of self-irony. "When I had bad news for Dinitz, I was not above ascribing it to bureaucratic stalemate or unfortunate decisions by superiors," Kissinger admitted. But he acknowledged Dinitz too as a great artist at reaching Congress and the media; adding that both he and Dinitz were only doing their jobs, and neither fooled the other for a moment.[85] Predictably, the hero of Nixon's memoirs is Nixon, but his account is characteristically unblemished by generosity, let alone self-irony. " 'Defense is putting up all kinds of obstacles," the former president quoted Kissinger. 'Tell Schlesinger to speed it up,' " he quoted himself.[86]

Each version, in fact, is plausible. Yet ironically, each is about equally misleading for reasons of perspective policy priorities and objective reality than personal duplicity or ill will. Even I.L. Kenen, the founding father of AIPAC and one of the all-time masters of congressional pulse-taking, was to concede post facto that neither Kissinger nor the military was to blame. On the contrary, he reported, he had it on good authority from Israeli airmen that General George Brown, the Air Force chief of staff, had been "ready and eager" to resupply Israel from the beginning.[87] If bureaucratic inertia, domestic priorities, and logistics all played their role in obstructing the airlift, the biggest dilemma was a matter of political choice: how to aid Israel without being conspicuous and without helping too much. Both Kissinger and Schlesinger publicly acknowledged delay by choice as a way of effecting an early cease-fire.[88] In the end, it took the Soviet airlift, the changing tides of battle, the changing tides of domestic opinion, and a good deal of improvisation before both problems were solved.

Israeli airlift capacity was the first obvious problem, even after agreement on how and where the planes, with their markings painted over, could land. But the issue was already double: whether Israel's tiny civil air fleet could actually carry what was needed, and whether it could do so with minimal damage to U.S. credibility. It was soon clear that the answer to both questions was no; local reporters spotted Israeli planes almost on arrival in Virginia, just as local reporters were to discover Israeli ships at the U.S. Army docks in Bremerhaven a few weeks later. But by now it hardly mattered. By the end of the week, the immensity of Israeli need; the risks of Israeli panic to the point of nuclear consequences;[89] the magnitude of the Soviet investment in the resupply of their clients; and not least an impending speech by Jackson were all seen as reasons to change the rules of détente and U.S. commitment.

The interim low-cost solution seemed to be an ad hoc charter service of the kind Americans had flown in Southeast Asia and were to fly again in Nicaragua. Yet this turned out to be no solution either. Even Kissinger had to concede that commercial carriers, and their insurers, were reluctant to face the risks; the Pentagon was reluctant to pressure the charter companies; and the Department of Transportation was clearly reluctant to take on the challenges of ad hoc military transport.[90] This left the option of direct U.S. military transport, be it as far as the Azores or all the way to Israel; landing rights en route; and access to U.S. depots. For good reasons, there was continued hesitation to commit U.S. planes in numbers or on courses where they might be seen.

Save for the Germans, Dutch, and Portuguese,[91] the allies were demonstratively unaccommodating. *Mutatis mutandis,* the same considerations that inhibited the United States naturally extended to third parties, particularly those, like all European NATO members, who imported all their oil. The Germans "were willing to permit major diversions of NATO-committed arms to Israel, provided it were done without direct identification of Germany as the geographical source," Ambassador Martin Hillenbrand recalled years later. They were obviously unwilling to be embarrassed as they were on October 24, when Israeli vessels at the U.S. Army docks in Bremerhaven were discovered by not only local security agencies but the local press. It did not make things easier that the incumbent government of Chancellor Willy Brandt was disposed to regard itself a representative of those Germans who had been liberated, not conquered, in 1945, and was concerned for its dignity as an ally.

Horst Ehmke, at the time Brandt's chief of staff, acknowledged the right of the United States to the use of its depots, the Bremerhaven docks, and the air base at Ramstein. "But if this has something to do with NATO, they could at least consult us first," he declared. A victim, as he saw it, of "Henry Kissinger's proclivity for hanky-panky, and his unwillingness to use established channels of communication," Hillenbrand was called in by senior officials to explain the inexplicable. The next day, the Foreign Office delivered a statement, reaffirming the Federal Republic's de jure neutrality.[92]

The real issues had been political all along. As late as October 12, the administration still favored caution. From October 13, when Nixon personally intervened to order activation of "everything that flies," it favored action, despite Saudi threats and even actual anticipation of oil cuts. Yet at stake as before were means, not ends. The idea, as Eban understood it, was to create a military situation that would constitute an "incentive for a cease-fire." It was only consistent under the circumstances to lean explicitly on Portugal and implicitly on West Germany. It was equally consistent to extend $2.2 billion in aid to Israel, two-thirds of it an outright grant. Not only was the package conceived as a carrot to Israel, it was intended to impress both the Soviets and American Jews—although the collateral offense to Saudi Arabia's King Faisal, which led in turn to the oil boycott, later caused Kissinger to acknowledge it as a major mistake.[93]

In the wake of the war, there was inevitable speculation about the respective roles of such self-evidently interested parties as the Jewish lobby and the oil industry. Kissinger's tactic of blaming Schlesinger, reinforced ad hoc by such random outbursts as General George Brown's intimation that the Jews controlled the banks and media, focused attention on the bureaucrats too. It had never been a secret, after all, that there were officials in the State Department who believed that Israel was getting only what it deserved. It was no secret either that there had always been officers in the Pentagon who were more disposed to see Israel as a liability than an asset, and regarded it since the airlift in much the way the three bears regarded Goldilocks.[94]

Yet the bureaucratic impact on what really happened seems substantially overrated. Even Kenen, not usually a man to underestimate his role, acknowledged that "Kissinger was more persuasive than I" when it came to getting the House, by a vote of 364–52, and the Senate, by a vote of 64–9, to appropriate the Israeli aid package without conditions.[95] A moment of truth for U.S. foreign policy, the October war in this sense was also a confirmation that the natural forces of constitutional gravitation continued to operate. Even on the threshold of exemplary crisis, the executive branch remained more equal than the others when it came to the existential questions of war and peace.

With respect to these, both Nixon and Kissinger received the foreign ministers of Morocco, Algeria, Saudi Arabia, and Kuwait on October 17 to reassure them of the U.S. intention to link a cease-fire to settlement on the basis of Resolution 242. But Kissinger also avoided commitments on the Sinai, let alone the traditional Arab position on repatriation of the Palestinians, while nonetheless emphasizing Israeli dependency on U.S. resupply; U.S. interest in avoiding any superpower confrontation; and, not least, good relations with Sadat.

Meanwhile, in contact with Egypt since the second day of the war, Kissinger made certain that the contacts continued. "The U.S. side will make a major effort as soon as hostilities are terminated to assist in bringing a just and lasting peace to the Middle East," he informed Sadat on October 14. Within a day, Sadat had been on the wire with an invitation to visit Cairo.[96]

By this time, Egyptian advances had been stopped for good, and advancing Israeli forces had already crossed to the west bank of the canal. But while the impact of the airlift was fundamental, its major significance was political rather than directly strategic. The war with Syria had been settled by October 10. The decision to cross the canal, under discussion since October 11, was in place by October 14, that is, before the first C-5 arrived. By the end of that day, the Egyptians had lost almost a third of their tanks, the Israelis only ten of some seven hundred. Arguably, Israeli plans were contingent on U.S. resupply, but they reflected an accurate assessment of U.S. intentions.

Sensitive again to the sound of running clocks, Israelis were already thinking ahead to the final whistle, and a victory beyond what Americans were likely to countenance. Under the circumstances, the U.S. airlift put the Soviets on the alert, the Egyptians at risk, and the Israelis at the long term mercy of their suppliers. Yet ironically, it also put them in a position to do what Kissinger, let alone Moscow, was determined to prevent.[97] After first overestimating Israel, Americans were hesitant to appreciate the change. But remarkably, the Egyptians were slow to see it too, despite the arrival of an anxious Kosygin on October 16. Only after seeing aerial photos of the battle area on October 18 could Sadat be persuaded of the need for an early cease-fire.[98] Yet it was only the next day, Israeli forces seventeen miles west of the canal, that Soviet anxiety finally registered in Washington.

Invited to receive Soviet Foreign Minister Andrei Gromyko or fly to Moscow himself for "urgent consultations," Kissinger chose the latter, after congratulating his colleagues on "the best-run crisis ever." He took his time to get there, armed with a stern letter from Nixon to Brezhnev that conveyed personal greetings "from Pat and me to him and Mrs. Brezhnev" and effectively conferred power of attorney on Kissinger.[99] In the meantime, Arab oil producers had announced production cuts, and both Libya and Abu Dhabi had imposed a boycott on the United States. By the time Kissinger arrived in Moscow, Nixon's "Saturday night massacre" had precipitated a constitutional crisis, and the Saudis had announced an oil embargo that sorted the Dutch and Americans into enemies, the British and French into friends, and the Germans, Italians, and Japanese into neutrals. At least in theory, friends were to get full deliveries, enemies no deliveries, and there would be monthly cuts of 5 percent for neutrals till they presumably reached zero or a new understanding of their best interests.[100]

By now, the Soviets were as eager to stop the war immediately as the Israelis were to carry on a little longer. Paradoxically, Kissinger regarded his mandate as burdensome or worse, since it cost him the option of stalling for instructions from Washington. A follow-up message from Nixon only complicated things further. The Soviets were to be included, not excluded, the president wanted Brezhnev informed. Keen to take personal control of the negotiations, give the Israelis a little more time, and put off the Security Council till the superpowers reached agreement, Kissinger effectively waived the president's instructions.[101]

The joint product, adopted by the Security Council as Resolution 338 at 12:52 A.M. on October 22, 1973, not only reflected Kissinger's intentions but was, he believed, the best deal obtainable. It provided for a cease-fire within twelve hours, implementation of Resolution 242 "in all its parts," and negotiations between the parties immediate and concurrent with the cease-fire. Both guarantors undertook to see that the cease-fire was carried out. Obviously apprehensive of more delay, Soviet negotiators had by now dropped their demands for Israeli withdrawal to the pre-1967 borders. For the first time, they had even agreed to the principle of negotiations "between the parties concerned under appropriate auspices," code for direct negotiations. Meir, who was informed but not consulted, was nonetheless upset, both by the fait accompli, and the "indecent speed" with which it happened. Yet, given the immense Israeli dependence on U.S. supplies, influence, and goodwill, and a personal appeal from the president of the United States himself, she could hardly say no. Instead, she demanded that Kissinger stop off for explanation en route back to Washington.[102]

On his arrival at Ben-Gurion Airport, Kissinger was applauded by hundreds of war-weary Israelis,[103] but there were no ovations in Jerusalem. International realities and domestic politics alike, he observed later, had taught Israelis to say no to U.S. initiatives until "everyone has reached a state of exhaustion that deprives the conclusion of exaltation and even good will." The United States might otherwise conclude that its client was docile, while domestic adversaries might infer that the government was weak, he reported. "In the final analysis, to put it bluntly, the fate of small countries always rests with the superpowers, and they always have their own interests to guard," Meir recalled in turn.[104] Kissinger's visit was clearly no pleasure for either of them.

In the course of their conversations, Kissinger emphasized that another three days' fighting risked destruction of U.S. credibility in the Arab world and a superpower crisis. Meir, no less emphatic, demanded to know if there were a Soviet-U.S. plan for imposing borders, whether and how a cease-fire was to be linked to a prisoner exchange, and where and when negotiations under "appropriate auspices" were to take place. With Resolution 242 conspicuous on the agenda, and the Israeli general election rescheduled for December 31, she was in no hurry. En route to the airport, Kissinger begged Eban to push Meir for an early Geneva conference. Pictures of Arab and Israeli negotiators around the same table could hardly hurt her campaign, he argued.[105]

Seemingly resolved, the crisis reerupted unexpectedly within hours of Kissinger's return to Washington. Conversations with the military had, in fact, been ambiguous on both sides. Senior Israeli officers had apparently led Kissinger to understand that a climactic victory over Egypt could take as many as twelve or as few as three days. "In Vietnam the cease-fire didn't come into effect when it was supposed to either," Kissinger reportedly replied—or at least listened to others say it without contradiction. It was also unclear who was to police the cease-fire.[106]

As Israeli forces resumed—or continued—closing in on the Egyptian Third Army, the Soviets grew so concerned that Brezhnev reached for the hotline for the first time in Nixon's presidency. Within a few hours, he had appealed to Nixon twice and, even more remarkably, to Kissinger directly. Soviet credibility was obviously at stake. But, as Sadat appealed frantically for U.S. help, U.S. credibility was at issue too. "There were limits beyond which we could not go, with all our friendship for Israel," Kissinger told Dinitz, "and one of them was to make the leader of another superpower look like an idiot."[107] On October 23, Security Council Resolution 339 called for another cease-fire with authorized observers and restoration of the previous day's status quo. But Israeli units continued to advance.

By October 24, Sadat was in regular contact with Nixon about the survival of Resolution 339, and Kissinger with Dobrynin on the survival of Resolution 338. That afternoon it was reported in Washington that Sadat had publicly appealed to both superpowers for troops to supervise the cease-fire. It was only that evening, however, with the arrival of a new and urgent message from Brezhnev, that Americans once again found themselves at the brink. Amplified by suspension of the Soviet airlift, with its implied signal that the planes were being readied to carry troops, the message threatened unilateral action if the United States should "find it impossible to act jointly." Kissinger reacted characteristically to the challenge. "We were heading into what could have become the gravest foreign policy crisis of the Nixon Presidency," he recalled, "because it involved a direct confrontation of the superpowers . . . with a President overwhelmed by his persecution and with a Congress that had just, in the War Powers Act, restricted the President's authority to use military force."[108]

At 10:40 P.M., while Nixon slept, Kissinger convened a "meeting of principals," that is, Schlesinger, Colby, Moorer, and senior aides. When they emerged at 2:00 A.M., on October 25, they had put U.S. forces not already at a comparable or higher alert status on DefCon 3, the highest state of peacetime readiness. As Europeans had learned to expect of Washington in such situations, NATO was informed but not consulted. Though the psychic reverberations were considerable, the practical implications were relatively modest. The Air Force's Strategic Air Command was advanced a stage from its previous 4. Because of Vietnam, DefCon 3 was the normal status for Pacific Command. Polaris submarines, whose status was usually between 3 and 2, were also set at 3. The Sixth Fleet in the Mediterranean remained at 2. On grounds, as Kissinger noted, that "two could play chicken," the meeting also authorized naval movements in the Mediterranean, and drafted a message to Brezhnev, informing him that unilateral action would have "incalculable consequences."[109]

A few hours later, to Kissinger's horror, the decision was on the morning news. After an extended conference with Nixon, he proceeded to congressional briefings later that morning, where he found "these distinguished men" at once "supportive, rudderless and ambivalent." At his own press conference that noon, he was himself dismayed and testy when questioners suggested the alert had anything to do with Watergate. On the other hand, his reaction implied that he was not surprised. "One cannot have crises of authority in a society for a period of months without paying a price somewhere along the line," he acknowledged.[110]

Though Watergate was hardly something any presidential appointee could disregard, and there was understandable public reluctance to believe the alert was called entirely on its merits, the dismay had some foundation. For rather different reasons from Kissinger's, Nixon too denied any connection when addressing himself to the Middle East, the question of judicial access to the famous White House tapes, and the appointment of a new special prosecutor respectively, at a press conference on October 26, the day the alert was canceled. It was his first press conference since October 3.

Meanwhile, both superpowers had agreed in the Security Council to Resolution 340. The text, reflecting Nixon's preferences to a greater degree than Brezhnev's, authorized a U.N. Emergency Force without superpower representation to police the cease-fire. "Demanding" and no longer "urging" reinstatement of the cease-fire lines of October 22, it also called for implementation of Resolution 338. "It will be necessary for all sides to make substantial concessions," Kissinger had declared. "The problem will be to relate the Arab concern over—for the sovereignty over the territories—to the Israeli concern for secure boundaries."[111]

As Kissinger himself noted, the president "knew better than his critics" why

Watergate had little direct impact in the night of October 24–25.[112] Crisis past, the president also had every reason to view with alarm post facto, the better to point with pride to how the crisis confirmed U.S. capacity to act and his own capacity to "do what was right."[113] As Kissinger also noted, Nixon was delighted with the outcome of the global alert. Ready one moment to summon the major news organizations to call attention to his decisiveness and indispensability, the president had been ready a moment later to "get the whole bunch" of Jewish leaders in a room, remind them they were Americans first, and ask rhetorically, "Who is going to save Israel and who will save it in the future?"[114]

The answer to that was reasonably clear too, just as it was reasonably clear what had finally resolved the three-week crisis. Faced with what it saw as an existential challenge to its role in the world, in Europe, and the Middle East, the administration had stood firm in support of Israel, détente, containment, and regional equilibrium respectively, ultimately balancing each against the other. "We had supported Israel throughout the war for many historical, moral and strategic reasons," Kissinger observed. "And we had just run the risk of war with the Soviet Union, amidst the domestic crisis of Watergate." But "our shared interests did not embrace the elimination of the (Egyptian) Third Army," he added.[115]

It was equally important, in the administration's worldview, that Americans, not the Soviets, save the Egyptians under siege. Brezhnev's note of October 24 was "very firm" and "left very little to the imagination," Nixon declared at his press conference. At the same time, in a region where things rarely move at right angles, as Thomas L. Friedman observed years later, this could be understood as both more and less than traditional Cold War rhetoric. If Nixon was resolved that the world should know that "the tougher it gets, the cooler I get," he also acknowledged explicitly and audibly that "without détente, we might have had a major conflict in the Middle East"; that no one could afford a war there; and that differences there must not be allowed "to jeopardize even greater interests," for example, in European détente and nuclear arms control.

As Nixon further acknowledged, there was also the question of oil. Japan and Europe got 80 percent of their oil from the Middle East, the president emphasized. Without a settlement, both "would have frozen to death this winter,"[116] in what had been intended as recently as April to be a "Year of Europe." But this hardly meant that Europe was grateful. On the contrary, oil was now a solvent of such unanticipated effectiveness that when Washington called, Brussels put it on "hold." Kissinger had been trying for two weeks to elicit an invitation to meet European Community foreign ministers, the State Department announced in early December. They were still waiting for an answer.[117]

So regarded, DefCon 3 was at least as much a signal to the Israelis as to the Soviet Union.[118] In any case, it was surely no coincidence that the principal Israelis should recall it as such. In Moshe Dayan's version, corroborated by Kissinger, the Americans made clear to Dinitz that they would consider destruction of the Egyptian Third Army a blow to U.S. prestige, irrespective of who violated the original cease-fire. There was no threat to interrupt the airlift. But there were no concessions either: if the Israelis refused to allow the Egyptians to resupply their troops, Dayan understood the Americans to say, they would find themselves "in a crisis situation with the United States." In fact, Kissinger indicated, the Americans themselves would resupply the Egyptians if the Israelis left no other option.[119]

For her own obvious reasons, Meir emphasized U.S. pressure when the cabinet convened in the night of October 25. The meeting then continued until 4:00 A.M. "When we knew that the United States had decided on a deterrent alert, we were profoundly heartened and impressed," Eban reported. "On the other hand, our need to take American wishes into account was now more acute." Given the choice of greater military victory or continuation of good relations with the United States, the Israelis consciously opted for the latter, he said.[120]

Meir tootled along in apparent, if reluctant, harmony. Her ambivalence was actually at the heart of Ben-Gurion's legacy. From the beginning of Zionist settlement, it had been Labor's policy to make facts. From the beginnings of Zionist foreign policy, it had also been Labor's policy to face them. Meir could acknowledge Kissinger's goodwill and even good work.[121] In the rapidly fading afterglow of June 11, 1967, and painfully throbbing aftershock of October 6, 1973, she could hardly help but acknowledge Israeli dependence. But there was no obligation to like it. Israel's recovery had been a function of U.S. support and supply. Israel's inability to reestablish and even exceed the status quo had also been a function of U.S. support and supply. Nixon's decision of October 24, as she referred to it, had been dangerous, courageous and correct, Meir concluded for the record. Its consequences also put Israel on the spot.

For the moment, at least, Meir both faced facts and made them. The Israelis accepted the new cease-fire. They also remained in their positions. "There is nothing to be ashamed of when a small country like Israel, in this situation, has to give in sometimes to the United States," she told her cabinet.[122] But it was harder to say if she really believed it.

"My ultimate responsibility was as Secretary of State of the United States, not as psychiatrist to the government of Israel," Kissinger observed. "With the utmost reluctance I decided that my duty was to force a showdown."[123] An Israeli observer was reminded of prewar Poland. Just as Poland's Marshal Josef Pilsudski had once managed to extract his country's independence from the German defeat of Russia and the Allied defeat of Germany, so, he noted, had Sadat now managed to get the Soviets to deter Israel and the Americans to deter the Soviet Union. In the process, he observed, the United States had come full circle not only once but twice. As in 1954, Washington was prepared to take a chance on Egypt. As in 1969, it was again disposed to ask Israelis to surrender land for peace.[124]

8

Step by Step

This time, to a point and for awhile, the quest for Arab-Israeli peace, "balance," even new friends and influence in the Middle East seemed actually to pay off. Between fall 1973 and spring 1979, "the peace process," as it was now called,[1] produced a series of successes, even triumphs, like none before, or any that would follow for years afterward. By now, it appeared, U.S. diplomacy had established a kind of pattern. Republican or Democratic, new administrations fantasized about grand designs and comprehensive solutions on taking office, but sooner or later, they settled for what they could get.

For years, it was assumed, the solution would be a settlement with Jordan. From the 1940s on, both Jerusalem and Washington took it practically on faith that the little kingdom, precariously wedged between an explosive Syria and a baleful Egypt, was both the anchor and the last best hope of Arab moderation. Now, to the amazement of all and the dismay of many, the payoff turned out to be what the Nixon administration, in its inimitable idiom, might have called "the big enchilada." From Truman to Kennedy, from Farouk to Nasser, Egypt had persistently evaded the grasp of the United States. Now, under Sadat, it advanced, step by step, into the arms of two of the century's least popular administrations. Washington, Jerusalem, and Moscow alike saw the new relationship as Cold War politics by other means, but Cairo's calculus could hardly have been more different. It was Egypt's decision to pursue another round with Israel that brought the Cold War to the Middle East in the 1950s. Twenty years later, it was as plausible to argue that it was Cairo's decision to opt out of Cold War politics that led to an Israeli-Egyptian peace.

Within five years, the cumulative results of U.S. brokerage included five major agreements, four of them between Egypt and Israel. In the aftermath of the 1978 Camp David Accords and the 1979 Israeli-Egyptian peace, U.S. policymakers tried hard to build on their foundations, just as they had once sought to clone the Marshall Plan, NATO, or the 1953 coup that restored the shah of Iran. Yet sometimes calamitously, sometimes anticlimactically, each new failure only confirmed the uniqueness of the original success.

Ironically, just as the United States had once set out to rebuild a battered Europe and reconstruct the world economy in the aftermath of World War II, it had also set out to guide the Middle East from colonial darkness to postimperial light. Yet in all those years, neither Republicans nor Democrats had even been able to get Arabs and Israelis to meet in public. Since then, Americans had learned something about the Middle East and the realities of global power. In the process, the nominally imperial presidency had lost its luster, while neoconservative evangelists deplored détente and what they increasingly saw as the unresisted ascendance of a *pax sovietica*.

Now, in the aftermath of Watergate and Southeast Asia, even the traditional shout of "Bear!" had seemingly lost its resonance. From Cambodia and Cyprus to Angola and the Horn of Africa, Kissinger himself urged new commitments on a reluctant Congress.[2] Yet the Middle East seemed not only to contradict the secretary's forebodings but to resist the thitherto accepted laws of political gravity.

Successively and cumulatively, the successes of 1973–1979 tested truths about the U.S. role, the U.S. and regional political process, and even the nature of power itself, which had thitherto been held to be self-evident. Even as they proclaimed and conceded the declining hegemony of the United States, first Kissinger, then his Democratic successors, descended from airplanes with pieces of Middle Eastern peace, snatched from the wreckage of their own global scenarios and grand designs. Persuaded for good reasons that peace was cheaper than war, they then persuaded an otherwise reluctant Congress to advance the necessary capital.

Meanwhile, as objects, beneficiaries, and practitioners of what was now known as "public diplomacy," Israelis and Egyptians accomplished what Dulles and Eisenhower once urged, and Ben-Gurion and Nasser had considered and rejected, some twenty years before. This time they not only allowed Americans to get them to settle, they persuaded the United States to underwrite the settlement, and incidentally replace their arsenals. It was almost as though, by making peace with one another, they were doing something nice for the United States. At the same time, they learned to shake hands, and even smile on camera, while Americans, from the White House lawn to the kitchen television, looked on and liked what they saw.

In this respect too, the peace process was as rich in contrasts and paradoxes as the classical movie travelogue, and the itinerary as remarkable as the destination. Recalling an earlier generation's "open covenants, openly arrived at" in ways that would never have occurred to President Wilson, the new U.S. policy reflected at once the impact of technology, the weight of historical memory, and the compelling need for public support. Neither the jet engine, the communications satellite, nor the contingencies of network news producers explain in themselves the dynamics of shuttle diplomacy[3] or the success of Camp David. But it is hard to see how either shuttle diplomacy or Camp David would have worked without them.

At home, where the president, the courts, and the Congress were playing out their respective roles in the most remarkable constitutional drama since the Civil War, the media took on the role of Nemesis, the goddess of retribution. Yet under way with Kissinger, they were not only a willing instrument of diplomacy but an airborne chorus. Aboard the secretary's plane, the wire services, the networks, the newsmagazines, the national press were all in attendance, as many as twenty at a time. Clad only in the translucent persona of a "senior American official," Kissinger himself appeared from time to time to brief them.[4] Still more correspondents followed on commercial aircraft.

If China-Kissinger had been a diplomatic practitioner of classical discretion and cunning, Middle East-Kissinger was now a global presence. Given the nature of his constituencies, both foreign and domestic, it was a virtual condition of success that his shuttles be seen around the region, and his message heard around the world. No one, least of all his critics, denied his virtuosity. From palaces, airport lounges, and even Golda Meir's kitchen, the impact on anyone who owned a television was almost instantaneous. Aware of their responsibilities and alert to their opportunities both as witnesses to, and actors in, a unique political pageant, the reporters left a trail of instant history, curbside futurology, and even creative fiction.[5]

Israeli writers tended to deep skepticism, even overt pessimism, both with respect to the achievement and the U.S. role. Their ambivalence about Kissinger, as an American and as a fellow Jew, stands out especially against the shrewd and generous appreciations of Israeli politics, motives, and primal fears that constitute some of the most eloquent passages of Kissinger's memoirs.[6] Almost irrespective of differences with one another, their message was consistently ambivalent, even abrasive. "Incrementalism as a concept has utterly failed," wrote Amos Perlmutter in a book that appeared the same year as Camp David. Instead, he argued for a new Geneva conference as the last best hope of peace at just about the moment the Carter administration was abandoning the idea, "With no reasonable alternative to continuing support by the United States, Israel could not afford to stand back and make a critical judgment of U.S. policy as expressed by Kissinger," wrote Matti Golan of *Ha'aretz*. He nonetheless believed his country had been suborned to U.S. ends, and that the belligerents would have done better if they had just been left to themselves.[7]

For Americans, on the other hand, Kissinger was nothing less than fascinating: the Harvard professor, German-Jewish intellectual, not to mention secretary of state, as culture hero. Save, perhaps, for his fellow immigré, Albert Einstein, a generation earlier, there had never been anything like him. Like Woody Allen, whose screen persona as streetwise intellectual *nebbish* also captured the public imagination, Kissinger seemed a figure both mythical and prototypical, as generationally Jewish-American as a Saul Bellow novel. Yet his magic had all but vanished within a year or two of what so recently seemed his finest hours. In June 1974 *Newsweek* portrayed him as Super-K in flight. Only a few years later, a resourceful editorial cartoonist showed him outside a phone booth, looking thoughtfully at his undershorts.[8] By election year 1976, his achievements were practically regarded as a political liability.

By this time, neither eviction of Soviet influence from Egypt nor effective exclusion of the Soviet Union from regional diplomacy were a shield against angry neoconservatives. On the contrary, the secretary's Cassandran warnings only encouraged his critics, many of them Jews and former Democrats. Facing new Soviet initiatives in Angola, Ethiopia, and other hitherto inaccessible corners of the Third World, they now weighed Kissinger in the balance, and found him wanting.

The neoconservative critique fell particularly hard on the Middle East. Since 1970, the administration had viewed détente as the very premise of success there. Yet for Kissinger's critics, the fact that the Soviet Union seemed to see it that way too[9] was only confirmation of their worst suspicions. They tended accordingly to see Israel as a neo-Czechoslovakia, and Kissinger himself as a neo-appeaser. A few years later, they were equally hard on Carter as his successes in one regional conflict

were eclipsed by the real and present dangers of another. In the aftermath of the
revolution in Iran and the Soviet invasion of Afghanistan, they were then co-opted
as insiders in a new Republican administration by a president, who, like so many
of them, was also a former Democrat.[10]

Among the oddest contrasts to both previous and subsequent experience was
the distribution of rewards and honors, including the Nobel Peace Prize. In 1950,
Ralph Bunche, now nearly forgotten, had been the first American to receive it for
his brokerage of armistice agreements between Israel and Lebanon, Syria and
Egypt.[11] In 1973, the prize went to Kissinger—but for efforts to make peace in Vietnam that collapsed within three years of their negotiation. Yet by this time, even
the Syrian-Israeli disengagement had become a feature of the Middle Eastern landscape, and Kissinger's efforts to disengage Israel and Egypt had established a platform for the breakthroughs of 1978–1979. These, in turn, earned a Nobel Peace
Prize for Egypt's President Anwar al-Sadat and Israel's Prime Minister Menahim
Begin. But there was no prize at all for Carter, who both brought them together and
kept them there till they had reached agreement.

Arguably, no secretary of state on record nor any president since Truman had
better reason to be proud of their achievements in the Middle East. Eisenhower,
who succeeded Truman, built on sand. Reagan, who succeeded Carter, left an
unmatched trail of disaster from Beirut to Tehran. Yet paradoxically, the collected
alarums and embarrassments of the Middle East left Eisenhower undented, and
Reagan survived debacles that might have got Carter impeached.

By contrast, in early 1976, Ford's campaign advisors warned against returning
fire when Reagan challenged "Ford-Kissinger" foreign policy, and Ford himself
retreated from the very word *détente* at a meeting in Peoria.[12] Four years later,
Reagan's own new Republican administration successively appointed General
Alexander Haig its first secretary of state, and Robert C. "Bud" McFarlane as its
second national security advisor; both were Kissinger protégés. After their fashion,
both were also to distinguish themselves in the Middle East as accessories to ill-
considered, and even disastrous, Israeli initiatives. But the new administration
demonstratively avoided Kissinger.

As always, it was easy to explain in retrospect why what previously failed had
now succeeded with such surpassing brilliance. As so often in history, war had once
again been both catalyst and agent of international change. Each in his way, a
resourceful secretary of state and a tenacious president had seen their chance to
guide the process, but a changing Egypt and a changing Israel were crucial factors.

Since Gamal Abdel Nasser's ascent to power in the heady 1950s, Egyptians had
seen the future, and it didn't work. The legendary Soviet arms deal of 1955 had led
to military disaster. The resulting dependency on the Soviet Union had been as
damaging in its way as the old relationship to Britain. Arab nationalism and the
bloody arabesques of regional politics led to successive humiliations in Syria and
the Yemen. The conflict with Israel was a disaster unto itself. Not only had it led to
the loss of considerable territory and a major source of revenue, it was a body blow
to Egyptian prestige and self-assurance, leaving the country systemically vulnerable
to the seductions and provocations of trigger-happy neighbors.

Although no one could say for sure what Arab socialism meant in theory, it was clear from experience that it meant stagnation and dictatorship in practice. Cost-benefit analyses of the Aswan high dam, perhaps the revolution's most potent symbol and one of the great achievements in the history of civil engineering, remained a matter of debate. But what was clear, at least, was that it had failed to keep pace with the needs of a population growing at 2 to 3 percent a year. "We're like Bangladesh, and Cairo is like Calcutta," Egypt's Foreign Minister Boutros Ghali reportedly told Israel's defense minister only hours after Sadat had flown to Jerusalem to end the conflict.[13] In a world where Egyptians suspected fellow Arabs of a willingness to fight to the last Egyptian, both political and economic necessity made October 1973 Egypt's war to end all wars.

For Israel too, the postwar reconsiderations reflected fatigue and doubt. For hundreds of thousands of new immigrants, the 1950s meant austerity and challenge beyond anything known recently in western Europe. But they were also years of consensus and purpose; of impressive, even dramatic growth; of marked gains in real income; and a price stability later generations could only envy.[14] These too had become a casualty of the wars. If consumer durables were a problem—and fewer than 34 percent of all households in 1958 could so much as claim a refrigerator—élan, solidarity, national identity were not. For a majority of Israelis, the day-to-day challenges of housing, job, and security did wonders to concentrate the mind.

In the longer run, it was practically inevitable that there would be problems with the non-European immigrants who now constituted what was called a Second Israel. Like Irish or Sicilian peasants in Yankee New England, their exodus from Morocco or the Yemen had not been simply a matter of miles but of worlds and centuries. For many, their most challenging adjustment was learning to live with fellow Jews from Europe, who ignored and patronized them. Meanwhile the armistice lines separated yet another Israel, the Arabs who remained in 1948, from Gaza and the West Bank, but for the moment, they too could be ignored and marginalized.

Confident in their arms, their ingenuity, the rightness of their cause, and the legitimacy of their political establishment, Israelis addressed the priorities of national and economic survival with sovereign self-assurance. Their independence was all the more remarkable in a country whose exports paid for less than a third of its imports. Arguably, the Labor Zionism that was their prevailing creed was as unrealistic, anachronistic, even counterproductive as the socialist and nationalist utopias that intoxicated their Arab neighbors. The contingencies of national survival had nonetheless made Israelis very good at war, and their skill at war had in many ways become an alternative to politics. Israelis learned from experience how to coexist with their neighbors and, when necessary, how to fight them. But virtually nothing in their collective national history had taught either side to address the other as an equal.[15]

Though Israelis were understandably reluctant to see the connection, the crisis of 1973 was as much a testimonial to their successes as their failures. In the Israel of 1974, 94 percent of all households owned refrigerators, and exports covered up to half of imports, but the consensus and self-assurance of the earlier austerity were gone.

For all the rigor of the early years, defense and police made up as relatively little as 23.2% of public spending, and only once exceeded 30% in the first decade of independence. Now, in the five years after 1970, defense and police averaged over 38% of public spending, and only once fell below 32%. The relative weight of defense in the overall economy grew even more impressively. Before 1961, defense constituted about 8% of GNP; between 1962 and 1966, about 10%. Despite "extended but defensible borders, huge quantities of captured equipment and a weakened enemy," Eitan Berglas observed, the 1967 war was followed by the most dramatic increase in defense expenditure to date. From 1968 to 1972, defense spending grew to at least 21% of GNP; after 1973, to at least 28%. Between 1970 and 1975, official figures reported average defense spending at nearly 27% of GNP, 23% minus U.S. military grants, 22% minus all U.S. grants. By comparison, U.S. defense spending in the same period averaged about 32% of federal spending but less than 6.5% of GNP.[16]

Of course, it was as much a fact of life as ever that Israelis, of all nations, could not afford to lose a war, but despite their understandable anxiety, there had never been a serious threat of military defeat. Both numbers and geography favored a strategy of initiative and preemption. Supply was inevitably a matter of constant concern. In a tiny, densely populated country where work force and armed force were virtually identical, attrition was a perennial nightmare. Yet even in 1973, when Israelis lost the initiative in ways that haunted them for years afterward, they had nonetheless emerged as military victors. On the contrary, for all their doubts, the October war confirmed that they were as good at war as ever. What was new was a degree of logistical dependency and political isolation that increasingly made victory in the old sense unaffordable.

This was where the United States came in. As only an indignant superpower can, the United States had lowered the boom on its closest allies and Israel too between November 1956 and early 1957. Declaring the Sinai invasion an unacceptable threat to U.S. values and interests, it not only halted but reversed the adventure with minimal regard for both foreign and domestic sensibilities. Secure in his public popularity, his personal conviction and the unchallengeable superiority of his political firepower, Eisenhower met little more than token resistance. On the contrary, an ambivalent Congress, a still-undeveloped Jewish lobby, and a concerned but largely unfocused public opinion acceded, and even applauded, as the president threatened to destroy the pound sterling, and suspend aid to Israel.[17] British resistance crumbled in days. The French followed shortly. After an initial show of defiance, Israelis were hesitant to risk what, despite all political reservations, was still their major, and only reliable, source of long-term foreign support.

Despite obvious continuities of anxiety, virtually none of these conditions obtained after the Yom Kippur War. In 1973 as in 1956, Washington was fearful where further Middle Eastern hostilities might lead; concerned to spare Egypt further humiliation; and resolved to stop its allies short of "victory." To achieve this end, it was prepared to work de facto with the Soviets—whose regional presence and influence in the region it was nonetheless determined to limit, if not eradicate altogether.

What was new was the odd package of vulnerabilities and strengths that now energized, inhibited, and motivated U.S. policy almost interchangeably. This time, for all its huge arsenal, the United States was no longer the cop on the block, and still less an Olympian neutral. Vietnam, the Nixon Doctrine, and the administration's own view of the world precluded any show of cool objectivity, let alone of neo-Wilsonian outrage. In practice, if not in law, Israel had become an ally. Even a Republican White House acknowledged now that U.S.-Israeli links were no longer discretionary. Yet this time, paradoxically, Egypt's president was not showing the United States the door. On the contrary, he was pushing it open till the hinges squeaked, and waving for attention.

Meanwhile, the Soviet situation too had changed. In 1956, the Soviet military reach extended to Budapest. By 1973, it extended to Alexandria and Cairo. Yet a twenty-year speculation in Middle Eastern futures had paid off in liabilities Krushchev never dreamed of. For all the embarrassments Sadat now heaped on Moscow, Egypt held its onetime patrons hostage. Like it or not, the Soviets could no more leave Egypt to another drubbing than the United States could walk away from Israel.

If no longer sovereign in the sense they believed themselves to be in 1956, Europeans were no longer acquiescent either. In 1950, oil accounted for 10 percent of Europe's energy requirements, coal for 75 percent. By 1970, oil supplied 60 percent of the energy needs of vastly larger European economies, while coal's share had fallen to a third.[18] In 1973, with block-long lines at every gas station, the United States was hard-pressed even to help itself. "You can't send us oil in CARE packages," one European told an American colleague. Even the dollar was swinging in the wind, after being cut loose from its postwar moorings by a Republican president.

The status of the presidency was itself a measure of how things had changed since the days when presidents could still be heroes, and Congress protected domestic producers against cheap foreign oil. In 1956, a majority of Americans might have nodded indulgently if President Eisenhower had told them that the world was flat. By late 1973, a majority of Americans might have asked for a second opinion if President Nixon told them it was raining.

Kissinger's agenda reflected the new circumstances. Long-term, his mandate called for global settlement as per Resolution 338. But what mattered was the short term, before the guns again went off and the global fuse again began to burn. This time it was crucial that both sides win something without damage to détente; essential that allies remain on board, and that oil resume its flow to Rotterdam from aggrieved and emboldened Middle East producers; crucial that a Congress, less and less supportive of one of history's least popular presidents, should nonetheless support his foreign policy in the wake of the least popular foreign war of the United States. Not least, as Kissinger himself noted, it was necessary, to persuade "a prickly, proud and somewhat overwrought friendly nation . . . not to persist on a course promising great domestic benefits in the runup to an election."[19]

It followed from his agenda that the next steps, resupply of the entrapped Egyptian army, disengagement of both Israeli and Egyptian forces, and exchange of prisoners, were at once their own reward and down payment on a larger process. Though the execution of what followed was to be endlessly subtle, elaborate, even improvisatory, at least the premises were clear from the start. In important ways, each side had reached its limits. Neither could "win." Both wanted something only the other could give. Each regarded the other with all but absolute distrust and fear.

In their hearts, both sides really believed in a zero-sum game, where any concession was the other's gain, and where no imaginable gain could match the sacrifices it required. "Comprehensive" solution, as once envisaged in Resolution 242, inconclusively pursued in the Rogers Plan, and now resurrected in Resolution 338, was universally seen to be a phantom. A lifelong student of politics between nations, Kissinger was skeptical of such things in general and particular. He was assumed to believe that such conflicts had no comprehensive solutions. Even the pursuit of one was only an incentive for each side to reaffirm the status quo.[20] For Egyptians, an international conference was tantamount to a Syrian veto. For Israelis, whose memories reached back at least as far as Rhodes and Lausanne, it was just another hopeless match. Like OPEC, a conference promised an iron front of naysayers, each ostentatiously committed to the Palestinian cause, and demonstratively concerned to keep his neighbor from temptation, on one side. Like the United Nations, it meant an isolated Israel on the other. The Soviets would, of course, be right behind the Arabs. On the other hand, Israel would be virtually shackled to an ambivalent United States, while choruses of Europeans implored Israelis to forsake "intransigence" for "reasonableness" on territorial concessions and the status of the Palestinians.

Yet, after its fashion each side did believe in the United States, whose leaders were eager to show some tangible progress, whatever their skepticism about how to achieve it. If the best, that is, a "comprehensive," settlement was out, there was still room at least for the good. The idea, according to Kissinger, was to approach "the Middle East problem in individual and therefore manageable segments." In more or less consecutive order, this meant conciliating "moderate" Arabs, restoring the oil flow, preempting allies, dealing ad hoc with the bellingerents, isolating the Soviets, preserving détente, and avoiding major confrontation with both Israeli and domestic opinion.

But perhaps above all, it meant taking personal charge.[21] The operative principle was a kind of diplomatic judo, where even apparent handicaps could be turned to practical advantage. Only the United States could meet at least some expectations of virtually all the interested parties: aid for the Israelis, land for the Arabs, oil for the West Europeans, an international conference with its acknowledged superpower parity for the Soviets, and all, the administration could argue, in the best interest of the United States.

The Israeli-U.S. relationship was an obvious case. If it made the United States more vulnerable than any other foreign power to the October war and its global fallout, it also made the United States uniquely qualified to tidy up when the shooting stopped. If the Arabs wanted to reverse the 1967 war by fighting, the Soviets could naturally supply the weapons. But if they wanted their land back without another war, and were unwilling, as they had been since 1948, to talk directly to Israelis, they had no choice but to talk to the United States. In the process, the United States might even emerge the peaceful winner of what had just recently seemed the most threatening international confrontation since the Cuban missile crisis.

"Perhaps the most important ingredient," Nadav Safran noted, "was the success of the United States in conveying to the Arab side *at one and the same time* the sense that it was able to move Israel and that such a feat was by no means easy."[22] To Edward R. F. Sheehan, a sometime journalist and novelist who followed the secretary's entourage, Kissinger's performance was nature imitating art. In principle, Sheehan noted, his diplomacy recalled the matchmaker who offers a poor man Lord Rothschild's daughter as his son's bride. He then offers Lord Rothschild a vice president of the World Bank as his daughter's fiancé. He then offers the World Bank Lord Rothschild's son-in-law as its new vice president.[23]

Kissinger's strategy proceeded logically from similar premises. *If* Israel wanted peace, it would have to pay in land. *If* the Arabs wanted land—not to mention security from both the Soviets and one another—they would have to pay in oil, and some accommodation of Israel. *If* Europeans wanted oil, they would have to accept U.S. leadership. *If* the Russians wanted negotiated nuclear parity, most favored nation status, or any other emblem of superpower symmetry, they would have to yield to the United States in the Middle East. *If* Americans wanted the Soviets out of the Middle East, they would have to accept détente.[24]

His function, as Kissinger regularly emphasized, was making clear to each side the goals that moved, and the constraints that inhibited, the other, then explaining to each the goals he wanted to reach himself.[25] But there were no doubts either about the goals that moved, and the constraints that obtained on, the United States. The peace conference, which Kissinger acknowledged as a "seeming contradiction," was an example. "We strove to assemble a multilateral conference, but our purpose was to use it as a framework for an essentially bilateral diplomacy," he commented.[26] The idea, in effect, was to win Soviet cooperation for an endeavor that would make further cooperation unnecessary.

The constraints were not only inherent in U.S. politics, they derived from the role itself. Israel alone, as Kissinger noted, demanded almost antithetical things of the United States. It wanted support for an Israeli position that was itself driven toward intransigence by domestic politics. It then wanted the United States to persuade the Arabs to sit down and conclude a peace.[27] In the well-established tradition of the Eastern Question, both sides welcomed and even demanded, while also resisting, external action. In differing degrees, both demanded that the broker also play the role of guarantor. Both continued acting independently. Both appealed directly and indirectly to foreign, especially U.S., constituencies over which Kissinger had limited control.

The long-term paradox of U.S. mediation, as Michael Handel observed, was its very success. Step by step, its price, both in aid to Israel and to Arab clients, made it progressively easier for Israel to resist U.S. wishes, while practically assuring Moscow's continued support of Arab radicals.[28] At the same time, contrary to all previous wisdom on the sources and nature of presidential power,[29] Watergate seemed to be not only no handicap but a positive advantage. The facts of political life made Nixon "almost fanatically avid for success in the Middle East," Abba Eban recalled.[30] Yet it was at once Nixon's glory and his trump that neither Arabs nor Israelis, Soviets nor Chinese, European allies nor domestic Democrats could afford to let his foreign policy fail.

Not only was disengagement of forces the only case in which U.S. mediation was unsolicited by both parties, it was the only case in which it was overtly resented by one of them. To the pleasant surprise of the Americans, Sadat was again resilient beyond expectation. He could hardly be unaware of the capacity of the United States to unleash the Israelis on his isolated army. He also accepted the special relationship of the United States to Israel as given, abandoned any illusions that Resolution 242 would be instantly fulfilled, and allowed Kissinger time to pursue a more substantial Israeli withdrawal. The long-term goal, both men agreed, was "mutually assured borders."[31]

Paradoxically, it was the aggrieved and embattled Israelis who now presented the major obstacle. By deliberately avoiding the big issues, step-by-step diplomacy seemed actually to favor their position. And yet, as Sheehan observed, even Kissinger's prodigious salesmanship was never quite enough to persuade them it was in their interest.[32] Direct bilateral talks between Israeli and Egyptian military delegations under General Aharon Yariv and General Abdel Ghany el-Gamasy were a test case of the inherent trade-offs. Convened in a tent on the Cairo-Suez road, the negotiators took one another's measure, established personal rapport, then hung tough on the relative priorities of prisoner exchange versus resupply of the besieged Egyptian army.

Meanwhile, Meir and Kissinger raged and haggled with each other on whether, how, and to what end both countries should be nice to Egypt. In the end, the generals reached agreement after eighteen meetings. Without U.S. mediation, they were even ready to go further, but they were whistled back by Kissinger. "If you take Henry out of context, he's an abomination," one of the secretary's friends explained to Sheehan.[33] The Israeli-Egyptian agreement was nonetheless a watershed after five weeks of existential panic.

But context was, of course, the point. The impending Geneva conference—of which Kissinger, in fact, expected very little—was crucial to his strategy. Potentially, Yariv and Gamasy were robbing the conference of something it could usefully talk about. This might thereby advance the agenda prematurely to the issue of peace negotiations as such, which in turn could jeopardize the entire intricate process. Only two months later, Kissinger himself was to mediate a rather similar arrangement to what was envisaged by Yariv and Gamasy, but no one could foresee this in November.

Ironically, Israel's Labor government turned out to be at least as interested in Geneva as the U.S. secretary of state. Shocked and frightened by their equivocal victory, and battered in their self-esteem, the Israelis were at the same time engaged in an election campaign and a national self-examination. Fairly or not, the incumbent lions, Meir and Moshe Dayan, were blamed for the war. For the first time, the opposition Likud was more or less coherently organized around the war's only hero, Ariel Sharon.

For the moment, it was the peace issue that put Geneva at the top of Labor's platform. The party had little choice but to run as peacemaker, and incidentally custodian of good relations with the United States. This still left the question of terms, for example, the role of the U.N. secretary general; identification of, and Red Cross access to, Israeli prisoners in Syrian hands; and the always vexing question of the Palestinians. Unsurprisingly, the Arabs demanded a Palestinian presence at Geneva. For the first time, the United States had not said no—at least in as many words. But there was less to the statement than met the eye. In principle, the United States declared the Palestinians to be an inter-Arab, not an international, concern. In his draft invitation, Kissinger again fudged the question by proclaiming Palestinian participation an unresolved matter to be discussed after the conference opened. Yet even accommodation of the Palestinians as a procedural issue was more than the Israeli political traffic would allow.[34]

As Kissinger arrived in Israel in mid-December via Algeria, Syria, Egypt, Saudi Arabia, and Jordan, there was another scene from Shakespeare. He was met at the airport by demonstrators bearing messages like "America—You too, Brutus," and "Kissinger Abandoned Formosa—Us Next?" It was, Bernard and Marvin Kalb observed, "like negotiating with a whole country."[35] In his meetings with the Israelis, the secretary turned up his sense of urgency to full volume, warning what would happen if Israel stayed away from Geneva, but, yielding to "ordeal by exegesis," he also backed down on the Palestinians. The Israelis agreed to tolerate them as part of a Jordanian delegation. They were adamant about a Palestinian delegation as such, let alone an invitation to the PLO. For "Palestinians," Kissinger accordingly substituted "other participants from the Middle East area." The day before the conference, he then added a secret memorandum, in effect conferring an Israeli veto on the PLO.[36]

When the delegates finally convened in Geneva on December 21, 1973, the conference fulfilled the modest expectations, both positive and negative, that were placed in it. The Israelis came; the Syrians stayed away; both Jordanian and Egyptian speakers lambasted Israel; the Arabs avoided the secretary general's cocktail party where they might be seen in the company of Israelis; there were formal presentations by both the Soviet and U.S. foreign ministers, and no one left prematurely.[37]

Ten days later, Israelis went to the polls. For one last time, the incumbents squeaked to victory, but there was little room for self-congratulation, and the outcome was hardly a mandate for the doves. Though disappointed by the outcome, Likud did especially well among young, army-age voters, and made significant gains among Oriental immigrants, thitherto respectful of Labor's legendary patronage machine.[38] The Israeli opposition, Eban reflected grimly, seemed almost unconcerned that Israel was negotiating with the United States as well as Egypt, and indifferent to whether Israel continued to enjoy U.S. aid and support.[39]

Despite Watergate, Kissinger, Dayan, and Sadat needed only a few more weeks between them to dispatch the Geneva conference and advance the course of disengagement beyond anything imaginable just weeks before. Perhaps it was because "the Arab states could not admit the impotence of their deus ex machina nor the Israelis the potential weakness of their protector," Kissinger mused.[40] This time, the crucial idea was Dayan's. Opposed to the idea of Israeli forces at the canal since 1967, he perceived them as a standing provocation to the Egyptians and warned consistently that they were a strategic liability.[41] He now proposed a U.N. buffer force and a phased withdrawal. Like Sadat, he was in no hurry for resumption in Geneva. Like Sadat, he also favored quick agreement. The fragile economy and the polarized state of domestic politics were both incentives for Israeli action. Sadat too had reason to look for quick results. The nominal victor in October, he still had Israeli forces sixty miles from Cairo, an Egyptian army under their control, and Suez City at their mercy. He also saw no reason to involve the Soviets.

Both sides were only too happy to make use of the good offices of the United States. The mediation, of course, was Kissinger's. First there was an agreement with Sadat on disengagement and limitation of forces. The Israelis would withdraw to the Sinai passes. The Egyptians would remain on the east bank. There would be a U.N. buffer force between them. To shield the Egyptian president against charges of yielding to Israel, the two men then devised a fig leaf: Sadat's voluntary concessions, communicated to the United States, would then be communicated further ad lib. The next step was naturally to get Israel to accede to its first voluntary withdrawal in nearly twenty years without first having obtained direct negotiations, termination of belligerency, or explicit access to a newly reopened canal. The whole process took five days, and yielded two documents. The first was an agreement, officially signed by Israel and Egypt. The second, Kissinger's invention, was a letter of understanding to both governments, defining the limitations each had agreed to, for example, that Egypt had agreed to clear the canal, rebuild the adjacent cities, and allow transit of Israeli cargo. There were assurances of long-term military aid, U.S. aerial surveillance, and guaranteed passage of the Strait of Bab el-Mandeb in the bargain.[42]

The next step was sure to be harder. The oil embargo, relations with Syria, relations with Jordan, and the future of the Palestinians were all still unresolved. In one way or another, they were also connected. Of the three, the oil boycott proved the easiest to deal with. The Saudis, a U.S. client since the beginnings of their national existence, wanted something for the Syrians but were also reluctant to antagonize the traditional patron that protected them from what they saw as a satanic world of communists, Zionists, and Arab radicals.

On the other hand, most Arabs now dreamed dreams of what their petrodollars would buy them, and even officially radical and anti-American Algerians were keen for U.S. recognition and commerce. A judicious bit of shadowboxing helped. If Egypt, Algeria, Saudi Arabia, and Syria wanted the United States to move Israel, Nixon and Kissinger let it be known, they had no interest in making things hard for Nixon and Kissinger. The United States was Syria's best diplomatic hope, and Algeria's best potential customer. By 1976, the United States had, in fact, become the largest consumer of Algerian oil, and imported about a quarter of Algeria's natural gas production. A huge commitment to Saudi industrialization, accompanied by a huge infusion of modern weaponry, brought the Saudis around.[43]

To the relief of Europe, the United States, and Israel too, the embargo was finally lifted in mid-March 1974. The very point of the exercise had been to make things tough on the West, and so put intolerable pressure on the Israelis. Israeli strategists played for time, yielding piecemeal concessions and accommodations until the threat receded. Given their choices, it was only logical that accommodation should become a function of distance. Relative at least to the alternatives, the easiest choice was Egypt, where strategic space was great and ideological commitment minimal. Next came Syria, where the strategic margins were far tighter and political differences intractable. Yet the hardest case was Jordan, despite face-to-face contacts as far back as the war of independence, and an implicit Israeli commitment to defend the little kingdom against Egypt, Syria, Iraq, and the PLO reaching back as far as 1958.[44] Under other circumstances, right-wing Israelis lost no opportunity to call Jordan "the" Palestinian state. In 1970, Israelis could, in fact, have let it become one. Instead, they had all but intervened directly to save Hussein.

Yet, to the extent Jordan could claim some higher purpose, its existence was inextricably entangled in Palestine, including Jerusalem. Given his role as direct descendant of the Prophet, not to mention great grandson of the man who had lost Mecca and Medina, Hussein could hardly surrender it without a fight. The case for intervention and annexation after 1948 was based on the premise that Transjordan's king was king of Palestine and Jerusalem—and, naturally, that Palestinians were ready to accept him. Even after the debacle of 1967, it was Israel's premise that the West Bank was still under Jordanian law. By what claim was the West Bank occupied territory, after all, if not from Jordan? Yet the days of Hashemite monopoly were long past. Now the PLO, Egypt, and Syria too competed for the market. In the quest for the consent of the governed, the only effective test was who was most likely to move the Israelis.[45]

On the face of it, Jordan was still the most credible candidate. Yet since at least 1967, its choices had become strictly defensive. In 1973, Jordan avoided the new war with Israel, but, in its way, the outcome was as fateful as it had been six years before. Then too disengagement had enjoyed high priority, but this time there were no Jordanians to disengage. Inevitably, the belligerents, Egypt and Syria, were now the main contenders for Kissinger's attention. As he repeatedly pointed out to Israeli leaders, American Jews, and anyone else who cared to listen, there was also a powerful case for dealing with Jordan while it still had some authority in the territories. But the argument cut no ice. Since October, Israeli views had hardly changed, despite Jordanian abstention. What had changed was the nation's belief in itself, or at least its government. Between 1967 and 1970, government approval ratings had averaged 70 to 80 percent. In the aftermath of October's debacle, they now hovered around 50 percent. Before the war, Israelis opposed concessions because they felt strong. Now they opposed them because they felt weak, and the mediator could hardly be expected to risk attainable deals with Egypt and Syria for the sake of an unattainable deal with Jordan. According to Kissinger, Meir and her colleagues begged that he not even mention in public that the issue was discussed.[46]

This led to Syria. Cease-fire or not, the fire on the Golan had never really ceased. Both Kissinger and the Israelis had reason to fear that it could ignite another, larger round, Even if not, Israeli troops were still pinned down in a miniwar of attrition. There were still Israeli prisoners in Syria to assure attention in Jerusalem. On the other hand, Syria was now alone, with Israeli troops within artillery range of Damascus, and no recourse to Egypt, the oil producers, or neighboring Iraq. Despite already stormy relations between the two regimes, Iraq had dispatched three divisions in October, but it then withdrew them after Syria's "defeatist" accession to Resolution 338. In concert with Iran, both Kissinger and Israel nonetheless took care to keep Iraqis busy by increasing aid to rebellious Kurds in northern Iraq. Then, in March 1975, Iraq and Iran reached their own rapprochement. At that point, Iraq too drifted out of the Soviet orbit, which was fine with Kissinger, and Syria came to the aid of the Kurds.[47]

Israel too had reasons to come around, including the continuing costs of mobilization, the prisoners in Syrian hands, structural support for the agreement with Egypt, and, not least, U.S. urging. Even a severely weakened Nixon left no doubt that aid was linked to compliance. The presidential option to waive payment on some 70 percent of a $2.2 billion military aid package was only one obvious incentive. Meanwhile, however disingenuously, the next year's budget foresaw substantial cuts in aid to Israel—and with rather similar packages for Jordan and Egypt.[48]

Incentives or not, the Syrian-Israeli disengagement proved labor-intensive beyond anything yet, involving 30 days of shuttle diplomacy, 130 hours of face-to-face talks between Kissinger and Syria's President Hafiz el-Asad, and as many as 26 arrivals and departures at Damascus airport alone.[49] Characteristically, it took five weeks just to resolve the chicken-egg problem of prisoners and disengagement. Clearly trying to exploit its military advantage, Israel demanded a list of prisoners before presenting a proposal. Reluctant to surrender what little he had, Asad demanded a proposal before yielding a list of prisoners. The solution, as usual, was Kissinger himself, who personally agreed to carry and exchange the documents.[50]

It hardly helped that the Israeli government and Labor party were now in a state of crisis, only worsened in early April 1974 by the interim report of the Agranat commission on the causes of the war. Fairly or not, its findings placed exclusive blame on the military, yet the public furor that followed its release led directly to Dayan's, and indirectly to Meir's, resignation on April 11.[51] Israelis could console themselves that they were just part of the trend in a worldwide season of political collapse. Concurrent with the troubles in Israel, governments were sagging to their knees in London and even Luxembourg, while leaders as formidable as Meir were forced from the scene in Bonn and Washington. But there was a time when Labor, like U.S. Democrats, could deal with such things with the oligarchical self-assurance of a party accustomed to power. Those days were now gone, and with them the consensus they represented.

If coalition-building was always something of a psychodrama, the new style of consensus-building was itself more strenuous than anything to date. The first native-born Israeli to reach the top and tentatively hailed as the leader of a new generation, Meir's presumptive successor, Yitzhak Rabin, emerged the winner by a slim majority on April 22. But it was victory by default for the hero of one war back, a junior member and political outsider, who had made his career outside politics as chief of staff and ambassador to Washington. Anxious to restore equilibrium, his party hastened to flank him with the "dovish" Yigal Allon and "hawkish" Shimon Peres as foreign and defense minister respectively.

Contemporaries, peers, and rivals, they were an uncomfortable triumvirate. Even the election itself was a signal of crisis, the first of its kind in the party's history.[52] It was May 19 before the Central Committee agreed to form a government—with a one-vote majority in a chamber of 120, and without its traditional partner, the National Religious party, which was now vehemently opposed to territorial concessions on the West Bank.[53] It was June 3 before the cabinet was sworn in. By this time the thirty-day shuttle had come and gone.[54]

As in January, the outcome stood or fell on Kissinger's ability to persuade both parties they had something to gain from the process. Both the issues and solution were similar too: territory, security, and limitation of arms, contingent on a phased withdrawal and a U.N. presence. But this time Kissinger was facing incomparably smaller tolerances in a space perhaps fifteen by thirty miles. Save for Kissinger himself, with his concern for protecting the new relationship with Egypt, and the embattled Nixon, who was frantic for any success at all, there was rather less sense of urgency too, and there were powerful incentives for both sides to hang tough. For Syria, there was twice-conquered territory to recover, and the need to prove that the October war had not been fought for nothing. For Israel, there were settlements and terrain to protect, whose strategic importance to the people living both on and below the Golan Heights was real and present to them in ways the Sinai was not. Unsurprisingly, neither side was in a giving mood.

The common denominator was Kuneitra, the devastated little town of 20,000 that had been the administrative center of the Golan Heights. Syria wanted it back. From the beginning, Israel was willing to surrender it, but it was no less determined, as Matti Golan reported, to sell it street by street. This meant two weeks more to reach agreement on such issues as where to draw the line, and whether the U.N. presence should be active (as the Israelis wanted) or passive (as the Syrians wanted). In the end, it was agreed to fudge the latter issue, while negotiating the former in increments of hundreds of meters.[55] In 1919, President Wilson took five weeks to negotiate the Treaty of Versailles. In 1945, President Truman took four weeks to negotiate the Potsdam Accords, including two weeks at sea. By comparison, Kissinger had now been away from Washington for five weeks, while the disintegration of the presidency seemed only to accelerate. Yet he was exasperated by speculations that he was only keeping his distance from Watergate, and irritated again by Nixon's hints that Kissinger's absence proved Nixon was still in charge.[56]

What eventually brought the Syrians around was the bleakness of the alternatives. Kissinger could get them a deal with the Israelis, or they could try to do it themselves. What worked on Israel was the usual combination of carrots and sticks: assured delivery of a very large package of tanks and armored personnel carriers; plus transformation of credits into grants; plus the risk that Egypt—and the Soviet Union—might come to Syria's aid in the event of new hostilities; plus Kissinger's threat to make Israel publicly responsible for the impasse, and go home. The trade-off, Kissinger argued, was military advantage for political gain. But political gain was a relative thing in a polarized Israel, where Golan settlers shouted "Jew boy" at a U.S. secretary of state, and a precarious cabinet feared the voters at least as much as it did the United States.[57]

In the end, there was a settlement, but, like the terrain itself, it was uphill beyond all previous experience. Why, Israelis asked with some reason, did they have to pay when Syria started the war? Why, a testy Kissinger replied with some reason, did he have to invest the dignity of his office in running around like a "rug merchant" to broker a few hundred meters of contested territory? Stalled and frustrated, the secretary looked to Nixon, Sadat, the Algerians, and the Saudis for support. Meanwhile, intent on appearing hawkisher than thou in the eyes of their peers and fellow citizens, Israelis looked suspiciously at one another, while Palestinian terrorists did their murderous best to disrupt the negotiations with border raids from Lebanon. In April, they attacked a northern settlement town with the loss of eighteen Israeli lives. A month later, they seized a hundred Israeli schoolchildren. Among the costs were twenty-four young Israeli lives, and sixty-three Israeli wounded. But the effort failed to stall the talks.[58]

What made the difference, in Nadav Safran's terms, was the gradual transformation of Kissinger's role from intermediary to moderator to mediator, and even beyond. Confining himself at first to reporting positions, he had progressively come to interpret them, and then to advance his own "United States proposals," both real and cosmetic.[59] In practice, this meant political pressure on the Israelis, but it also meant a growing list of U.S. commitments. In the wake of Palestinian attacks, for instance, he committed the United States to political support for Israeli action in the—virtually self-evident—event of Israeli retaliation.

The Golan settlement led to the U.S. waiver of the remaining $500 million due on the emergency shipments of 1973. Directly in its aftermath, Israelis requested five more such grants of $1.5 million each, and sent Peres to Washington with a newly revised procurement schedule.[60] At the same time, the United States and Syria resumed diplomatic relations for the first time since 1967. In his memoirs eight years later, Kissinger still basked in his achievement. If Syria and Israel could reach an agreement, he argued "there were no ideological obstacles to peace talks with any other Arab state." But the agreement, he added, also confirmed how Soviet influence had declined. This was true and not true, for all that whole caravans of Arab leaders now trooped demonstratively to Washington, while Soviet leaders circled the Middle East, in quest of a place to land.[61]

Soviet policy was admittedly an anthology of dilemmas. Too conservative to satisfy Arab rejectionists, the Soviets had too little to offer Arab conservatives. Legitimation of their role in the region required détente, yet regional influence required the Arabs. Just as U.S. influence on Arabs presupposed an ability to pressure Israel, Soviet influence on Arabs presupposed an ability to pressure the United States on behalf of Syria and the PLO, their own mutual ambivalence notwithstanding. In a speech in September 1974, Soviet President Nikolay Podgorny finally acknowledged a Palestinian right to statehood for the first time—"in one form or another."[62] The formula was not really so different from formulas concocted by Americans a year or two later, and it was another four years before the Soviet Union finally acknowledged the PLO as "sole legitimate representative." It nonetheless entailed the risk of another no-win conflict, and incidentally jeopardized détente. Yet the Soviets were not about to tolerate a *pax americana.*[63]

As intricately busy as a Steinberg cartoon, Kissinger's diplomacy all but kicked sand in Soviet faces, restoring choices and dynamism to U.S. policy in a part of the world where they had only recently seemed as unlikely as summer rain. When Nixon toured the Middle East in June 1974, the visit was remarkable for the very fact it happened. Not long before, official Washington had even balked at receiving an Israeli head of state. Now save for President Roosevelt's wartime summit in Cairo, it was the first time a U.S. president had been seen officially in Egypt, and the first presidential visit ever to Syria, let alone to Israel.

Acknowledging the new possibilities in his way, the president even offered Egypt a nuclear reactor—for peaceful purposes, it was naturally understood.[64] Acknowledging the new possibilities in their way, as many as seven million Egyptians, perhaps a sixth of the population, dutifully lined the route to cheer the official party. Though Syrian-U.S. relations had not been officially resumed, there was then a warm reception in Damascus.

Acknowledging the new possibilities in yet another way, Israelis were more reserved, not only about the idea of an U.S. reactor in Egyptian hands but about learning of it from the newspapers. Reportedly, the president responded by offering his hosts a reactor too. He then urged them to negotiate with Hussein while they still had the chance. When the talk turned to terrorism, Nixon leaped from his seat with an imaginary machine-gun, Chicago-gangland fashion, to show his hosts how it should be dealt with.[65] Significantly, the reception in Jerusalem was the most restrained of the tour.

Still, for all his prodigies of skill and energy, Kissinger had at best bought time. He had not brought the Peaceable Kingdom, or even peace. As he himself conceded, he had little more in mind. "In most periods of history, peace had been a precarious state and not the millennial disappearance of all tensions that so many Israelis envisaged," he told Yigal Allon, his onetime student and now Israel's new foreign minister.[66] There was no hint that he saw his own times as exceptional. For all the media glitz and technical virtuosity, his goals were correspondingly modest. The idea was to lower or remove a few obstacles without adding new ones; then, all things being equal, to advance toward peace in further increments. But this, in turn, required Israelis to define peace as they had in 1967, and a majority of Americans still did: territorial compromise, partition of Palestine, normal relations in return for land.

This only led back to the familiar dilemmas. Geneva was no more attractive than before. For the moment, there was nowhere else to go with Syria. Egypt might be eager to proceed, but this was just another argument for caution, if Egyptian self-isolation and yet another special relationship were not to create new obstacles. This again left Jordan as the logical alternative, but contingent on Israeli stamina as well as Israeli consent. Did Rabin have "Golda's guts," Sadat asked Kissinger?[67] This was imaginable, but it was clear from the start that he lacked her majority, her personal authority, and her political capital. All of Rabin's predecessors had been pioneers, party leaders, defense ministers, kibbutz and trade union insiders, in combination, and all at once. Rabin was none of the above.

Already an elaborate compromise between increasingly centrifugal wings and factions of the Labor party, his cabinet was also hoping to co-opt the National Religious party as a hedge and last defense against a wall-to-wall national government that would, by definition, include the opposition. "After Jordan comes the PLO" was one side of the coin. "After Labor comes Likud" was the other. Either way, Jordan was a formidable obstacle. On the one hand, Rabin's government stood or fell on its ability to conduct successful negotiations. On the other, it was committed in advance to new elections in the event of territorial concessions to Jordan. Each in his way, his colleagues already constituted a veto. A dove by the standards of the 1980s, when he successively served as prime minister, foreign minister, and finance minister in coalitions with the Likud, Peres was a hawk by the standard of the mid-

1970s, opposed to all territorial concessions. Allon, who favored a Jordanian-Palestinian federation in Gaza and the populated areas of the West Bank, but Israeli retention of strategic positions in and above the Jordan Valley, was the most dovish of the governing triumvirate. Rabin favored more talks with Egypt that would spare the new elections that potentially turned him into a lame duck before he had even taken flight.[68]

Under the circumstances, talks with Jordan could have little appeal for either side. If Jordan's only chance was to preempt the PLO, Israel's only chance was to persuade a reluctant electorate of what it wanted least to hear. Already edgy over concessions to Syria and Egypt, large numbers of Israelis also considered the West Bank Israel, either in toto or considerable part. Over the course of the disengagement negotiations, support for its retention had actually increased.[69] In contrast to the earlier disengagement rounds, there was little sense of urgency or drama. In the Sinai, a large Israeli army had been tied down. On the Golan, Israeli troops had still been under fire. On the West Bank, Israelis still felt thoroughly in control. Meanwhile, the heavy breathing of European oil consumers had subsided too.

This left little for Israel to offer Kissinger, and little in turn for him to offer Hussein. In the final throes of a unique constitutional crisis, the Nixon administration was in any case concerned with other things, though Israeli-U.S. shadowboxing continued inconclusively through the summer. When Kissinger returned in October 1974 for yet another tour of the Middle East, he tried to persuade Sadat to support Hussein, and so hold off the PLO. But there was little Sadat could do, and little reason that he should try, when PLO success in Jordan could well favor another round of U.S.-mediated Israeli withdrawal from Egypt. At the summit in Rabat the same month, Morocco, Arab leaders quizzed Hussein about commitments from Kissinger and the likelihood of Israeli withdrawal. The answer to both was zero. Sincerely or disingenuously, Arab leaders therewith declared the PLO "sole representative of the Palestinian people," effectively letting Israelis off the hook.[70] The decision also eliminated any further possibility of new talks in Geneva, where the Americans saw no reason to surrender the diplomatic initiative to the Soviets, and the Israelis had no intention of appearing with the PLO. A few days after Rabat, the National Religious party joined the Israeli government.

In November, to the horror of Israelis and American Jews alike, Arafat, in uniform, *kaffiyeh,* and pistol holster, was invited to address the General Assembly of the United Nations at its annual session. The vote in favor was 105–3—the Dominican Republic, Bolivia, and the United States—with twenty abstentions. The only nonmember to have been similarly invited was Pope Paul VI eight years before. Israelis were not impressed by the implied equation. Shortly afterward, by an 89–37 majority with eight abstentions, the General Assembly recognized the Palestinian right to nationhood plus homes and property in Israel. Though there was euphoria on the West Bank, the sudden legitimation of the PLO required it to face dilemmas inherent from the start. Nationhood where, for example, given the inconclusive cartography of more than half a century? In all of Palestine? In part of Palestine before—or after—1948? In part of Palestine since 1967?[71]

But this hardly made the U.S. options easier. Like bicyclists obliged to move on or fall off, policymakers were increasingly left with little choice but a new Israeli-

Egyptian initiative. Yet for both foreign and domestic reasons, it was more and more like riding in sand. Unsurprisingly, the Syrians opposed negotiations that would carry Egypt still further along its separate course. Relations with the Soviet Union too were cooling appreciably as the Soviets again pushed for Geneva, and Congress exasperated Kissinger by linking trade concessions to liberalized emigration of Soviet Jews to Israel. Despite their legendary resonance in Congress, the Israelis, kept their distance, reluctant, on the one hand, to antagonize the Soviets, who signed the exit visas, and reluctant, on the other, to antagonize the Congress and the Nixon administration that signed the checks. For their part, the Soviets refused to be held hostage by Congress, détente or no détente. As a result, the deal fell through, and emigration fell with it.[72]

The conjunctions of détente and global conflict, Cold War and hot war, Jews and Arabs, embargoes and petrodollars only added to a sense of bafflement, even betrayal. Like television images of burning flags in foreign hands, the inflated price of oil was itself a psychic provocation. Accustomed to victory, intolerant of ambiguity, and hooked on their cars like no other society, Americans increasingly sought comfort in verbal hawkishness, aimed almost interchangeably at the Soviets, the Arabs and, occasionally, the Jews. At the same time, world power was losing its savor even as the imperial presidency was losing its glow. "No more Munichs" and "No more Vietnams" were both the order of the day.

In October 1973, a frustrated Congress imposed unprecedented statutory limits on the president's ability to commit troops abroad, then overrode his veto by substantial majorities. Within eighteen months, it had stopped funding war in Southeast Asia. In 1974, Congress also imposed its say on arms sales. Thereafter, on sales exceeding $25 million—little more than the cost of one new F-15 jet fighter—the president was obliged to notify both houses of the terms of sale and the weapons involved. Barring declaration of an emergency, Congress would then have twenty, later thirty, days to exercise a veto. In December 1975, Congress retreated from Africa too, rejecting Kissinger's pleas to take up arms in Angola's covertly internationalized civil war. Surveys showed Americans opposed by a 65–22 margin to military aid in general, and by 74–17 to more aid for Southeast Asia.[73]

What about the Middle East where, in contrast to other places, Americans were neither clearly dovish nor hawkish? Though unfamiliar fault lines appeared increasingly in Israel, the Democratic party, and even the American-Jewish community, the targets proved elusive and unfocused. By margins as high as three to one, Americans blamed foreign producers for inflation, recession, and oil shortages. But by 62–24, they also equated Israel's friendship with its need for U.S. arms, and agreed by 48–33 that "Israel seems to feel the United States will back them up no matter what they do." Revealingly, only one in four Americans was willing to send troops, even "if Israel were being defeated by the Arabs." Yet Americans favored military aid to Israel by the same margin, for all that only 34 percent were confident that Israel would win another war.[74]

In January 1975, a robust strategic debate erupted in *Commentary,* an intellectual monthly published and heavily subsidized by the American Jewish Committee. It was initiated by Robert Tucker, a political scientist at the Johns Hopkins University School for Advanced International Studies in Washington. Tucker proposed an imaginative scenario for U.S. military intervention in the Gulf in the event of a real Arab effort to cut oil supplies. His article reverberated for weeks in the journals of opinion and the letters columns of *Commentary* itself. In one or another incarnation, the scheme resurfaced through the rest of the decade in a cascade of plans and projects for regional alliances, joint maneuvers, and rapid deployment forces. In an interview with *Business Week* that made the White House sweat,[75] Kissinger himself dropped elliptical hints that force was an option. At least in theory, this was surely true. The interview was also clearly meant to influence foreign opinion, but it hardly meant that Americans, in or out of Congress, were keen to go. On the contrary, polls showed 58–25 opposition.[76]

In a report submitted to the Senate Foreign Relations Committee in May, Senator George McGovern declared the idea of a Gulf invasion "sheer stupidity." The first presidential candidate since Kennedy with a distinguished combat record, he had also been buried by Nixon's reelection landslide. Admired and suspected for his dovishness, McGovern favored prudence across the Middle East. The United States could not impose peace, he emphasized. On the other hand, it continued to play an indispensable role.

For McGovern, the Golan, Gaza, and the Sinai had the makings of a "next Sarajevo." The United States was vitally interested in the survival and security of an independent Israel, he stressed, but Americans were doing "a good friend" no service by supporting an unyielding position. If the United States was responsible for making clear to Arabs that Israel could never be destroyed in war, it was also responsible for making clear to Israelis that peace required Arab assent and cooperation, and that there could be no peace without Palestinian consent.

Unlike many Americans, McGovern was undismayed by the idea of Palestinian rights and Arab investments. Americans themselves should know how productive and vulnerable foreign investments could be, he contended. What Israel wanted, he reported after conversations with Rabin, was "a long-term, Congressionally endorsed promise to maintain a steady and varied supply of modern weapons." What Sadat envisioned were U.S. guarantees for both Israel and Egypt. McGovern was not averse to either. He himself proposed returning to Geneva, and pursuit of a comprehensive settlement as a matter of "American selective interests." In fact, this was more or less consistent with public opinion. By two to one Americans already saw Egypt as "reasonable," and of the 55 percent who knew who Sadat was, 69 percent also took a favorable view of him. Americans even seemed ready to talk to Arafat, if only on grounds that Kissinger already conferred with thugs.

At the same time, McGovern also favored Palestinian self-determination, economic aid for the West Bank and Gaza, and even talks with the PLO, though "without any implication of recognition and with the express proviso that the PLO explicitly repudiate all further acts of terrorism."[77] Fourteen years later, this actually became U.S. policy, though even then it was both tentative and transient. But then and after, such a position was decidedly not a mainstream taste. On the eve of Sinai II, more than half of a national sample opposed pressuring Israel to surrender occupied territory, and nearly two-thirds of Americans opposed surrendering it to Arafat.[78]

Both American Jews and visiting Israelis nonetheless feared a backlash. They even believed they spotted one in November 1974 when General George Brown, the chairman of the Joint Chiefs of Staff, set off a ministorm with an outburst at Duke University. Jews "own, you know, the banks in this country, the newspapers," Brown informed his listeners. A loyal accessory to the airlift only a year before, he worried what would happen if the Arabs again switched off the oil spigots, and brooded about the cost of Israel's shopping lists to the military inventories of the United States. A new embargo, he told his audience, might move Americans "to get tough minded enough to set down the Jewish influence in this country and break that lobby." Though it took a month for the report of his speech to surface in Washington, the story set off a furor. Brown was promptly summoned to the White House, where the new president, Gerald Ford, told him to shut up.[79]

In fact, as surveys consistently confirmed, the worry was misplaced. By 45–42, Jewish respondents assumed that non-Jews found it "proper and right" for Brown to say what he did. In fact, by 61–19, a national sample of non-Jews found Brown's remarks "improper and wrong." Asked how Americans would choose between oil and Israel, a cross-section of Jewish respondents assumed by 45–34 that the country would opt for oil. Yet interviews in December 1973 confirmed support for Israel at circa 50 percent, its highest level since June 1967. A year later, it had even gone up, while sympathy for Arabs in general stagnated around 7 percent. Remaining respondents split more or less evenly into neutrals and undecided. Still more remarkably, Americans firmly disagreed with the proposition "We need Arab oil for our gasoline shortage so we had better find ways to get along with the Arabs, even if that means supporting Israel less." In fact, the margin of disagreement had actually risen between January 1974 and February 1975, from 61 percent to 68 percent.

Rather more challenging to policymakers than public views on the Mideast per se was the steady erosion of détente and the ascendancy of neoconservatism among both opinion makers and opinion consumers. "I hear the Russians have sent the Arabs all their latest planes and missiles," an Ohio mechanic told a Lou Harris interviewer. "So we better do the same, or Israel will be wiped out, and Russia will take over the whole area."[80]

A bellwether coalition with roots in every administration since World War II, the neoconservatives included old-line Republicans and New Deal Democrats, union officials and Wall Street bankers, academics and CEOs. Their reservations about détente had less to do with its failures than the successes they consistently saw as placebos. They were particularly concerned with the Middle East and arms control. As anxious as Kissinger that the United States was in retreat while Soviet power was inexorably on the march, they nonetheless reached significantly different conclusions on what to do about it.

For neoconservatives, many of them children of the fateful 1930s, the Soviet Union had again joined forces with the "proletarian" regimes against the "imperialist" democracies, just as it had conspired with the Germans on the eve of World War II.[81] Third World preferences for "socialism," single-party military dictatorships, and "anti-Zionism" seemed only further confirmation that dictatorship again was on the march. From London to Paris to Bonn to Rome, it seemed equally clear that the appeasers were again in the saddle. Under the circumstances, Europe's capitulation and the progressive isolation of both the United States and Israel could be taken for givens. But the particular neoconservative quarrel with Kissinger was that Israel was also under pressure from its only ally, the United States.[82]

Declaring him too soft on an implacable and expansionist adversary determined to get its hand on the oil spigot, and too hard on a well-armed, well-situated, well-motivated democratic ally that any rational policy would regard as a natural asset, neoconservatives regarded détente as the root of all geostrategic evil.[83] Solid or not, the case for a natural Israeli-U.S. alliance had hardly changed since Ben-Gurion and Sharett had advanced it in the 1950s. What had changed was its reception among establishmentarian Americans, who would once have dismissed it out of hand, and the fact that Jews, outsiders in the 1950s, had now become part of that very establishment.

It was just one of the many ironies of neoconservatism that its target should be Kissinger, a natural conservative with a unique sensitivity to power. It was another irony that so many Jews—William Safire of the *New York Times,* Norman Podhoretz of *Commentary,* Martin Peretz of the *New Republic,* the veteran publicist Irving Kristol, or Eugene V. Debs Rostow, a former dean of Yale Law school with a long career in public service—should now play conservative Ahab to Kissinger's Moby Dick. But it was still another irony that Syrians and Israelis alike continued to see Kissinger as the very personification of U.S. policy at a time when not only they but increasing numbers of Americans were coming to question his judgment, his character, or both.[84]

Seen from Kissinger's perspective, the decline of détente, paradoxically, was now an incentive to try again in the Middle East, just as the ascendancy of détente had been an incentive for the United States to keep its distance from the region a long half decade earlier. Like his critics, Kissinger agreed that things were tough. The ten-year investment of the United States in Vietnam was about to crumble. He himself not only feared the worst of the revolution in Portugal but almost made it self-fulfilling.[85] He was appalled when Congress cut off arms to Turkey after its intervention in Cyprus. The decline of détente, as he saw it, was reason for more, not less, U.S. activity in one of the few parts of the world where the dollar, superior military technology, plus well-established relationships with Turkey, Iran, Saudi Arabia, Jordan, *and* Israel, still gave the United States a comparative advantage.

Yet even Kissinger could hardly deny that the material was becoming more and more intractable. Rabin tipped his hand in a December 1974 interview with *Ha'aretz,* Israel's leading daily. Given the mid-term prognosis, he explained, the wisest course was procrastination until the West unhooked itself from Arab oil. This, in turn, meant working with the United States to separate Egypt from the Soviet Union and Syria respectively. Till this was achieved, a general settlement would have to wait, in part by Israel's choice, in part for lack of consensus among the interested parties. The Israeli-Egyptian asymmetries were themselves an example of the problem confronting U.S. diplomacy. Israel wanted a political settlement, Egypt a military agreement. Israel wanted nonbelligerency, Egypt the recovery of its land—understood, at least, as the Sinai passes and the Abu Rodeis oil fields. Israel wanted a commitment for up to twelve years, Egypt for as few as three. Israeli negotiators needed to cover their electoral flanks, Egyptians to stay in step with fellow Arabs.

The domestic climate alone was far from propitious for a new initiative. Washington was in obvious need of a success. By the end of Kissinger's latest shuttle, Rabin's popularity had also sunk to record levels. By spring 1975, the negotiations had stalled, leaving a trail of competitive recriminations.[86] Israel was unyielding on territory, Egypt on nonbelligerency. But it was the Israelis who made the veins throb in American foreheads. "Their tactics frustrated the Egyptians and made me mad as hell," Ford recalled in his memoirs.[87] In a last-ditch effort to make his point, he threatened to "reassess" U.S. policy in the event of a breakdown. The United States was unwilling to finance a deadlock prejudicial to its interests, the president announced.[88] The note only made the Israelis tougher.

Grim, resigned, then furious, Kissinger spelled out his view of the consequences after a day-tour of Masada, the mountaintop fortress where Jewish zealots had once held out to the death against Roman besiegers. He then made sure that the world learn what he said.[89] Failure to reach agreement, first with Jordan, then Egypt, meant the end of U.S. credibility with Arab clients, he told the Israeli cabinet. This could only mean a bigger role for the Palestinians, linkage of Sinai and the Golan, renewed Arab unity, recovery of Soviet influence, even a return to Geneva. This, in turn, could only mean reduced U.S. influence on the diplomatic process, reduced insulation against global pressures and increased pressure on Israel to return to the 1967 borders. "It's tragic to see people dooming themselves to a course of unbelievable peril," he concluded.[90]

The next day, there were unusually emotional airport farewells, and the secretary returned to Washington, where he was demonstratively received on the White House lawn. The day after, Ford and Kissinger briefed congressional leaders. Senator Henry M. Jackson of Washington, a hard-line Democrat and already a candidate for his party's presidential nomination, proclaimed the end of shuttle diplomacy and called for a return to the conference table. Addressing the American Society of Newspaper Editors, Kissinger was reminded of an anecdote from World War II, when someone had allegedly proposed heating the ocean to boil enemy submarines to the surface. "So the man was asked how to do this," Kissinger recalled, "and he said, 'I have given you the idea, the technical implementation is up to you.'"[91]

There followed a kind of public colloquium on U.S. policy, whose intent, at least, was pressure exceeding any since 1957.[92] A huge Israeli aid request was deliberately left hanging; a quasi-embargo was imposed on sale of the F-15, the latest U.S. jet fighter, though training of flight crews continued; and delivery of Lance missiles was suspended, though their conventionally armed warheads continued to be produced.[93] The reassessment, as it was euphemistically called, included a near-cavalcade of Jewish and congressional leaders, academic experts, and assorted wise men, whose collective experience extended back to the Roosevelt administration. Options included a comprehensive solution, and explicit U.S. guarantees to be negotiated in Geneva; a quasi-comprehensive settlement with Egypt to include exchange of most of the Sinai for "political non-belligerency"; and then, if all else failed, a return to step-by-step diplomacy. The wise men and experts leaned strongly to the first option. Kissinger, while noncommittal, was at least not averse to talking about it. "The American political situation is so fluid at this moment, we can afford to do the right thing," he told Edward Sheehan. At the same time, to Sheehan's bemusement, he seemed to preclude any role for the Soviets and Palestinians a priori.[94]

Not for the first time, the battle for U.S. policy reflected the contingencies of the presidential calendar, but it was significantly influenced, if not won, on the playing fields of Capitol Hill. Although "no hearings had been held, no debate conducted, nor had the Administration been invited to prevent its views," as a sheepish signatory later recalled,[95] seventy-six U.S. senators heeded Israeli cries with a letter to the president just two months after the collapse of the latest shuttle. Their message was "defensible" frontiers, direct negotiations, and a "level of military and economic support adequate to deter a renewal of war by Israel's neighbors." Even the dovish McGovern was among the signatories, though he was quick to point out elsewhere that the existing borders were not defensible "but a virtual assurance of continued conflict."[96] For the vast majority, on the other hand, "defensible" meant what Israel's government said it did, which in practice meant the status quo.

Among the nonsignatories was J. William Fulbright, still chairman of the Senate Foreign Relations Committee, who saw the letter as a one-way ticket to disaster. The itinerary, as he spelled it out in the *Washington Star,* included a new war, a new Israeli victory, and a new embargo, in the near future. These then led, to a European recession and a U.S. invasion of the Persian Gulf by 1976; endemic oil crisis by 1977; escalating Arab terrorism by 1978, and a perpendicular decline in support for both Israel and the president by 1979. By 1980, Fulbright continued, dovish Democratic presidential candidates would be asking Israel to withdraw to the partition lines of 1947, perhaps in exchange for a U.S. guarantee. But he himself would oppose them, he added, in part out of loyalty to Resolution 242, in part because someone had to support the president.[97]

Recalling the grand finale of Meredith Willson's musical *The Music Man,* State Department officials jocularly referred to the collective authors of the Senate letter as "The seventy-six Trombones." But years of Middle East diplomacy had also taught some respect for the mighty sound of Congress. Depending on taste and perspective, the letter was viewed as an assurance, a blank check, and a line in the sand.[98] In July, Congress struck again, this time against a contracted sale of Hawk air-defense missiles to Jordan. The transaction itself was a lesson in Middle East politics, Washington style. Convinced that the Israelis had Congress in their pocket, the administration delayed notification of the sale until the eve of Congress's summer break. Upset by the sale, but no less upset by administration tactics, Congress instead dug in till Kissinger himself was forced to intervene. It was mid-September before the deal was made on Congress's terms.[99] By that time, Kissinger's Middle Eastern *chef d'oeuvre,* Sinai II, was also signed and sealed.

Meanwhile, each in their way, both Israelis and Arabs did their bit to break the deadlock. It was true that Israel was well-stocked with arms, while Syria was only marginally above, and Egypt below its prewar strength. It was also true that Israel's refusal to back down in March had been a brilliant public success. It was true again that the electorate and public opinion were badly polarized on the inevitable trade-offs of U.S. aid for Israeli-held territory. Kissinger's visits in August and September 1975 were accompanied by nasty, even violent anti-American demonstrations in Jerusalem and Tel-Aviv as hawks and nationalists, secular and religious, took to the streets with the *obbligato* choruses of "Jew Boy, Go Home" that now seemed to go with such occasions.[100]

What Israel was not well stocked with was money or self-assurance. Senior Israeli officials never forgot that there were endemic frictions in the Pentagon and State Department that not even Congress could always be relied on to reverse. The Finance Ministry perennially reminded the cabinet that there might be ways to stockpile arms, there were no known ways to stockpile credits. The credit deficit, U.S. hints to return to Geneva, and a general failure to reach consensus on any other option, all moved Israel increasingly toward the deal with the Egypt that Rabin claimed to favor all along.

From an Israeli point of view, a *Pax Americana* was unappealing for the very reasons it was attractive to the Arabs, that is, it acknowledged, even legitimated U.S. pressure on Israel. Any alternative involving the United Nations was a slippery slope toward what many Israelis tended to see as a cloaca. From its record high in November 1947, Israeli regard for the international body had slipped to Dead Sea levels, as Third World majorities tilted reflexively to the Arabs and the Palestinians. In summer 1975, there was even Arab pressure to suspend Israel from U.N. activity. The Israelis countered by threatening disqualification of the truce-keeping bodies in the Sinai and on the Golan.[101]

As an immediately affected party, Sadat too had little sympathy or interest in such things. On the contrary, he had virtually staked his regime on the ability of the United States to deliver the goods. Despite Kissinger's worst fears, Egypt's military option was receding over the horizon. Battle cries from the Syrians and PLO could only make things worse by involving Egypt in a new war in the wrong place at the wrong time. Their insistence on Arab unanimity in Geneva meant stalemate or a confrontation that, in turn, allowed Israel to stand pat or procrastinate indefinitely. Meanwhile, Egypt's population grew while its economy crumbled.

Actually, each party was now at the mercy of the other. The United States needed to prove it could move Israel. Sadat needed something to show for his victories—and concessions—since the October war. The Israelis had little choice but to respond to the sticks and carrots, or suffer the *faits accomplis* of others. In ways unimaginable in March, the successful resumption in summer could actually be traced to the earlier failure. Israel scaled back its political demands on Egypt. Egypt conceded nonbelligerency in all but name, and agreed to U.S. surveillance of the Sinai passes. The United States showered rewards on both sides, arms for the one, the promise of wholesale economic aid and eventual recovery of its original border for the other.

Officially signed in Geneva on September 4, 1975 the accord was significant for the agreement between the parties. The Israelis surrendered oil and land. The Egyptians allowed nonmilitary cargoes through the newly reopened canal. Both sides agreed to resolve future conflicts by peaceful means. The U.N. force remained in place between clearly designated military deployments. Each side would maintain a surveillance station, with supplementary stations established and manned by American civilians, contingent on congressional approval. The agreement was to be valid for three years, unless extended or superseded by a new one.

Still more significant were U.S. commitments to each side, but especially Israel. Officially secret, they appeared in the *New York Times* and *Washington Post* a few weeks later. The Egyptians were assured that the Americans would try to resume negotiations between Syria and Israel; would help with the early-warning system in the buffer zone; and would consult with Egypt in the event of Israeli violations. U.S. commitments to Israel included a de facto Israeli veto on resumption of the Geneva conference and admission there of any "additional state, group or organization," that is, the PLO; nonrecognition and no negotiation with the PLO until it recognized Israel's right to exist and accepted Resolutions 242 and 338; U.S. efforts to assure that any "substantive negotiations" in Geneva would be on a bilateral basis; and U.S. opposition in the Security Council to any initiative likely to change Resolutions 242 and 338 "in ways which are incompatible with the original purpose."[102]

Most remarkable was the agreement signed by Kissinger and Allon on September 1 that constituted the first formal, public, written commitment of the United States to Israeli security since the creation of the state. The United States therewith undertook "to be fully responsive, within the limits of its resources and Congressional authorization and appropriation, on an on-going and long-term basis to Israel's military equipment and other defense requirements, to its energy requirements and to its economic needs." Practical results included a U.S. guarantee of Israel's oil supply, with assured support of right of passage through the Straits of Bab el-Mandeb and Gibraltar, and in the event of "threats to Israel's security or sovereignty by a world power."

It also meant immediate release of all previously suspended arms transfers; $1.5 billion in immediate military credits, with half again as much in economic aid; and open-ended assurances of about $1 million in military credits, plus economic aid for the three-year duration of the accords. It was further understood that circa $150 million, 10 percent of the basic package, would fund Israeli domestic arms production, an arrangement without precedent.

Whether, how, and to what extent this was actually binding was arguable. Kissinger and his staff were up day and night, qualifying verbs, battling for escape clauses.[103] Significantly, there was no effort to propose it to the Senate as a treaty. For all that it was now general usage to call Israel an "ally," it was hardly a coincidence that the Senate and successive administrations had dodged the question of formal alliance since Israel's independence. Not only did alliance imply treaties, and the two-thirds majorities constitutionally required for ratification, it also invited debate on things both sides agreed were best left undebated. For an obvious example, alliance meant guarantees. Guarantees, of course, presupposed mutually agreed borders.

European experience suggested how daunting such agreement could be, even in a part of the world where Americans had twice fought world wars, and committed themselves to their first "entangling alliance." The test case was Germany, divided de facto in 1945 into three parts. Not only had postwar West Germans not recognized the East German state created by the Soviets in the Soviet zone of occupation, they had also not acknowledged the border revisions that assigned once-German territories to Poland, Czechoslovakia, and the Soviet Union. Before the Western Allies could commit themselves to the defense of Germany, there obviously had to be an agreement on what was to be defended. Before extending the umbrella, and admitting the Federal Republic to the Western Alliance, they accordingly asked West Germans to renounce their claim to the old eastern territories.

West Germany was still incapable of self-defense, its sovereignty qualified by international agreement. Its cabinets were well-established, its chancellor both popular and passionately pro-Western. Both the zonal boundaries and the Western borders were recognized and well defined in international law. Large contingents of foreign troops precluded independent action. Despite twelve million refugees, most Germans had already written off the eastern territories. There was certainly no will or taste for "armed struggle." Yet domestic politics made public commitment impossible, even with respect to the world's supermost superpower, whose support most Germans wanted.[104]

Before and after Kissinger, a debate on Israel's borders could only be tougher. Though none of Israel's borders was, or ever had been, mutually and permanently accepted, its sovereignty was unqualified. By U.N. resolution, the status of Israel's borders was also subject to negotiation with its neighbors, not the United States. There were no foreign troops on Israel's soil. There were few foreign constraints on Israeli decision making. Historical experience repeatedly confirmed that its strategy and policy were intended to assure that accomplished missions led to accomplished facts. At the same time, its fractious politics and passionate commitment to keep at least some of the Occupied Territories guaranteed that a treaty debate in both countries would be brutal, nasty, and long.

What was feasible, on the other hand, not least on the eve of an election year, was a pragmatic commitment. Sinai II, it was argued, made Israel secure and strong. It was therefore an incentive to comply with Resolution 242. It therefore advanced the cause of peace. The logic of this was at least debatable. "I honestly believe that aid in the magnitude being requested by the Administration . . . is more likely than not to encourage the continuing belief within Israel that it has more time than in fact is available to achieve resolution of basic questions in the Golan and the West Bank . . . ," Congressman David Obey, a Wisconsin Democrat, informed the House Appropriations Committee after visiting the Middle East in August 1975. He then proposed to cut the proposed appropriations by $200 million, even invoking Israel's chief of staff, Mordechai Gur, to make his case that Israel could already defend itself against all comers.[105]

Voting with Obey were several of the most respected members of the House, among them Lee Hamilton of Indiana, whose Europe and Middle East subcommittee was equally critical of open-ended commitments to Iran and Saudi Arabia. In 1973, Hamilton had proposed to cut aid to Israel by $500 million. As a group, Obey's supporters were slightly more liberal and substantially more midwestern than the House mean. They also came from districts with few or no Jews. But there were only thirty-one of them.[106] Eventually, the credits won by big majorities with one qualification. Kissinger had proposed to offer Israel the Pershing missile, an intermediate-range weapon designed for nuclear warheads and central Europe. That idea was dropped by mutual consent.[107] The rest, as codified in a memorandum of understanding, assured Israel several hundred M-60 tanks and heavy artillery, twenty-five F-15s, the Lance, various new precision-guided missiles and laser-guided "smart bombs," and the latest in electronic warfare technology.

Considering the cost of failure, the successful conclusion of Sinai II set off ripples of relief but not exhilaration. Celebration was strictly pro forma. Surely among the most expensive agreements per capita the United States had ever reached with a foreign government, it left trails of ambivalence on all sides. In one way or another, it had transformed Israeli-U.S. relations. Yet for all its prodigies of pressure and co-optation, ingenuity and high purpose, it had not, it seemed, advanced the cause of Israeli-Arab peace. Both sides believed with some sincerity that they had sacrificed a lot for a little. From an Egyptian perspective, there were still Israeli troops and settlements on Egyptian territory, Egyptian and Syrian orbits were increasingly divergent, and there was nothing to show for the Palestinians at all. For their part, Israelis did not have peace, explicit nonbelligerency, or even face-to-face negotiations to show for the surrender of hard-won ground. On the eve of ratification, Likud and the religious parties rallied some twenty-five thousand supporters in Jerusalem for public protests, and forty-three members of the Knesset ultimately voted against the agreement.

Nominally, each side had at least been negotiating indirectly with the other, but as skeptics on both sides now argued, they were really negotiating their respective, even Faustian, bargains with the United States. At least post facto, Rabin acknowledged a "moment of gratification." Sinai II, he explained to the American journalist, Milton Viorst, proved to the Arabs that they could never win by force. Since that was the necessary condition of any settlement, it left them only the choice of negotiation through Washington, which in turn meant "a tremendous achievement" for Kissinger.[108]

Israelis tended more generally to regard the enormous package of aid and commitments—"in the neighborhood of $2 billion in military and economic aid with some new military hardware," as Matti Golan laconically described it—as a kind of consolation prize, if not an covert bribe.[109] Above all, there was the question of where to go next, not least in a country, as Kissinger himself described Israel, that had no foreign policy, only domestic politics. Dayan was deeply critical of the political and economic costs of Israel's increasing dependence on U.S. conventional arms. Instead, he favored nuclear deterrence, combined with new territorial concessions to both Egypt and Syria, contingent on nonbelligerency. Moshe Arens of the opposition Likud was equally opposed to further concessions, be they to Washington or Cairo. His alternative was increased domestic arms production, even at the cost of national austerity.[110] But Israelis were disinclined to trade butter for guns, when they could continue to enjoy both by act of Congress.

After their fashion, Americans shared the same ambivalence. If a 30 km. withdrawal cost $2.5 billion, some asked, what would peace cost? The attendant choices were especially burdensome for Democrats in the aftermath of Vietnam. Anxious to cut defense spending and foreign military assistance, reduce arms exports, and generally break the Cold War habit after a generation of global activism, they were also hesitant to undercut Israel, expose a flank in the Middle East, and offend their traditional Jewish constituency.

In July 1975, twenty-eight congressmen, twenty-three of them Democrats, acted out the resulting dilemmas. They first voted against the annual Foreign Assistance Appropriations Act. They then informed the White House that their action "should not be construed as a vote against aid for the state of Israel." Among the signatories were some of the chamber's most visible doves, including Christopher Dodd, Tom Harkin, Otis Pike, and Pat Schroeder. But only a year later, after the leadership had hitched Sinai II to a new foreign aid bill, fourteen of the twenty-eight voted in favor, among them the later U.S. Senators Dodd and Harkin.[111] With House funding in jeopardy, Thomas P. "Tip" O'Neill, the majority leader and later Speaker, then linked Sinai II to appropriations not only for job and education programs but even the Tennessee Valley Authority. Sure enough, this paid off too. In July 1976, O'Neill's otherwise vulnerable amendment carried by 213–203.[112] Expensive or not, the House vote proved at least that Sinai II was good politics. But it also confirmed that, step by step, U.S. policy had again reached an impasse.

9

A Piece of Peace

The question, as usual, was where to go from there. Kissinger himself conceded the limits of Sinai II in a speech to the Greater Cincinnati Chamber of Commerce on September 16, 1975. "I want to emphasize that the United States did not help negotiate this agreement in order to put an end to the process of peace but to give it new impetus," he told the U.N. General Assembly a few days later. There were unusual opportunities for progress, he added hopefully, but they had to be seized before they disappeared.

It was clear, for all that, that the opportunities were both indeterminate and open-ended. "Impeccable" execution of the Sinai accords was a first condition, the secretary emphasized. Washington was prepared to "make a serious effort to encourage negotiations between Syria and Israel," he continued bravely. But the third course, involving exploration of "possibilities for perhaps a more informal multilateral meeting to assess conditions and discuss the future," already led into the mists. "We have no preference for any particular procedure," the secretary added. Acknowledging superpower concurrence that another war in the region would be disastrous, and the persisting willingness of the United Nations to dispatch *casques bleues,* he let it be known that the United States was prepared to pursue "whatever process seems most promising."

What exactly did he intend by the "multilateral meeting?" CBS's veteran diplomatic correspondent Richard Hottelet asked him the next day. The idea was basically exploratory, the secretary repeated. In principle, it was addressed to the states of the Geneva conference, but there was nothing binding about that. Anyone interested was welcome. The object was to make things move. What was not at issue were ideas, he added. The United States had these too. It was just that no one had replied to them.[1]

In fact, things did move, but hardly in a direction Americans welcomed. In late October 1975, the *New York Times* noted that "most delegates" joined in a standing ovation for Anwar al-Sadat when he appeared with his wife and daughters at the U.N. General Assembly. On November 10 the General Assembly passed Resolution 3379. The text, and the majority behind it, were guaranteed to confirm the worst possible expectations of Israelis, American Jews, and the almost exclusively Western interests associated with them. Harking back to a U.N. declaration on racial discrimination in 1963, and "taking note" of a variety of Third World rhetorical exercises since December 1973 that linked Israel to colonialism, South

240

Africa, apartheid, and so on, a 72–35 majority "determined" that "zionism is a form of racism and racial discrimination." There were thirty-two abstentions. Only one developed country, the Soviet Union, was among the twenty-five sponsors. Of the other twenty-four, twenty-one were Moslem, nineteen of them Arab.[2] The resolution remained in place for 16 years.

The next day, Luxembourg's Gaston Thorn, the General Assembly's president, deplored the impact of the resolution "on the climate of conciliation" thitherto established. Called to task for violating the neutrality of the presidency, he qualified that he had spoken only as Luxembourg's prime minister. He then apologized to the Arab League, which accepted his apology. In a furious speech a few weeks later, the chief U.S. delegate, Daniel Patrick Moynihan, declared the General Assembly a "theater of the absurd," and blasted its majority for even presuming to judge what constituted consent of the governed. There were only twenty-eight or twenty-nine functioning representative democracies in the world, he declared emphatically, and one of them, Switzerland, was not even a member of the General Assembly.[3] Meanwhile, the PLO delegation, a nominal observer of the General Assembly, was scheduled for speaking time as though it were a member.

Within its inevitable constraints, Washington moved too. In his speech to the General Assembly, even Kissinger now referred to "the legitimate rights of the Palestinians." The oracularism was deliberate. What rights? Which Palestinians? Legitimated by whom by virtue of what? In a world of new realities and precarious détente, the formula nonetheless acknowledged that Palestinians, like the (East) German Democratic Republic with which the United States had recently exchanged ambassadors, or the People's Republic of China, which Nixon and Kissinger had only discovered in living memory, now existed without quotation marks.

Only two days after Resolution 3379, Harold Saunders testified before the Mideast subcommittee of the House Committee on Foreign Affairs. One of the younger generation of old Middle East hands, Saunders had begun in the comparative antiquity of the Johnson years. He then served in Nixon's White House, before proceeding, with Kissinger, to the State Department, where he now served as deputy assistant secretary for Near Eastern and South Asian affairs. In September 1970, he had been an observer-participant in the Jordan crisis.

It was hardly by chance that his subject was the Palestinians. "It is a fact that many of the 3 million or so people who call themselves Palestinians today increasingly regard themselves as having their own identity as a people and desire a voice in determining their political status," he told his listeners. It was, he emphasized with the gravity of someone who knew whereof he spoke, "another interest that must be taken into account."

He acknowledged that the PLO was itself "ambivalent" about options that now extended more or less officially from "armed struggle" to propagation of a "secular-democratic," that is, binational but predominantly Arab, state in Palestine. But the choices of the United States were scarcely easier. On the one hand, both the Arab League and General Assembly now recognized the PLO as the sole representative of the Palestinian people. On the other, the PLO not only refused to recognize Israel, a U.N. member, but to accept Security Council resolutions 242 and 338, which were the presumable basis of any negotiations. Israel, for its part, refused to recognize the PLO "or the idea of a separate Palestinian entity."

"We cannot envision or urge a negotiation between two parties as long as one professes to hold the objective of eliminating the other," Saunders conceded. There was also the matter of terrorism. "It seems to us that there must be some assurance if Palestinians are drawn into the negotiating process that these practices will be curbed," he added. The message was nonetheless clear. A "diplomatic process which will help bring forth a reasonable definition of Palestinian interests" was "a first step" toward Middle Eastern peace. The question, he declared, was how, not whether.[4]

As both Israeli and American-Jewish reaction confirmed, this was not a popular position, but neither was it a particularly daring one. Even as Saunders spoke, an unchallengeably establishmentarian and almost ostentatiously ecumenical study group was presenting quite similar conclusions after conferring intermittently for half a year at Washington's Brookings Institution.[5] Of its members, four would serve in the next administration, and two, Zbigniew Brzezinski and William Quandt, would be directly involved in its efforts to turn their report into practice.

Artfully composed of Jews and Arabs, Democrats and Republicans, old and younger Middle East hands, and veterans or inside observers of five administrations, the group agreed with Kissinger that step-by-step had run its course. But their conclusions were not Kissingerian. Since neither Syrian-Israeli nor Jordanian-Israeli talks showed any promise, they concluded, the next step had to be comprehensive. Presumably, it also had to include the Soviet Union, if only because of the Soviet Union's "considerable capacity for complicating or even for blocking either further interim steps or progress toward an overall settlement."[6]

Whether by means of a general conference or multilateral meetings in Geneva, the process, in effect, would have to address everything at once: boundaries, security, guarantees, diplomatic relations, Palestine, Jerusalem. The "primary basis for a settlement," the rapporteurs declared, was a "negotiated and agreed tradeoff between the Israeli requirement for peace and security and the Arab requirement for evacuation of territories occupied in 1967 and for Palestinian self-determination."[7]

The rest was negotiable. On the most contentious issues, the conferees spelled out their differences on a kind of menu. After a quarter century's bitter experience, a short list of minimal, even negative, conditions, constituted the lowest common denominator on Jerusalem. There was no longer even a hint left of the U.N.-administered free city envisaged in 1947. Holy sites should be accessible and under the custody of their respective religionists, the authors contended; there should be no barriers to movement within the city; each national group "should, if it so desires, have substantial political autonomy within the area where it predominates."[8]

Palestine was seen alternatively as an independent state or a voluntary adjunct to a federation with Jordan, but it was agreed that either course should require resettlement of refugees, and "reasonable" compensation, both for Palestinians once resident in Israel, and Jews once resident in Arab states. The conferees also agreed that any Palestinian representatives would have to accept "the equal right to self-determination of Israel and Jordan."[9]

But whatever the outcome and destination, any settlement would clearly have to be multilateral and multistage, "reinforced and supplemented" by "safeguards, assurances, guarantees and assistance," military included.[10] It was hardly surprising that the rapporteurs saw the role of the United States as bigger than most, while the collateral roles of Congress, the United Nations, the Soviet Union, and other powers were left purposefully vague. But although the circumstances could be described both as propitious and precarious, with no apparent sense of contradiction, it was taken practically for granted that the affected parties shared a common desire for peace,[11] that they were presumably prepared to act on it, and that voters at home might even be willing to honor their government's effort to help.

At the same time, the random interactions of social change, economic turmoil, White House conspiracy, Middle Eastern turbulence, and the unpaid bills from a generation of global activism, had transformed the foreign policy landscape beyond anything imaginable ten or even four years earlier. Vietnam divided the Democrats. Détente, in turn, divided the Republicans. The rolling thunder of an impending election only added to the dissonance as hawks and doves lined up on both sides.

The eruption of the Lebanese civil war in 1975 could be seen as a kind of not-so-distant early warning of the Middle Eastern future. As recently as 1958, it still appeared that such things could be managed successfully, and even bloodlessly, with little more than a timely show of the flag. Not only had Eisenhower dispatched a unit of Marines, he even brought them home again without injury or incident, while Israel kept its distance. Now, in a scene reminiscent by turns of Miami Beach and Stalingrad, Beirut showed every promise of becoming the heart of darkness, where some adolescents in green fatigues and running shoes ran around with Kalashnikovs, while others in string bikinis sunned themselves on beaches. Seemingly distinguishable only by one another, the contending factions tangled obscurely amid the shattered buildings, burned-out cars, maimed children, and ululating mothers of an open-ended war of all against all. The problem, as so often in the Middle East, was that their tribal warfare merged increasingly with world politics, while willingly and reluctantly, external powers became parties and accessories to their tribal wars.

Lebanon, it now appeared, posed impossible choices for nearly everyone. For the United States, the trade-offs included concerns for Lebanon's integrity and an Israel under fire from PLO encampments just across the border. For the Soviets, they included the future of détente and commitments to both Syria and the PLO. For Syria, they included renewed claims to Arab leadership; traditional aspirations to influence in Lebanon and Jordan; fear of isolation as Egypt went its separate way; and strategic encirclement if PLO activism should provoke Israel to invade Lebanon. At this point, ironically, the Syrians, like the Israelis, even found themselves allied with Lebanese Christians against the PLO. But irrespective of the company Damascus now kept, Israelis were bound to fear a Syrian protectorate on their northern border as much as they feared the PLO.[12]

Of course, with Republicans arrayed against détente, Democrats inclined to dovishness, and cascades of latest-model U.S. arms still coursing toward Iran and Saudi Arabia, they could hardly help brood about Americans too. By now, according to Ezer Weizmann, Israel's new defense minister, an estimated 20 percent of his country's military capacity was directly underwritten by the United States.[13] The question was price, both economic and political. Since 1967, ascendant hawks had regarded territorial control *and* U.S. weapons as the premise of Israeli security. Détente implied a choice of either-or. So, in their respective ways, did Democratic victory and the ascendancy of the Republican Right. For Israelis, disposed to see a Republican president and Democratic Congress as the best defender of their interests, Ford was at least a lesser evil in the White House. The president's vulnerability, not only to the Democrats but to his party's Right, was therefore just one more constraint on a Labor government that was itself increasingly embattled from both the dovish Left and hawkish Right.[14]

For the first time since the 1940s, there were even hairline cracks in the American-Jewish community, but as any Israeli could confirm, they only matched the corresponding cracks in Israel. In April 1978, a "committee of eight" American-Jewish leaders presented Prime Minister Menahem Begin with polling data "and other evidence" that Israel was losing congressional and public support, and thirty-six prominent American Jews, including the Nobel laureates Kenneth Arrow and Saul Bellow, ten rabbis, and a supporting cast of outstanding intellectuals, publicly urged Israeli moderation. The same month, twenty-five to thirty thousand Israelis demonstrated in Tel Aviv's Kings of Israel Square in support of the dovish Peace Now movement. From the *New York Times* to the *Jerusalem Post,* Americans on both sides bombarded one another with display ads and manifestos.[15]

Paradoxically, it often seemed that the actual facts of Israeli life were almost irrelevant to the vast majority of American Jews, whose relationship to Israel was at once philanthropic, abstract, and existential.[16] Mattityahu Peled, a retired Israeli general who spent 1975 at Harvard, and toured the United States to make the case for negotiating with the Arabs, went home convinced that American Jews were "more Israeli than the Israelis" on security. Though there was substantially less dissent in the United States than Israel, the organized establishment, both Israeli and American, nonetheless reacted to what little there was as to a mouse that roared.

The object, and test case, was Breira (alternative), a name deliberately chosen as counterpoint to Ayn Breira (There is no alternative), a slogan from the 1948 war. But in contrast to the assimilationist-establishmentarian American Council on Judaism a generation earlier, members of the new organization were consistently unestablishmentarian, self-confidently Jewish, even Hebrew-speaking. In contrast to the vast majority of American Jews, many were also uncommonly familiar with the Israeli scene. But official Israel hardly saw this as a point in their favor. Rabin reportedly saw Breira as both a challenge and an embarrassment.[17] For a Labor government already skidding toward disaster,[18] and disposed to assume that those not for it were against it, Breira's dissent was, at least, inopportune.

Conceived in 1973 as the Project of Concern in Israeli-Diaspora Relations, Breira had grown by the mid-1970s to an organization of perhaps a thousand. But unlike the established Jewish organizations grouped since the 1950s in the Conference of Presidents of Major Jewish Organizations, its constituency tended to be young and campus-based. By 1975, it had been invited to testify before Senator George McGovern's subcommittee of the Senate Foreign Relations Committee, in company with past and future cabinet members, high-profile academics, and the chairman of the Conference of Presidents of Major Jewish Organizations.[19]

In November 1976, two Breira board members were among five American Jews to do privately what Kissinger had committed their government not to do. At a meeting in Washington arranged by the American Friends Service Committee, they conferred with representatives of the PLO. The Palestinians arrived *ex officio,* among them Dr. Issam Sartawi, who was assassinated in 1983 for endorsing recognition of Israel. Though the Jewish participants represented such mainstream organizations as B'nai B'rith, the American Jewish Congress, and the National Council of Jewish Women, as well as Breira, they were at pains to emphasize that they had come as individuals. But it was Breira that drew the heaviest fire after Arthur Waskow, one of its founding fathers, reported publicly on the meeting in the *New York Times.*[20]

Breira's critics, of whom there were many, pointed demonstratively to its countercultural origins in the peace and civil rights movements of the 1960s.[21] Yet whatever its past, delegates to its first—and last—national meeting at the National 4-H Center in suburban Chevy Chase, Maryland, made clear by their dress, demeanor, even haircuts that sober and experienced grown-ups—the writer Irving Howe, the Harvard sociologist Nathan Glazer, Rabbi Arnold Jacob Wolf—now set the tone.

Of thirty-eight executive board members listed on the letterhead in 1976, eighteen, in fact, were rabbis, for all that their names, which included Gerry, Doug, Chuck, and Buzz, reflected a provenance rather different from that of their Israeli counterparts. Yet Breira positions hardly differed from views then common to official Washington, the editorial board of the *New York Times,* and so establishmentarian an Israeli as Abba Eban. Over its two-year existence, contributors to "interChange," its little monthly newsletter, included Balfour Brickner, a prominent Reform rabbi; Boaz Evron, a respected Israeli journalist; Naomi Chazan, the daughter of a former Israeli ambassador to the United States; Jacob Neusner, an acknowledged authority on Jewish philosophy and literature; Melvin Urofsky, a historian of American Zionism; the Middle East scholars Don Peretz and Barry Rubin; and Stephen S. Rosenfeld, an editorial writer for the *Washington Post.*

The venom unleashed on Breira made it easy to see the confrontation as a war among the Jews, or conspiracy against dissent.[22] There was something to both, but neither was an end in itself, despite the passion expended on them. Both were subsumed in far larger debates on the meaning of Vietnam, the lessons of the October war, and other tectonic changes in a world Americans and Israelis alike found increasingly perplexing. Within three years of Breira's appearance before McGovern's subcommittee, three of the subcommittee's liberal Democratic members, including Wyoming's Gale McGee, Iowa's Dick Clark, and McGovern himself, had been swept to defeat by Republican conservatives, at least in part for their ostensible softness, both foreign and domestic. (Meanwhile, Hubert Humphrey, the subcommittee's fourth Democrat, had died.) For reasons believed linked to his views on Palestinians, one of its two Republicans, Charles Percy of Illinois, had also lost.[23] By now, Breira too had been effectively ostracized, its funding dried, and its membership scattered. Meanwhile, Israel, recently perceived as a tiny, independent, social democratic commonwealth, had come to be seen, by no means invidiously, as a bulwark against détente and even liberalism.

For their part, Israelis were generally happy with the role. Once again, the United States was their best hope and biggest problem. But by that time, both Israeli and U.S. foreign policy were under new management. In November 1976, Americans had elected Jimmy Carter, a Cold War–weary liberal Democrat and Southern Baptist, with serious reservations about the course of U.S. foreign policy. In May 1977, Israelis elected Begin, the lifelong Revisionist, after almost thirty years of Labor leadership.

The collapse of Rabin's coalition in December 1976 was itself a kind of metaphor for the current state of Israeli-U.S. relations. The occasion was the arrival and presentation to the Israeli defense forces of their first three F-15s just a little too close to sunset on a winter Friday afternoon. Rabin and his ministers rejoiced in the coming of the planes, the latest advance in both their own arsenal and that of the United States. The perennially contentious religious establishment rejoiced in the chance to score points off one another. The following Tuesday, a tiny religious party produced a no-confidence motion, noting that the ceremony had caused ministers to get home late for the Sabbath. Though associated with Rabin's government, nine of ten deputies from the National Religious party (NRP) abstained from the vote that followed. The government scraped by, but an exasperated Rabin dismissed the NRP's three ministers. The parliamentary process then went its inexorable way.[24]

Given the respective premises of the new governments in Jerusalem and Washington, it could be reasonably assumed that they were on collision courses. Where the political map of the Middle East was concerned, Carter's bible was the Brookings study, Stuart Eizenstat, the new president's domestic policy advisor, later told an interviewer.[25] For generically similar purposes, the new Israeli prime minister's bible appeared to be the Bible. "These are not occupied territories," Begin told reporters at an improvised press conference only two days after his election victory. "You've used this expression for ten years, but from May 1977, I hope you'll start using the word liberated territories." The site of the exchange was Kadum, a settlement Rabin's government had tried unsuccessfully to declare illegal. The settlers, many of them veterans of the 1973 war, called themselves Gush Emunim, League of the Faithful. A spin-off of traditional religious Zionism, they were entirely European-descended. Like Begin, who traced his political identity to the liberal nationalism of Garibaldi, the settlers too evoked odd European reminiscences—in this case of the poet Gabriele D'Annunzio and the romantic irridentists who followed him to Fiume after World War I in order to embarrass the government in Rome. The new encampment too had been a challenge, in this case to Labor's pragmatic reluctance to settle Arab-populated areas.[26]

After a lifetime in the political wilderness, Begin seemed the unlikeliest of victors. Head of a perennial minority party that had only recently escaped financial scandal, and was now trying to redress its cash-flow problem in the United States, the new prime minister was also recovering from a major heart attack.[27] Although conducted in Begin's name, the campaign had actually been managed by Weizman, a nephew of the founding father, and a retired air force general. Described by one

British reporter as "an Israeli de Gaulle" waiting "to be called to save the nation," he himself acknowledged the irony of his situation as a Weizman among the heirs of Vladimir Jabotinsky.[28]

Three things helped win the election, he later told an interviewer. One was that Moshe Dayan still ran on Labor's ticket, the second that Ariel Sharon ran on his own ticket, the third that Begin was in the hospital.[29] Likud strategy was ingeniously calculated to assure that Begin would be seen without being heard. Campaign handlers took care that traditional bloody shirts—the *Altalena* episode, biblical rights, the Land of Israel—remained securely in the closet. Instead, they targeted accelerating inflation, national frustration, and partisan dissension, not to mention what Rabin, at least, regarded as mindless knocks from Washington.[30] As more than half a century of Labor hegemony crumbled amidst allegations of high living, and both personal and institutional financial scandals, Likud campaign spots offered voters an honest man, playing with his grandchildren.[31]

When the ballots were counted, there were doubts whether it was even a victory for Begin, but everyone agreed it was a debacle for Labor. Like American Democrats just a few years earlier, Labor voters had declared their independence. Almost a third of them took refuge in a liberal opposition party, newly founded by the archaeologist and former chief of staff Yigael Yadin and Amnon Rubinstein, a former dean of the Tel Aviv law school. Their defection dropped Labor to second place with about a quarter of the total vote. Meanwhile, Likud had gained almost a quarter, winning about a third of the total votes, and thus becoming the strongest party in the Knesset. With 11.5 percent, Yadin and Rubinstein came in third. The religious parties held their own.[32]

In principle, similar shifts had already been spotted from Scandinavia to California. But in Israel they were favored and amplified by idiosyncrasies of ethnicity and class that transformed the election of a government into a kind of plebiscite on the nature of the country. Signal or protest, the returns confirmed that an era was over. Not only did they make Begin Israel's first non-Labor prime minister, they arguably made him the father of a new republic.

With the support of a European-descended, white-collar, professional "first Israel," who saw him as one of their own, Yadin was among the winners. But it was the "second Israel," the Middle Eastern and North African immigrants of the late 1940s and early 1950s, who elected Begin. Still smarting from the indignities of an immigrant generation, they rallied to Begin as a fellow outsider and observant Jew, his inevitable tie and white shirt, Polish good manners, and predilection for Latin notwithstanding.[33] Their choice turned the floating vote into a torrent. Since 1973, almost half the electorate had switched parties, but, as subsequent elections only confirmed, the heavy traffic was moving to the right. In towns established before 1948, where Labor losses exceeded 15 percent, Yadin was the principal beneficiary. In the new towns, where Oriental voters were more heavily represented and Labor losses approached 17 percent, the principal beneficiary was Likud.

It took Begin barely a month to form a government, a brisk pace by Israeli standards. Though Yadin was later to join with U.S. encouragement, initial support came almost entirely from the Likud and the like-minded religious parties that till now had been allies of Labor.[34] There was a determined display of continuity in the prime minister's office, where four senior officials were kept over from the previous administration. The new government was nonetheless the furthest right to date, leavened only by two maverick deputies, each constituting a party of one. In his way, each also testified to the idiosyncrasies of democracy Israeli style. The first, Shmuel Flatto-Sharon, was a fugitive from French justice. Though his priority concern was presumably avoiding extradition, he had made such a nice impression promising largesse to the development towns that he actually outpolled the more famous General Ariel Sharon. The second, elected again on the Labor list, was the new government's foreign minister, Moshe Dayan.

There were differing versions about who talked to whom,[35] but it was hardly surprising that Labor, Herut, and Begin's Liberal partners alike were outraged. The Dayan appointment displayed not only the new prime minister's underestimated capacity for pragmatism but his concern for U.S. opinion. After a conclusive interview at Begin's hospital bedside, Dayan accepted. A man, as a biographer notes, "who attached great importance to words,"[36] the new prime minister told Dayan what he wanted to hear. Israeli sovereignty would not be extended to the "administered" territories, that is, the West Bank and Gaza, while peace negotiations were in progress. Israel would return to Geneva on the basis of Resolution 242. There would be no change in the status of the Arabs in the West Bank and Gaza, that is, they would continue to send representatives to the Jordanian parliament, and receive Arab subsidies through Amman. There would also be no organized Jewish services on the Temple Mount, the site of Jerusalem's great mosques and once of Solomon's temple.[37]

On the other hand, as events confirmed, Begin understood Resolution 242 quite differently than did his predecessors and official Washington.[38] Whatever his reservations about sovereignty, Dayan too believed in settlements, "strategic borders," and a Greater Israel. His personal creation, the deliberate ambiguity of Israeli occupation policy in the West Bank after 1967, had been designed to help achieve them.[39] Could he really say no, Dayan wrote a critic, when he had a solution; could act only as a member of the government; and when the alternative to peace was war? Would a Begin government be better without him?[40]

In its idiosyncratic way, the U.S. campaign was also a kind of plebiscite on foreign policy. Though each party tended to support détente, Republicans leaned, as usual, toward a more or less conservative version of realpolitik; Democrats echoed an earlier idealism. If Ford, the incumbent Republican, defended arms control, Carter, his Democratic challenger, made arms sales a priority target and underscored human rights.

Like the obligatory campaign appearances in synagogues and delicatessens, Israel was both a consensus issue and a specialty item. Republicans pointed pridefully to their role in preserving regional peace and stability, then affirmed their commitment to Israel. Democrats undertook to pursue "a just and lasting peace," then declared that "a firm commitment to the independence and security" of Israel was its "cornerstone."

"Face-to-face negotiations" appeared in both platforms. But Republicans linked these to support for Israel, and linked this, in turn, to pursuit of regional peace. Democrats, while favoring pragmatism, pledged first to oppose the isolation of Israel, and then imposition of terms. Both texts affirmed their opposition to "boycotts." But the Republican referent was the threat to oil; the Democratic referent a threat to "friendly countries." Although neither platform even hinted at Palestine or Palestinians, only the Democrats explicitly opposed the "recognition of terrorist groups which refuse to acknowledge their adversary's right to exist." They even promised to move the U.S. embassy from Tel Aviv to Jerusalem. Republicans pledged their continuing commitment to "the balance of power in the Mediterranean region."[41]

Kissinger's sagging fortunes were a telling indication of how much had changed in four years. *Time* magazine even reported formation of a group called "American Jews Against Ford," whose stated goal was "to change the kind of thinking that leads to sellouts." Running against both Ford and Kissinger, California's Governor Ronald Reagan came within 117 of 2,257 delegates—4 percent—of dumping the president at the nominating convention. But Carter, who had impressed his presumptive national security advisor only the year before by speaking "forcefully and clearly on behalf of a fair Middle East settlement" at a meeting in Japan,[42] made sure to keep his distance too. If elected, he would "make sure Dr. Henry Kissinger is removed as secretary of state," he reportedly told "Israeli political leaders in the strongest terms."[43]

As usual in election years, foreign policy ran in place, but Ford himself warned Sadat to expect no action until the campaign was over.[44] Though specifically "Jewish" issues were marginal, both sides worked hard for the Jewish vote. On the eve of the election, the administration approved new credits and even hardware for Israel, including indiscriminately lethal cluster-bomb units for which even the Pentagon had trouble finding a use.[45] But anticipating a hope that was to be among the administration's many disappointments and anticlimaxes, its presumptive vice president, Walter Mondale, also urged an end to the cresting tide of arms sales—though especially to Saudi Arabia.[46]

Yet it was the challenger's handlers who rubbed their jaws after their man landed a potential knockout punch in the campaign's foreign policy debate in San Francisco. In a legendary gaffe, Ford denied that Poland was dominated by Soviet influence. He then compounded it with a declaration of support for legislation penalizing U.S. companies complicit in the Arab boycott. Carter sailed enthusiastically into both claims. In reality, he pointed out, the administration had done everything it could to stop antiboycott legislation, and had no intention of releasing the names of cooperating companies.[47] Campaign aides watching in Atlanta only deplored what they feared might seem counterproductive aggressiveness.[48]

In the event, the Jewish vote sufficed to turn a narrow popular plurality into a substantial electoral majority. New York alone made the difference, Carter's pollster reportedly told him on election night. If Jews had voted for Carter with the same circumspection as other American whites, he would have lost by 103 electoral votes. In the end, it was estimated that Carter, like Truman, carried about 75 percent of the Jewish vote, up 10 percent from McGovern's dismal showing four years earlier. It was estimated that 63 percent of his campaign money was Jewish too, yet commentators were right to note the softness. During the primary season, Carter's Jewish vote lagged well behind his popular vote, and Jewish money was estimated at less than 20 percent of his total contributions. One could only guess how he felt about a constituency that considered him their last alternative.[49]

Though hard-pressed to claim a specific mandate, the new president nonetheless made his priorities clear within weeks of his inauguration. For the first time in memory, a first family walked home from the Capitol. A statement of personal style, the gesture was also a public signal to a nation that not only continued to lead the world in fuel consumption but had actually increased oil imports since October 1973. Then about 35 percent of total consumption, they now amounted to nearly half. Barely two weeks later, Carter appeared for a nationally televised speech, conspicuously clad in a sweater. There could hardly have been a more dramatic contrast to Nixon, a man reportedly so fond of the fireplace that he turned up the White House air conditioning so he could enjoy a fire in summer. If the Republican platform declared an oil boycott "a hostile act,"[50] the new president declared conservation "the moral equivalent of war," and invested vast amounts of political capital in a bitterly divisive struggle to reverse the country's appetite for imports.[51]

About six weeks later, at a town meeting in Clinton, Massachusetts, there was another new departure, as the president for the first time spelled out his Middle East policy in public. As before, the first steps included Arab recognition of Israel and a negotiated package of mutually recognized borders. But there was a third element too, reflective of a southern president marked by the civil rights movement, sincerely concerned for human rights, and temperamentally disposed to link the predicaments of Palestinians and black Americans.[52] It was "a homeland . . . for the Palestinian refugees, who have suffered for many, many years." The most explicit reference by any president to date, it came as a surprise to Secretary of State Cyrus Vance, National Security Advisor Zbigniew Brzezinski, and PLO Chairman Yassir Arafat alike.[53] The next day, inadvertently, the president even shook hands with the PLO representative, who appeared in the receiving line after Carter's speech at the United Nations. Both were embarrassed, Carter noted in his diary.[54]

Just five days after Begin's election, Carter spelled out his view of the world before a graduation audience at the University of Notre Dame. "I believe we can have a foreign policy that is democratic, that is based on fundamental values, and that uses power and influence, which we have, for human purposes," he declared. He therefore intended to emphasize human rights; wider cooperation on such global issues as Third World poverty and nuclear proliferation, nuclear arms control, and "lasting peace in the Middle East." The "historic friendship" of the United States for Israel, Carter added, was neither dependent on "domestic politics" nor affected by "changes in leadership."[55]

Already anticipated by Vance in a preelection overview, the new policy was a medley of intellectual conviction, perceived opportunity, and trial balloon. The Middle East was also among Brzezinski's priorities. Barely settled in their new offices, the two men dispatched their respective staffers—Alfred Atherton, now assistant secretary for Near East and South Asia, Harold Saunders, now director of State Department I&R, and William B. Quandt, now National Security Council staff member for the Middle East—to draft strategies. The alternatives were prudently hedged. The first favored "damage limitation." The second, candidly anticipating the wear and tear it could cause on Israeli-U.S. relations, advocated activism. But risks and all, it was clear from the administration's earliest discussions that Carter, Vance, Brzezinski, and the staffers themselves preferred the second course. By February 1977, Vance was en route to the Middle East for a first round of talks.

Between March and May, Carter too made the round of Middle Eastern leaders. He later recalled his first meeting with Sadat as "a shining light." Sadat, in turn, apostrophized Carter as "a great statesman," "a sweet man," even an "inspiration."[56] But it was increasingly obvious that Sadat and Carter were responding to different clocks and calendars. Heir to one of the world's historic centers of gravity, yet painfully sensitive to pressures from the street and the army, Sadat had already decided that peace was both a means and an end in itself. Taking for given that only the United States could deliver peace *and* arms *and* economic aid, he now pursued a relationship both comparable to, and functionally linked with, Israel's.

For Washington, on the other hand, Egyptian support had become both a nuisance and a free good. For an administration concerned to deter the hazards of another war and oil embargo, neither a special relationship with Egypt nor a separate peace was a plausible goal. By definition, any comprehensive settlement required Saudi Arabia, Jordan, Syria, even the PLO. This, in turn, meant moving Israel. Given the special importance of Syria, Carter was even willing to meet its president on neutral ground en route from the London economic summit. Carter's *tour d'horizon* therefore included a three-and-a-half-hour interview with Hafiz al-Asad in Geneva, as well as talks with Sadat and King Hussein in Washington.

The review was occasion for both hope and sobriety. Yet as always, the lowest common denominator of any comprehensive solution seemed to be U.S. pressure on Israel. The more he dealt with Arab leaders, Carter noted, "the more disparity I discovered between their private assurances and their public comments."[57] At the same time, even before the coming of Begin, it was clear that the Israelis were reluctant to move; and that trial balloons—including constraints on both deliveries of the new cluster bombs to Israel and sale of U.S.-equipped Israeli planes to Ecuador—would draw flak from the American-Jewish establishment. Most ominous, perhaps, were hints passed on by knowledgeable American Jews that the administration was believed responsive to pressure.[58]

In a way, the coming of Begin made things clearer, though hardly simpler. "It was frightening to watch his adamant position on issues that must be resolved if a Middle Eastern peace settlement is going to be realized," Carter noted apprehensively after listening to Begin on ABC's "Issues and Answers."[59] Yet contrary to prevailing wisdom outside and even inside Israel, there was more to the new prime minister than an idiosyncratic view of history[60] and a predilection for legalism that would regularly bring U.S. negotiators to a tight-jawed simmer. Consistently anti-Soviet, though hardly more so than Sadat, he was equally consistent about Gaza and, especially, the West Bank.[61] On the other hand, within only a few months of taking office, his relative detachment about the Sinai and even Golan had led, via Romania, Morocco, and possibly even India and Iran, to the most serious contacts with Egypt since the 1950s.[62]

Given the reputation that preceded him, his inaugural appearance in Washington came almost as a relief. Of Carter's stated priorities—a comprehensive peace, with unrestricted trade and open borders, based on Resolution 242; Israeli withdrawal from the Occupied Territories and a Palestinian "entity"—Begin claimed to support all but the last. He also listened "closely," if unresponsively, as Carter explained why, in the view of the United States, West Bank settlements were both counterproductive and in violation of international law. He then went home and legalized three settlements the Rabin government had previously declared illegal. No agreements were violated, but it was not a friendly signal.[63]

Begin's deep distrust and adamant hostility to the PLO was only one of an aggregate of differences that divided not only Israel from the Arabs but the Arab states from one another and the PLO, and the PLO within itself. As so often, even nominally procedural differences, like one or several Arab delegations, inclusion of Palestinians in a unified or a Jordanian delegation, early or deferred reference to the Palestinian issue, assumed near-existential meaning. In response to a hint from the PLO, Carter went so far as to take a cue from Israel's former Foreign Minister Yigal Allon. If the PLO would recognize Resolution 242, the United States would talk to the PLO, the president publicly declared in early August 1977. He was even prepared to let the PLO amend the reference to "refugees."[64]

In fact, the PLO agreed to nothing, nor were the Syrians inclined to let them. Summoned to Egypt and Saudi Arabia, Arafat seemed ready to agree to Resolution 242. Then, to the despair of Carter, Vance, and the Saudis, the PLO council said no by a 12–4 vote at a meeting in Damascus.[65] Meanwhile, Begin announced construction of three more West Bank settlements, emphasizing his opposition to a unified Arab delegation and the PLO in any form. Seen through Israeli eyes, the new settlement policy was something of a compromise by a government determined to make facts but reluctant to jeopardize the peace process.[66] But seen through increasingly bloodshot U.S. eyes, it was open provocation. He was unwilling to maintain a policy "in which in effect we are financing their conquests and they simply defy us," Carter reportedly told a staff meeting in late August.[67]

Not only did American Jews reply in kind, they seemed to grow even more ambivalent as senior officials and Jewish staffers tried to sell administration policy. "Now, people think that you are pushing Israel to sit down and recognize the PLO . . . ," a representative of the *Texas Jewish Post* informed Carter at a press conference in mid-September. "With all due respect, that's one of the most distorted assessments of my own policy that I've ever heard," the president replied.[68]

Reflecting the heat both at home and abroad, the administration's grand design underwent a subtle change. Once envisaged as the finale to a process already brokered and negotiated in advance, Geneva now began to look like a real conference. This was in part because the administration was unwilling to give up its hopes for achieving something. "As cochairman of the Geneva conference, the United States has a special responsibility for the success of the conference," the State Department earnestly reaffirmed.[69] But the transformation was also an acknowledgement that the parties were so clearly unable to agree in advance among themselves.

In mid-September, Dayan returned to Washington via Morocco. Carter later recalled the meeting as "surprisingly productive," but Dayan recalled it as "most unpleasant." In the president's version, Dayan was "even" flexible on the Palestinians, prepared to accept a joint Arab delegation at an opening session in Geneva; PLO members as part of the Jordanian delegation in the negotiations that followed;

with a separate multinational group to discuss the Palestinian question. In Dayan's version, not only Carter had been hostile and reproachful but also Mondale, "who at other times and on other occasions had been helpful." Dayan himself was implacable. Israel would discuss the West Bank "only with representatives of the Jordan government and the Arab inhabitants of that territory," he emphasized before leaving for the annual round of Israel Bond and United Jewish Appeal meetings.[70]

Interviews with the Egyptian and Syrian foreign ministers were no more successful. Carter could hardly ask Syria and Jordan to come to Geneva to watch Egypt sign a peace treaty; he could hardly make U.S. policy without support of the Jewish community, Congress, and the public; he could hardly ask Egypt to accept a Syrian veto, Carter told them successively. Both only came away persuaded of the president's weakness. Meanwhile, Jordan's foreign minister rejected any effort to include the PLO in a Jordanian delegation.[71]

On October 1, 1977, after a meeting between Vance and the Soviet foreign minister Andrei Gromyko, the Americans dropped the third shoe in conjunction with a working paper, laying out procedure for a conference. Since a joint communiqué was normal at such meetings, the administration saw the statement as routine. In it, Vance and Gromyko declared their intention to reconvene the Geneva conference "not later than" December with representatives of all parties involved "including those of the Palestinian people." That Vance found the Soviet draft unexpectedly forthcoming was only another argument for making their agreement public.

The statement confirmed that comprehensive settlement was a common goal; that this required withdrawal of Israeli forces from territories occupied in 1967; and that "resolution of the Palestinian question, including . . . the legitimate rights of the Palestinian people," termination of the state of war, and "normal peaceful relations" based on "mutual recognition of . . . sovereignty, territorial integrity and political independence" were also necessary elements. Although the statement envisaged the possibility of demilitarized zones, U.N. forces and international guarantees, it referred neither to the PLO nor to a Palestinian state, though also not to Resolution 242. One ostensibly new formulation, "legitimate rights of the Palestinian people," progressed beyond the 1967 text, but it seems also to have had no special meaning.[72] Two years before Kissinger had used an almost identical phrase before without noticeable reaction.

Apart from co-optation of the Soviets, the strategic purpose of the statement seems actually to have been to bring pressure on Syria to show up in Geneva, and on the PLO to accede to the meeting. But in Jerusalem the statement was read as a direct assault on Kissinger's 1975 Memorandum of Agreement, a joint declaration of intent to impose a superpower settlement, and de facto announcement of a Palestinian state. Dayan's access to an advance text, and the administration's failure to consult or brief Congress only added to the impact. The fallout descended on the White House, where the mail room acknowledged receipt of over 3,500 telegrams. The blast—from Israel, American Jews, organized labor, members of Congress, and indignantly pro-Israel and anti-Soviet neoconservatives—reverberated for days.[73] Yet it came as a complete surprise.

In the aftershock of the joint statement, Carter and Dayan met again, this time in New York. It was another strenuous session. To Begin's alarm, Dayan conceded the principle of Palestinian membership in a unified Arab delegation, but there were no concessions on a Palestinian state or the 1967 borders. "Let's talk politics," Carter had said. It was understood that Carter would avoid domestic confrontation of the kind that preceded Sinai II if Dayan would reassure American Jews.

Procedural issues were addressed in a working paper. There was also agreement on a "minute," confirming Israel's right to screen Palestinian participants. The working paper allowed for bilateral working groups, Palestinian participation in discussions on the occupied territories, and even discussion of refugee issues "on terms to be agreed upon." The joint statement, released the next day, affirmed only that acceptance of the superpower statement was "not a prerequisite for the reconvening and conduct of the Geneva conference." But irrespective of substance, it seemed to suggest that Carter had caved in.[74]

The communiqué had its effect both in Israel and Egypt, but neither was what the administration had in mind. With its whiff of superpower condominium and external imposition of terms, it may well have played a major part in Yadin's decision to join the Begin cabinet, both to compensate its heavy rightward list and to support the government against external pressure. Acknowledging their differences on both settlements and territorial concessions, the parties agreed nonetheless that there would be no Palestinian state and no return to the 1967 borders. Labor protested Dayan's ostensible concessions. The march of the United States to Geneva nonetheless helped bring about the toughest Israeli government since Begin's election.[75]

In Egypt, it was the combination of the communiqué, the original working paper, and its revision that did their work. Sadat seemed at first to conclude that the United States had again changed the rules to the advantage of Syria and the Soviet Union. It was bad enough that this implied an external veto on bilateral, that is, Israeli-Egyptian, decisions. It was worse that it might cause Israelis to boycott the conference, where Sadat had assumed they would agree to a U.S. plan. The new working paper only compounded the damage. No Arab government would buy a package that was now understood as an Israeli-U.S. package. In any event, the Syrians were bound to resent that the PLO had vanished from the text, and they themselves from official discussion of the issue. Searching for a way to square vicious circles, Carter proposed instead that the Geneva conference reconvene and adopt its own procedures. The appearance of Arab states would itself confirm their recognition of Israel, he argued. Sadat appealed for reconsideration. Carter replied with a hand-written, hand-delivered appeal for support.[76]

Sadat's answer was a month in coming, but was then among the century's great surprises. Encouraged by Israeli-Egyptian contacts in Morocco, and a conversation with Romania's President Nicolae Ceausescu, who had meanwhile met Begin, he announced his willingness on November 9, 1977, to go to Jerusalem. A few days later, in seemingly concurrent interviews, Walter Cronkite of CBS reported Sadat's interest in, and Begin's willingness to issue, an invitation. On the evening of November 19, with what seemed like half of Israel waiting on the tarmac to receive him, and the other half glued to their television sets, Sadat landed at Israel's Ben-Gurion Airport. With the eyes of the world upon him, and a new foreign minister to replace the one who just resigned, he was then whisked off to Jerusalem. There, in a visit rich in firsts, he addressed the Knesset, and agreed to be interviewed with Begin by Barbara Walters of ABC. A contrast in every way to the familiar image of the Arab terrorist or oil sheikh, he was plainly very good at television.[77] For the moment, Americans could only look on in wonder—or, in the case of official Washington, with an odd combination of fascination, ambivalence, and envy. "Sadat's initiative compelled us to reappraise our position," Brzezinski recalled with becoming understatement.[78]

Yet for all that Sadat had changed the role of the United States, it was soon clear that it was as crucial as before. In return for Palestinian self-determination and Israeli withdrawal on all fronts, Sadat was prepared to offer peace, normal relations, even proud isolation from the other Arab states. Begin countered with phased withdrawal from the Sinai; "home rule" for the West Bank and Gaza; a new settlement near Jerusalem; even, to the common consternation of the Egyptians, Americans, and many Israelis, four new settlements in the Sinai. Intended to put pressure on Egypt, the settlements were Sharon's idea, but they were approved by Dayan. Challenged by Americans on Dayan's commitment of September 1977 to suspend new settlements for a year, Begin replied that year referred only to the remainder of 1977 as opposed to the twelve months ending in September 1978. It was depressingly clear, as Weizman noted, that bilateral talks were a dialogue of the deaf.[79] Between mid-January and September 1978, the relationship was to approach the brink four times in four quite different venues.

That the relationship nonetheless continued had a lot to do with Washington's unique capacity for good offices, and its concern that the talks not collapse. Apparently unneeded and unwanted as *maître de plaisir* at a diplomatic gala in Geneva, or as guarantor of an eventual settlement,[80] the United States was still the only possible banker, broker, counselor, mediator, even obstetrician, of an agreement between Israel and Egypt. The calendar alone confirmed how Washington had become the midpoint between their capitals. In December, Vance visited the Middle East and Begin visited Washington. In January 1978, Carter visited the Middle East. In February, Dayan and Sadat visited Washington. In March and again in May, Begin visited Washington too.

By this time, the administration was engaged on a dozen fronts from strategic arms control to the impending bankruptcy of New York City. "It's hard to concentrate on anything except Panama," the president noted in his diary only days before Begin's arrival.[81] With twenty senators up for reelection, the Panama Canal treaty was touch and go, a natural target for the Republican Right and a hostage to pro-Israel Democrats. It was to clear the Senate with one vote to spare.

A comprehensive package of arms transfers, including the F-15s Carter had promised Saudi Arabia's King Khalid in January, and the F-5E's that Sadat had unexpectedly requested in February, was another whopping claim on political capital. Warned and presumably aware of the domestic hazards if it proceeded,[82] but no less aware of the diplomatic costs if it backed down, the administration resolved to risk the sale: seventy-five F-16s plus fifteen more F-15s for Israel; sixty F-15s for Saudi Arabia, plus fifty F-5E's for Egypt. Though Begin urged prior approval of the Israeli share, Vance held firm. If any part were rejected, he told Congress, the administration would withdraw the package.[83] The four-month debate that followed was memorably nasty. The administration presented the plane sales as a confidence builder on all sides, and therefore an incentive to peacemaking. It also denied any intent to pressure Israel. It was nonetheless suspected, and even circumstantially confirmed, that members of the administration intended the package not only for just that purpose but as a deliberate showdown with the Jewish lobby and a test of Israel's influence in Congress. Assigned to explain the sale to the president's Jewish constituency, Mark Siegel, the White House liaison to the Jewish community, instead resigned in protest.

The pressure was hardly exaggerated, but it poured in from all sides. Before the debate was over, no fewer than three Saudi princes had toured offices in the Capitol. Sadat too met with both House and Senate committees, while Dayan convened what one participant called "a private rump session of the Senate Foreign Relations Committee," and Begin declared the sale an attempt to impose peace terms. The debate was a dilemma for Israelis. Forced to choose between planes in the hand and defeat of the package, Weizman appeared to favor the former, Dayan the latter. Begin, who, according to Carter, had never even mentioned the sales in two days of talks,[84] appeared to be on both sides. As Congress reacted with growing distaste and impatience, even Weizman wondered if Israel's opposition was well advised. U.S. arms, he noted plausibly, meant U.S. influence, just as Soviet arms had meant Soviet influence.[85] Carter made the same point in a strong letter to every senator and selected members of the House, and senior officials lobbied for weeks. In the end, the package passed, and the president declared it a pyrrhic victory. But he still had political problems among American Jews, he later acknowledged discreetly. Shortly after the arms sale, Democratic fund-raisers in Los Angeles and New York were, in fact, called off because of cancellations.[86]

Efforts to push the Israelis on their settlement policy and interpretation of Resolution 242 had meanwhile only increased the tension and frustration. Well aware that the Palestinian issue was poison, the administration had chosen to mount its campaign instead on land and peace, and aim it both at Israel and the home front. Israeli ambivalence was hardly a secret; though majorities still favored settlement and retention of occupied territories, Sadat's *coup de théâtre* had reduced support for both to post-1967 lows.[87] American-Jewish ambivalence was even more pronounced. "For thirty years we have been building for Israel the image of a peace-loving country," one American-Jewish leader told an interviewer from *Ha'aretz*. "Begin destroyed this image in three months." His reservations were reportedly confirmed in a poll of 150 American Jewish leaders, commissioned by the Begin government, and then not published. By a three-quarter majority, the sample group had called on Israel for moderation.[88]

The confrontation led to a dialogue approaching psychodrama between American Jews, whose generic American liberalism was literally foreign to most Israelis, and Israelis, whose belief in the land was literally foreign to most American Jews.[89] Dayan, who virtually personified the history of Jewish Palestine, was understandably bitter about American Jews telling *him* that Israeli settlement policy was "sabotaging Zionism." Yet he conceded himself that he got nowhere with American audiences, while Sadat, the first "good" Arab most Americans had consciously encountered, was stealing the show. Weizman, another walking personification of

Jewish settlement, was also impressed by his meetings with American Jews. But in contrast to Dayan, the experience caused him to reflect. Israeli policy would lead to anti-Semitism, some of his listeners had told him tearfully. What an irony, Weizman thought, if Israel, the sanctuary for persecuted Jews, should now cause Jews in other places to be persecuted.[90]

American-Jewish diffidence nonetheless had limits. Reluctant to stand tall against their government, American Jews were also unwilling to be a weapon against Israel—above all in public. Largely impervious to all save the most abstract Israeli landscapes, they could still respond at least to *Fiddler on the Roof.* Appealing for Israeli-U.S. partnership in a world of Soviet brutality and expansionism, summoning up visions of a postsocialist, entrepreneurial Israel, and inevitably recalling the Holocaust, Begin knew better than most what made American Jews resonate. Folk memories of the Russia from which so many came and nightly news clips of the ecumenical slaughter in a Lebanon once regarded as the region's prototypical "secular-democratic" state only reinforced his message.

Carter knew it too. "I told him that peace in the Middle East was in his hands, that he had a unique opportunity to either bring it into being or kill it," he noted after another acid meeting with Begin in 1978. The occasion was the thirtieth anniversary of Israeli independence. To honor it, the president had invited 200 rabbis to the White House; he found 1,200 people waiting at the gate. At a hastily improvised ceremony on the south lawn, the two men delivered what Carter remembered as "brief but somewhat emotional" speeches, and shook hands with every guest. While acknowledging "transient" differences to a titter from the audience, the president not only assured Israel of the continued and permanent support of the United States, he offered to create a commission for a U.S. memorial to victims of the Holocaust. But his efforts had "very little serious effect either in the Middle East or within our own country," he noted.[91]

Already vulnerable to historical memory and media image, the administration's strategy was only the more vulnerable to events themselves. There were credible cases to be made that the accretion of Soviet clients in Africa meant only a further burden for Moscow; that the recently negotiated Helsinki accords were a positive Western gain; that the Syrian presence in Lebanon was Asad's tar baby, and still another millstone around the neck of the PLO. Yet just as in 1970, when Palestinian activists declared war on the Rogers Plan by hijacking airliners, the promiscuous violence the PLO called "armed struggle" seemed only to vindicate Israeli intransigence.

On March 11, 1978, members of Fatah, the PLO's dominant component, landed south of Haifa. Their mission was to seize a Tel Aviv hotel and take tourists hostage to force the release of terrorists held from earlier incidents. In the ensuing chase and shoot-out, thirty-four Israelis were killed, most of them civilians, and seventy-four were wounded. Begin, whose approval ratings had declined from almost 80 percent in December to under 60 percent by mid-March, delayed a scheduled trip to Washington. Weizman returned from New York. Three days later, Israeli forces invaded Lebanon. Before the exercise was over, between ten and thirty thousand troops had reportedly been involved, anywhere from a hundred thousand to a quarter of a million people had been left homeless, and hundreds, perhaps even thousands of noncombatants had been killed, some by a local militia under the command of Major Saad Haddad, an Israeli client.

The outcome was something of a disappointment to Haddad, who had hoped to be allowed to join the battle, and to Maronite leaders in the North, who reportedly had hoped Israeli troops would continue toward Beirut and Syrian positions in the Bekaa Valley. But the Israelis were not yet prepared to fight Syria for the Christians. Knowing what to expect, most Palestinian guerrillas, of course, had already left with time to spare. A few days later, under pressure from the United States and reservations from Israel, the United Nations dispatched a peacekeeping force that the Soviets had obviously chosen not to veto, notwithstanding their liaison with the Syrians and ongoing dalliance with the PLO.

Not least in view of past speculations on the Litani as an Israeli-Lebanese border, and Israel's full-scale invasion of Lebanon in 1982, there was a variety of post facto interpretations to explain the ferocity of intervention. But almost irrespective of Israeli motives, the Carter administration was bound to respond. What set off alarms was not only what Washington saw as overreaction, and fear for its impact on Egypt, but the use of U.S. equipment, including the controversial cluster bombs, and fear for its impact on Congress. After Israeli withdrawal, some equipment actually remained in the custody of Haddad's militia. The Israeli claim of defensive use was barely acceptable, but transfer to proxies was a clear violation of the end-use provisions of the Arms Export Control Act. Impatient with Israeli denials and sensitive to congressional heat, Carter reportedly produced satellite photos to make his point, and Vance intervened in force. Begin removed the equipment just as he had removed the troops, but it still seemed to Vance that any possible Israeli accommodation on either the West Bank or the Palestinians had been just another casualty of the terrorist incident.[92]

Already badly wilted, the previous November's euphoria was an obvious casualty too. Sadat and Begin had stopped speaking directly after their turn-of-the-year meeting in Ismailia. Since then, their foreign ministers too had stalled. At a midsummer conference at Britain's Leeds Castle, Vance considered it significant that he had even persuaded the respective delegations to eat together.[93] Once again, Washington huddled for reassessment. "There was only one thing to do, as dismal and unpleasant as the prospect seemed," Carter concluded after a thorough review. "I would try to bring Sadat and Begin together for an extensive bargaining session with me."[94]

Once more, Vance set off for the Middle East, this time with handwritten notes from Carter, inviting Sadat, Begin, and their wives, to an open-ended summit at Camp David. Each was allowed a maximum of eight associates and advisors. Both accepted without apparent reservations. All three then set about to pick their delegations. The Israeli team was remarkable for its inclusion of the briskly pragmatic Avraham Tamir, the only active general on any delegation, and two legal advisors, including Attorney General Aharon Barak, who was to be one of the acknowledged heroes of the conference.[95] It was also notable for at least one omission, the relatively dovish Yadin, now deputy prime minister. Sadat leaned heavily on his foreign office. But in contrast to the contentious and egalitarian Israelis,[96] it was clear that he made the big decisions himself, if necessary, in splendid isolation.

The Carter team included Vance and Brzezinski, as well as their associates, but without need for formal congressional ratification, it was drawn entirely from the White House and State Department. Softened up by intimations of high risks if the stalemate continued, congressional leaders, with the exception of Sen. Henry Jackson, were nonetheless generally supportive. Still, there was a counterflow of warnings from people Carter described as "closest advisers and friends." Each, he noted, could invent a dozen plausible scenarios for failure.

Persuaded he could do something useful, aware of his need for success, and confident it was worth the effort, Carter dug in, becoming, as he later wrote, "as stubborn as at any other time I can remember." It was hard to think of any precedent for an equivalent presidential commitment. In 1905, Theodore Roosevelt had invited Russian and Japanese delegations to Portsmouth, New Hampshire, to negotiate an end to the Russo-Japanese War. His mediation had incidentally won him a Nobel Peace Prize, though, as he later conceded, it had also made him unpopular in Russia and Japan. But Roosevelt had kept to his estate on Long Island, and mediated from a distance. This, as Vance noted, was neither Carter's style nor strategy.[97]

Also in contrast to 1905, when it was hard to see that any obvious U.S. interest was riding on the outcome, the stakes in 1978 could hardly have been higher, not least for Carter himself. Of course, Begin was the most vulnerable to charges of obstructionism if the conference failed. He then risked backlash not only from Congress, American public opinion, perhaps even American Jews but from his colleagues Weizman and Dayan, who clearly wanted peace with Egypt. Still, he was probably the likeliest of the three principals to walk away without domestic damage. Sadat, in turn, would have fences to mend and debts to pay. Egypt's position would be difficult as ever. But as long as he brought an agreement with Carter, Sadat could afford to come home without one with Begin. For Carter, on the other hand, who had practically staked his presidency on Middle East peace, a break with Begin and agreement with Sadat were both losers. The precariousness of his domestic position could meanwhile be read in the weekly ratings. Only a year after the administration took office, approval had fallen from 77 percent to circa 50 percent.[98]

In August 1978, Vance, Atherton, Quandt, and Saunders withdrew to W. Averell Harriman's Virginia estate to prepare strategy memos, briefing papers, and personality profiles for every contingency. A legendary consumer, the president then hauled the documents along on a family fishing vacation in Wyoming. Their eyes fixed on the Palestinian deadlock, members of the briefing team were little concerned with the Sinai as such. On the other hand, as one paper even confirmed by its title, they regarded "The Sinai/West Bank Relationship" as "The Pivotal Issue." The best that could be managed, Vance believed, was a breach in the negotiating impasse that would bring in Jordan, let the foreign ministers negotiate, and establish the basis for a Sinai agreement. Carter was struck by his advisors' bureaucratic caution. Although he was admittedly uncertain how to get there, his own goal was "a written agreement for peace between Egypt and Israel with an agenda for implementation of its terms during the succeeding months." Given the risk of failure and embarrassment the administration confronted already, he thought there was little to lose by aiming for success.[99]

By the time Carter returned to Washington, it was agreed that the conference would meet for three days—or "as long as a week if we were making good progress"; that Mondale would take charge in the president's absence; that every effort would be taken to maximize physical well-being and minimize distraction; and that issues, so far as possible, would be confronted face to face. For good measure, Carter also checked in with Ed Sanders, the latest White House liaison with the Jewish community, and packed an annotated Bible, "which I predicted—accurately, as it turned out—would be needed in my discussions with Prime Minister Begin."[100]

As the meeting approached, Carter, characteristically, made lists. The first consisted of issues seemingly decided already, for example, that Jerusalem would not be redivided, Israeli access to the Suez Canal, termination of Egypt's economic boycott and the state of war, inclusion of Jordan and the Palestinians in future negotiations, phased implementation of any agreements, and an Israeli security presence on the West Bank. A second consisted of issues believed partially resolved but still contested, such as a common understanding of Resolution 242; the extent of normal relations between Egypt and Israel; the political status of the Palestinians, given the negotiators' common opposition to a Palestinian state; and Israel's declared, but ambiguous, willingness to end military rule in the West Bank and Gaza. That left the unqualified problems, including dismantlement of Israeli settlements on Egyptian soil, a ban on new settlements anywhere, application of Resolution 242 to the West Bank, a Palestinian role in future negotiations, an Arab role in Jerusalem, and the nature of any final agreement. From there on, Carter recalled, he was reminded of how men are believed to feel before going into battle, or how he and his submarine shipmates used to feel before putting out to sea.[101]

In the days that followed, working days of epic length save for formal accommodation of the Jewish Sabbath, the principals struggled with themselves and one another in a social landscape as self-contained as an ocean liner and as assertively American as Carter could make it. To minimize leaks, Carter's press secretary, Jody Powell, spoke for all three delegations. But to his exasperation, it was agreed that nothing of substance would be said until the meeting ended.[102]

Meanwhile, the delegations schemed, bargained, speculated, and worried. Though Mrs. Sadat was in Paris, both Carter and Begin brought their wives, and Carter brought his daughter. When it was over, the participants remembered billiards, tennis, bicycles, forest walks, and prayer, some warmly, some ambivalently. There had been endless movies for those with time to watch them; universally admired kabobs and shashlik from the Filipino mess attendants; and grimly competitive chess between Begin and Brzezinski, with differing versions of who won. There had also been two entertainments, both improbably martial. The first, a "silent drill" by an elaborately trained marine contingent, made Dayan uncomfortable. The other was a slightly ambiguous tour of the Gettysburg battlefield, that had the same effect.[103] Throughout, Carter opted for tennis shorts and jeans, Sadat for casual elegance. Apparently for reasons of principle, only Begin consistently wore a tie.[104]

As Carter was more poignantly aware than most, the outcome fell short not only of the generous hopes his administration had once brought to office but even its scaled-down expectations. Yet the participants' memoirs confirm their awareness of making history and Carter's and Quandt's day-by-day accounts can even be read as a kind of thirteen-day Genesis, in which, to be sure, it was long after the first day before there were signs of light. Still, in the end, most of the conferees found the outcome good, and even the exception, Egypt's Foreign Minister Mohamed Ibrahim Kamel, who submitted his resignation at the end of the twelfth day,[105] conveyed a sense of presence at a creation.

From its beginning on September 5, as Quandt noted, the conference was a kind of reprise of the previous eighteen months. But it was now open-ended, the tempo was drastically accelerated, and the carefully created external environment, which buffered the distractions and temptations of domestic politics, also increased the impact of the participants on one another. The one exception, ironically, was the two principals on whose account the exercise had been arranged. "Those of us who were at Camp David really got to know one another," Carter was to note, "that is, everyone except Begin and Sadat."[106]

Soon after arrival, Begin met Carter. The next morning, Sadat conferred with him too. That afternoon Sadat met Begin in Carter's presence, but it was already clear that the next day would be difficult. That night, Carter, watched *Shane,* the classic movie western, featuring Alan Ladd as a kind of mediator in white buckskins.[107] On Thursday, the conference's third day, Sadat and Begin met twice for the kind of discussions diplomatic communiqués refer to as frank and open. The third-day meetings were their last until the conference ended. Sadat, in fact, had almost left on day eleven. Dispatched to the scene by a white-faced Vance, Carter had even dressed for the occasion, he told Brzezinski, before asking him to change his mind. Leaving now would not only wreck the peace effort and Egyptian-U.S. relationship, he reportedly told Sadat. It would also finish off his presidency and end their friendship.[108]

The contested issues were hardly a surprise. But the Americans were clearly startled by Israel's determination to keep the Sinai settlements and air bases, just in case. Although Begin promised "full autonomy" in the West Bank and Gaza, there was a serious question of what he meant. The Israeli interpretation of Resolution 242 was another obvious difference. The "inadmissibility of acquisition of territory by war" was a good principle, Begin agreed, but what if the war had been defensive, and the territories in question were acquired for defense?[109]

Sadat's opener was another shocker. Not only did it call for full Israeli withdrawal, dismantlement of settlements, and transfer of Gaza and the West Bank to Egypt and Jordan, as necessary conditions of any agreement, it demanded a ban on nuclear weapons, return or compensation of Palestinian refugees, and indemnification of Egypt for oil and war damage. To Carter's relief, Sadat then spelled out his fallback positions, but he insisted that Begin first reply to the Egyptian terms. As Carter anticipated, the Israelis were stunned and infuriated, and the next day's confrontations left him in a quandary. By evening of the third day, a member of the Israeli delegation had already approached Quandt to get across to Carter how important it was to keep Begin and Sadat apart.[110]

From here, it was clear that both the U.S. role and the influence of Begin's colleagues would be crucial to a successful outcome. Sadat, Carter noted, realized early that it was good to be on the president's side, leaving Begin in the cold. Now Begin too was catching on. "I will never personally recommend that the settlements in the

Sinai be dismantled," he told Carter on day four. A delighted Carter registered the shift: "never recommend" was not inalterable opposition to removal. Ignoring Begin's reservations, Carter then announced a new procedure. The Americans would prepare their own proposal, and present it to both sides. Carter would then negotiate the best possible compromise between them. Sadat agreed. Any reasonable proposal was fine with him, he said, providing it respected the land and sovereignty of the Golan and Sinai.[111]

By the fourth night, Saunders was at work on the first of twenty-three versions of what was eventually to be a two-part document. At this point, Israeli-U.S. bargaining began in earnest, and the Egyptians grew steadily grimmer. Returning from a morning bike ride early on day eight, Carter saw Sadat on his front porch in a heated exchange with his advisors. The Israeli strategy, the Americans plausibly inferred, was classical *do ut des.* They would dig in on the West Bank, Gaza, and the Palestinian issues, then come around on the Sinai, contingent on the outcome. Meanwhile, the Americans huffed and puffed at both Egyptian and Israeli positions on settlements, autonomy, Jerusalem, even the definition of *Palestinian.* "Bilateral issues between Egypt and Israel," Vance noted, "seemed relatively simple by comparison."[112]

On day nine, even the generally sanguine Carter briefly lost his poise after meeting almost eleven hours with Barak and Osama el-Baz, Egypt's under secretary of foreign affairs. The procedure—intense direct negotiation between a head of state, who incidentally happened to be president of the world's supermost superpower, and two technical experts, each charged with selling the product post facto to his respective political master—was a phenomenon in itself. In an apparent reversal of policy, el-Baz had then unexpectedly denied Israel's right to be a party to decisions on refugees entering the West Bank. But under pressure from Carter, he conceded the idea was his own. Carter demanded to see Sadat. Though it was still relatively early, lights were on in the Egyptian cabin, and Sadat was known for working late, the Egyptians replied that he had gone to bed, leaving instructions not to be awakened. Normally a sound sleeper, Carter woke abruptly at 4:00 A.M., called Brzezinski and the Secret Service, and ordered reinforced security around Sadat's cabin.[113]

The next day, to Carter's vast relief, Sadat turned up as usual, but the negotiations seemed to have reached full deadlock. That morning there was a bruising confrontation between Dayan and Sadat over Israeli settlements in the Sinai. That evening there was another between Vance and Begin over the latest U.S. formula on Jerusalem and the Palestinians. Ordinarily among the most self-controlled of men, even Vance turned red, waved his arms, and raised his voice, Dayan remembered.[114]

With claustrophobia setting in, Carter now faced the classic choice of whether to aim high and miss, or take his chances on the art of the possible. Two big issues remained: total Israeli evacuation of the Sinai, and the future of the West Bank and Gaza. Theoretically, as Quandt noted, Carter could hold firm on both. He could then let the conference fail, report to Congress and the nation on what had and could have been accomplished, and try to turn the heat on Begin. The alternative was to try to solve one issue at the expense of the other, and so end up with an agreement.[115]

Carter asked Quandt to draft a fall-back speech, just in case. But he also invited a last best effort from Sadat and Begin, and set a deadline. Sinai was the first problem to yield to the president's timetable. At Weizman's suggestion, Vance and Secretary of Defense Harold Brown agreed that the United States would advance Israel $3 billion in concessional loans to replace the Sinai airfields with new bases in the Negev. With Dayan about to leave, Tamir then proposed to brief Sharon, who, in turn, would encourage Begin to evacuate the Sinai settlements.[116] Sharon agreed to call. Soon afterward, Begin grimly agreed to waive party discipline and submit the question to the Knesset within two weeks in the form that Carter demanded. To Weizman's bemusement, Begin yielded again on "legitimate rights of the Palestinian people." Considering that "legitimate" derived from the Latin *lex,* he reflected, illegitimate rights were a contradiction in terms. There was a last furious confrontation over Jerusalem, resolved by an exchange of letters, confirming established positions.[117]

That still left the question of settlements in the West Bank. Glazed with fatigue, Carter was convinced he had got Begin to suspend settlement, contingent henceforth on agreement between the parties. He therefore failed to react the next day when Begin produced a statement, suspending it for only three months.[118] Instead, he turned to Sadat, agreeing that Begin would confirm the presumed understanding post facto.[119] Agreement in hand, the principals then returned to Washington to preempt the network season openers with the signing ceremony. It became clear only some days later to what extent the understanding had been a misunderstanding, but by now it was too late to do anything about it. "If the U.S. President wanted clear and specific commitments from us, he should have . . . tried to get them before the signing," Dayan remembered testily. "[H]e could not now blame us but only himself."[120]

The next evening, Carter appeared before a joint session of Congress, with Sadat and Begin conspicuously in tow. His speech included tributes to both men and to Vance, as well as citations from the 85th Psalm and the Sermon on the Mount. There were fourteen interruptions for applause. But there was no applause for either of two explications of how the agreement could contribute to solution of the Palestinian problem.[121] At a White House reception for American-Jewish leaders, Carter was nonetheless warmly congratulated by the guests. Their warmth was all the more welcome for being so rare, he recalled.[122]

Later, Dayan was to charge the Americans with superficial understanding of the Middle East, and Carter noted how Begin was already savaging their historic agreement. "Begin wanted to keep two things: the peace with Egypt—and the West Bank," he remembered.[123] This, in fact, was true. Yet both Israelis and Americans, each for their own reasons, had cause to point with pride. The accords, as Vance argued, opened the way to a watershed peace between Israel and Egypt. Despite the many issues still awaiting resolution, the accords also caused the Israelis to admit, at least, that there was a Palestinian problem, and established a process for addressing it.

According to the new agreement, negotiations on "the Palestinian problem in all its aspects" were supposed to take place within three years, on the basis of Resolution 242 "in all its parts." After a five-year transitional period, these were then to "determine the final status of the West Bank and Gaza and its relationship with its neighbors." Jordan too was invited to accede to the accords, and Palestinians "as mutually agreed" were to be allowed to join the Jordanian delegation.

In the aftermath, Begin stayed behind to present his own version of the agreement to American audiences. Unsurprisingly, he minimized those elements that either the Jordanians or Palestinians might have seen as bluffs waiting to be called. Meanwhile, Dayan and Weizman returned directly to Israel to report to their colleagues. Holding his ground against all comers at a marathon cabinet meeting a few days later, Begin won 11–2. Before coherent opposition could form, he then reconvened the Knesset for what turned out to be a seventeen-hour debate.

Deputies sat tight as Dayan challenged critics to offer a better alternative. But despite fears that Egyptian-Israeli agreement could set a precedent for the West Bank, and anxieties that Camp David was a first step toward Palestinian statehood, they accepted the accords, and agreed, contingent on satisfactory peace terms, to evacuate the Sinai settlements. The majority was 84–19, with seventeen abstentions. Only forty-seven of the eighty-four yeas came from government deputies; the nays, including Moshe Arens, the later defense and foreign minister, and abstentions, including Yitzhak Shamir, the later prime minister, came almost entirely from the prime minister's Herut and the National Religious party.[124]

Despite U.S. hopes of finishing by Christmas, and even election day, 1978, delivery of an Israeli-Egyptian peace treaty took another six months, and intermittently threatened to break down altogether. Things began bravely enough. In the afterglow of Camp David, the State Department prepared a U.S. draft, the procedure that worked so well before. On October 12, Israelis and Egyptians returned to Washington with Camp David veterans—including Dayan; Weizman; Boutros Ghali, later U.N. Secretary General and then Egypt's minister of state for foreign affairs; and El-Baz—well represented in each delegation. Carter received them *ex officio* at the White House before dispatching them to Blair House across the street, where Vance and Atherton took charge.

It was plain from the beginning that there would be trouble on two fronts. One was the conjunction of Israeli-Egyptian and Israeli-Palestinian issues. The other was "priority of obligations," that is, whether a treaty with Israel superseded existing Egyptian commitments to Arab states. A seemingly technical problem, it was to pursue negotiators for months till they finally reached agreement in a virtuoso compromise. The final version recalled Dr. Doolittle's pushmi-pullyu. "The parties undertake to fulfill in good faith their obligations under this Treaty, without regard to action or inaction of any other party, and independently of any instrument external to this Treaty," declared Article VI(2). "It is agreed by the Parties that there is no assertion that this Treaty prevails over other Treaties or agreements or that other Treaties or agreements prevail over this Treaty," declared the Agreed Minute appended to it.[125]

By late October, the negotiators seemed nonetheless to have reached substantial agreement, at least on most other Israeli-Egyptian issues.[126] Yet on closer inspection, there was less to this too than met the eye. It was true, for example, that the negotiators had made progress on—or at least successfully fudged—some basic issues, in part with the help of an increasingly frazzled Carter. The president was even willing to listen, if not respond, to an Israeli request for aid in moving bases—though he made it emphatically clear that he would not recommend aid for liquidating settlements he considered illegal in the first place.[127] It was also true that the negotiators had found a common language scarcely imaginable a year before. But selling the product at home was another matter, not least for the Americans, whose support was as crucial as ever. There, three rather different but inevitably complementary factors stood in the way like so many angels with flaming swords. One was the inherent recalcitrance of the issues; the second, external circumstances; the third, domestic politics.

For Sadat, who had already lost two foreign ministers, the peace process meant not only trouble with Egypt's political class but potential isolation from the Arab world, with incalculable political and economic consequences. Without oil, timber, minerals, or industrial base, with fifty million citizens already crowded into 4 percent of its land mass, and over a million new births per year, Egypt depended on Saudi subsidies and remittances from vulnerable *Gastarbeiter*. Like the accrued cost of five wars, the handout economy too was part of Nasser's legacy. The peace offensive was intended from the start to yield a peace dividend. But an all-too-separate peace was inherently counterproductive. On November 5, an Arab summit in Baghdad attacked Camp David, and threatened to move the Arab League offices from Cairo if Egypt and Israel concluded peace. It then sent a delegation to Sadat, who refused to receive them.

Lebanon was already a black hole, whose dense hot hatreds drew their energy from the entire region. By now, Iran too had begun to smolder. On the fourth day of Camp David, the shah's police shot hundreds—perhaps even thousands—of demonstrators. The slaughter was later recalled as the "Black Monday" of a revolution soon felt around the world. By the end of 1978, the Gaza–West Bank linkage seemed even more crucial than before to Sadat's credibility, both at home and abroad. Was it in Israel's interest to see Egypt isolated, and the Gulf states replace Egyptian *Gastarbeiter* with Koreans and Pakistanis? Mustafa Khalil, Egypt's new foreign minister, asked Dayan in Brussels in late December. "Priority of obligations" was crucial too. Was it not in the interest of Israel—and of the United States—that Egypt become, and remain, allied with moderate Arab states?

What if Syria attacked Israel on the Golan? Dayan inquired. Egypt would support Syria, Khalil replied, but not fight. To Dayan, such a "golden mean whereby Egypt could both remain in the Arab anti-Israel camp and yet sign a peace treaty with us" seemed about as likely as squaring the circle—though this was no reason not to try it, he added.[128] In the event, the Egyptians proved as good as their word. Only weeks after evacuating the last Sinai settlement in 1982, Israel invaded Lebanon, where it confronted a deeply ambivalent Syria. Yet Egypt held firm, despite Sadat's assassination less than a year before.

On the other hand, the Israeli position was hardly less contradictory. It could be argued, as many Israelis did argue, that civil war in Lebanon, revolution in Iran, anxiety in Egypt, vulnerability in the Gulf, and ambivalence in Washington were all reasons to push for peace while the going was good—and without making things harder for Sadat and Carter. Yet there were plenty of Israelis as ready to argue the contrary. As Jews, Sharon told Vance in December, Israelis owed nothing to anybody.[129] Was Sadat in trouble? All the more reason to drive a tough deal with him, or avoid one altogether. Was the United States in danger of being crowded from the region? All the more reason to support Israel as its only ally.[130] Did Egypt need Saudi or Jordanian, let alone Syrian or Palestinian, support? All the more reason to separate an Israeli-Egyptian treaty from the West Bank and Gaza, rather than let other Arabs hold it hostage.

For Israelis in general, the negotiations were a moment of truth, and an exercise in self-discovery. Dayan recalled a revealing meeting in Vance's office in the otherwise deserted State Department on Armistice Day night 1978. What was on his mind, the secretary explained, was not just another working session but history. If the negotiators failed, future generations would blame them. As so often, Dayan sat silent. It was U.S. policy that caused the impasse, he thought to himself. Let the United States solve it. Then Barak spoke up. Only a few weeks before, he had trumped the president of the United States on "priority of obligations" by slipping off to New Haven to confer with the flower of Yale Law School, including Eugene Rostow, its former dean and a former under secretary of state. He returned with a reading that vindicated the Israeli position. Yet now, to the apparent surprise of his colleagues, it was Barak who informed them that they "would neither be understood nor forgiven" if they failed to reach agreement "because of a few words in a clause."[131]

Yet for Begin, the peace process meant not only a state of cold war with his closest peers but even with himself. He had not become prime minister, he might have paraphrased Churchill, in order to liquidate the Israeli empire. In any case, if there were to be concessions, the vote on Camp David was reason to make sure his cabinet shared the lumps. Besides, just as his own readings of Camp David predictably infuriated the White House, U.S. readings, intended to massage Hussein and the Palestinians, predictably alarmed Israelis.

That the American signals also failed to reach their goal was both ironic and familiar. In fact, according to Carter, Arafat had reportedly signaled the Saudis, asking that Hussein represent the Palestinians in the Camp David process. "But none of the Arabs was willing to move . . . unless Arafat was willing to take the responsibility himself—and he chose not to," Carter added.[132] Irrespective of effect, the U.S. signals nonetheless confirmed the Israelis' worst suspicions. Weizman and especially Dayan felt the consequences as far away as Washington. Lifelong hawks of purest pedigree and veterans of every war since independence, they were now under pressure from their colleagues in Jerusalem to prove they were not incurable doves.

In late October, Zevulun Hammer, Begin's education minister and a leader of the National Religious party, even threatened to quit the government. With Egyptians and Americans on one flank, and his colleagues on another, Dayan pulled off yet another feat of tactical virtuosity, getting Begin to co-opt Barak again for the negotiating team. But he also proposed adding to the West Bank settlements, not least as a signal to the Americans. They would be angry, he noted, but that was the point. "I have to tell you with gravest concern and regret that taking this step at this time will have the most serious consequences for our relationship," Carter replied in his own hand. The next day, the Nobel committee declared Begin and Sadat, but not Carter, winners of that year's peace prize.[133]

As Begin knew as well as anyone, the U.S. political calendar was now imposing its own logic. Within a week, the prime minister was in New York, demanding revisions the Americans knew Cairo would never accept. He then, disarmingly, requested a substantial loan, repayable at 2–4 percent over twenty-five years. The next day, both Carter and Begin dutifully appeared together at a New York fundraiser where they shook hands and said hello in the presence of witnesses. As wails of consternation echoed back from the Israeli finance ministry, Dayan was then obliged to report to Vance that what the Israelis had really requested was a grant. At a staff meeting November 8, Carter counted at least eight deviations between his and Begin's understanding of Camp David. If all the Israelis wanted was a separate peace, a free hand in the West Bank, and U.S. money, Brzezinski favored hanging tough. According to the national security advisor, Carter first accused him of brutal frankness and oversimplification. He then agreed with him.[134]

By now, Carter too was in heavy weather. Only a day after the negotiators convened at Blair House, the administration's energy bill had cleared the House by a single, Republican, vote, 207–206. The deepening turmoil in Iran had already pushed spot-market oil prices 20 percent above OPEC levels, while Americans refused to cut imports, helping drive prices still higher.[135]

The rest of the foreign policy agenda was no help either. The Panama Canal treaty was a victory, but hardly a crowd pleaser in a country turning grim and mean under the impact of rising prices and foreign frustrations. Normal relations with China were thirty years overdue, but neither politically nor morally easy after a thirty-year liaison with Taiwan. Another legacy of previous administrations, the strategic arms talks, too were red meat for the nation's hawks. Carter's evident sympathy with Egyptian positions, and his audible frustration with Begin hardly made his situation easier. In mid-December 1978, thirty-three of the thirty-six American Jews who had urged moderation on Begin in April now wrote Carter that they found his position unacceptable.[136] "By late 1978, with the congressional elections near and with the Presidential season gradually beginning," Mondale already favored "a rather passive U.S. posture," Brzezinski noted. Just as Rabin had once wanted Nixon to win, he concluded, Begin wanted Carter to lose.[137]

Yet, as Quandt acknowledged, the last thing anybody needed was a new confrontation, for example over his own proposal to cut U.S. aid for each new Israeli settlement.[138] By now, the administration had virtually given up on Lebanon. Totally unanticipated, Iran's revolution too was a total bafflement. With the region in general nearly out of control, and himself as badly in need of success as Sadat, Carter reached a lonely decision as he had the previous summer. After one more tough meeting with Begin in early March 1979, he decided to intervene again in person, but in Egypt and Israel, not at home. "My proposal was an act of desperation," he candidly acknowledged.[139] Once more, the Americans revised their text, already garnished with a trail of interpretive codicils. This time the Israeli cabinet accepted it.

Welcomed in the grand manner in Egypt on March 7, the U.S. delegation was received with full but icy honors in Israel three days later. Begin refused to be rushed. Instead, he demonstratively took Carter to the Holocaust memorial, Yad vaShem, and the graves of Herzl and Jabotinsky, before once more going over the text with the intensity of a literary critic. Within a day of arrival, the whole U.S. delegation—Carter, Vance, Brown, Brzezinski, Atherton, Saunders, Quandt, and Ambassador Samuel Lewis—found itself thumbing in thesauruses and dictionaries.[140] That night, after a joyless banquet in the Knesset and a token performance by Isaac Stern, the cabinet convened until 5:30 A.M. After meeting inconclusively the next day with the cabinet, Carter then appeared with Begin at an uproarious special session of the Knesset, where Vance was appalled, Dayan embarrassed, and Begin confided to Carter his pride in "this display of democracy at work."[141] By late afternoon, a deeply disappointed Carter was ready to go home with no further meetings scheduled. Powell, hedging preemptively at his evening briefings, encouraged correspondents to do the same.

Dayan, the strategist, had meanwhile called Vance, the lawyer. There were still two issues waiting to be settled. One was Egypt's demand for early elections and a special status in Gaza. The Egyptians could make their case at the autonomy talks, Dayan argued. With normalization, they could also enter Gaza just as Israelis could visit Cairo. The other problem was Sinai oil. Israel wanted an explicit stipulation of its right to buy from Egypt, and of assured U.S. delivery, if all else failed. Begin and Carter accepted both proposals.[142] As Carter confirmed the next day from Cairo, they were also fine with Sadat.

So suddenly had things changed that reporters felt misled. Carter also resented charges that the treaties had been "'bought' at a price of $10 to $20 billion." But years later, Seymour Hersh reported plausibly that Carter had decided in March to allow Israeli's access to the high-resolution, real-time satellite photos that were the glory of U.S. intelligence. In addition, as part of a 1979 supplementary military aid package proposed in May, Secretary of Defense Harold Brown announced $3 billion in military aid for Israel, including $800 million to replace the Sinai air bases. Over three months that summer, letters of offer were also issued or accepted on $900 million worth of weapons and systems; F-16 deliveries were accelerated; and there were further commitments, inconceivable ten years earlier, of cooperative R&D.[143]

On March 14, the Israeli cabinet approved the treaty, including nine main articles, three annexes, and a preamble that demonstratively hitched it to Camp David and Resolutions 242 and 338.[144] On March 20, after sixteen hours of debate, the Knesset ratified it too by 95–18. On March 26, the treaty and an Israeli-U.S. memorandum of understanding were then signed in Washington, the former, though not the latter, in the presence of some 1,600 invited guests. Among them were Weizman's son, the victim of an Egyptian bullet in 1970, and Sadat's son. They embraced. Carter found the ceremony "very satisfactory," even "thrilling." Addressed as "Moishe" by the Jews and "General" by the non-Jews, Dayan found it hot and noisy. Bored and tired, he drifted off early for his hotel.[145] Two years later, Israelis again went to the polls and Begin formed a new cabinet. But this time, neither the saturnine Dayan nor the ebullient Weizman were in it, and Carter too had returned involuntarily to private life.

10

Perpetuum Stabile?

By now, events and Menahem Begin too were in the saddle, and gravity was taking over. Successive presidential envoys did their best to keep things moving Carter's way—or at least to cushion the blow if things went wrong.[1] The first, Robert Strauss, a former chairman of the Democratic National Committee, who was later to become U.S. ambassador to the Soviet Union under a Republican president, was renowned as a master of political ways and means. The second, Sol Linowitz, had recently piloted the Panama Canal treaties into port after a voyage begun under Lyndon Johnson. It was hardly an accident that both men were Jews, Democrats, and highly regarded in Washington, but these were qualities that now cut little ice in Jerusalem. On the contrary, both men's frustrations were just a measure of the growing distance not only between Jerusalem and Washington but within Jerusalem itself. Although Palestinian autonomy was still high priority in Washington, peace for Begin's men began and ended with Egypt. More and more impatient with his government's inertia, Moshe Dayan resigned as foreign minister in October 1979. He was succeeded by the hard-line Yitzhak Shamir. A half year later, an equally frustrated Ezer Weizman left the Defense Ministry, where Begin himself replaced him. Before the year was over, he was then thrown out of Herut after supporting a close no-confidence motion on economic policy.

Each in their respective ways, Israel and Egypt appeared to have taken all the chances they chose to take before Israel's scheduled departure from the Sinai on April 25, 1982. With both parties resolved to haul their prize ashore, Egypt was neither prepared nor probably able to lean on Jordan or the Palestinians but was intent within its limits on keeping Israel sweet. Meanwhile, as both Begin and Carter knew full well, electoral clocks were running in both their countries. Begin, who had presumably got all he wanted from Camp David, had no further cause to upset domestic partners. Carter had every reason to avoid upsetting domestic constituents.

And yet, as the president noted ruefully, "there seemed to be no way I could stay out of Middle East affairs."[2] Even the sudden embarrassment and resignation of Andrew Young in August 1979 was an example of what made abstinence impossible. A veteran of the civil rights movement and a former U.S. representative, Young was the administration's ambassador to the United Nations. In this capacity, he had recently talked with Ibrahim Terzi, the PLO observer at the United Nations, in apparent violation of U.S. policy. He had also reported as much to

Yehuda Blum, the Israeli ambassador to the United Nations, and the Israelis tipped off *Newsweek.*

What compounded Young's offense was that he seemed to have deliberately misled the State Department, already reported unhappy with his conduct in office. Despite his efforts to minimize the shock, his resignation was seen almost automatically as a confrontation between blacks and Jews, and therefore bad news for an administration that needed the votes of both. Though he really had been under Jewish fire, Jewish organizations were defensive. Not only had Young been a charter member of Black Americans for Support of Israel (BASIC), he had cosponsored a House resolution calling for reconsideration of U.S. membership if the United Nations excluded Israel. He had also criticized PLO terrorism and rejection of Resolution 242.

Expressions of concern and solidarity soon came pouring in from a black community with its own frustrations and its own need to stand up and be counted. In the aftermath of the resignation, various black leaders toured the Middle East. To Dayan's regret, Begin refused so much as to see the Reverend Jesse Jackson. On the other hand, Jackson was welcomed enthusiastically by the PLO in Beirut, where the reception included not only embraces and a bagpipe band but even the now obligatory chorus of "We Shall Overcome."[3] According to a Lou Harris poll, at least 40 percent of black respondents saw Young as a victim of both Jewish and Israeli pressures. Though a bare majority of blacks indicated more sympathy for Israel than the PLO, two-thirds of them, compared to one-third of whites, also agreed that Young had been right to talk to Terzi.[4]

A further triumph of inadvertence followed in early March. For neither the first nor last time, the issue was Jerusalem, this time in the context of a new Security Council resolution condemning Israeli settlements in the Occupied Territories. Unsurprisingly, the Israelis were passionately opposed. Consistent with previous policy, the president opted for abstention. But Cyrus Vance and Donald McHenry, Young's successor, favored a positive vote, providing the offending passages were amended to omit Jerusalem. Understanding this condition to be met, Vance appealed to Carter, who let him instruct McHenry accordingly. Minus a U.S. veto, the resolution passed unopposed. But it was soon discovered that six references to Jerusalem had survived the drafting process, that the Israelis were irate, and that the administration was once again in trouble. After a long night meeting with Vice President Walter Mondale, Robert Strauss, and Hamilton Jordan, Carter's principal aide, a mortified Vance agreed to retract the vote. It was then left to Carter to explain away the error, and affirm that the U.S. position was unchanged. This seemed only to compound error with irresolution. The impact was immediately visible in voter surveys that neither a flying squad of cabinet-level Jewish surrogates nor broadsides of television spots with reminiscences of Camp David could correct. When the votes were counted in the New York Democratic primary a few weeks later, the challenger, Senator Edward Kennedy, had swamped the president by a margin of nearly three to two. Carter was unflinchingly explicit in linking both New York and a collateral rout in Connecticut to the bungled vote on Jerusalem.[5] But these were only symptoms.

The real problems were specific to both the times and a region where flocks of postwar chickens were coming home to roost.[6] Iran alone was an open-ended disaster. A fervid brew of real grievance and indigenous psychodrama, its revolution had become the most baffling in memory. It was only another irony that "the Great Satan," as Tehran now called the United States, was personified by the most sincerely religious president in memory.

Anti-American, anti-Western, anticommunist, antisecular and fervently anti-Zionist, revolutionary Iran not only challenged both superpowers, it rattled the region and shook the world. With Israel, Arab kings, and clients in general looking to Washington for cues, Americans had two theoretical choices. They could stand by a longtime client with the usual ineffectual appeal for reforms. Or they could deal as best they could with the winners. In the event, neither course showed much promise. Unable, and at root unwilling, to save a shah identified with the United States since the 1940s, official Washington was equally hard put to find a viable alternative or a credible interlocutor among the shah's successors.

Like China in the 1940s, Cuba in the 1950s, and Vietnam in recent memory, the collapse of so visible a client was a symbolic El Dorado for the administration's many critics. But it was the ill-advised, if innocently intended, decision to allow the shah into the country for medical treatment that flung the door wide open to Nemesis. On November 4, 1979, a few days after his arrival in New York, demonstrators in Tehran overran the U.S. embassy, and seized the last seventy-five representatives of what had once been a staff of eleven hundred. It would be Inauguration Day 1981 before the bulk of the hostages would be released, and then under circumstances that still smelled odd a decade later.[7]

With the eyes of the world, and certainly the country, upon it, the administration again faced two choices. If only for the sake of global credibility, it could come out swinging. Not least for the sake of the hostages, it could also impose economic sanctions while reserving further action. The chosen course, involving frozen assets, rhetorical forbearance, conspicuous solicitude for hostage families, high-level contingency planning, endless negotiations, fierce publicity, an abortive rescue attempt, and, above all, high-profile presidential involvement, had elements of both. But seen from among the ubiquitous yellow ribbons that bloomed spontaneously around the country, administration handling of the hostage crisis seemed only one more confirmation of what seemed in turn its intrinsic haplessness.

The Soviet invasion of Afghanistan on December 27 only complicated things again. Like earlier Soviet interventions in Czechoslovakia, Hungary, and East Germany, it was arguable that this one, too, was limited both in scale and purpose. There was also evidence that the Soviets tried to say so.[8] Yet it was equally true that Afghanistan was not now, and had never been, an acknowledged member of the Soviet bloc, and that Moscow's claims of fraternal support were strikingly disingenuous, even by prevailing standards. The first such exercise since World War II in which Soviet troops had crossed borders to change, and not maintain, the status quo, the invasion awakened historical memories of the Eastern Question, warmwater ports, the Thin Red Line, the Great Game, and the Khyber Pass. Carter replied with a limited—and unpopular—grain embargo and a symbolic boycott of the summer Olympics in Moscow. Like three postwar presidents before him, he also issued a doctrine. At once a reminiscence of Eisenhower's Doctrine, a reaffirmation of Truman's, and a qualified revision of Nixon's, the Carter Doctrine reserved strategic initiative to the United States in the event of an "attempt by any outside force to gain control of the Persian Gulf region . . . . ."[9]

Yet for a White House held hostage by Shi'ite mullahs and an administration just weeks from the Iowa caucuses, virtually any course now seemed a loser.[10] As seen from Riyadh, Jerusalem, and even Europe, looking the other way could be seen as ineptitude or capitulation. But intervention was hardly more attractive. Not only could it be regarded as the moral equivalent, and therefore a kind of post facto ratification, of the Soviet action in Afghanistan; it could also be seen by agitated Moslems as further evidence that the superpowers were interchangeable when it came to invading their territory. There was also the further risk that, with communist clients active again in Iran, the Soviets might even exploit U.S. intervention there for an intervention of their own.

For a nation torn once again between the presumptive lessons of Munich and the presumptive lessons of Vietnam, the presidential campaign tended increasingly to become a kind of plebiscite on the president himself. As always, the impact of foreign policy was debatable. The Iraqi invasion of Iran on September 22, 1980, was a test case. In the aftermath of the election, White House aides conceded wistfully, they had expected the combination of war and energy crunch to refocus the campaign on foreign policy, with the usual advantage to the incumbent. Sure enough, even the hint of a hostage release left deep marks on the Wisconsin primary, and Republicans admitted their fear of an "October surprise."[11]

Yet, in fact, the Gulf war scarcely caused a ripple.[12] It was also hard to gainsay the impact of Reagan's peroration, perhaps the most memorable moment of the campaign, at the candidates' debate in Cleveland. "Are you better off than you were four years ago?" he asked. "Is it easier for you to go and buy things . . . ? Is there more or less unemployment . . .? Is America as respected throughout the world as it was? Do you feel that our security is as safe, that we're as strong as we were four years ago?" It was revealing enough of the nation's mood that opinion makers reacted with smirks, not sympathy, when Carter referred to his daughter's concern about nuclear weapons.[13]

Though hard to read as a secular mandate for Reagan, the 51–41 outcome, with 7 percent for the third candidate, John Anderson, was certainly a thumping defeat for Carter. Liberals yearned for a renascent liberal, hawks for an ascendant hawk. A qualified combination of liberal *and* hawk, Jewish voters were marginal but interesting, both to the candidates and the outcome. It was clear from Kennedy's appearance at a suburban New Jersey synagogue in May 1980 that a large and establishmentarian Reform Jewish audience still yearned to vote for him. Presumably for their own reasons, as well as those that put off other people, Jews also avoided John Connally, the free-spending Democrat turned Republican, after the former Texas governor and secretary of the treasury proposed a land-for-peace package in a speech in Philadelphia in October 1979.[14]

Yet in contrast to earlier campaigns, most Republicans made a serious effort to attract Jews, as did Anderson, a former Republican U.S. congressman from northern Illinois who had once favored writing Christianity into the Constitution. Despite the rather substantial differences of priority and purpose that were to distinguish the new administration from its predecessor, emphatic support for Israel was common to both major campaigns, with only differences of nuance. Arguably, Reagan's denial that West Bank settlements were illegal[15] was a nuance of some magnitude after thirteen years of U.S. declarations to the contrary, but there was no way for the embattled Carter to exploit it without risking a net loss of support.

The returns made clear that neither the Jews nor Camp David had done much for Carter. Not only was his estimated 45% share of the Jewish vote barely 60% of what he had carried four years earlier, it was a new low for a Democrat. On the other hand, although Reagan's estimated 35% was a new high for Republicans, it was well below the estimated 45% of Catholics, and 60% of whites and Protestants, who voted for him too. Still, one atypical but unusually purposeful and increasingly influential Jewish constituency, the Hassidim of Borough Park, had gone for Reagan by 63%. They thus outvoted the Protestant fundamentalists who supported Reagan by an estimated 60%.[16] Closely linked to Israeli communities that, in turn, were closely linked to Begin, the American Orthodox had become a factor to contend with.

Like none since 1953, the new administration took office resolved to take arms, buy arms, and sell arms after what Reagan declared an era of "vacillation, appeasement and aimlessness."[17] What was probably the gaudiest display of political intellectuals since the coming of Kennedy could itself be taken as a signal of intent. Yet from the administration's earliest days, there was a fundamental tension between conservatives and *neo*conservatives, rhetoric and policy, action and inertia that was to perplex and exasperate insiders and outsiders for the next eight years, and both baffle and terrify foreign observers.[18]

The inherent contradictions were nowhere more obvious than in the Middle East, where four major conflicts—the war between Iran and Iraq, the civil war in Lebanon, the Arab-Israeli conflict, and the struggle for Afghanistan—now merged and collided. A liberal Democrat turned hard-line Republican, who had lived through World War II; a "Hollywood poolside Zionist," who had resigned from a Los Angeles country club in 1948 to protest exclusion of Jewish members, and signed a bill into law in 1971 authorizing California banks and lending agencies to buy Israel bonds; lodestar to a whole new movement of passionately pro-Israel Protestant fundamentalists, Reagan was temperamentally devoted to Israel for reasons as diverse as his biography and constituency.[19] Yet, as the admiring syndicated columnists, Rowland Evans and Robert Novak, noted in a campaign portrait, "there had always been a higher commitment in his world view: to stop Soviet aggression."

It was unclear, under such circumstances, where the Middle East fit in the new administration's grand design. Their minds, for the most part, on other things, the new men took office less with a policy than with an anthology of archetypes that were to contend and coexist till their return to private life. Some, like the new defense secretary, Caspar Weinberger, brought theirs from the Eisenhower-Dulles years. Others, like the new secretary of state, Alexander Haig, inherited theirs from Nixon and Kissinger. There were even traces of the "region-for-itself" model, preferred by the Carter administration and traditionally favored at least in corners of the State Department. But although no one challenged Camp David, none put the region at the top of the list. Revealingly, it was mid-February before the new administration even named an assistant secretary of state for Near Eastern affairs. It took still longer to find a senior staff member on the area for the National Security Council, and there was no successor at all for Linowitz, the U.S. representative to the stillborn autonomy talks.[20]

In debut statements before congressional committees and talk-show panels, successive members of the new administration confidently linked Soviet expansionism, Islamic fundamentalism, and Palestinian terror in defining priorities. Haig noted in his memoirs, "In reality, this was one consolidated fear: that terrorism and fundamentalism would so destabilize the region that the Soviets would either subvert the Islamic movement . . . or seize control of Iran and possibly the whole gulf. . . ."[21] Save, perhaps, as an existing feature in the landscape—"the only operative game in town," as Assistant Secretary of State Nicholas Veliotes called it—pursuit of Camp David was not among the priorities. For Israeli hawks, this could only be good news: a clear disavowal of the previous administration's fixation on settlements, autonomy and land for peace. But it was potential bad news too, to the extent it refocused Washington's gaze on what Reagan referred to at a press conference in October 1981 as the "very key" role of the Saudis. "I think that maybe they could be of help broadening the representation of the Palestinians," the president added.

The "Arab-Israeli question" had to be seen "in a strategic framework that recognizes and is responsible to the *larger threat* of Soviet expansionism," Rick Burt, the new director of the State Department's Bureau of Political-Military Affairs explained to a House subcommittee.[22] The administration's difficulties in dealing with an arms-sales challenge, a potential confrontation in Lebanon, and an impressive display of Israeli unilateralism made evident, if not entirely clear, what this could mean in practice.

Ironically, the arms transfer was a Carter legacy, going back to the sale in 1978 of sixty-two F-15s to Saudi Arabia. The Saudis now wanted aerial refueling support to extend their range, plus air-to-air missiles and bomb racks to increase their effectiveness. In response to the civil war in Yemen and the new war in the Gulf, Washington had deployed several latest-model AWACS (advance warning and control) planes to Saudi Arabia in 1979–1980 to keep track of occurrences on the ground, and guard against attack. Now the Saudis expressed interest in acquiring an AWACS too. Haig, who was not opposed per se, had been appropriately briefed by his predecessors on the impending sales. What was clear neither to him nor, he believed, to his predecessors, was the Pentagon's determination to sell the most advanced AWACS in its inventory. Since the package required congressional concurrence within thirty days of formal announcement, a political general of Haig's experience needed no AWACS to see trouble coming. He nonetheless believed that the administration should proceed, and that the sale could be made palatable to Israel.[23]

Haig's position was hardly the Israeli position. Especially with an election on the horizon, AWACS alone assured a battle. Within weeks of inauguration day, AIPAC had informed Edwin Meese, the new presidential counsel, of its intention to "fight all the way." Yet without effective coordination between White House, State Department, and Defense Department, and with the president's staff in hot pursuit of the tax cut, budget cuts, and increased military spending that had so tire-lessly been declared the pillars of "the Reagan revolution," the administration seemed both hell-bent to proceed anyway, and practically oblivious to the growing resistance.

With inadvertent humor, the National Security Council approved the package on April 1. Though the official announcement followed only three weeks later, the decision was leaked within a day, just as Haig prepared to leave for the Middle East. By early April 1981, forty-four members of the Senate and seventy-seven members of the House, a number of them prominent Republicans, had already taken the floor to register their opposition. On June 24, thirty-four Democrats and twenty-four Republicans advised the president to "refrain from sending this proposal to Congress." At the suggestion of Howard Baker, the Senate majority leader, the administration agreed instead to delay official action until after the Israeli elections June 30. Meanwhile, the White House would presumably attend to changing minds, while responding as best it could to quite different events in the Middle East.

Like other crises before and more to follow, the heart of the new crisis was Leb-anon, where Israel had theorized for decades about common interests with the Maronite Christians, who had historically dominated the country. Fearful of Syrian domination and eager to get the PLO out of the country, the principal Maronite party, The Phalange, had, in turn, been signaling Israelis since at least the mid-1970s. With a presidential election coming due, the Phalangists now aimed for Zahle, a major Christian center in the Bekaa Valley where Lebanon, Syria, Israel, and the occupied Golan, met. As could be expected, the Syrians replied in force, at the same time both signaling and reserving their intent to deploy latest model Soviet SAM-6 air-defense missiles against the Israelis. Despite severe Israeli suspicions that the Phalangists were really trying to provoke Israeli intervention, the Israeli cabinet authorized a strike at Syrian positions. While the Phalangists withdrew discreetly, Israeli pilots shot down two Syrian helicopters carrying troops. In the shadow of the Holocaust, Israel could not allow the Syrians to do to the Maronites what the Germans had done to the Jews, Begin explained to Samuel Lewis, the U.S. ambassador. When the Syrians replied by deploying missiles in what the Israelis understood as violation of a five-year tacit understanding on mutual nonengagement in Lebanon, Begin really was provoked. Unless the missiles were removed, Israel would destroy them, he announced at a Likud convention. But for bad weather, there would actu-ally have been a strike on April 30, he later told the Knesset.[24]

The crisis was as much a moment of truth for Washington as it was for Israel, but different truths stood toe to toe. Given the inevitable threat to Israeli-Egyptian peace and the inherent risk of escalation, there was little enthusiasm for a war between Israeli and Syrian. But there was equally little for leaving Israel under PLO guns and so appearing to concede points to the Soviet-supported Syrians. After a half decade of averted eyes and ad hoc crisis management, there were even those, as Veliotes later told a congressional panel, who were prepared "to address Lebanon as Lebanon."[25]

For both global and regional reasons, the State Department leaned increasingly toward a comprehensive solution that would include removal of Syrian troops, Soviet missiles, PLO weapons, *and* the Israeli presence. As usual, the problem was distinguishing effects from causes, and eggs from chickens. Deeply divided on which should come first, the White House settled on Philip Habib, a retired career diplomat of Lebanese origin, for an open-ended shuttle mission as special presidential envoy. Initially dispatched to restrain Israel, persuade the Christians to negotiate with Syria, and warn the Syrians to pull back their missiles,[26] he was neither successful nor unsuccessful enough to justify bringing him home. Instead, like a kind of perambulant crisis center, he remained in place for the duration of the U.S. engagement in Lebanon, while his mission grew and metamorphized.

By this time, Israeli attention was elsewhere. At least for the moment, Israel could live with the Syrian missiles, its leaders decided. But similar restraint did not apply to other targets. On May 29 and June 2, Israeli planes bombed Palestinian positions in Lebanon. They then resumed the pounding after the June election. The attacks caused the PLO to target the Israeli coastal resort of Nahariya. Despite misgivings in both the military and the cabinet, Israeli planes replied by striking PLO headquarters in downtown Beirut, with substantial civilian casualties. This led, in turn, to a barrage of some twelve hundred Palestinian shells and rockets on some thirty Israeli communities in the course of a twelve-day skirmish across the Lebanese border.

The exchange was a pyrrhic victory and a turning point for both Israel and the PLO.[27] Viewed from Beirut, Israel's hugely superior firepower cost the PLO not only most of the guns and rocket launchers it had assembled at much effort and expense, but any remaining sympathy among Lebanese, who had long learned to see Chairman Yasir Arafat's gunmen as an overbearing nuisance, and now came increasingly to see them as a menace.[28] Yet the outcome was a dilemma for both sides. As usual, the PLO was overwhelmingly outgunned, but it also faced its more radical members, increasingly disposed to see Arafat as a paper tiger. Israelis, in turn, had proven again they could deliver on target. An unprecedented wave of refugees made nonetheless clear that Israel was vulnerable, and civilian morale a hostage to PLO guns.

Faced with their respective dilemmas, both sides settled for what Reagan was to call "our cease-fire,"[29] mediated by the Saudis, the United Nations, and Habib. But this was no long-term solution for a PLO as committed as ever to "armed struggle," nor for an Israel more determined than ever to deal with the Occupied Territories without the PLO. It was bad enough for Israelis that the cease-fire applied only to southern Lebanon; still worse that their forces had failed to "win" and therefore, in the symbolic calculus of irregular warfare, had "lost." But perhaps worst of all from Begin's perspective was that the cease-fire implied de facto recognition of the PLO. "There is a dialogue through this confrontation," Arafat noted cheerfully in an American television interview. "What does this mean?"[30]

Yet that was just one front. On June 7, 1981, three days after a Sadat visit to Israel, and three weeks before the Israeli election,[16] U.S.-supplied Israeli F-15s and F-16s loaded with U.S.-supplied bombs had overflown Saudi territory to strike Osiraq, the French-built Iraqi nuclear installation near Baghdad. Reportedly, they even navigated with the aid of U.S.-supplied satellite photographs, acquired through regular channels.[31] Remarkably, considering both the cause and the outcome, hardly anyone seemed even to notice that U.S. AWACS already in Saudi Arabia failed to detect the Israeli planes.[32]

Despite its opportune timing, Israelis had been planning the raid for months, though political support was reserved, even in Begin's cabinet. Yet as with Israel's invasion of Lebanon a year later, cabinet skeptics were no match for Shamir, Chief of Staff Rafael Eitan, Begin, and Sharon.[33] According to the Israelis, who seemed both well informed and far more cautious about Iraqi developments than their U.S. peers,[34] Osiraq was approaching activation.

Shocked, indignant, and bitter, the White House seemed nonetheless surprised by what it took for a first case of unannounced Israeli unilateralism. Yet the surprise itself was surprising. Though Israeli and U.S. analysts differed on the actual state of the project, there was agreement that the Iraqi reactor was designed to yield weapons-grade uranium. Given its own concerns about proliferation, and about the heavy involvement of France and Italy, both NATO members, in Osiraq's construction and operation, Washington had actually been aware of the problem since at least fall 1979, when the Israelis began to press it in public, in diplomatic conversations, and in systematic sabotage of the project's European sources.[35]

By election time 1980, the subject had become a staple of Israeli-U.S. conversations, a major item in reports from Tel Aviv, a further source of friction between the United States and France and Italy, and a matter of some contention between Brzezinkski's NSC staff and the State Department. On the eve of the new administration, Lewis recalled, he knew for a fact that his top-security reports on Osiraq were among briefing materials awaiting the transition teams.[36] In fact, he added, the Israelis stopped talking about Osiraq only in January 1981 after Washington, for whatever reason, had failed to answer. He later reproached himself for failing to recognize the silence itself as a message. Robert Hunter, a former member of Brzezinski's staff, also recalled raising the issue with his successor. The Israelis would act on their own unless the United States took action, he said he warned him.[37]

It was imaginable that the new administration opted for complicity by omission, leaving the initiative to the Israelis, while reserving post facto censure. According to the Israeli author, Shlomo Nakdimon, the failure of the United States to move the French and Italians had come up when Haig visited the Middle East in April. Begin, he speculates, might have understood Haig's admission of defeat as a signal to go ahead.[38] But clumsy management of the AWACS sale, neglect of the deadlocked autonomy talks, and its centrifugal style in general, make it at least as plausible that hot pursuit of rather different priorities caused the Administration first to default, and then to respond ad hoc, to the Iraqi challenge. Hunter agreed that the new men may have known more than they were telling, but both he and Lewis preferred to attribute the subsequent embarrassments to Murphy's Law and the proverbial confusions of the Reagan White House.

In any case, with the AWACS sale still hanging fire and friendly Arabs clucking portentously, there was no reason to doubt the sincerity of Pentagon indignation about the Osiraq raid. Given the awkwardness and inconvenience of the trade-offs it imposed on him, there was little reason to doubt Haig's sincerity either. "Not only could the United States not condone the raid, it would have to take some action against Israel," he noted in his memoirs. "Yet my feelings were mixed," he added. His ambivalence was presumably shared by the White House.[39]

Reminded by Lewis of the prehistory of discussions, the White House settled on sanctions, with the State Department in charge of details. Once again, there was pro forma investigation of Israel's use of U.S. weapons under the Arms Export Control Act. Shipment of four new F-16s, already paid for by the Israelis, was also suspended for two months, and the United States voted with the rest of the Security Council to condemn the raid.[40] Yet Israeli irritation too was understandable. The issue was not new. Washington had not been left in the dark. There was no reason that Israelis should know that briefing materials might never have reached their intended readers. There were also precedents enough in the history of the relationship for Israelis to infer that silence meant yes.

On June 30, 1981, barely three weeks after the raid, Israelis went to the polls, but in contrast to four years earlier, Begin was now the featured attraction. With inflation at 130 percent, his government had barely survived a confidence vote the previous November. As late as April, polls could be read to show Labor ahead, and even approaching an absolute majority, but a third to half of the electorate was still undecided. Then came the missile crisis and Osiraq. Labor's Chaim Herzog, the later president of the state, and Shimon Peres, the later prime minister, were volubly critical of the raid, but voters liked it. They were even happier with an expansive program of subsidized loans and savings, and a tax cut of Reaganesque dimension, undertaken since January by Yoram Aridor, Begin's finance minister. By some estimates, the volume of buying and selling that resulted constituted 10 percent of GNP. Importers had to charter extra air-freight capacity to supply 100,000 new television sets, 20,000 new home appliances, and 5,000 new cars for the consumer binge that followed.[41]

Beyond any election yet, the campaign both revealed and exploited fault lines of culture, ethnicity, and class dating back to the beginnings of the state. Among the casualties was the barrier between verbal violence, a traditional staple of Israeli democracy, and physical violence, which now exceeded anything to date. Regularly pelted with eggs and tomatoes, and systematically harassed at rallies in Jerusalem, Kiryat Shmona, and Petach Tikvah, Peres appealed to the virtues of the pioneer past, while the novelist A. B. Yehoshua deplored the "mob." Begin sneered back at "lovely souls," and made clear how he, who had already stood firm against Germans, communists, Arabs, and, not incidentally, Labor, would also stand firm against Syrian SAMs and PLO Katyushas.[42] "Begin, King of Israel," supporters roared in acknowledgment.

As in 1977, the outcome was equivocal, but this time it was a virtual dead heat. Of the new Knesset's 120 members, 48 were from Likud, 47 from Labor. The aggregate religious vote remained almost constant too, declining by only a seat, from 17 to 16. But similar numbers concealed increasingly different constituencies. Reflecting the relative youth and growing numbers of the Sephardi population,[43] Likud outpolled Labor in all voter cohorts from age eighteen to forty-nine. It also appeared that more than a third of Likud voters came from Asia and Africa, and nearly half were Israeli-born. By contrast, scarcely a quarter of Labor's voters came from Asia and Africa, and only 40 percent were native Israelis. At the same time, the traditionally conservative ranks of the National Religious party shrank by 50 percent. The defectors instead took their votes to fundamentalist, radical, and ethnic competitors, such as *Agudat Israel, Tehiya,* and the Moroccan-born Aharon Abu-Hatzeira's *Tami,* which was itself to bring down the government and force early elections three years later.[44]

The emergent cabinet list left no doubt who was in charge. Save for Sharon as minister of defense, the new government was overwhelmingly civilian. Yet, conventional wisdom to the contrary, civilian predominance marked another long step to the right. After more than thirty years in the desert, Herut had reached the political Promised Land with representatives in the prime minister's office, and the ministries of finance, defense, and foreign affairs. Cost what it might in money, public tolerance and even American-Jewish sympathy, Begin was now willing to render as much unto the religious parties as was needed to reach his goal. Of eighty-three provisions in the new coalition agreement, thirty dealt with religion. Among them were military exemptions for religious students; possible amendment of the Law of Return to exclude immigrants of non-Jewish birth who had been converted by non-Orthodox rabbis; and, despite painful losses of revenue, suspension of port activity and El Al flights on the Sabbath.[45]

Meanwhile, as Begin looked once again to Egypt and an impending visit to the United States, the administration returned to the Saudi arms sale. Given the summer's events and growing concern for administration credibility, both the Saudis and the White House saw it increasingly as a matter of principle. Yet administration lobbying seemed only to have made things worse. Concern for Jewish constituents and a subliminal residue of anti-Arab resentment aside, the opposition advanced behind two arguments: the ostensible risks to Israel's security per se, and the risks to U.S. security in the event that Saudi Arabia were to become "another Iran." As late as October, the combination of arguments seemed insuperable. What turned it around was in part a formidable lobbying campaign by Boeing and United Technologies, both with vast and demonstrable interests in plane sales, and oil companies like Mobil, with their stake in Saudi oil.[46]

But the decisive weapon was the president himself. Fred Dutton, the Saudi lobbyist in Washington, was among the first to say as much in public. "If I had my way, I'd have bumper stickers all over town that say 'Reagan or Begin,' " he declared in an interview.[47] "It is not the business of any other nation to make American foreign policy," Reagan himself declared on October 1, 1981, at what he jocularly referred to as his "annual" news conference. It could also be seen as the opening shot of the administration's counteroffensive.[48] As expected, the House, whose Democratic majority had survived the previous November's earthquake, still rejected the sale by 301–111. The Senate was more vulnerable, not least after Reagan personally conferred with forty-three Republican members on October 7, the day after Sadat's assassination. Before the final vote October 28, Reagan had conferred with as much as two-thirds of the Senate, earnestly reassuring them that "we were completely dedicated to the preservation of the state of Israel."[49] The newly Republican Senate began to come around.

In the nature of things, this could hardly save Sadat. But it sufficed for the moment to save Reagan's face. On October 29, when the sale finally came up in the

Senate, it carried by two. Among the majority were ten signatories of the letter protesting the sale the previous June, nine of them Republicans. Among the nine was Roger Jepsen, a believing Reaganite and ostentatiously born-again fundamentalist from Iowa, who had pledged only the previous May to oppose the sale in a keynote speech to the annual AIPAC convention.[50]

The payoff appeared in August, and again at an Arab summit in Fez, Morocco, in November, when Saudi Arabia's crown prince, and later king, Fahd, proposed a peace plan. It included Israeli withdrawal from all occupied territories, dismantlement of all settlements, and a PLO-governed state. An Arab maximalist reading of Resolution 242, combined with the Rabat resolution of a few years earlier, Fahd's proposal omitted any reference to Israel per se. It nonetheless marked another step on the long march from 1967 and the no-man's-land of Khartoum. The proposal could also be seen as a Palestinian trial balloon. But by Saudi standards, it was a gesture of some courage.[51]

In the event, the implied recognition of Israel, contained in the formula "the Security Council will guarantee peace for all states of the region," divided the PLO leadership and led to de facto Syrian veto.[52] It could be taken for granted that Israel would reject it too, not only because of what it proposed but because of its "comprehensive" approach, which clearly and intentionally set off the Saudi plan from Camp David.[53] But Washington was the immediate addressee. Delicately avoiding names, Haig conceded his dismay that Reagan "was induced" to speak approvingly of the Fahd plan in the afterglow of the AWACS battle. It showed "that they recognize Israel as a nation to be negotiated with," the president told reporters.[54] When King Hussein arrived in Washington a few days later, Haig had already made sure that Reagan reaffirmed Camp David, while taking care himself to tell Fahd that the United States regarded his plan as impractical.[55]

Shortly afterward, in what was generally understood as a kind of consolation prize for the AWACS sale, Israel became the beneficiary of a Memorandum of Understanding (MOU). As it happened, the ceremony took place the same day that Reagan also signed a presidential "finding," informing Congress of his intention to send covert aid to the Nicaraguan Contras. Though each engagement seemed discrete, and at least a continent apart, they were eventually to merge in ways that no one yet imagined.

Conceived in what appears to have been a rather typical liaison between an eager Begin and an accommodating Reagan, the MOU was effectively left on the Pentagon's doorstep, where Ariel Sharon and Defense Secretary Weinberger assumed formal custody, with photographers excluded. The arrangement subsumed an existing Defense Trade Initiative that was apparently Haig's idea. To prime Israeli pumps and encourage efficiencies of scale, it was agreed that the Pentagon would buy up to $200 million in Israeli products a year. "Reaffirm[ing] the common bonds of friendship between the United States and Israel," the document otherwise envisioned "joint military exercises as agreed on by the parties," "joint readiness activities," and "other areas . . . , as may be jointly agreed" to "deter all threats from the Soviet Union in the region."[56]

What this might mean was deliberately left spongy. But whatever it meant, it was assumed to mean far more to Israelis than to Americans. "The advantage of having the MOU," according to one American observer, was that at long last those factions in the administration that were determined upon a strategic relationship with Israel could now wave the all-important piece of paper in dealing with the opposition in other parts of the government." According to one Begin supporter, the document could even be read to Israel's disadvantage. Israel was now committed to come to the aid of the United States against the Soviet Union, he argued. There was no corresponding U.S. commitment to come to Israel's aid in the event of attack by Arab rejectionists.[57]

Within days, such questions had become theoretical. On December 14, 1981, Begin moved again. This time it was decided that "the law, jurisdiction and administration of the State [of Israel] shall apply to the Golan Heights," that is, that the territory was therewith effectively annexed.[58] With the PLO still standing tall in Lebanon, Israeli policy going nowhere in Gaza and the West Bank, and both the United States and the Israeli opposition determined to avoid confrontations with Sadat's successors, there were inevitably speculations about his motives. Some saw it as a gesture to his hard right wing, already showing withdrawal symptoms as the April date with Egypt approached. Others saw it as a test of Sadat's successors and another way of saying there would be no more land for peace.[59] Actually, all three readings were plausible. Like other decisions soon to follow, the quasi-annexation surprised even the Israeli cabinet, but with government forces intact, and the opposition badly divided, it sailed through the Knesset 61–21. The army was then ordered preemptively to concentrate forces on the northern borders.

Predictably, reaction was quite different in a Washington that had not been warned or asked; that believed it deserved better of an ally; and that anyway had its official hands full with the Polish declaration of martial law. This time, Weinberger and Haig were furious in tandem, and James Reston of the *New York Times* quoted "senior American officials" who "feel Mr. Begin is a certified disaster for Israel and the rest of the world." Soon afterward, Reagan suspended the freshly minted MOU, and Lewis was summoned to Begin's office for a performance the prime minister later repeated for reporters. "Are we a vassal state? Are we a banana republic?" he demanded of the U.S. ambassador. Lewis replied dutifully that reinstatement of the MOU depended on progress in the autonomy talks and what happened in Lebanon. "The people of Israel lived without the MOU for 3700 years, and will continue to live without it for another 3700 years," Begin answered.[60]

There were by now at least two schools on how to proceed in Lebanon. Both of them Labor spokesmen and former chiefs of staff, Rabin and Mordechai Gur were skeptical that a large military operation could solve the problem. However reluctantly, they instead endorsed the existing cease-fire. An alternative course, already anticipated in Israel's support for Major Saad Haddad's indigenous "South Lebanese army," the Israeli incursion in 1978, and a staff plan called "Little Pines," was the creation of a "security zone" in southern Lebanon. But "Big Pines," a plan for operations as far north as Beirut, was an option that Sharon had been spelling out for staff officers since at least October. Contingent in part on the Lebanese political calendar, which called for election of a new president in September, the goal was nothing less than a full-scale Israeli invasion to drive the PLO out of Lebanon. The Israelis would then, in effect, remake the country in cooperation with Bashir

Gemayel's Maronite Christian Phalangists. On December 20, still warm from his assault on Lewis, Begin let Sharon brief Israel's most hawkish cabinet. Maps in hand, Sharon produced a war plan clearly directed at the Beirut-Damascus highway, with the additional option of landing Israeli troops north of Beirut. To the surprise of both men, the presentation met unexpected resistance that led, in turn, to a change of tactics. Thereafter briefings were to be selective, with a preference for *faits accomplis.* But the goals remained unchanged. "I want Arafat in his bunker!" Begin told a military visitor, who called on him a few days later.[61]

By now, U.S. officials may actually have had a better idea what was going on than the Israeli cabinet or public. In spring, when NBC's John Chancellor unveiled Israeli plans on the network's evening news, even the U.S. public got a look. According to the well-informed Israeli journalists Ze'ev Schiff and Ehud Ya'ari, Sharon had already proposed an implicit division of strategic labor when he visited the Pentagon in November 1981. The United States, in effect, would take care of Africa; Israel would attend to Soviet clients in the Middle East, that is, Syria and the PLO. Asserting that he expressed only personal views, Sharon had then briefed Habib and associates in early December. Both were suitably appalled.

In February 1982, with the approval of Begin and Shamir, the Israeli position was then aired again, this time by Yehoshua Saguy, Israel's chief of military intelligence. In the wake of a PLO incursion from Jordan, Saguy came to Washington to sound out Haig on what he considered grounds for war. Like a second Lyndon Johnson in a remake of 1967, the secretary of state replied that the United States would tolerate no more than a "strictly proportional response" to " 'an internationally recognized provocation.' " For its part, the United States would ask the Jordanians and Syrians to urge restraint on the PLO.[62]

Meanwhile, with no occasion for warm feelings on either side, the once-unimaginable outbreak of peace between Egypt and Israel went almost unnoticed but for a well-calculated media production by Israeli intransigents. Apart from a contested beachfront at Taba, which was to haunt Israeli-Egyptian relations for years afterward,[63] Israeli withdrawal was accomplished on schedule. But each in their way, the Egyptians, *Gush Emunim,* and Herut secessionists from the new secular-ultranationalist *Tehiya,* made sure there would be no relief or catharsis. In March an estimated forty thousand Jewish demonstrators assembled for a rally at the Western Wall. On the eve of the final evacuation, a few thousand supporters, mostly religious students, then occupied the settlement town of Yamit for a last symbolic defense. Though there were no serious injuries, unarmed soldiers had to haul them out of Yamit before the inevitable television cameras. There were light fines for resisting the army, but nothing approaching the draconic sanctions inflicted almost simultaneously on the protesting Druse on the Golan, who were refusing to accept Israeli IDs. Contrary to the terms of the peace treaty, Sharon then ordered the evacuated town to be bulldozed.[64]

Unquantifiable by its nature, the "Yamit trauma" was nonetheless accepted as fact by a government even more indulgent than before of settler activism in the Occupied Territories, and by settlers, who saw it as proof of their isolation from mainstream Israel. Thitherto officially nonpartisan, some now opted for party politics. The result was a surge of far-right electoral activity in a system congenial to sectarianism, and increasingly vulnerable to minority veto. Others, including twenty-five charged two years later with placing bombs under Arab buses, opted for direct action. Only after their arrest was it discovered that they had also carried out well-publicized assaults on West Bank mayors and an Islamic college. A few had even conspired to seize the Temple Mount and blow up the Moslem shrines.[65]

For a government challenged to defend its flanks and assert its authority, the campaign in Lebanon could increasingly be seen as a way to do both. At a two-and-a-half-hour meeting on May 25, 1982, Sharon conferred again with Weinberger, then with Haig, who by now had become Israel's preferred American. Weinberger seems only to have threatened further sanctions. Far from working as a deterrent on Sharon's return to Jerusalem, the threat may imaginably have worked as a plus, just as early reinstatement of the MOU might have worked as a restraint.

Haig was more accommodating. A man who had learned his Middle East from Kissinger, he was also persuaded of the need for radical change in Lebanon. "The time has come to take concerted action in support of both Lebanon's territorial integrity . . . and a strong central government . . . ," he told the Chicago Council on Foreign Relations on May 26.[66] By his own account, he was considering an international conference even before the war began. Given his reactions a few weeks later, it seems likely that he was also thinking of ways to turn an Israeli invasion to strategic advantage.[67] In any case, his message, which was not no, seems to have been exactly what Sharon had come to hear. A military operation had to be quick and clean, and in response to a clear provocation, Haig told him. Even now, a hard ultimatum from Reagan might have had some effect on the impending war. But there was no real chance of this. Instead, it was agreed that Haig would state Reagan's position in a letter to Begin, expressing U.S. concern and urging "absolute restraint."[68]

In the absence of a clearly visible red light, all that was needed was a cause. This was delivered June 3 when the Israeli ambassador in London was struck down in a professionally planned attack. Police soon established that one of the assailants was a cousin of Sabri al-Banna (Abu Nidal), who had broken with Arafat some years earlier, and now seemed, by turns, to be both a Syrian and an Iraqi client. The assassins had also been armed by the Iraqi embassy, and both previous and future targets included regular representatives of the PLO. Apart from revenge for the Israeli raid on Osiraq, the attack could be seen as a deliberate Iraqi provocation, whose primary addresses were Arafat, still clutching to his cease-fire, and Syria, Iraq's neighbor and enemy. Both would inevitably come under pressure to respond if the Israelis invaded. Apprehensive of Israeli intentions, suspicious of Arab governments, and concerned to make a serious impression on Washington, Arafat predictably, and even plausibly, denied responsibility for the London attack. There was no patience in Israel for such nuances. Hints of Palestinian-U.S. flirtations may even have added to the Israeli sense of urgency.[69]

Instead, the cabinet agreed on June 4 to bomb West Beirut. The PLO predictably replied by resuming fire on Israeli settlements in the Galilee. Challenged, provoked, and angered by the course of events, and successively reassured by Begin,

Sharon, and Chief of Staff Eitan that "Operation Peace for Galilee" was all that its name implied, the ministers then assented, with only token opposition. Labor fell in with the consensus, voting with the majority for limited military action.[70]

Public opinion was no obstacle either. By the end of June, according to one poll, over 77 percent of Israelis agreed that the war was justified. Support for Begin, while far behind, had risen over 10 percent within a month. By July, support for the war was even higher. Consciously or not, Israelis thus acceded in their first unambiguously discretionary war and, to the dismay of many, their first-ever siege of an Arab capital.[71] In reply to appeals from both Lewis and Reagan, Begin emphatically denied any territorial designs. On the contrary, he reaffirmed Israel's goal to "push the terrorists north to a distance of 40 km.," and added his hope for a peace treaty with "a free and independent Lebanon."[72]

Measured against all previous experience, the relative, if qualified, moderation of the superpowers was another reassurance to Israeli policymakers. Seeking to put the squeeze on Israel, Pentagon officials invoked the self-defense provisions of the Arms Export Control Act, and even submitted to State a list of U.S.-supplied equipment Israel was believed to have used in Lebanon. But although this led in July to a suspension of cluster-bomb deliveries, State was outstandingly deliberate in forwarding its report to Congress. Persuaded that the war was an opportunity as well as a risk, both Haig and William Casey, the director of central intelligence, agreed that the war should be turned to the advantage of the United States.[73]

The fault line was visible in Reagan's first public pronouncement. Returning via London from the annual world economic summit, he told members of Parliament that the fighting had to stop. It was also necessary to "stamp out the scourge of terrorism that in the Middle East makes war an ever-present threat," he added, to what sounded like a cue from Haig. At the United Nations, Ambassador Jeane J. Kirkpatrick voted with everyone else for Israeli withdrawal and a general cease-fire. But for Haig, she would presumably have been instructed a few days later to condemn Israel and threaten sanctions too.[74] Instead, Haig urged Reagan to take to the hot line to urge Soviet pressure on the Syrians for a cease-fire. He then appealed personally to Begin, while Habib appealed to Asad.

U.S. policy by now was in full-throated cacophony, and Habib's effectiveness too was bruised. Even as he waited in Damascus with a personal message from Begin, Israeli forces were engaging the Syrians, smashing the tanks and missiles that were the pride of Soviet technology, and destroying or damaging up to 30 percent of the Syrian planes entering Lebanese air space.[75] Undeterred by superpower diplomacy, Syrian arms, or domestic opinion, Israeli forces meanwhile continued advancing northward, just as Sharon intended, though resistance was substantially stiffer than any foreseen by Rosy Scenario. On June 13, Gemayel's miltia greeted them on the outskirts of the capital. An apparent surprise even to Begin, who continued to deny their presence there to Habib, Israeli troops and journalists then entered the city.

The Israelis' arrival in East Beirut opened a new phase in the war. Yet the intended victory was still out of reach. Sharon was now in effective control of most of Lebanon. He and Begin had also won tactical victories over more skeptical colleagues, the cabinet, the opposition, both superpowers, the Syrians, and all other

Arabs. But they had not yet overcome the PLO. Yet for all the smouldering grievances against its presence that allowed even Moslems to welcome Israelis as liberators, there was little in the way of practical help to expect from the Lebanese. Ironically, for reasons Israelis persistently failed to understand,[76] this reticence even
included the Phalangists they now regarded as their clients and allies. Solicitous of
Arab opinion and the parliamentary majority needed to make Gemayel president,
the Phalangists were out to use the Israelis, not to join them. Meanwhile, a week's
fighting had cost Israel an estimated 170 dead and 700 wounded. This was the
equivalent of 10,000 American dead and 40,000 wounded, Haig noted, and no one
could guess what it might cost to assault West Beirut.

Politically unable either to call it a victory and come home, or to face the price
of urban warfare, the Israelis instead took recourse in a nine-week siege, while the
PLO hung on. As early as July 3, Lewis informed Begin of U.S. willingness to send
marines to buffer PLO withdrawal as part of a multinational force. Yet, as Habib
and a trail of international mediators sought to sell their package, Sharon only continued turning up the heat. From August 1, Israeli bombing escalated, while troops
advanced toward the heart of the city, and Reagan repeatedly pressed restraint on
a furious Begin. On August 12, with his staff demanding intervention and a senior
aide even threatening to resign, Reagan even called in person. "Menachem, this is
a holocaust," he told the Israeli prime minister. "Mr. President," Begin replied with
heaviest irony, "I think I know what a holocaust is." He nonetheless returned the
call in twenty minutes to report that he had ordered Sharon to stop the bombing.[77]
On the other hand, while a threat to recall Habib may have had some effect, threats
to cut aid were neither effective nor credible, not least after a delegation of American Jews emerged from the White House on August 5 to report that the president
was not considering sanctions.[78]

August 12 was nonetheless a watershed for both sides. Faced with almost una-
mimous cabinet opposition, Sharon was divested of authority to use the air force,
a precedent unique in Israeli military history, while the government acceded to
terms Habib proposed, including orderly PLO withdrawal from Lebanon.[79] By
now, it had long been clear to the PLO leadership that the situation was hopeless.
Surrounded by Lebanese hostility, Arab reserve, and Israeli firepower, they had little to look forward to but more and worse. A familiar handicap, Arafat's reluctance
to pronounce the magic words "Resolution 242," assured that there would be no
political concessions, let alone recognition, from the United States. Help from Arab
governments, let alone the Soviet Union, was as unlikely as a snowfall.[80] Yet only
on August 21, after extended discussions, negotiations, and final appeals, did evacuation of the PLO's ragtag little army finally start. All the while, the rest of the world
watched on television what was happening on both sides in more or less real time.[81]

For a democracy with a citizen soldiery, a free press, and an active public opinion, heavily dependent on another democracy with a free press and an active public
opinion, the siege of Lebanon was a Hobson's choice. As was ruefully noted afterward, three more or less concurrent wars of large and comprehensive bloodiness
were not seen on television. With easy control of access to the war zone, professional forces under their command, and a sharp sense of how Americans had
reacted to Vietnam, British officials imposed virtually total control on news from

the Falklands. Both Iraq and Iran assured that Gulf war pictures were also both scarce and selective, while Soviet viewers were unlikely to see much real news from Afghanistan.

Yet, irrespective of intention, honest reporting from Beirut was hardly simple either. Ordinarily a high-risk occupation, fearless reporting had meanwhile become a virtual oxymoron. "Every reporter," the *New York Times*'s correspondent Tom Friedman recalled, "was aware that for $1.98 and ten Green Stamps anyone could have you killed."[82] But in its current situation, it was hardly in the PLO's interest to kill reporters. On the contrary, it was a matter of the greatest urgency to make a good impression. From here on, the conjunction of fear and objective journalism could only work to the advantage of the PLO.

"The American," as one Israeli editor observed, "thinks he is a camera."[83] American editors were bound to see Arafat as news by definition, a kind of walking war goal and a natural target for inherently competitive correspondents. But from the reporter's perspective, he was also worth talking to as the Other Side of a Story Israel was trying hard to keep untold; and because official Washington, which was what the press was demonstratively resolved to show it was not, had refused to talk to him since 1975. Reduced to images of an embattled Arafat kissing babies, or surrounded by desperate and adoring constituents, arrayed alone against one of the world's most formidable military forces, the resulting news judgment too reflected a kind of censorship: the PLO as it wished to be seen. But it was not a kind that easily allowed for formal acknowledgement.

Israel was different. Briefers, trying to get across the official position, met increasing resistance, and military censorship was both a given and a source of contention, after an Israeli censor refused to approve an ABC interview with Arafat for transmission from Israel. NBC seems to have made a particular point of drawing attention to the censor, but in a situation where reporters could drive to the war from the airport and file, if necessary from Damascus or Cyprus, Israeli control of access to the war zone was effectively impossible. With a citizen army in the field and domestic consensus sliding by July, media management was another problem. Begin, Sharon, and Eitan notwithstanding, the results of the two most recent general elections, let alone the genesis and course of the war itself, were evidence enough that Israel had no party line or long-term policy. Civilians in uniform like everyone else, press officers improvised, while Israeli journalists like Schiff pursued the story with exemplary authority and courage. A major military power with state-of-the-art weaponry facing fifteen thousand irregulars in a city of some half a million, the Israelis thus unwittingly followed the French in Algeria and the Americans in Vietnam in a war that could not be concealed, prettified, or won.

By the time Begin reached Washington on June 21, 1982, for what he hoped would be an unmediated tête-à-tête, the first-name bonhomie of a few months earlier[84] had vanished in an unseasonable frost. Unless the shooting stopped, it was reported, there were indications the president might not receive him at all. Instead, the two leaders met in the presence of Sam Lewis, called home from Israel, and Moshe Arens, now ambassador to Washington. Reagan read aloud from file cards, prepared for him by the NSC staff. As was obviously planned, the Oval Office meeting ended before Begin could even get the floor. In the presence of aides, the talks then continued acerbically in the Cabinet Room. Although Begin acceded equivocally to a promise not to invade Beirut, the perpendicular decline of cordiality was apparent not only in the omission of the customary presidential luncheon toast but even the public exchange that followed the meeting. Confining himself to six circumspect sentences on the integrity of Lebanon and security of Israel, Reagan acknowledged that it was "worthwhile" having "Prime Minister Begin" at the White House. It was a misnomer that Israel had invaded Lebanon, Begin replied defensively. *Invasion* implied territorial ambitions; Israel had none. He envisaged a time when "Lebanon and Israel will sign a peace treaty and live in peace forever."[85]

U.S. coherence, Israeli consensus, and Israeli-U.S. relations withered apace. Even as Begin and Reagan agreed provisionally on Israeli restraint, and Bashir Gemayel's candidacy for the Lebanese presidency,[86] Weinberger, Vice President George Bush, and Senator Charles Percy, chairman of the Foreign Relations Committee, were arriving in Riyadh to pass on a rather different message to the Saudis. Officially, the occasion was King Khalid's funeral; unofficially, it was a chance to assure the hosts of the determination of the United States to keep the heat on Israel. Meanwhile, Habib, in Beirut, was trying to leverage Israeli pressure into PLO withdrawal. By early July, Haig was convinced that contrary signals had snatched defeat from the jaws of victory. In effect, both he and others argued, U.S. confusion only encouraged the PLO to play for time; it thus robbed the opportunity afforded by the Israeli invasion of an attainable political victory.

A few days after the Saudi funeral, Haig himself was fired. His forced resignation, combined with the nomination of George Shultz as his successor, seemed a signal in itself.[87] Fairly or otherwise, attention now turned to Shultz's relationship with Bechtel, the expansive California contracting firm with its extensive Arab connections. In contrast to his predecessor's emphasis on the Soviet Union, the new secretary also stressed Lebanon at his confirmation hearings. Like a distant echo of Harold Saunders, in 1975, he even referred to "the legitimate needs and problems of the Palestinian people" as "a central reality of the Middle East."[88]

Meanwhile, on the face of it, Beirut remained what it had been for years. Yet till now, for the most part, the principal actors had been indigenous "Christians" and "Moslems," "leftists" and "rightists," Shiites and Druse, whatever the tags might mean. Now, thirty-four years after the first war for Palestine, and fifteen years after the spectacular third, Israelis and Palestinians had taken over the Lebanese stage in roles no casting agency could have imagined in 1948 or 1967. For the next ten weeks, with correspondents, editors, even anchormen personally on the scene, the national media of the United States literally brought the story home in all its savage ambiguity: "Thousands reported killed," "Beirut civilians injured by Israeli attacks," "Israeli soldiers greeted like heroes in S Lebanon," "PLO forces are rooted in residential areas," "Bombing in Beirut damages home for retarded," "Israelis admit to using US cluster bombs," "Pressure grows in Israel to bring soldiers home," "UN urges Israel to restore water, food supplies to Beirut," "American woman, recently in Beirut, recounts horrors," "Israel attacks residential areas of Beirut," "Poll shows Israelis oppose Beirut invasion," "Lebanese parliament refuses to elect new pres.," "Am, Israeli Jews question Begin's policies."[89] In the first major war of portable cameras and real-time transmission by satellite, it was only a matter of weeks before the story itself became the story.

Spontaneous and manipulative, clumsy, sinister, sometimes cynical, but almost always sincerely revealing of what the user believed to be at stake, the story was invariably served up in a dense shroud of association and analogy. The associations extended from Vietnam and Hiroshima to the thug republics of the Caribbean. But not only did the Holocaust predominate, this time, a first time, its imagery was systematically appropriated and applied by both sides.

"In a war whose aim is to annihilate the leader of the terrorists in West Beirut, I feel like one who has sent an army to Berlin to annihilate Hitler in the bunker," Begin declared in a letter to Reagan.[90] Though presented with incomparably more sophistication, the argument could be found again in Norman Podhoretz's critique both of the media and critics of the war. Deliberately titled "J'accuse," after Emile Zola's famous Dreyfusard call to arms of the 1890s, the piece was a kind of neo-conservative credo.[91] Beirut, in Podhoretz's perspective, was where the brutal experiences of a century—the czars and Weimar, appeasement and the Cold War, totalitarianism and Third World nationalism—now intersected, with Israel as the last best hope of Western democracy, and the PLO as the direct and demonstrable heirs of Stalin, Hitler, and the Kishinev *pogromchiki*.

Stung and infuriated by Israeli policy, others replied by equating Beirut with Warsaw, Palestinians with Jews, the PLO in 1982 with the Warsaw ghetto rising of 1943, the Israelis with Germans, and Begin himself with Hitler. Advanced among others by the novelist John Le Carré, the columnist Nicholas von Hoffmann, and the cartoonist Patrick Oliphant, the counterrhetoric was sometimes vicious, and often naive.[92]

"It was a hard summer for Israel's image," the American journalist, Milton Viorst, noted in the aftermath of the siege. For some Israelis, including oppositionists like the Labor deputy Dov Ben-Meir, it even had the look of a conspiracy. Israel faced three enemies in Lebanon, Ben-Meir declared on the floor of the Knesset: the PLO, the Syrians, and the international media.[93] But it was hard for reporters too to get it right. Significantly, skirmishing on the third front continued well after the battle for Lebanon had stopped. A summer later, the alleged bias of the Western media was the subject of a conference in Jerusalem, where one Israeli official pointed to "irreparable damage."[94] In the aftermath of an official investigation that found Sharon officially, if indirectly, responsible for the slaughter of Palestinian civilians in the Sabra and Shatila refugee camps after the end of the siege in September, the former defense minister even carried his cause to a New York courtroom. There he sued *Time* for libel, on grounds of what turned out to be a reporter's citation of a nonexistent document. For failing to prove malicious intent as required by U.S. law, his case was eventually dismissed. But as with the war itself, while both sides claimed victory, it was hard to see a real winner.[95]

The U.S. media emerged from the experience reflective, even defensive, once the shooting stopped. In every sense the editors and reporters most intensively watched and appealed to over the course of the long hot summer, they displayed a humility not always typical of their profession. Stung by charges of anti-Israel bias, Ben Bradlee, the executive editor of the *Washington Post,* even invited a representative of the Jewish Community Council to sit in the newsroom for a week, for the most part at the foreign desk. Jim Hoagland, the *Post*'s foreign editor, confirmed that there was also a regular "dialogue" with Arab-American groups. The rules stipulated that the observer would neither write about his experience nor comment publicly before a given day's paper appeared but report only to his officers and directors. According to Hoagland, the observer emerged from the experience undecided if there were bias or not.[96]

Yet many reporters agreed they had let early refugee and casualty figures—from PLO sources, as it turned out—be wildly, and uncritically, abused. In part by deliberate intent of the camera-conscious Arafat, in part by normal exposure to the homeless, bereaved, and distraught, they had also transformed the Palestinian image in ways the Israeli government was powerless to block. "Thanks largely to TV," one B'nai B'rith official noted, "there is a growing recognition in the Jewish community that these are human beings who love, kiss, weep, and have wives."[97]

In the nature of that conflict, the Palestinian gain was Israel's loss. Revealingly, one of the war's most celebrated media confrontations was also one of its most inadvertently ambiguous. "Israeli planes, gunboats and artillery rained indiscriminate shellfire all across West Beirut today," Tom Friedman, the resident correspondent, reported to the *New York Times* on August 4. But the adjective was gone when the paper appeared the next morning. *Indiscriminate* was a word that did not belong in news stories, his editors decided. Friedman shot back at furious length. Transmitted on an open Reuters wire in full view of colleagues from across the profession, his reply was exploited as proof that the *Times* was protecting Israel. Yet, as Friedman himself took pains to explain, he was really trying to spell out the difference between the day before, and the sixty-three days before that, when Israeli fire had *not* been indiscriminate.[98]

Six weeks later, correspondent and editors again agreed on what news was fit to print. By this time, the siege was over; the Palestinians had agreed to withdraw from Lebanon; Bashir Gemayel had first been elected president, then assassinated; and Israeli troops had stood by in West Beirut as vengeful Phalangists slaughtered Palestinians in the Sabra and Shatila refugee camps. Friedman's reconstruction of the massacre appeared on four pages of the *Times*'s huge Sunday edition. Written in what he himself acknowledged as a spasm of Jewish outrage, it won him a Pulitzer for international reporting. Yet once again, he was careful to distinguish shades of black. One of the reasons the Palestinians had been so vulnerable to the Phalangists, Friedman surmised on the basis of both interviews and historical experience, was that they did *not* regard the Israelis as "monsters," and believed themselves under their protection.[99]

Vindication of sorts, the reporting of the war drew fire from both Arab-American and Jewish-American sides. Excepting only the *Christian Science Monitor,* the Arab-American Anti-Discrimination Committee unabashedly noted a "pro-Israeli bias" in all major dailies, combined with "inaccurate and demeaning caricatures" of Moslems, Arabs, and Palestinians. On the other hand, Martin Peretz of the *New Republic,* who wrote early, and Podhoretz, who wrote at considerable length, saw a systemic bias that included such Jewish critics of the war as Meg Greenfield, the *Newsweek* columnist and editorial page editor of the *Washington Post;* Anthony

Lewis, the editorial page columnist of the *New York Times;* and Nat Hentoff, a columnist for the *Village Voice.* Their common grievance, Podhoretz proposed, was that a democratic Israel had succeeded to do in Lebanon what Americans had failed to do in Vietnam. He concluded that Israel's adversaries were guilty not only of anti-Semitism but of "faithlessness to the interests of the United States" and even "the values of Western civilization."[100]

There were also those who thought the press had done pretty well, among them Ghassan Bishara, the Washington correspondent of a West Bank Palestinian paper, and Milton Viorst, an American Jewish free-lance with extensive Middle Eastern experience. "For performance under fire, readers and viewers could have asked for little more," Roger Morris concluded in the *Columbia Journalism Review.*[101] But exceptions aside, there was at least a sediment of residual ambivalence.

Was the symmetrical backlash a proof of objectivity, or only that the media had not done very well with the story? There was introspection about hidden, even subliminal, agendas too. It was argued with some reason that the media had held Israelis to standards not otherwise applied to "Syrians, Yemenis, or Ugandans"; that Americans tended by nature to believe that "violence never solves anything" and that conflicts should be talked out; and that perceptions and coverage of Lebanon had been colored by the putative "lessons" of Vietnam in ways that obscured the basic differences.[102]

As Morris and others noticed, the blind spots were instructive too. There had been few stories on Congress, a body whose goodwill had always been of great interest to Israel. There was little attention to the Occupied Territories, and especially the West Bank, a crucial audience for both Israel and the PLO. There was little perception of the good life that survived intact in much of Christian Lebanon, and that was itself an important clue to what the conflict was about. Perhaps most typically, there was little sense of the context or historical, cultural, and political background of a region where the United States had been heavily engaged since World War II, where U.S. policymakers had fared little better than American reporters, and that most Americans found perennially baffling.

Survey data reflected the dips and curves,[103] but perhaps above all, they reflected the bafflement. Depending on the sample and question, Americans both approved and opposed the raids on Osiraq and Beirut. Yet, although a third believed that Israel threatened U.S. interests and almost two-thirds favored Reagan's embargo of F-16s, over 70 percent favored maintaining or increasing military aid to Israel. In general, the polls made clear that sympathy for Israel had declined significantly since the day, so long yet not so long ago, when Begin, Sadat, and Carter had joined hands at the White House. Yet as late as August 1982, and well into the siege of Beirut, sympathy for Israel was consistently three to five times greater than sympathy for Arabs, though declining numbers expressed much sympathy for Begin. On the eve of Israel's withdrawal from the Sinai, absolute majorities of Americans saw Egypt and Israel as almost equally reliable allies. But on the eve of the war in Lebanon two months later, Israel was seen as a substantially stronger ally, and respondents by a margin of 44–21 saw Israel as likelier to fight for the United States.

The war in Lebanon was something else again. Of those with views, only minorities approved of the invasion, though, as a qualified comfort to the State Department, a thin majority agreed that the war would be "justified" if it succeeded in getting foreign powers out of Lebanon. According to a Harris poll in July, similar majorities agreed that "Israel was right to take defensive action" and that "Israel was wrong to go to war and kill thousands of Lebanese civilians." By early August, approval of the war had declined to 30:60. Yet when Harris combined an earlier question with a new one, similar majorities recorded their disapproval of killing "thousands of Lebanese civilians," and their approval of crushing the PLO, "since the PLO has sworn to destroy Israel and is an international terrorist organization." According to a *Washington Post*-ABC News poll on the eve of the PLO withdrawal, respondents regarded as "aware" supported the Israeli invasion by 52–38; those recorded as "unaware" opposed it by 43–28.

There was no question that Sabra and Shatila left their mark on Americans' perceptions, though even here, the Arabs were still losers. But the real loser was Israel. *Newsweek*-Gallup, after reporting a 49–10 margin of sympathy for Israel a year before, now reported a difference of 32–28; *Washington Post*-ABC, which had reported 52–18 a month before, now reported 48–27. Four days after the massacres, 70 percent agreed that "Begin's policies are hurting support for Israel in the U.S." In August 1981, a near majority of 47–34 told Harris interviewers that the "PLO should not be dealt with because they are armed by the Russians and are trained in terrorist tactics in Russia and Libya." In August 1982, a near majority of 48–42 told *Newsweek*-Gallup that "the United States [should] talk directly with the PLO as the representative of the Palestinian people." But respondents also discriminated nicely, when asked, between "Palestinian," "PLO," and "Arafat." In the wake of the PLO evacuation, a Yankelovich poll showed a 10-point gain in sympathy for Palestinians, a 26-point loss in sympathy for the PLO, and a 29-point loss for Arafat. A few weeks later, according to a Chicago Council on Foreign Relations poll, he was only slightly ahead of Iran's Khomeini as the international figure Americans most loved to hate.[104]

Only months later did sympathy for Israel again come around to earlier levels. In part, this reflected acknowledgment and respect for the public protests and official inquiry that forced Sharon's resignation from the cabinet. At least as important was the cumulative impact of terrorist assaults on the U.S. embassy in Beirut, the marine contingent at the Beirut airport, a TWA airliner en route from Athens to Rome, and the *Achille Lauro,* an Italian cruise ship. Back to 1981 levels within three months of the Beirut massacres, sympathy for Israel peaked at 64 percent after the attack on the *Achille Lauro* in October 1985.

Guided neither by the sovereign vision of a Kissinger or Carter nor driven or significantly inhibited by public opinion, policy tended as often to follow as to lead. Over time, it appeared that the State Department was dominant. But both process and product were frequently reactive, and seemed sometimes positively aleatory. Reagan's peace initiative of September 1, 1982, was a prime example. It was identified with Shultz, who even consulted Henry Kissinger, and left messages for Arafat, suggesting that accession to Resolution 242 would lead to contacts.[105] But the spadework went back at least to the previous spring. The new initiative was neither an improvisation nor a break with previous policy. A conscious challenge to the Israeli right-wing thesis that Jordan was "the" Palestinian state, its first premise was preservation of the Hashemite status quo, with King Hussein as a party to the settlement. The second premise was political status for the Palestinians without concurrent recognition of the PLO.

"The Lebanon war, tragic as it was, has left us with a new opportunity for Middle East peace," Reagan declared. "The question now is how to reconcile Israel's legitimate security concerns with the legitimate rights of the Palestinians." Any solution, he acknowledged gingerly, would require concessions from all sides, including the Arab states, but he emphasized that Jerusalem "must remain undivided," and that the United States "would oppose any proposal—from any party and at any point in the negotiating process—that threatens the security of Israel." Harking back to Camp David, he nonetheless urged Israel to stop further settlement and confer autonomy on the Palestinians for a five-year transitional period. He then moved beyond Resolution 242 and Camp David. Not only did he oppose both "Israeli sovereignty or permanent control" and "an independent Palestinian state in the West Bank and Gaza," he now proposed a specific alternative with a long history of its own. "It is the firm view of the United States that self-government by the Palestinians of the West Bank and Gaza in association with Jordan offers the best chance," Reagan stated.[106]

Arriving at the prime minister's door without advance warning, Ambassador Samuel Lewis presented an advance text to Begin on August 31. It was clear almost instantly that the initiative was going nowhere. Begin, predictably, was one major obstacle. Allowing himself what must surely have seemed a triumphant and well-earned vacation, his first in five years, Begin could only be shocked by what his ultimate ally appeared to have in store for him. He had not been consulted. Demobilization of the troops and consolidation of the putative victory were inevitable and urgent priorities. Renewed demands for suspension of West Bank settlement and territorial concession can only have struck him as a provocation. Within ten days of Reagan's speech, he had mobilized his cabinet, then the Knesset, to record their opposition, while Begin himself, in a published interview, denounced U.S. interference in Israel's internal affairs.[107]

The other predictable obstacle was the Arabs. Challenged and invited to Amman by Hussein's representatives, Arafat chose instead to play for time, while an Arab summit reaffirmed the Fahd plan of 1974 a few days after Reagan's speech. In October 1983, Arafat reappeared in Amman for the first time in twelve years. With the Black September of Jordan's civil war thirteen years behind, Hussein now needed and wanted a mandate from Arafat, though it only promised trouble with the Syrians. As he had already been for years, and certainly been all summer, Arafat was eager too for acceptance by the United States. Like the Americans he regularly conferred with, Hussein was persuaded that acceptance of Resolution 242 was the key to any progress. Yet even after still another watershed debacle, Arafat hesitated. Compliance with the Reagan initiative meant trouble with the Syrians. Above all, it meant trouble with his own disaffected troops. In April 1983, after months of inconclusive negotiations with a frustrated Hussein, he finally flew to Kuwait to try to sell a package, part Reagan, part Fahd, to Fatah and the PLO Council. Both dismissed it out of hand. At this point, Jordan too dismissed the Reagan initiative.[108]

As U.S. attention switched instead to Lebanon, Beirut seemed more than ever a heart of darkness. If only by virtue of Israeli acquiescence, Amin Gemayel had succeeded his dead brother as latest incumbent of his country's traditionally Christian presidency. He was, as Friedman noted, a man with "all of Bashir's weaknesses and none of his strengths."[109] If only by virtue of bad conscience for the refugee camp massacres that had followed U.S. withdrawal, Reagan had meanwhile recommitted the marine contingent. A component of an international force, its role was understood as neutral, "with the mission of enabling the Lebanese government to restore full sovereignty over its capital, the essential precondition for extending its control over the entire country."[110]

But there was nothing very neutral about Amin Gemayel, nor Syria's Asad, nor Begin. Each had his own expectations, both of Gemayel and one another. Wisely or otherwise, it was understandable that Begin wanted a peace treaty with Lebanon. In a sense, it was what the war was all about. Asad's resistance was predictable too. He opposed the treaty for the same reasons Israelis and Americans favored it. In the nature of his situation, Gemayel's position was in the middle. Resolved to maintain traditional Christian hegemony, above all over the Druse and Shiites on the lower rungs of the Lebanese totem pole, he was no less eager to keep Syria at bay, and the Israelis at a distance. To clear the country of foreign armies, and presumably make Lebanon safe for the Lebanese, this thus required a U.S. guarantee. The same was true, of course, of the peace between Egypt and Israel. But unlike Egypt, which was large, physically distant, and disposed to peace for its own reasons, Lebanon remained endlessly penetrable and vulnerable, a medley of civil wars, which outsiders were invariably unable to win or to resist.

In practice, this required a rather different order of U.S. commitment from observers in the Sinai, or even money in the bank. It presumed Washington's ability and willingness to deter and, if necessary, confront Gemayel's adversaries—and their willingness to be thus confronted and deterred. As few Americans yet understood, but some would soon learn, this meant a formal linkage between Israeli-Lebanese peace and U.S. willingness to defend such a settlement against Syrians, supported by the Soviet Union, and Lebanese Shiites, supported by the implacably anti-American Khomeini.

Unsurprisingly, U.S. special envoy Habib preferred a pragmatic security agreement for South Lebanon, negotiated with U.S. mediation. But Sharon had other plans, and Gemayel acceded. In late December 1982, formal peace talks opened. A U.S. delegation was demonstratively present. Meanwhile Lebanese and Israeli negotiators worked out their own terms in private. In March 1983, after three months of strenuous deadlock, Shultz invited the respective foreign ministers to Washington for a week of talks. In April, a terrorist bomb blew up the U.S. embassy in Beirut, killing sixty-three. Among them were seventeen Americans, including Robert Ames, the CIA's chief Middle East analyst, Casey's de facto liaison officer to the PLO, and an unofficial adviser to Shultz.[111]

Two days after the embassy bombing, Shultz returned to the Middle East in person with a draft agreement acceptable to the Israeli cabinet. He then tried to sell it to Damascus, but Asad, whose views had thitherto not been requested, declared it a capitulation to Israel. On May 17, Israeli and Lebanese representatives nonetheless signed the agreement. It stipulated a territorial status quo, mutual regard for sovereignty, and a 45 km "security zone" in southern Lebanon; and provided for trade, an Israeli "liaison" office in Beirut, and an end to the state of war. The arrangement survived pro forma, but unobserved, for ten months. The Lebanese then declared it void.[112]

Seen from a distance, it seemed a no-lose proposition for Israel. If observed, the treaty was its own reward. If not, it was an excuse to remain in Lebanon. But for many Moslems, it was de facto confirmation of their worst suspicions, and for Asad a chance to score on many fronts, including Israel, the United States, PLO.[113] The paradoxical result was more war, not less. By this time, the Soviets had rearmed the Syrians, and the Lebanese had resumed their tribal warfare with familiar gusto. Israelis, who had imprudently put themselves between their Phalangist clients and embattled Druse in the Shuf Mountains, learned gradually and painfully that they had even alienated people who once welcomed them as liberators. They then redeployed southward, where they became a target for the Palestinian refugees and furious Shiites of what Ze'ev Schiff called a potential "North Bank."[114]

Starting in September 1983, offshore U.S. forces began to intervene as well. U.S. fire was seen in part as support for the legitimate authorities, in part as an intended show of credibility after a terrorist bomb destroyed the marine barracks at the Beirut airport, in part as a message to Syria. In the process, the marines became parties, then targets, of the civil war in Lebanon. Only in early 1984, an election year in both the United States and Israel, were they finally transferred offshore. The ships then sailed away, though only after the sixteen-inch guns of the battleship *New Jersey* poured nearly three hundred shells on Shiite camps and villages. But it was dreadfully clear that they had not made peace. "Marines" and "New Jersey," the TWA hijackers shouted a year later at their baffled and terrified hostages.[115]

"The struggle for peace is indivisible." Reagan declared after the marine barracks bombing in October 1983. "The United States will not be intimidated by terrorists," he added.[116] At other times in other places, the decision to pull out might well have cost a Democrat his political life. Yet, by now, with Congress restive, such different Republican Senators as Charles Mathias, Howard Baker, and Barry Goldwater calling for withdrawal, the Pentagon anxious about wrong wars in the wrong place at the wrong time, and the conservative columnists in full agreement, there was a powerful case for cutting losses. Polls showed most Americans positively grateful to be out.[117] A few weeks later, Democrats in the New York presidential primary made traditional noises about moving the U.S. embassy from Tel Aviv to Jerusalem, but none demanded to know "Who lost Lebanon?" or brandished Reagan's Churchillian speeches.

Israeli viewers chuckled indulgently at the folkways of U.S. politics, then turned again to the real news, which was the sudden collapse of their government. If Americans still groped in the shadow of Vietnam, the Israeli scene increasingly recalled Athens after the Sicilian expedition. Domestic consensus was in tatters. Begin had withdrawn from public life in a state of clinical depression. Annual inflation was approaching 300 percent. Two-thirds of the national budget was allocated to defense and service on public debt. Health fees were up, imports down, and a state that had once set out to be a social democratic light unto the nations had imposed a system of fees on secondary education. Ironically, for reasons of thrift, the finance ministry even demanded a one-year freeze on West Bank settlements.[118] In the aftermath of the election, the Israelis too withdrew from Lebanon.

Like a kind of Middle Eastern *Rashomon* in an adaptation by Thomas Hobbes, the legacy of the war was an object lesson, cautionary tale, and puzzle for Americans, Israelis, Palestinians, and Lebanese. In a Lebanon plunged again into sectarian mayhem, presidential authority first retreated to the grounds of the presidential palace, then vanished altogether. In ever-surprising combinations, Shi'ites now battled Shi'ites, and Christians Christians, while Shi'ite militiamen blockaded and brutalized Sabra and Shatila. Eventually, in the aftermath of the Gulf war, Iraq joined as patron of the Lebanese Christians, happily appropriating the country as a theater for its own proxy war with Syria. Apart from a residual South Lebanese "security zone," Israelis once again chose to defend their interests from the air. As before in Iran when a Democrat was in the White House, alienated Shi'ites now made their point by taking U.S. hostages in Lebanon. Now under a Republican president, most remaining Americans followed the marines in an evacuation only slightly less total than the withdrawal from Vietnam.

The PLO was an even more obvious loser. Driven from Beirut as it had already been from Amman and Cairo, it now was scattered from Tunis to Damascus. Like Napoleon from Elba, Arafat briefly returned in late 1982 from Syria to northern Lebanon, where he arrayed his battered loyalists against the Syrians, rebellious Palestinians, Lebanese militiamen, and the Israelis. Now it was the Syrians, and his own disaffected followers, who drove him out of Lebanon. The latest setbacks led to new flirtations with Egypt and Jordan. Yet, as so often in the past, there was no consummation. Shunned by the United States and Israel, Arafat seemed increasingly peripheral, even to fellow Arabs. At a summit in Amman in November 1987, Arab leaders virtually ignored the Palestinians while brooding over the fallout from Iraq's continuing war with Iran. Syptomatically, even the obligatory formula "sole, legitimate representative of the Palestinian people," which had been one of the PLO's proudest achievements, was missing from the English-language version of the final communiqué. In December 1987, when the occupied territories then rebelled, as much against the PLO's irrelevance as the hated Israeli occupation, Arafat had to scramble to catch up with his followers. By summer 1991, after still another war in the Gulf had incapacitated Iraq and so doused the final flickers of Palestinian resistance, a reconstituted Lebanese army went to work on PLO guerrillas in southern Lebanon.

By such a course, it could be argued that "Peace for Galilee" had at least attained a semblance of the promised peace for Galilee. Yet this hardly made Israelis winners, or assured the promised peace for Israel. Locked in perennial conflict with the Palestinians of the Occupied Territories, and what appeared to be perennial deadlock with one another, Israelis quarreled vainly and endlessly over formulas and initiatives for talks with Egypt, Jordan, and even selected Palestinians, while dividing power between Likud and Labor. After another deadlocked election in 1984, the prevailing consensus took the form of a power-sharing arrangement unique in parliamentary history. It at least allowed Israelis to address the Lebanese quagmire and impending economic collapse, before Prime Minister Shimon Peres became Foreign Minister Shimon Peres in 1986. But it also politicized, complicated, and envenomed even such basic decisions as the appointment of a new ambassador to Washington, and virtually precluded any common position on the future of the territories. Political inertia thus assured continued settlement and occupation of the West Bank and Gaza, the continuing rage and desperation of the Palestinians who lived there, and, not least, a dependence on the United States of a nature, magnitude, and ambivalence remarkable even by previous standards.

Yet at the same time, in new and unanticipated ways, the dependency had become explicit and mutual. With hostages in Lebanon, Soviets in Afghanistan, Khomeini in Iran, a seemingly endless war in the Gulf, and the unresolved conflict in the territories, the United States wanted a lot of Israel too. From the very beginning, the relationship had been seen as special from both sides. Now, after more than forty years, an elaborate construction of sticks and carrots, favors and expectations, loose ends and mutual ambivalence confirmed and bore witness to how special it had become.

11

Afterthoughts

All appearances to the contrary, four eventful decades only confirmed the continuities, tensions, even paradoxes of Israeli-U.S. relations. Over forty years, Israelis
and Americans had learned a lot about themselves and each another.[1] Regularly
euphemized as "normalization," the results were both good news and bad news.
More than forty years' experience seemed to suggest that U.S. support was most
certain when Israel was endangered. Yet paradoxically, Israel had rarely seemed so
vulnerable as when an Egyptian president proposed to make peace. In contrast to
their other neighbors, Israelis had thitherto at least been willing to talk to anyone
at any time. Now, as the bangs of the *intifada* followed the whimpers of Lebanon,
even this had become a matter of furious contention. Given the choice of settlement
or settlements, the choice seemed loud and clear. Not only did Israelis no longer
believe that negotiations were possible, they no longer seemed even to care.

Still, the more things changed, the more some really did remain the same. Over
the history of the relationship, three themes stood out with particular prominence.
None had lost its salience. Yet each, while valid unto itself, was also a function of
the others.

The first, the existence of a sovereign Jewish national state in what was once
called Palestine, was unchanged and unchallenged since Israel's independence.
Like the freedom of West Berlin, it had become a measure of U.S. credibility. But
it was also a matter of principle. Americans supported Israel's survival and had
repeatedly risked war to prove it. Yet apart from the Sinai, Israel's borders were as
unresolved as ever, not only between Israel and its neighbors but between Israelis
and Americans. Over four decades, Washington had abstained, intervened, ca-
joled, and threatened, officially and unofficially, multilaterally and unilaterally,
grimly and hopefully, while the state of war continued. Meanwhile Israel sought to
define itself, first tentatively, then with increasing self-assurance and even aggressiveness, within borders that nonetheless remained provisional.

In part in anticipation, in part for sheer lack, of a negotiated settlement,
UNSCOP plus forty had thus come to mean an aggregate of armistice lines: 1948–
1949; augmented by previously Syrian-, Jordanian-, and Egyptian-administered
territories acquired in 1967 and 1973; supplemented by a juridically indeterminate
"security zone" in southern Lebanon created since 1978. But this was assertion,
and self-assertion. As Washington invariably remembered, and Jerusalem seldom
forgot, it was subject as always to revision. For all its deliberate imprecision, Res-

olution 242 too had been a matter of principle since 1967. Each in his way, both Carter and Reagan confirmed that Americans had not changed their reading of the text. Before and after Camp David, as one author turned policymaker noted, this meant that peace was linked to territory, and that Americans continued to consider the status of the Golan, Gaza, the West Bank, even Jerusalem, as negotiable in principle as the Sinai.[2]

The second major theme was Israel's status as an ally or, as per the formula that had become virtually automatic since the middle 1970s, its utility as a "strategic asset." Unlike the first, the second theme was equivocal from the beginning. For most of the forty years since Israel's independence, the global struggle called the Cold War formed the context of the relationship, but the postcolonial Middle East that began to emerge in the early 1950s was just as pertinent. Was support for Israel an interest in itself, and good for U.S. interests? Or was it a handicap both in the region and beyond it? Successive administrations, agencies, advocates, and constituencies had reached quite different conclusions on such questions, some of them at once. Seemingly piecemeal and ad hoc, contingent on political mood and circumstance, Carter Democrats differed from Truman Democrats, Nixon and Reagan Republicans from Eisenhower Republicans, Haig's State Department from Rusk's and Rogers's State Department, Casey's CIA from Allen Dulles's CIA. But for forty years, the question itself had been a constant.

The third persisting theme, for Americans no less than Israelis, was Israel's place in a region where three continents, many different painful histories, and 65 percent of the world's proven oil reserves now intersected. A world-class arms race since the early 1950s only confirmed the cumulative impact of demography and cultural despair, oil wealth and religious fervor, geopolitics and unrequited nationalism on a part of the world where all six combined and collided in ever-more-volatile combinations. Between 1973 and 1983 alone, arms spending in constant dollars had risen from $23.8 billion to $60.9 billion. Between 1983 and 1990, the curve continued to rise. Of the world's top-ten arms consumers, seven were Middle Eastern. Of these—Saudi Arabia, Iraq, Iran, Afghanistan, Syria, Egypt, and Libya—six were formally or nominally at war with Israel. Between 1987 and 1990 alone, Americans sold $30.7 billion, the Soviet Union $17.5 billion, in state-of-the-art weaponry to Middle Eastern clients. Unaffected by their mutual détente, the superpowers thus helped the region hold its place as the world's biggest arms bazaar, accounting for more than half of global sales.[3]

As always, the regional arms race reflected a political landscape unlike any other. Sometimes believed monolithic, sometimes anarchic, the Middle East was actually neither. Instead, it was a region whose natural dynamics rendered it as attractive, yet resistant, to aspiring hegemons as the Europe of Richelieu or Bismarck. Since the beginning of history, it had been catnip to foreign armies, whose artifacts could be seen in the great museums of Jerusalem, Cairo, and Baghdad alike. Yet Assyrian or Persian, Hellenic or Roman, Byzantine or Arab, Ottoman, Romanov, British, or French, regional motives and experience seemed as constant and familiar as the great river valleys at the heart of the region's political geography. Jerusalem was a practical example. Over four thousand years, the city had been besieged and conquered thirty-seven times. Over the same period, soldiers had variously fought with bronze and steel, spears and cordite, chariots and diesel engines. But relative to the contending sovereignties of the Nile and the Fertile Crescent, the city remained where it had been in biblical times.[4]

Reluctantly heedful of the same imperatives that moved their predecessors, Americans had joined the game since World War II. The experience was not much fun. Suez alone had changed the regional scene beyond all recognition. With their eccentric maps and compasses, Americans scrambled as best they could to shape the landscape, and find their way in the unfamiliar topography. Five presidential "doctrines" since 1947 testified to the resulting shocks and improvisations. In the forty years between the Truman Doctrine and Irangate, Iran and Lebanon had come and gone as U.S. clients, Egypt had switched from "their" to "our" side, and Syria and Iraq had marched to many drummers. Oil had nonetheless flowed with minimal interruption; Soviet communism had lost the little allure it had for the successor states of World War I; and reports of the death of these nominally fragile sovereignties had proved consistently exaggerated.

Some questions consistently refused to go away. One was whether the partition of Palestine had been a transitional phase or a necessary condition of Jewish statehood. Another was whether the United States could be both a friend of Israel and an honest broker between Jews and Arabs. A third was what to do about the people, twice displaced since 1948, whom even Israelis had since learned to call Palestinians. But perhaps most important for Israeli-U.S. relations were the nature and viability of Israel, and its significance and attractiveness to the Americans, whose money and support had become so crucial to its future.

Measured by aid levels, memoranda of understanding, and the conventional rituals of U.S. electoral politics, the relationship had seemingly become more special than ever. Yet measured by votes with the feet and even checkbook, the news was mixed for both countries. Since 1948, only 50,000 of some 6 million American Jews had emigrated to Israel. Of these, increasing numbers also came from the religious and nationalist Right and ultra-Right. Among them was the forthrightly annexationist and Arab-bashing Rabbi Meir Kahane, whose message that democracy was bad for Jews, and that all Palestinians should be driven across the Jordan, even got him elected to the Knesset. By comparison, as many as 300,000 of 3.5 million Israeli Jews, many professional and most unpolitical, had settled by 1990 as permanent or semipermanent residents of the United States. By the same token, congressional appropriations since 1975 had attained, and remained at, record levels. But American-Jewish investors had shown themselves consistently unresponsive to Israeli appeals for U.S. investment; as many as three-quarters of all American Jews had never even visited Israel as tourists; and United Jewish Appeal contributions, as measured in constant dollars, had peaked in 1974.[5]

Since then, those with a taste for Clausewitz, Thucydides, or the prophet Jeremiah, whose self-lacerating lamentations are read in darkened synagogues every year on the anniversary of the fall of Jerusalem to the Babylonians, could subsume the basic issues in a master theme. This was the perennial question of how people should define, achieve, and pay for their security. But, as always, the master theme could be reduced to questions that might be asked in turn of any state-to-state relationship. What is this about? Whom does it involve? Who's in charge? What are the choices? Who are the winners—or losers? Which are the means, and which the ends? How much is this worth, and to whom?

Perennially difficult to answer, the questions, at least, had once seemed relatively simple. Now such tests and challenges as free trade and strategic understandings, the Lavi aircraft and the Arrow missile, the end of the Cold War and wars in the Persian Gulf, an American-Jewish spy and a constitutional psychodrama, the Palestinian *intifada* and the multilateral "peace process" suggested that even these had become peculiarly elusive. But they at least illuminated the trade-offs and mechanisms that had come to make the relationship so special.

An indirect legacy of Lebanon, a report by the U.S. General Accounting office (GAO) was itself both a benchmark and CAT scan of the strategic relationship both countries now claimed to take for given. Even more remarkably, it seemed to be the first such survey ever. Officially intended for Congress, the body traditionally most sensitive to Israeli concerns, its specific addressees were Senator Charles Percy, the Illinois Republican who was chairman of the Foreign Relations Committee, and Clement J. Zablocki, the Wisconsin Democrat who was chairman of its House counterpart. Since neither was an uncritical supporter of Israel, and since both seemed keen to find a source immune to the conflicted priorities of official Washington, the report was remarkable even for its authorship. Clad in a reassuring image of green eyeshades, sleeve garters, and calf-length socks, the GAO was clearly seen as a professional, nonpartisan, even unpolitical guide in what the text itself acknowledged as an intensely political environment. Sometime after its official release, an earlier draft was leaked to the American-Arab Anti-Discrimination Committee, a Washington-based policy lobby. Rather grandly but misleadingly identified as the "uncensored" version, this then appeared in a modest edition, with supporting text from two Palestinian academics, and an introduction by Elmer Berger, the veteran anti-Zionist, who had once presided over the American Council on Judaism.[6] But for those already disposed to worry that there was something rotten in the state of Israeli-U.S. relations, the official version was potent enough.

In effect, the report was an anatomy of two dilemmas, one a U.S. dilemma, one Israeli. The first, as the financial history of recent decades made clear in a variety of other ways, was inherent in the nature of foreign aid. Borrowers depend on lenders, but also vice versa. The larger the loan, the greater the dependency of both. Default threatens lenders as well as borrowers. Political lending only complicates choices. What applies to real estate, business, and economic development loans, applies all the more to loans on national security.

As an earlier generation might have remembered from the European Recovery, also known as the Marshall, Plan of 1948, political loans follow political logic. Originally keen on interest-paying loans and lots of federal buying in their districts, Congress soon realized that European recovery was really the goal. Political ends had then caused revision of the economic means: more grants, instead of loans, to minimize interest payments; more offshore deals, instead of domestic purchases, to cut costs and maximize comparative advantage.[7]

Though no one thought or dared to ask it, the question was whether Israeli security might be a comparable case. In principle, the Israelis offered their growth potential, productivity, and export capacity as collateral on U.S. loans, but the only really commensurate payoff was political, not commercial. The real collateral was Israel's security. A securer Israel, ran the argument, meant a securer United States. Any aid bill stood or fell on the willingness of a Congress, including a Senate that had never ratified a formal defense pact, to take this as given.

The second dilemma was the soaring cost of independence. In an age of missiles and avionics, military technology had long become interchangeable with high technology. Even superpowers now took it for given that lead times were long, research costs formidable, development costs prohibitive, and unit costs sky-high.[8] The global arms bazaar confirmed how affordable domestic production all but demanded foreign sales. What applied to rich, developed Sweden, France, and Britain inevitably applied to Israel.

Geography, politics, and history only sharpened the Israeli dilemma. Israel governments could neither afford nor neglect to go it alone. But for the first Czech arms deal of spring 1948, the state might never have been created. The second Czech arms deal, the basis of the Soviet sale to Egypt in 1955, caused something like an existential crisis. Before and after 1967, reliance on France exacted its price. In October 1973, the whether and when of U.S. resupply had caused another national drama. Domestic production seemed an obvious course. In practice, it only meant new dependencies on foreign technology and capital.

Methodical as bookkeepers, the GAO authors spelled out the consequences. How would aid to Israel affect global and regional arms races? they asked. What would happen if other countries asked, and got, similar considerations from the United States? To what extent were U.S. commitments likely to become self-perpetuating as Israel confronted the costs of repayment?

Since 1948, the authors reported, the United States had invested some $25 billion as part of a "commitment to Israel's continued national existence." Rooted in "shared cultural, religious, moral and political values" that presumably went back to the beginnings of Israeli statehood, the bulk of U.S. aid had nonetheless been spent since 1974. Although, as they noted, the aggregate was unrelated to "any specific agreement such as a mutual security pact," about two-thirds of all aid consisted of military assistance. Since the end of the Vietnam war, Israel had actually consumed more such assistance than any other country. Since 1974, about half of it had been in grants, yet the totals only seemed likely to go higher, the report concluded.[9]

The findings revealed and documented a truly impressive degree of dependency. In 1982, Israel's defense spending was already estimated at 21.3% of GNP, and defense and "debt alignment" constituted 57% of its total budget. By 1987, nearly 60% of government research money went into military research and development.[10] Both an effect and a cause of Israeli defense policy, military or defense-related industries were reported to employ a fifth of the work force. U.S. aid constituted 12% of Israel's GNP. A third of the Israeli defense budget between 1977 and 1981, U.S. aid funded 37% of it in 1982. Projections for the following years rose as high as 50%.[11]

The authors also noted a series of statutory concessions and accommodations unique to, or born of, Israeli-U.S. programs. Conceived to relieve the service burden on the beneficiaries, they were thus designed to maximize Israeli bang per U.S.

buck. In contrast to earlier beneficiaries, for example, Israelis enjoyed "cash-flow financing." This allowed them to invest successive grants in new contracts rather than commit the money to existing ones. The United States had also underwritten Israeli redeployment in the Sinai, replaced existing bases with some of the world's most modern underground airfields, and left behind an entire fleet of building equipment. In addition, Israel had been allowed 40-percent write-offs on loans; economic aid untied to specific projects; trade offset agreements that linked U.S. aid to assured U.S. purchases of Israeli goods, and access to technologies that contributed to Israel's own export potential.

Consistent with their mandate, the authors feared for the precedents. Egypt and Turkey, they noted, already benefited from considerations first extended to Israel. There was also the vexed question of political and economic trade-offs. On the one hand, liberalized terms of payment meant Israelis could buy more in the United States. On the other, they meant less interest income for U.S. taxpayers. Actually, as the report acknowledged, Israelis were generally good about their obligations. There was nonetheless a strong hint of approval for Secretary of the Treasury Donald Regan in a paragraph deleted from the official version. Regan, the authors noted, had refused to advance release of appropriated aid so Israelis could bank the money and earn interest before spending it. "Congress authorized a specified amount of assistance, . . . 'not that amount, plus interest,'" the authors quoted an unnamed Treasury official.[12]

More significant and interesting were the familiar contours of Catch-22. These took three roughly complementary and interactive forms. One was the familiar ratchet effect of arming potentially adversarial Middle Eastern clients, at the risk of losing business to competitors, including Moscow. Twice since 1978, U.S. administrations had delivered arms packages to Jordan and Saudi Arabia, the report observed. Intended to defend both clients against their Iranian and Arab neighbors, they were incidentally supposed to stabilize the region. Yet each time, the outcome seemed to be increased aid to Israel. An extra $300 million as compensation for the famous AWACS sale, as another deleted paragraph noted, was a practical example. In U.S. perspective, Egypt was now on "our" side, as Jordan and Saudi Arabia had been for years. Yet Israelis saw two of the three—along with Iraq and Syria—as immediate threats, and even Egypt was still considered potentially threatening pending further experience with the peace treaty.

In effect, the system was open-ended. Predictably, Americans tended to be more sanguine about Israeli security than the Israelis, though CIA and State Department sources were less confident than their Pentagon colleagues about the longer-term prospects. In Washington's view, Israeli leadership, motivation, morale, and training sufficed to overcome a handicap of 3:1. But the Arab advantage already exceeded that, the Israelis answered, and would only get worse if Americans continued selling arms to Arabs. Fearful of casualties in the event of another war, they accordingly requested more aid of the United States. Fearful with reason of Israeli preemption, the Americans gave serious consideration to the new requests. But, in the logic of Camp David, they then made sure that Egypt got more too.[13]

The impact of aid on the U.S. economy was a second familiar problem. The concern took two forms. One was debt service, the other job loss and potential competition. Unlike Israel's economy, the authors estimated, Israel's military debt was likely to grow by about 25 percent over the next decade.[14] Policy options included commercial loans, refinancing, debt forgiveness, and direct investment in the Israeli economy with the goal of making the economy more competitive, and thereby making Israel less dependent on aid.

But this only meant more dilemmas. Congress could agree to an indirect loss by letting Israel pay more for commercial loans. Or it could squeeze the federal budget to extend the current cheaper ones—in fact, squeeze it twice, since Egypt would claim equivalent terms to Israel's. Alternatively, it could forgive the loans or advance new money to repay the old ones. Other possibilities included leaving ill enough alone; letting other U.S. clients spend U.S. aid money in Israel, or making Israel efficient enough to compete with the Pentagon in hitherto U.S. markets, for example, in Latin America.[15]

Arms exports were already an Israeli growth industry: up 15% in 1974, 80% in 1975, 85% in 1976. As export-dependent and technology-conscious as Singapore, Hongkong, or Taiwan, Israeli producers nonetheless aimed for different targets. Since the mid-1960s Israelis had regularly invested as much as 3% of their GNP in research and development (R&D). They thus put themselves in a league with Japan and Germany, and ahead of the United States, Britain, and France. By 1991, the investment paid off in high-tech products that already constituted about 40% of industrial exports. By the mid-1990s, it was hoped, this figure would rise to about 60%—a matter of some importance to a work force heavily tilted toward technicians, professionals, and academics.[16]

Yet, as the GAO report itself confirmed, both R&D and high-tech exports were heavily mortgaged to a sector remarkable for both its political and economic vicissitudes. In 1982, arms were believed to constitute a fourth to a third of all industrial, and 10 percent of total, exports. By comparison, Britain and the United States sold about a quarter of their defense production abroad; Israelis, half or more. Meanwhile, the high-tech share of industrial exports had risen from less than 1 percent in the early 1970s to a third of the total in 1981. By 1987, Israel Aircraft Industries (IAI) alone reported sales of $1 billion, $650 million of it in exports to some sixty countries. By 1990, Israel—exceeded only by the vastly larger Soviet Union, the United States, Britain, France, and China—had become the sixth-leading purveyor of arms to Asia, Africa, and Latin America. But even this was no assurance that the industry turned a profit.[17]

It was only another Israeli paradox that the road to self-reliance led to new dependencies. Even Israelis acknowledged that a third of their technological exports required imported components, and that 35 percent of the electronic expertise they invested in their fastest-growing industry had been acquired for licensed production from the United States.[18]

The Lavi (Lion) was a kind of metaphor of the choices facing both partners. Conceived in the mid-1970s, it was still intended in 1979 as a low-cost, low-technology, ground support replacement for U.S. A-4s and Israeli Kfirs. At least initially, both Israeli and U.S. officials inclined to support a program that would enhance Israeli's industrial base and self-sufficiency, while incidentally employing twenty thousand aircraft workers. Development costs, financed with U.S. military assistance, were estimated at $750 million, unit costs per plane at about $7 million.

Four years later, this already looked quite different. By 1983, the cost of development had doubled, and the estimated unit cost of the new design had risen by more than half. It also appeared that its Pratt and Whitney engine, Lear Siegler avionics, and Grumman airframe technology, plus weapons systems, would all be U.S. imports or U.S.-licensed, U.S.-financed, Israeli-produced U.S. technologies. Factored for development and production costs, the cost of a single plane was now estimated at $15.5 million, compared to $12 million for the U.S. Air Force's latest F-16. To this point, neither U.S. nor European makers showed any interest in participation, though Pratt and Whitney was later to buy a minority share of the company proposed to produce the engines.[19] Exports would arguably lower the unit prices on the estimated four hundred planes Israel wanted for itself, but in succeeding years, the projected Israeli order fell as low as seventy-five, while production costs mounted and budgets sagged.[20] Arguably, foreign sales might yet make up the difference, but this already led to screwy logic with regard to a plane proposed for local needs. It also inevitably led to more political problems, since the need for foreign sales could only make the Lavi compete with U.S. and European products. Yet, the plane's U.S. contents would surely subject foreign sales to U.S. approval.

Israeli politicians and officials argued strenuously for both the psychic and the economic benefits of the Lavi. It would maintain Israel's vulnerable technological advantage, they insisted. It would obviate the need of the United States to sell Arab clients its most modern fighters on grounds that Israel already had them. It would support an advanced domestic aircraft industry with all its collateral benefits, including some twenty thousand jobs. It would keep engineers from emigrating. It was even asserted that it would generate an estimated thirty-seven thousand jobs and $1.5 billion in spending in the United States. U.S. officials replied that the Lavi was "an unwise use" of defense funds—though this paragraph too was deleted from the official version.[21] It was clear that they understood quite well how suspension of U.S. aid could kill the whole program with indeterminate political consequences.

At this point the battle was joined, not least in Israel itself, where the state comptroller had declared the project a "fait accompli" as early as 1981.[22] Under pressure, Defense Minister Ariel Sharon had eventually commissioned a cost-benefit analysis. But the options were deliberately limited: building the Lavi, coproducing it with the United States, or buying an alternative. No one, it seemed, had ever asked about its impact on alternative projects, the other military services, or the economy as a whole.

By 1984, Israeli inflation had reached 450 percent, and government deficits constituted 17 percent of GNP (compared to 5 percent in the United States). A year later, research and development costs on the Lavi had reached $2 billion, the estimated cost of the program had reached $9 billion, and the plane's unit cost was now believed to exceed $20 million. By now, two former air force chiefs of staff had turned against the project, including Ezer Weizman, who had once helped launch it. Yet despite resistance from General Dynamics, Northrop, Lockheed, the Pentagon, and organized labor, there was virtually no resistance in Congress, where one man's cost overrun was widely seen as another man's test of loyalty to Israel. By 1987, not only had Congress invested $1.75 billion in the Lavi but the administration had reversed Pentagon policy so Israel could invest U.S. military aid directly in the project.[23]

In the end, it took a combination of Israeli and U.S. flak to shoot it down. If friends of the Lavi like Moshe Arens, a former defense minister and professional aeronautical engineer, saw the Lavi as Israel's economic salvation, some of the country's top managers increasingly viewed it as a black hole, or what one called "a lion that may eat all the other small animals." Labor, skills, and capital lavished on the Lavi, Arens argued, were only lost to electronic, robotic, ballistic, optical, and metallurgical products that Israel could use, make, and sell competitively.

Meanwhile, as U.S. trade and budget deficits soared to record levels, Washington too read the handwriting on the financial walls. Among the consequences were the budget-freezing Gramm-Rudman-Hollings bill and audible threats both to and from the Pentagon. Applicable to all categories of federal spending, Gramm-Rudman-Hollings ended the bull years at the Pentagon, and effectively cut aid to Israel by denying adjustments for inflation. If Israel continued developing the Lavi, "the Defense Dept. will be far less enthusiastic about carrying out other cooperative arrangements," one senior official told *Aviation Week,* where his threat was certain to be seen and understood.[24] Under such circumstances, a high-performance Israeli warplane, funded to 90 percent with U.S. money, was bound to lose some teflon.

But Americans also took care to flash the occasional carrot. A letter from Ambassador Thomas Pickering to all cabinet members reportedly assured $100 million for continued research in advanced aircraft technology, and increased the amount of military aid convertible into local currency to $400 million, about 20 percent of the total. In September 1987, by 12–11, with one abstention, the minister of health who had thitherto supported it, the cabinet voted to kill the Laos. Arens resigned in protest, and IAI employees broke through a fence, manhandled officials, blockaded plant gates and highways, temporarily obstructed a runway at Ben-Gurion Airport, and threatened to bring down the government in demonstrations that recalled the evacuation of Yamit. Job losses were projected at four thousand; it was, in fact an underestimate. But two years later, the aircraft division of IAI was largely engaged in subcontract projects for various commercial and military aerospace programs, mainly U.S.[25]

As with Yamit, there was rather less to the show than met the eye. Though of arguable gauge and denier, at least two nets were already in place. In 1985, the United States officially invited Israel to take part in the Strategic Defense Initiative (SDI) or "Star Wars." It was widely assumed that participation would give Israel access to what were intended to be some of the world's most advanced military technologies. Though some expressed reservations on both moral and political grounds, a large majority of Israel's military-intellectual complex was clearly delighted. In May 1986, U.S. and Israeli officials concluded a new Memorandum of Understanding to govern their cooperation. It was also reported that the U.S. Army, Navy, and Air Force were looking for cooperative programs of their own, some in such advanced areas as avionics, weaponry, and remotely piloted vehicles.

The new MOU followed closely on similar agreements with Britain and West

Germany, both NATO allies. Within a year, contracts with Israeli firms had already reached a volume of $10.8 million, compared with $2.3 million in Italy, $28.9 million in Britain, and $48.2 million in West Germany. At least pro forma, the arrangement allowed for Israeli as well as U.S. financing; reserved ownership of U.S.-funded projects to the United States, and imposed limits on third-party transfers. Pentagon officials emphasized that coordinated, as opposed to subcontracted, development was new territory, and warned that congressional sensitivities would require Israeli firms to work closely with U.S. counterparts if they hoped to get contracts.[26]

By early December 1987, only a few months after cancellation of the Lavi, the enterprise was already in familiar trouble. IAI was now hard at work on a antitactical missile called the Arrow. The first Western system of its kind, the Arrow was at the same time an authentic Third World weapon, conceived for a strategic landscape where short- and intermediate-range ballistic missiles had now become cheap and readily available, while peace had not. Its obvious purpose was to intercept such short-range Soviet-made missiles as the Scud and SS-21 missiles launched from Iraq and Syria.[27] The Israelis demanded that the United States fund up to 90 percent of a thirty-month, $125 million demonstration experiment, yet neither the U.S. Army, which the Israelis regarded as a presumptive customer, nor SDI, whose budget was already being squeezed, were keen to support it. Congress, which had recently put up an extra $75 million in aid, was supportive. But there was no consensus either on a proposed Pentagon formula calling on the United States to put up 90 percent—50 percent of it in cash, with 40 percent more from Israel's $1.8 billion in U.S. foreign military sales (FMS) credits—with the rest to come from Israel. The army, it was noted, was already having a hard time supporting the advanced PAC-2 version of Raytheon's U.S.-made Patriot.[28]

Second thoughts had clearly been thought when Yitzak Rabin, now Israel's defense minister, arrived in Washington a few weeks later to sign yet another MOU. The new version, valid for ten years, effectively put Israel in a class with Sweden, Australia, and the NATO allies—though, on obvious political grounds, Egypt too was reported to be a candidate for equal status. It was also agreed that 80 percent of the Arrow test would be funded by SDI. Israel would then pay the balance without resort to FMS credits. Ironically, Israel anticipated at least $3 million more in incremental aid from West Germany, which had become its largest scientific partner, and was also both another ally and a potential competitor of the United States. The Germans too had been quick to join SDI. Eager to make Daimler-Benz a major producer of electronics, aircraft, and jet engines, they now co-opted Israel as an accessory to the biggest German-based armaments group since Krupp.[29]

In August 1990, the Arrow was finally tested, about two weeks after Iraq's invasion of Kuwait, and a day after Iraq's President Saddam Hussein had threatened to attack Israel with missiles. Though Americans were skeptical about its radar, command-and-control equipment, and other technical specifications, Israeli officials considered the test a success. Yet the Arrow already showed promise of recapitulating the history of the Lavi. Its development had already consumed about $158 million, 81 percent of it U.S. money. Even Israelis admitted that budget shortfalls could delay its operational deployment until the mid or late 1990s.[30]

The military operations that broke out a few months later thus tested priorities of almost every kind. Among the contending claims on budget makers, policy planners, and strategic thinkers alike was $37 million to resettle new Soviet-Jewish immigrants. The wave was expected to reach a million, in U.S. terms the equivalent of resettling the population of France. By summer 1991, several hundred thousand immigrants from the Soviet Union, as well as thousands more from Ethiopia, had already poured into the country.

Depending on perspective, the new immigrants were either a new Israeli-U.S. dilemma or another variation of an old one. Haunted by the differential between Palestinian birthrates and their own, Israelis had long understood that demography too was security.[31] Now, for the first time since the Bolshevik revolution, Jews were both eager and able to leave the Soviet Union. Israelis not only wanted their skills and numbers but were prepared to fight to get them. Not least under pressure from Israel, Washington, with the support of major Jewish groups, agreed in 1989 to limit Soviet-Jewish immigration to the United States to 40,000 a year.

Considering the actual preferences of large numbers of Soviet-Jewish immigrants, and the origins and original choice of large numbers of American Jews, the decision was as morally equivocal as the immigrant policy of 1947.[32] In the event, as they had been forty years before, the immigrants, who were Israel's long-term hope, were also its short-term nightmare. And once again, the United States seemed the only solution: in this case, as guarantor of $10 billion in loans to underwrite resettlement.

Since the 1960s, France had resettled a million of its own citizens from North Africa. Since the 1980s, West Germans had resettled hundreds of thousands of ethnic Germans from eastern Europe. By July 1990, American Jews had privately pledged $600 million to resettle Soviet Jews in Israel, but this was scarcely a fraction of the $20 billion believed to be required for such a project. It was hard to think of any precedent for what was now proposed. Declaring it in the donor's interest as well as its own, and thus, incidentally updating the old Zionist joke, one country asked another to help resettle immigrants from a third.[33] In fact, there might have been a precedent had Saudi Arabia or Kuwait ever seen fit to resettle Palestinians in Syria, Egypt, or Iraq. But since 1948, such ideas had been dismissed out of hand.

In its way, the Gulf war was also a test of the Arrow. About a year before the war began, Israel acquired a battery of U.S.-made Patriots, and subsequently ordered two more. But the battery was not yet operational in January 1991. Targeted by Iraqi Scuds fired at random from mobile launchers, Israelis now huddled in the shadow of U.S. missile batteries, rushed to the scene and operated by Israeli-American and all-Israeli crews. For those mindful of precedent, this was the first time that Israel had ever been directly defended by U.S. troops.

Amidst the fog of war, there were choruses of enthusiasm for the Patriot's effectiveness,[34] but the perspective changed as the fog lifted, assisted by questioning from Congressman Les Aspin's Democratic-controlled House Armed Services Committee. Over the war's six weeks, Patriot batteries fired 158 missiles at 47 Scuds. Yet there were dramatic differences in the assessment of the impact. According to U.S. claims soon after the war, Patriots had intercepted 45 of the 47 incoming missiles, while both Raytheon and the Israeli government reported 44 percent destruction of their warheads. Later analyses, presumably from partisans of Arrow—and contested by other Israelis, presumably partial to Patriot—estimated that warhead destruction had been as low as 0–20 percent.[35] In some cases, Israelis charged, Patriots had even increased the damage—in part by diverting missiles from heading harmlessly off course or into the sea; in part because debris from both missiles combined to form a double hazard.[36]

Arguably, the longer-range and higher-speed Arrow might have minimized the damage. This presupposed that the system was available and affordable; that its superiority to the Patriot was generally recognized and acknowledged; that there was money to build it in adequate numbers; and that Americans were willing to pay what it required.[37] But all of this was large and speculative. As with the Lavi, the problem of the Arrow was of cost rather than quality, and the paradoxes it posed were both stark and familiar. Of course, Israel could not afford its failure. But could it also afford its success? By 1989, defense had declined from 13 percent to under 10 percent of GNP, and from 30 percent to under 20 percent of the current budget. Yet defense plus debt service now came to 70 percent of the budget.

"The defense industry will always lead in technology in Israel," Rabin told an interviewer, but there was a distant echo of the Red Queen's message to Alice about running as fast as one could to stay in the same place. Though budget cuts had reduced defense employment by fourteen thousand, including six thousand jobs at IAI alone, Israeli industries now produced a world-class line of military exports, including missiles for both attacking and defending ships, television- and laser-guided bombs and infrared guided missiles, multimode and phased-array radars, active and passive early warning systems, an airborne search-and-rescue system, and a startling variety of avionic and electro-optical systems. Both a space satellite and main battle tank were already in the works. Of total output, as much as 65 percent to 75 percent was intended for sale abroad. Yet the fewest of Israeli defense companies acknowledged they were really making money. Tadiran, a major electronics manufacturer, seemed more typical. With about half its effort invested in defense, the company generated a turnover of almost $1 billion in 1988, but still lost $10 million that year.[38]

Did such projects make Israel more or less secure? Did their attendant costs make Israel less or more dependent? And anyway, as Henry Kissinger had once asked of nuclear superiority, what was such technical superiority good for? Was it a substitute for peace, the equivalent of peace, a necessary condition for achieving peace? "Can honour set to a leg?" as Falstaff asked.[39] Could technical superiority achieved at such a price promote the general welfare? Was it even, necessarily, the best way to provide for the common defense?

As U.S. diplomatic pressure resumed in the aftermath of still another war, and Soviet immigrants began arriving in hundreds of thousands, Israel bonds fell to BBB, Standard & Poor's lowest rating.[40] Yet the questions were as inevitable and unresolved as ever. The free trade agreement, concluded in 1985, reflected the same conundrums in a different form. It was no coincidence that hearings on the measure coincided with an Israeli economic crisis, including zero growth, roaring inflation, hopeful plans for an export-driven recovery, and a record request for U.S. aid.[41] The very purpose of the agreement, Oregon's Republican Senator Robert Packwood emphasized as the hearings convened, was to "encourage development in Israel that hopefully will lessen its dependence on U.S. aid."

The parade of witnesses before the House Ways and Means Committee and the Senate Finance Committee profiled the interests at stake. Though a 422–0 House majority sent its own emphatic message, the California Almond Growers Exchange, the California Avocado Commission, the California-Arizona Citrus League, the Florida Fruit and Vegetable Association, the American Textile Manufacturers Institute, the U.S. Bromine Alliance, and the Leather Products Coalition appeared pro forma to express concern, and even organized labor, for all its traditional friendliness to Israel, expressed reservations. No major business group—the U.S. Chamber of Commerce, the National Association of Manufacturers, not to mention the Emergency Committee for U.S. Trade—appeared to speak at all. On the other hand, AIPAC, the Zionist Organization of America, and the National Association of Arab-Americans were conspicuously represented.[42]

From an Israeli perspective, the agreement was at once shrewd, courageous, and incalculable in its impact. A market of marginal interest to Americans, Israel was at least of interest to Israelis, whose unassuming local products had once been viewed as the triumph of Zionist socialism. At least in theory, free trade would seem to mean an avalanche of superior consumer goods in a market already addicted to imports. By leveling both tariff and nontariff barriers between the two countries, the free trade agreement seemed to make Israel duty-free for U.S. products and a kind of fifty-first state.[43]

The agreement was novel in two ways. As the first of its kind in a program of bilateral trade liberalizations, it became a precedent for subsequent U.S. free trade agreements with Canada and Mexico. Unlike any free trade agreement to date, it also included services. Though the paragraphs on services were not legally binding, they applied, at least in principle, to such sectors as law, transportation, tourism, banking, communications, insurance, consulting, computer services, and advertising, subject only to such limits—though these could, of course, be considerable—as might be imposed by regulatory bodies. Government procurement too was officially bilateralized. This made U.S. companies eligible not only to compete with local suppliers for contracts of $50,000 and up but to submit their bids to the Ministry of Defense. Since Israel had enjoyed a free trade agreement with the European Community (EC) since the middle 1970s, and EC producers claimed half the Israeli market, equal access to Israel was a marginal payoff for aspiring U.S. exporters. At least as interesting in the increasingly contentious world of global trade was Israel's utility as a bridge to the EC. One of the agreement's particular virtues, as one U.S. official pointed out, was as a vehicle for expanded licensing, joint ventures, and cooperative research and development. By 1989, Israeli officials were even beating the bushes in pursuit of bilateral arrangements with U.S. states.[44]

By 1989, politics, Israeli industrial development, the weak dollar, and the free trade agreement had all combined to make the United States Israel's biggest trading partner with an 18 percent share of the market, despite purchase taxes from 5 percent to 220 percent and special levies on food and farm products. By comparison, Israel's share of the U.S. market amounted to about 0.5 percent, the equivalent, for yet another standard of measurement, of the Soviet Union's. Contrary to earlier

expectations that free trade would mean an avalanche of Crest and Colgate, Marl-
boros and bourbon, Head & Shoulders and Selsun Blue, the real growth sectors
appeared to be computers and telecommunications, including a Voice of America
transmitter. With its 50 percent market share, the United States was Israel's biggest
foreign supplier of computers, peripherals, and software. By 1991, as the price of
oil rose in response to the Gulf war and streams of Soviet immigrants descended on
Israel, U.S. Commerce Department officials saw bright prospects for coal and housing materials, as well as the usual high-tech products.[45]

The constitutional mare's nest, known somewhat awkwardly as the Iran-Contra
affair, and officially documented in a sprawling mass of presidential commission
findings, congressional inquiries, and judicial transcripts,[46] illuminated a rather different kind of Israeli-U.S. exchange. Seemingly unique, it was also, as Yagil Weinberg observed, a manifestation of two established policies: Israel's role as a U.S.
proxy, and both countries' concern with international terrorism.[47] In fact, the Iran
and Contra segments were actually discrete, born of rather different expectations
and circumstances in very different parts of the world. But Israel was somehow
common to both, and the functional links between them, and the identity of many
of the actors, exposed a dimension of Israeli-U.S. relations that again revealed how
special the relationship had become.[48]

The Contra part came first. Since taking office in 1981, the Reagan administration had made things as hard as possible for the revolutionary regime in Nicaragua,
which sought aid and support from the Soviet Union and Cuba, and itself supported
a similarly minded movement in neighboring El Salvador. Yet presidential intentions and administration efforts had consistently run into congressional opposition
that virtually precluded direct assistance to Contras, as the Nicaraguan opposition
was called, and sought to cut covert assistance too.

In early 1983, it occurred to Robert C. McFarlane, then Reagan's national security advisor, that it might be possible to circumvent Congress via Israel. Isolated as
always, the Jewish state was generically interested in making itself useful to other
countries, but it took a specific interest in agricultural affairs and water resource
development in the Caribbean. McFarlane wondered if Israel might advance an
increment of its growing aid package for use in Central America. He even considered subcontracting Contra support in its entirety, and proposed as much to his
counterpart, David Kimche, the director general of the Israeli Foreign Ministry and
a former deputy director of the Mossad. The idea also appealed to William J. Casey.
As director of central intelligence, Casey wondered incidentally if the Israelis might
sell captured weapons from Lebanon for transfer to the Contras. Without a word
to the State Department, a member of the NSC staff even visited Jerusalem to propose the idea to the Foreign Ministry, but at this point, the Israelis rejected it. Familiar with the uncoordinated polyphony in Washington, and hardly unpracticed in
such things themselves, they also contacted Ambassador Samuel Lewis for corrob-
oration and further information. Knowing nothing of the matter, Lewis then notified Secretary of State George Shultz. The secretary was understandably upset.[49]

The second point of entry was rather more complicated. Between them, the revolution in Iran and the U.S. intervention in Lebanon had reduced U.S. influence,
and even the U.S. presence, in both countries to nearly zero. But neither could be

simply written off for at least three reasons. Irrespective of the regime in power, Iran was still on the Soviet border; still at the head of the Gulf, where whatever might happen in Tehran would be felt in all directions; and still a major producer of oil in a world that depended on it. Lebanon too continued to matter, if only because of American hostages—academics, journalists, clergymen, even the CIA station chief—who were at least an indirect legacy of U.S. intervention. A third reason for interest was that Iran and Lebanon intersected. Radical Shi'ite activism was yet another legacy of the wars in Lebanon, the hostages were held by radical Shi'ites, and it was assumed that the captors could at least be influenced from Tehran.

The Iran end of the Iran-Contra affair seemed to begin with a memo to McFarlane in early 1984, inviting new thoughts on Iran after Khomeini. Though at first hypothetical, these thoughts had led by the end of the year to preliminary talks in the demimonde of the international arms bazaar. From there, they led to Israel. Till 1979, Israel too had maintained a visible presence in Tehran. Since the revolution, Israelis, among them Kimche, Ya'acov Nimrodi, and Adolph (Al) Schwimmer, had, like the Americans, maintained their traditional contacts. Nimrodi, once military attaché in Tehran, had since gone into private business, becoming one of Israel's richest men. The U.S.-born Schwimmer, who had run planes to the Haganah in 1948, had later been invited by Shimon Peres to found IAI. Unlike U.S. policy, which had become even more adamantly anti-Iran since the disasters of 1983, Israeli policy was pragmatic. Money was money. There were still Jews in Iran. There was also the war with Iraq. Israel, as most Israelis saw it, had little to gain from an Iranian victory, but it had plenty to lose from an Iranian defeat. By early 1985, despite U.S. policy that included censure of allies, Israelis and Iranians were negotiating earnestly, if inconclusively, through Adnan Kashoggi, a Saudi, and Manucher Ghorbanifar, an Iranian middleman, on indirect sales of U.S. arms to Iran.

The next step, again arranged through McFarlane, linked Iran to Israel to the United States. Michael Ledeen, a part-time consultant with a connection to Peres, who was now prime minister, proposed an Israel-U.S. intelligence exchange. But for a last-minute cancellation, Tehran would actually have bought a consignment of Israeli-made arms. Instead, it appeared, the Iranians wanted U.S.-made, precision-guided, TOW missiles. At this point, Kimche arrived in Washington to confer with McFarlane. By mid-July, McFarlane claimed to have learned from the Israelis that a deal was on the horizon, including release of the hostages, dialogue with the West, even a new regime in Tehran, in return for one hundred TOW missiles via Israel. Throughout there was an almost touching credulousness on the part of men who believed themselves uncommonly experienced in the ways of the world. Eager to meet U.S. needs and prove themselves the partner they both claimed and were genuinely believed to be, Israelis passed on what they got from their middlemen or Iranian sources. Hopelessly out of touch with the Iranian scene, and eager to please a president deeply sensitive to the hostages,[50] the Americans were equally eager to believe the Israelis.

Duly endorsed by a president only just recovering from surgery, the result was a deal in August-September 1985. It was generally understood that the hostages were the payoff. Taking for given that the Israelis knew what they were doing, the

United States agreed to countenance continued "dialogue" between Israelis and Iranians, and to allow Israel to sell U.S. arms to Iran. Israel wanted a stalemate in the war, more U.S. influence in Tehran, and reduced Iranian support for terrorism, Kimche explained to McFarlane. It also wanted assurances that anything sold to Iran would be quickly replaced; that Shultz was aware of what was going on; and that any deal was authorized by Reagan.

The first delivery, of 96 Israeli-owned TOW missiles, took place in August. Even the financing was an illumination. Ghorbanifar, who collected $1,217,410 for arranging the deal, charged the Iranians $18,000, and paid the Israelis $10,000 per missile, although the Israeli Defense Ministry had wanted $12,000, the expected cost of replacement. To the apparent embarrassment of Ghorbanifar and the Israelis alike, there was no immediate release of hostages; actually, the CIA station chief in Lebanon was now dead. This led to a heated meeting in Paris, where it was agreed to try again. In mid-September, an Israeli-chartered plane delivered another 408 missiles; a Presbyterian missionary was released in Lebanon; Ghorbanifar passed on another $290,000 to Nimrodi and Schwimmer, his Israeli intermediaries, to cover transport costs; and Iran transferred another $5 million to Ghorbanifar's account in Switzerland.

By now there was understandable sentiment for disengaging further dealings from the question of hostages. But with fourteen Israelis including two soldiers imprisoned in Lebanon, it was Nimrodi and Schwimmer who opposed the suggestion, while the Americans clearly assumed that Reagan too was primarily concerned with the hostages. Ledeen, still a part-time consultant, accordingly prevailed on Kimche, the senior official in the Israeli foreign ministry, to come to Washington to persuade McFarlane to carry on with the job, while two new actors appeared on the stage, both keen for new joint ventures. One of them, Marine Lt. Col. Oliver North, was a junior member of the NSC staff, already deeply engaged in Nicaragua. The other, Amiram Nir, a former Israeli journalist turned political appointee, was advisor on counterterrorism to Peres. By late 1985, both men were busy with elaborate schemes for an operation in Lebanon, in which Israel was to be both "conduit" and partner.

At the same time, it was agreed to let Iran buy another hundred Hawks in return for four hostages. Israel would supply the missiles from current inventories. It would then buy current models with the proceeds, incidentally paying in cash to avoid attention from auditors, for example, at the GAO. At this point, things started to go wrong. Suspicious Portuguese authorities refused to let the plane land in Lisbon, the intended point of transshipment from Tel Aviv to Tehran. Rabin, for the first time, requested U.S. intercession. There were open-ended ambiguities about the cargo, terms of payment, and the release of hostages. What followed seems to have been a tangle of James Bond and Inspector Clouzot. Unexpectedly, inadequate numbers of obsolescent missiles arrived in Tehran at vast expense via reluctantly extended Turkish airspace on U.S. transport from Frankfurt via Tel Aviv. While an indignant Schwimmer and Nimrodi were left to deal with the consequences in Geneva, the Iranians believed themselves bilked. There was no release of hostages. The Americans grimly resolved to proceed—but minus Kimche, Schwimmer, and Nimrodi.

On the other hand, there seemed to be no substitute for Israel. This time the novelty was Nir, who took over as Peres's proxy, in much the same way that North took over as McFarlane's. And just as the Americans excluded such responsible agencies as State, Defense, the CIA, and the Joint Chiefs of Staff, the Israelis, meaning Peres and Rabin, effectively excluded the Mossad and the Foreign Ministry, which was currently in Likud hands.

In January 1986, Nir again surfaced in Washington, this time with a plan approved by Peres and Rabin. The Israelis were now prepared to sell materiel unilaterally with the long-term goal of creating dependencies and changing the Tehran regime. A first intimation of the later linkage to the Contras, there was even a hint of turning a profit on the deal for use elsewhere. If the scheme worked, the Americans would recover their hostages at the cost of replacing four thousand Israeli TOWs, to be sure, with a more recent model. If not, the Israelis would lose the five hundred, admittedly obsolescent, TOWs that constituted the projected first installment. Opposed by his secretaries of state and defense, but supported by Admiral John Poindexter, his new national security advisor, and his director of central intelligence, Reagan agreed. But there was again a revealing delay while the parties bargained about money and scrutinized the law. This time, it was decided, the missiles would come from U.S. stocks. This meant a direct transaction, whose proceeds would finally link Iran and Nicaragua, but its primary goal was discretion, if not overt obstruction, since it was believed that third-party transfer, that is, from Israel to Iran, required congressional notification.[51]

In the end, missiles were actually shipped, and there were elaborate negotiations for other materials, including spare parts for Hawk missiles and even radars. On the other hand, Israel was still needed as cover and intermediary, just as Nir was still needed as middleman between Ghorbanifar and the Americans. This led some Americans to suspect that Ghorbanifar must at least be an Israeli agent, and to confirm several in their conviction that the whole operation would be better off without both him and Nir.

When an U.S. group, including McFarlane and North, showed up in Tehran in May, they brought a chocolate-covered cake from Tel Aviv. They also brought Nir, whom they described to Iranians as another American, as a quasi-member of the delegation. Neither side is likely to have had a very clear idea to whom it was talking. It was also unclear what each had to offer. Israel and the Americans were arguably at cross-purposes. It was uncertain how much influence the Iranians actually had in Lebanon. It was equally questionable how the Americans could help the Iranians with their real concerns: high-tech weaponry, release of Shi'ite prisoners held in Kuwait, and the personal defeat of Iraq's President Saddam Hussein.

Under the circumstances, the meeting can only have disappointed both. It soon became fairly obvious that the Americans, let alone Israelis, were not about to get their Lebanese hostages. It was equally apparent that the Iranians had more urgent things to think about than the Soviet threat the Americans persisted in talking about. Hardly conciliatory to start with, they could only grow tougher as they realized they had been had. Ghorbanifar alone had apparently overcharged them by 600 percent for spare parts. In violation of all political logic, it soon appeared that the Americans, both public and private, were in it for the money too. For their part, the Americans brooded and simmered over Nir's failure to deliver another freed hostage. Like a kind of Entebbe in reverse, the release was to have coincided with the July 4 centennial of the Statue of Liberty.[52]

Remarkably, the dealing still continued, in part as a reflex of Reagan's preoccupation with the hostages, in part as an implicit concession that military options would only be worse. An apparent vindication of Nir and Ghorbanifar, there was even another hostage to show for the effort, this time a Catholic priest released in late July. To judge from a briefing for Vice President George Bush in Jerusalem a few days later, Nir himself seems to have had few illusions about what was happening. If, as the Americans demanded, the Iranians surrendered the hostages at once, it meant the end of the arms relationship. As though to prove the point, two more U.S. hostages were taken in Lebanon to replace those released earlier. But eager at least to be rid of Ghorbanifar, the Americans only opened a "second channel." This time it consisted of Richard Secord, a retired air force major general, now in business for himself, and his partner Albert Hakim, a former Iranian national.

Unsurprisingly, U.S. unilateralism was both threatening and offensive to the Israelis, who considered themselves full partners. When Peres appeared in Washington in September, North and Poindexter agreed that the president would thank him for Israel's assistance, and assure him that the Israeli hostages would be included in any future deals. But Nir was deliberately excluded from the "second channel." Meanwhile, Rabin had offered to make available a consignment of captured Soviet arms to the Contras.

In late October, another five hundred TOWs left for Tehran on a camouflaged Israeli plane; in November a third, and last, U.S. hostage was released in Beirut. For all the elaborate projections of long-term influence and strategic dialogue, there was little else to show for the effort than money en route to Swiss bank accounts. Shortly afterward, mentions of McFarlane's May 1985 mission to Tehran began to appear in Lebanese papers, and questions began to be asked in Washington. Each for his own reasons, Poindexter and Shultz were quick to blame Israel. So, of course, were North and Attorney General Edwin Meese, who relied on North for information. Through the resignations and revelations that followed, it therefore remained a kind of party line that the Israelis were the cause of the embarrassment, that Israel had also made a profit on the deal, and that it had voluntarily passed on some of the money to the Contras.

Yet it was hard to explain why North and Poindexter were in trouble if everything was Israel's fault. Peres complained to Meese, and Nir complained to North. There was no public correction, but the congressional inquiry that followed at least produced a candid exchange. "Was one of the reasons for wanting to have Israel involved so that we could say it was Israel that was selling, and Israel, everyone knows, sells arms?" asked Arthur Liman, the chief committee counsel. "Well," North replied, "Israel was already involved . . . we did not want the U.S. government's hand, or role in this activity, exposed, and thus . . . as I said earlier, we tried to mirror the Israeli model."[53]

Like Irangate, the affair of Jonathan Jay Pollard was another mirror, whose reflections were neither flattering nor comforting to either side Hired as a naval intelligence analyst in 1979, Pollard was arrested in November 1985, and charged with spying for Israel. By the time of his arrest, his Israeli handlers, alerted by Pollard, had already left the country. Most were covered by diplomatic immunity, but his contact, a much-decorated Israeli air force colonel, who might one day have become chief of staff, was later indicted in absentia on three charges of espionage. This too was a first.

Despite an attempted plea bargain, Pollard himself was sentenced in March 1987 to life imprisonment. It was less than two weeks after the so-called Tower Commission report that was the first to illuminate Irangate. It was assumed that a forty-six-page memo from Caspar Weinberger, Pollard's nominal employer, played an important role in his sentence. Embarrassed by not only Irangate but a profusion of other concurrent espionage cases,[54] and no great friend of Israeli-U.S. closeness anyway, Weinberger testified that Pollard had damaged U.S. foreign policy and caused "significant harm" to national security.[55]

As it happened, the Pollard affair too linked Iran and the Caribbean. Transferred as watch officer to the Anti-Terrorist Alert Center newly created by the Naval Investigative Service (NIS) in 1984, and then cleared for "top secret" and "special compartmented information," Pollard had been assigned to the Caribbean/Continental United States desk. At least in theory, his mandate confined him to regional files, but it took only a short time to parlay the global dimensions of terrorism with his generous clearance and the astonishing porosity of the security system.[56] Caribbean or no Caribbean, the combination allowed him plausible access to the most classified Middle East material until his arrest in November 1985.

Although it was never conclusively proven that Pollard's access was open-ended, it was prudently assumed that he had compromised the whole system.[57] Initially, he chose material himself, but later it was his handlers who chose materials, almost as though they were ordering from a menu. They thus revealed so intimate a knowledge of U.S. classified materials that U.S. investigators continued long afterward to suspect the existence of a second Pollard.[58]

Virtually concurrent with the Kimche-McFarlane meeting in summer 1985, Pollard was also asked for suggestions on how Iran might defend its Kharg Island oil-loading facilities against Iraqi air attack. He proposed arming Iran, for example with the French-made Cactus system. Given the wheelings and dealings already in progress but yet to be revealed, his defensiveness in later interviews was both ironic and slightly comic. Arming Iran "may not, on first sight, seem acceptable to many Americans, who are accustomed to a more idealistic foreign policy," but for Israel it was "a modern-day version of 'the enemy of my enemy is my friend,'" he solemnly explained to his biographer, Wolf Blitzer, then Washington correspondent of the *Jerusalem Post*.[59]

Although the Iran-Caribbean link was fortuitous, the other issues were not. Among them were the reciprocity, mutual confidence, political accountability, and compatibility of interests at the heart of the Israeli-U.S. relationship. The same conjunction of fortuitousness and essence was basic to the affair's very origins. A seemingly random conjunction of individuals, it was also a test of mutual trust and primary loyalties between Israel and non-Israeli Jews. These issues went back to the origins of the state, and even of Zionism. Within living memory of all the major actors, they had also been at the heart of one of Israel's formative traumas, the Lavon affair.

The new affair began in early 1984 when Pollard learned through a friend that Aviem Sella, a senior colonel in the Israeli air force, was in New York. Already well known at home, Sella had led the raid on Osiraq. As a hero-worshipful American Jew, Pollard was eager to meet a real Israeli hero, but he also knew already that he wanted to spy for Israel. The friend arranged their introduction in good faith. Without it, there might conceivably have been no affair.

For all their individuality, both men were also generic figures, distinguishable only in nuance from thousands of their contemporaries. Each in his way represented a distinct, if interdependent, milieu and generation. Professional, middle-class, middlewestern, and barely thirty, Pollard was an unmistakable product of the professional, middle-class American-Jewish culture, down even to his minimal command of Hebrew. Tough, ambitious, perhaps a decade older than Pollard and native-born to Ben-Gurion's Israel, Sella too seemed the unmistakable product of a generation that reached awareness between the Eichmann trial and 1967. Early in their relationship, he had proposed communicating with Pollard from neighborhood pay phones coded with letters of the Hebrew alphabet. "Pollard was pleased that he had mastered the Hebrew alphabet during his years in Hebrew School in South Bend," his biographer noted without apparent irony.[60]

Raised on the popular literature of the Holocaust, the Mossad, and Israeli heroism, Pollard seemed nonetheless as dedicated to the image of "a certain Israel" as Charles de Gaulle had been to the idea of "a certain France."[61] As a schoolboy, he had once even been to Israel. He came back deeply impressed. "Eventually," he told Blitzer, he had planned to settle there. Instead, he pursued a mainstream U.S. education at Stanford; at Notre Dame Law School, which he left early, and the Fletcher School of Law and Diplomacy, which he left before finishing his M.A. Contemporaries later recalled his passion for tabletop war games, and self-important fibs about links to the Mossad and an elite Golani brigade. None were true. But they were delivered with such bravado and implied confidentiality that some classmates wondered if there might not be at least a little truth to them.

It was only another of the affair's many ironies that Pollard had been rejected by the CIA, and regarded with suspicion by NIS for a show of dubious connections with South Africa. In 1981, he was turned down again, this time by AIPAC, where he applied for a job as a defense analyst. His interviewers recalled the meeting as "bizarre" and "off the wall."[62] Pollard's assertive display of his security clearance and his insistence that AIPAC was under surveillance only made them suspicious of entrapment. Later contacts left a similar impression with both Israelis and his superiors. "Are they really that stupid that they would hire Jay, of all people?" one asked.[63]

In fact, after the original schoolboy visit, he had never returned to Israel. He had also avoided any Jewish affiliation in college. Yet he not only regarded himself but was apparently regarded by others as "a knee-jerk Zionist." Meanwhile, while much of official Washington had learned to see the Israeli military as a standard for emulation, Israeli intelligence as a worker of wonders, and Israeli noses as exemplary in their hardness, Pollard, like many American Jews, continued to see Israel as Daniel in a den of Soviet-armed lions, its vulnerability unrelieved, its military security precarious. His job and security access only made him more convinced that the Pentagon, in defiance of stated policy, was denying Israel information crucial to its security. It was a conviction he apparently shared with Ariel Sharon.

While Pollard brooded, Sella, who already held a business degree, worked on a doctorate in computer science. But he also spoke at Israel Bond meetings, and kept in touch with Yosef Yagur, the science counselor at the Israeli consulate. Yagur, in turn, reported to a technical intelligence agency, known by its Hebrew acronym, LAKAM, in the Ministry of Defense. There the air force high command agreed to let Sella meet Pollard. The meeting made Sella, too, suspicious of entrapment. But the first delivery of documents, including a satellite photo of Osiraq after Sella's raid, seemed credible proof of Pollard's bona fides. From here, official responsibility devolved on Rafael Eitan. Once one of Adolf Eichmann's captors, liaison to Bashir Gemayel in the early 1980s, and a former director of the Mossad's operations branch, Eitan was a legendary spy in his own right. He had been passed over for the directorships of the two senior intelligence services, however, and even phased out as special advisor on terrorism to the prime minister when Peres, succeeding Itzak Shamir, replaced him with Nir. An old friend, associate and former business partner of Sharon, Eitan had thus ended up at LAKAM.

In the mirror world of intelligence and counterintelligence, Israelis inferred that Americans inferred that Israel had three priorities. The first was information on its Arab neighbors. The second was what could be learned about U.S. policy or decisions affecting Israel. The third was scientific and technological information from developed countries, including the United States. If this were true, and there was no reason to doubt it, Pollard was a potential window on all three, as well as a fourth that seems to have mattered particularly to Eitan. This was how much Americans knew about Israel.[64]

For a man with Eitan's memory, past, and likely scores to settle, the advent of Pollard must have seemed like a lottery ticket from providence. A Washington spy was an unacceptable risk for the establishmentarian Mossad, concerned for its traditional contacts with the CIA; for the raffish Eitan, on the other hand, an inside source in Washington was not just its own reward in the bureaucratic struggle of the fittest. It was also, his critics implied, revenge for the way Americans had dealt with Sharon in Lebanon.[65]

Once persuaded that Pollard was real, sincere, and uniquely well equipped to deliver what he promised, Eitan made sure that he was bought. Guided by Yagur, Pollard seems to have supplied an estimated 360 square feet of documents, as many as a thousand of them, some of book length. Among them were updates of national intelligence estimates, highest security satellite photos and communications codes, ship movements, detailed surveys of Soviet shipments to Syria and Iraq.[66] The volume alone must have employed a corps of analysts, but the quality can only have impressed and delighted readers in Tel Aviv and Jerusalem. Israel's longest-range air mission to date, the raid on PLO headquarters in Tunis on October 1, 1985, was reportedly based on Pollard-supplied material. Eitan, in return, provided a regular income, jewelry, an expansive travel allowance, and assurances of a new, Israeli identity for Pollard and his wife.

It seemed remarkable under such circumstances that it took so long to catch him. But when he was caught, even the arrest was an embarrassment. Demanding asylum, and even invoking the Law of Return, Pollard, his wife, and cat drove into the embassy compound in northwest Washington only to find the Israelis unyielding. There was a frantic exchange with security personnel. The car was then hustled out again, and into the arms of the FBI. Not surprisingly, Pollard felt betrayed. Yet the political logic was hardly mysterious. On the contrary, it was hard to see how the ambassador of a country so massively dependent on U.S. government aid and American-Jewish support could have done otherwise without putting both at serious risk.

Cold comfort to the Israelis, the dilemma would only have been worse, had Pollard chosen to remain silent rather than cooperate, plead guilty, and plea bargain, as his lawyers prevailed on him to do. Conviction, as Alan Dershowitz later argued, would then have required Israeli evidence. This would have confronted any Israeli government with a hopeless choice. Heavily dependent on U.S. aid and goodwill, it could require Eitan, Yagur, and other officials to appear in open court, subject to cross-examination. Or it could refuse to cooperate as, in effect, it did. Professionally brilliant, as one former U.S. intelligence officer noted, the operation was political lunacy.[67]

As it was, the political fallout was embarrassing enough. Summoned to the State Department, Ambassador Meir Rosenne denied that any Israelis had left the country. In Jerusalem, Peres, Rabin, and Shamir denied that they had ever heard of Pollard. No one seemed to have heard of Eitan. Still less had anyone heard of Sella, who was hustled out of Israel with a back-dated stamp in his passport before U.S. investigators arrived. Peres appointed a special commission of inquiry, including Avraham Shalom, head of the internal security service, Shin Beth. Shalom, who was forced from office for another cover-up two years later, acknowledged only that Pollard had volunteered, and insisted that the operation had been unauthorized. Rabin made sure the report was leaked to the *New York Times*. There was also a countersalvo about U.S. spying in Israel.[68]

While Peres assured full cooperation, including return of all documents, a parliamentary inquiry split 3:3 on party lines, and U.S. investigators even threatened to go home. Faced with the choice of coming clean or hanging tough, as Blitzer noted, Israelis did neither. Instead, they supplied enough material to convict Pollard—who pointed back at the Israelis—but too little to establish good faith. In the end, 163 of some thousand documents were returned, and LAKAM was dismantled. But there was hardly a trace of political, let alone juridical, accountability, and little public indignation.[69] On the contrary, Eitan, equipped with a golden parachute, landed as chairman of the board of Israeli Chemical Industries, the largest state-owned corporation. Despite U.S. indignation, Sella was promoted to brigadier general,[70] though he was later asked to step laterally off the escalator to head the military staff college.

Predictably, what embarrassed Israelis haunted and alarmed American Jews.

But the concurrent debate in the Knesset hardly helped. The issue "Who is a Jew?" was largely a coincidence. A longtime hobby horse of the religious parties with their monopoly status in Israeli law, it challenged the legitimacy of conversions by non-Orthodox rabbis. The idea was to disqualify the illegitimately converted as eligible immigrants. In practice, the proposed measure would have affected as few as fifty people a year, yet the impact was almost incalculable. In the end, the measure was beaten back, but intentionally or otherwise, the very question seemed to challenge the legitimacy and identity of American Jews.

Behind closed doors, American-Jewish leaders reportedly demanded that Eitan and Sella be disciplined, and accused Israeli leaders of "mishandling" the case. Revealingly, their discomfort—their "nervousness, insecurity and even cringing," as Shlomo Avineri, a political scientist at the Hebrew University and former director general of the Foreign Ministry called it in a "Letter to an American Friend" published in the *Jerusalem Post*—discomfited and irritated Israelis. Perhaps, Avineri suggested, American Jews were not as "free, secure and unmolested" as was generally assumed.[71]

Unlike most of the spies concurrently on trial, Pollard had at least spied for an ally. He had also pleaded guilty and cooperated with the prosecution. Yet the severity of his sentence recalled the Rosenbergs, who had been executed in the early 1950s for spying for the Soviet Union. Years passed before a word was even said in his defense. On the other hand, survey data made startlingly clear how much things had changed since the Rosenbergs, let alone since Captain Dreyfus, with whom Pollard was occasionally, if not very helpfully, compared.[72]

What was perhaps most interesting about the Pollard affair was the discrepancy between Jewish anxiety and the almost casual indifference of non-Jews. According to a CBS/*New York Times* poll, almost two-thirds of American Jews knew whom Pollard spied for. More than half the Jewish respondents also believed that Israel's involvement in Irangate and the Pollard affair would lead to increased anti-Semitism, yet only 18 percent of the non-Jewish respondents were even aware that Pollard had spied for Israel, and only a third believed the affair would lead to increased anti-Semitism. Perhaps most significant, large majorities of both Jews and non-Jews expected it all to blow over with minimal damage to Israeli-U.S. relations.[73]

A testimonial to the stability, maturity, and resilience of a forty-year relationship, this was true enough. But there were challenges far greater than Pollard just ahead. Within a year of his conviction, Palestinian rage and frustration had shaken the twenty-year Israeli-Arab status quo. Within little more than two years, communism had collapsed and the Cold War ended. Within a little less than four years, Iraq's abortive annexation of—and violent ejection from—Kuwait had seemingly left Iraq unchanged but transformed the regional landscape. Could Israeli-U.S. relations remain the same when the world around them had changed beyond recognition?

THE PAST AS PROLOGUE

Since the creation of Israel, three premises—the moral and psychic legacy of the Holocaust, the presumed affinities of what were now universally referred to as "Judaeo-Christian" values, and the exigencies of the Cold War—had defined and driven the relationship. Even after forty years, all three retained their evocative force. Yet the first, like all historical memories, was subject to passing time; the second, like all strategic arguments, to changing circumstance; the third, like all images, to new images, increasingly remote from the world of *Exodus,* embattled kibbutzniks, and blooming deserts. What would support, or replace, them in the familiar, yet unfamiliar, world coming up on the horizon?

To probe public memory of the Holocaust, as it had been commonly called since the 1960s,[1] was to probe the Israeli-U.S. relationship at its most visceral and vulnerable. A perennial challenge to the moral, historical, and political imagination, the Holocaust was also, in its ever-more-ritualized and -institutionalized form, an example of what the French writer Charles Péguy had in mind when he observed, during the Dreyfus affair, that *"Tout commence en mystique et finit en politique."* The Holocaust, as the Nuremberg tribunal determined in 1946, was a unique and singular crime against humanity. But, as much of the world systematically forgot, and Jews ever more insistently remembered, it was, above all, a singular crime against Jews. The result, in effect, was two different Holocausts, one Jewish, one extra- and even anti-Jewish, but each with its own political significance.

As a crime committed in real time in real places against real people, the meaning and enormity of the Holocaust had once seemed self-evident. To thousands of survivors, and millions of contemporaries, the correlations—Holocaust:Israel, death:redemption—were, in fact, so obvious as to need no iteration. But that was increasingly long ago, and there was no shortage of new candidates in the world since Auschwitz with their own legitimate claim on the world's conscience.

First published in 1957, Nathan Glazer's pioneer study of American-Jewish experience was a benchmark of public perception. Despite repeated references to Zionism, Glazer referred only once to the Holocaust, and even that was buried in the index.[2] Until the catharsis of the Adolf Eichmann trial in 1961, Israelis too seemed almost to behave as though the last word had been said.

As American-Jewish scholars like Leonard Fein, Arthur Hertzberg, and Jacob Neusner regularly noted, memory resurfaced only after the 1967 war. As it happened, its rediscovery coincided with the war's unliberating aftermath, and the collapse of the liberal consensus in the United States. In the process, the Holocaust became part of the American as well as the Israeli civic religion and its specific gravity only increased with the weight of official metaphor. By the 1980s, it appeared, the Holocaust had become the ultimate post facto case for Zionism, even, perhaps especially, for the heirs of Vladimir Jabotinsky, although they had always denied the connection. Lebanon confirmed how the Holocaust would be seen both as the premise of, and final justification for, Israel's actions.[3] Yet its psychopolitical function had grown consistently since the 1970s and especially since Begin's reelection in 1981.[4] In contrast to their socialist predecessors, with their secular faith in the land, the pioneer, and the renascent, Hebrew-speaking nation, post-Labour governments and even school reformers now implied that Jewish history was always and everywhere the same. Surrounded by Palestinians and perennially threatened by the 200 million Arabs who were their involuntary neighbors, even Israelis in Israel, it appeared, still lived in the Spain of Isabella the Catholic, the Russia of Alexander III, and the Europe of Heinrich Himmler.

Perhaps nothing was more revealing of the changing psychic state than the evolution of national images. Founded in the Jordan valley in 1909, Degania Aleph was the original kibbutz and a shrine of Labor Zionism. As such, it was the functional equivalent of the log cabin, as representative of Israel's origins as Mount Vernon or Independence Hall were of the United States. Now, the Israeli Defense Ministry ran effective, pageant-like military exercises for visitors in tourist buses, and Yad vaShem, the Holocaust memorial, was a constant in every itinerary.[5] No one any longer visited Degania.

Unlike any other country but Israel, the United States too internalized and institutionalized the Holocaust, but in a specifically American, and characteristically ambiguous, way. In 1980, by unanimous vote of Congress, Carter's 1978 initiative for a memorial had been institutionalized as the U.S. Holocaust Memorial Council. The United States Holocaust Memorial Museum was scheduled to open in 1993. Its venue was just off the Mall, four hundred yards from the Washington Monument, and virtually equidistant from the Lincoln Memorial and the rotunda of the National Archives, where visitors could look at the original Declaration of Independence and Constitution. There were no similar commissions or museums for other Nazi victims, or the Armenians, Cambodians, or victims of the Gulag, whose survivors also lived in the United States. Nor were there any such commissions or museums for descendants of the four million black slaves, or the tribes of what were previously known as Indians, but now increasingly known as Native Americans, who had at least as direct a claim on the U.S. conscience.

The museum's symbolism was accordingly both universal and particular. A permanent reminder of evil in human history, it was also, at least indirectly, a memorial to the ambiguous role of the United States in resisting and overcoming it. At the same time, it was a monument to the specific sensitivities of American Jews, who now constituted perhaps 2.5 percent of the U.S. population but, in 1987, constituted more than 5 percent of the U.S. House and 7 percent of the Senate. The Congressional figures were evidence in themselves that the United States had been good for Jews, as Jews freely acknowledged. Yet ironically, large numbers of them had come to associate their roots and even identity with the Holocaust.[6]

With ethnicity rediscovered as a vehicle of U.S. civic identity, the civil rights movement of the 1960s turned sour, and the U.N. General Assembly's 1975 "Zionism is racism" resolution still unrescinded, Jews bridled understandably and legitimately at efforts to hijack, co-opt, and, worst of all, to minimize the specifically

Jewish horror of the Holocaust. But was the Holocaust a relevant guide to Lebanon in 1982 or Gaza and the West Bank since 1967? "I repress an urge to shout 'Shut up, already' in the White House press room when Menahem Begin toasts an American president with a 15-minute lecture on the meaning of the Holocaust," one survivor noted coldly in the *Washington Post.* "Must every thought of compromise conjure up the ghost of appeasement in Munich?"[7]

Consistently more dovish than their Israeli counterparts, American Jews agreed by two-to-one pluralities that "Palestinians have a right to a homeland on the West Bank and Gaza, so long as it does not threaten Israel." By nine-to-one majorities they opposed forcible transfer of Palestinians from the West Bank. Barely a quarter favored expanded settlements, barely a fifth Israeli annexations. Yet Israelis also revealed considerable differences with one another, notwithstanding their government's seemingly immovable commitment to the status quo. What and how much varied with the question. But virtually every survey indicated that for no fewer than half, and as many as two thirds, of Israeli respondents, land for peace was not in itself an outlandish idea.[8]

A challenge both to Israeli democracy and "Judaeo-Christian" ethics, the question of learning from history led inevitably to that shared sense of "we" and "our" that had always been basic to the Israeli–American-Jewish relationship, and was a second operational premise of the Israeli-U.S. relationship. Had the "we" survived a generation of military occupation since 1967, fifteen years of righter-and-righter-wing governments since the election of Begin, the disillusionments of the war in Lebanon, and the shock of the Palestinian *intifada?*

The answers were at once reassuring and disquieting. Though Israel's style sometimes recalled Third Republican France and sometimes Weimar Germany, it remained a democracy by any real-world, and certainly any Middle Eastern, standard. Despite forty years of hot war and cold, it still assured its citizens, the Arab minority included, an enviably free press, an independent judiciary, and free and honest elections. In contrast to much of the postcolonial world, civilian control of the military had never even been in question either. For better or worse, majorities ruled, but majorities beholden to minorities in ways that thus assured them too their say.

On the other hand, it was hard to deny that the Occupied Territories remained almost literally lawless, unrelieved by even a mirage of political settlement. Confronted with a moral, political, and professional challenge unlike any they had yet encountered, citizen-officers and citizen-soldiers sought to defend themselves, restore order, and meet the expectations of their civilian masters, while maintaining their traditional self-respect.[9] While Labor pursued a "Jordanian solution," and Likud the status quo, the PLO, as always, balanced noncommittally on the rim of Resolution 242. In July 1988, a frustrated King Hussein withdrew all Jordanian subsidies and disavowed any further claim to the West Bank. His decision not only pulled the plug on both Israelis and Americans but added to the confused status of the territories. Acknowledged as Jordanian before June 1967, they presumably derived their legal status from their Jordanian sovereignty. Neither Jordanian, Israeli, nor Palestinian, their status seemed again as obscure as in 1947. Only minimally restrained by public opinion, Israeli courts, and the Geneva conventions, civil and military agencies, settlers, and peace groups filled the vacuum as they had for twenty years, hauling and tugging at people, land, and water ad hoc under the umbrella of statutes going back to the British Mandate and the Ottoman Empire.

Voting behavior and attitudinal surveys confirmed significant, if still subliminal, stresses. Israeli voters, like many Western electorates, had moved right since the 1970s. In important ways, Israeli and U.S. electorates saw eye to eye. For all their differences on particulars, Israeli governments and Republican administrations took compatible views of the world in general. "Israel, in a sense, earns its special status and relationship with the United States by giving aid and arms to regimes that Washington supports but cannot overtly assist because of concerns about its international image, U.S. public opinion, or congressional prohibitions," as one Israeli noted candidly.[10]

Yet American Jews were not only among the last holdout liberals of the United States, they continued to regard their liberalism as part of their identity. In 1988, Massachusetts's Governor Michael Dukakis carried a scant minority of states but an estimated 70 percent of the Jewish vote. If fundamentalist constituencies flocked to Reagan, and Begin delighted in their support, American Jews continued to vote Democratic, not least because of Reagan's fundamentalist constituents. Relations with South Africa, another issue between Jerusalem and Washington, a Republican White House and Democratic Congress, were another abrasive surface. Surveys regularly confirmed that Israelis, a majority in their country, were substantially less sympathetic toward individuals and minorities, and considerably less sensitive to civil rights and liberties than Americans in general, let alone American Jews.[11]

Like the war in Lebanon, the *intifada* seemed both a watershed and a catalyst of Israeli-U.S. differences. As in 1982, Israeli conduct and policy were again subject to daily review in every household with a television set. Once more, the result was heated debates on both the medium and the message, until the Israelis learned to keep camera crews out of the Occupied Territories. In February 1988, a dozen members of Congress met privately with the Israeli ambassador to express their concern about the beatings and shootings. A few weeks later, thirty senators of both parties, many with a long record of support for Israel, publicly censured Itzak Shamir's rejection of land for peace. Though Congress assured continued aid, Democratic conventions in ten states passed resolutions favoring Palestinian statehood and self-determination, and the issue was openly and aggressively debated at the Democratic national convention in Atlanta. Republicans made the same point in their own way. Itself a legacy of the Carter era, the State Department's annual human rights report unflinchingly recorded constraints on speech, press, and assembly, deportations, detentions without trial, and punitive destruction of Palestinian houses.[12] Reawakened to activity despite the conventional wisdom of an impending election, Secretary of State George Shultz opened a peace offensive. It was the first of its kind since the abortive Reagan initiative of September 1982.

Both American and Israeli opinion reflected a crumbling consensus. Depending on what they were asked, Americans reported increased and reduced sympathy for both sides, skepticism that either side was willing to make concessions, support for U.S. contacts with the PLO, and qualified toleration for a Palestinian state. The American-Jewish consensus too reflected the strain in irritable exchanges of state-

ments, display ads, conferences, public meetings, and op-ed pieces. Perception of
the media varied with religious affiliation: 80% of Orthodox Jews, 62% of Conservative Jews, 53% of Reform Jews, but only 42% of the unaffiliated Jews complained
of bias in media treatment of the story. But surveys also reported that only 22% of
American Jews now agreed that "they should not publicly criticize policies of the
Israel government." Asked for their impressions, 49% responded favorably to
Shamir and 57% to Shimon Peres, but 70% responded favorably to Shultz.[13]

With support and technical assistance from Sweden's Foreign Minister Sten
Andersson and Ambassador Wilhelm Wachtmeister, the Brookings Institution's
William Quandt, the Egyptians, and even increasingly anxious Soviets,[14] Shultz
marched discreetly but purposefully into the fractured consensus. Barely noted in
the United States, the changing nuances and newly audible overtones in the U.S.
position were nonetheless heard in Tunis. In mid-November 1988, a PLO delegation arrived in Stockholm to confer with a delegation of American Jews. Both
Americans—Stanley Sheinbaum, an old-time liberal Democratic activist from Los
Angeles, and Rita E. Hauser, a Republican lawyer from New York who had served
in the Nixon administration—were close to the International Center for Peace in
the Middle East, a peace lobby cofounded in 1982 by Abba Eban and French Prime
Minister Pierre Mendès-France. Hauser consulted Assistant Secretary of State
Richard Murphy, an old acquaintance. But if only to assure "plausible deniability,"
neither Eban nor any other Israeli was informed till the talks were over.

Before leaving again for home, the Americans had persuaded the PLO to risk
the thitherto impossible. A giant step toward acceptance of Resolution 242,
addressed to American Jews, it was still a giant step from Sadat's giant step to Jerusalem. For the first time, it nonetheless included recognition of "the existence of
Israel as a state in the region" and a "rejection and condemnation of terrorism in
all its forms," as conditions for a peace conference that would, in effect, be successor
to the abortive Geneva conference of 1973.[15] After extended introspection and consultation with his associates, Shultz decided against a visa that would allow Arafat
to address a special U.N. session in New York, but he was prepared to write Arafat
the speech he wanted to hear.

In early December 1988, when the Americans returned to Stockholm, they
found a Palestinian delegation, including Arafat, reluctantly willing to negotiate on
U.S. terms in anticipation of a summit between Reagan, President-elect George
Bush, and Soviet Party Chairman Mikhail Gorbachev. On December 14, at a press
conference in Geneva, Arafat finally pronounced what had come to be known as
"the words." Did he accept Resolution 242 unconditionally, he was asked? "Of
course," Arafat replied.[16] For the first time since 1975, there was no longer a formal
obstacle to official contacts between the United States and the PLO.

As news of the Stockholm meetings became public, a storm of protest
descended on the U.S. negotiators. It was predictable that Israelis would be indignant, but after forty years, it was surprising that they should be surprised. In fact, it
was the second time the United States had surprised Israel since the Reagan plan,
one senior diplomat complained to an American colleague. "Is this what you call
a strategic relationship?" he demanded. Like the related questions of shared values

and learning from history, the question was appropriate and legitimate. But the answer in this case was perhaps the clearest of all.

Jewish organizations joined the chorus of lamentation and reappraisal. Sheinbaum was accused of "Jewish self-laceration." Supported by two rabbis, a Los Angeles city council candidate even demanded that he resign as a regent of the University of California. For his part in the second round of talks, Menahem Rosensaft, chairman of the Zionist Labor movement of the United States and a member of the Conference of Presidents of Major American Jewish Organizations was almost deposed by indignant associates.[17] But in contrast to his luckless predecessors William Rogers and even Cyrus Vance, only the curtain fell on Shultz, whose initiative just went on without him after Shultz himself left office. Conventional wisdom to the contrary, American Jews now tended to look on or away. Bruised by the "Who is a Jew?" debate, they were also reluctant to challenge an irreproachably supportive secretary of state, just as Congress was hesitant to interfere with the peace process.

Meanwhile, the Iraqi-Iranian bloodletting ended in the Gulf, and communism ended in Europe. The end of the Cold War left one superpower where there had until now been two. If the impact could be felt as far away as Cambodia and southern Africa, it was no surprise that it should also be felt in the Middle East, where the winds of change now seemed to blow from all directions. The new and unprecedented surge of Soviet-Jewish emigration assured the creation of dilemmas that would be felt increasingly by both Arabs and Israelis. At the same time, after almost a quarter century, Czechs, Poles, and even the Soviet Union resumed relations with a previously isolated Israel, while Soviet aid to Arab clients ended about as precipitously as the Soviet Union itself. As Iran, China, North Korea, and indeterminate others moved to fill the gap left by the retreating Soviets, both the remaining and the disappearing superpower lost their appetite for regional involvements, but in different ways and with different consequences. For Russians, the Middle East—or at least renascent Islam—was closer now than ever. Kazakhstan alone, with its hitherto Soviet bombs, strategic location, and Russian majority presented challenges hitherto undreamed of. After more than a half century of world depression, world war, and ambivalent global responsibility, Americans too were torn between the dream that President George Bush now called a new world order and the yearning that President Warren G. Harding had once called returning to normalcy. Either way, even former hard-line Arabs saw little choice but to compete for United States favor. But neither, of course, did Israel, where successive premiers since at least the 1960s had done all they could to make their country a "strategic asset" in a Cold War that would presumably go on indefinitely.

In an unreconstructed Israel, where the end of the Cold War threatened the return of U.S. "even-handedness," and the end of Communism threatened reflexive spasms of traditional European anti-Semitism, the choice was bound to be as problematic as ever. More than half a year before the fall of the Berlin Wall, the stiff wind from Washington could already be felt in Jerusalem, where a cabinet comprising three present and former prime ministers, five ex-defense ministers, and three former chiefs of staff, again struggled against entropy. The outcome, the lowest common denominator acceptable both to Washington and their constituents, was a proposal for elections in the Occupied Territories that grimly avoided such basic issues as land for peace and the status of East Jerusalem. So regarded, the proposal, known hereafter as the Shamir Plan, was little more than an expression of willingness to talk about talks. At a central committee meeting of his party a few weeks later, Prime Minister Yitzhak Shamir capitulated to his later Housing Minister Ariel Sharon and Foreign Minister David Levi without even risking a floor fight. But to his discomfiture, Secretary of State James Baker and Egypt's President Hosni Mubarak each said yes to the plan, carefully adjusting it to preempt rejection by the PLO, while persuading the PLO not to let Shamir off the hook by saying no.

"[W]e approach what I think is a critical juncture in the Middle East," Shultz's successor, Baker, told AIPAC on May 22, 1989. A distant echo of Henry Byroade, his speech only confirmed how much the world had changed and how much the State Department had learned since 1954. Evidence in itself of how things had changed, as many as six of the younger officials around the secretary of state were now both Jewish and supportive of the U.S. initiative. Baker himself called attention to the magnitude of change. "[T]he globe is being transformed," he emphasized. This, he continued, marked "the wider context in which we and Israel must consider the peace process."

The principles he enumerated were an anthology of historical experience: a "step-by-step approach," involving face-to-face negotiations, based on Resolutions 242 and 338, perhaps in the context of a "properly-structured international conference . . . *at an appropriate time;*[4] ample provision for transitional arrangements and confidence-building; and no prior commitments either to permanent Israeli control or annexation or to an independent Palestinian state.

"We are not going to stop at the status quo," the secretary declared. The time had come for Israelis "to lay aside, once and for all, the unrealistic vision of a greater Israel"; for Palestinians to amend their covenant, and reach out to Israelis, and understand that no one was going to "'deliver'" Israel for them; for the Soviet Union to restore diplomatic relations with Israel and stop arming "countries like Libya."[18]

By early 1990, Israel's government had again collapsed, a victim of Shamir's own disavowal of the Shamir Plan. With Labor out, and Sharon, as minister of housing, responsible for settlements in the Occupied Territories, its successor was the rightest-wing cabinet in Israeli history. Not peace but settlement of Soviet refugees was Israel's highest priority, Shamir announced. In 1991, with the Gulf war behind it, the White House proposed, and Congress accepted, a provisional, but unmistakable, freeze on the $10 million in requested credits as a condition for Israel's participation in a peace conference. It thus made clear that, in its view, the questions of peace and resettlement were linked, but, for the moment, Shamir's implied either-or went unchallenged. Shortly afterward, and scarcely a year after Baker's AIPAC speech, supporters of Abul Abbas, a member of the PLO executive and the author of the 1985 assault on the *Achille Lauro,* attacked a Tel Aviv beach.

It was probable that the raid, which was intended to kill as many hostages as possible and threaten the U.S. embassy, came as a relief to many on both sides. Challenged from Washington, the PLO refused outright condemnation of both Abbas and the raid. The United States therewith suspended contacts. Soon afterward, Arafat was in Baghdad as a guest of the Iraqi government, Iraqi troops were in Kuwait not simply as occupiers but presumptive conquerors, and thousands of Palestinians were in the streets, roaring support for Saddam Hussein.

Among the casualties of the war that followed were as many as 100,000 Iraqis, the myth of Arab unity, Kuwaiti and Saudi toleration of Palestinians, Gulf subsidies for the PLO, what little remained of Arafat's credibility—and much conventional wisdom about the Israeli–United States strategic partnership, Israel's invulnerability, and the West Bank as a shield against external attack. By now, even Israelis fantasized about alternative relationships: with Europeans; with the Soviet Union, which had broken off relations in 1967; even with Arabs.[19]

While not in itself a casualty, the American domestic consensus was at least a flashing amber light. Given the Administration's skill and convictions, the rift between non-Jewish conservatives and Jewish *neo*-conservatives was of arguable importance to the future of the Republican party. But potentially at least, the rift between pro- and anti-war Democrats was as devastating as it had been in 1968. On the eve of the war, a representative liberal congressman, Iowa's Dave Nagle, was visibly. relieved, after a Friday night visit (apparently his first ever), to a synagogue to discover his Jewish constituents were not hellbent for early offensive operations. It was clear not only from his nervousness, but his very decision to appear, that this was not the message he had been hearing in Washington. Within the same weeks in November 1990, the Protestant National Council of Churches urged withdrawal of U.S. troops, the predominantly black National Baptist Convention, U.S.A., called for greater diplomatic efforts, and the National Council of Catholic Bishops asked audibly whether operations in the Gulf would constitute a "just" war. At the same time, the Council of Jewish Federations unanimously supported "a firm posture of opposition." Reflecting the realities of a volunteer army, blacks constituted 25 percent of U.S. forces in the Gulf, while Jews constituted 0.4 percent of the U.S. armed forces. There was no calculating the mischief, as Charles William Maynes noted, if blacks took the casualties while Jews supported the war.[20]

In fact, the American peace initiative not only survived virtually intact but, in November 1991, Soviets, Americans, Egyptians, Jordanians, Lebanese, Syrians, Israelis and Palestinians actually convened in Madrid around a common T-shaped table in the presence of 4500 journalists from around the world. Israelis and Egyptians aside, it was the first such face-to-face confrontation in forty-three years. Soon after, on December 16, 1991, the U.N. General Assembly decided, in a one-line resolution, "to revoke" its earlier equation of Zionism and racism. The vote was 111 to 25, with 13 abstentions and 17 states, including Egypt, Kuwait, and China, not voting. Among the 85 cosponsors were the Soviet Union and all its former satellites.

Since the history of diplomacy had nothing to show quite like it, it was unsurprising that the participants in Madrid seemed both flustered and apprehensive. As always, there seemed some awareness that outsiders could neither impose a solution nor could any be achieved without them. But as never before, there also seemed some shared sense of peril and opportunity, compounded, in turn, by tactical calculation. Some delegations—like Israel's, with its stake in a thaw both in Washington and Moscow—showed up because there seemed some chance of gain. Others—

like the Palestinians, who arrived as part of a Jordanian delegation on Israeli terms—appeared because there seemed little more to lose. Common to most, including the Syrians, was reluctance to antagonize the United States, a prudent wish to lay the blame on others if things went wrong, and a fear of what might happen in their absence.

Although no one made an offer that couldn't be refused, the conference nonetheless created precedents all sides would find difficult to undo. Not only the Palestinians but Shamir himself had accepted the Shamir—and Baker and Mubarak—Plan. Official hands, rather than fists, had been shaken on camera. No one had walked out despite calculated provocations from several sides. Considering the precedents since 1948, the conference was remarkable even for having happened. Palestinian negotiators returned, in fact, to an enthusiastic welcome, and Israeli polls reflected a changing climate. If only for the moment, it also seemed clear that the United States had achieved a predominance like none since Britain's in the early 1920s; that the myth of Arab unity was visibly, and perhaps irrevocably, fractured; and that such traditional brakes and vetoes as congressional counterpressures and the threat of government-busting defections on the far Israeli right had failed to work or even operate. Perhaps it was really true as Farouk Shara, the Syrian foreign minister plausibly observed, that Israelis were more dovish than their government, and the Arab world was the opposite.

If history was any guide, a successful outcome was still likely to call for Arab leaders as willing to take risks as Sadat had been in 1982; Israeli leaders as willing to face political, and even civil, confrontation as Ben-Gurion in 1948 and Begin in 1979 had been; and treaty-supported U.S. commitments on the scale of Camp David. But this time they were also likely to demand economic support on a scale far larger than the United States could—or perhaps would—now provide. The aid bill alone was therefore likely to require assistance from as far afield as the Gulf states, the European Community, and Japan. Any settlement was also likely to require prodigies of juridical invention to cover such equivocal issues as Palestinian sovereignty; joint management of water resources; trans-Jordanian movement of people, goods, and services; and the status of Jerusalem. Given the realities and eventualities of nuclear development, a viable balance of terror was another likely requirement in a region and system dramatically more complex than the relatively simple bipolarity of the Cold War. All the while, there would be innumerable incentives both inside and outside to pour new arms into a systemically contentious region whose oil continued to sustain the world economy, and whose Arab population alone was expected to double within a generation.[21]

Given the variety of potential vetoes from all sides, no one could say whether, let alone how, any of this might work. As always, three outcomes were theoretically possible. Things could get worse, but, in the short run, this was unlikely. Too many different actors now felt at home in the status quo. None could effect basic change unilaterally. Alternatively, things could remain the same, but, in the long run, this too was unlikely. In an area so intrinsically accident-prone, too many circles—spiraling demography, deficient water reserves, economic stagnation, political illegitimacy, cultural crisis—were too vicious and too interactive to remain in dependable equilibrium.

This left the third option, that things could get better. In fact, it now seemed, success might be the least or the lesser evil, something to be doggedly, pragmatically, even reluctantly pursued until it was finally, and in all likelihood joylessly, attained at the end of long, tough, and open-ended bargaining process. Yet stranger things had happened in a century that had already seen the collapse of a half dozen empires far older than the Arab-Israeli conflict, and the reconciliation of at least as many enmities as visceral as the enmity between Jews and Arabs. Given the alternatives and the calculability of rational interest, it also seemed worth it to many to try to slip through a window of opportunity that was unlikely to open again in their lifetimes.

Thanks to the commissions and omissions of so improbable a conjunction of characters as James Baker and Mikhail Gorbachev, Saddam Hussein and Yasir Arafat, Yitzhak Shamir and Ariel Sharon, it now seemed in the interest of both Israelis and Palestinians to settle as best they could, while they could, on whatever terms they could agree to between them. It seemed equally in the interest of Jordan, Egypt, Saudi Arabia, and the Gulf sheikhdoms to support and encourage such a settlement; and of the United States, the European Community, Japan, not to mention what was left of the Soviet Union, to do all they could to bring it about.

Ironically, the Russian, Ukrainian, and Moldavian Jews, who had once been the first best hope of Zionism, were now the latest, perhaps even the last, best hope for years to come of Israelis eager for freedom from the dilemmas of an endless military occupation. In fact, the new immigrants were a potential windfall for virtually everyone disposed to a negotiated settlement. For Israelis, they were an invigorating infusion of skills and talent; a cohort of new voters with the numbers, and just possibly the motivation, to move Israeli politics back toward the center; and a challenge amounting to a moment of truth. *If* resources were limited, as Israelis knew better than most, and as official Washington was resolved to prove; *if* the choice were between absorption of a million ex-Soviet immigrants outside the Occupied Territories and the extravagant subsidy of 200,000 settlers within them, there was, at least, no lack of clear alternatives. The 1992 election campaign was a test and a benchmark. For the opposition, the challenge was to pose alternatives. For the government parties, the challenge was to avoid them. As the outcome confirmed, the new immigrants constituted a formidable, and perhaps decisive, incentive for both Israelis and Palestinians to reconsider their options after decades of self-destructive irresolution.

Wherever the talks might lead, they showed promise of changing the regional scene more radically than anything since Israel's creation. Cold War or no Cold War, the conflict had served a multitude of governments for more than forty years as a *raison d'être* and a distraction. The Gulf War alone proved how the new climate continued to threaten still more of what the world had known for decades. Even in a post–Cold War world, an Arab-Israeli settlement was insufficient to assure the coming of the Peaceable Kingdom. But apart from being a good thing in itself, it was a necessary condition for the attainment of any regional good.

Yet such a settlement would inevitably demand of Israelis a thousand little steps and a giant leap of faith after forty years of war and isolation. On the long road from here to there, there would still be a thousand reasons to read both Jewish history and the current world scene as a succession of flashing amber lights. For many, at least, their message would be that Jews could only rely on themselves—and that even they could not always be depended on; that danger is perennial and ubiquitous; that it is always wrong to depend on others, and that the familiar risks of the status quo are preferable to the unknown risks of negotiated change. At the same time, the attentive and experienced Israeli traveller could hardly help notice that even the sovereignty of superpowers was no longer absolute; and that in any state worth living in, dependence and independence are inextricably linked, something Weizmann and Ben-Gurion had always known, and even Begin had come to learn.

Meanwhile, in much of the world, social peace and political stability, not to mention prosperity itself, would still depend on oil. With alternative fuels still over the horizon, but fissionable materials now more or less readily obtainable, rocket scientists increasingly fungible, missile technologies increasingly consumer-friendly, and arms suppliers increasingly competitive, the Middle East, and America's role in it, were likely to matter as much as ever. If only for this reason, Israeli-American relations were likely to matter as much as ever too, and a relationship that history has already made special would continue to be more special than most.

NOTES

Introduction, pp. ix–xiii

1. Walter Laqueur, *A History of Zionism* (New York, 1976); Nadav Safran, *Israel: The Embattled Ally* (Cambridge, 1978); Howard M. Sachar, *A History of Israel,* vol. 1 (New York 1979), vol. 2 (New York, 1988); Steven Spiegel, *The Other Israeli-Arab Conflict* (Chicago, 1986).

2. David Schoenbaum, " . . . or Lucky: Jordan—The Forgotten Crisis," *Foreign Policy,* Spring 1973; Seymour Hersh, *The Price of Power* (New York, 1983), p. 652n.

3. For an example, see Lorenzo Cremonesi's 1991 interview with Abu Malek, the thirty-three-year-old leader of the Palestinian Moslem group Hamas, believed to represent at least 30 percent of the people of the Occupied Territories. "Sadat was punished with death for his treason," Abu Malek declared. "The same will happen to the Syrian President Assad and to [Chairman of the Palestine Liberation Organization] Arafat." The only difference between Sadat and Arafat, he continued, is that the latter wears the *Keffiyah,* symbolizing Palestinian resistance. "Abu Malek, guida religiosa dell'Hamas: I1 traditore Arafat finirà come Sadat," *Corriere della Sera,* October 13, 1991.

4. Personal correspondence, September 11, 1991.

5. Thomas L. Friedman, *From Beirut to Jerusalem* (New York, 1990), pp. 3–18.

Chapter 1, pp. 3–5

1. For a comprehensive theoretical discussion of relationships, special and otherwise, see Lily Gardner Feldman, *The Special Relationship between West Germany and Israel* (Boston, 1984), chaps. 10–12.

2. Thomas A. Dine, "The Revolution in U.S.-Israel Relations," reprinted in *Journal of Palestine Studies,* Summer 1986, p. 138.

3. "Israel: U.S. Foreign Assistance Facts," Congressional Research Service Issue Brief (Washington, 1990), pp. 4–5; Eytan Gilboa, *American Public Opinion toward Israel and the Arab-Israeli Conflict* (Lexington, Mass., 1987), pp. 210–11.

4. Gilboa, *American Public Opinion,* chaps. 8–9. Cf. "American Support for Israel: Solid, but Not the Rock It Was," *New York Times,* July 9, 1990.

5. Gilboa, *American Public Opinion,* pp. 23–26, 223–28.

6. Interviewed on "Sixty Minutes," CBS, October 23, 1988.

7. "Israel Lobbying Group Found to Comply with Law," *New York Times,* December 22, 1990. The final report is on file with the Federal Election Commission as MUR 2804.

8. The contrary position can be argued too. See Wolf Blitzer, *Between Washington and Jerusalem* (New York, 1985), pp. 153–56.

9. In 1984, it was estimated that Jewish political action committees contributed $3.6 million to presidential and congressional candidates, including $1.8 million for Senate and $1.5 million for House candidates. It was also reported that Sen. Jesse Helms of North Carolina spent over $16 million to keep his seat in North Carolina, a smallish state with few Jews, and

that the average cost of running for one of the 435 House seats was $225,000, i.e., a total of $97,875,000. By that, admittedly arbitrary, standard, Jewish contributions made up about the same proportion of the total as do Jews in the general population. See Rochelle L. Stanfield, "O Israel!" *National Journal,* June 23, 1990; Edward Tivnan, *The Lobby* (New York, 1987), p. 188. Cf. Paul Findley, *They Dare to Speak Out* (Westport, Conn., 1985).

10. See David Schoenbaum, "The Iowa Senatorial Race," *Present Tense,* Summer 1984.

11. "PACs and Votes," *Issues* (Arab American Institute), November–December 1990, pp 10–11; *Time,* November 19, 1990, p. 43. Cf. *Economist,* November 10, 1990, p. 24.

12. Stanfield, "O Israel!," p. 1524. Cf. Gilboa, *American Public Opinion,* pp. 34–35, 285.

13. Blitzer, *Between Washington and Jerusalem,* chaps. 3–4.

14. George F. Kennan, *The Cloud of Danger* (Boston, 1977), pp. 82–85.

15. See *New York Times,* March 7, 1991.

16. See Michael Wolffsohn, *Israel: Polity, Society, Economy, 1882–1986* (Atlantic Highlands, N.J., 1987), pp. 5–6.

17. Cf. Henry Kissinger, *Years of Upheaval* (Boston, 1986), pp. 538–39.

18. Cf. Walter Laqueur, "Thirteen Theses on Zionism," in *A History of Zionism* (New York, 1976), pp. 589–99.

19. "By the second decade of Israel's existence, surely by the third, . . . Israel was the only Jewish community . . . that was calling on Jews elsewhere to save it from 'another Holocaust,' a threat that its very existence was supposed to avert. . . . [T]he nation was emerging as one of the 'developed' world's chronic mendicants." Howard M. Sachar, *A History of Israel,* vol. 2 (New York, 1988), pp. 253–54.

20. See Robert H. Abzug, *Inside the Vicious Heart* (New York, 1985), passim.

21. Thucycides, *The Peloponnesian War* (Harmandsworth, 1977), p. 403.

22. Kissinger, *Years of Upheaval,* pp. 483–84.

23. See George R. Stewart, *Names on the Land* (Boston, 1967), pp. 232–33.

24. See Peter Grose, *Israel in the Mind of America* (New York, 1983), prologue and chap. 1.

25. Cf. James A. Field, Jr., "Trade, Skills and Sympathy," pp. 1ff., and Bayard Dodge, "American Missionary Efforts in the Nineteenth and Early Twentieth Centuries," pp. 15ff., *Annals of the American Academy of Political and Social Science,* May 1972; William R. Polk, *The United States and the Arab World* (Cambridge, Mass., 1975), pp. 92, 106.

26. Grose, *Israel in the Mind of America,* p. 59.

27. George McGhee, *Envoy to the Middle World* (New York, 1983), pp. 7–9; Evan M. Wilson, *Decision on Palestine* (Stanford, 1979), p. 4.

28. Arthur Walworth, *Woodrow Wilson* (Baltimore 1969), 2: 108.

29. Lucy S. Dawidowicz, *Jews in America, 1881–1981* (New York, 1982), p. 167. Cf. Nathan Glazer, *American Judaism* (Chicago, 1972), p. 23; Irving Howe, *World of Our Fathers* (New York, 1976), p. 58.

30. Grose, *Israel in the Mind of America,* pp. 38–39.

31. Barbara W. Tuchman in Tuchman et al., *The Palestinian Question in American History* (New York, 1978), pp. 8ff.

32. Arcadius Kahan, *Essays in Jewish Social and Economic History* (Chicago, 1986), chaps. 4–6. Cf. Simon Kuznets, "Immigration of Russian Jews to the United States," *Perspectives in American History,* vol. 9, (1975).

33. Howe, *World of Our Fathers,* pp. 462ff.

34. See John Lewis Gaddis, *Russia, the Soviet Union and the United States* (New York, 1978), pp. 42–47.

35. Cf. Grose, *Israel in the Mind of America,* chap. 2; Lewis J. Paper, *Brandeis* (Englewood Cliffs, N.J., 1983), chaps. 15, 18.

36. Gaddis, *Russia, the Soviet Union and the United States,* pp. 43–44.

37. See Egmont Zechlin, *Die deutsche Politik und die Juden im Ersten Weltkrieg* (Goettingen, 1969), passim.

38. Cf. Isaiah Friedman, *The Question of Palestine* (New York, 1973), pp. 286–87; Leonard Stein, *The Balfour Declaration* (New York, 1961), pp. 533ff.; Ronald Sanders, *The High Walls of Jerusalem* (New York, 1983), p. 591.

39. Friedman, *Question of Palestine,* pp. 200–2; Stein, *Balfour Declaration,* pp. 422ff.

40. Grose, *Israel in the Mind of America,* pp. 69–70.

41. Laqueur, *A History of Zionism,* pp. 195–99.

42. Walter Laqueur and Barry Rubin (eds.), *The Israel-Arab Reader* (New York, 1984), pp. 21–22.

43. Ibid., p. 35.

44. Cf. Grose, *Israel in the Mind of America,* pp. 69–71.

45. Laqueur and Rubin, *Israel-Arab Reader,* p. 30. Cf. Grose, *Israel in the Mind of America,* pp. 87–90.

46. Cf. Frank Manuel, *The Realities of American-Palestine Relations* (Washington, 1949), p. 312; John DeNovo, *American Interests in the Middle East* (Minneapolis, 1963), pp. 169ff., 339–41; Philip J. Baram, *The Department of State in the Middle East* (Philadelphia, 1978), pp. 247–49.

47. See Irwin Oder, "American Zionism and the Congressional Resolution of 1922 on Palestine," *Publications of the American Jewish Historical Society,* no. 45 (1955).

48. Paper, *Brandeis,* p. 317.

49. Alan M. Kraut, *The Huddled Masses* (Arlington Heights, Ill., 1982), pp. 176–77.

50. Christopher Sykes, *Crossroads to Israel* (Bloomington, Ind., 1973), p. 102. Cf. Michael J. Cohen, *The Origins and Evolution of the Arab-Zionist Conflict* (Berkeley, 1987), pp. 84–87.

51. Laqueur, *History of Zionism,* pp. 466–68. Cf. Sykes, *Crossroads to Israel,* pp. 104–7; Norman Rose, *Lewis Namier and Zionism* (Oxford, 1980), pp. 40–41.

52. Quoted in Naomi W. Cohen, *The Year after the Riots* (Detroit, 1988), pp. 101–2.

53. In his introduction to the 1969 edition, Sheean takes rightful pride in a German police decree of 1940, making it a criminal offense to buy, sell, or read anything he wrote. Acknowledging how the world has changed in the thirty-five years since his book first appeared, he also equates "Communism, anti-Semitism, Zionism, nationalism, xenophobia, greed and the will to power" among the baleful constants. But he makes no effort to reconsider Zionism in the light of the Nazi persecution he was among the first to report, nor is there any reconsideration of Israel, despite the recent experience of the Six-Day War. See Vincent Sheean, *A Personal History* (New York, 1934), p. 372, and later editions.

54. Cohen, *Origins,* p. 74; Sykes, *Crossroads to Israel,* pp. 113–19; Laqueur, *History of Zionism,* pp. 491–93.

55. See Cohen, *Year after the Riots,* chap. 2–4.

56. Sykes, *Crossroads to Israel,* pp. 118–19; Laqueur, *History of Zionism,* pp. 493–94; Rose, *Lewis Namier and Zionism,* pp. 45–53; Cohen, *Origins,* p. 89.

57. Cf. Laqueur, *History of Zionism,* pp. 492–99; Laqueur and Rubin, *Israel-Arab Reader,* pp. 72–74.

58. A. J. Sherman, *Island Refuge* (Berkeley, 1973), p. 271.

59. Cf. Walter Laqueur, *The Terrible Secret* (Harmondsworth, 1982), passim.

60. Aaron Berman, *Nazism, The Jews and American Zionism* (Detroit, 1990) p. 23.

61. Cf. David S. Wyman, *The Abandonment of the Jews* (New York, 1984), pp. 311ff.; Howe, *World of Our Fathers,* pp. 72–74.

62. See Grose, *Israel in the Mind of America,* pp. 109–12; Edwin Black, *The Transfer*

Agreement (New York, 1984), passim; Leni Yahil, *The Holocaust* (London, 1990), pp. 100–4; Berman, *Nazism. The Jews and American Zionism,* pp. 36–40, 51ff.

63. Melvin I. Urofsky, *We Are One!* (Garden City, N.Y., 1978), pp. 4ff.

64. See Josef Bard, "Why Europe Dislikes the Jew," *Harper's,* March 1927. Cf. Lewis B. Namier, "Zionism," *New Statesman,* November 5, 1927; reprinted in *Skyscrapers and Other Essays* (London, 1931).

65. Quoted by Berman, *Nazism, the Jews and American Zionism,* p. 23; Robert E. Herzstein, *Roosevelt and Hitler* (New York, 1989), pp. 257, 400.

66. Cf. Shlomo Aronson, "Hitlers Judenpolitik, die Aliierten und die Juden," *Vierteljahrshefte für Zeitgeschichte,* January 1984, pp. 29–65.

67. Howe, *World of Our Fathers,* p. 393, Berman, *Nazism, The Jews and American Zionism,* p. 78.

68. Carl Herman Voss, "In Praise of Stephen S. Wise," *Moment,* July–August 1987, p. 51.

69. Aronson, "Hitler Judenpolitik," pp. 45–50. Cf. Christopher R. Browning, "The Decision Concerning the Final Solution," in François Furet (ed.), *Unanswered Questions* (New York, 1989); Hans Mommsen, "Die Realisierung des Utopischen: Die 'Endloesung der Judenfrage' im 'Dritten Reich'" in *Der Nationalsozialismus und die deutsche Gesellschaft* (Reinbek, 1991).

70. Berman, *Nazism, The Jews and American Zionism,* pp. 90–93.

71. *New York Times,* May 11–12, 1942.

72. Laqueur and Rubin, *Arab-Israeli Reader,* p. 79. Cf. Laqueur, *History of Zionism,* pp. 545–49; Dan Kurzman, *Ben-Gurion* (New York, 1983), pp. 236–37; Urofsky, *We Are One!,* pp. 4ff.

73. Urofsky, *We Are One!,* pp. 108–17. Cf. Laqueur, *History of Zionism,* pp. 552–53.

74. Zvi Ganin, *Truman, American Jewry and Israel* (New York, 1979), pp. 8ff. Cf. Dan Tschirgi, *The Politics of Indecision* (New York, 1983), pp. 51, 58–61.

75. I. L. Kenen, *Israel's Defense Line* (Buffalo, 1981), pp. 16ff.; Ganin, *Truman, American Jewry and Israel,* p. 5.

76. See Berman, *Nazism, The Jews and American Zionism,* pp. 119–21, 130.

77. See Ben Hecht, *Child of the Century* (New York, 1954), pp. 525ff. Cf. Urofsky, *We Are One!,* pp. 65ff.

78. Cf. Nahum Goldmann, *Mein Leben—USA, Europa, Israel* (Munich, 1981), pp. 67ff.

79. *Washington Post,* October 3, 1944. Cf. Michael J. Cohen, *Truman and Israel* (Berkeley, 1990), pp. 40–42.

80. Walter Clay Lowdermilk, *Palestine: Land of Promise* (New York, 1944).

81. Letter from Young Zionist Action Committee, January 23, 1945, and petition, State Department Central Files, Palestine and Israel [hereafter SDCF/PI] 1945–1949, reel 2. See Kenen, *Israel's Defense Line,* pp. vii–ix; George Norris, "TVA on the Jordan," *Nation,* May 20, 1944. Cf. Urofsky, *We Are One!,* pp. 30ff.; Grose, *Israel in the Mind of America,* p. 174; Berman, *Nazism, The Jews and American Zionism,* pp. 138–39.

82. Ganin, *Truman, American Jewry and Israel,* pp. xiii–xiv.

83. Grose, *Israel in the Mind of America,* pp. 174–75; Berman, op. cit., p. 132.

84. Dennis Deutsch, "The Palestine Question," in Robin Higham (ed.), *Intervention or Abstention* (Lexington, Ky., 1975), pp. 79ff.; J. Joseph Huthmacher, *Senator Robert F. Wagner and the Rise of Urban Liberalism* (New York, 1968), pp. 306ff. See Grose, *Israel in the Mind of America,* pp. 174–75. Cf. Urofsky, *We Are One!,* pp. 40ff.

85. Cohen, *Truman and Israel,* pp. 46–49; H. G. Nicholas (ed.), *Washington Despatches, 1941–1945* (Chicago, 1981), pp. 316–17, 325–26, 332–33, 479–80. Cf. Berman, *Nazism, The*

Jews and American Zionism, pp. 132–35; Tschirgi, *Politics of Indecision,* pp. 98–106, 110–13.

86. Urofsky, *We Are One!,* p. 91.

87. See Sol Bloom, *The Autobiography* (New York, 1948), passim.

88. Bloom and Stettinius, January 23, 1945, transcript in SDCF/PI 1945–1949, reel 2.

89. Huthmacher, *Senator Robert F. Wagner,* p. 307.

90. Wilson, *Decision on Palestine,* p. 59.

91. Naomi W. Cohen, *Not Free to Desist* (Philadelphia, 1972), p. 295.

92. See David Schoenbaum, "The World War II Allied Agreement on Occupation and Administration of Post-War Germany," in Alexander George, Alexander Dallin, and Phillip J. Farley (eds.) *U.S.-Soviet Security Cooperation* (New York, 1988).

93. Unsigned memo of January 8, 1945, SDCF/PI 1945–1949, reel 2; Wilson, *Decision on Palestine,* p. 49.

94. *The Conferences at Malta and Yalta, 1945, Foreign Relations of the United States* [hereafter FRUS] (Washington, 1955), p. 94. Cf. Ganin, *Truman, American Jewry and Israel,* p. 15.

95. Grose, *Israel in the Mind of America,* pp. 248–54. Cf. Irvine H. Anderson, *Aramco, the United States and Saudi Arabia* (Princeton, 1981), passim.

96. Memo of conversation, January 26, 1945, SDCF/PI 1945–1949, reel 2.

97. Berman, *Nazism, the Jews and American Zionism,* p. 156.

98. Nicholas, *Washington Dispatches,* p. 558.

Chapter 2

1. FRUS, *1948,* (Washington, 1976) vol. 5, no. 2, p. 1007.

2. Ibid., p. 975.

3. Harry S Truman, *Years of Trial and Hope* (New York, 1965), p. 198. Cf. Herbert Feis, *The Birth of Israel* (New York 1969), p. 21.

4. Moshe Davis "Reflections on Harry S Truman," in Allen Weinstein and Moshe Ma'oz (eds.), *Truman and the American Commitment to Israel* (Jerusalem, 1981), pp. 82ff.

5. See Truman, *Years of Trial and Hope,* pp. 159–99.

6. Robert Donovan, *Conflict and Crisis, 1945–1949* (New York, 1977), *Tumultuous Years, 1949–1953* (New York, 1982).

7. See Michael J. Cohen, *Truman and Israel* (Berkeley, 1990), p. 278. Cf. Peter Grose, *Israel in the Mind of America* (New York, 1983), p. 295.

8. Truman, *Years of Trial and Hope,* pp. 246, 271.

9. Zvi Ganin, "Truman, American Jewry and the Creation of Israel," in Allen Weinstein and Moshe Ma'oz (eds.), *Truman and the American Commitment to Israel* (Jerusalem, 1981), pp. 112–13.

10. Quoted by Grose, *Israel in the Mind of America,* p. 294.

11. FRUS, *1948,* vol. 5, no. 2, p. 1272.

12. Dean Acheson, *Present at the Creation* (New York 1969), p. 259. One of Bunche's contemporaries, who took the job himself, inferred that Bunche was reluctant to expose his family to the humiliations of daily life in Washington, which was still a heavily segregated southern city. Interview with George C. McGhee, summer 1987.

13. Margaret Truman. *Harry S Truman* (New York, 1973), p. xx

14. Robert H. Ferrell (ed.), *Off the Record* (Harmondsworth, 1982, p. 66.

15. Cf. Allan Bullock, *Ernest Bevin* (Oxford, 1983), p. 175; Michael J. Cohen, *Palestine*

and the Great Powers (Princeton, 1982), p. 58; W. Roger Louis, *The British Empire in the Middle East, 1945–1951* (Oxford, 1985), p. 391.

16. Virginia Gildersleeve, *Many a Good Crusade* (New York, 1955), pp. 181–82.

17. Personal correspondence from Mrs. Bernice Baron, January 12, 1987.

18. Joseph P. Lash, *Eleanor: The Years Alone* (New York, 1972), pp. 109ff., 114.

19. See Marion K. Sanders, *Dorothy Thompson* (Boston, 1973), pp. 320ff.

20. Murray Weisgal, . . . *So Far* (New York, 1971), p. 197.

21. Cf. Feis, *Birth of Israel*, pp. 24, 30–32, 50, 64–65; Donovan, *Conflict and Crisis*, pts. 2, 3.

22. Cf. I. L. Kenen, *Israel's Defense Line* (Buffalo, 1981), pp. 24ff.; 2 vi Ganin, *Truman, American Jews and Israel* (New York, 1979), pp. 25ff.

23. See Leonard Slater, *The Pledge* (New York, 1970), pp. 21–280.

24. Transcripts of April 4, 1945, April 3 and 4, 1946, SDCF/PI 1945–1949, reel 29.

25. Truman, *Years of Trial and Hope*, pp. 166–67.

26. Cf. Robert Abzug, *Inside the Vicious Heart* (New York, 1985), pp. 147–51.

27. Cf. Bullock, *Bevin*, pp. 170–72; Louis, *British Empire in the Middle East*, pp. 388ff.

28. Cf. Abraham L. Sachar, *The Redemption of the Unwanted* (New York, 1983), pp. 161–62; Grose, *Israel in the Mind of America*, pp. 197–98; Cohen, *Palestine and the Great Powers*, p. 56; Cohen, *Truman and Israel*, p. 111.

29. Thomas Albrich, *Exodus durch Oesterreich* (Innsbruck, 1987), pp. 196–97. Cf. Bullock, *Bevin*, p. 173; Cohen, *Palestine and the Great Powers*, p. 388; Sachar, *Redemption of the Unwanted*, p. 158.

30. Cf. Cohen, *Palestine and the Great Powers*, p. 57; Bullock, *Bevin*, p. 175.

31. Cohen, *Palestine and the Great Powers*, pp. 64–65; Bullock, *Bevin*, pp. 179–81; Grose, *Israel in the Mind of America*, pp. 202–3.

32. Quoted by Bullock, *Bevin*, p. 181.

33. Louis, *British Empire in the Middle East*, p. 421.

34. Ganin, *Truman*, pp. 44ff.

35. Cf. Albrich, *Exodus*, pp. 90–97; Cohen, *Palestine and the Great Powers*, pp. 101–2; Sachar, *Redemption of the Unwanted*, p. 202; Louis, *British Empire in the Middle East*, pp. 407–8.

36. See Louis, *British Empire in the Middle East*, pp. 412–13.

37. Bartley Crum, *Behind the Silken Curtain* (New York, 1947), pp. 7–8.

38. Ibid., p. 291.

39. R. H. S. Crossman, *Palestine Mission* (London, 1947), pp. 39–40.

40. Evan Wilson, *Decision on Palestine* (Stanford, 1979), p. 71.

41. Sachar, *Redemption of the Unwanted*, pp. 314–15.

42. Ibid., pp. 315–16. Cf. Louis, *British Empire in the Middle East*, p. 425.

43. Cf. Ganin, *Truman*, p. 74.

44. Louis, *British Empire in the Middle East*, p. 419. Cf. Cohen, *Palestine and the Great Powers*, pp. 109ff.; Bullock, *Bevin*, pp. 255ff.

45. Robert F. Drinan, *Honor the Promise* (New York, 1977), p. 74; Melvin I. Urofsky, *We Are One!* (Garden City, N.Y., 1978), p. 102. Cf. Bullock, *Bevin*, p. 278.

46. Cf. Richard N. Gardner, *Sterling-Dollar Diplomacy* (New York, 1969), p. 251; Ganin, *Truman*, pp. 72–73; Cohen, *Palestine and the Great Powers*, p. 118; Urofsky, *We Are One!*, pp. 127ff.

47. Bullock, *Bevin*, p. 165.

48. Ibid., p. 333.

49. Urofsky, *We Are One!*, p. 149.

50. Joint Intelligence Committee, May 18, 1946; request from H. Freeman Matthews,

June 6, 1946; reply from Chief of Staff, U.S. Army, June 19, 1946, with attached memos. Records of the Joint Chiefs of Staff [hereafter Records of the JCS], pt. 2, 1946–1953, Middle East, reel 1.

51. Albrich, *Exodus,* pp. 44ff., 113ff.

52. Cohen, *Palestine and the Great Powers,* p. 123.

53. Urofsky, *We Are One!,* p. 125.

54. Slater, *Pledge,* p. 294.

55. Quoted by Ganin, *Truman,* p. 65.

56. Louis, *British Empire in the Middle East,* p. 433; Cohen, *Palestine and the Great Powers,* p. 122.

57. Cf. Louis, *British Empire in the Middle East,* p. 435; Cohen, *Palestine and the Great Powers,* p. 122.

58. For a credible account of the bombing, see Eric Silver, *Begin* (New York, 1984), pp. 66–73.

59. Reprinted by John Bowyer Bell, *Terror out of Zion* (New York, 1977), between p. 252 and p. 254.

60. Cf. Silver, *Begin,* pp. 81–85.

61. Cf. Bell, *Terror out of Zion,* pp. 169–73; Cohen, *Palestine and the Great Powers,* pp. 90–93.

62. Louis, *British Empire in the Middle East,* p. 449. Cf. Cohen, *Palestine and the Great Powers,* pp. 137–34.

63. Cf. Louis, *British Empire in the Middle East,* pp. 437–38.

64. Henry A. Wallace, *The Price of Vision* (Boston, 1973), p. 603.

65. Ibid., p. 607.

66. Ganin, *Truman,* p. 30; Cohen, *Truman and Israel,* p. 135.

67. Louis, *British Empire in the Middle East,* p. 433.

68. Quoted in Wallace, *Price of Vision,* p. 605.

69. Cf. Sachar, *Redemption of the Unwanted,* pp. 192–99, Grose, *Israel in the Mind of America,* pp. 218–22.

70. Cf. Cohen, *Palestine and the Great Powers,* pp. 129–32; Ganin, *Truman,* pp. 80ff.

71. Cf. Nahum Goldmann, *Mein Leben—USA, Europa, Israel,* (Munich, 1980), pp. 159ff.; Ganin, *Truman,* pp. 90ff.; Cohen, *Palestine and the Great Powers,* pp. 141–47; Cohen, *Truman and Israel,* pp. 135–37.

72. Naomi W. Cohen, *Not Free to Desist* (Philadelphia, 1972), pp. 298ff. Cf. Goldmann, *Mein Leben—USA,* pp. 159ff.

73. Cf. Ganin, *Truman,* pp. 90ff.; Cohen, *Palestine and the Great Powers,* pp. 147–51; Cohen, *Truman and Israel,* pp. 140–41; Louis, *British Empire in the Middle East,* pp. 440–41.

74. Cf. Donovan, *Conflict,* pp. 229–38.

75. Ibid., pp. 321–22. Cf. Cohen, *Palestine and the Great Powers,* p. 167.

76. Cf. Bullock, *Bevin,* pp. 305–6; Louis, *British Empire in the Middle East,* pp. 442–43; Cohen, *Truman and Israel,* p. 145.

77. Wilson, *Decision on Palestine,* pp. 96ff.

78. Cf. Bullock, *Bevin,* pp. 343–44.

79. Cf. Grose, *Israel in the Mind of America,* pp. 233–36; Bullock, *Bevin,* pp. 366–67.

80. Cf. Louis, *British Empire in the Middle East,* pp. 465ff.

81. Quoted, ibid., p. 433.

82. FRUS, *1947,* (Washington, 1976) vol. 5, pp. 1014–15; quoted by Bullock, *Bevin,* p. 364.

83. See Reports from U.S. Consul General, Jerusalem, of September 27, 1946, and August 27, 1947, SDCF/PI 1945–1949, reel 2.

84. Eliahu Elath, "The 14th of May 1948 in Washington, D.C." in Allen Weinstein and Moshe Ma'oz (eds.), *Truman and the American Commitment to Israel* (Jerusalem, 1981), pp. 109–10.

85. Memo of April 4, 1947, Marshall-Lovett Memoranda to President Truman 1947–1948, reel 1, National Archives 27343. (Hereafter Marshall-Lovett Memoranda.)

86. Cf. Louis, *British Empire in the Middle East,* pp. 468–69; Feis, *Birth of Israel,* p. 77.

87. Memos of July 10 and 18, 1947, Marshall-Lovett Memoranda.

88. Cf. Bullock, *Bevin,* pp. 446–50; Cohen, *Palestine and the Great Powers,* pp. 250–59. In 1988, in the early stages of the Palestinian *intifada,* the Palestine Liberation Organization undertook a deliberate reprise, announcing plans to launch a "Ship of Return" from Cyprus to the now-Israeli port of Haifa with recent deportees from the Israeli-occupied territories. This time, Israelis saw to it that the ship was rendered unseaworthy before it even weighed anchor, and the PLO was unable to find another ship before the international press corps disbanded and went home. See Ze'ev Schiff and Ehud Ya'ari, *The Intifada* (New York, 1990), pp. 171–72.

89. Proposed supplement to report, October 8, 1947, Records of the JCS, pt. 2, 1946–1953, Middle East, reel 1.

90. Cohen, *Palestine and the Great Powers,* pp. 46–48; "Memorandum by the President's Special Counsel (Clifford) to President Truman," March 8, 1948, FRUS 1948, vol. 5, no. 2, pp. 690ff.

91. Memos of September 24 and October 10, and recommendations of October 21, 1947, Records of the JCS, pt. 2, 1946–1953, Middle East, reel 1.

92. "The Current Situation in the Mediterranean and the Near East," October 17, 1947, CIA Research Reports, Middle East, 1946–1976, reel 1, and "The Current Situation in Palestine," October 20, 1947, ibid., reel 3.

93. See David Niles, "Memorandum for the President," July 29, 1947, reprinted in Sachar, *Redemption of the Unwanted,* pp. 320–21; Ganin, *Truman,* pp. 125ff.

94. Cf. Lash, *Eleanor,* pp. 122ff.; Ganin, *Truman,* p. 129. See Bohlen memo to Lovett of November 19, Weizmann letter to Morgenthau of November 20, and Michael Comay letter to Bernard Gering of December 3, reprinted in Michael J. Cohen (ed.), *United Nations Discussions on Palestine, 1947* (New York, 1987), pp. 143, 145, 186.

95. Cf. Ganin, *Truman,* p. 130; Feis, *Birth of Israel,* pp. 45–46. Cf. Cohen, *Truman and Israel,* pp. 159–61.

96. See Lovett to Truman, December 10, 1947, Marshall-Lovett Memoranda. Cf. Cohen, *Palestine and the Great Powers,* pp. 296–98; Urofsky, *We Are One!,* pp. 245ff.; Goldmann, *Mein Leben—USA,* p. 184; Sachar, *Redemption of the Unwanted,* pp. 221–23; Donovan, *Conflict,* pp. 328–31; Zvi Ganin, "The Limits of American Jewish Political Power," *Jewish Social Studies* 39 (1977): 8; Emanuel Neumann, *In the Arena* (New York, 1976), pp. 251–52; Cohen, *Truman and Israel,* pp. 168–70.

97. Edward B. Glick, *Latin America and the Palestine Question* (New York, 1958), pp. 105ff.; Jorge Garcia-Granados, *The Birth of Israel* (New York, 1949), p. 259.

98. Acheson, *Present at the Creation,* p. 259.

99. Memo from the Chief of Naval Operations, February 7, 1948; draft for the Secretary of Defense, February 17, 1948; memo from Gen. Gruenther, March 31, 1948, Records of the JCS, pt. 2, 1946–1953, Middle East, reel 1.

100. FRUS, *1948,* vol. 5, no. 2, p. 657.

101. Ibid., pp. 617–25.

102. Walter Millis (ed.), *The Forrestal Diaries* (New York, 1951), p. 357.

103. FRUS, *1948*, vol. 5, no. 2, pp. 805–6.

104. Robert Divine, *Foreign Policy and U.S. Presidential Elections* (New York, 1974), p. 174.

105. Ibid., pp. 176–77; Cohen, *Truman and Israel*, p. 179.

106. Diary entry for March 20, 1948, in Ferrell, *Off the Record*, p. 127.

107. See memo from Leonard C. Meeker to Ernest Gross, "Formulation of United States policy on Palestine, January to April 1948," November 5, 1948, SDCF/PI 1945–1949, reel 2. Cf. Cohen, *Truman and Israel*, pp. 188–98.

108. See Avi Shlaim, *Collusion across the Jordan* (New York, 1988), pp. 188ff.

109. Arnold Rogow, *James Forrestal* (New York, 1963), p. 359.

110. Cf. Teddy Kollek, *For Jerusalem* (New York, 1978), pp. 67ff.; Slater, *Pledge*, pp. 320–27.

111. See chapter 11.

112. Editorial Note, FRUS, *1948*, vol. 5, no. 2, p. 993.

113. Cf. Feis, *Birth of Israel*, p. 61; Ian Bickerton, "Truman, the Creation of Israel and the Liberal Tradition," in Allen Weinstein and Moshe Ma'oz (eds.), *Truman and the American Commitment to Israel* (Jerusalem, 1981), pp. 103–4; Ganin, *Truman*, p. 188; Cohen, *Palestine and the Great Powers*, pp. 389–90; Cohen, *Truman and Israel*, pp. 215–22.

114. FRUS, *1948*, vol. 5, no. 2, p. 1222.

115. Ibid., p. 1251. Cf. Lash, *Eleanor*, pp. 134–35.

116. Truman, *Years of Trial and Hope*, p. 197.

117. FRUS, *1948*, vol. 5, no. 2, p. 1661.

Chapter 3

1. In conversation with the author, Iowa City, December 1990.

2. Quoted in Naomi W. Cohen, *Not Free to Desist* (Philadelphia, 1972), pp. 309ff. Cf. Charles S. Liebman, *Pressure without Sanctions* (Rutherford, N.J., 1977), pp. 118–30; Alan Lesser, *Israel's Impact* (Lanham, Md., 1984), pp. 49ff.

3. See Melvin I. Urofsky, *We Are One!* (Garden City, N.Y., 1978), p. 273.

4. Ibid., p. x.

5. Quoted in Itamar Rabinovich and Jehuda Reinharz (eds.), *Israel in the Middle East* (New York, 1984), pp. 375, 377.

6. Both illuminating and funny is a 1953 exchange of letters between a concerned Brooklyn mother, whose daughters were attending a Labor Zionist summer camp, and the Israel desk officer at the State Department. The woman attached her daughter's report of the May Day celebration at a kibbutz in the Upper Galilee, where the red flag had been prominently displayed. Despite the girl's reminder that her mother should "never forget that Israel is a democratic state," the woman wanted more information. Was there any danger, she asked, that "the girls might come back to America with communistice [*sic*] leanings?" Referring to the *American Jewish Yearbook* as his source, the desk officer reported that the sponsoring organization had shut down its camp for prospective immigrants in 1951, and now prepared American visitors for active participation in American Jewish community life. "In Israel, as in a number of other countries, May 1 is celebrated by non-communist socialist and workers' groups as well as communists," he added reassuringly. Letter from Mrs. Ethel Zukor of May 11, 1953, reply from Fred E. Weller, May 21, 1953, SDCF P/I, 1950–1954.

7. Cf. Lesser, *Israel's Impact*, pp. xviiff., 1–49; Emanuel Neumann, *In the Arena* (New York, 1976), pp. 270ff.; Dan Kurzman, *Ben-Gurion* (New York, 1983), pp. 334–35; "The

Israel Government's Economic Conference with Representatives of American Jewry," Richard Ford to State Department, September 7, 1950, SDCF P/I 1950–1954.

8. Cf. Urofsky, *We Are One!,* pp. 202–3, 227ff.; Lesser, *Israel's Impact,* pp. 193–213.

9. Joseph P. Lash, *Eleanor: The Years Alone* (New York, 1972), p. 137; Urofsky, *We Are One!,* p. 201.

10. Virginia Gildersleeve, *Many a Good Crusade* (New York, 1955), pp. 409ff.

11. See Kermit Roosevelt, *Countercoup* (New York, 1979); Miles Copeland, *The Game of Nations* (New York, 1969).

12. Marion K. Sanders, *Dorothy Thompson,* pp. 335ff.; letter to President Johnson of March 21, 1967, from Rabbi Philip A. Bernstein, American-Israel Public Affairs Committee; memo and draft letter of March 29, 1967, to Walt Rostow from Benjamin H. Read, with draft letter of reply, National Security Files, Isreal, 1963–69.

13. Reader's letter from Dorothy Thompson, *New York Times,* July 29, 1951.

14. Rusk to Clifford, September 2, 1949, SDCF P/I, 1945–1949.

15. Richard Ford to State Department, September 25, 1950, SDCF P/I, 1950–1954.

16. FRUS, *1948,* vol. 5, no. 2, p. 1179; McDonald reply to report from Harold [*sic*] Hoskins, November 24, 1950, SDCF P/I 1950–1954, reel 2; James G. McDonald, *My Mission in Israel* (New York, 1951), p. 153.

17. McDonald, *My Mission in Israel,* pp. 225ff.

18. Sheldon D. Engelmayer and Robert J. Wagman, *Hubert Humphrey* (New York 1978), pp. 187–91.

19. "The Current Situation in Palestine," July 18, 1949, CIA Research Reports, Middle East, 1946–1976, reel 3.

20. Memo of August 7, 1949, Records of the JCS, pt. 2, 1946–1953, Middle East, reel 2.

21. Cf. memo from Under Secretary of State Webb to Under Secretary of Defense Lovett, February 11, 1952, and Lovett reply of April 19, 1952, SDCF P/I 1950–1954, reel 6.

22. FRUS, *1949,* Washington, 1977, vol. 6, p. 695.

23. Ibid., p. 732.

24. Ibid., p. 787.

25. Eric Silver, *Begin* (New York, 1984), pp. 98ff.

26. FRUS, *1949,* p. 1019.

27. Ibid., p. 1251.

28. Forrestal to Lovett, October 21, 1948, Records of the JCS, pt. 2, 1946–1953, Middle East, reel 2. Cf. Saadia Touval, *The Peace Brokers* (Princeton, 1982), p. 41.

29. FRUS, *1949,* pp. 733, 1508–9.

30. Ibid., p. 1596. Cf. Itamar Rabinovich, *The Road Not Taken* (New York and Oxford, 1991), passim.

31. Memo of April 23, 1950, SDCF P/I 1950–1954, reel 2; Ben-Gurion to Acheson, May 31, 1951, ibid., reel 6. Cf. Teddy Kollek, *For Jerusalem* (New York, 1978), pp. 91ff. Cf. Touval, *Peace Brokers,* pp. 84, 94–103.

32. Kenneth W. Bilby, *New Star in the Near East* (New York, 1951), pp. 258ff.

33. Tom Segev, *The First Israelis* (New York, 1985), p. 290.

34. Abba Eban, *An Autobiography* (New York, 1977), pp. 154ff.

35. Walter Eytan, *The First Ten Years* (New York, 1958), pp. 9–10.

36. "Current Situation in Palestine," CIA Research Reports.

37. Quoted in Lesser, *Israel's Impact,* p. 11.

38. See SDCF P/I 1945–1949, reel 29, passim.

39. Ibid., reel 23.

40. Segev, *First Israelis,* pp. 273–78.

41. Ibid., pp. 273ff. Cf. Stewart Steven, *The Spymasters of Israel* (New York, 1980), p. 53; Kurzman, *Ben-Gurion,* pp. 305, 340.

42. Michael Brecher, *Decisions in Israel's Foreign Policy* (New Haven, 1975), pp. 111–16; FRUS, *1951,* vol. 3 (Washington, 1982), p. 1824; Ben-Gurion telegrams of November 12, 1952, SDCF P/I 1950–1954, reel 6.

43. Cable from Richard Ford, October 5, 1949, SDCF P/I 1945–1949, reel 2.

44. Brecher, *Decision in Israel's Foreign Policy,* pp. 8ff.

45. Ibid, p. 342.

46. Segev, *First Israelis,* pp. 296–97.

47. Urofsky, *We Are One!,* p. 201.

48. Eytan, *First Ten Years,* pp. 209ff.

49. McDonald dispatch of April 24, 1950, SDCF P/I 1950–1954, reel 2.

50. Telegram, Ford to State Department, September 9, 1949, SDCF P/I 1945–1949, reel 22.

51. Truman speech to National Jewish Welfare Board, October 17, 1952, SDCF P/I 1950–1954, reel 2.

52. Engelmayer and Wagman, *Humphrey,* pp. 159–63.

53. Andrei Zhdanov, "The International Situation," in *The Strategy and Tactics of World Communism,* 80th Cong., 2d sess., 1948, H. Doc. 619, supp. 1, pp. 218–30.

54. FRUS, *1949,* p. 1533.

55. Cf. Isaac Deutscher, *Stalin* (New York, 1967), pp. 604–9.

56. Lesser, *Israel's Impact,* p. 276.

57. Senate Committee on Foreign Relations and Senate Committee on Armed Services, *Hearings, Mutual Security Act of 1951,* 82nd Cong., second sess., 1951, S. Doc. 1762, pp. 739–40.

58. Text in FRUS, *1950,* vol. 5, (Washington, 1978), pp. 167–68.

59. See NSC staff study, March 4, 1952, Records of the JCS, pt. 2, 1946–1953, Middle East, reel 2.

60. "Command Structure in the Middle East," May 23, 1951, *FRUS, 1951* vol. 5 (Washington, 1982), pp. 144–45.

61. Acheson to Javits, January 12, 1950, SDCF P/I 1950–1954, reel 1.

62. FRUS *1951,* vol. 5, pp. 670, 686.

63. "Difficult Position of Israel," Memorandum of Conversation, December 27, 1950, SDCF P/I 1950–1954.

64. Cf. Letter from Daniel Goott, Office of Assistant Secretary for Economic Affairs, to Martin Koppel, Retail Men's Wear, Sporting Goods and Accessories Employees Union, Local No. 721, August 15, 1951, SDCF P/I 1950–1954.

65. Cf. FRUS, *1951,* vol. 5, p. 606; Kollek, *For Jerusalem,* pp. 99–100.

66. FRUS, *1951,* vol. 5, pp. 608–10.

67. Acheson cable, January 31, 1951; "Foreign Assistance for Israel," February 24, 1951; "Outline Analysis of Factors Concerning Israel: Grant Aid Request," undated; "Grant-aid to Israel," April 5, 1951; dispatch from Ambassador Davis, November 6, 1951, SCDF P/I 1950–1954, reel 2.

68. FRUS, *1951,* vol. 5, p. 605.

69. Ibid., pp. 630–31, 669–70, 748–50.

70. Cf. Brecher, *Decisions in Israel's Foreign Policy,* p. 78; Lily Gardner Feldman, *The Special Relationship between West Germany and Israel* (Boston, 1984), pp. 49ff.

71. Cf. Michael Wolffsohn, "Die Wiedergutmachung und der Westen," in "Aus Politik und Zeitgeschichte," *Das Parlament,* April 18, 1987, and "Das Deutsch-Israelische Wied-

ergutmachungsabkommen von 1952 in internationalen Zusammenhang," *Vierteljahrshefte für Zeitgeschichte,* October 1988, pp. 693–708; Norbert Frei, "Wiedergutmachungspolitik im Urteil der amerikanischen Oeffentlichkeit," in Ludolf Herbst and Constantin Goschler (eds.), *Wiedergutmachung in der Bundesrepublik Deutschland* (Munich, 1989), pp. 215ff.; Brecher, *Decisions in Israel's Foreign Policy,* pp. 78ff.; Feldman, *Special Relationship,* pp. 63ff., FRUS, *1952–1954* (Washington, 1986), vol. 9, pp. 913–14, 918–20, 936–37, 942–43; Goldmann, *Mein Leben als deutscher Jude* (Munich, 1980), pp. 393–94, 413–14; Hans-Peter Schwarz, *Adenauer* (Stuttgart, 1986), pp. 897–906.

72. Feldman, *Special Relationship,* p. 81.

73. NSC staff study (draft), March 4, 1952, Records of the JCS, pt. 2, 1946–1953, Middle East, reel 2.

74. Memo from Israeli embassy of January 9, 1953, SDCF P/I 1950–1954, reel 11.

75. FRUS, *1952–1954,* vol. 9, p. 2.

76. The full text of the speech can be found in the *Department of State Bulletin,* June 15, 1953, pp. 831–35.

77. James M. Ludlow and Pinhas Eliav, memo of conversation, June 3, 1953, SDCF P/I 1950–1954, reel 6.

Chapter 4

1. Cf. Wolfgang Leonhard, *The Kremlin after Stalin* (New York, 1962), passim; Arnulf Baring, *Revolution in East Germany* (Ithaca, 1972), passim; Coral Bell, *Negotiation from Strength* (New York, 1963), passim; John Lewis Gaddis, *Strategies of Containment* (New York, 1982), chap. 5.

2. Isaac Alteras, "Eisenhower, American Jewry and Israel," *American Jewish Archives, 1985,* pp. 257ff.

3. Aide-memoir [*sic*] by the ambassador of Israel, February 11, 1953; "United States-Israel relations including Israeli concern over press reports of a change in U.S. policies for the Near East," memorandum of conversation, March 6, 1953, SDCF P/I 1950–1954.

4. For U.S. policy in Iran, see George C. McGhee, *Envoy to the Middle World* (New York, 1983), chaps. 27, 31; Kermit Roosevelt, *Countercoup* (New York, 1979), passim.

5. For Middle Eastern dirty tricks, cf. Miles Copeland, *The Game of Nations* (New York, 1969), passim; Wilbur Crane Eveland, *Ropes of Sand* (New York, 1980), passim.

6. FRUS, *1952–1954* (Washington, 1986), vol. 9 p. 36.

7. Cf. Michael Brecher, *Decisions in Israel's Foreign Policy* (New Haven, 1975), p. 33.

8. Communication to journalists, July 1953; and embassy telegram, October 7, 1953, SDCF P/I 1950–1954, reel 6.

9. Telegram No. 1209 from Ambassador Davis, January 28, 1953, SDCF P/I 1950–1054.

10. FRUS, *1952–1954,* p. 31.

11. "American-Israel Relations," memorandum of conversation, May 13, 1954, SDCF P/I 1950–54.

12. FRUS, *1952–1954,* p. 39.

13. "The Middle East in New Pespective," *Department of State Bulletin,* April 26, 1954, pp. 628–33; *New York Times,* May 2, 1954.

14. FRUS, *1952–1954,* vol. 9, pp. 1557–61.

15. Personal letter from Teddy Kollek to Parker T. Hart, April 25, 1954, SDCF P/I 1950–1954.

16. "Memorandum to Hon. Sherman Adams," May 24, 1954; "Memorandum for the the Honorable Walter Bedell Smith," June 3, 1954; and attached documents and "Memo to the Files," June 22, 1954, SDCF P/I 1950–54.

17. FRUS, *1950–1954,* vol. 9, p. 526.

18. Joint Embassy-TCA Message, June 26, 1953; "Israel's financial crisis (July 1953)," June 29, 1953; and Joint State-DMS Message, July 15, 1953, SDCF P/I 1950–1954.

19. Joint State-DMS message, June 22, 1953 (signed) Dulles; embassy telegrams #164 and #194, August 5 and 12, 1953; "Confidential Security Information, Amembassy Tel Aviv Tecto 70," undated, (signed) Stassen; "An Israeli Reaction to Limitation on Use MSA Funds," August 18, 1953; and embassy telegram 270, August 26, 1953, SDCF P/I 1950–1954.

20. Cf. I. L. Kenen, *Israel's Defense Line* (Buffalo, 1981), pp. 92ff.; Ze'ev Schiff, *A History of the Israeli Army* (New York, 1985), pp. 73–76. Letters from Sen. Homer Ferguson of September 21 and Sen. Hubert Humphrey of September 22, 1953, SDCF P/I 1950–1954. Ferguson inquiry to Dulles, October 11, 1954; Dulles reply October 19; cover note and hand-out from Bernard Katzen to Roderic L. O'Connor, October 21; and note to Ferguson from John W. Hanes, Jr., October 21, Special Assistants Chronological Series, October 1954, John Foster Dulles Files, Princeton University Library.

21. Letters from various members of Congress; telegram from Adams to Hadassah conference; Stassen to Dulles, November 30, 1953; memo from O. L. Troxel, Jr., to Parker T. Hart, "Loss of Influence over Israeli Financial Developments," February 8, 1954, SDCF P/I 1950–54, reel 7.

22. Cf. Rashid Khalidi, "Consequences of the Suez Crisis in the Arab World," in W. Roger Louis and Roger Owen (eds.), *Suez 1956: The Crisis and Its Consequences* (New York, 1989), pp. 377–392.

23. FRUS, *1952–54,* vol. 9, pp. 1348–53.

24. See Brecher, *Decisions in Israel's Foreign Policy,* pp. 193–206.

25. Cf. Shimon Shamir, "The Collapse of Project Alpha," in William Roger Louis and Roger Owen (eds.), *Suez 1956: The Crisis and Its Consequences* (Oxford, 1989), pp. 73–100; Elmore Jackson, *Middle East Mission: The Story of a Major Bid for Peace in the Time of Nasser and Ben-Gurion* (New York, 1983).

26. "The General [Dayan] inquired if Israel would be required to pay for the improvement of United States relations with Egypt by giving up a corridor through the Negev. (Mr. Byroade expressed astonishment at the suggestion.)" Memo, "Israel," July 16, 1954, SDCF P/I 1950–1954.

27. Shamir, "Collapse of Project Alpha," pp. 9ff.; Mordechai Bar-on, "David Ben-Gurion and the Sèvres Collusion," in W. Roger Louis and Roger Owen, *Suez 1956: The Crisis and Its Consequences* (Oxford, 1989), pp. 145–60.

28. Evelyn Shuckburgh, *Descent to Suez* (London, 1986), p. 258.

29. Ibid., pp. 264–65.

30. See Uri Ra'anan, *The USSR Arms the Third World* (Cambridge, 1969).

31. Cf. Mohammed Heikal, *The Sphinx and the Commissar* (New York, 1978), pp. 56–65.

32. Memo from Philip H. Trezise, IR, "Soviet Arms Offer to Egypt," September 6, 1955, with attached report, "The Soviet Arms Offer to Egypt," SDCF P/I 1950–1954.

33. Shuckburgh, *Descent to Suez,* p. 279. Cf. Shamir, "Collapse of Project Alpha," pp. 11ff.

34. Shuckburgh, *Descent to Suez,* p. 293.

35. Cf. Amos Perlmutter, *Israel: The Partitioned State* (New York, 1985), pp. 156–57.

36. FRUS, 1952–1954, vol. 9, pp. 29–30.

37. Quoted in Itamar Rabinovich and Jehuda Reinharz, (eds.), *Israel in the Middle East* (New York, 1984), p. 82.

38. Ibid., p. 97.

39. Schiff, *History of the Israeli Army,* p. 69.

40. Cf. Perlmutter, *Israel,* pp. 170–73.

41. Thus, for example, several of his major speeches, like, e.g., Churchill's, were issued on commercial LPs.

42. See memo for Assistant Chief of Staff, G-2; message for Maj. General Clovis Byers from Gen. Hull, June 19, 1953, and top-secret reply from Hull to Byers, June 22, 1953; letter from Eban to Smith, June 10, 1953, memo from Smith to Jernegan, June 15, 1953, and Jernegan reply to Smith, June 22, 1953; memo for Smith of August 27, 1953, with attached draft from Byroade of reply to Eban, SDCF P/I 1950–1954.

43. Memo, "Arms for Israel," November 15, 1953, SDCF P/I 1950–1954.

44. Saadia Touval, *The Peace Brokers* (Princeton, 1982), pp. 114ff.

45. See memo, "Military Supplies for the Arab States," February 1, 1954; "Israel's Request for 24 Sabre Jets" etc., May 24, 1954; memo, Byroade to Dulles, "Israel request to purchase American jet aircraft," June 3, 1954; letter from VADM A. C. Davis to Eban, July 9, 1954; telegram to Middle East embassies on conversation between Eban and Dulles, August 7, 1954; memo, Dulles to Byroade, August 9, 1954; memo, Jernegan to Dulles, "Military Superiority of Israel in the Near East," September 28, 1954, SDCF P/I 1950–1954.

46. Gideon Rafael, *Destination Peace* (New York, 1981), pp. 35ff.

47. Touval, *Peace Brokers,* pp. 120ff.

48. Robert H. Ferrell (ed.), *The Eisenhower Diaries* (New York, 1981), p. 308. Many years later, Anderson was convicted of tax fraud.

49. Donald Neff, *Warriors at Suez* (New York, 1981), pp. 130ff.

50. Rafael, *Destination Peace,* pp. 40–44.

51. Schiff, *History of the Israeli Army,* pp. 68–85.

52. Cf. Stewart Steven, *The Spymasters of Israel* (New York, 1980), p. 66.

53. Ibid., pp. 194–96, Perlmutter, *Israel,* pp. 163–87. Cf. Ehud Ya'ari, "The Challenge of the Fedayeen," in Itamar Rabinovich and Jehuda Reinharz (eds.), *Israel in the Middle East* (New York, 1984), pp. 77–80.

54. National Security estimate, August 18, 1953, FRUS, *1952–54,* pp. 1284–85.

55. Cf. Selwyn Ilan Troen, "The Sinai Campaign as a 'War of No Alternative,' " in Troen and Moshe Shemesh (eds.), *The Suez-Sinai Crisis, 1956* (London, 1990), p. 181.

56. Moshe Sharett, "The Soviet Union and the Czech Arms Deal" in Itamar Rabinovich and Jehuda Reinharz, (eds.), *Israel in the Middle East* (New York, 1984), pp. 92–95. Cf. Rafael, *Destination Peace,* pp. 40–44.

57. See Yaacov Herzog, "The Background to the Sinai Campaign" in Itamar Rabinovich and Jehuda Reinharz, (eds.), *Israel in the Middle East* (New York, 1984), p. 100.

58. Personal correspondence with one of the authors, September 9, 1986.

59. "The Outlook for U.S. Interests in the Middle East," Intelligence Report 7074, State Department Intelligence and Research, November 14, 1955.

60. Abba Eban, *An Autobiography* (New York, 1977), p. 197.

61. See Sylvia K. Crosbie, *A Tacit Alliance* (Princeton, 1974), pp. 1–20.

62. Cf. Matti Golan, *Shimon Peres* (London, 1982), pp. 38ff.

63. See Pierre Péan, *Les deux Bombes* (Paris, 1982), pp. 33–34. Cf. Miles Kahler, *Decolonization in Britain and France* (Princeton, 1984), pp. 223ff.

64. Cf. Jean-Paul Cointet, "Guy Mollet, the French Government and the SFIO," in

Selwyn Ilan Troen and Moshe Shemesh, *The Suez-Sinai Crisis, 1956* (London, 1990), pp. 127ff.

65. Abel Thomas, *Comment Israël fut Savvé* (Paris, 1978).

66. See Ben-Gurion diary, entry of December 29, 1956, in Selwyn I. Troen and Moshe Shemesh, *The Suez-Sinai Crisis, 1956* (London, 1990), pp. 328–29.

67. Cf. Neff, *Warriors at Suez*, p. 159; Dwight D. Eisenhower, *Waging Peace* (New York, 1965), pp. 20ff.; Crosbie, *Tacit Alliance*, pp. 63ff.; Golan, *Peres*, pp. 41ff.; Shimon Peres, *David's Sling* (London, 1970), pp. 53ff.

68. Cf. Emmet John Hughes, *The Ordeal of Power* (New York, 1963); Neff, *Warriors at Suez*, p. 126.

69. Cf. Chester Cooper, *The Lion's Last Roar* (New York, 1978), pp. 95–96; Sherman Adams, *Firsthand Report* (New York, 1961), pp. 247ff.; Robert R. Bowie, "Dulles and the Suez Crisis" in W. Roger Louis and Roger Owen, *Suez 1956: The Crisis and Its Consequences* (Oxford, 1989), pp. 189–214.

70. Cf. Anthony Adamthwaite, "Suez Revisited," *International Affairs*, Summer 1988.

71. Bar-on, "Ben-Gurion and the Sèvres Collusion," pp. 10ff.

72. Neff, *Warriors at Suez*, pp. 343–44.

73. See Eisenhower, *Waging Peace*, pp. 56ff.; Ferrell, *Eisenhower Diaries*, pp. 331–32; Schiff, *History of the Israeli Army*, p. 94.

74. On the homeward flight from Sèvres, Dayan doodled a cartoon of a large and well-turned-out English gentleman and French lady looking down on a little Israeli figure in shorts, with his back to the Nile somewhere deep in the Sinai. "After you!" they are saying. Reproduced in Selwyn I. Troen and Jehuda Shemesh, *The Suez-Sinai Crisis, 1956* (London, 1990), p. 193.

75. See Ben-Gurion diary, October 22, 1956, pp. 305–9. Cf. Bar-on, "Ben-Gurion and the Sevres Collusion"; Dan Kurzman, *Ben-Gurion* (new York, 1983), p. 388.

76. Baron-on, "Ben-Gurion and the Sevres Collusion"; Schiff, *History of the Israeli Army*, p. 94.

77. FRUS, *1955–1957*, vol. 16, *Suez Crisis, July 26-December 31, 1956* (Washington, 1990), pp. 833–39.

78. Eisenhower, *Waging Peace*, pp. 98–99; Hughes, *Ordeal of Power*, pp. 212–13.

79. FRUS, *1955–1957*, vol. 16, p. 849.

80. Robert Griffith (ed.), *Ike's Letters to a Friend* (Lawrence, Kan., 1984), pp. 174–76. Cf. Adams, *Firsthand Report*, p. 256; Rafael, *Destination Peace*, pp. 58–59.

81. Cf. Hugh Thomas, *The Suez Affair* (London, 1967), pp. 142, 147.

82. FRUS, *1955–1957*, vol. 16, pp. 852, 881–82.

83. Quoted in Neff, *Warriors and Suez*, p. 365.

84. FRUS, *1955–1957*, vol. 16, p. 885.

85. Ibid., pp. 860, 901, 909, 912–13.

86. Cf. Cooper, *Lion's Last Roar*, p. 185; Alteras, "Eisenhower, American Jewry and Israel," pp. 266–67.

87. Eban, *Autobiography*, p. 213. Cf. Emanuel Neumann, *In the Arena* (New York, 1976), p. 294.

88. Neumann, *In the Arena*, appendix, pp. 356–59; Alteras, "Eisenhower, American Jewry and Israel," pp. 265–66.

89. Eban, *Autobiography*, pp. 217–18.

90 Cf. Diane B. Kunz, "The Importance of Having Money," in W. Roger Louis and Roger Owen, (eds.), *Suez 1956: The Crisis and Its Consequences* (Oxford, 1989), pp. 215–232.

91. Eban, *Autobiography*, pp. 228ff.

92. Cf. Cooper, *Lion's Last Roar,* pp. 250ff.; FRUS, *1955–1957,* vol. 16, p. 1050.

93. FRUS, *1955–1957,* vol. 16, p. 1051.

94. See ibid., pp. 1038ff.

95. Ibid., p. 1340.

96. Ibid., p. 1297. Cf. Eisenhower, *Waging Peace,* pp. 115–16.

97. FRUS, *1955–1957,* vol. 16, p. 1343.

98. Eban, *Autobiography,* pp. 234ff.

99. Adams, *Firsthand Report,* pp. 271ff.; Eisenhower, *Waging Peace,* pp. 177ff. Cf. Cooper, *Lion's Last Roar,* pp. 244ff.

100. See FRUS, *1955–1957,* vol. 17, *Arab-Israeli Dispute 1957* (Washington, 1990), p. 46.

101. Ibid., pp. 78–79.

102. See ibid., p. 199.

103. Ibid., pp. 136–37, 183.

104. Ibid., p. 239.

105. Ibid., pp. 142–43.

106. Ibid., pp. 167, 172.

107. Golda Meir, *My Life* (New York, 1975), p. 306.

108. FRUS, *1955–1957,* vol. 17, pp. 132–34. The text can also be found as Appendix J in Eisenhower, *Waging Peace,* pp. 684–85. See Alteras, "Eisenhower, American Jewry and Israel," p. 268.

109. Eban, *Autobiography,* p. 240.

110. See Eisenhower, *Waging Peace,* pp. 183ff.; Eban, *Autobiography,* pp. 238ff.

111. Richard M. Nixon, *RM* (New York, 1978), p. 179.

112. Minutes can be found in FRUS, *1955–1957,* vol. 17, pp. 214ff.

113. Ibid., p. 220.

114. Ibid., p. 223. Cf. Adams, *Firsthand Report,* pp. 284ff.; George Kent, "Congress and American Middle East Policy," in Willard A. Beling (ed.), *The Middle East: Quest for an American Policy* (Albany, 1973), p. 294.

115. FRUS, *1955–1957,* vol. 17, p. 224.

116. Hughes, *Ordeal of Power,* pp. 218–19; Eisenhower, *Waging Peace,* pp. 187ff.

117. Quoted by Alteras, "Eisenhower, American Jewry and Israel," p. 271. On Strauss and Jews, Seymour M. Hersh, *The Samson Option,* New York, 1991, Chapter 7.

118. FRUS, *1955–1957,* vol. 17, pp. 254–67.

119. See ibid., pp. 285ff., 296.

120. Christian Pineau, *1956, Suez* (Paris, 1976), pp. 214ff. Cf. Cooper, *Lion's Last Roar,* pp. 252–53.

121. Eban, *Autobiography,* p. 251.

122. FRUS, *1955–1957,* vol. 17, p. 331.

123. See ibid., pp. 293, 325.

124. Ibid., pp. 348, 359.

125. Meir, *My Life,* pp. 306–8; Rafael, *Destination Peace,* pp. 62ff.; Eban, *Autobiography,* pp. 252ff.

126. Cf. Kent, "Congress and American Middle East Policy," pp. 287ff.; Walter Eytan, *The First Ten Years* (New York, 1958), pp. 154ff.

127. Cf. Alan Dowty, *Middle East Crisis* (Berkeley, 1984), p. 41.

128. Briefing of July 14, 1958, CIA Research Reports, Middle East, 1946–1976, reel 1.

129. William B. Quandt, "Lebanon, 1958, and Jordan, 1970" in Barry M. Blechman and Stephen S. Kaplan (eds.), *Force without War* (Washington, 1978), p. 237.

130. Eisenhower, *Waging Peace,* p. 269.

131. Quandt, "Lebanon, 1958," p. 36.

132. Dowty, *Middle East Crisis,* p. 58.

Chapter 5

1. Cf. Hugh Thomas, *The Suez Affair* (London, 1967), pp. 142, 147.

2. Pierre Péan, *Les deux Bombes* (Paris, 1982), pp. 77ff.

3. See Amos Perlmutter et al., *Two Minutes over Baghdad* (London, 1982), pp. 25ff.; Hersh, *The Samson Option,* p. 66.

4. Peter Pry, *Israel's Nuclear Arsenal* (Boulder, Colo., 1984), pp. 12–13; Hersh, *The Samson Option,* op. cit. Chapters 2, 3, and 5.

5. Memorandum of conversation, "Prospects for non-proliferation agreement," July 13, 1965, National Security Files 1963–1969 (microform), Israel (Fredrick, Md., 1982).

6. Pry, *Israel's Nuclear Arsenal,* pp. 8–9.

7. Cf. Frank Barnaby, *The Invisible Bomb* (London, 1989), pp. 4–12; William B. Bader, *The United States and the Spread of Nuclear Weapons* (New York, 1968), pp. 88ff.; Stanley A. Blumberg and Gwinn Owens, *The Survival Factor* (New York, 1981), p. 293; Dan Kurzman, *Ben-Gurion* (New York, 1983), pp. 414–15; Sylvia K. Crosbie, *A Tacit Alliance* (Princeton, 1974), pp. 181ff.

8. Abba Eban, *An Autobiography* (New York, 1977), p. 251.

9. Cf. Ambassador Badeau to Department of State, May 3, 1963, reprinted in Mordechai Gazit, *President Kennedy's Policy toward the Arab States and Israel* (Tel-Aviv, 1983), pp. 85–86; Mohammed Heikal, *The Cairo Documents* (New York, 1973), p. 207.

10. Shimon Peres, *David's Sling* (London, 1970), p. 105.

11. Agency for International Development, *U.S. Overseas Loans and Grants, July 1, 1945–June 30, 1972* (Washington, May 1973); Defense Security Assistance Agency, *Military Assistance and Foreign Military Sales Facts* (Washington, April 1973); Department of State, *Communist States and Developing Countries: Aid and Trade in 1972* (Washington, 1973).

12. Hal Saunders to Rostow, November 19, 1966; Ambassador Barbour to State Department et al., October 19, 1966, National Security Files, Israel 1963–69: Israel.

13. Gideon Rafael, *Destination Peace* (New York, 1981), pp. 118ff.

14. Cf. Eban, *Autobiography,* pp. 200, 264.

15. Matti Golan, *Shimon Peres* (London, 1982), p. 57. Cf. Peres, *David's Sling,* pp. 36–41.

16. Cf. Ze'ev Schiff, *A History of the Israeli Army* (New York, 1985), pp. 99, 115–23.

17. See Golan, *Peres,* pp. 61ff.; Peres, *David's Sling,* p. 146.

18. Cf. Crosbie, *Tacit Alliance,* pp. 122ff.

19. Catherine McArdle Kelleher, *Germany and the Politics of Nuclear Weapons* (New York, 1975), p. 151.

20. Quoted in Michael Wolffsohn, *Ewige Schuld?* (Munich, 1988), p. 139. Cf. Franz Josef Strauss, *Die Erinnerungen,* Berlin 1991, pp. 378–84.

21. See J. C. Hurewitz, *Middle East Politics: The Military Dimension* (New York, 1969), pp. 479–80.

22. Golan, *Peres,* pp. 111ff.; Peres, *David's Sling,* pp. 76ff. Cf. Peres, *David's Sling,* pp. 67ff.; Wolffsohn, *Ewige Schuld?,* pp. 30–32; Seymour Freidin and George Bailey, *The Experts* (New York, 1968), pp. 381–82.

23. See Theodore C. Sorensen, *Kennedy* (New York, 1965), passim; Arthur M. Schlesinger, Jr., *A Thousand Days* (Boston, 1965), passim.

24. Gazit, *President Kennedy's Policy,* p. 56.

25. Eban, *Autobiography,* pp. 262–63. Cf. Heikal, *Cairo Documents,* p. 128.

26. Walter Laqueur to the author, personal correspondence, October 30, 1991.

27. *New York Times,* June 5, 1956. According to Stefan Staszewski, a former Warsaw party official, he personally handed the text to Western correspondents. Teresa Toranska, *"Them"* (New York, 1987), pp. 173–74. But according to Ray Cline, a retired official of the CIA, the *Times* version came directly from the CIA. Ray Cline, *The CIA under Reagan, Bush and Casey* (Washington, 1981), p. 187.

28. John Ranelagh, *The Agency* (New York, 1986), pp. 285–86; Yossi Melman and Dan Raviv, *The Imperfect Spies* (London, 1989), p. 80. Cf. Thomas Power, *The Man Who Kept the Secrets* (New York, 1979), pp. 80, 322n. 5; Stephen E. Ambrose, *Ike's Spies* (New York, 1981), pp. 236–37.

29. "James Angleton, Counterintelligence Figure, Dies," *New York Times,* May 12, 1987; Melman and Raviv, *Imperfect Spies,* pp. 81–82. Cf. William B. Quandt, *Decade of Decisions* (Berkeley, 1977), p. 75n. 5; Hersh, *The Samson Complex,* pp. 5–6, 144–48.

30. See Power, *Man Who Kept the Secrets,* p. 321n. 36.

31. Stewart Steven, *The Spymasters of Israel* (New York, 1980), pp. 95–98, 181.

32. Gazit, *President Kennedy's Policy,* p. 57.

33. Cf. Heikal, *Cairo Documents,* pp. 136ff.

34. Gazit, *President Kennedy's Policy,* pp. 13ff., 33–34.

35. Melvin I. Urofsky, *We Are One!* (Garden City, N.Y., 1978), p. 333; Kurzman, *Ben-Gurion,* p. 416.

36. The president's conversation with the United Arab Republic Ambassador, May 4, 1961, reprinted in Gazit, *President Kennedy's Policy,* p. 69.

37. The interview took place on August 11, 1961, but was published on November 24, 1963, after Kennedy's assassination.

38. Bowles to president, secretary of state, et al., February 21, 1962, reprinted in Gazit, *President Kennedy's Policy,* pp. 74–83.

39. Ibid., p. 82. Cf. Kennedy conversation with UAR ambassador, May 4, 1961, ibid., pp. 67ff.

40. Ibid., p. 16. Cf. Heikal, *Cairo Documents,* pp. 192, 206; reports of April 23, 1963, CIA Research Reports, Middle East, 1946–1976, reel 1.

41. Badeau to State Department, May 3, 1963, reprinted in Gazit, *President Kennedy's Policy,* p. 85. Cf. Heikal, *Cairo Documents,* pp. 189ff.

42. Rusk to Kennedy, January 30, 1961; "President's Conversation," May 4, 1961; CIA memorandum, "Consequences of Israeli Acquisition of Nuclear Capability," March 6, 1963, reprinted in Gazit, *President Kennedy's Policy,* pp. 89, 70, 116ff.

43. Kurzman, *Ben-Gurion,* pp. 415–16; Gazit, *President Kennedy's Policy,* pp. 36–39. Golan, *Peres,* p. 115. Cf. memorandum of meeting with Golda Meir, August 21, 1962; State Department brief re Dr. Johnson's meeting with Kennedy, February 5, 1963; report by U.S. ambassador in Israel re meeting with Ben-Gurion, April 3, 1963, reprinted in Gazit, *President Kennedy's Policy,* pp. 107–8, 123–33.

44. Department of State memorandum of conversation with Israel embassy re joint military balance meeting, July 6, 1962, reprinted ibid., pp. 97–102.

45. William P. Bundy's report on conversation with Shimon Peres, May 23, 1962, reprinted ibid., p. 94.

46. Memorandum of conversation between Kennedy and Golda Meir, December 27, 1962, reprinted ibid., p. 113. Cf. Hersh, *The Samson Option,* pp. 117–18.

47. See Shai Feldman, *Israeli Nuclear Deterrence* (New York, 1982), p. 211; Cf. Hersh, *The Samson Option,* pp. 109–11.

48. Ibid., pp. 113, 46–7; "How We Have Helped Israel," May 19, 1966, NSC films. See Golda Meir, *My Life* (New York, 1975), pp. 311–13.

49. Mission by Presidential Envoy Myer Feldman to Israel, August 16, 1962; instructions to inform British prime minister, August 17, 1962; British Bloodhound Missile suggested as alternative, August 18, 1962; memorandum of meeting with Israeli leaders, August 19, 1962, reprinted in Gazit, *President Kennedy's Policy,* pp. 103–8.

50. Cf. ibid., p. 30; Heikal, *Cairo Documents,* pp. 204–5, 213ff.

51. Kurzman, *Ben-Gurion,* pp. 438–40; Steven, *Spymasters of Israel,* pp. 136–39.

52. Ben-Gurion letter to Kennedy re Arab Tripartite Union, April 26, 1963, quoted in Gazit, *President Kennedy's Policy toward the Arab States and Israel.*

53. Cf. Peres, *David's Sling,* pp. 92ff.; Golan, *Peres,* pp. 117–20.

54. Special Memorandum No. 6-64, Office of National Estimates, February 25, 1964, NSC films. Remarks in New York City at the dinner of the Weizmann Institute of Science, February 6, 1964, *Public Papers of the Presidents: Lyndon B. Johnson, 1963–1964* (Washington 1965), pp. 270–71.

55. Memorandum of conversation, February 25, 1965, NSC films.

56. Memorandum for Mr. McGeorge Bundy, June 9, 1964, and attached joint communiqué; memorandum of conversation, "Difficulties in Desalination Joint Venture," July 16, 1964; cf. embassy telegram on Peres-Talbot talks, June 5, 1964, ibid.

57. White House press release, October 26, 1964; memorandum for Mr. W. W. Rostow, "Status of Israeli Desalting," April 22, 1966; H. S. Rowen, "Comment on Israel's Water Problem," July 21, 1966; background paper, "What the U.S. has Done for Israel," attached to memorandum for the president, "Talking Points for President Shazar," August 1, 1966; memorandum for the president, "Next Steps on Israeli Desalting," August 12, 1966, ibid.

58. Memorandum from Ball to McGeorge Bundy, January 27, 1964, ibid.

59. Office of National Estimates, February 25, 1964; Rowan memorandum for the president, March 25, 1964; memoranda for the secretary of defense, January 18 and March 12, 1964, ibid.

60. Memorandum for the president, May 11, 1964, ibid.

61 See memorandum for the president, "Our Commitments to Israel", May 19, 1967, with attached bar graphs, ibid.

62. Fouad Ajami, *The Arab Predicament* (Cambridge, 1981), p. xiii; Malcolm H. Kerr, *The Arab Cold War* (London, 1971), p. 115.

63. "List of Reassuring Moves We Might Make to Eshkol," April 30, 1964; conversation with Israeli Ambassador, May 12, 1964; embassy cable, May 16, 1964; background paper, May 28, 1964, NSC Films.

64. Peres, *David's Sling,* p. 101.

65. Thus the memoirs of George McGhee, at the time U.S. ambassador to West Germany, say nothing at all about the German-Israeli arms deal apropos U.S. efforts to increase German support for the war in Vietnam and share the costs of U.S. troops in Germany; and Wolffsohn cites as his source the anonymous notes of a German cabinet member. See George C. McGhee, *At the Creation of a New Germany* (New Haven, 1989), pp. 143–49; Michael Wolffsohn, "Von der verordneten zur freiwilligen 'Vergangenheitsbewältigung,'" *German Studies Review,* 1989.

66. See note from Komer to Bundy, December 18, 1965, NSC films.

67. Interview with Horst Osterfeld, Bonn, February 21, 1989.

68. See memorandum for Mr. Bundy, Arab-Israeli problems, March 8, 1965; memorandum for the president, "Talking Points for President Shazar," August 1, 1966," and attached background paper "What the U.S. Has Done for Israel," NSC films.

69. Rusk to Tel Aviv embassy, October 30, 1964; cf. Barbour to Rusk, October 14 and 21, 1964, NSC films.

70. Kurt Birrenbach, *Meine Sondermissionen* (Duesseldorf, 1984), pp. 101–5.

71. Ibid., pp. 96ff. Cf. Wolffsohn, "Von der verordneten zur freiwilligen."

72. Memo from Komer to Bundy, March 19, 1965.

73. Memorandum for Mr. Bundy, March 8, 1965; memorandum of conversation between Harman and Harriman, March 15, 1965, ibid.

74. Department circular 1976, April 26, 1965, ibid.

75. Memorandum of conversation, Israeli arms procurement, May 19, 1965; memorandum of conversation, views of Congressman Ogden Reid, May 25, 1965, ibid.

76. Background paper, "U.S. Arms Sales to Israel," attached to memorandum for the president, "Talking Points for President Shazar," August 1, 1966, ibid.

77. Memorandum for the president, "Israel Program," May 26, 1966, ibid.

78. See memorandum for Mr. Walt W. Rostow, "Israel's 'New Economic Policy' and The Problems of Success," September 27, 1966, ibid.

79. Memorandum for the president, "Talking Points for President Shazar," August 1, 1966, ibid.

80. Embassy telegram, April 26, 1966, ibid.

81. Memorandum for secretary of state from vice president, March 15, 1966, and attached reply, undated; Humphrey to Rusk, May 1, 1966; Rostow to Johnson, June 10 1966; memorandum for the president, "Talking Points for President Shazar," August 1, 1966, ibid.

82. "How We Have Helped Israel," May 19, 1966, ibid.

83. Rostow, "Memorandum for the President," May 21, 1966, ibid.

84. Presidential toast for the dinner honoring President Shazar, August 26, 1966, ibid.

85. Klutznick to Abraham Feinberg, September 19, 1966; Feinberg to Klutznick, September 21, 1966; Arvey to Watson, September 26, 1966, ibid.

86. Memorandum to secretary of state, secretary of defense, April 20, 1967, ibid.

87. Quoted in Sydney D. Bailey, *The Making of Resolution 242* (Dordrecht, 1985), p. 10; Theodore Draper, *Israel and World Politics* (New York, 1968), p. 4.

88. Kerr, *Arab Cold War,* p. 114.

89. Cf. ibid., pp. 121–27.

90. Cf. Bailey, *Making of Resolution 242,* pp. 16ff.

91. The narrative and chronology of events leading up to the outbreak of war on June 5, 1967, is based largely on Michael Brecher, *Decisions in Crisis* (Berkeley, 1980), pp. 42–50, 104–170.

92. Memorandum for the president, "Our Commitments to Israel," May 19, 1967, NSC films.

93. Eban, *Autobiography,* p. 326.

94. E. V. Rostow, *Peace in the Balance* (New York, 1972), pp. 254ff.

95. Interview with Brecher, cited Becher, *Decisions in Crisis,* ibid., p. 125.

96. Cf. Bailey, *Making of Resolution 242,* p. 44.

97. Eban, *Autobiography,* p. 355. Cf. Brecher, *Decisions in Crisis,* pp. 131–32; Rafael, *Destination Peace,* p. 143.

98. Cf. Walter Laqueur, *The Road to Jerusalem* (New York, 1968), p. 136.

99. W. W. Rostow, *The Diffusion of Power* (New York, 1972), p. 417.

100. Quotes in Draper, *Israel and World Politics,* p. 230; Beate Bumbacher, *Die USA und Nasser* (Wiesbaden, 1987), p. 273. Cf. W. Rostow, *Diffusion of Power,* p. 416.

101. Draper, *Israel and World Politics,* p. 62.

102. Interview with Benjamin Geist, quoted in Brecher, *Decisions in Crisis,* p. 153.

103. Cf. Bailey, *Making of Resolution 242,* p. 56.

104. Cf. E. Rostow, *Peace in the Balance,* p. 261; W. Rostow, *Diffusion of Power,* p. 417.

105. Cf. Eban, *Autobiography,* pp. 385ff.

106. Cf. Bumbacher, *Die USA und Nasser,* passim.

107. W. Rostow, *Diffusion of Power,* pp. 418–19.

108. Cf. Draper, *Israel and World Politics,* p. 134.

Chapter 6

1. McPherson himself found it hard to account for the appointment, save that he had worked on civil rights, worked with Jewish liberals, administered several foreign programs, "and was a pretty good schmoozer, as the expression goes." There also seems to have been no suitable Jewish candidate on the White House staff who was either interested or available. "The impression I have is that I simply reached up one day and found the 'Jewish affairs' hat on my head," he recalled. Personal correspondence, June 8, 1989.

2. Ze'ev Schiff, *A History of the Israeli Army* (New York, 1985), p. 137; Lyndon B. Johnson, *The Vantage Point* (New York, 1971), p. 287.

3. William B. Quandt, *Decade of Decisions* (Berkeley, 1977), pp. 63–64; Schiff, *History of the Israeli Army,* pp. 132–33, 141–43; Gideon Rafael, *Destination Peace* (New York, 1981), p. 168.

4. Schiff, *History of the Israeli Army,* p. 131.

5. Harry McPherson, *A Political Education* (Boston, 1972), pp. 413–15.

6. Johnson, *Vantage Point,* pp. 298–99.

7. "The Middle East," memo of conversation, October 24, 1967, National Security files, 1963–69, Israel films. cf. William B. Quandt, "Lyndon Johnson and the June 1967 War," *Middle East Journal,* Spring, 1992.

8. Johnson, *Vantage Point,* p. 297.

9. Walt W. Rostow, *The Diffusion of Power* (New York, 1972), p. 417.

10. Cf. Quandt, *Decade of Decisions,* p. 54.

11. Ibid., p. 58.

12. Johnson, *Vantage Point,* p. 287. Cf. E. V. Rostow, *Peace in the Balance* (New York, 1972), p. 250.

13. Robert S. McNamara, *Blundering into Disaster* (New York, 1986), p. 11.

14. Cf. Schiff, *History of the Israeli Army,* p. 131.

15. Quandt, *Decade of Decisions,* p. 61; Harold H. Saunders, "Regulating Soviet-U.S. Competition in the Arab-Israeli Arena," in Alexander L. George, Philip J. Farley, and Alexander Dallin (eds.), *U.S.-Soviet Security Cooperation* (New York, 1988), p. 551.

16. McNamara, *Blundering into Disaster,* pp. 11ff. Cf. Quandt, *Decade of Decisions,* pp. 62–63; Sydney D. Bailey, *The Making of Resolution 242* (Dordrecht, 1985), pp. 70ff.; Johnson, *Vantage Point,* pp. 298ff.

17. W. Rostow, *Diffusion of Power,* p. 419; Johnson, *Vantage Point,* p. 300; Abba Eban, *An Autobiography* (New York, 1977), pp. 417–18.

18. Phil G. Goulding, *Confirm or Deny* (New York, 1970), pp. 96ff.; James M. Ennes, Jr., *Assault on the Liberty* (New York, 1979), pp. 64, 76–78; Bailey, *Making of Resolution 242,* pp. 81–82; Johnson, *Vantage Point,* pp. 300–1.

19. Goulding, *Confirm or Deny,* pp. 123ff.

20. See Stewart Steven, *The Spymasters of Israel* (New York, 1980), pp. 193–94; Wilbur Crane Eveland, *Ropes of Sand* (New York, 1980), pp. 324–25.

21. Ennes, *Assault on the Liberty,* pp. 46–57.

22. Cf. Schiff, *History of the Israeli Army*, pp. 139–40.

23. See Ennes, *Assault on the Liberty*, pp. 143, 206ff.; Eveland, *Ropes of Sand*, pp. 324–25.

24. A. M. Rosenthal, "Not the Way to Tell the Liberty Story," *International Herald-Tribune*, November 9–10, 1991.

25. Eban, *Autobiography*, p. 421. See Steven, *Spymasters of Israel*, pp. 195–96; Ennes, *Assault on the Liberty*, Appendices R-T, pp. 284ff.

26. Eban, *Autobiography*, p. 421.

27. Schiff, *History of the Israeli Army*, p. 140.

28. Johnson, *Vantage Point*, p. 302; McNamara, *Blundering into Disaster*, pp. 11ff.

29. Rafael, *Destination Peace*, pp. 164–65. Cf. Bailey, *Making of Resolution 242*, pp. 88, 171; W. Rostow, *Diffusion of Power*, pp. 418–19; Quandt, *Decade of Decisions*, p. 63.

30. See Matti Golan, *The Secret Conversations of Henry Kissinger* (New York, 1976), p. 147.

31. Charles E. Silberman, *A Certain People* (New York, 1985), p. 185; Melvin I. Urofsky, *We Are One!* (Garden City, N.Y., 1978), p. 352; "Talking Points for Prime Minister Eshkol," memorandum for the president, January 5, 1968, National Security Files 1963–69; Israel Films.

32. McPherson, *Political Education*, p. 415.

33. Cf. Bailey, *Making of Resolution 242*, p. 115.

34. Rafael, *Destination Peace*, p. 169.

35. Cf. Rael Jean Isaac, *Israel Divided* (Baltimore, 1976), p. 104; Shlomo Aronson, *Conflict and Bargaining in the Middle East* (Baltimore, 1978), pp. 79–81, 85–87; Don Peretz, "Israeli Foreign Policymaking," in R. D. McLaurin, Don Peretz, and Lewis W. Snider (eds.), *Middle East Foreign Policy* (New York, 1982), pp. 148–49.

36. Isaac, *Israel Divided*, pp. 20ff.; Ian S. Lustick, *For the Land and the Lord* (New York, 1988), pp. 29ff.; Michael Wolffsohn, *Politik in Israel* (Opladen, 1983), pp. 251ff.

37. Memorandum to the secretary of defense JCSM 373–67 with appendix, "Discussion of Key Israeli border areas," June 29, 1967.

38. Survey data can be found in Michael Wolffsohn, *Politik in Israel*, pp. 95–97.

39. Ibid., p. 177; Eban, *Autobiography*, p. 435; memorandum of conversation, Congressman Joshua Eilbert and Harold H. Saunders, February 1, 1968, National Security Files, 1963–69; Israel.

40. *Public Papers of the Presidents: Lyndon B. Johnson, 1967* (Washington, 1968), p. 602.

41. Ibid., p. 612.

42. Ibid., p. 627.

43. Ibid., pp. 632–33.

44. Bailey, *Making of Resolution 242*, p. 110; *Public Papers: Johnson, 1967*, p. 652; Saunders, "Regulating Soviet-U.S. Competition," p. 551.

45. Rafael, *Destination Peace*, p. 179.

46. Eban, *Autobiography*, p. 442.

47. Bailey, *Making of Resolution 242*, p. 173.

48. Arthur J. Goldberg, "Negotiating History of Resolution 242," in Lord Caradon et al., *U.N. Security Council Resolution 242: A Case Study in Diplomatic Ambiguity* (Washington, 1981), p. 23.

49. Eban, *Autobiography*, p. 442. Cf. Bailey, *Making of Resolution 242*, pp. 126ff.

50. Cf. Bailey, *Making of Resolution 242*, p. 173.

51. See *Keesing's Contemporary Archives* (London, 1967), September 23–30, 1967, p. 22276.

52. Yitzhak Rabin, *The Rabin Memoirs* (Boston, 1979), pp. 135ff.

53. See draft telegram to U.S. embassy, Tel Aviv, September 14; information memorandum from Battle to Rusk, "Economic Situation of Israel," September 18; Saunders to W. W. Rostow, September 20, 1967, National Security Files, 1963–69; Israel.

54. "Talking Points for Visit of Foreign Minister Eban," October 23–24, 1967; "The Middle East," memorandum of conversation, October 24, 1967, National Security Files, 1963–69, Israel, Rafael, *Destination Peace,* p. 185.

55. See W. W. Rostow to president, October 9 and 10, 1967, transcript of press and radio news briefing, October 24, 1967, National Security Files, 1963–69, Israel.

56. Cf. Abba Eban, "Jarring, Lyndon Johnson, Richard Nixon and '242,'" in Lord Caradon et al., *U.N. Security Council Resolution 242: A Case Study in Diplomatic Ambiguity* (Washington, D.C., 1981), p. 48.

57. Henry Kissinger, *Years of Upheaval* (Boston, 1982), p. 197.

58. Cf. Saadia Touval, *The Peace Brokers,* (Princeton, 1982), p. 142.

59. See Caradon, "Security Council Resolution," p. 13; Goldberg, "Negotiating History," pp. 22–23; Mohamed H. El-Zayyat, "An Arab Viewpoint," pp. 32–34; Eban, "Jarring, Lyndon Johnson, Richard Nixon," p. 49, in Lord Caradon et al., *U.N. Security Council Resolution 242: A Case Study in Diplomatic Ambiguity* (Washington, D.C., 1981).

60. A table of alternative proposals can be found in Bailey, *Making of Resolution 242,* pp. 205–7. Cf. Quandt, *Decade of Decisions,* p. 65.

61. Statement issued by the Palestine Liberation Organization rejecting U.N. Resolution 242, Cairo, November 23, 1967, reprinted in Yehuda Lukacs (ed.), *Documents on the Israeli-Palestinian Conflict, 1967–1983* (Cambridge, 1984), pp. 138–39.

62. Rafael, *Destination Peace,* pp. 197–98.

63. Aronson, *Conflict and Bargaining,* pp. 89–90.

64. Memorandum of conversation, Congressman Joshua Eilberg and Harold H. Saunders, February 1, and memorandum for Barefoot Sanders, February 15, 1968, National Security Files, 1963–69; Israel.

65. Memorandum for the president, "Talking Points for Prime Minister Eshkol," January 5, and draft toasts and correspondence, January 5–8, 1968, National Security Files, 1963–69; Israel.

66. "Yitzhak Rabin had many extraordinary qualities, but the gift of human relations was not one of them. If he had been handed the entire United States Strategic Air Command as a free gift, he would have a) affected the attitude that at last Israel was getting its due, and b) found some technical shortcoming in the airplanes that made his accepting them a reluctant concession to us." Henry Kissinger, *The White House Years* (Boston, 1979), p. 568.

67. Rabin, *Memoirs,* p. 100.

68. Ibid., pp. 126–30.

69. Ibid., p. 123.

70. Cf. Charles H. Wagner, "Elite American Newspaper Opinion and the Middle East," in Willard A. Beling, *The Middle East: Quest for an American Policy* (Albany, 1973), pp. 306ff.

71. Cf. Theodore Draper, *Israel and World Politics* (New York, 1968), p. 117.

72. Quoted in Urofsky, *We Are One!,* p. 361.

73. Silberman, *Certain People,* p. 202. See Wagner, "Elite American Newspaper Opinion," pp. 317ff.

74. George Kent, "Congress and American Middle East Policy," in Willard A. Beling, *The Middle East: Quest for an American Policy* (Albany, 1973), pp. 294ff.; "Proposal for American Graduate School," memorandum for the president, October 16, and "American Graduate School at the Weizmann Institute," memorandum for Walt Rostow, October 28, 1968, National Security Files, 1963–69: Israel.

75. See Elaine Davenport, Paul Eddy, and Peter Gillmann, *The Plumbat Affair* (Philadelphia, 1978), pp. 11–97, 162–82; Yossi Melman and Dan Raviv, *Every Spy a Prince* (Boston, 1990), pp. 196–99, Hersh, *The Sampon Option,* op. cit., pp. 187–89 and 241ff.

76. Rabin, *Memoirs,* pp. 141–42; Paul C. Warnke, personal correspondence, February 3, 1987. The misrepresentation of Warnke's name, presumably as the result of a translator's unchecked retransliteration of a Hebrew transliteration; the implausibility of demanding a statement "whose answer would have been obvious to me and others in the Johnson administration," and Rabin's imprecision on the actual date of the sale, do not enhance the credibility of Rabin's version. Cf. Quandt, *Decade of Decisions,* pp. 66–67; Rabin, *Memoirs,* p. 131; Hersh, *The Samson Option,* op. cit., pp. 189–91.

77. Eban, *Autobiography,* pp. 457ff. Cf. Touval, *Peace Brokers,* p. 149.

78. Shai Feldman, *Israeli Nuclear Deterrence* (New York, 1982), pp. 214ff. Cf. McGeorge Bundy, *Danger and Survival* (New York, 1988), pp. 505–14. Hersh, *The Samson Option,* op. cit., pp. 209ff. Richard H. Ullman, "The Covert French Connection," Foreign Policy, Summer 1989.

79. Touval, *Peace Brokers,* p. 134.

80. See Urofsky, *We Are One!,* pp. 389ff. Cf. William Safire, *Before the Fall* (New York, 1975), pp. 564ff.

81. Safire, *Before the Fall,* pp. 570ff.

82. Richard Nixon, *RM* (New York, 1978), p. 435.

83. See Stephen E. Ambrose, *Nixon: The Triumph of a Politician* (New York, 1989), pp. 272–73, 457.

84. Kissinger, *White House Years,* p. 370.

85. Kissinger, *Years of Upheaval,* p. 202.

86. Seymour M. Hersh, *The Price of Power* (New York, 1983), p. 214.

87. Cf. Tad Szulc, *The Illusion of Peace* (New York, 1978), pp. 39ff.

88. Marvin Kalb and Bernard Kalb, *Kissinger* (Boston, 1974), pp. 186ff.

89. Kissinger, *White House Years,* p. 348.

90. Eban, *Autobiography,* pp. 462ff.

91. Ibid., pp. 568ff.; Kissinger, *Years of Upheaval,* p. 203; Hersh, *Price of Power,* p. 214.

92. Nixon, *RM,* pp. 479ff. Cf. Quandt, *Decade of Decisions,* p. 97; Kissinger, *White House Years,* pp. 563ff.

93. Nixon, *RM,* p. 476.

94. Cf. Quandt, *Decade of Decisions,* p. 78.

95. Ibid.

96. News conference, January 27, 1969, text in *Department of State Bulletin,* February 17, 1969, pp. 142–43. Cf. Nixon, *RM,* p. 476.

97. Kissinger, *White House Years,* pp. 378–79. Cf. Hassanain Haykal, "The Strategy of the War of Attrition," in Walter Laqueur and Barry Rubin, (eds.) *The Israel-Arab Reader* (New York, 1984), pp. 414–27.

98. Arnold Hottinger, *Die Araber vor ihrer Zukunft* (Paderborn, 1989), p. 135.

99. Cf. Amos Perlmutter, *Israel: The Partitioned State,* pp. 201ff.; Aronson, *Conflict and Bargaining,* pp. 100ff. Cf. Hersh, *Price of Power,* p. 219.

100. Rabin, *Memoirs,* p. 157. Cf. Milton Viorst, *Sands of Sorrow* (New York, 1987), pp. 127–28.

101. Rabin, *Memoirs,* p. 162.

102. Nixon, *RM,* pp. 478ff. Cf. Kissinger, *White House Years,* pp. 364ff.; Szulc, *Illusion of Peace,* pp. 100ff.

103. Rabin, *Memoirs,* pp. 148, 162. Cf. Rafael, *Destination Peace,* pp. 209ff.

104. "Informal Remarks in Guam with Newsmen," July 25, 1969, and "Address to the

Nation on the War in Vietnam," November 3, 1969, in *Public Papers of the Presidents: Richard Nixon, 1969* (Washington, 1971), pp. 548, 905. Cf. Franz Schurmann, *The Foreign Politics of Richard Nixon* (Berkeley, 1987), pp. 34–37.

105. Cf. Quandt, *Decade of Decisions*, pp. 120–21.

106. Cf. Hersh, *Price of Power*, p. 225.

107. Schiff, *History of the Israeli Army*, pp. 185–86; Eban, *Autobiography*, p. 465; Rafael, *Destination Peace*, p. 205; Aronson, *Conflict and Bargaining*, pp. 116–17. Cf. Hersh, *Price of Power*, pp. 217ff.

108. Walter Laqueur, *Confrontation* (London, 1974), p. 4.

109. Cf. Alexander L. George, "Missed Opportunities for Crisis Prevention," in George, *Managing U.S.-Soviet Rivalry* (Boulder, Colo., 1983), pp. 196–98.

110. Nixon, *RM*, pp. 479ff.; Kissinger, *White House Years*, pp. 560ff.; Quandt, *Decade of Decisions*, pp. 94ff.

111. Rabin, *Memoirs*, p. 168.

112. Rafael, *Destination Peace*, pp. 216–17.

113. Nixon, *RM*, pp. 481–82.

114. Golda Meir, *My Life* (New York, 1975), p. 384; Aronson, *Conflict and Bargaining*, p. 120.

115. Eban, *Autobiography*, p. 466; Rafael, *Destination Peace*, pp. 221ff.

116. Kalb and Kalb, *Kissinger*, p. 195; Kissinger, *White House Years*, p. 578; Szulc, *Illusion of Peace*, pp. 312ff.; Hersh, *Price of Power*, pp. 228–29.

117. Rabin, *Memoirs*, p. 177; Michael Brecher, *Decisions in Israel's Foreign Policy* (New Haven, 1975), p. 489; Touval, *Peace Brokers*, pp. 171–72.

118. Kissinger, *White House Years*, pp. 583–84.

119. Touval, *Peace Brokers*, p. 173; Aronson, *Conflict and Bargaining*, p. 121; Rabin, *Memoirs*, p. 177; Brecher, *Decisions in Israel's Foreign Policy*, p. 491.

120. Cf. Quandt, *Decade of Decisions*, pp. 101–2; Touval, *Peace Brokers*, pp. 169–75; Aronson, *Conflict and Bargaining*, pp. 125–29; Brecher, *Decisions in Israel's Foreign Policy*, pp. 495ff.; Kissinger, *White House Years*, pp. 584ff.; Kalb and Kalb, *Kissinger*, p. 195; Rabin, *Memoirs*, pp. 175ff.; Eric Silver, *Begin* (New York, 1984), p. 140.

121. Eban, *Autobiography*, p. 466. Cf. Rafael, *Destination Peace*, p. 229.

122. Nixon, *RM*, p. 482.

123. Aronson, *Conflict and Bargaining*, p. 129.

124. Cf. Quandt, *Decade of Decisions*, p. 107; Aronson, *Conflict and Bargaining*, pp. 129–30.

125. Szulc, *Illusion of Peace*, p. 319.

126. See Kissinger, *White House Years*, pp. 589–90.

127. Nixon, *RM*, p. 482.

128. Palestinian National Covenant, 1968, reprinted in Lukacs, *Documents on the Israeli-Palestinian Conflict*, pp. 139–43.

129. Patrick Seale, *Asad: The Struggle for the Middle East* (London, 1988), p. 157.

130. Kissinger, *White House Years*, p. 577.

131. Szulc, *Illusion of Peace*, p. 312.

132. Hersh, *Price of Power*, pp. 235–36.

133. Cf. Alan Dowty, *Middle East Crisis* (Berkeley, 1984), pp. 127–29.

134. Kissinger, *White House Years*, p. 606.

135. Meir, *My Life*, p. 386.

136. Nixon, *RM*, pp. 484–85.

137. Quandt, *Decade of Decisions*, p. 119. Cf. David Schoenbaum, ". . . or Lucky? Jordan—The Forgotten Crisis," *Foreign Policy*, Spring 1973, pp. 171ff.

138. Kissinger, *White House Years,* pp. 620ff.; Rabin, *Memoirs,* pp. 187–88; Kalb and Kalb, *Kissinger,* p. 202.

139. Dowty, *Middle East Crisis,* p. 183.

140. Ibid., p. 158.

141. The Kalbs assert that Nixon agreed to an unequivocal guarantee against both Egyptian and Soviet attack, though "there was no time to put this extraordinary understanding into writing." Kalb and Kalb, *Kissinger* p. 206. Dowty, on the other hand, is at least skeptical of any such explicit guarantee, not least on the basis of interviewees who believe they would have known of it. Dowty, *Middle East Crisis,* p. 173.

142. Kissinger, *White House Years,* pp. 626–27.

143. See Dowty, *Middle East Crisis,* p. 179.

144. Cf. Henry Brandon, "Were We Masterful . . .," *Foreign Policy,* Spring 1973, pp. 158ff.; Dowty, *Middle East Crisis,* p. 177.

145. See John Edwards, *Superweapon* (New York, 1982), pp. 67ff.

146. Patrick Seale, *Asad: The Struggle for the Middle East* (London, 1988), p. 162.

147. Ibid., pp. 157ff.; Moshe Ma'oz, *The Sphinx of Damascus* (London, 1988), p. 39.

148. See Hersh, *Price of Power,* pp. 240ff.; Quandt, *Decade of Decisions,* pp. 124–25.

149. Kissinger, *White House Years,* p. 631.

150. Cf. Dowty, *Middle East Crisis,* p. 178.

151. See Quandt, *Decade of Decisions,* pp. 123ff.; William B. Quandt, "Lebanon, 1958, and Jordan, 1970," in Barry M. Blechman and Stephen S. Kaplan (eds.), *Force Without War,* pp. 287–88.

Chapter 7

1. Robert J. Lieber, *The Oil Decade* (Lanham, Md., 1986), p. 20.

2. Yitzak Rabin, *The Rabin Memoirs* (Boston, 1979), pp. 222ff.

3. See "The Agranat Commission Report," in Walter Laqueur and Barry Rubin (eds.), *The Israel-Arab Reader* (New York, 1984), pp. 487ff.

4. See Lieber, *Oil Decade,* pp. 21ff.

5. Cf. Raymond L. Garthoff, *Détente and Confrontation* (Washington, D.C., 1985), pp. 25–68.

6. Lawrence L. Whetten, "The Arab-Israeli Dispute," in Gregory Treverton (ed.), *Crisis Management and the Superpowers in the Middle East* (Aldershot, Hants, 1983), p. 69.

7. Cf. Yehoshua Arieli, "Annexation and Democracy," in Walter Laqueur and Barry Rubin, *The Israel-Arab Reader* (New York, 1984), pp. 445ff.

8. Yehoshafat Harkabi, "Comment," in "The Changing Strategic Landscape," pt. 3, Adelphi Papers 237, (London, Spring 1989), p. 22. Cf. "Israel's Fateful Hour" (Yehoshafat Harkabi, interviewed by Robert I. Friedman), *World Policy Journal,* Spring 1989, pp. 360ff.

9. Henry Kissinger, *Years of Upheaval* (Boston, 1986), p. 199.

10. See Cecil Hourani, "The Moment of Truth," in Walter Laqueur and Barry Rubin (eds.), *The Israel-Arab Reader* (New York, 1984), pp. 244ff.

11. Cf. Moshe Ma'oz, *The Sphinx of Damascus* (London, 1988), pp. 84, 87.

12. Mohammed Heikal, *The Road to Ramadan* (London 1975), p. 111.

13. Ibid., pp. 122ff. Cf. Michael I. Handel, *The Diplomacy of Surprise* (Cambridge, 1981), pp. 243–47.

14. See Patrick Seale, *Asad: The Struggle for the Middle East,* (London, 1988), pp. 163–65; Ma'oz, *Sphinx of Damascus,* pp. 39–40.

15. Quoted in Perlmutter, *Israel: The Partitioned State,* p. 225.

16. Kissinger, *Years of Upheaval,* p. 220.

17. Cf. Peter Pry, *Israel's Nuclear Arsenal* (Boulder, Colo., 1984), pp. 19ff.; Hersh, *The Samson Option,* op. cit., ch. 13.

18. Nadav Safran, *Israel: The Embattled Ally* (Cambridge, 1978), p. 573.

19. Tad Szulc, *The Illusion of Peace* (New York, 1978), p. 333; William B. Quandt, *Decade of Decisions* (Berkeley, 1977), p. 163.

20. Perlmutter, *Israel: The Partitioned State,* p. 212.

21. Ibid., pp. 201–4; Don Peretz, "Israeli Foreign Policy Making" in McLaurin et al. (eds.), *Middle East Foreign Policy,* pp. 177–78; Michael Wolffsohn, *Israel: Policy, Society, Economy, 1882–1986* (Atlantic Highlands, N.J., 1987), pp. 212–13, 239.

22. Rael Jean Isaac, *Israel Divided* (Baltimore, 1976), p. 47; Wolffsohn, *Israel,* p. 97.

23. See Shlomo Aronson, *Conflict and Bargaining in the Middle East* (Baltimore, 1978), pp. 135–39.

24. Paul Johnson, *A History of the Jews* (New York, 1987), p. 529; Wolffsohn, *Israel,* p. 126.

25. Wolffsohn, *Israel,* p. 95.

26. Edward R. F. Sheehan, *The Arabs, Israelis and Kissinger* (New York, 1976), p. 160.

27. Cf. Gideon Rafael, *Destination Peace* (New York, 1981), p. 259.

28. Cf. Walter Laqueur, *Confrontation* (London, 1974), pp. 84–85; Matti Golan, *The Secret Conversations of Henry Kissinger* (New York, 1976), p. 147; Wolffsohn, *Israel,* p. 235.

29. Cf. Aronson, *Conflict and Bargaining,* pp. 139–41; Handel, *Diplomacy of Surprise,* p. 255; Saadia Touval, *The Peace Brokers* (Princeton, 1982), 178–79.

30. William B. Quandt, *Decade of Decisions* (Berkeley, 1977), p. 134.

31. Heikal, *Road to Ramadan,* pp. 115–16.

32. Quoted by Handel, *Diplomacy of Surprise,* p. 257.

33. Ibid., p. 263.

34. Ibid., pp. 257–60.

35. Touval, *Peace Brokers,* pp. 157ff.; Quandt, *Decade of Decisions,* pp. 133–35.

36. See Rabin, *Memoirs,* pp. 194ff.; Abba Eban, *An Autobiography* (New York, 1977), p. 474.

37. Kissinger, *Years of Upheaval,* p. 201.

38. Ibid., pp. 206–7.

39. Cf. Quandt, *Decade of Decisions,* pp. 143ff.; Heikal, *Road to Ramadan,* pp. 140–41, 152–55; Rabin, *Memoirs,* p. 201; Touval, *Peace Brokers,* pp. 182ff.; Henry Kissinger, *The White House Years* (Boston, 1979), pp. 1287–88.

40. Cf. Quandt, *Decade of Decisions,* p. 147; Seymour Hersh, *The Price of Power* (New York, 1983), pp. 407ff.; Rabin, *Memoirs,* p. 232.

41. See Touval, *Peace Brokers,* pp. 192–94. Cf. David Pollock, *The Politics of Pressure,* (Westport, Conn., 1982), pp. 112, 126–27.

42. Cf. Handel, *Diplomacy of Surprise,* pp. 268–71; Heikal, *Road to Ramadan,* pp. 161–81.

43. See Hersh, *Price of Power,* pp. 407ff.; Szulc, *Illusion of Peace,* pp. 725ff.

44. Kissinger, *White House Years,* p. 1285.

45. See Peter Mangold, "The Soviet Record in the Middle East," in Gregory F. Treverton, (ed.) *Crisis Management and the Superpowers in the Middle East,* Aldershot, Hanto and Montclair, NJ, 1983, pp. 89ff.

46. See George Ball, *The Past Has Another Pattern* (New York, 1982), pp. 136, 138.

47. J. William Fulbright, *The Crippled Giant* (New York, 1972), pp. 107, 131–32, 135.

48. Ibid., p. 109.

49. Ibid., pp. 147–48.

50. Hersh, *Price of Power*, pp. 410ff.

51. Ibid., pp. 407ff.

52. See Henry Kissinger, "The White Revolutionary," *Daedalus,* Summer 1968; Richard Nixon, *RM* (New York, 1978), pp. 371–74, 681, 768. Cf. Franz Schurmann, *The Foreign Politics of Richard Nixon* (Berkeley, 1987), p. 51.

53. Kissinger, *White House Years*, p. 1279.

54. Ibid., p. 1289.

55. Cf. Handel, *Diplomacy of Surprise*, pp. 278–79.

56. Ibid., pp. 276–77; Quandt, *Decade of Decisions*, pp. 152–53.

57. Kissinger, *Years of Upheaval*, p. 212.

58. Ibid., pp. 221–22; Marvin Kalb and Bernard Kalb, *Kissinger* (Boston, 1974), pp. 450ff.; Shlomo Slonim, *United States-Israel Relations* (Jerusalem, 1974), p. 28.

59. Quoted in Quandt, *Decade of Decisions*, p. 157.

60. William B. Quandt, "U.S. Energy Policy and the Arab-Israeli Conflict," in Naiem A. Sherbiny and Mark A. Tessler (eds.), *Arab Oil* (New York, 1976), pp. 281–84.

61. Cf. Quandt, *Decade of Decisions*, pp. 159–62; Garthoff, *Détente and Confrontation,* pp. 362–63.

62. Whetten says October 2, Seale October 4. See Seale, *Asad*, pp. 193–94; Whetten, "Arab-Israeli Dispute," pp. 67–69. Cf. Moshe Ma'oz, *The Sphinx of Damascus* (London, 1988), p. 90; Aronson, *Conflict and Bargaining*, pp. 165–66.

63. Heikal, *Road to Ramadan*, p. 181; Seale, *Asad*, p. 195; Ma'oz, *Sphinx of Damascus*, p. 86.

64. Heikal, *Road to Ramadan*, p. 207; Seale, *Asad*, pp. 204–5; Ze'ev Schiff, *A History of the Israeli Army* (New York, 1985), pp. 213–15.

65. Cf. Richard K. Betts, *Surprise Attack* (Washington, 1982); Roberta Wohlstetter, *Pearl Harbor* (Stanford, 1962); W. F. D. Deakin and Richard Storry, *The Case of Richard Sorge* (New York, 1966), passim.

66. Cf. Seale, *Asad*, pp. 199–200; Garthoff, *Détente and Confrontation*, p. 368.

67. Kissinger, *Years of Upheaval*, p. 459.

68. Ibid., pp. 461ff., Cf. Alan Dowty, *Middle East Crisis* (Berkeley, 1984), pp. 204–10. Cf. Aronson, *Conflict and Bargaining*, pp. 164–65; Garthoff, *Détente and Confrontation*, pp. 367–68.

69. See Brecher, *Decisions in Crisis* (Berkeley, 1980), pp. 53–67; Nixon, *RM,* p. 920; Szulc, *Illusion of Peace*, p. 728; Kalb and Kalb, *Kissinger,* pp. 454ff.; Schiff, *History of the Israeli Army*, pp. 209–13.

70. Cf. Matti Golan, *The Secret Conversations of Henry Kissinger* (New York, 1976), pp. 35, 43–44; Schiff, *History of the Israeli Army*, pp. 212–13; Brecher, *Decisions in Crisis*, pp. 177–78.

71. Cf. Golda Meir, *My Life* (New York, 1975), pp. 427ff.; Eban, *Autobiography*, p. 502; Kissinger, *Years of Upheaval*, p. 477.

72. Kalb and Kalb, *Kissinger,* p. 459; Kissinger, *Years of Upheaval*, pp. 450ff.; Quandt, *Decade of Decisions*, p. 166.

73. Kissinger, *Years of Upheaval*, pp. 458–59; Dowty, *Middle East Crisis*, p. 211. Cf. Quandt, *Decade of Decisions*, p. 170; Brecher, *Decisions in Crisis*, p. 201; Chaim Herzog, *The War of Atonement* (Boston, 1975), p. 278.

74. Cf. Dowty, *Middle East Crisis*, p. 202.

75. Kissinger, *Years of Upheaval*, pp. 478; Eban, *Autobiography*, p. 512; Elmo Zumwalt, *On Watch* (New York, 1976), p. 435. Cf. Robert G. Weinland, "Superpower Naval Diplomacy in the October 1973 Arab-Israeli War" (Center for Naval Analyses, June 1978), pp. 36ff.

76. Nixon, *RM,* pp. 920ff.; Kissinger, *Years of Upheaval,* p. 459; Dowty, *Middle East Crisis,* pp. 227–30.

77. Meir, *My Life,* pp. 427ff.; Quandt, *Decade of Decisions,* pp. 174–75; Kissinger, *Years of Upheaval,* p. 480; Dowty, *Middle East Crisis,* p. 229; Schiff, *History of the Israeli Army,* p. 216; Amos Perlmutter et al., *Two Minutes over Baghdad* (London, 1982), pp. 46–47; Hersh, *The Samson Option,* op. cit., Ch. 17.

78. Golan, *Secret Conversations,* pp. 66–67; Meir, *My Life,* pp. 430ff.

79. Nixon refers in his memoirs to "an operation bigger than the Berlin airlift," but this is a considerable exaggeration, despite the vastly greater distances involved. In September 1948, British and American fliers averaged 4,641 tons daily on the routes between Berlin and the Western zones, and on one memorable day, September 18, reached 6,988 tons in planes of dramatically smaller cargo capacity than the C-5s and C-141s of a generation later. Quandt, *Decade of Decisions,* p. 185 n. 46; Nixon, *RM,* pp. 927ff. Cf. Ann Tusa and John Tusa, *The Berlin Blockade* (London, 1988), pp. 234–35.

80. Anne Hessing Cahn, "United States Arms to the Middle East, 1967–1976," in Milton Leitenberg and Gabriel Sheffer (eds.), *Great Power Intervention in the Middle East* (New York, 1979), p. 122.

81. See Kalb and Kalb, *Kissinger,* pp. 465ff.

82. See Szulc, *Illusion of Peace,* pp. 735ff.

83. See Golan, *Secret Conversations,* pp. 57–62.

84. Zumwalt, *On Watch,* pp. 434–35.

85. Kissinger, *Years of Upheaval,* p. 485.

86. Nixon, *RM,* pp. 924ff.

87. Cf. Dowty, *Middle East Crisis,* pp. 237ff.; Sheehan, *Arabs, Israelis,* p. 33; Eban, *Autobiography,* pp. 517–18; I.L. Kenen, *Israel's Defense Line* (Buffalo, 1981), pp. 303–4.

88. Quoted in Dowty, *Middle East Crisis,* pp. 233–34.

89. Cf. Pry, *Israel's Nuclear Arsenal,* pp. 30–31; Dowty, *Middle East Crisis,* p. 244.

90. Kissinger, *Years of Upheaval,* p. 501.

91. Though each for quite different reasons. The Dutch were traditionally pro-Israel. West Germans, for historical and security reasons, were considerate alike of Israel and the United States. Portugal wanted and needed U.S. aid—and incidentally found itself vulnerable to congressional sanctions because of its policies in Mozambique and Angola. The question of Israeli resupply was thus linked to an appeal to Sen. Hubert Humphrey, for twenty-five years a bellwether liberal and friend of Israel, to go easy on Portugal. Dowty, *Middle East Crisis,* p. 267.

92. Interview with Horst Ehmke, June 14, 1989; personal correspondence from Ambassador Martin J. Hillenbrand, March 9, 1987; David Schoenbaum, "West Germany and Israel," *Present Tense,* Autumn 1974, pp. 41ff.; Rolf Vogel, ed., *Der Deutsch-Israelische Dialog* (Munich, 1987), vol. 1, pp. 465–66.

93. Sheehan, *Arabs, Israelis,* pp. 69–70.

94. See Zumwalt, *On Watch,* pp. 441–42.

95. Kenen, *Israel's Defense Line,* p. 314. Cf. Dowty, *Middle East Crisis,* pp. 237ff.; Saad Ibrahim, "American Domestic Forces and the October War," *Journal of Palestine Studies,* Autumn 1974, pp. 65–67.

96. Quandt, *Decade of Decisions,* pp. 183, 188–89; Dowty, *Middle East Crisis,* pp. 264–70; Sheehan, *Arabs, Israelis,* pp. 34–35; Szulc, *Illusion of Peace,* p. 742; Heikal, *Road to Ramadan,* pp. 233–34.

97. Cf. Quandt, *Decade of Decisions,* p. 184 n. 44; Herzog, *War of Atonement,* pp. 202–3; Aronson, *Conflict and Bargaining,* pp. 184–85; Szulc, *Illusion of Peace,* p. 739; Schiff, *History of the Israeli Army,* p. 223; Dowty, *Middle East Crisis,* p. 252.

98. Heikal, *Road to Ramadan,* p. 235.

99. Nixon, *RM,* p. 933.

100. Ibid., pp. 192–93; Dowty, *Middle East Crisis,* pp. 252–53; Kalb and Kalb, *Kissinger,* pp. 482ff.; Lieber, *Oil Decade,* p. 17; Aronson, *Conflict and Bargaining,* p. 187.

101. Quandt, *Decade of Decisions,* p. 191; Kissinger, *Years of Upheaval,* pp. 544ff.; Garthoff, *Détente and Confrontation,* pp. 370–71.

102. Kalb and Kalb, *Kissinger,* pp. 484–86; Golan, *Secret Conversations,* pp. 76–82; Aronson, *Conflict and Bargaining,* pp. 186–87; Garthoff, *Détente and Confrontation,* p. 373; Quandt, *Decade of Decisions,* pp. 192–93; Brecher, *Decisions,* pp. 222–23; Kissinger, *Years of Upheaval,* p. 552; Meir, *My Life,* p. 438; Eban, *Autobiography,* p. 531; Nixon, *RM,* p. 936.

103. Golan, *Secret Conversations,* pp. 82–83; Kalb and Kalb, *Kissinger,* pp. 436ff.

104. Kissinger, *Years of Upheaval,* pp. 538–39; Meir, *My Life,* p. 438.

105. Golan, *Secret Conversations,* pp. 82–87; Eban, *Autobiography,* pp. 532–33. Cf. Aronson, *Conflict and Bargaining,* pp. 188–89; Quandt, *Decade of Decisions,* pp. 193–94.

106. Aronson, *Conflict and Bargaining,* pp. 189–90; Golan, *Secret Conversations,* pp. 86–87.

107. Kissinger, *Years of Upheaval,* p. 575.

108. Ibid., p. 581; Garthoff, *Détente and Confrontation,* pp. 376ff.; Quandt, *Decade of Decisions,* pp. 194–95.

109. Kalb and Kalb, *Kissinger,* p. 491; Kissinger, *Years of Upheaval,* pp. 586ff.

110. Quoted in Quandt, *Decade of Decisions,* p. 199. Cf. Kissinger, *Years of Upheaval,* pp. 588ff.; Kalb and Kalb, *Kissinger,* pp. 495ff.

111. Quoted in Quandt, *Decade of Decisions,* p. 200.

112. Kissinger, *Years of Upheaval,* pp. 597–98.

113. Of sixteen questions asked, eleven had directly or indirectly to do with Watergate. See The President's News Conference of October 26, 1973, *Public Papers of the Presidents: Richard Nixon, 1973* (Washington, 1975), pp. 896–906.

114. Kissinger, *Years of Upheaval,* p. 601.

115. Ibid., p. 602.

116. President's news conference, *Public Papers: Nixon, 1973.*

117. *New York Times,* December 6, 1973.

118. Cf. Harold H. Saunders, "Regulating Soviet-U.S. Competition in the Arab-Israeli Arena," in Alexander George, Alexander Dallin, and Philip J. Farley (eds.) *U.S.-Soviet Security Cooperation* (New York, 1988), p. 562; Garthoff, *Détente and Confrontation,* pp. 383–85.

119. Quoted in Brecher, *Decisions,* pp. 226–27; Kissinger, *Years of Upheaval,* p. 604. Cf. Quandt, *Decade of Decisions,* p. 198 n. 71; Sheehan, *Arabs, Israelis,* pp. 36–37.

120. Eban, *Autobiography,* p. 535. Cf. Rafael, *Destination Peace,* p. 311.

121. Eban, *Autobiography,* p. 541.

122. Meir, *My Life,* pp. 440–41; Aronson, *Conflict and Bargaining,* p. 197.

123. Kissinger, *Years of Upheaval,* pp. 608–9.

124. Slonim, *United States-Israel Relations,* p. 42.

Chapter 8

1. See Harold H. Saunders, *The Other Walls* (Washington, 1985), pp. 3–4.

2. See Thomas M. Franck and Edward Weisband, *Foreign Policy by Congress* (New York, 1979), pp. 13–57.

3. According to Kissinger, Assistant Secretary Joseph J. Sisco devised the phrase—an

allusion to the Eastern Airlines shuttle between New York and Washington—as he welcomed reporters back on the plane for the flight from Tel Aviv to Aswan, January 13, 1974. Henry Kissinger, *Years of Upheaval* (Boston, 1986), p. 818.

4. Ibid. pp. 820–21. Cf. William R. Brown, *The Last Crusade* (Chicago, 1980), pp. 313–21.

5. See Edward R.F. Sheehan, *The Arabs, Israelis and Kissinger* (New York, 1976); Marvin Kalb and Bernard Kalb, *Kissinger* (Boston, 1974); Richard Valeriani, *Travels with Henry* (New York, 1979); Marvin Kalb and Ted Koppel, *In the National Interest* (New York, 1977).

6. "The problem thus boiled down to a challenge as old as international relations themselves. In an interdependent world, each nation must adjust goals and policies to some extent to those of others; no country has the possibility of acting as if only its preferences mattered. For many a decade, Arab intransigence and Soviet pressure had created the illusion that Israel did not have to conduct a foreign policy, only a defense policy. But the October war and Egypt's turn toward moderation had ended that simple state of affairs. Golda was railing not against America's strategy but against a new, more complicated, reality." Kissinger, *Years of Upheaval,* p. 621. Cf. pp. 483–84, 622–24, 789–90.

7. Amos Perlmutter, *Politics and the Military in Israel* (London, 1978), p. 162; Matti Golan, *The Secret Conversations of Henry Kissinger* (New York, 1976), p. 255.

8. *Newsweek,* cover, June 10, 1974. See Sheehan, *Arabs, Israelis,* p. 129. Cf. Valeriani, *Travels with Henry,* pp. 1–42.

9. See Galia Golan, *Yom Kippur and After* (New York, 1977), pp. 145–46.

10. On the origin and impact of the neoconservatives, see Coral Bell, *The Reagan Paradox* (New Brunswick, N.J., 1989), pp. 9–16.

11. Cf. Saadia Touval, *The Peace Brokers* (Princeton, 1982), pp. 54–75.

12. Raymond L. Garthoff, *Détente and Confrontation* (Washington, 1985), pp. 547–48.

13. Cf. Richard Elliot Benedick, "The High Dam and the Transformation of the Nile," *Middle East Journal,* Spring 1979, pp. 119–44; Ezer Weizman, *The Battle for Peace* (Toronto, 1981), p. 60.

14. Michael Wolffsohn, *Israel: Polity, Society, Economy, 1882–1986* (Atlantic Highlands, N.J., 1987), p. 212.

15. "Soon we encountered a methodological problem. . . . We had had much experience involving war. . . . But what indicated peace? We had seen a form of Arab expression that was different. . . . But could we ignore the possibility that such talk might be Arab propaganda intended to dull our senses and deceive us?" Quoted from a lecture by Shlomo Gazit, director of Israeli intelligence, 1974–1979, Michael I. Handel, *The Diplomacy of Surprise* (Cambridge, 1981), p. 298.

16. By considering the additional costs of conscription, reserve duty, casualties, stockpiling, requisition of land for military use, etc., Eitan Berglas argues credibly that the official figures are actually underreported, and that the increases after the 1967 and 1973 wars are "certainly" understated. Cf. "Defense and the Economy: The Israeli Experience," Maurice Falk Institute for Economic Research in Israel, Discussion Paper No. 83.01 (Jerusalem, January 1983), pp. 11–14, 18–23; Wolffsohn, *Israel,* pp. 235–36; John Lewis Gaddis, *Strategies of Containment* (New York, 1982), p. 359.

17. I.L. Kenen, *Israel's Defense Line* (Buffalo, 1981), pp. 135ff.; George Ball, *The Past Has Another Pattern* (New York, 1982), pp. 176–78. Cf. Diane B. Kunz, "The Importance of Having Money," in W. Roger Louis and Roger Owen, *Suez 1956* (New York, 1988); FRUS, *1955–1957* (Washington, 1990), vol. 16, pp. 833ff.

18. Robert J. Lieber, *The Oil Decade* (Lanham, Md., 1986), p. 14.

19. Kissinger, *Years of Upheaval,* p. 603.

20. See ibid., p. 615. Cf. Touval, *Peace Brokers,* p. 273; Sheehan, *Arabs, Israelis,* p. 114;

Golan, *Secret Conversations,* p. 210; William B. Quandt, *Decade of Decisions* (Berkeley, 1977), p. 209.

21. Quoted by Touval, *Peace Brokers,* p. 272. Cf. Quandt, *Decade of Decisions,* p. 210.

22. Nadav Safran, *Israel: The Embattled Ally* (Cambridge, 1978), p. 534. Cf. Kissinger, *Years of Upheaval,* p. 624.

23. Sheehan, *Arabs, Israelis,* pp. 129–30.

24. "There was a . . . mounting clamor that in some undefinable way we were being gulled by the Soviets. The opposite was true. . . . An end to détente would have triggered the Soviets into a political assault on us in the Middle East." Kissinger, *Years of Upheaval,* p. 594.

25. Ibid., pp. 1053–54.

26. Ibid., p. 755.

27. Ibid., p. 619.

28. See Handel, *Diplomacy of Surprise,* p. 307. Cf. Brown, *Last Crusade,* pp. 143–45; Milton Viorst, *Sands of Sorrow* (New York, 1987), pp. 30–31.

29. See Richard E. Neustadt, *Presidential Power* (New York, 1980).

30. Abba Eban, *An Autobiography* (New York, 1977), p. 576.

31. See Kissinger, *Years of Upheaval,* pp. 767–70. Cf. Quandt, *Decade of Decisions,* pp. 216–18; Sheehan, *Arabs, Israelis,* pp. 48ff.

32. Sheehan, *Arabs, Israelis,* p. 225. "I felt that if he wanted to sell us a car with a wheel missing, he would achieve his purpose by an eloquent and cogent eulogy of the three wheels that remained." Eban, *Autobiography,* p. 562.

33. Sheehan, *Arabs, Israelis,* p. 81. Cf. Golan, *The Secret Conversations,* pp. 120–21; Quandt, *Decade of Decisions,* p. 220; Safran, *Israel,* p. 512.

34. Kissinger, *Years of Upheaval,* pp. 628, 758–59; Sheehan, *Arabs, Israelis,* p. 49.

35. Kalb and Kalb, *Kissinger,* p. 526; Golan, *Secret Conversations,* p. 151.

36. Kissinger, *Years of Upheaval,* p. 790; Quandt, *Decade of Decisions,* p. 23. Cf. Golan, *Secret Conversations,* pp. 152–56; Sheehan, *Arabs, Israelis,* pp. 84–85, 101–5, 109.

37. See Safran, *Israel,* pp. 520–21; Kissinger, *Years of Upheaval,* pp. 792–98; Golan, *Secret Conversations,* pp. 122–42.

38. Eric Silver, *Begin* (New York, 1984), p. 147; Sasson Sofer, *Begin* (Oxford, 1988), pp. 92–93; Golan, *Secret Conversations,* pp. 131–32.

39. Eban, *Autobiography,* p. 560.

40. Kissinger, *Years of Upheaval,* p. 798.

41. See Moshe Dayan, *Breakthrough* (New York, 1981), pp. 88–89.

42. Ibid., pp. 809ff. Cf. Safran, *Israel,* pp. 521–27; Sheehan, *Arabs, Israelis,* pp. 109–12; Golan, *Secret Conversations,* pp. 158–78; Touval, *Peace Brokers,* pp. 245–48.

43. See Kissinger, *Years of Upheaval,* pp. 892–95, 945–53, 974–76. Cf. Sheehan, *Arabs, Israelis,* pp. 84–85, 115; Brown, *Last Crusade,* pp. 231–41.

44. Cf. Touval, *Peace Brokers,* p. 51.

45. Cf. Sheehan, *Arabs, Israelis* pp. 138–47; Quandt, *Decade of Decisions,* p. 234.

46. Rael Jean Isaac, *Israel Divided* (Baltimore, 1976), pp. 152–53; Kissinger, *Years of Upheaval,* p. 977.

47. See Garthoff, *Détente and Confrontation,* p. 469. Cf. Patrick Seale, *Asad: The Struggle for the Middle East* (London, 1988), p. 243; Moshe Ma'oz, *The Sphinx of Damascus* (London, 1988), p. 113.

48. Cf. Touval, *Peace Brokers* p. 251; Quandt, *Decade of Decisions,* p. 235; Seale, *Asad,* p. 247.

49. Seale, *Asad,* p. 244.

50. Kissinger, *Years of Upheaval,* pp. 958, 960–62. Cf. Seale, *Asad,* pp. 240–41.

51. The text is reprinted in Itamar Rabinovich and Jehuda Reinharz (eds.) *Israel in the Middle East* (New York, 1984), pp. 254ff. Cf. Motti Ashkenazi, "The Protest Movements in the Aftermath of the 1973 War," ibid., pp. 260ff.; Yitzak Rabin, *The Rabin Memoirs* (Boston, 1979), p. 238; Isaac, *Israel Divided*, pp. 141–42; Golan, *Secret Conversations*, pp. 185–88.

52. Cf. Shlomo Aronson, *Conflict and Bargaining in the Middle East* (Baltimore, 1978), pp. 232–38; Perlmutter, *Politics*, pp. 195–96.

53. Cf. Isaac, *Israel Divided*, pp. 200–1.

54. In his memoirs, Rabin dispatches the shuttle in one independent clause and one full sentence, all but implying that he regarded the Syrian disengagement as a distraction from the more serious business of negotiating with the National Religious party. Rabin, *Memoirs*, p. 240.

55. The fudge was even visible in the name, United Nations Disengagement Observer Force, as opposed to the United Nations Emergency Force in the Sinai. Cf. Touval, *Peace Brokers*, p. 254; Golan, *Secret Conversations*, p. 211.

56. Kissinger, *Years of Upheaval*, p. 1090.

57. Sheehan, *Arabs, Israelis*, pp. 119–22.

58. The morning after the school attack, Kissinger reported an exchange with an employee at his hotel. What was the man willing to give up, Kissinger had asked? Nothing, the man replied. Did that mean he ought to give up the negotiations, Kissinger continued? "Absolutely not," the Israeli answered. "I am willing to give ten years of my life for peace." How many kilometers would the Israeli give up, Kissinger persisted? Not a kilometer, the man insisted. Kissinger, *Years of Upheaval*, p. 1054. Cf. Sheehan, *Arabs, Israelis*, p. 125; Golan, *Secret Conversations*, p. 203.

59. Safran, *Israel*, p. 531. Cf. Kissinger, *Years of Upheaval*, pp. 1084, 1093.

60. See David Pollock, *The Politics of Pressure* (Westport, Conn., 1982), pp. 180–81.

61. Even literally. According to Kissinger, the Syrians let Soviet Foreign Minister Gromyko circle Damascus for forty-five minutes before allowing him to land in an obscure corner of the airport. They then dispatched a deputy foreign minister to receive him. They then fed Kissinger his dinner. Kissinger, *Years of Upheaval*, pp. 1109, 1099–1100.

62. Galia Golan, *The Soviet Union and the Palestine Liberation Organization* (New York, 1980), pp. 55–56.

63. Cf. Garthoff, *Détente and Confrontation*, pp. 469–71; Galia Golan, *Yom Kippur*, pp. 248–49, and *Soviet Union*, p. 14; Perlmutter, *Politics*, pp. 145–47.

64. Kissinger, *Years of Upheaval*, pp. 1129.

65. Quandt, *Decade of Decisions*, p. 248. Cf. Golan, *Secret Conversations*, pp. 214, 216.

66. Kissinger, *Years of Upheaval*, p. 1085.

67. Ibid., p. 1108.

68. See Yigal Allon, "The West Bank and Gaza within the Framework of a Middle East Peace Settlement," in Itamar Rabinovich and Jehuda Reinharz (eds.), *Israel in the Middle East* (New York, 1984), pp. 277–80.

69. Wolffsohn, *Israel*, p. 75.

70. See "Resolutions at Rabat," reprinted in Itamar Rabinovich and Jehuda Reinharz, (eds.), *Israel in the Middle East* (New York, 1984), pp. 307–9.

71. Cf. Brown, *Last Crusade*, pp. 124–29.

72. See Paula Stern, *Water's Edge* (Westport, Conn., 1979), pp. 6–7, 65–66, 74–76, 217–18. Cf. Kissinger, *Years of Upheaval*, pp. 985–98; Thomas M. Franck and Edward Weisband, *Foreign Policy by Congress* (New York, 1979), pp. 103, 314 n. 129.

73. Franck and Weisband, *Foreign Policy by Congress*, pp. 98–100.

74. Louis Harris, "Oil or Israel," *New York Times Magazine*, April 6, 1975.

75. Ron Nissen, *It Sure Looks Different from the Inside* (Chicago, 1978), pp. 143–47.

76. Robert Tucker, "Oil, the Issue of American Intervention," *Commentary*, January 1975; Letters, *Commentary*, April 1975, pp. 4–21; *Business Week*, January 13, 1975; Harris, "Oil or Israel." Cf. Nissen, *It Sure Looks Different*, pp. 143–47.

77. George S. McGovern, "Realities in the Middle East," Report to the Senate Foreign Relations Committee (Washington, D.C., 1975).

78. Harris, "Oil or Israel."

79. Nissen, *It Sure Looks Different*, pp. 41–43.

80. Ibid.

81. See Arnold Wolfers, *Britain and France between Two Wars* (New York, 1966), p. 130.

82. Cf. Garthoff, *Détente and Confrontation*, pp. 405–8; Samuel F. Wells, Jr., "Sounding the Tocsin," *International Security*, Fall 1979, pp. 148–51.

83. See Joseph Churba, *The Politics of Defeat* (New York, 1977), with introduction by Adm. Elmo R. Zumwalt, Jr., for a representative statement of the argument.

84. Cf. Golan, *Secret Conversations*, passim; Seale, *Asad*, pp. 226–49.

85. See Tad Szulc, "Lisbon and Washington," *Foreign Policy*, Winter 1975–1976.

86. Cf. Quandt, *Decade of Decisions*, p. 267; Sheehan, *Arabs, Israelis*, pp. 162–63; Golan, *Secret Conversations*, p. 242; Aronson, *Conflict and Bargaining*, pp. 284–87; Touval, *Peace Brokers*, pp. 267–71; Safran, *Israel*, p. 547.

87. Gerald R. Ford, *A Time to Heal* (New York, 1979), p. 247.

88. Quoted in Rabin, *Memoirs*, p. 256. Cf. Sheehan, *Arabs, Israelis*, p. 159.

89. "Aftermath: The Sheehan Affair," *Foreign Policy*, Summer 1976. Cf. Valeriani, *Travels with Henry*, p. 233.

90. Sheehan, *Arabs, Israelis*, p. 162.

91. Quoted in Valeriani, *Travels with Henry*, p. 234.

92. Ford, *Time to Heal*, p. 247. Cf. Golan, *Secret Conversations*, p. 241; Rabin, *Memoirs*, p. 258; Valeriani, *Travels with Henry*, p. 231; Abraham Ben-Zvi, *Alliance Politics and the Limits of Influence* (Tel Aviv, 1984), pp. 12–21.

93. Pollock, *Politics of Pressure*, pp. 185–87.

94. Sheehan, *Arabs, Israelis*, pp. 166–67.

95. Charles McC. Mathias, "Ethnic Groups and Foreign Policy," *Foreign Affairs*, Summer 1981, p. 993.

96. Reprinted in Marvin C. Feuerwerger, *Congress and Israel* (Westport, Conn., 1979), p. 206. Cf. Sheehan, *Arabs, Israelis*, p. 175–76, Rabin, *Memoirs*, p. 262–63; Ford, *Time to Heal*, p. 287.

97. *Washington Star*, July 13, 1975, reprinted in Sheehan, *Arabs, Israelis*, pp. 261ff.

98. See Feuerwerger, *Congress and Israel*, pp. 41, 171; Quandt, *Decade of Decisions*, p. 270.

99. Franck and Weisband, *Foreign Policy by Congress*, pp. 100–3. Cf. Feuerwerger, *Congress and Israel*, pp. 155–56 n. 33; Pollock, *Politics of Pressure*, p. 188.

100. Sheehan, *Arabs, Israelis*, p. 183; Perlmutter, *Politics*, pp. 176–77; Valeriani, *Travels with Henry*, p. 235.

101. Safran, *Israel*, pp. 552–53; Pollock, *Politics of Pressure*, pp. 189–90; Brown, *Last Crusade*, p. 159.

102. The full texts of the agreements, including annexes and memoranda, are reprinted in Sheehan, *Arabs, Israelis*, pp. 245–57. Cf. Quandt, *Decade of Decisions*, pp. 274–75.

103. Cf. Sheehan, *Arabs, Israelis*, pp. 187–88; Duncan L. Clarke, "Entanglement, The Commitment to Israel," in Yehuda Lukacs and Abdalla M. Battah (eds.), *The Arab-Israeli Conflict* (Boulder, Colo., 1988), pp. 220–23.

104. Cf. Karl Kaiser, "Konrad Adenauer und die Oder-Neisse Linie," *Die Zeit,* September 29, 1989.

105. Quoted in Feuerwerger, *Congress and Israel,* p. 117–18.

106. Ibid., pp. 119–26.

107. Pollock, *Politics of Pressure,* p. 190; Aronson, *Conflict and Bargaining,* p. 306; Quandt, *Decade of Decisions,* p. 279.

108. Rabin, *Memoirs,* p. 274; Viorst, *Sands of Sorrow,* p. 211.

109. Golan, *Secret Conversations,* p. 248.

110. Aronson, *Conflict and Bargaining,* p. 310.

111. Cited in Feuerwerger, *Congress and Israel,* pp. 209–10.

112. Ibid., pp. 127–37.

Chapter 9

1. See Department of State *Bulletin* 1975, pp. 499, 545–53, 553–54.

2. The text is reprinted *inter alia* in Itamar Rabinovich and Jehuda Reinharz, (eds.), *Israel in the Middle East* (New York, 1984), p. 310. Cf. Daniel Patrick Moynihan, *A Dangerous Place* (Boston, 1978), chap. 9.

3. See *New York Times,* November 12 and 14, and December 18, 1975.

4. The text of Saunders's statement can be found in the *Department of State Bulletin,* 1975, pp. 797–802.

5. *Toward Peace in the Middle East* (Washington, D.C., 1975).

6. Ibid., p. 16.

7. Ibid., p. 8.

8. Ibid., pp. 12–13.

9. Ibid., pp. 10–11.

10. Ibid., p. 14.

11. See ibid. pp. 6–7. Cf. Martin Indyk, *To the Ends of the Earth* (Cambridge, 1984), pp. 15–16.

12. Cf. Helena Cobban, *Modern Lebanon* (London, 1985), chap. 6; Itamar Rabinovich, *The War for Lebanon* (Ithaca, 1985), chap. 2; David Gilmour, *Lebanon: The Fractured Country* (Oxford, 1983), chaps. 8–9; Jonathan C. Randal, *Going All the Way* (New York, 1984) pp. 195–96; Moshe Ma'oz, *The Sphinx of Damascus* (London, 1988), chap. 10; Patrick Seale, *Asad: The Struggle for the Middle East* (London, 1988), chaps. 16–17.

13. Indyk, *To the Ends of the Earth,* p. 8; Ezer Weizman, *The Battle for Peace* (Toronto, 1981), p. 245.

14. Cf. Shlomo Aronson, *Conflict and Bargaining in the Middle East* (Baltimore, 1978), pp. 307–8.

15. *New York Times,* April 21, 1978, p. 1; *American Jewish Year Book, 1980* (New York, 1979), pp. 104–7. Cf. Rael Jean Isaac, *Israel Divided* (Baltimore, 1976), passim

16. Cf. Charles S. Liebman, *The Ambivalent American Jew* (Philadelphia, 1973), pp. 88ff. For a thoughtful overview of the Israeli-U.S. relationship, see Joyce Starr, *Kissing Through Glass* (Chicago, 1990), passim. For an authoritative and intelligent comparative study of Israeli-Jewish and American-Jewish relations, see Stephen M. Cohen and Charles S. Liebman, *Two Worlds of Judaism* (New Haven, 1990), passim.

17. Cf. Edward Tivnan, *The Lobby* (New York, 1987), p. 94.

18. Cf. Aronson, *Conflict and Bargaining,* pp. 320–30; C. Paul Bradley, *Parliamentary Elections in Israel* (Grantham, N.H., 1985), pp. 48–50.

19. See statement and testimony of Bob Loeb, Breira's executive director, in Senate Committee on Foreign Relations, Subcommittee on Middle and Near East and South Asian Affairs, *Hearings: Priorities for Peace in the Middle East,* July 23–24, 1975 (Washington, 1975), p. 33. Other witnesses included Arthur Goldberg, the former U.N. ambassador, secretary of labor, and Supreme Court justice; Philip Klutznick, later President Carter's secretary of commerce; the Middle East scholars Hisham Sharabi of Georgetown, Nadav Safran of Harvard, and Bernard Lewis of Princeton; and John C. Campbell of the Council on Foreign Relations.

20. Arthur Waskow, "Talking with the PLO," *New York Times,* December 16, 1976.

21. See Rael Jean Isaac, "Breira: Counsel for Judaism" (Americans for a Safe Israel, n.d.); Joseph Shattan, "Why Breira?" *Commentary,* April 1977, pp. 60ff.; Letters, *Commentary,* June 1977, pp. 4–31.

22. Tivnan, *The Lobby,* pp. 91–96. Cf. Carolyn Toll, "American Jews and the Middle East Dilemma," *Progressive,* August 1979, pp. 28–35.

23. Cf. Tivnan, *Lobby,* pp. 189–91; Russell Warren Howe and Sarah Hayes Trott, *The Power Peddlers* (New York, 1977), pp. 275–77.

24. See Yitzak Rabin, *The Rabin Memoirs* (Boston, 1979), pp. 290–91.

25. Peter Evan Bass, "The Anti-Politics of Presidential Leadership" (senior thesis, Woodrow Wilson School, Princeton, 1985), p. 61.

26. Quoted by Eric Silver, *Begin* (New York, 1984), p. 160. Cf. Aronson, *Conflict and Bargaining,* pp. 324–25; Yael Yishai, *Land or Peace* (Stanford, 1987), pp. 48–53; Ian S. Lustick, *For the Land and the Lord,* (New York, 1988), pp. 44ff.; Milton Viorst, *Sands of Sorrow* (New York, 1987), p. 214.

27. See Leon Charney, *Special Counsel* (New York, 1984), pp. 96–97.

28. Silver, *Begin,* p. 110; Ezer Weizman, *The Battle for Peace* (Toronto, 1981), pp. 43–49.

29. Ilan Peleg, *Begin's Foreign Policy, 1977–1983* (Boulder, Colo., 1987), p. 135 n. 10.

30. See Michael I. Handel, *The Diplomacy of Surprise* (Cambridge, 1981), pp. 299–300. Cf. William B. Quandt, *Camp David* (Washington, 1986), pp. 48–49.

31. Silver, *Begin,* pp. 153–54. Cf. Sasson Sofer, *Begin* (Oxford, 1988), p. 93; Aronson, *Conflict and Bargaining,* p. 337.

32. See Bradley, *Parliamentary Elections,* p. 60; Michael Wolffsohn, *Israel: Polity, Society, Economy, 1882–1986* (Atlantic Highlands, N.J., 1987), p. 20. Cf. Dan V. Segre, *A Crisis of Identity* (New York, 1980), chap. 8; Maurice M. Roumani, "The Ethnic Factor in Israel's Foreign Policy," in Bernard Reich and Gershon R. Kieval (eds.), *Israeli National Security Policy* (New York, 1988), pp. 83–96.

33. For a vivid and credible first-person impression of the immigrant milieu the new voters came from, see Naomi Shepherd, *Alarms and Excursions* (London, 1990), chap. 3. For Begin's weakness for Latin, see Jimmy Carter, *Keeping Faith* (Toronto, 1982), p. 344; Weizman, *Battle for Peace,* p. 353.

34. Cf. Silver, *Begin,* pp. 164–66.

35. Ibid., pp. 162–63; Moshe Dayan, *Breakthrough* (New York, 1981), p. 1. Cf. Peleg, *Begin's Foreign Policy,* pp. 98–99.

36. Sofer, *Begin,* p. 218.

37. Dayan, *Breakthrough,* pp. 4–5. Cf. Sofer, *Begin,* p. 178; Peleg, *Begin's Foreign Policy,* p. 99.

38. Cf. Quandt, *Camp David,* p. 184; Dayan, *Breakthrough,* p. 124.

39. Cf. Yishai, *Land or Peace,* pp. 63–67.

40. Quoted by Silver, *Begin,* p. 162.

41. The full texts can be found in Donald Bruce Johnson (ed.), *National Party Platforms,* vol. 2, *1960–1976* (Urbana, 1978), pp. 944, 990–91.

42. Zbigniew Brzezinski, *Power and Principle* (New York, 1985), p. 5.

43. Quoted by Thomas L. Friedman, "Traces Jewish Resentment of Kissinger to Frustration," *Des Moines Register,* August 22, 1976.

44. Quandt, *Camp David,* p. 33.

45. David Pollock. *The Politics of Pressure* (Westport, Conn., 1982), p. 197.

46. Elizabeth Drew, *American Journal* (New York, 1977), p. 454.

47. Cf. Howe and Trott, *Power Peddlers,* pp. 302–5.

48. Jules Witcover, *Maratthon* (New York, 1977), 605–6. Cf. Drew, *American Journal,* p. 464; Martin Schram, *Running for President, 1976* (New York, 1977), p. 318; Carter, *Keeping Faith,* pp. 277–78.

49. See Bass, "Anti-Politics of Presidential Leadership," pp. 15–19, 23–38.

50. Johnson, *National Party Platforms,* p. 991.

51. Carter, *Keeping Faith,* pp. 93–94, 278.

52. See Quandt, *Camp David,* p. 31.

53. Ibid., pp. 48, 60.

54. Quoted from *Weekly Compilation of Presidential Documents,* March 21, 1977, p. 361. See Carter, *Keeping Faith,* p. 281.

55. *Public Papers of the Presidents: Jimmy Carter, 1977,* vol. 1, (Washington, 1977), pp. 954–962.

56. Carter, *Keeping Faith,* p. 282; Indyk, *To the Ends of the Earth,* p. 23.

57. Carter, *Keeping Faith,* p. 286. Cf. Quandt, *Camp David,* p. 61.

58. Cf. Cyrus Vance, *Hard Choices* (New York, 1983), pp. 163–80; Brzezinski, *Power and Principle,* pp. 85ff.; Carter, *Keeping Faith* pp. 273–88; Quandt, *Camp David,* chap. 3; Bass, "Anti-Politics of Presidential Leadership," pp. 70ff.; Pollock, *Politics of Pressure,* pp. 234–35.

59. Carter, *Keeping Faith,* p. 288.

60. Ibid., chap. 3.

61. Cf. Peleg, *Begin's Foreign Policy,* chap. 4.

62. See Handel, *Diplomacy of Surprise,* pp. 301–5; Dayan, *Breakthrough,* chaps. 3–4. Cf. Seale, *Asad,* p. 303.

63. See Carter, *Keeping Faith,* pp. 291; Quandt, *Camp David,* pp. 81–83; Vance, *Hard Choices,* pp. 180–84; Brzezinski, *Power and Principle,* pp. 97–101.

64. See Quandt, *Camp David,* pp. 85, 91. Cf. Brzezinski, *Power and Principle,* pp. 101ff.

65. Quandt, *Camp David,* pp. 100–3. Cf. Vance, *Hard Choices,* p. 189.

66. Cf. Yishai, *Land or Peace,* pp. 53ff.

67. See Brzezinski, *Power and Principle,* p. 105. By mid-September, temperatures had moderated, but there was still a perceptible glow in the State Department statement of September 12: "[T]he status of the Palestinians must be settled," it declared, if other issues were to be solved. "This means that the Palestinians must be involved in the peacemaking process." The statement added that all parties to the peace conference would have to adhere to Resolutions 242 and 338, "which presently form the only agreed basis for negotiations." *Department of State Bulletin,* October 10, 1977, p. 463.

68. *Department of State Bulletin,* October 24, 1977, pp. 570–71. Cf. Bass, "Anti-Politics of Presidential Leadership," pp. 73–77.

69. *Department of State Bulletin,* October 10, 1977, p. 463.

70. Carter, *Keeping Faith,* pp. 292–93; Dayan, *Breakthrough,* pp. 55–64. Cf. Vance, *Hard Choices,* p. 191; Quandt, *Camp David,* pp. 111–14.

71. Quandt, *Camp David,* pp. 114–17, 121.

72. The text can be found in the *Department of State Bulletin,* November 7, 1990, pp. 639–49. Cf. Vance, *Hard Choices,* p. 192; Raymond L. Garthoff, *Détente and Confrontation* (Washington, D.C., 1985), pp. 580–81; Galia Golan, *The Soviet Union and the Palestine Liberation Organization* (New York, 1980), pp. 138–40; Brzezinski, *Power and Principle,* pp. 107–8.

73. A statement by Rabbi Alexander Schindler, chairman of the Conference of Presidents of Major American Jewish Organizations, is typical. "We are profoundly disturbed by the joint U.S.-Soviet statement which, on its face, represents an abandonment of America's historic commitment to the security and survival of Israel," he declared. Quoted by Handel, *Diplomacy of Surprise,* p. 315. Cf. Bass, "Anti-Politics of Presidential Leadership," pp. 78ff.; Tivnan, *Lobby,* pp. 119–20; Melvin A. Friedlander, *Sadat and Begin* (Boulder, Colo., 1983), pp. 59–61; Abraham Ben-Zvi, *Alliance Politics and the Limits of Influence* (Tel Aviv, 1984), pp. 29ff.

74. *Department of State Bulletin,* November 7, 1977, p. 640. Cf. Dayan, *Breakthrough,* pp. 66–71; Brzezinski, *Power and Principle,* pp. 109–10; Quandt, *Camp David,* pp. 125–31.

75. Dayan, *Breakthrough,* pp. 72–74. Cf. Friedlander, *Sadat and Begin,* pp. 64–65; Bernard Reich, *The United States and Israel* (New York, 1984), pp. 54–56.

76. Carter, *Keeping Faith,* p. 295; Quandt, *Camp David,* pp. 137–39; Indyk, *To tne Ends of the Earth,* pp. 43–45.

77. Av Westin, *Newswatch* (New York, 1982), pp. 138–39. Cf. Edwin Diamond, *Sign Off* (Cambridge, 1982), pp. 102–3.

78. Brzezinski, *Power and Principle,* p. 112. "One cannot help but admire a leader who is willing to take such risks on behalf of a higher cause," he also noted. "My only regret is that Carter is not doing it." Ibid., p. 111.

79. Weizman, *Battle for Peace,* p. 132. Cf. ibid., pp. 143–47, Dayan, *Breakthrough,* pp. 115–16; Quandt, *Camp David,* pp. 161–62.

80. See Dayan, *Breakthrough,* pp. 62–63. Cf. Quandt, *Camp David,* p. 242.

81. Carter, *Keeping Faith,* p. 171.

82. See Quandt, *Camp David,* p. 188.

83. Vance, *Hard Choices,* p. 205.

84. See "Interview with the President," *Public Papers of the Presidents: Jimmy Carter, 1978,* vol. 1 (Washington, 1979), pp. 807–9.

85. Cf. Bass, "Anti-Politics of Presidential Leadership," pp. 90ff.; Tivnan, *Lobby,* pp. 124–28; Quandt, *Camp David,* pp. 188, 191; Thomas M. Franck and Edward Weisband, *Foreign Policy by Congress* (New York, 1979), pp. 184–85, 190; Pollock, *Politics of Pressure,* pp. 237–41; Weizman, *Battle for Peace,* pp. 242–44.

86. See "Middle East Arms Sales: Letter to Members of Congress," *Public Papers: Carter, 1978,* vol. 1, May 12, 1978, pp. 896–97.

87. See Yishai, *Land or Peace,* pp. 174–79.

88. Tivnan, *Lobby,* pp. 123–24.

89. For a helpful discussion, with illuminating survey data, see Charles S. Liebman and Stephen Cohen, *Two Worlds of Judaism* (New Haven, 1990), chps. 2–3.

90. Dayan, *Breakthrough,* pp. 115–18; Weizman, *Battle for Peace,* p. 249.

91. Carter, *Keeping Faith,* p. 313. See *Public Papers: Carter, 1978,* vol. 1, May 1, 1978, pp. 812–14.

92. See Vance, *Hard Choices,* pp. 208–9; Carter, *Keeping Faith,* pp. 310–11; Galia Golan, *Soviet Union and the Palestine Liberation Organization,* pp. 204–7. Cf. Walid Khalidi, *Conflict and Violence in Lebanon* (Cambridge, 1979), pp. 123–30; Beate Hamizrachi, *The Emergence of the South Lebanon Security Belt* (Westport, Conn, 1988), chap. 18.

93. Vance, *Hard Choices*, p. 215.

94. Carter, *Keeping Faith*, p. 316.

95. See Vance, *Hard Choices*, p. 223; Brzezinski, *Power and Principle*, p. 269; Quandt, *Camp David*, p. 233; Dayan, *Breakthrough*, p. 156; Silver, *Begin*, pp. 195–96.

96. Cf. Dayan, *Breakthrough*, pp. 153–54.

97. Vance, *Hard Choices*, p. 218. Roosevelt added that he found the unpopularity "perfectly natural," and "did not resent it in the least." Theodore Roosevelt, *An Autobiography* (New York, 1926), p. 529.

98. Cf. Quandt, *Camp David*, p. 208; Friedlander, *Sadat and Begin*, pp. 207–8; Weizman, *Battle for Peace*, p. 341. Cf. Bass, "Anti-Politics of Presidential Leadership," pp. 99ff.

99. Carter, *Keeping Faith*, pp. 315–17, 321; Quandt, *Camp David*, pp. 209–17. Cf. Vance, *Hard Choices*, pp. 216–17; Brzezinski, *Power and Principle*, pp. 249–52; Quandt, *Camp David*, pp. 214–15.

100. Carter, *Keeping Faith*, p. 322.

101. Ibid., pp. 322–23, 327.

102. Vance, *Hard Choices*, p. 219; Carter, *Keeping Faith*, pp. 317–18. Cf. Jody Powell, *The Other Side of the Story* (New York, 1984), pp. 59ff.

103. See Carter, *Keeping Faith*, p. 372; Powell, *Other Side*, pp. 75–77; Dayan, *Breakthrough*, pp. 170–71.

104. See Weizman, *Battle for Peace*, pp. 344–47; Brzezinski, *Power and Principle*, p. 259; Avraham Tamir, *A Soldier in Search of Peace* (New York, 1988), p. 32; Dayan, *Breakthrough*, p. 169; Carter, *Keeping Faith*, pp. 324, 331–32; Silver, *Begin*, p. 192.

105. Mohamed Ibrahim Kamil, *The Camp David Accords* (London 1986), pp. 361–69.

106. Carter, *Keeping Faith*, p. 402.

107. Ibid. p. 346.

108. Brzezinski, *Power and Principle*, pp. 271–72. Cf. Carter, *Keeping Faith*, pp. 392–93; Vance, *Hard Choices*, p. 224; Quandt, *Camp David*, pp. 238–39.

109. See Carter, *Keeping Faith*, pp. 336, 374–75. Cf. Weizman, *Battle for Peace*, pp. 346, 365; Dayan, *Breakthrough*, pp. 166–67.

110. Carter, *Keeping Faith*, pp. 345–59; Quandt, *Camp David*, p. 224; Dayan, *Breakthrough*, pp. 161–63; Weizman, *Battle for Peace*, pp. 351–53.

111. Carter, *Keeping Faith*, pp. 365–68. Cf. Vance, *Hard Choices*, p. 219.

112. Vance, *Hard Choices*, p. 222. Cf. Weizman, *Battle for Peace*, pp. 367–69.

113. Carter, *Keeping Faith*, pp. 388–89; Brzezinski, *Power and Principle*, p. 265.

114. Dayan, *Breakthrough*, pp. 171–74. Cf. Kamil, *Camp David Accords*, pp. 349–52; Brzezinski, *Power and Principle*, p. 267.

115. Quandt, *Camp David*, pp. 235–36.

116. Weizman, *Battle for Peace*, pp. 370–71; Brzezinski, *Power and Principle*, p. 267. See "Letter from Secretary of Defense Harold Brown to Israeli Defense Minister Ezer Weizman, accompanying the documents agreed to at Camp David," released September 29, 1978, reprinted in Quandt, *Camp David*, p. 387. Cf. ibid., p. 371.

117. Carter, *Keeping Faith*, pp. 396, 400–1. See "Letter from Israeli Prime Minister Menachem Begin to President Jimmy Carter, September 17, 1978";"Letter from President Jimmy Carter to Israeli Prime Minister Menachem Begin, September 22, 1978";"Letter from Israeli Prime Minister Menachem Begin to President Jimmy Carter, September 17, 1978";"Letter from President Jimmy Carter to Egyptian President Anwar el Sadat, September 22, 1978," reprinted in Quandt, *Camp David*, pp. 383, 385–86. Cf. Weizman, *Battle for Peace*, p. 373; Dayan, *Breakthrough*, pp. 176ff.; Brzezinski, *Power and Principle*, p. 270; Vance, *Hard Choices*, pp. 225–26; Quandt, *Camp David*, p. 252; Tamir, *Soldier in Search of Peace*, pp. 37–38.

118. Carter, *Keeping Faith,* pp. 397, 400–1; Tamir, *Soldier in Search of Peace,* pp. 38–39; Quandt, *Camp David,* pp. 253, 163–64; Dayan, *Breakthrough,* pp. 181–88; Brezinski, *Power and Principle,* p. 273; Silver, *Begin,* pp. 199–200; Vance, *Hard Choices,* p. 228.

119. The full text of the accords and supplementary letters can be found *inter alia* in *Public Papers of the Presidents: Jimmy Carter, 1978,* vol. 2 (Washington, 1979), pp. 1523–28, 1566–68.

120. Dayan, *Breakthrough,* p. 229.

121. "Address by the President of the United States," *Congressional Record,* 95th Cong., 2d sess., September 13–20, 1978, vol. 124, pt. 22, pp. 29926–17.

122. Vance, *Hard Choices,* pp. 228–29; Carter, *Keeping Faith,* pp. 404–6. Cf. Quandt, *Camp David,* pp. 254–58.

123. Dayan, *Breakthrough,* p. 166; Carter, *Keeping Faith,* p. 405. Weizman, on the other hand, declared himself "full of admiration for the American president," and admired the unanimity, preparation and efficiency of the American delegation. Weizman, *Battle for Peace,* pp. 362–63.

124. See Dayan, *Breakthrough,* chap. 15. Cf. Friedlander, *Sadat and Begin,* pp. 238–43; Silver, *Begin,* p. 205.

125. Reprinted in Quandt, *Camp David,* pp. 400, 402.

126. "My prediction is that the Egyptian-Israeli treaty negotiations will be concluded within ten days . . . ," Quandt wrote Brzezinski on October 31. "[D]epending on how Begin reacts," he qualified. Quandt, *Camp David,* p. 278. Cf. Tamir, *Soldier in Search of Peace,* pp. 45–48.

127. Carter, *Keeping Faith,* p. 408; Dayan, *Breakthrough,* p. 214. Cf. Quandt, *Camp David,* pp. 273–74.

128. Dayan, *Breakthrough,* pp. 253–54.

129. Cited by Quandt, *Camp David,* p. 289.

130. Cf. Vance, *Hard Choices,* pp. 243–44; Quandt, *Camp David,* p. 298.

131. Dayan, *Breakthrough,* pp. 219, 240–41; Quandt, *Camp David,* p. 274. Though there is no reference to the meeting in Vance's memoirs, he confirmed Dayan's version in a personal correspondence of February 15, 1991. "It was a very interesting—perhaps historic—meeting," he added.

132. See Carter, *Keeping Faith,* pp. 405–6, 408–9, 412; Quandt, *Camp David,* pp. 263–64, and appendix, "American Answers to Jordanian Questions, October 1978," ibid., pp. 388–96; Vance, *Hard Choices,* pp. 233–34.

133. Dayan, *Breakthrough,* pp. 209–10, 225. Cf. Friedlander, *Sadat and Begin,* pp. 253–55; Quandt, *Camp David,* pp. 276–77.

134. Dayan, *Breakthrough,* pp. 232–34; Vance, *Hard Choices,* p. 236; Brzezinski, *Power and Principle,* p. 276; Quandt, *Camp David,* pp. 280–81.

135. See Carter, *Keeping Faith,* pp. 102–6; Ethan B. Kapstein, *The Insecure Alliance* (New York, 1990), pp. 185–91.

136. *American Jewish Year Book, 1980,* p. 113.

137. Brzezinski, *Power and Principle,* p. 35. Cf. ibid., p. 279; Quandt, *Camp David,* p. 298.

138. See Quandt, *Camp David,* p. 296.

139. Carter, *Keeping Faith,* p. 416. Cf. Powell, *Other Side,* p. 93.

140. Quandt, *Camp David,* p. 306.

141. Carter, *Keeping Faith,* p. 423; Vance, *Hard Choices,* p. 248; Dayan, *Breakthrough,* pp. 274–75.

142. Dayan, *Breakthrough,* pp. 276–77; Vance, *Hard Choices,* pp. 249–51; Quandt, *Camp David,* pp. 309–10.

143. Carter, *Keeping Faith,* p. 426; Powell, *Other Side,* pp. 94–102; Pollock, *Politics of Pressure,* pp. 243–44; Hersh, *The Samson Option,* op. cit., pp. 3–6.

144. The full texts of the treaty, annexes, and letters are reprinted in Quandt, *Camp David,* pp. 397ff.

145. Carter,*Keeping Faith,* p. 427; Dayan, *Breakthrough,* p. 281.

Chapter 10

1. "I . . . want Strauss to be up front because I need him as a political shield," Carter reportedly declared at a staff meeting in August 1979. Zbigniew Brzezinski, *Power and Principle* (New York, 1985), p. 439.

2. Jimmy Carter, *Keeping Faith* (Toronto, 1982), p. 491.

3. Thomas L. Friedman, *From Beirut to Jerusalem* (New York, 1989), p. 123; Robert G. Weisbord and Richard J. Kazarian, *Israel in the Black American Perspective* (Westport, Conn., 1985), pp. 141ff.

4. See Weisbord and Kazarian, *Israel in the Black American Perspective,* pp. 121ff. Cf. Eytan Gilboa, *American Public Opinion toward Israel and the Arab-Israeli Conflict* (Lexington, Mass., 1987), pp. 276–77; Carter, *Keeping Faith* p. 491.

5. Brzezinski, *Power and Principle,* pp. 441–42; Carter, *Keeping Faith,* pp. 492–94; "Israeli Settlements and the Status of Jerusalem," March 3, 1980, *Public Papers of the Presidents: Jimmy Carter, 1980–1981,* vol. 1 (Washington, 1981), p. 426. Cf. Elizabeth Drew, *Portrait of an Election* (New York, 1981), pp. 143–44; Jonathan Moore (ed.), *The Campaign for President* (Cambridge, 1981), p. 75.

6. See David Schoenbaum, "Passing the Buck(s)," *Foreign Policy,* Spring 1979.

7. See Gary Sick, "The Election Story of the Decade," *New York Times,* April 15, 1991; "The Election Held Hostage," on "Frontline" (WGBH Educational Foundation), April 16, 1991. For a contrary view from Carter's White House counsel, see Lloyd Cutler, "The 'October Surprise' Made Unsurprising," *New York Times,* May 15, 1991.

8. See Raymond L. Garthoff, *Detente and Confrontation* (Washington, 1985), pp. 915ff.

9. "State of the Union," January 23, 1981, *Public Papers: Carter,* vol. 1, p. 197. Cf. Garthoff, *Détente and Confrontation,* pp. 971ff.; Brzezinski, *Power and Principle,* pp. 426ff.

10. See Hedley Donovan, *Roosevelt to Reagan* (New York, 1985), pp. 169ff.

11. Ibid., pp. 79, 224–27.

23. Moore, *Campaign for President,* p. 228.

13. A full text can be found in Richard Harwood (ed.), *The Pursuit of the Presidency, 1980* (New York, 1980), pp. 359ff.

14. John F. Stacks, *Watershed* (New York, 1981), pp. 56, 63, 141–142, 171–72.

15. Rowland Evans and Robert Novak, *The Reagan Revolution* (New York, 1981), p. 177.

16. Drew, *Portrait,* pp. 324–25; Harwood, *Pursuit of the Presidency,* p. 330. Cf. Clifford W. Brown, Jr., and Robert J. Walker (ed.), *A Campaign of Ideas* (Westport, Conn., 1984), pp. 250–53.

17. Quoted by Evans and Novak, *Reagan Revolution,* p. 159.

18. A practical case is Joseph Churba, a former Pentagon official, who seems at least to have influenced an op-ed piece that appeared under Reagan's byline in the *Washington Post* of August 15, 1979. The article emphasized Israel's attractiveness as a "strategic asset." On the other hand, as Quandt has noted, there were no references at all to "Camp David," "peace process," or "negotiations." In 1980, Churba was a Reagan campaign advisor. Yet four years later, he was the author of *The American Retreat* (Chicago, 1984), whose third chapter, "Mis-

handling the Israeli Asset," argues sadly that, "except for the rhetoric," Reagan's policy had become "identical with the Carter administration." See ibid., p. 26; William B. Quandt, "U.S. Policy toward the Arab-Israeli Conflict," in Quandt, (ed.), *The Middle East: Ten Years after Camp David* (Washington, 1988), pp. 361–62. Cf. Coral Bell, *The Reagan Paradox* (New Brunswick, N.J., 1989), passim.

19. Quoted by Bell, *Reagan Paradox,* p. 16. Wolf Blitzer, *Between Washington and Jerusalem* (New York, 1985), p. 238. Cf. Lou Cannon, *President Reagan* (New York, 1991), pp. 390–91.

20. Evans and Novak, *Reagan Revolution,* p. 177. Cf. Bernard Reich, *The United States and Israel* (New York, 1984), pp. 87ff.

21. See Alexander M. Haig, Jr., *Caveat* (New York, 1984), pp. 169–71.

22. Quoted in Abraham Ben-Zvi, "The Reagan Presidency and the Palestinian Predicament," CSS Paper No. 16 (Tel Aviv, September 1982), pp. 7ff., 13ff., 25ff.

23. Haig, *Caveat,* pp. 174–75.

24. Ze'ev Schiff and Ehud Ya'ari, *Israel's Lebanon War* (New York, 1984), pp. 32–35; Itamar Rabinovich, *The War for Lebanon* (Ithaca, 1985), pp. 114–20; Patrick Seale, *Asad: The Struggle for the Middle East* (London, 1988), pp. 368–73; Yair Evron, *War and Intervention in Lebanon* (London, 1987), pp. 93–97; Eric Silver, *Begin* (New York, 1984), pp. 216–17.

25. Haig, *Caveat,* p. 331. Veliotes quoted by R. D. McLaurin, "Lebanon and the United States," in R. D. McLaurin (ed.), *Lebanon and the World in the 1980s* (College Park, Md., 1983), p. 105.

26. See Raymond Tanter, *Who's at the Helm?* (Boulder, Colo., 1990), pp. 5–59.

27. See Schiff and Ya'ari, *Israel's Lebanon War,* pp. 35–7; Rashid Khalidi, *Under Siege* (New York, 1986), pp. 36–39; Rabinovich, *War for Lebanon,* p. 120; Evron, *War and Intervention,* pp. 119–20; Avraham Tamir, *A Soldier in Search of Peace* (New York, 1988), p. 117.

28. See Khalidi, *Under Siege,* pp. 20–27.

29. President's news conference, May 13, 1982, *Public Papers of the Presidents: Ronald Reagan, 1982,* vol. 2 (Washington, 1983), p. 621.

30. Andrew Gowers and Tony Walker, *Behind the Myth* (London, 1990), p. 191.

31. Bob Woodward, *Veil* (New York, 1987), p. 161; Hersh, *The Samson Option,* op. cit., pp. 8ff.

32. See Edward Tivnan, *The Lobby* (New York, 1987), p. 152.

33. Silver, *Begin,* pp. 218–19; Ilan Peleg, *Begin's Foreign Policy, 1977–*(Boulder, Colo., 1987), pp. 185–190.

34. See Shai Feldman, *Israeli Nuclear Deterrence* (New York, 1982), pp. 73–78.

35. See Yossi Melman and Dan Raviv, *Every Spy a Prince* (Boston, 1990), pp. 268–70.

36. Interview with Ambassador Samuel Lewis, June 21, 1991. See Samuel Lewis, "The United States and Israel," in William B. Quandt, *The Middle East: Ten Years after Camp David* (Washington, D.C., 1988), p. 231. Cf. Shlomo Nakdimon, *First Strike* (New York, 1987), pp. 173–77.

37. According to Hunter, he also warned that Sadat had cause to fear for his life unless the United States could win a few points for him from the Israelis. Interview with Robert E. Hunter, June 4, 1991.

38. But there is no mention of this in Haig's memoirs. Nakdimon, *First Strike,* pp. 186–87.

39. Haig, *Caveat,* pp. 183–84. Cf. Hersh, *The Samson Option,* op. cit., pp. 8–9.

40. Cf. Tanter, *Who's at the Helm?,* pp. 155–56.

41. C. Paul Bradley, *Parliamentary Elections in Israel* (Grantham, N.H., 1985), pp. 98–99; Silver, *Begin,* pp. 213–16.

42. Myron J. Aronoff, *Israeli Visions and Divisions* (New Brunswick, N.J. 1989), pp. 30–33; Bradley, *Parliamentary Elections,* pp. 108–9; Sasson Sofer, *Begin* (Oxford, 1988), p. 205.

43. Asher Arian, "Political Images and Ethnic Polarization," in Howard R. Penniman and Daniel J. Elazar (eds.), *Israel at the Polls, 1981* (Washington, 1986), pp. 130–33.

44. Efraim Torgovnik, "Party Organization and Electoral Alignment," and Shmuel Sandler, "The Religious Parties," in Howard R. Penniman and Daniel J. Elazar, (eds.), *Israel at the Polls, 1981* (Washington, 1986), pp. 49–50, 105–10. Cf. Avraham Diskin, "The Jewish Ethnic Vote," and Yochanan Peres and Sara Shemer, "The Ethnic Factor in Elections," in Dan Caspi et al. (eds.), *The Roots of Begin's Success* (New York, 1984); Bradley, *Parliamentary Elections,* pp. 116–17.

45. See Bradley, *Parliamentary Elections,* pp. 124–31; Silver, *Begin,* p. 221.

46. See Nimrod Novik, *The United States and Israel* (Boulder, Colo., 1986), pp. 127–29.

47. Quoted by Tivnan, *Lobby,* p. 143.

48. President's news conference, October 1, 1981, *Public Papers of the Presidents: Ronald Reagan, 1981* (Washington, 1982), p. 867.

49. "Interview with Members of the Editorial Board of the New York Post," March 23, 1982, *Public Papers: Reagan, 1982,* vol. 2, p. 366. Cannon, *Reagan,* pp. 392–93.

50. See Mitchell Bard, "Ethnic Group Influence on Middle East Policy," in Mohammed E. Ahrari (ed.), *Ethnic Groups and U.S. Foreign Policy* (Westport, Conn., 1987), pp. 59–62. Cf. Tivnan, *Lobby,* pp. 156–60.

51. See Anthony H. Cordesman, *Western Security Interests in Saudi Arabia* (London, 1987), pp. 44–45; Gowers and Walker, *Behind the Myth,* p. 191.

52. See Seale, *Begin,* p. 403; Moshe Ma'oz, *The Sphinx of Damascus* (London, 1988), p. 165.

53. See Rabinovich, *War for Lebanon,* pp. 129–30.

54. "Exchange with Reporters," October 29, 1981, *Public Papers: Reagan, 1981,* p. 1000. Cf. "Remarks and a Question and Answer Session," October 28, 1981, ibid., p. 995.

55. Haig, *Caveat,* p. 327.

56. The published text can be found in Walter Laqueur and Barry Rubin (eds.), *The Israel-Arab Reader* (New York, 1984), pp. 633–34, and the *New York Times* of December 1, 1981. The arrangement for defense purchases is deleted from "U.S. Assistance to the State of Israel," a report by the General Accounting Office, published as GAO/ID-83-51 (Washington, June 24, 1983), but it is included in a draft published by Mohamed El-Khawas et al., *American Aid to Israel* (Brattleboro, Vt., 1984), p. 154.

57. See Haig, *Caveat,* pp. 328–29; Lewis, "United States and Israel," pp. 234–35; Ze'ev Schiff and Ehud Ya'ari, *Israel's Lebanon War* (New York, 1984), p. 64. Cf. Bernard Reich, "Israeli Foreign Policy and the 1981 Election," in Howard M. Penniman and Daniel J. Elazar (eds.), *Israel at the Polls, 1981* (Washington, 1986), pp. 233–34; Harvey Sicherman, "'A Perilous Partnership,'" in Nimrod Novik (ed.), *Israel in U.S. Foreign and Security Policies,* Jaffee Center for Strategic Studies, Paper No. 21 (Tel Aviv, November 1983); Peleg, *Begin's Foreign Policy,* pp. 201–21; Churba, *American Retreat,* pp. 29–31.

58. The text of the law can be found in Laqueur and Rubin, *Israel-Arab Reader,* pp. 634–35.

59. Peleg, *Begin's Foreign Policy,* pp. 190–95; Rabinovich, *War for Lebanon,* pp. 130–31; Reich, "Israeli Foreign Policy," p. 234; Silver, *Begin,* p. 247.

60. Lewis, "United States and Israel," pp. 235–36; Haig, *Caveat,* p. 329; Silver, *Begin,* pp. 245–46.

61. Schiff and Yaari, *Israeli's Lebanon War,* pp. 39ff.; Lewis, "United States and Israel," p. 237; Rabinovich, *War for Lebanon,* p. 123.

62. See Haig, *Caveat,* pp. 332–33.

63. Tamir, *Soldier in Search of Peace,* chap. 6.

64. Tamir, *Soldier in Search of Peace,* pp. 65–66; Ian S. Lustick, *For the Land and the Lord* (New York, 1988), pp. 59–62; Rafik Halabi, *The West Bank Story* (Orlando, Fla., 1985), pp. 297–99.

65. Lustick, *For the Land and the Lord,* pp. 69–70; Yael Yishai, *Land or Peace,* Stanford, 1987), p. 147; Peleg, *Begin's Foreign Policy,* p. 155.

66. The complete text can be found in *Department of State Bulletin,* July 1982, pp. 44–47.

67. Haig, *Caveat,* pp. 334, 342–43. Cf. Tanter, *Who's at the Helm?,* pp. 117–19.

68. Schiff and Ya'ari, *Israel's Lebanon War,* pp. 72–76; Lewis, "United States and Israel," p. 238; Haig, *Caveat,* pp. 335; Ariel Sharon, *Warrior* (New York, 1989), pp. 450–51; Tanter, *Who's at the Helm?,* pp. 108–13. Cf. Ze'ev Schiff, "The Green Light," *Foreign Policy,* Spring 1983.

69. Gowers and Walker, *Behind the Myth,* p. 205; Janet Wallach and John Wallach, *Arafat* (New York, 1990), pp. 363–67.

70. Schiff and Ya'ari, *Israel's Lebanon War,* pp. 97–106. Cf. Shai Feldman and Heda Rechnitz-Kijner, "Deception, Consensus and War," Jaffee Center for Strategic Studies, Paper No. 27, (Tel Aviv, October 1984), pp. 29–33, 41–43; Evron, *War and Intervention,* p. 128.

71. Feldman and Rechnitz-Kijner, "Deception, Consensus and War," p. 62.

72. Quoted by Evron, *War and Intervention,* p. 126.

73. See Tanter, *Who's at the Helm?,* pp. 120–24, 154–59. Cf. Woodward, *Veil,* p. 217.

74. Address to Members of the British Parliament," June 8, 1982, *Public Papers of the Presidents: Ronald Reagan, 1982,* vol. 1 (Washington, 1983), p. 745; Haig, *Caveat,* pp. 334–40.

75. Schiff and Ya'ari, *Israel's Lebanon War,* pp. 166–69.

76. For an observer's view, cf. Friedman, *From Beirut to Jerusalem,* pp. 134–41.

77. Cannon, *Reagan,* pp. 400–1. Cf. White House statement, August 12, 1982, *Department of State Bulletin,* September 1982, p. 22.

78. See Tanter, *Who's at the Helm?,* pp. 183–91, 200–1.

79. Schiff and Ya'ari, *Israel's Lebanon War,* pp. 225–27.

80. Khalidi, *Under Siege,* pp. 164–65.

81. Haig, *Caveat,* p. 341. Cf. Evron, *War and Intervention,* pp. 139–42.

82. Friedman, *From Beirut to Jerusalem,* p. 170.

83. Quoted by Milton Viorst, "The Media Front," *Channels,* November–December 1982, p. 90. For a comparison of the "American" style of the *New York Times* versus the "European" style of *Le Monde,* see Raymond Stock, "Prestige Press at War," *Middle East Journal,* Summer 1985.

84. For a practical example, see the "Dear Menachem" salutation and signature of "Ron" in "Letter to Prime Minister Menachem Begin," February 16, 1982, *Public Papers: Reagan, 1982,* vol. 2, p. 177.

85. Remarks of the president and Prime Minister Menachem Begin of Israel following their meetings, June 21, 1982, ibid. p. 799. See Cannon, *Reagan,* pp. 395–97. Cf. Blitzer, *Between Washington and Jerusalem,* p. 248–49.

86. Schiff and Ya'ari, *Israel's Lebanon War,* pp. 202–3.

87. Haig, *Caveat,* pp. 342–43; Tanter, *Who's at the Helm?,* pp. 134–42. Cf. Rabinovich, *War for Lebanon,* p. 140; Lewis, "United States and Israel," pp. 238–39.

88. Senate Committee on Foreign Relations, *Hearings: Nomination of George P. Schultz,* 97th Cong. 1982, p. 11.

89. Examples for June-July 1982 drawn from *CBS News Index, 1982* (Sanford, N.C., 1983), pp. 451–53.

90. Quoted by Sofer, *Begin,* p. 210.

91. Norman Podhoretz, "J'accuse," *Commentary,* September 1982. See also Robert W. Tucker, "Lebanon: The Case for the War," *Commentary,* October 1982, and "The Response to 'J'accuse,'" *Commentary,* December 1982.

92. Citations of von Hoffmann et al. in Podhoretz, "J'accuse." For a less sophisticated example, the University of Iowa chapter of the PLO-sponsored General Union of Palestinian Students displayed a homemade campus poster showing sketches of Hitler and Begin with the message, "I can't tell any more which is which."

93. Viorst, "Media Front," pp. 89ff.

94. Quoted by Raymond Stock, "Prestige Press at War," *Middle East Journal,* Summer 1985, p. 318.

95. Cf. Uri Dan, *Blood Libel* (New York, 1987), passim; Renata Adler, *Reckless Disregard* (New York, 1986), passim.

96. *Editor & Publisher,* November 20, 1982, p. 33.

97. Quoted by Viorst, "Media Front," p. 92.

98. Friedman, *From Beirut to Jerusalem,* p. 83. Cf. Stock, "Prestige Press at War," pp. 327–28; Roger Morris, "Beirut—and the Press—under Siege," *Columbia Journalism Review,* November-December 1982, p. 30.

99. *New York Times,* September 26, 1991; Friedman, *From Beirut to Jerusalem,* pp. 164–66; Stock, "Prestige Press at War," pp. 330–31.

100. Podhoretz, "J'accuse." An anthology of media criticism and self-criticism, including Podhoretz's article, can be found in Landrum R. Bolling (ed.), *Reporters under Fire* (Boulder, Colo., 1985), pp. 45–93. Cf. "ADL Faults Networks' News Coverage of Lebanon," *Broadcasting,* October 25, 1982, pp. 28–29.

101. Milton Viorst, quoted in Bolling, *Reporters under Fire,* p. 23; Ghassan Bishara of Al Fajr, quoted, ibid., pp. 30–31. Morris, "Beirut—and the Press—under Siege," p. 33.

102. Joshua Muravchik, "Misreporting Lebanon," *Policy Review,* Winter 1983, pp. 63–64.

103. Unless otherwise indicated, all of the surveys quoted below can be found in Gilboa, *American Public Opinion,* chap. 4.

104. Ibid., pp. 184–87. Cf. Tanter, *Who's at the Helm?,* pp. 172–75.

105. Wallach and Wallach, *Arafat,* pp. 373–77.

106. The text can be found in the *Department of State Bulletin,* September 1982, pp. 23–25. On its origins, see Tanter, *Who's at the Helm?,* pp. 89–93.

107. Lewis, "United States and Israel," pp. 246–47; Reich, *United States and Israel,* p. 122–25.

108. Gowers and Walker, *Behind the Myth,* pp. 223–25; Wallach and Wallach, *Arafat,* p. 377; Seale, *Asad,* pp. 402–4. A text of the Jordanian rejection can be found in Walter Laqueur and Barry Rubin (eds.), *The Israel-Arab Reader* (New York, 1984), pp. 686–91.

109. Friedman, *From Beirut to Jerusalem,* p. 177. For a similar and plausible estimation by William Casey, director of the CIA, see Woodward, *Veil,* p. 244.

110. "Address to the Nation Announcing the Formation of a New Multinational Force in Lebanon," *Public Papers: Reagan, 1982,* pp. 1187–89.

111. Woodward, *Veil,* pp. 245–46; Wallach and Wallach, *Arafat,* pp. 341ff.; Gowers and Walker, *Behind the Myth,* p. 166; Seale, *Asad,* p. 406.

112. Tamir, *Soldier in Search of Peace,* pp. 141ff.; Reich, *United States and Israel,* pp. 133–38; William B. Quandt, "Reagan's Lebanon Policy," *Middle East Journal,* Spring 1984, pp. 237ff.

113. See Augustus Richard Norton, *Amal and the Shi'a* (Austin, Tex., 1987), pp. 96–97. Cf. Seale, *Asad,* pp. 394ff.; Ma'oz, *Sphinx of Damascus,* pp. 173–74.

114. Ze'ev Schiff, "Lebanon: Motivations and Interests in Israel's Policy," *Middle East Journal,* Spring 1984, p. 227.

115. See Cannon, *Reagan,* p. 605.

116. "Remarks and a Question-and-Answer Session with Regional Editors and Broadcasters on the Situation in Lebanon," October 24, 1983, *Public Papers of the Presidents: Ronald Reagan, 1983,* (Washington, 1985), p. 1501.

117. Gilboa, *American Public Opinion,* pp. 152–55.

118. See Rabinovitz, *War for Lebanon,* pp. 183ff.; Evron, *War and Intervention,* pp. 163ff.; Bradley, *Parlimentary Elections,* pp. 147–48.

Chapter 11

1. For a thoughtful revisionist overview of Jewish history, see David Biale, *Power and Powerlessness in Jewish History* (New York, 1986), passim. For a grim survey and melancholy projection of Israeli-Jewish, and particularly Israeli-American Jewish relations, see David Vital, *The Future of the Jews* (Cambridge, 1990), passim. For an alternative, and rather more hopeful perspective, cf. Leonard Fein, *Where Are We?* (New York, 1988).

2. See Richard N. Haass, *Conflicts Unending* (New Haven, 1990), pp. 30ff.

3. Cited by Anthony H. Cordesman, "The Middle East and the Cost of the Politics of Force," *Middle East Journal,* Winter 1986, p. 6; Richard F. Grimmett, "Conventional Arms Transfers to the Third World, 1983–1990," Congressional Research Service (Washington, August 2, 1991), passim.

4. Meron Benvenisti, *Jerusalem, the Torn City* (Minneapolis, 1976), p. vii. See L. Carl Brown, *International Politics and the Middle East* (Princeton, 1984), passim.

5. Stuart E. Eizenstat, "Loving Israel—Warts and All," *Foreign Policy,* Winter 1990–1991, p. 91. Cf. Thomas L. Friedman, "America in the Mind of Israel," *New York Times Magazine,* May 25, 1987.

6. "The "uncensored" version includes a number of paragraphs explicitly deleted from the official text, but, as in many documents of this kind, the deletions testify as much to bureaucratic sensitivities as to any real and present danger. The official text also includes material missing from the "uncensored" version. The interested reader is best advised to look at both. "U.S. Assistance to the State of Israel"; *Report of the Comptroller General of the United States,* "U.S. Assistance to Israel, General Accounting Office, United States, June 24, 1983, Washington 1983, and Mohamed El-Khawas and Samir Abed-Rabbo (eds.), *American Aid to Israel, Nature and Impact,* Brattleboro, VT, 1984.

7. See Hadley Arkes, *Bureaucracy, the Marshall Plan and the National Interest* (Princeton, 1972), pp. 250ff.

8. See Donald E. Fink, "Lavi: A Tough Decision," *Aviation Week & Space Technology,* September 7, 1987.

9. "U.S. Assistance," pp. 1–3.

10. "Defence Research Still Sacrosanct," *Nature,* June 18, 1987.

11. "U.S. Assistance," pp. 7, 34–35.

12. *American Aid to Israel,* p. 168.

13. Ibid., pp. 39, 131–33.

14. "U.S. Assistance," p. 38.

15. See Bishara Bahbah, *Israel and Latin America* (New York, 1986), passim.

16. In the late 1980s the highly skilled were believed to constitute about a quarter of the work force. Because almost a quarter of the new Soviet immigration was assumed to consist of engineers, their arrival was thus expected to increase the proportion of the highly skilled to a third. Hugh Carnegy, "Striving for a Leading Edge," *Financial Times,* August 20, 1991.

17. Grimmett, "Conventional Arms Transfers," p. 65. See Aaron S. Klieman, *Israel's Global Reach* (Washington, 1985), pp. 58ff.; James J. Harford, "Israeli Aeronautics after Lavi," *Aerospace America,* November 1988, p. 8.

18. "U.S. Assistance," p. 43.

19. Stewart Reiser, *The Israeli Arms Industry* (New York, 1989), pp. 176–77.

20. Michael Mecham, "U.S. Increases Pressure on Israel to Abandon Lavi," *Aviation Week & Space Technology,* August 17, 1987, p. 21; David Brown, "Israelis Review Decisions That Led to Lavi Cancellation," ibid., September 14, 1987, p. 22.

21. "U.S. Assistance," p. 58. Cf. *American Aid to Israel,* p. 165; Duncan L. Clarke and Alan S. Cohen, "The United States, Israel and the Lavi Fighter," *Middle East Journal,* Winter 1986, p. 18.

22. Quoted in Reiser, *Israeli Arms Industry,* p. 171.

23. Clarke and Cohen, "United States, Israel, and the Lavi," pp. 28–30; Edward Tivnan, *The Lobby* (New York, 1987), pp. 195–96; Reiser, *Israeli Arms Industry,* pp. 178–79.

24. Mecham, "U.S. Increases Pressure."

25. "Decision to Cancel Lavi Divides Israel," *Aviation Week & Space Technology,* September 7, 1987, p. 22; *Nature,* September 10, 1987, p. 94; Brian Wanstall, "Life after Lavi," *Interavia,* July 1989, p. 725.

26. Nechemia Meyers, "Israel Attracted by Spin-off," *Nature,* April 25, 1985, p. 660; "Israel Signs Agreement for SDI Cooperation," *Aviation Week and Space Technology,* May 12, 1986; James K. Gordon, "U.S., Israel Attempt to Expand Defense Research Cooperation," ibid., June 16, 1986; "Taking a Share of the SDI Bounty," *Nature,* June 18, 1987.

27. See Janne E. Nolan, *Trappings of Power,* (Washington, 1991), pp. 75–81.

28. "Funding Problems Dampen U.S. Support for Israeli Arrow Missile," *Aviation Week & Space Technology,* December 7, 1987.

29. "U.S., Israel to Test Arrow Antitactical Missile," *Aviation Week & Space Technology,* December 21, 1987; Reiser, *Israeli Arms Industry,* pp. 237–38.

30. "Burnishing Israel's Arrow," *Economist,* July 18, 1990, p. 34; "Israel Successfully Launches First Antiballistic Missile," *Aviation Week & Space Technology,* August 13, 1990; David Nordell, "Israel Tests 'Star Wars' Rocket," *New Scientist,* August 18, 1990.

31. See Nick Eberstadt and Eric Breindel, "Commentary: The Population Factor in the Middle East," *International Security,* Spring 1979.

32. See "Exit for Soviet Jews, Conflict for Americans," *New York Times,* August 14, 1988.

33. The joke, in its original form, defines Zionism as one Jew soliciting money from a second Jew to send a third Jew to Palestine. See Leon Hadar, "Reforming Israel before It's Too Late," *Foreign Policy,* Winter 1990–91, pp. 125–27; "Cutting the Uncuttable," *Economist,* August 3, 1991.

34. See "Patriot System Exceeds Army's Expectations," and "Joint U.S.-Israeli Forces Use Patriots to Defend Against Iraqi Scud Missiles," *Aviation Week & Space Technology,* January 28, 1991; "U.S. Army Patriot Proven in New Role as Anti-Tactical Ballistic Missile Weapon," ibid., February 18, 1991.

35. "Israelis Question Effectiveness of Patriot Missiles," *International Herald-Tribune,* November 2–3, 1991.

36. "Patriot Missile, High-Tech Hero in Gulf, Comes under Attack as Less than Scud's

Worst Enemy," *Wall Street Journal,* April 15, 1991; "Did Patriot Missiles Work? Not So Well, Scientists Say," *New York Times,* April 17, 1991. Cf. Caspar Weinberger, "How the Patriot Almost Lost the War," *Forbes,* May 27, 1991.

37. Measured against the Clausewitzian standard that arms should be an extension of policy, and means should be proportional with ends, it also presupposed that missile defense was a either cost-effective supplement, or a cost-effective alternative, to deterrence and diplomacy. The question of supplements, while plausible, only led back to the Lavi question, i.e., whether a country in Israel's situation could afford to build one on its own. The question of alternatives, on the other hand, like all hypotheticals and incommensurates, was untestable and unprovable, but it was arguable, at least, that the Iraqis had been effectively deterred by the threat of nuclear retaliation. Cf. Seymour Hersh, *The Samson Option* (New York, 1991), epilogue. It was also arguable that the Scud attacks had been neither more nor less than a political provocation, designed to drag Israel into the war, and so legitimate Iraqi leadership; and that a different Israeli policy might have denied Saddam Hussein the Palestinian cause, which was among his few effective political weapons. But just as it did in 1973, when public debate focused on negligent intelligence rather than the possibility of negligent politics, debate in 1991 too tended to focus on alternative weapons systems rather than alternative military or political strategies.

38. Wanstall, "Life after Lavi," p. 726.

39. Shakespeare, *Henry IV,* pt. 1, act 5, 1.

40. "Economists Assessing Gains If Arab-Israeli Boycott Ends," *New York Times,* July 25, 1991.

41. Hobart Rowan, "Israel's Embattled Economy," *Washington Post,* March 14, 1985.

42. House Committee on Ways and Means, *Hearing: United States-Israel Free Trade Area Agreement,* March 6, 1985; Senate Committee on Finance, *Hearing: Proposed United States-Israel Free Trade Agreement,* March 20, 1985; *New York Times,* May 8, 1985.

43. See Barry Chamish and Edwin E. Bobrow, "The Pros and Cons of Marketing in Israel," *S&MM,* August 12, 1985.

44. "Israel: A Bridge to the European Market," *Global Trade,* January 1989, p. 14.

45. See "Proposed U.S.-Israel Free Trade Area Is Initialed," *Business America,* March 18, 1985; "The U.S.-Israel Free Trade Area Agreement," "Free Trade Area Agreement Eases Barriers," "Free Trade Area Agreement Enhances Israeli Market," ibid., June 24, 1985; "Israel: Free Trade Agreement Paves Way," ibid., April 25, 1988; "Israel: Trade Continues to Grow," ibid., April 10, 1989; "Israel: U.S. Market Share Grows," ibid., April 23, 1990; "Israel: Demand Is Strong for Both High and Low-Tech Items," ibid., September 25, 1989; "An Update for American Exporters," ibid., January 14, 1991; "Israel: High-Technology Products Continue to Be Best Prospects," ibid., April 22, 1991.

46. See "Report of the President's Special Review Board" (Washington, Feburary 26, 1987). There are twenty-seven volumes total of published testimony and depositions before the House and Senate select committees.

47. Yagil Weinberg, "The Iran-Contra Crisis and Its Impact on U.S.-Israeli Counterterrorism Cooperation" in Neil C. Livingstone and Terrell E. Arnold (eds.), *Beyond the Iran-Contra Crisis* (Lexington, Mass., 1988).

48. The account that follows is heavily indebted to Theodore Draper, *A Very Thin Line* (New York, 1991), passim. Cf. Yassi Melman and Dan Raviv, *Every Spy a Prince* (Boston, 1990), chap. 15; Samuel Segev, *The Iranian Triangle* (New York, 1988), passim; Ian Black and Benny Morris, *Israel's Secret Wars* (New York, 1991), pp. 427ff.

49. Cf. Lou Cannon, *President Reagan* (New York, 1991), pp. 384–85.

50. Ibid., pp. 609ff.

51. Ibid., pp. 635–37.

52. Ibid., pp. 655ff.

53. Quoted by Andrew Cockburn and Leslie Cockburn, *Dangerous Liaisons* (New York, 1991), p. 345.

54. See Thomas B. Allen and Norman Polmar, *Merchants of Treason* (New York, 1988), passim.

55. See Wolf Blitzer, *Territory of Lies* (New York, 1989), pp. 223ff. Cf. Draper, *Very Thin Line*, pp. 258–59, 555–57.

56. Why, a supervisor wanted to know some months before Pollard's arrest, would a Caribbean analyst need top-secret materials on the most advanced Soviet weapons systems being supplied to the Arabs? Because they were background for a study of terrorist activity in the Caribbean, Pollard replied. Since the supervisor then dropped the matter, he evidently found the answer satisfactory. Blitzer, *Territory of Lies*, p. 108

57. Bob Woodward, *Veil* (New York, 1987), p. 478

58. Black and Morris, *Israel's Secret Wars*, p. 425; Allen and Polmar, *Merchants of Treason*, p. 296; Melman and Raviv, *Every Spy a Prince*, p. 313.

59. A keen reader of spy novels who seemed to speak the argot of neoconservative geopolitics as his native language, Pollard added that it was also "a little-known tenet of U.S. strategic policy that the territorial integrity of Iran must be maintained so as to prevent a vacuum from arising, which could facilitate a Soviet advance to the Indian Ocean."

60. Blitzer. *Territory of Lies.*, p. 76.

61. Charles de Gaulle, *Memoires de Guerre: L'Appel 1940–42* (Paris, 1954,, p. 1

62. Blitzer, *Territory of Lies*, p. 54.

63. Ibid., p. 122.

64. Melman and Raviv, *Every Spy a Prince*, pp. 307–8, 318, Blitzer, *Territory of Lies*, p. 165.

65. Black and Morris, *Israel's Secret Wars*, p. 423.

66. According to Seymour Hersh, the material also included information that made it possible for Israelis to target the Soviet Union. Hersh, *Samson Option*, pp. 285ff.

67. Alan M. Dershowitz, *Chutzpah* (Boston, 1991), pp. 286–87; George A. Carver, Jr., "Official Rogues," *New Republic*, April 13, 1991.

68. See Wolf Blitzer, "I Spy, You Spy," *New Republic*, April 13, 1991.

69. Cf. Yoel Marcus, "The Politics of Secrecy and Silence," *Newsweek*, March 30, 1987.

70. John Felton, "Israel Promoted Key Figure," *Congressional Quarterly Weekly Report*, March 14, 1987.

71. "Strains in the Family," *Newsweek*, March 30, 1987. Cf. Annette Dulzin, "The Spy and the American Jew," *New York Times*, July 9, 1986; Dershowitz, *Chutzpah*, pp. 289–312.

72. Dershowitz, *Chutzpah*, p. 284.

73. "Poll Shows Jews and Non-Jews Differ on Pollard," *New York Times*, April 12, 1987.

The Past as Prologue

1. Though *sho'ah,* its Hebrew equivalent, had been used since the early 1940, no one could say for certain when or how the term had gained general currency. But that it had, and that its use had become a cause for introspection, was itself a reflection of how perceptions and self-perceptions had changed since the creation of the Jewish state. See "Holocaust," in Israel Gutman et al., *Encyclopedia of the Holocaust,* vol. 2 (New York, 1990), p. 681. Revealing in itself, the short and rather inconclusive article "Holocaust" is followed by a long article, "Holocaust, Denial of," as well as references to the articles "Holocaust Art," "Holocaust Education," "Holocaust Film," and "Holocaust Memorials and Museums."

2. A reflection on its energizing impact on postwar Jewish activism, the reference had instead been subsumed under Zionism. Nathan Glazer, *American Judaism* (Chicago, 1972), pp. 114–15 and index. Cf. second revised edition (Chicago, 1972), pp. 114–15 and index.

3. Jacob Neusner, "How the Extermination of Jewry Became 'The Holocaust,'" in *Stranger at Home* (Chicago, 1981), pp. 82ff.; Leonard Fein, *Where Are We?* (New York, 1988), pp. 59–61.

4. It seemed hardly an accident that the war in Lebanon was accompanied by a fierce historiographical reprise of the anguished debates of the 1930s and 1940s. In September 1982, the same month, as it happened, as the refugee camp massacres in Lebanon, a compulsory course on the Holocaust was then introduced into Israeli high school curricula. In contrast to courses in other countries, the thirty-hour syllabus was supposed to focus not on individual victims, perpetrators, or bystanders but on "collective, national" answers to "the meanings and implications of the Holocaust." "Education on the Holocaust," Gutman et al., *Encyclopedia of the Holocaust,* p. 423.

5. "In Avi[em Sella], Jay finally had someone who could value and discuss the things he cared about, from Israel's strategic planning to the Holocaust," Blitzer reported after a conversation with Pollard's wife. Wolf Blitzer, *A Territory of Lies* (New York, 1989), p. 136. On the other hand, while a plausible characterization of Pollard, it may or may not have done full justice to Israeli air force colonels. Cf. Friedman's conversation with a "Colonel Z," appalled that the air force had commissioned a "Holocaust quiz," in Thomas L. Friedman, *From Beirut to Jerusalem* (New York, 1990), pp. 282–83.

6. See Neusner, "How the Extermination," pp. 88ff. Cf. Fein, *Where Are We?,* chaps. 4, 7.

7. Charles Fenyvesi, "Holocaust: A Survivor's Thoughts," *Washington Post,* April 11, 1983

8. See Saul Friedlander, *Reflections of Nazism* (New York, 1984), passim; David Shipler, *Arab and Jew* (New York, 1986), chap. 12; Stuart Eizenstat, "Loving Israel—Warts and All," *Foreign Policy,* Winter 1990–1991, pp. 96–97; Leon Hadar, "Reforming Israel before It's Too Late," *Foreign Policy,* Winter 1990–1991, pp. 124.

9. See Ze'ev Schiff and Ehud Ya'ari, *The Intifada* (New York, 1990), pp. 164–69, 325–26. Cf. Tom Farer, "Israel's Unlawful Occupation," Foreign Policy, Spring 1991.

10. Yagil Weinberg, "The Iran-Contra Crisis and Its Impact on U.S.-Israeli Counterterrorism Cooperation," in Neil C. Livingstone and Terrell E. Arnold (eds.), *Beyond the Iran-Contra Crisis* (Lexington, Mass., 1988), p. 175.

11. Charles S. Liebman and Stephen Cohen, *Two Worlds of Judaism* (New Haven, 1990), chaps. 3, 5. Cf. Fein, *Where Are We?,* pp. 222ff.; Eizenstat, "Loving Israel," pp. 95–96.

12. Department of State, *Country Reports on Human Rights Practices for 1988* (Washington, February 1989), pp. 1366ff.

13. See Don Peretz, *Intifada* (Boulder, Colo., 1990), pp. 173ff.

14. See Schiff and Ya'ari, *Intifada,* pp. 310–15.

15. Peretz, *Intifada* p. 230.

16. Ibid., pp. 182ff.; Janet Wallach and John Wallach, *Arafat* (New York, 1990), chap. 22; interview with Rita E. Hauser, May 30, 1989.

17. *Los Angeles Times,* December 16, 1988; Schiff and Ya'ari, *Intifada,* pp. 305–6.

18. The text is reprinted in Peretz, *Intifada,* pp. 225–29.

19. Hadar, "Reforming Israel," p. 113; Moshe Ma'oz, "Iraq: Strategic Opening for Israel," *New York Times,* August 9, 1990.

20. Charles William Maynes, "A Necessary War?" *Foreign Policy,* Spring 1991, pp. 169–70.

21. See "When History Passes by," *Economist,* May 12, 1990.

BIBLIOGRAPHY

Public Documents, Printed and Microfilmed

Agency for International Development. *U.S. Overseas Loans and Grants, July 1, 1945-June 30, 1972.* Washington, May 1973.

CIA Research Reports. Middle East. 1946–1976.

The Conferences at Malta and Yalta, 1945. Foreign Relations of the United States (Washington, 1955).

Defense Security Assistance Agency. *Military Assistance and Foreign Military Sales Facts.* Washington, April 1973.

Department of Commerce. *Global Trade.*

Department of State Bulletin.

Department of State. *Communist States and Developing Countries: Aid and Trade in 1972.* Washington, 1973.

Department of State. *Country Reports on Human Rights Practices for 1988.* Washington, February 1989.

Federal Election Commission. File MUR 2804.

Foreign Relations of the United States, 1947, vol. 5. Washington, 1971.

Foreign Relations of the United States, 1948, vol. 5, no. 2. Washington, 1976.

Richard F. Grimmett. "Conventional Arms Transfers to the Third World, 1983–90." Congressional Research Service, Washington, August 2, 1991.

"Israel: U.S. Foreign Assistance Facts." Congressional Research Service Issue Brief. Washington, 1990.

George S. McGovern, "Realities in the Middle East." Report to the Senate Foreign Relations Committee. Washington, 1975.

Marshall-Lovett Memoranda to President Truman, 1947–1948. National Archives 27343.

Mutual Security Act of 1951. Hearings, Senate Committee on Foreign Relations and Committee on Armed Forces. Washington, 1951.

National Security Files, Israel, 1963–1969. National Archives Microfilms.

Nomination of George P. Shultz. Hearings, Senate Committee on Foreign Relations. Washington, 1982.

"The Outlook for U.S. Interests in the Middle East." Intelligence Report 7074. State Department Intelligence and Research, 1955.

Priorities for Peace in the Middle East. Hearings, House Committee on Foreign Affairs, Subcommittee on Middle and Near East and South Asian Affairs, July 23–24, 1975. Washington, 1975.

Proposed United States-Israel Free Trade Agreement. Hearing, Senate Committee on Finance, March 20, 1985. Washington, 1985.

Public Papers of the Presidents: Lyndon Johnson, 1963–1964 (Washington, 1965); *Lyndon Johnson, 1967* (Washington, 1968); *Richard Nixon, 1969* (Washington, 1971); *Richard Nixon, 1973* (Washington, 1975); *Jimmy Carter, 1977* (Washington, 1977); *Jimmy Carter, 1978* (Washington, 1979); *Jimmy Carter, 1980–1981* (Washington,

1981); *Ronald Reagan, 1981* (Washington, 1982); *Ronald Reagan, 1982* (Washington, 1983); *Ronald Reagan, 1983* (Washington, 1985).

Records of the Joint Chiefs of Staff, part 2, 1946–1953: ME, National Archives Microfilms.

Report of the Comptroller General of the United States, "U.S. Assistance to Israel," General Accounting Office, United States, June 24, 1983, Washington, 1983.

State Department Central Files 1945–1949. Reels 2, 22, 23, 29, National Archives Microfilms.

State Department Central Files 1950–1954. Reels 1, 2, 6, 7, 10, 11, National Archives Microfilms.

The Strategy and Tactics of World Communism. H. Doc. 619. Washington, 1948.

Suez Crisis, July 16–December 31, 1956. Foreign Relations of the United States, 1955–1957, vol. XVI, 1990. Washington, 1990.

United States-Israel Free Trade Area Agreement. Hearing, House Committee on Ways and Means, March 6, 1985. Washington, 1985.

Books

Abzug, Robert H. *Inside the Vicious Heart.* New York, 1985.

Acheson, Dean. *Present at the Creation.* New York, 1969.

Adams, Sherman. *Firsthand Report.* New York, 1961.

Adler, Renata. *Reckless Disregard.* New York, 1986.

Ajami, Fouad. *The Arab Predicament.* Cambridge, 1981.

Albrich, Thomas. *Exodus durch Oesterreich.* Innsbruck, 1987.

Allen, Thomas B., and Norman Polmar. *Merchants of Treason.* New York, 1988.

Ambrose, Stephen E. *Ike's Spies.* New York, 1981.

———. *Nixon: The Triumph of a Politician,* New York, 1989.

Anderson, Irvine H. *Aramco, the United States and Saudi-Arabia.* Princeton, 1981.

Arkes, Hadley. *Bureaucracy, the Marshall Plan and the National Interest.* Princeton, 1972.

Aronoff, Myron J. *Israeli Visions and Divisions.* New Brunswick, N.J., 1989.

Aronson, Shlomo. *Conflict and Bargaining in the Middle East.* Baltimore, 1978.

Bader, William B. *The United States and the Spread of Nuclear Weapons.* New York, 1968.

Bahbah, Bishara. *Israel and Latin America,* New York, 1986.

Bailey, Sydney D. *The Making of Resolution 242.* Dordrecht, 1985.

Ball, George. *The Past Has Another Pattern.* New York, 1982.

Baram, Philip J. *The Department of State in the Middle East.* Philadelphia, 1978.

Baring, Arnulf. *Revolution in East Germany.* Ithaca, 1972.

Barnaby, Frank. *The Invisible Bomb.* London, 1989.

Bass, Peter Evan. "The Anti-Politics of Presidential Leadership." Senior thesis, Woodrov Wilson School, Princeton University, 1985.

Bell, Coral. *Negotiation from Strength.* New York, 1963.

Bell, Coral. *The Reagan Paradox.* New Brunswick, N.J., 1989.

Bell, John Bowyer. *Terror out of Zion.* New York, 1977.

Benvenisti, Meron. *Jerusalem, the Torn City.* Minneapolis, 1976.

Ben-Zvi, Abraham. *Alliance Politics and the Limits of Influence.* Tel Aviv, 1984.

Berman, Aaron. *Nazism, the Jews and American Zionism.* Detroit, 1990.

Betts, Richard K. *Surprise Attack.* Washington, 1982.

Biale, David. *Power and Powerlessness in Jewish History.* New York, 1986.

Bilby, Kenneth W. *New Star in the Near East.* New York, 1951.

Birrenbach, Kurt. *Meine Sondermissionen.* Duesseldorf, 1984.

Black, Edwin. *The Transfer Agreement.* New York, 1984.

Black, Ian, and Benny Morris. *Israel's Secret Wars.* New York, 1991.

Blitzer, Wolf. *Between Washington and Jerusalem.* New York, 1985.

Blitzer, Wolf. *A Territory of Lies.* New York, 1989.

Bloom, Sol. *The Autobiography.* New York, 1948.

Blumberg, Stanley A., and Gwinn Owens. *The Survival Factor.* New York, 1981.

Bolling, Landrum R. (ed.). *Reporters under Fire.* Boulder, Colo., 1985.

Bradley, C. Paul. *Parliamentary Elections in Israel.* Grantham, N.H., 1985.

Brecher, Michael. *Decisions in Israel's Foreign Policy.* New Haven, 1975.

———. *Decisions in Crisis.* Berkeley, 1980.

Brown, Clifford W., Jr., and Robert J. Walker (eds.). *A Campaign of Ideas.* Westport, Conn., 1984.

Brown, L. Carl. *International Politics and the Middle East.* Princeton, 1984.

Brown, William R. *The Last Crusade.* Chicago, 1980.

Brzezinski, Zbigniew. *Power and Principle.* New York, 1985.

Bullock, Allan. *Ernest Bevin.* Oxford, 1983.

Bumbacher, Beate. *Die USA und Nasser.* Wiesbaden, 1987.

Bundy, McGeorge. *Danger and Survival.* New York, 1988.

Cannon, Lou. *President Reagan.* New York, 1991.

Carter, Jimmy. *Keeping Faith.* Toronto, 1982.

Charney, Leon. *Special Counsel.* New York, 1984.

Churba, Joseph. *The Politics of Defeat.* New York, 1977.

———. *The American Retreat.* Chicago, 1984.

Cline, Ray. *The CIA under Reagan, Bush and Casey.* Washington, 1981.

Cobban, Helena. *Modern Lebanon.* London, 1985.

Cockburn, Andrew, and Leslie Cockburn. *Dangerous Liaisons.* New York, 1991.

Michael J. Cohen. *Palestine and the Great Powers.* Princeton, 1982.

———. *The Origins and Evolution of the Arab-Zionist Conflict.* Berkeley, 1987.

———. *Truman and Israel.* Berkeley, 1990.

———, ed. *United Nations Discussions on Palestine 1947.* New York, 1987.

Cohen, Naomi W. *Not Free to Desist.* Philadelphia, 1972.

———. *The Year after the Riots.* Detroit, 1988.

Cooper, Chester. *The Lion's Last Roar.* New York, 1978.

Copeland, Miles. *The Game of Nations.* New York, 1969.

Cordesman, Anthony H. *Western Security Interests in Saudi Arabia.* London, 1987.

Crosbie, Sylvia K. *A Tacit Alliance.* Princeton, 1974.

Crossman, R.H.S. *Palestine Mission.* London, 1947.

Crum, Bartley. *Behind the Silken Curtain.* New York, 1947.

Dan, Uri. *Blood Libel.* New York, 1987.

Davenport, Elaine, Paul Eddy, and Peter Gillmann. *The Plumbat Affair.* Philadelphia, 1978.

Davidowicz, Lucy S. *Jews in America, 1881–1981.* New York, 1982.

Dayan, Moshe. *Breakthrough.* New York, 1981.

Deakin, W.F.D., and Richard Storry. *The Case of Richard Sorge.* New York, 1966.

DeNovo, John. *American Interests in the Middle East.* Minneapolis, 1963.

Dershowitz, Alan M. *Chutzpah.* Boston, 1991.

Deutscher, Isaac. *Stalin.* New York, 1967.

Diamond, Edwin. *Sign Off.* Cambridge, 1982.

Divine, Robert. *Foreign Policy and U.S. Presidential Elections.* New York, 1974.

Donovan, Hedley. *Roosevelt to Reagan.* New York, 1985.

Donovan, Robert. *Conflict and Crisis, 1945–1949.* New York, 1977.

————. *Tumultuous Years, 1949–1953.* New York, 1982.

Dowty, Alan. *Middle East Crisis.* Berkeley, 1984.

Draper, Theodore. *Israel and World Politics.* New York, 1968.

————. *A Very Thin Line.* New York, 1991.

Drew, Elizabeth, *American Journal,* New York, 1977.

————. *Portrait of an Election.* New York, 1981.

Drinan, Robert F. *Honor the Promise.* New York, 1977.

Eban, Abba. *An Autobiography.* New York, 1977.

Edwards, John. *Superweapon.* New York, 1982.

Eisenhower, Dwight D. *Waging Peace.* New York, 1965.

Engelmayer, Sheldon D., and Robert J. Wagman. *Hubert Humphrey.* New York, 1978.

Ennes, James M., Jr. *Assault on the Liberty.* New York, 1979.

Evans, Rowland, and Robert Novak. *The Reagan Revolution.* New York, 1981.

Eveland, Wilbur Crane. *Ropes of Sand.* New York, 1980.

Evron, Yair. *War and Intervention in Lebanon.* London, 1987.

Eytan, Walter. *The First Ten Years.* New York, 1958.

Fein, Leonard. *Where Are We? New York, 1988.*

Feis, Herbert. *The Birth of Israel.* New York, 1969.

Feldman, Lily Gardner. *The Special Relationship between West Germany and Israel.* Boston, 1984.

Feldman, Shai. *Israeli Nuclear Deterrence.* New York, 1982.

Ferrell, Robert H. (ed.). *The Eisenhower Diaries,* New York, 1981.

————, (ed.). *Off the Record.* Harmondsworth, 1982.

Feuerwerger, Marvin C. *Congress and Israel.* Westport, Conn., 1979.

Findley, Paul. *They Dare to Speak Out.* Westport, Conn., 1985.

Ford, Gerald R. *A Time to Heal.* New York, 1979.

Franck, Thomas M., and Edward Weisband. *Foreign Policy by Congress.* New York, 1979.

Freidin, Seymour, and George Bailey. *The Experts.* New York, 1968.

Friedlander, Melvin A. *Sadat and Begin.* Boulder, Colo., 1983.

Friedlander, Saul. *Reflections of Nazism.* New York, 1984.

Friedman, Isaiah. *The Question of Palestine.* New York, 1973.

Friedman, Thomas L. *From Beirut to Jerusalem.* New York, 1989.

Fulbright, J. William. *The Crippled Giant.* New York, 1972.

Gaddis, John Lewis. *Russia, the Soviet Union and the United States.* New York, 1978.

————. *Strategies of Containment.* New York, 1982.

Ganin, Zvi. *Truman, American Jews and Israel.* New York, 1979.

Garcia-Granados, Jorge. *The Birth of Israel.* New York, 1949.

Gardner, Richard N. *Sterling-Dollar Diplomacy.* New York, 1969.

Garthoff, Raymond L. *Détente and Confrontation,* Washington, 1985.

Gazit, Mordechai. *President Kennedy's Policy toward the Arab States and Israel.* Tel Aviv, 1983.

Gilboa, Eytan. *American Public Opinion toward Israel and the Arab-Israeli Conflict.* Lexington, Mass., 1987.

Gildersleeve, Virginia. *Many a Good Crusade.* New York, 1955.

Gilmour, David. *The Fractured Country.* Oxford, 1983.

Glaser, Nathan. *American Judaism.* Chicago, 1972.

Glick, Edward B. *Latin America and the Palestine Question.* New York, 1958.

Golan, Galia. *Yom Kippur and After.* New York, 1977.

————. *The Soviet Union and the Palestine Liberation Organization.* New York, 1980.

Golan, Matti. *The Secret Conversations of Henry Kissinger.* New York, 1976.

————. *Shimon Peres.* London, 1982.
Goldmann, Nahum. *Mein Leben als deutscher Jude.* Munich, 1980.
————. *Mein Leben—USA, Europa, Israel.* Munich, Vienna, 1981.
Goulding, Phil G. *Confirm or Deny.* New York, 1970.
Gowers, Andrew, and Tony Walker. *Behind the Myth.* London, 1990.
Griffith, Robert (ed.). *Ike's Letters to a Friend.* Lawrence, Kan., 1984.
Grose, Peter. *Israel in the Mind of America.* New York, 1983.
Gutman, Israel, et al. *Encyclopedia of the Holocaust.* New York, 1990.
Haass, Richard N. *Conflicts Unending.* New Haven, 1990.
Haig, Alexander M., Jr. *Caveat.* New York, 1984.
Halabi, Rafik. *The West Bank Story.* Orlando, Fla., 1985.
Hamizrachi, Beate. *The Emergence of the South Lebanon Security Belt.* Westport, Conn., 1988.
Handel, Michael I. *The Diplomacy of Surprise.* Cambridge, 1981.
Harwood, Richard (ed.). *The Pursuit of the Presidency, 1980.* New York, 1980.
Hecht, Ben. *Child of the Century.* New York, 1954.
Heikal, Mohammed. *The Cairo Documents.* New York, 1973.
————. *The Road to Ramadan.* London, 1975.
————. *The Sphinx and the Commissar.* New York, 1978.
Hersh, Seymour. *The Price of Power.* New York, 1983.
————. *The Samson Option,* New York, 1991.
Herzog, Chaim. *The War of Atonement.* Boston, 1975.
Herzstein, Robert E. *Roosevelt and Hitler.* New York, 1989.
Hottinger, Arnold. *Die Araber vor ihrer Zukunft.* Paderborn, 1989.
Howe, Irving. *World of Our Fathers.* New York, 1976.
Howe, Russell Warren, and Sarah Hayes Trott. *The Power Peddlers.* New York, 1977.
Hughes, Emmet John. *The Ordeal of Power.* New York, 1963.
Hurewitz, J.C. *Middle East Politics: The Military Dimension.* New York, 1969.
Huthmacher, Joseph. *Senator Robert F. Wagner and the Rise of Urban Liberalism.* New York, 1968.
Indyk, Martin. *To the ends of the Earth.* Cambridge, 1984.
Isaac, Rael Jean. *Israel Divided,* Baltimore, 1976.
Jackson, Elmore. *Middle East Mission: The Story of a Major Bid for Peace in the Time of Nasser and Ben-Gurion.* New York, 1983.
Johnson, Donald Bruce (ed.). *National Party Platforms.* Vol. 2, *1960–1976.* Urbana, 1978.
Johnson, Lyndon B. *The Vantage Point.* New York, 1971.
Johnson, Paul. *A History of the Jews.* New York, 1987.
Kahan, Arcadius. *Essays in Jewish Social and Economic History.* Chicago, 1986.
Kahler, Miles. *Decolonization in Britain and France.* Princeton, 1984.
Kalb, Marvin, and Bernard Kalb. *Kissinger.* Boston, 1974.
Kalb, Marvin, and Ted Koppel. *In the National Interest.* New York, 1977.
Kamil, Mohamed Ibrahim. *The Camp David Accords.* London, 1986.
Kapstein, Ethan B. *The Insecure Alliance.* New York, 1990.
Kelleher, Catherine McArdle. *Germany and the Politics of Nuclear Weapons.* New York, 1975.
Kenen, I. L. *Israel's Defense Line.* Buffalo, 1981.
Kennan, George F. *The Cloud of Danger.* Boston, 1977.
Kerr, Malcolm H. *The Arab Cold War.* London, 1971.
Khalidi, Rashid. *Under Siege.* New York, 1986.
Khalidi, Walid. *Conflict and Violence in Lebanon.* Cambridge, 1979.

El-Khawas, Mohamed. *American Aid to Israel*. Brattleboro, Vt., 1984.

Kissinger, Henry. *The White House Years*. Boston, 1979.

———. *Years of Upheaval*. Boston, 1986.

Klieman, Aaron S. *Israel's Global Reach*. Washington, 1985.

Kollek, Teddy. *For Jerusalem*. New York, 1978.

Kraut, Alan M. *The Huddled Masses*. Arlington Heights, Ill., 1982.

Kurzman, Dan. *Ben-Gurion*. New York, 1983.

Laqueur, Walter, *The Road to Jerusalem*. New York, 1968.

———. *Confrontation*. London, 1974.

———. *A History of Zionism*. New York, 1976.

———. *The Terrible Secret*. Harmondsworth, 1982.

———, and Barry Rubin (eds.). *The Israel-Arab Reader*. New York, 1984.

Lash, Joseph P. *Eleanor: The Years Alone*. New York, 1972.

Leonhard, Wolfgang. *The Kremlin after Stalin*. New York, 1962.

Lesser, Alan. *Israel's Impact*. Lanham, Md., 1984.

Lieber, Robert J. *The Oil Decade*. Lanham, Md, 1986.

Liebman, Charles S. *The Ambivalent American Jew*. Philadelphia, 1973.

———. *Pressure without Sanctions*. Rutherford, N.J., 1977.

———, and Stephen Cohen. *Two Worlds of Judaism*. New Haven, 1990.

Louis, W. Roger. *The British Empire in the Middle East, 1945–1951*. Oxford, 1985.

Lowdermilk, Walter Clay. *Palestine: Land of Promise*. New York, 1944.

Lukacs, Yehuda (ed.). *Documents on the Israeli-Palestinian Conflict, 1967–1983*. Cambridge, 1984.

Lustick, Ian S. *For the Land and the Lord*. New York, 1988.

McDonald, James G. *My Mission in Israel*. New York, 1951.

McGhee, George C. *Envoy to the Middle World*. New York, 1983.

———. *At the Creation of a New Germany*. New Haven, 1989.

McNamara, Robert S. *Blundering into Disaster*. New York, 1986.

McPherson, Harry. *A Political Education*. Boston, 1972.

Manuel, Frank. *The Realities of American-Palestine Relations*. Washington, 1949.

Ma'oz, Moshe. *The Sphinx of Damascus*. London, 1988.

Meir, Golda. *My Life*. New York, 1975.

Melman Yossi, and Dan Raviv. *The Imperfect Spies*. London, 1989.

———. *Every Spy a Prince*. Boston, 1990.

Millis, Walter (ed.). *The Forrestal Diaries*. New York, 1951.

Mommsen, Hans. *Der Nationalsozialismus und die Deutsche Gesellschaft*. Reinbek, 1991.

Moore, Jonathan. *The Campaign for President*. Cambridge, 1981.

Moynihan, Daniel Patrick. *A Dangerous Place*. Boston, 1978.

Nakdimon, Shlomo. *First Strike*. New York, 1987.

Neff, Donald. *Warriors at Suez*. New York, 1981.

Neumann, Emanuel. *In the Arena*. New York, 1976.

Neusner, Jacob. *Stranger at Home*. Chicago, 1981.

Neustadt, Richard E. *Presidential Power*. New York, 1980.

Nicholas, Herbert G. (ed.). *Washington Despatches, 1941–1945*. Chicago, 1981.

Nissen, Ron. *It Sure Looks Different from the Inside*. Chicago, 1978.

Nixon, Richard M. *RM*. New York, 1978.

Nolan, Janne E. *Trappings of Power*. Washington, 1991.

Norton, Augustus Richard. *Amal and the Shi'a*. Austin, Tex., 1987.

Novik, Nimrod. *The United States and Israel*. Boulder, Colo., 1986.

Paper, Lewis J. *Brandeis*. Englewood Cliffs, N.J., 1983.

Peán, Pierre. *Les deux Bombes.* Paris, 1982.

Peleg, Ilan. *Begin's Foreign Policy, 1977–1983.* Boulder, Colo., 1987.

Peres, Shimon. *David's Sling.* London, 1970.

Peretz, Don. *Intifada.* Boulder, Colo., 1990.

Perlmutter, Amos. *Politics and the Military in Israel.* London, 1978.

———. *Israel: The Partitioned State.* New York, 1985.

——— et al. *Two Minutes over Baghdad.* London, 1982.

Pineau, Christian. *1956, Suez.* Paris, 1976.

Polk, William R. *The United States and the Arab World.* Cambridge, 1975.

Pollock, David. *The Politics of Pressure.* Westport, Conn., 1982.

Powell, Jody. *The Other Side of the Story.* New York, 1984.

Power, Thomas. *The Man Who Kept the Secrets.* New York, 1979.

Pry, Peter. *Israel's Nuclear Arsenal.* Boulder, Colo., 1984.

Quandt, William B. *Decade of Decisions.* Berkeley, 1977.

———. *Camp David.* Washington, 1986.

Ra'anan, Uri. *The USSR Arms the Third World.* Cambridge, 1969.

Rabin, Yitzhak. *The Rabin Memoirs.* Boston, 1979.

Rabinovich, Itamar. *The Road Not Taken.* New York, 1991.

———. *The War for Lebanon.* Ithaca, 1985.

———, and Jehuda Reinharz (eds.). *Israel in the Middle East.* New York, 1984.

Rafael, Gideon. *Destination Peace.* New York, 1981.

Randal, Jonathan C. *Going All the Way.* New York, 1984.

Ranelagh, John. *The Agency.* New York, 1986.

Reich, Bernard. *The United States and Israel.* New York, 1984.

Reiser, Stewart. *The Israeli Arms Industry.* New York, 1989.

Rogow, Arnold. *James Forrestal.* New York, 1963.

Roosevelt, Kermit. *Countercoup.* New York, 1979.

Roosevelt, Theodore. *An Autobiography.* New York, 1926.

Rose, Norman. *Lewis Namier and Zionism.* Oxford, 1980.

Rostow, E. V. *Peace in the Balance.* New York, 1972.

Rostow, W. W. *The Diffusion of Power.* New York, 1972.

Sachar, Abraham. *The Redemption of the Unwanted.* New York, 1983.

Sachar, Howard. *A History of Israel.* Vol. 1, New York, 1979; vol. 2, New York, 1988.

Safire, William. *Before the Fall.* New York, 1975.

Safran, Nadav. *Israel: The Embattled Ally.* Cambridge, 1978.

Sanders, Marion K. *Dorothy Thompson.* Boston, 1973.

Sanders, Ronald. *The High Walls of Jerusalem.* New York, 1983.

Saunders, Harold H. *The Other Walls.* Washington, 1985.

Schiff, Ze'ev. *A History of the Israeli Army.* New York, 1985.

———, and Ehud Ya'ari. *Israel's Lebanon War.* New York, 1984.

———. *The Intifada.* New York, 1990.

Schlesinger, Arthur M., Jr. *A Thousand Days.* Boston, 1965.

Schram, Martin. *Running for President 1976.* New York, 1977.

Schurmann, Franz. *The Foreign Politics of Richard Nixon.* Berkeley, 1987.

Schwarz, Hans-Peter. *Adenauer.* Stuttgart, 1986.

Seale, Patrick. *Asad: The Struggle for the Middle East.* London, 1988.

Segev, Samuel. *The Iranian Triangle.* New York, 1988.

Segev, Tom. *The First Israelis.* New York, 1985.

Segre, Dan. *A Crisis of Identity.* New York, 1980.

Sharon, Ariel. *Warrior.* New York, 1989.

Sheean, Vincent. *A Personal History.* New York, 1934.

Sheehan, Edward R. F. *The Arabs, Israelis and Kissinger.* New York, 1976.

Shepherd, Naomi. *Alarms and Excursions.* London, 1990.

Sherman, A. J. *Island Refuge.* Berkeley, 1973.

Shipler, David. *Arab and Jew.* New York, 1986.

Shlaim, Avi. *Collusion across the Jordan.* New York, 1988.

Shuckburgh, Evelyn. *Descent to Suez.* London, 1986.

Silberman, Charles E. *A Certain People.* New York, 1985.

Silver, Eric. *Begin.* New York, 1984.

Slater, Leonard. *The Pledge.* New York, 1970.

Slonim, Shlomo. *United States-Israel Relations.* Jerusalem, 1974.

Sofer, Sasson. *Begin.* Oxford, 1988.

Sorensen, Theodore C. *Kennedy.* New York, 1965.

Spiegel, Steven. *The Other Israeli-Arab Conflict.* Chicago, 1986.

Stacks, John F. *Watershed.* New York, 1981.

Starr, Joyce. *Kissing Through Glass.* Chicago, 1990.

Stein, Leonard. *The Balfour Declaration.* New York, 1961.

Stern, Paula. *Water's Edge.* Westport, Conn., 1979.

Steven, Stewart. *The Spymasters of Israel.* New York, 1980.

Stewart, George R. *Names on the Land.* Boston, 1967.

Sykes, Christopher. *Crossroads to Israel.* Bloomington, Ind., 1973.

Szulc, Tad. *The Illusion of Peace.* New York, 1978.

Tamir, Avraham. *A Soldier in Search of Peace.* New York, 1988.

Tanter, Raymond. *Who's at the Helm?* Boulder, Colo., 1990.

Thomas, Abel. *Comment Israël fût Sauvé.* Paris, 1978.

Thomas, Hugh. *The Suez Affair.* London, 1967.

Thucydides. *The Peloponnesian War.* Harmondsworth, 1977.

Tivnan, Edward. *The Lobby.* New York, 1987.

Toranska, Teresa. *"Them".* New York, 1987.

Touval, Saadia. *The Peace Brokers.* Princeton, 1982.

Toward Peace in the Middle East. Washington, 1975.

Troen, Selwem I. and Moshe Shemesh. *The Suez-Sinai Crisis, 1956.* London, 1990.

Truman, Harry S. *Years of Trial and Hope.* New York, 1965.

Tschirgi, Dan. *The Politics of Indecision.* New York, 1983.

Tuchman, Barbara W., et al. *The Palestinian Question in American History.* New York, 1978.

Tusa, Ann, and John Tusa. *The Berlin Blockade.* London, 1988.

Urofsky, Melvin I. *We Are One!.* Garden City, N.Y., 1978.

Valeriani, Richard. *Travels with Henry.* New York, 1979.

Vance, Cyrus. *Hard Choices.* New York, 1983.

Viorst, Milton. *Sands of Sorrow.* New York, 1987.

Vital, David. *The Future of the Jews.* Cambridge, 1990.

Vogel, Rolf (ed.). *Der Deutsch-Israelische Dialog.* Vol. 1. Munich, 1987.

Wallace, Henry A. *The Price of Vision.* Boston, 1973.

Wallach, Janet, and John Wallach. *Arafat.* New York, 1990.

Walworth, Arthur. *Woodrow Wilson.* Baltimore, 1969.

Weisbord, Robert G., and Richard J. Kazarian. *Israel in the Black American Perspective.* Westport, Conn., 1985.

Weisgal, Murray. . . . *So Far.* New York, 1971.

Weizman, Ezer. *The Battle for Peace.* Toronto, 1981.

Westin, Av. *Newswatch.* New York, 1982.

Wilson, Evan. *Decision on Palestine.* Stanford, 1979.

Witcover, Jules. *Marathon.* New York, 1977.

Wohlstetter, Roberta. *Pearl Harbor.* Stanford, 1962.

Wolfers, Arnold. *Britain and France between Two Wars.* New York, 1966.

Wolffsohn, Michael. *Israel: Polity, Society, Economy, 1882–1986.* Atlantic Highlands, N.J., 1987.

———. *Ewige Schuld?.* Munich, 1988.

———. *Politik in Israel,* Opladen, 1983.

Woodward, Bob. *Veil.* New York, 1987.

Wyman, David. *The Abandonment of the Jews.* New York, 1984.

Yahil, Leni. *The Holocaust.* London, 1990.

Yishai, Yael. *Land or Peace.* Stanford, 1987.

Zechlin, Egmont. *Die deutsche Politik und die Juden im Ersten Weltkrieg.* Goettingen, 1969.

Zumwalt, Elmo. *On Watch.* New York, 1976.

Articles

Adamthwaite, Anthony. "Suez Revisited." *International Affairs,* Summer 1988.

"Aftermath: The Sheehan Affair." *Foreign Policy,* Summer 1976.

Alteras, Isaac. "Eisenhower, American Jewry and Israel." *American Jewish Archives,* 1985.

Arian, Asher. "Political Images and Ethnic Polarization." In Howard R. Penniman and Daniel J. Elazar (eds.), *Israel and the Polls, 1981.* Washington, 1986.

Aronson, Shlomo. "Hitlers Judenpolitik, die Aliierten und die Juden." *Vierteljahrshefte für Zeitgeschichte,* January 1984.

Bard, Josef. "Why Europe Dislikes the Jew." *Harper's,* March 1927.

Bard, Mitchell. "Ethnic Group Influence on Middle East Policy." In Mohammed E. Ahrari (ed.), *Ethnic Groups and U.S. Foreign Policy.* Westport, Conn., 1987.

Bar-on, Mordechai. "David Ben-Gurion and the Sèvres Collusion." In W. Roger Louis and Roger Owen (eds.), *Suez 1956: The Crisis and Its Consequences.* New York, 1989.

Benedick, Richard Elliot. "The High Dam and the Transformation of the Nile." *Middle East Journal,* Spring 1979.

Ben-Zvi, Abraham. "The Reagan Presidency and the Palestinian Predicament." CSS Paper No. 16, Tel Aviv, September 1982.

Berglas, Eitan. "Defense and the Economy: The Israeli Experience." Maurice Falk Institute for Economic Research in Israel, Discussion Paper No. 83.01. Jerusalem, January 1983.

Bickerton, Ian. "Truman, the Creation of Israel and the Liberal Tradition." In Allen Weinstein and Moshe Ma'oz (eds.), *Truman and the American Commitment to Israel.* Jerusalem, 1981.

Bowie, Robert. "Dulles and the Suez Crisis." In W. Roger Louis and Roger Owens (eds.), *Suez 1956: The Crisis and Its Consequences.* New York, 1989.

Brandon, Henry. "Were We Masterful . . ." *Foreign Policy,* Spring 1973.

Browning, Christopher R. "The Decision Concerning the Final Solution." In François Furet (ed.), *Unanswered Questions.* New York, 1989.

Cahn, Anne Hessing. "United States Arms to the Middle East 1967–1976." In Milton Leitenberg and Gabriel Sheffer (eds.), *Great Power Intervention in the Middle East.* New York, 1979.

Clarke, Duncan L. "Entanglement: The Commitment to israel." In Yehuda Lukacs and Abdalla M. Battah (eds.), *The Arab-Israeli Conflict.* Boulder, Colo., 1988.

Clarke, Duncan L., and Alan S. Cohen. "The United States, Israel and the Lavi Fighter." *Middle East Journal,* Winter 1986.

Cointet, Jean-Paul. "Guy Mollet, the French Government and the SFIP." In Selwyn Ilan Troen and Moshe Shemesh, *The Suez-Sinai Crisis, 1956.* London, 1990.

Cordesman, Anthony H. "The Middle East and the Cost of the Politics of Force." *Middle East Journal,* Winter 1986.

Cremonesi, Lorenzo. Interview with Sheikh Abu Malek. *Corriere della Sera,* October 13, 1991.

Davis, Moshe. "Reflections on Harry S. Truman." In Allen Weinstein and Moshe Ma'oz (eds.), *Truman and the American Commitment to Israel.* Jerusalem, 1981.

Deutsch, Dennis. "The Palestine Question." In Robin Higham (ed.), *Intervention or Abstention.* Lexington, Ky., 1975.

Dine, Thomas A. "The Revolution in U.S.-Israel Relations." *Journal of Palestine Studies,* Summer 1986.

Dodge, Bayard. "American Missionary Efforts in the Nineteenth and Early Twentieth Centuries." *Annals of the American Academy of Political and Social Science,* May 1972.

Eban, Abba. "Jarring, Lyndon Johnson, Richard Nixon and '242'" in Lord Caradon et al., *U.N. Security Council, Resolution 242,* Washington, 1981.

Eberstadt, Nick, and Eric Breindel. "The Population Factor in the Middle East." *International Security,* Spring 1979.

Eizenstat, Stuart E. "Loving Israel—Warts and All." *Foreign Policy,* Winter 1990–1991.

Elath, Eliahu. "The 14th of May 1948 in Washington, D.C.," in Allen Weinstein and Moshe Ma'oz (eds.), *Truman and the American Commitment to Israel,* Jerusalem, 1981.

Farer, Tom. "Israel's Unlawful Occupation," *Foreign Policy,* Spring 1991.

Feldman, Shai, and Heda Rechnitz-Kijner. "Deception, Consensus and War," Jaffee Center for Strategic Studies, Paper No. 27. Tel Aviv, October 1984.

Field, James A., Jr. "Trade, Skills and Sympathy." *Annals of the American Academy of Political and Social Science,* May 1972.

Fink, Donald E. "Lavi: A Tough Decision." *Aviation Week,* September 7, 1987.

Frei, Norbert. "Wiedergutmachungspolitik im Urteil der amerikanischen Oeffentlichkeit." In Ludolf Herbst and Constantin Goschler (eds.), *Wiedergutmachung in der Bundesrepublik Deutschland.* Munich, 1989.

Friedman, Thomas L. "America in the Mind of Israel." *New York Times magazine,* May 25, 1987.

Ganin, Zvi. "The Limits of American Jewish Political Power." *Jewish Social Studies,* vol. 39, 1977.

———. "Truman, American Jewry and the Creation of Israel." In Allen Weinstein and Moshe Ma'oz (eds.), *Truman and the American Commitment to Israel.* Jerusalem, 1981.

George, Alexander. "Missed Opportunities for Crisis Prevention." In Alexander L. George (ed.), *Managing U.S.-Soviet Rivalry.* Boulder, Colo., 1983.

Goldberg, Arthur J. "Negotiating History of Resolution 242." In Lord Caradon et al. *U.N. Security Council Resolution 242.* Washington, 1981.

Hadar, Leon. "Reforming Israel Before It's Too Late." *Foreign Policy,* Winter 1990–1991.

Harford, James J. "Israeli Aeronautics after Lavi." *Aerospace America,* November 1988.

Harkabi, Yehoshafat. "Comment." In "The Changing Strategic Landscape," pt 3, Adelphi Papers 237. London, Spring 1989.

———. Interview with Robert I. Friedman. *World Policy Journal,* Spring 1989.

Harris, Louis. "Oil or Israel." *New York Times Magazine,* April 6, 1975.

Ibrahim, Saad. "American Domestic Forces and the October War." *Journal of Palestine Studies,* Autumn 1974.

Kaiser, Karl. "Konrad Adenauer und die Oder-Neisse Line." *Die Zeit,* September 29, 1989.

Kent, George. "Congress and American Middle East Policy." In Willard A. Beling, (ed.), *The Middle East: Quest for an American Policy.* Albany, 1973.

Khalidi, Rashid. "Consequences of the Suez Crisis in the Arab World." In W. Roger Louis and Roger Owen (eds.), *Suez 1956: The Crisis and Its Consequences* Oxford, 1989.

Kissinger, Henry. "The White Revolutionary." *Daedalus,* Summer 1968.

Kunz, Diane B. "The Importance of Having Money." In W. Roger Louis and Roger Owen, *Suez 1956.* New York, 1989.

Kuznets, Simon. "Immigration of Russian Jews to the United States." *Perspectives in American History,* vol. 9, 1975.

Lewis, Samuel. "The United States and Israel." In William B. Quandt (ed.), *The Middle East: Ten Years after Camp David.* Washington, 1988.

McLaurin, R. D. "Lebanon and the United States." In R. D. McLaurin (ed.) *Lebanon and the World in the 1980s.* College Park, Md., 1983.

Mathias, Charles McC. "Ethnic Groups and Foreign Policy." *Foreign Affairs,* Summer 1981.

Morris, Roger. "Beirut—and the Press—under Siege." *Columbia Journalism Review,* November-December 1982.

Muravchik, Joshua. "Misreporting Lebanon." *Policy Review,* Winter 1983.

Namier Lewis B. "Zionism." *New Statesman,* November 5, 1927.

Norris, George. "TVA on the Jordan." *Nation,* May 20, 1944.

Oder, Irving. "American Zionism and the Congressional Resolution of 1922 on Palestine." *Publications of the American Jewish Historical Society,* no. 45, 1955.

Peres, Yochanan, and Sara Shemer. "The Ethnic Factor in Elections." In Don Caspi et al. (eds.), *The Roots of Begin's Success.* New York, 1984.

Peretz, Don. "Israel Foreign Policymaking." In R.D. McLaurin, Don Peretz, and Lewis W. Snider, *Middle East Foreign Policy.* New York, 1982.

Podhoretz, Norman. "J'accuse." *Commentary,* September 1982.

Quandt, William B. "U.S. Energy Policy and the Arab-Israeli Conflict." In Naiem A. Sherbiny and Mark A. Tessler (eds.), *Arab Oil.* New York, 1976.

———. "Lebanon, 1958, and Jordan, 1970." In Barry M. Blechman and Stephen S. Kaplan (eds.), *Force without War.* Washington, 1978.

———. "Reagan's Lebanon Policy." *Middle East Journal,* Spring 1984.

———. "U.S. Policy toward the Arab-Israeli Conflict." In Quandt (ed.), *The Middle East: Ten Years after Camp David.* Washington, 1988.

———. "Lyndon Johnson and the June 1967 War." *Middle East Journal,* Spring 1992.

Reich, Bernard. "Israeli Foreign Policy and the 1981 Election," in Howard M. Penniman and David J. Elazar, *Israel at the Polls, 1981.* Washington, 1986.

Roumani, Maurice M. "The Ethnic Factor in Israel's Foreign Policy." In Bernard Reich and Gershon R. Kieval (eds.), *Israeli National Security Policy.* New York, 1988.

Sandler, Shmuel. "The Religious Parties." In Howard R. Penniman and Daniel J. Elazar (eds.), *Israel at the Polls, 1981.* Washington, 1986.

Saunders, Harold, H. "Regulating Soviet-U.S. Competition in the Arab-Israeli Arena." In Alexander George, Alexander Dallin, and Philip J. Farley (eds.), *U.S.-Soviet Security Cooperation.* New York, 1988.

Schiff, Ze'ev. "The Green Light." *Foreign Policy,* Spring 1983.

———. "Lebanon: Motivations and Interests in Israel's Policy." *Middle East Journal,* Spring 1984.

Schoenbaum, David. ". . . or Lucky: Jordan—The Forgotten Crisis." *Foreign Policy,* Spring 1973.

———. "West Germany and Israel." *Present Tense,* Autumn 1974.

———. "Passing the Buck(s)." *Foreign Policy,* Spring 1979.

———. "The Iowa Senatorial Race." *Present Tense,* Summer 1984.

———. "The World War II Allied Agreement on Occupation and Administration of Post-War Germany." In Alexander George, Alexander Dallin, Philip J. Farley (eds.), *U.S.-Soviet Security Cooperation.* New York, 1988.

Shamir, Simon. "The Collapse of Project Alpha." In W. Roger Louis and Roger Owen (eds.), *Suez 1956: The Crisis and its Consequences.* New York, 1989.

Shattan, Joseph. "Why Breira." *Commentary,* June 1977.

Sicherman, Harvey. "A Perilous Partnership." In Nimrod Novik (ed.), *Israel in U.S. Foreign and Security Policies.* Jaffee Center for Strategic Studies, Paper No. 21. Tel Aviv, November 1983.

Stanfield, Rochelle L. "O Israel!" *National Journal,* June 23, 1990.

Stock, Raymond. "Prestige Press at War." *Middle East Journal,* Summer 1985.

Szulc, Tad. "Lisbon and Washington." *Foreign Policy,* Winter 1975–1976.

Toll, Carolyn. "American Jews and the Middle East Dilemma." *Progressive,* August 1979.

Torgovnik, Efraim. "Party Organization and Electoral Alignment." In Howard R. Penniman and Daniel J. Elazar, *Israel at the Polls, 1981.* Washington, 1986.

Troen, Selwyn Ilan. "The Sinai Campaign as a 'War of No Alternative,'" in Troen and Moshe Shemesh (eds.), *The Suez-Sinai Crisis, 1956.* London, 1990.

Tuchman, Barbara W., et al., *The Palestinian Question in American History.* New York, 1978.

Tucker, Robert. "Oil, the Issue of American Intervention." *Commentary,* January 1975.

———. "Lebanon, the Case for the War." *Commentary,* October 1982.

Ullman, Richard H. "The Covert French Connection." *Foreign Policy,* Summer 1989.

Viorst, Milton. "The Media Front." *Channels,* November-December 1982.

Voss, Carl Herman. "In Praise of Stephen S. Wise." *Moment,* July-August 1987.

Wagner, Charles H. "Elite American Newspaper Opinion and The Middle East," in Willard A. Beling (ed.), *The Middle East Quest for an American Policy.* Albany, 1973.

Weinberg, Yagil. "The Iran-Contra Crisis and Its Impact on U.S.-Israeli Counterterrorism Cooperation." In Neil C. Livingstone and Terrell E. Arnold (eds.), *Beyond the Iran-Contra Crisis.* Lexington, Mass., 1988.

Weinland, Robert G. "Superpower Naval Diplomacy in the October 1973 Arab-Israeli War." Center for Naval Analyses, June 1978.

Wells, Samuel F., Jr. "Sounding the Tocsin." *International Security,* Fall 1979.

Whetten, Lawrence L. "The Arab-Israeli Dispute." In Gregory Treverton (ed.), *Crisis Management and the Superpowers in the Middle East.* Aldershot, Hants., 1983.

Wolffsohn, Michael. "Die Wiedergutmachung und der Westen." In "Aus Politik und Zeitgeschichte." Das Parlament, April 18, 1987.

———. "Das Deutsch-Israelische Wiedergutmachungsabkommen," *Vierteljahrshefte für Zeitgeschichte,* October 1988.

———. "Von der verordneten zur freiwilligen 'Vergangenheitsbewältigung.'" *German Studies Review,* 1989.

Other Sources

Aviation Week
American Jewish Yearbook
Business Week
Congressional Quarterly
Des Moines Register
The Economist
Editor & Publisher
Financial Times
Forbes
"Frontline," WGBH
Interavia
International Herald-Tribune
Issues
Keesing's Contemporary Archives
Los Angeles Times
Nature
New Republic
New Scientist
Newsweek
New York Times
"Sixty Minutes," CBS
S&MM
Time
Wall Street Journal
Washington Post

Index

Abbas, Abul, 326
Abdullah, King of Jordan, 59–60, 70–72, 178, 190
Abu-Hatzeira, Aharon, 279
Acheson, Dean, 27, 36, 39, 47–49, 52, 70, 75, 85–88, 175
Achille Lauro, x, 291, 326
Adams, Sherman, 96, 99
Adenauer, Konrad, 9, 87–89, 130–31
Adler, Mortimer, 28
Agnew, Spiro T., 199, 202
Aiken, George, 193
Algeria, 111, 150, 162, 172, 205, 221–22, 225
Allen, George, 121–22
Allon, Yigal, xii, 126, 160, 172, 224, 227, 236, 252
Alsop, Joseph, 167
American Council for Judaism, 26–27, 30, 37, 63, 66, 92, 96, 244
American Friends of the Middle East, 66–67
American Israel Public Affairs Committee (AIPAC), 4–6, 203, 274, 280
American Jewish Committee, 14–15, 26, 31, 49, 66, 229
American Jewish Conference, 26–27
American Jews, 5–6, 14, 16, 21–31, 60, 63–64, 68, 91, 205, 255–56, 285, 323–25; and Carter, 252, 256, 260, 263; and Eisenhower administration, 96–97; German, 13, 16; and Holocaust, 321–22; immigration, 11–14, 19, 22, 41, 43–44; immigration to Israel, 64, 299; investment in Israel, 299; and Israel, financial support, 60–61, 63–65, 75, 79, 122, 147, 159, 187, 299, 307; and Israeli Jews, 95–97; and Johnson, 141–42, 147–48; and Kennedy, 133–34; and neoconservatism, 231–32; and 1967 War, 151, 159, 168; and Nixon, 148, 176; and Palestine, 27, 57–58; and peace process, 244–45, 256, 260; and PLO, 245, 324–25; political power, 5–6, 13–14, 24, 28–29, 58, 95, 133–34, 167, 169–70, 249, 272–73; population, 13–15; and Roosevelt, 24, 95; and Soviet Jews, 148; and Suez, 115–17, 128; and Zionism, 14–15, 19–21, 26–27, 37, 48–49
American Labor party, 58
American League for a Free Palestine, 27
American Palestine Committee, 28
American Zionist Emergency Council (AZEC), 26, 28–29
Ames, Robert, 293
Amit, Meir, 152

Anderson, Clinton, 48
Anderson, John, 272
Anderson, Robert, 107, 109, 118, 127, 152
Andersson, Sten, 324
Angleton, James Jesus, 3, 132
Arab-American Anti-Discrimination Committee, 289, 300
Arab Higher Committee, 60
Arab League, 60, 71–72, 100, 241, 265
Arafat, Yasir, 182, 186, 197, 228, 230, 252, 266, 276, 282–83, 285–86, 291–92, 295
Arens, Moshe, 264, 286, 304–5
Aridor, Yoram, 278
Arrow, Kenneth, 244
Arrow missile, 300, 306–8
Arvey, Jacob M., 148
Asad, Hafiz al-, 179, 181–82, 186, 198, 224, 251, 284, 293–94
Aspin, Les, 307
Atalena, 70, 247
Atherton, Alfred, 200, 250, 259, 268
Atomic Energy Commission, 92, 122
Atoms for Peace plan, 126
Attlee, Clement, 40, 44, 49–50
Austin, Warren, 38, 55, 58–59, 61
Australia, 84, 117, 152
Austria, 40–41, 45
Avineri, Shlomo, 319

Badeau, John, 135
Baghdad Pact, 84, 103, 109, 124, 192
Baker, Howard, 275, 294
Baker, James, 326, 328–29
Balfour, Arthur, 16–17, 20, 192
Balfour Declaration, xii, 8–9, 17–21, 29–30
Ball, George, 5, 140, 193
Banna, Sabri al-, 283
Barak, Aharon, 258, 262, 266
Barbour, Walworth, 136, 147, 154–55, 162
Baruch, Bernard, 56
Baz, Osama el-, 262
Begin, Menahem, 44, 46–47, 51, 70, 104, 152, 160, 166, 176, 214, 244, 246–48, 250, 254–68, 270, 273, 275, 277–79, 282–88, 291, 293–94, 321, 323, 330
Beirut, 4, 11, 17, 168, 197, 285–88, 290, 292–93
Bell, David, 146
Ben-Gurion, David, 4, 25–26, 39–40, 45, 60–61, 63–65, 70, 73, 75–78, 85, 87, 89, 94–96, 104–

395

Ben-Gurion, David (*Continued*)
   5, 107–9, 111, 114–18, 120, 122–23, 125–27,
   129–31, 134–36, 138, 188, 210, 212, 232, 328,
   330
Ben-Meir, David, 288
Bennike, Maj. Gen. Yagn, 98–99
Ben-tov, Mordechai, 33
Berger, Elmer, 66, 300
Berglas, Eitan, 216
Bergson, Peter, 27–28, 30, 37
Bergus, Donald, 195
Berle, Adolph, 56
Bernadotte, Folke, 61, 70–71
Bernstein, Philip S., 66
Bevin, Ernest, 40–41, 43–44, 50–51
Bilby, Kenneth, 73
Biltmore conference, 8–9, 24–27, 33, 48
Birrenbach, Kurt, 143
Bishara, Ghassan, 290
Black Americans for Support of Israel (BASIC),
   270
Blaustein, Jacob, 64, 88, 101, 117
Bliss, Howard, 17
Blitzer, Wolf, 315–16, 318
Bloom, Sol, 30–31
Blum, Yehuda, 270
B'nai B'Rith, 245, 289
Boehm, Franz, 88
Bohlen, Charles E., 56, 59
Borchgrave, Arnaud de, 190
Boschwitz, Rudy, 5–6
Boumedienne, Houari, 162
Boutros Ghali, 215, 264
Bowles, Chester, 135
Bradlee, Ben, 288–89
Brandeis, Louis D., 15, 17–18, 25, 27
Brandt, Willy, 204
Breira, 244–45
Brezhnev, Leonid, 198, 206–9
Brickner, Balfour, 245
Brown, George, 203, 205, 231, 268
Brown, Harold, 263, 268
Brzezinski, Zbigniew, 242, 250, 255, 258–62,
   267–68, 277
Buckley, William F., 167–68
Bull, Odd, 149
Bunche, Ralph, 36, 191, 214
Bundy, McGeorge, 138, 143, 156
Bundy, William P., 137
Bunker, Ellsworth, 140
Burns, Arthur, 170
Burt, Richard, 274
Bush, George, 287, 314, 325
Byrnes, James F., 42, 48
Byroade, Henry, 86–89, 95–96, 104, 106, 326

Camp David Accords, xiii, 211–12, 258–69, 273,
   292, 298
Canada, 4, 41, 152, 164, 309
Caradon, Lord, 164–65

Cardozo, Benjamin, 170
Carter, Jimmy, 191, 213–14, 246, 248–73, 291,
   298
Casey, William, 284, 293, 310
Ceaucescu, Nicolae, 254
Celler, Emanuel, 99
Chandler, Albert, 28
Chapman, Oscar, 72–73
Chazan, Naomi, 245
China, 11, 56, 77, 89, 113, 185, 191, 196, 267,
   271
Christian Council on Palestine, 28
Churchill, Winston, 20, 40, 47, 51, 143
CIA, 3, 55, 66, 69, 74–76, 98, 101, 103, 107–9,
   132–33, 136, 152, 158–60, 169, 177–78, 191,
   316
Clapp, Gordon, 72, 100
Clark, Dick, 245
Clausewitz, Carl von, xi, 299
Clay, Lucius D., 59, 118
Clements, William, 202
Clifford, Clark, 34, 54, 56, 58, 61, 67, 156–57
Cline, Ray, 199
Coffin, Henry Sloane, 37
Colby, William, 200, 208
Cold War, 6–7, 57, 81–85, 109–10, 123, 125,
   129, 171, 174–75, 192–95, 211, 298
Committee for Justice and Peace in the Holy
   Land, 65–66
Conference of Presidents of Major Jewish
   Organizations, 6, 244, 325
Connally, John, 272
Connally, Tom, 42
Copeland, Miles, 132
Council of Jewish Federations, 60, 327
Cox, Archibald, 200
Cox, Oscar, 31
Crane, Charles, 17
Cronkite, Walter, 254
Crossman, R.H.S., 42–43
Crum, Bartley, 41–43, 49, 80
Cuba, 56, 61, 131, 134, 136, 150, 156, 218, 271
Cunningham, Alan, 47
Czechoslovakia, 54, 59–60, 77–78, 88, 117, 168,
   237

Davis, Monett, 68–69, 86, 94–95
Dayan, Moshe, 106–7, 114–15, 126, 130, 132,
   143, 152, 155, 158–59, 166, 172, 176, 186,
   189, 201, 209–10, 220–22, 224, 247–48, 252–
   56, 259–60, 262–70
Dean, Arthur H., 118
Democratic party, 29; and American Jews, 13–
   14, 92, 95, 167, 169, 239, 270, 273; and Israel,
   8, 67, 102, 166–67, 229, 238–39, 243–44, 248–
   49, 323
Dershowitz, Alan, 318
desalinization projects, 127, 139–40, 166
Dewey, Thomas E., 49, 55, 60, 62, 96–97, 117
Diaspora Jews, 63–64, 95–97

Dimona nuclear reactor, 126–27, 136, 140, 187
Dine, Thomas A., 4
Dinitz, Simcha, 199–201, 203, 207, 209
displaced persons (DPs), 35, 39–40; Anglo-U.S. commission, 41–42, 45–48, 68
Dissentchik, Arieh, 126
Dobrynin, Anatoly, 161, 191, 199–200
Dodd, Christopher, 239
Donovan, Robert, 35
Douglas, Helen Gahagan, 28
Douglas, Paul, 81, 85–86
Draper, Theodore, 149
Dubinsky, David, 44
Dukakis, Michael, 323
Dulles, Allen, 18, 109, 123, 132
Dulles, John Foster, 3, 18, 55, 62, 66, 93–103, 106–7, 109, 112–13, 115–22, 124, 129, 131–32, 135, 212, 391
Dutton, Fred, 279

East Germany, 92–93, 131, 143, 237
Eban, Abba, xiii, 71, 74, 78, 87, 92, 97, 99, 105, 111, 114, 117–18, 120, 122–23, 132, 147, 150–52, 155–57, 159–63, 165–69, 172, 176–77, 199–200, 204, 207, 210, 219, 221, 245, 324
Eden, Anthony, 110, 112, 115–16, 118, 135
Egypt, 107, 111–13, 134–35, 138, 165, 183, 215, 230, 235, 265; aid from United States, 85, 92, 133, 135; arms sales to, 144, 174, 255; and Gaza, 72, 118, 120, 122; German scientists in, 127–28, 138; and Great Britain, 50, 101–3, 105, 114; and Israel, 69, 78, 100–1, 107–8, 113–23, 127–28, 169, 172–73, 177–78, 185, 188–91, 211–12, 222, 228, 232–33, 235, 238, 282, 293; and Jordan, 56, 135, 152; and Negev, 71, 101–2; and 1967 War, 150, 152–53, 156; and nuclear power, 227; and Palestinians, 71–72, 108; and peace process, 211, 214–15, 221–22, 227–28, 232–33, 260–61; Soviet personnel in, 174–76, 196–97; and Soviet Union, 102–3, 108–9, 112–13, 115, 123, 127–28, 163, 172–73, 175–78, 191, 198, 207, 217, 232; and Suez Canal negotiations, 188–91; and Syria, 127–28, 138, 150, 185, 198, 225, 228, 265; and United States, 90, 99, 105, 107, 133–36, 142–43, 156, 174, 196–97, 209–10, 251, 255, 302; and Yemen, 127–28, and Yom Kippur War, 186, 198–210
Ehmke, Horst, 204
Eilat, 101, 139, 160
Eilberg, Joshua, 160, 166
Einstein, Albert, 28, 42, 213
Eisenhower, Dwight D., 4, 44, 54–55, 60, 77, 91–98, 101–3, 107, 109, 111–12, 114–24, 126–27, 151, 192, 212, 216–17
Eisenstat, Stuart, 246
Eitan, Rafael, 277, 284, 286, 317–19
Elazar, David, 159
Elon, Amos, 134
El Salvador, 56, 310
Epstein (Elath), Eliahu, 49, 52

Erhard, Ludwig, 142–43
Erler, Fritz, 131
Eshkol, Levi, 97, 126, 137, 140–47, 149, 151–52, 154, 165–66
Ethridge, Mark, 127
Evans, Rowland, 273
Evron, Ephraim, 151, 154–55
Export-Import Bank, 39, 76, 85
Eytan, Walter, 63, 70, 74

Fahd, King of Saudi Arabia, 280, 292
Faisal, King of Saudi Arabia, 197–99, 205
Farouk, King of Egypt, 71, 84–85, 90
Fatah, 197, 256–57, 292
Fein, Leonard, 320
Feinberg, Abraham, 133
Feisal, Emir, 17
Feldman, Lily Gardner, 89
Feldman, Myer, 133–34, 136–38, 140, 154
Ferguson, Homer, 98
Finney, John W., 145
Firestone, Harvey, 56
Fish, Hamilton, 19
Flatto-Sharon, Shmuel, 248
Ford, Gerald R., 175, 214, 231, 233, 248–249
Ford, Richard, 79
Forrestal, James V., 47, 58, 71
Fosdick, Harry Emerson, 37
Foster, William C., 126
France, 6–8, 23, 56, 63–64, 82–83, 97, 111–17, 126–27, 152, 171, 206, 216, 277, 307; aircraft sales to Israel, 107–9, 111–13, 171; and Israel, 111–17, 125, 130, 164, 171, 187
Frankfurter, Felix, 17–18, 27, 129, 170
Friedman, Thomas L., xiii, 209, 286, 289, 293
Friedrich, Carl J., 28
Fulbright, J. William, 3, 121, 124, 193–95, 234

Gaddis, John Lewis, x
Gahal, 152, 160, 177
Gallili, Israel, 172
Gamasy, Abdel Ghany el-, 220
Gandhi, Mohandas K., 51
Garcia-Granados, Jorge, 53, 56
Garment, Leonard, 170
Gaza, 72, 101, 108, 114–15, 118–20, 122–23, 127, 160, 228, 230; and peace process, 228, 251, 255, 261–64, 266, 268, 281, 292, 298
Gazit, Mordechai, 131, 133
Gemayel, Amin, 293
Gemayel, Bashir, 281–82, 284–85, 287, 289, 293, 317
Geneva conference, 220–21, 228–30, 235–36, 252–55, 324
George, Walter F., 49, 116
Gerstenmaier, Eugen, 143
Ghandi, Indira, 164
Ghorbanifar, Manucher, 311–14
Gildersleeve, Virginia, 37, 65–66
Gillette, Guy, 27
Glazer, Nathan, 245, 320

Golan, Matti, 130, 202–3, 213, 225, 238
Golan Heights, 8, 159, 181, 198–99, 223, 225, 228, 230, 235, 237, 281; and peace process, 225–26, 262, 298
Gold, Ernest, 65
Goldberg, Arthur, 156, 159, 161–62
Goldmann, Nahum, 24, 27, 48–49, 87–89
Goldwater, Barry, 98, 175, 294
Goodpaster, Andrew, 151
Gorbachev, Mikhail, 324, 329
Goulding, Phil, 157
Grady, Henry F., 46–47
Graham, Billy, 175
Great Britain, 8, 21–22, 24, 29–30, 40–42, 46–47, 50–52, 54, 59–60, 63–64, 75, 82–84, 101–3, 105, 113–17, 124–26, 164–65, 206, 216, 305–6; and Israel, 105, 114–17; and Palestine, 15–22, 24, 29, 39, 42–43, 45–46, 49–51, 53–54; and United States, 6–7, 21, 29, 42–43, 49–52, 84
Greece, 34, 45, 51–52, 56, 81, 98
Green, William, 28
Greenfield, Meg, 289
Greenspun, Hank, 60
Grew, Joseph, 40
Gromyko, Andrei, 161, 206, 253
Grose, Peter, 29
Gruenther, Alfred, 125
Grunich, Fred, 76–77
Gur, Mordechai, 201, 237, 281
Gush Emunim, 246, 282

Habib, Philip, 276, 284–85, 287, 293
Haddad, Saad, 256–57, 281
Haig, Alexander, 214, 273–75, 277–78, 280–82, 284–85, 287
Hakim, Albert, 314
Hamilton, Lee, 237
Hamilton, Thomas J., 56
Hammarskjold, Dag, 119, 122
Hammer, Zevulun, 266
Handel, Michael, 219
Handlin, Oscar, 66
Hannegan, Robert E., 49
Harkabi, Yehoshafat, 185
Harkin, Tom, 5–6, 239
Harman, Avraham, 136–37, 141, 151
Harrel, Isser, 132, 138
Harriman, W. Averell, 75, 102, 139–40, 143–45, 259
Harrison, Earl, 40
Hart, Parker T., 96
Hauser, Rita E., 324
Heikal, Mohammed, 135, 189–90, 198
Helms, Richard, 169
Henderson, Loy, 42, 55, 59, 98
Hersh, Seymour, 191, 195
Herut, 77, 264, 279, 282
Herzl, Theodor, xi, 11, 14–15, 268
Herzog, Chaim, 85, 106, 278
Hickenlooper, Bourke, 82

Hilldring, John H., 45, 55–56, 70, 76
Hillenbrand, Martin, 204
Hitler, Adolf, 21–25, 51
Hoagland, Jim, 289
Holocaust, 6, 8–9, 24–25, 257, 285, 288, 320–22
Hoover, Herbert, 129
Hoover, Herbert, Jr., 112
Hopkins, Harry, 48
Horowitz, David, 87
Hourani, Albert, 42
Howe, Irving, 245
Hughes, Emmet John, 121
Humphrey, George, 116
Humphrey, Hubert, xi, 3, 69, 79–80, 98, 146–47, 153, 156, 169, 245
Hunter, Robert, 277
Hussein, King, 112, 123, 133, 153, 162–63, 171, 178–82, 186, 199, 223, 227–28, 251, 280, 292
Hussein, Saddam, 306, 313, 327, 329
Husseini, Haj-Amin al-, 20, 24, 60

Ibn Saud, 32
India, 46, 50–51, 54, 164
Iran, 46, 54, 66, 89–90, 93, 98, 118, 223–24, 232, 237, 265, 267, 271–74, 286, 299, 310–14; revolution, 7, 214, 267; and United States, 34, 52, 89–90, 98, 243
Iran-Contra Affair, 60, 310–14
Iraq, 23, 54, 84, 114, 127, 133, 138, 178, 180, 188, 223–24, 272–73, 286, 295; and Israel, 7, 68, 276–77, 306; nuclear weapons, 187, 276–77; revolution in, 133, 178; and Soviet Union, 7, 128, 224; and United States, 95, 106, 109–10
Irgun, 44, 46–47, 51
Israel, 70, 76–78, 80, 85, 130, 148–49, 157–59, 180–81, 275–76; and American Jews, financial support, 60–61, 63–65, 75, 79, 122, 147, 159, 187, 299, 307; and American Jews, immigration to, 64, 299; and American liberals, 80–81, 167, 193, 195, 323; armistice agreements, 104–5; bonds, 64–65, 86, 308; borders, 67, 69–70, 74–75, 166, 237, 297–98; border wars, 105, 107; covert operations, 107–8; defense budget, 146, 172, 187, 189, 215–16, 294, 301, 308; defense industry, 303; deficit, 79, 97; and Egypt, 69, 78, 100–1, 107–8, 113–23, 127–28, 169, 172–75, 177–78, 185, 188–91, 211–12, 222, 228, 232–33, 238, 282, 293; elections, 172, 221, 224, 246–47, 278, 294–95; external debt, 146, 301–3; and France, 111–17, 125, 130, 164, 171, 187; and Gaza, 119–20, 127, 228; and German reparations, 86–89; and Great Britain, 105, 114–17; immigrants to, 64, 73, 79–80, 96, 121–22, 188, 215, 229, 307, 326; inflation, 294, 304, 308; intelligence, 132, 199, 314–19; investment in, 187–88; and Iran-Contra affair, 60, 310–14; and Iraq, 7, 68, 276–77, 306; and Jordan, 70, 105, 114, 141, 163, 166, 178, 227–28; and Jordan River water, 100, 127, 137; and Lebanon, 69–70, 197, 275–76; loans, 76, 85, 146; and neoconservatives,

232, 288; neutrality, 77–78; and 1967 War, 150–60; and nuclear nonproliferation treaty, 166, 169; nuclear program, 126–27, 136, 139–40, 146, 169, 187; and oil, 118, 236; and Palestinian refugees, 71–72, 80; politics, 7, 104–5, 123, 220, 227–28, 238, 247–48, 269, 221–22; and Soviet Union, 77–78, 81, 110, 326; as strategic asset of United States, 6–7, 68–69, 75, 81–83, 108, 131–33, 298; and Suez, 113–23, 216; and Suez Canal, 166, 169, 172, 177, 191, 260; and Syria, 69–70, 111, 141, 149–50, 159–60, 181, 214, 223–24, 275–76; and third world, 77–78, 183; U. S. public support for, 3–5, 65, 73–74, 79–81, 193–94, 229–31, 290–97, 297; and United Nations, 67, 73, 77, 97–99, 105, 144, 237, 240–41, 321–22; and Vietnam, 146–47, 149, 166, 168; War of Independence, 60–63; water supplies, 91, 99–101, 127, 139–40, 144–45; and West Germany, 130–31, 142–43, 236–37; and Yemen, 141; and Yom Kippur War, 183–210; and Zionism, 63–64

Israel Aircraft Industries, 60, 303, 305–6, 308, 311
Israeli Army, 39, 45, 57, 60–61, 76–77
Israeli Foreign Ministry, 63–64, 74, 78, 97–98, 174
Italy, 40–41, 63–64, 152, 206, 277
Ives, Irving, 99

Jabotinsky, Vladimir, 20, 27, 104, 246, 268, 321
Jackson, Elmore, 107
Jackson, Henry M., 175, 195, 203–4, 259
Jackson, Jesse, 3, 270
Jacobson, Eddie, 34–35, 37–38, 58
Japan, 24, 29–30, 36, 206
Jarring, Gunnar, 165–66, 169–71, 176, 189–90
Javits, Jacob, 85, 99, 129
Jepsen, Roger, 5–6, 280
Jeremiah, Book of, 299
Jernegan, John, 106
Jerusalem, 8, 15, 19–21, 67, 70–71, 78, 81, 94, 159–60, 165, 223, 242, 248, 270, 298–99, 326
Jewish Agency, 20, 22, 24–25, 27–28, 39–41, 45, 48–49, 59
Jewish Community Council, 289
Johnson, Herschel, 55–56
Johnson, Lyndon B., 34, 66, 98, 129, 135, 137–40, 142–44, 147–48, 150–51, 153–56, 159–63, 165–69, 269
Johnston, Eric, 28, 100, 127, 139, 144
Jordan, 4, 67, 115–16, 144–45, 147, 165, 178, 180, 221, 228; arms sales to, 144–45, 162, 166, 234, 302; and Egypt, 56, 135, 152; and Great Britain, 105, 114–15, 124; and Israel, 70, 105, 114, 141, 163, 166, 178, 227–28; and Jordan River water, 100, 144–45; and 1967 War, 152–53; and Palestinians, 178–82, 223, 227–28, 242, 253, 291–92, 322–23; and peace process, 211, 223, 227–28, 260; and Syria, 149–50, 180–81, 243; and United States, 94, 123–24,

133, 144, 163, 166; and West Bank, 72, 145, 223; and Yom Kippur War, 199, 201
Jordan, Hamilton, 270

Kahane, Meir, 299
Kalb, Bernard, 201–3, 221
Kalb, Marvin, 201–3, 221
Kamel, Mohammed Ibrahim, 134, 261
Kaplan, Eliezar, 64
Kashoggi, Adnan, 311
Katzenbach, Nicholas, 156
Keating, Kenneth, 199
Kenen, I. L., 98, 203, 205
Kennan, George, 7, 12, 57–58, 61, 116, 135
Kennedy, Edward, 270, 272
Kennedy, John F., 60, 98, 129, 131, 133–39, 141–42, 230, 273
Kennedy, Robert F., 138, 167
Kerr, Malcolm, 149
Khalid, King of Saudi Arabia, 255, 287
Khalil, Mustafa, 265
Khomeini, Ayatollah, 291, 293, 311
Khruschev, Nikita S., 112–13, 125, 132, 134
Kimche, David, 310–12, 315
King, Henry C., 17
Kirkpatrick, Jeanne J., 284
Kishinev, xi
Kissinger, Henry, xiii, 10, 71, 80, 164, 167, 170, 173, 175–77, 179–81, 185–88, 191–92, 195–97, 199–206, 212–13, 217–21, 229–30, 232, 236, 249, 291, 308
Klutznick, Philip M., 148
Knowland, William, 120, 129
Kollek, Teddy, 76, 85–86, 96–97, 138
Komer, Robert, 143–45
Kook, Hillel, 27–28
Kosygin, Alexei, 156, 159, 161–62, 186, 206
Kristol, Irving, 232
Kuwait, 144, 162, 205, 327

Labor party (Israel), 7, 60, 172, 187, 210, 220–21, 224, 227–28, 244, 247–48, 278–79, 284, 322
Laird, Melvin, 179, 181
Lansing, Robert, 17
Laqueur, Walter, ix
Lavi aircraft, 300, 303–5
Lavon, Pinhas, 107–8, 316
League of Nations, 18–19, 68
Lebanon, 71, 100, 226, 275, 299; civil war, 243, 257, 265, 273; Eisenhower administration intervention, 123–24, 132; invasion by Israel, 4, 257–58, 265, 281–96; and Israel, 69–70, 197, 275–76; and PLO, 258–59, 276, 281–87, 289, 291, 295; and Syria, 69–70, 243, 256, 258, 275–76, 284, 293–94; and United States, 99, 132, 294–95
Le Carré, John, 288
Ledeen, Michael, 311–12
Lehman, Herbert H., 44, 49
Levi, David, 326
Lewis, Anthony, 289–90

Lewis, Samuel, 284–86, 292, 310
Liberia, 11, 56, 68
Liberty incident, 157–59
Libya, 162, 171, 173, 206, 326
Likud, 220–21, 227, 238, 247, 275, 278–79, 313, 322
Liman, Arthur, 314
Linowitz, Sol, 269, 274
Lippmann, Walter, 116
Lloyd-George, David, 20
Lodge, Henry Cabot, Jr., 115–16, 119–21, 123
Lodge, Henry Cabot, Sr., 18–19
Long, Breckinridge, 22
Lovett, Robert A., 34, 56, 59
Lowdermilk, Walter Clay, 28, 37, 42, 72, 100, 139
Lowenthal, Max, 56
Lucas, Scott, 28

McClintock, Robert, 58, 124
McCloskey, Robert, 163
McCloy, John J., 87–88, 118, 142–43
McCormick, Cyrus, 11
McDonald, James G., 68–69, 74, 79, 81
McDonald, Ramsay, 20–21
McFarlane, Robert C. "Bud," 214, 310–14
McGee, Gale, 245
McGhee, George C., 85
McGovern, George C., 169, 193, 230, 244–45
McHenry, Donald, 270
MacLeish, Archibald, 39
McNamara, Patrick V., 98
McNamara, Robert S., 142, 148, 153–54, 156–57, 160, 169
McNary, Charles, 28
McPherson, Harry, 154–55, 159
Madrid conference, 327–28
Mann, Thomas, x
Mansfield, Mike, 160
Marcus, David (Mickey), 60, 76
Marshall, George C., 30, 34, 36, 53, 55, 59, 75, 85
Marshall Plan, 52, 59, 88, 211
Mathias, Charles, 294
Matthews, H. Freeman, 44
Maynes, Charles William, 327
Mead, James, 47, 49
Meany, George, 129, 175
Meese, Edwin, 274, 314
Meir, Golda, 4, 60, 79, 118, 120, 122–23, 126, 136–38, 144, 170, 172–73, 176–77, 180, 190, 197, 201, 206–7, 210, 213, 220, 223–24, 227
Mexico, 5, 56, 152, 309
Mollet, Guy, 114, 116–18, 125, 135
Molotov, V. M., 109
Mondale, Walter, 249, 252, 259, 267, 270
Moorer, Thomas, 200, 203
Morgan, J. P., 11
Morgenthau, Hans, 28
Morgenthau, Henry, Jr., 39–40, 65
Morgenthau. Henry, Sr., 13
Morocco, 188, 205, 215, 251–52, 254

Morris, Roger, 170, 290
Morrison, Herbert, 46–47
Moynihan, Daniel Patrick, 241
Mubarak, Hosni, 326, 328
Murphy, Richard, 324
Murphy, Robert, 118, 120, 124
Murray, Philip, 28

Nagle, David, 327
Nahal-Soreq research reactor, 126
Nakdimon, Shlomo, 277
Nasser, Gamal Abdel, 101–3, 107, 112–13, 115, 117–18, 124–25, 128, 133, 135, 138, 142–43, 150, 152, 162, 165, 174, 178, 186, 190, 212, 214, 265
National Jewish Welfare Board, 79
National Religious party, 224, 227–28, 246, 264, 266, 268, 279
National Security Council, 90–91, 97, 99, 108, 121–22, 178, 275, 277
National Student Association, 66
NATO, 69, 81, 84–85, 109, 130, 151, 204, 277
Negev, 56, 62, 71, 101–2
Netherlands, 152, 206
Neumann, Emanuel, 28, 56, 117
Neusner, Jacob, 245, 320
New Zealand, 84, 117, 152
Nicaragua, 56, 280, 310–14
Nidal, Abu, 283
Niebuhr, Reinhold, 28
Niles, David, 48–49, 56, 77
Nimrodi, Ya'acov, 311
Nir, Amiram, 312–14, 317
Nitze, Paul, 84, 86
Nixon, Richard M., 27–28, 116, 120, 135, 148, 170–73, 175–81, 191, 195–209, 217, 219, 225–27, 250
Norris, George, 28
North, Oliver, 312–14
Novak, Robert, 273

Obey, David, 237–38
Occupied Territories, 162, 165, 185–86, 188, 254, 270, 282–83, 290, 295–97, 326
October War. *See* Yom Kippur War
Oliphant, Patrick, 190, 288
O'Neill, Thomas P. "Tip," 239
Organization of Petroleum Exporting Countries (OPEC), 184, 218
Osiraq reactor attack, 187, 276–78, 290, 316–17

Packwood, Robert, 308–9
Palestine, 15–17, 27, 35, 40–46, 50, and Great Britain, 15–22, 24, 29, 39, 42–43, 45–46, 49–51, 53–54; Jewish immigration to, 21–26, 35–36, 40–46, 49, 52–53; Jewish terrorism, 37, 51; riots, 19–21; and Soviet Union, 42, 54–55, 57–58; and United Nations, 8, 47, 49, 51–57; and United States, 3, 16–19, 37–39, 52–53; and

Zionism, 25–26, 43–45, 48–49, 56, 63. *See also* Palestine partition; Palestinians

Palestine Liberation Organization (PLO), x, 141, 149–50, 165, 172, 179, 181–82, 226–28, 236, 245, 253–54, 280, 327; and American Jews, 245, 324–25; and Lebanon, 258–59, 276; Pahlavi, Rezo, Shah of Iran, 66, 93, 118, 211, 271, 281–87, 289, 291, 295; and peace process, 252–53, 280; and Syria, 149–50, 179–82, 254, 280; terrorism, 186, 256–57, 326–27; and United Nations, 228, 241, 269–70, and United States, 230, 241–42, 252

Palestine partition, 4, 22, 49–50, 54–56, 58; and Great Britain, 44, 47

Palestinians, 70, 72, 102, 134, 136, 165, 179, 226, 250, 254; and American Jews, 323–25; and Arabs, 140, 295; and Jordan, 178–82, 223, 227–28, 242, 253, 291–92, 322–23; and peace process, 221, 260, 263–64, 266; refugees, 68, 71, 101, 134, 136–37, 161; self-determination, 70, 160; terrorism, 179–80, 186, 197, 225–26, 256–57, 291, 326; and United Nations, 140, 165, 228–29; and United States, 72, 230, 241–42

Palmach, 76–77, 104

Passfield, Lord, 20

Patterson, Robert, 49

Paul VI, 228

Peace Now movement, 244

Peǵuy, Charles, 320

Peled, Mattiyahu, 244

Percy, Charles, 245, 287, 300

Peres, Shimon, 102, 126, 128, 224, 226–28, 278, 295, 311, 313–14, 317–18, 324; and arms, 111–12, 129–31, 137–38

Peretz, Don, 245

Peretz, Martin, 232, 289

Perkins, Frances, 31

Perlmutter, Amos, 213

Persian Gulf war, 300, 310, 327, 329

Phleger, Herman, 118

Pickering, Thomas, 305

Pike, Otis, 239

Pilsudski, Josef, 210

Pineau, Christian, 112, 122

Podgorny, Nikolay, 226

Podhoretz, Norman, 232, 288–90

Poindexter, John, 313–14

Point Four Aid Program, 85–86

Poland, 3, 16, 22, 40, 77, 88, 114, 132, 210, 237

Poling, Daniel, 28

Pollard, Jonathan Jay, 314–19

Pompidou, Georges, 171, 175

Popular Front for the Liberation of Palestine (PFLP), 179

Powell, Jody, 260, 268

President's Foreign Intelligence Advisory Board, 156

Price, Melvin, 98

Project Alpha, 101–2

Proskauer, Joseph M., 49, 117

Qaddafi, Muammar, 173

Quandt, William B., 242, 250, 259–63, 267–68, 324

Rabb, Max, 92

Rabin, Yitzhak, 144, 162, 167–69, 173, 175–78, 181, 183, 191, 199, 224, 227, 238, 244, 246, 267, 281, 306, 308, 312–13, 318

Rafael, Gideon, 154, 175

Rayburn, Sam, 121, 124

Reagan, Ronald, xii, 214, 249, 272–74, 276, 279–80, 283–84, 286–88, 291–92, 294, 298, 311–14, 323–24

Regan, Donald, 302

Reid, Ogden, 136, 145

Republican party, 29, 48–49, 55, 243; and American Jews, 13–14, 92, 167, 170, 272–73; and Israel, 8, 66, 81–82, 244, 248–49

Reston, James, 120, 190, 281

Ribicoff, Abraham, 133

Richardson, Eliot, 179

Rogers, William P., 127, 172–73, 176–78, 181, 191, 195, 325

Rogers Plan, 173, 177, 179, 187, 189, 218, 256

Rogow, Arnold, 60

Roosevelt, Eleanor, 22, 31, 37, 55, 65, 116

Roosevelt, Franklin D., 4, 12, 24, 31–33, 42, 48–49, 135, 226

Roosevelt, Kermit, 65–66, 132

Roosevelt, Theodore, 13–14, 65, 259

Rosenfeld, Stephen, 245

Rosenman, Samuel I., 31, 49

Rosenne, Meir, 318

Rosensaft, Menahem, 325

Rosenwald, Lessing, 26–27

Rostow, Eugene V. Debs, 38–39, 150–52, 156, 232, 266

Rostow, Walt Whitman, 128, 135, 140, 146–48, 150–52, 154–56, 166

Rowan, Carl, 140

Rowen, H. S., 140

Rubin, Barry, 245

Rubinstein, Amnon, 247

Rush, Kenneth, 200

Rusk, Dean, 52–53, 58–59, 61, 67, 136, 142–43, 145, 147–48, 151, 153, 155–56, 159–61, 169

Russell, Francis, 97, 101–2

Russell, Richard B., 121, 123

Sabra and Shatilla refugee camps, Beirut, 288–89, 291, 295

Sachar, Howard, ix

Sadat, Anwar al-, xiii, 186, 189–90, 195–98, 205–7, 210–11, 214, 217, 220–22, 225, 227–28, 235, 240, 251, 254–55, 258, 261–62, 265, 279, 328

Safire, William, 170, 232

Safran, Nadav, ix, 219, 226

Saguy, Yehoshua, 282

St. Antony's College Oxford, xi

Sanders, Barefoot, 166

Sanders, Ed, 260
Sapir, Pinhas, 126
Sartawi, Issam, 245
Saud, King, 118, 124
Saudi Arabia, 68, 103, 118, 135, 199, 204–6, 221, 232, 237, 274, 277, 280, 287; oil, 47, 54, 66, 162, 197–98, 204–6, 279; U. S. arms sales to, 112, 243, 255, 274–75, 279, 302; and United States, 32, 54, 118, 124, 222–23
Saunders, Harold, 128, 152, 166, 241–42, 250, 259, 262, 268, 287
Schaeffer, Fritz, 89
Schiff, Jacob, 13
Schiff, Ze'ev, 158, 286
Schlesinger, Arthur M., Jr., 28, 131
Schlesinger, James, 200–3, 205, 208
Schmidt, Helmut, 9
Schroeder, Gerhard, 142
Schroeder, Pat, 239
Schumacher, Kurt, 88
Schwimmer, Al, 60, 311–12
Scott, Hugh, 27
Secord, Richard, 314
Sella, Aviem, 316–19
Shalom, Avraham, 318
Shamir, Yitzhak, 61, 164, 269, 277, 282, 317–18, 323–24, 326, 328–29
Shara, Farouk, 328
Sharett, Moshe, 65, 78, 85–86, 94–95, 102, 104–5, 107–9, 111, 128–29, 232
Sharon, Ariel, 99, 220, 247–48, 255, 265–66, 277, 279–86, 288–89, 291, 293, 304–5, 217, 326, 329
Shazar, Zalman, 146–48
Sheean, Vincent, 21
Sheehan, Edward R. F., 219–20, 234
Sheinbaum, Stanley, 324
Shermann, A. J., xiii
Shuckburgh, Evelyn, 102–3
Shultz, George, 287, 291–94, 310, 314, 323, 325, 342
Shuqairi, Ahmad, 141, 150
Sidney, Sylvia, 27
Siegel, Mark, 256
Silver, Hillel, 26, 30, 48, 92, 97
Sinai, 9, 70, 114–15, 117–18, 123, 150, 156, 160, 198–99, 201, 228, 230, 235, 255, 256, 259, 262–64
Sioux City, xi
Sisco, Joseph, 173, 177–78, 181, 189, 191, 195, 199-200
Six-Day War, xiii, 149–53, 186–87, 320
Smith, Walter Bedell, 97, 106, 118, 122
Snyder, John, 48–49
Sokolsky, George, 65
Sorensen, Theodore C., 131
Soviet Union, 7, 19, 22–23, 29–30, 46, 52, 81, 103, 110, 114, 116, 128, 144–45, 149, 157, 175–76, 184–85, 192, 224, 226, 285; and Afghanistan, 7, 214, 271–72; and Arabs, 32, 55, 81, 164, 219; arms sales to Egypt, 108–110,

127–28, 163, 198, 214; and Egypt, 102–3, 108–10, 112–13, 115, 123, 127–28, 163, 172–73, 175–78, 191, 196–198, 207–8, 217, 233; and Iraq, 7, 128, 224; and Israel, 77–78, 81, 110, 326; Jews, 148–49, 171, 229; and Mideast, 51, 75, 84, 109–10, 191–95, 226; and 1967 War, 150–53, 156–57, 159, 164; and Palestine, 42, 54–55, 57–58; and peace process, 229, 242; and PLO, 226, 253; recognition of Israel, 60–61; and Suez, 115–17, 125; and Syria, 103, 123, 127–28, 182, 198, 226, 232, 294; and United States, 52, 75, 81–82, 109, 156–57, 163; and Yom Kippur War, 198–201, 203–4, 206–10
Spellman, Francis, 71, 78
Spiegel, Steven, ix-x
Stalin, Josef, 32, 77, 81, 92, 132, 143
Stassen, Harold, 98–99, 116
Stein, Herbert, 170
Stettinius, Edward R., Jr., 30–31, 56
Stevenson, Adlai, 92, 102, 116, 129, 134, 193
Stimson, Henry, 30
Strategic Defense Initiative, Israel and, 77, 305–6
Straus, Oscar, 13–14
Strauss, Franz Josef, 130–31
Strauss, Lewis L., 92, 122
Strauss, Robert, 269–70
Suez Canal, 82, 101, 105, 159, 188–91, 199, 222, 235, 260; and Israel, 166, 169–72, 177, 191, 260
Suez Crisis, 6–7, 113–23, 128–29, 131–32, 216, 299
Sulzberger, Arthur Hays, 27, 75
Sykes, Christopher, 19
Symington, Stuart, 129
Syria, 71–72, 100, 127, 138, 144, 149–50, 221; and Egypt, 127–28, 138, 150, 185, 225, 228, 265; and Golan Heights, 181, 198–99, 223, 225; and Israel, 69–70, 111, 141, 149–50, 159–60, 181, 214, 223–24, 275–76; and Jordan, 149–50, 180–81, 243; and Lebanon, 69–70, 243, 256, 258, 275–76, 284, 293–94; and 1967 War, 149–50, 158–59; and peace process, 222–25, 228–29; and PLO, 149–50, 179–82, 254, 280; and Soviet Union, 103, 123, 127–28, 182, 198, 226, 232, 294; and United States, 69, 72, 99, 109, 158, 226–27, 251; and Yom Kippur War, 199, 201, 205
Szulc, Tad, 178, 191, 202–3

Taft, Robert A., 30, 42, 48, 81–82, 85–86, 98
Talbot, Phillips, 141
Tamir, Avraham, 258
Terzi, Ibrahim, 269–70
Third World, 84, 93, 128, 133–34, 183, 235, 240–41, 250
Thomas, Abel, 111–12
Thompson, Dorothy, 37, 66–67
Thompson, Llewellyn, 156
Thorn, Gaston, 241
Thucydides, xi, 10, 299

Tillich, Paul, 28
Tocqueville, Alexis de, 11, 141
Tripartite Declaration, 82–85, 91, 103, 106, 108, 110, 112, 115, 117, 137, 161
Truman, Harry S., 4, 28, 33–36, 39–40, 42–43, 45–46, 47–50, 55–61, 71, 74, 78–79, 88, 129, 225, 249
Tubman, William V. S., 56
Tucker, Robert, 229–30
Turkey, 5, 34, 44–46, 51–52, 81, 84, 98, 110, 180, 232, 302

Ulbricht, Walter, 143
United Arab Republic, 127–28, 133, 135
United Jewish Appeal (UJA), 22, 45, 63, 65, 86, 98, 253, 299
United Nations, 35, 38, 70–73, 162–63, 192–95, 218, 222, 225, 235–236, 243, 270, 284; and Israel, 67, 73, 77, 97–99, 105, 144, 237, 240–41, 321–22; and Jerusalem, 70–71, 78, 81; and 1967 War, 150–51, 156–57, 164–65; and Palestine, 8, 47, 49, 51–57; and Palestinians, 136, 140, 165, 228; resolution 242, 165–66, 171, 176–77, 179, 190, 205–7, 218, 234, 236, 248, 251–52, 256, 260, 263–64, 268, 280, 291, 297–98, 324, 326; resolution 338, 206–8, 218–19, 223, 236, 268, 326; resolution 339, 207, 240–41; and Suez, 115–16, 119, 121–22; and United States, 52–56, 59, 121; and Yom Kippur War, 199–200, 206–8
United Nations Security Council, 58–59, 115–16
United Nations Special Committee on Palestine (UNSCOP), 53–57, 67, 69, 73
United States, 5–7, 11–12, 14–17, 23, 46, 57–58, 81, 95–96, 99–101, 106–9, 113, 125, 143–46, 169, 184–85, 232; 274–275, 106–7, 111, 129–30, 136–38, 140–41, 143–46, 162–63, 166; aid to Israel, 4, 7, 9, 69, 75, 85–86, 90–91, 95, 97–100, 103–4, 123, 140–41, 146–49, 166, 168–169, 197, 205, 233, 236, 299–303, 308; arms embargo to Israel, 57, 60, 67, 78, 82, 137, 162–63; arms sales to Israel, 106–7, 111, 129–30, 136–38, 140–41, 143–46, 162–63, 166, 168–69, 173, 186–87, 191, 200–2, 233, 236–38, 268; and displaced persons, 40–42, 45–46; and Egypt, 90, 99, 105, 107, 133–36, 142–43, 156, 174, 196–97, 209–10, 251, 255, 302; free trade agreement with Israel, 308–10; and Great Britain, 6–7, 21, 29, 42–43, 49–52, 84; and Greece, 52, 81; historical landscape and Israel-United States relations, 10–17; and Iran, 34, 52, 89–90, 98, 243; Iraq, 95, 106, 109–110; and Israeli nuclear program, 126–27, 136; and Jerusalem, policy on, 67–68, 70–71; and Jordan, 94, 123–24, 133, 144, 163, 166; and Lebanon, 99, 132, 294–95; Mideast policy, 66–67, 118–19, 160–62; military liaison with Israel, 76–77; neoconservatives, 213–14, 231–32, 273, 288; and 1967 War, 150–60; and Palestine, 16–19, 33, 37–39, 52–62; and Palestinians, 35, 72, 197, 230, 241–42; peace

initiatives in Mideast, 69–70, 107, 165–67; and PLO, 230, 242–43, 252; public support for Israel, 3–5, 65, 73–74, 79–81, 193–94, 229–31, 290–91, 297; recognition of Israel, 8, 34, 59–61, 67–68, 74, 79; and Soviet Union, 52, 75, 81–82, 109, 156–57, 163; and Suez, 113–23, 131–32; and Syria, 69, 72, 99, 158, 226–27, 251; and Third World, 133–34; and Turkey, 52, 81; and United Nations, 52–56, 59, 121; and West Germany, 9, 142–43; as world power, 74–75; and World War II, 24–33; and Yom Kippur War, 198–210, 216
U.S. Congress, 5–6, 18–19, 22, 28–30, 42, 44, 46, 49–50, 52, 83, 113, 118–21, 124, 132, 151–53, 155–56, 168, 205, 217, 229, 234, 243, 255–56, 275, 279–80, 294, 304–5, 308–9; and aid to Israel, 85–86, 98, 140–41, 146, 159, 168, 205, 239; and arms sales to Israel, 162–63, 187, 236–39
U.S. Defense Department, 145–46, 148, 291–92
U.S. Joint Chiefs of Staff, 44–45, 54–55, 57, 69, 76, 140, 151
U.S. Naval War College, xi, xii
U.S. State Department, 11–13, 17–18, 21–22, 24, 32–33, 35–36, 43, 50, 54 57–59, 61, 67–69, 76, 86, 91, 99, 103, 109, 115–16, 142–43, 145–46, 171, 177–78, 191, 274–76, 278, 326
Urofsky, Melvin, 245

Vance, Cyrus, 250, 252–53, 255, 258–59, 261–63, 265–68, 270, 325
Vandenberg, Arthur, 42
Veliotes, Nicholas, 274–75
Vietnam, 9, 46, 118, 131, 139, 142, 146–47, 149, 166–67, 172–74, 185, 187, 193, 196–97, 217, 232, 238, 271
Viorst, Milton, 238, 288, 290
von Hoffman, Nicholas, 288

Wachtmeister, Wilhelm, 324
Wagner, Robert F., Sr., 28, 30–32, 42, 47
Wallace, Henry A., 39, 47–48, 58, 62, 80
Warnke, Paul C., 169
Washington, George, 10–11
Waskow, Arthur, 245
Watergate, 27, 196, 200, 208–9, 212
Watson, Marvin, 148
Webb, Sidney, 20
Weinberg, Yagil, 310
Weinberger, Caspar, 273, 280–82, 287, 315
Weisgal, Murray, 37
Weizman, Ezer, 246–47, 255, 259, 263–64, 268–69, 304
Weizmann, Chaim, 4, 16–17, 20–21, 25, 34, 37, 40, 56, 58–59, 78–79, 105, 330
Weizmann Institute, 126, 146, 159, 168
Welles, Sumner, 27–28, 52
Wellstone, Paul, 5–6
West Bank, 70, 72, 145, 160, 223–24, 237, 273, 283; and peace process, 228, 248, 251–53, 255, 259–64, 266–67, 281, 292, 298

West Germany, 5, 9, 93, 109, 142–43, 152, 206, 305–6, 307; arms transfers to Israel, 130–31, 142–43; and Israel, 130–31, 142–43; and Israel, 130–31, 142–43, 236–37; reparations to Israel, 86–89; and Yom Kippur War airlift, 204–5
Wheeler, Earle G., 151–52, 160
Willkie, Wendell, 42
Wilson, E. M., 33
Wilson, Evan, 43
Wilson, Woodrow, xi, 9, 12–13, 16–17, 31, 117, 212, 225
Wise, Stephen S., 13, 18, 24, 27, 30–31, 36, 44
Wolf, Arnold Jacob, 245
Woodrow Wilson Center, xi
World Jewish Congress, 87
World War I, 12, 15–17, 23
World War II, 12, 24–33

Yadin, Yigael, 77, 247, 254
Yagur, Yosef, 317
Yariv, Aharon, 154, 230
Yemen, 127–28, 141, 188, 215
Yom Kippur War, 183–210
Young, Andrew 269–70
Yugoslavia, 54, 89, 134–35

Zablocki, Clement J., 300
Zhdanov, Andrei, 81
Zionism, 8, 14–15, 17, 19–21, 25–29, 33, 37–38, 43–45, 47–49, 56, 63, 320–21; Revisionists, 20, 25–29, 37, 128
Zionist Organization of America, 15, 19, 28–29, 31, 98, 309
Zumwalt, Elmo, 203